The Practice of Research in
CRIMINOLOGY and
CRIMINAL JUSTICE

Second Edition

PINE FORGE PRESS TITLES OF RELATED INTEREST IN RESEARCH METHODS AND STATISTICS

Investigating the Social World: The Process and Practice of Research, Third Edition by Russell K. Schutt

Investigating the Social World: The Process and Practice of Research, Third Edition, with Student Version of SPSS v.10.0, by Russell K. Schutt

Making Sense of the Social World: Methods of Investigation by Daniel F. Chambliss and Russell K. Schutt

Social Statistics for a Diverse Society, Third Edition by Chava Frankfort-Nachmias and Anna Leon-Guerrero

Social Statistics for a Diverse Society, Third Edition with Student Version of SPSS v.11.0 by Chava Frankfort-Nachmias and Anna Leon-Guerrero

Adventures in Social Research: Data Analysis Using SPSS for Windows, Fifth Edition by Earl Babbie, Fred Halley, and Jeanne Zaino

Adventures in Social Research: Data Analysis Using SPSS for Windows, with Student Version of SPSS v.11.0, Fifth Edition by Earl Babbie, Fred Halley, and Jeanne Zaino

Adventures in Criminal Justice Research: Data Analysis for Windows: Using SPSS Versions 11.0/11.5, or Higher, Fourth Edition by George Dowdall, Kim Loggio, Earl Babbie, and Fred Halley

Theory-Based Data Analysis for the Social Sciences by Carol Anashensel

Multiple Regression: A Primer by Paul Allison

A Guide to Field Research by Carol A. Bailey

Designing Surveys: A Guide to Decisions and Procedures by Ronald F. Czaja and Johnny Blair

Experimental Design and the Analysis of Variance by Robert K. Leik

How Sampling Works by Richard Maisel and Caroline Hodges Persell

Exploring Social Issues: Using SPSS for Windows 95 by Joseph Healey, John Boli, Earl Babbie, and Fred Halley

Constructing Social Research: The Unity and Diversity of Method by Charles C. Ragin

The Practice of Research in
CRIMINOLOGY and CRIMINAL JUSTICE

Second Edition

RONET BACHMAN • RUSSELL K. SCHUTT

University of Delaware   University of Massachusetts, Boston

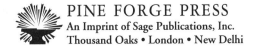

PINE FORGE PRESS
An Imprint of Sage Publications, Inc.
Thousand Oaks • London • New Delhi

For information:

 Pine Forge Press
A Sage Publications Company
2455 Teller Road
Thousand Oaks, California 91320
E-mail: order@sagepub.com

Sage Publications Ltd.
6 Bonhill Street
London EC2A 4PU
United Kingdom

Sage Publications India Pvt. Ltd.
B-42 Panchsheel Enclave
Post Box 4109
New Delhi 110 017 India

Printed in the United States of America

Library of Congress Cataloging-in-Publication Data

Bachman, Ronet.
The practice of research in criminology and criminal justice /
by Ronet Bachman and Russell K. Schutt.–2nd ed.
    p. cm.
Includes bibliographical references and index.
ISBN 0-7619-2877-4 (Pbk.)
  1. Criminology-Research. 2. Criminal justice, Administration of-Research.
I. Schutt, Russell K. II. Title.
HV6024.5.B33 2003
364′.07′2—dc211

2003000231

04 10 9 8 7 6 5 4 3 2

Acquiring Editor:	Jerry Westby
Editorial Assistant:	Vonessa Vondera
Production Editor:	Diana E. Axelsen
Copy Editor:	Toni Zuccarini Ackley
Typesetter:	C&M Digitals (P) Ltd.
Indexer:	Mary Mortensen
Cover Designer:	Michelle Lee
CD-ROM Production:	Eclectic Media

BRIEF CONTENTS

DETAILED CONTENTS

ABOUT THE AUTHORS

Ronet Bachman, Ph.D., is Professor of Sociology and Criminal Justice at the University of Delaware. She is coauthor of *Statistical Methods for Crime and Criminal Justice* and coeditor of *Explaining Crime and Criminology: Essays in Contemporary Criminal Theory*. In addition, she is author of *Death and Violence on the Reservation,* coauthor of *Stress, Culture, and Aggression in the United States,* and coauthor of *Murder American Style*, as well as numerous articles and papers that examine the epidemiology and etiology of violence, with particular emphasis on women and minority populations.

Russell K. Schutt, Ph.D., is Professor of Sociology at the University of Massachusetts, Boston. Author of *Investigating the Social World: The Process and Practice of Research* (3rd ed.) and *Organization in a Changing Environment,* coauthor of *Responding to the Homeless: Policy and Practice*, and coeditor of *The Organizational Response to Social Problems,* he has written numerous journal articles on organizations, law, homelessness, mental health, and teaching research methods. His research experience includes federally funded studies of housing options for severely mentally ill persons, surveys of homeless persons and service personnel, multi-method investigations of organizational change, and secondary analyses of juvenile justice decision making and craft union practices. He has recently been a lecturer in the Department of Psychiatry at the Harvard Medical School.

In loving memory of two pioneer women who instilled in me the importance
of education and lifelong learning:

To my great aunt, Martha Geiken Lund, 1912–2002

and

To my grandmother, Anna Geiken Bachman, 1907–1989.

—R.B.

To my wife, Elizabeth.

—R.K.S.

PREFACE

$\mathbf{O}$ne of the most important aspects of teaching a research methods course is conveying to students the vital role that research plays in our discipline. After years of teaching courses in research methods, we have found that the best avenue for achieving this goal has been to link the teaching of key topics to contemporary research examples in the discipline. By combining discussions of research techniques with practical research examples from the field, students not only learn how to conduct research, but they also learn why it is important to do so. The second edition of *The Practice of Research in Criminology and Criminal Justice* has evolved from comments from students in the classroom, insightful reviews from those who teach research methods courses, and our own continuing learning experience as scholars and teachers.

The purpose of this book is to introduce you to the scientific methods of research in criminology and criminal justice and show how they are actually used. Each chapter in this book combines instruction in research methods with investigations of key research questions in our field: What are the causes of violent crime? What is the best police response to intimate partner violence? How do gang members perceive their world? Are boot camps effective in reducing recidivism? Do community police officers perceive their roles as different from regular patrol officers?

You will learn not only the skills necessary for conducting research but also the means necessary to evaluate research done by others. You will learn to ask many questions before determining that research-based conclusions are appropriate and valid. What did the researchers set out to investigate? How were people or places selected for the study? What were the phenomena being studied, and how were they measured or defined? How was information analyzed? Throughout this book, you will learn what questions to ask when critiquing a research study and how to evaluate the answers.

Another goal of this book is to train you to actually do research. Substantive examples will help you see how methods are used in practice. Exercises at the end of each chapter give you a way to try different methods alone or in a group. A checklist for research proposals will chart a course for you when you plan more ambitious studies. But research methods cannot be learned by rote and applied mechanically. Thus, you will learn the benefits and liabilities of each major approach to research and why employing a combination of them is often preferable. You will come to appreciate why the results of particular research studies must always be interpreted within the context of prior research and through the lens of social and criminological theory.

ORGANIZATION OF THE BOOK

The way this book is organized reflects our beliefs in making research methods interesting, teaching students how to critique research, and viewing specific research techniques as parts of an integrated research strategy. The first two chapters introduce the why and how of research in general. Chapter 1 shows how research has helped us understand the magnitude of and the factors related to youth violence. Chapter 2 illustrates the basic stages of research with a series of experiments on the police response to intimate partner violence. Chapters 3 and 4 discuss how to evaluate the way researchers design their measures and draw their samples.

Chapters 5 through 8 present the four most important methods of data collection: experiments, surveys, qualitative methods (including participant observation, intensive interviews, and focus groups), and secondary data analysis (including historical and comparative research, content analysis, and crime mapping). The substantive studies in these chapters show how these methods have been used to improve our understanding of criminal justice–related issues, including the factors related to violence, how question wording affects estimates of victimization in surveys, how gang members perceive their world, how community police officers describe their role in comparison to regular patrol officers, the perceptions of jurors who have participated in a death penalty case, and the effects of war on violence in a cross-national comparison, to name just a few of the examples provided.

Chapter 9 provides a review of how research methods are used in the criminology field for evaluation research. In this chapter, you will see how various methods have been used to investigate the effects of several programs and policies, including problem-oriented policing, boot camps, rape-reform legislation, and mandatory sentencing laws.

Because it is important that students understand the merits of both qualitative and quantitative methodologies, Chapter 10 includes a unique "integration and review" that illustrates the value of multiple methods. This chapter examines studies that combine methods or investigate social processes within larger contexts.

Chapter 11 presents the basic statistical methods used to analyze the results of quantitative studies in a descriptive manner. We will work through an analysis of survey data on self-reported delinquency to see how these statistics are used to answer actual research questions. Chapter 12 provides an overview of the main types of written reports used in criminology and criminal justice. You will learn the required sections of a research proposal and paper along with the peer review process that actually accompanies such endeavors.

DISTINCTIVE FEATURES OF THE SECOND EDITION

The most distinctive feature of this text compared to others in the field continues to be the integration into each chapter of in-depth substantive research examples from the real world. Examples from the literature are not simply dropped here and there to keep students' attention. Rather, each chapter presents a particular research method in the context of a substantive research story. As such, this book's success is due in no small measure to the availability in the research literature of so many excellent examples. The following points are additional strengths of this text along with some new innovations in this edition:

A new chapter on secondary data analysis including discussions of crime mapping, content analysis, and historical and comparative research methods. Examples from the literature in this chapter include a historical analysis of the Martinsville Seven, who were executed for rape in Virginia in 1951; a secondary analysis of existing data from the ICPSR; a cross-national study of violence; a content analysis of real-life crime shows on television; and a study that utilizes crime mapping techniques to study gang-related homicide in St. Louis.

Examples of criminological research as they occur in real-world settings. We include interesting studies taken from the literature on a variety of topics including the causes and correlates of violence, the efficacy of arrest for intimate partner assault, the perceptions of police officers regarding community policing, and an investigation into the lives of gang members, to name just a few. These real-world research examples illustrate the exigencies and complexities that shape the application of research methods.

Increased attention to qualitative methods. Qualitative and quantitative methods are contrasted in Chapter 1, and most other chapters include a special section on qualitative approaches. Chapter 7, which is devoted exclusively to qualitative methods, has been expanded and updated; Chapter 8, devoted to secondary data analysis, expands on this discussion by providing illustrations of other qualitative methods including content analysis.

Ethical concerns and ethical decision making. Every step in the research process raises ethical concerns, so ethics should be treated in tandem with the study of specific methods. You will find ethics introduced in Chapter 2 and reviewed in each subsequent chapter in the context of each method of data collection, data analysis, and reporting.

Useful instructional software. The enclosed disk has been edited extensively to improve ease of use. You should spend enough time with these lessons to become comfortable with the basic research concepts presented.

End-of-chapter exercises. In addition to individual and group projects, each chapter includes exercises to give you experience in data analysis using SPSS, the statistical software for the social sciences. Each chapter also provides updated end-of-chapter Web exercises. Plus, a new section has been added to each chapter to guide you through the preparation of a research proposal. A demo of the HyperRESEARCH software is included on the CD-ROM, along with a new appendix (Appendix F) that describes how to use it to analyze qualitative data.

Aids to effective study. Lists of main points and key terms provide quick summaries at the end of each chapter. In addition, key terms are highlighted in boldface type when first introduced and defined in the text. Definitions for them can also be found in the glossary/index at the end of the book. The instructor's manual includes more exercises that have been specially designed for collaborative group work inside and outside the classroom. Appendix A, "Finding Information," provides up-to-date information about using the Internet.

If this book communicates the excitement of research and the importance of evaluating carefully the methods we use in research, then we have succeeded in representing what social scientists interested in issues related to criminal justice and criminology do. We think it conveys the latest developments in research methodology, and thereby demonstrates that researchers are committed to evaluating and improving their own methods of investigation.

We hope you enjoy learning how to investigate research questions related to criminal justice and criminology and perhaps do some research of your own along the way. We guarantee that the knowledge you develop about research methods will serve you well throughout your education, in your career, and in your community.

A NOTE ABOUT USING SPSS AND HyperRESEARCH

To carry out the SPSS exercises at the end of each chapter and in Appendix D, you must have SPSS installed on your computer. The CD-ROM included with this text includes several subsets of data, including data from the National Crime Victimization Survey and the Uniform Crime Reports. Appendix D will get you up and running with SPSS for Windows; you can then spend as much time as you like exploring the data sets provided, or even use your own data. You can also carry out analyses of the General Social Survey (GSS) at the Berkeley Web site: http://sda.berkeley.edu:7502/archive.htm.

Appendix F contains a detailed discussion of what it is like to do qualitative research with the statistical software package HyperRESEARCH. In this appendix, you will learn how to begin a simple project in HyperRESEARCH by creating and managing data and ideas, coding, linking, modeling, and asking questions about your narrative data.

ACKNOWLEDGMENTS

We must first acknowledge our gratitude to Jerry Westby, whose hard work and guidance on this project are unrivaled. His attention to detail and his tenacity for tracking down even the most remote suggestions have truly been remarkable. We are also indebted to Toni Zuccarini Ackley for her meticulous copy editing of the text. Also contributing vitally to this book were other exceptional members of the Pine Forge Press team, including Diana Axelsen, who marshaled the text through production, and Vonessa Vondera, who managed the communication between all parties.

Gratitude also goes to the reviewers of this work including Cathy Couglan, Texas Christian University; Lucy Hochstein, Radford University; Mark Winton, University of Central Florida; Stephen Haas, Marshall University; Hank J. Brightman, Saint Peter's College; Eric Metchick, Salem State College; Kristen Kuehnle, Salem State College; Wilson R. Palacios, University of South Florida; and Phyllis B. Gerstenfeld, California State University–Stanislaus. Andre Rosay also provided an extensive and invaluable review of the first edition of this text. We also thank Lindsay R. Reed and Hanna S. Scott for their diligence and hard work in writing the instructor's manual, Ann Dupuis and Sharlene Hesse-Biber for the appendix on HyperRESEARCH software, Lisa M. Gilman for the appendix on SPSS, and Heather Albertson and Kathryn Stoeckert for additional interactive exercises.

We continue to be indebted to the many students we have had an opportunity to teach and mentor, at both the undergraduate and graduate levels. In many respects, this book could not have been written without these ongoing reciprocal teaching and learning experiences. You inspire us to become better teachers!

Ronet is also indebted to the support group that started after the members endured graduate school together; we get together for a retreat one weekend of the year (14 years and counting!) for guidance, support, and laughter: Dianne Carmody, Gerry King, Peggy Plass, and Barbara Wauchope. You are the most amazing women in the world, and I am so blessed to have you in my life. To Alex Alvarez, my other kindred spirit in the world for all his support and guidance; to my mother and best friend, Jan, who remains my primary inspiration; and to my father, Ron, and my stepfather, Bill, for unfailing support.

Of course, such endeavors would not be possible without a supportive and nurturing department. Ronet would like to thank her chair, Joel Best, for his unique style of leadership that is always filled with humor and a critical eye. She is also fortunate to work in a department with many first-rate scholars, several of whom have become close friends, including Anne Bowler, Michelle Meloy, Susan Miller, and Eric Rise. Thanks for your unwavering support.

And most important, we both wish to thank our spouses, Raymond Paternoster and Elizabeth Schutt, for their love and support (and editorship!), and our children, John and Julia, for all the remarkable joy they have brought to our lives.

SCIENCE, SOCIETY, AND CRIMINOLOGICAL RESEARCH

$\mathbf{B}$y now the scenario is common knowledge—on April 20, 1999, Eric Harris and Dylan Klebold turned Columbine High School, in suburban Colorado, into the scene of the deadliest school shooting in American history. After killing 12 students and a teacher, the youths apparently shot themselves in the head. In the end, 15 people were dead and 28 were injured. After the blood bath, police found the school in Littleton littered with bombs and other booby traps. Harris and Klebold were not typical terrorists. They were apparently bright young men who became social outcasts at their school, affiliated with a group known as the Trenchcoat Mafia, whose outward symbols included dark trenchcoats, dark sunglasses, and berets—part of a larger group described as "Goths." But signs of trouble were evident to many before the killings. Harris's Web pages were filled with images of fire, skulls, devils, and weapons and included recipes for and sketches of pipe bombs. The two young men also wrote poetry about death for their English class and made a video about guns for a video class.

The Littleton horror was simply the latest in a string of school shootings in 1998 and 1999. In the spring of 1998, in Jonesboro, Arkansas, two prepubescent boys decided that the best way to deal with girls who might have minds of their own was to shoot them. After pulling the school's fire alarm, the boys sat in the trees awaiting their targets. When the students filed out of the school, the boys opened fire, killing four students and a teacher. In the months that followed, three students were killed and five were injured in West Paducah, Kentucky, when another student shot them as they left a prayer meeting. In Edinboro, Pennsylvania, a student gunned down a teacher and wounded two classmates. And in Springfield, Oregon, a disgruntled student brought a rifle into the cafeteria at Thurston High School and fired indiscriminately into a crowd, killing 2 students and wounding 22 others. These were not inner-city schools riddled with economic deprivation and disorganization; they were all schools in quiet towns where violence, at least publicly displayed violence, was rare.

Each of these school shootings caused a media frenzy. Headlines such as "The School Violence Crisis" and "School Crime Epidemic" were plastered across national newspapers and weekly news journals. From a statistical standpoint, these headlines seemed a little late, particularly because the juvenile arrest rate for murder had been declining. In addition, the thousands of other shootings that occurred in less privileged communities during the same time rarely made the national news. For example, there were no such declarations when an 11-year-old boy was shot and killed in Chicago because he had allegedly shorted an 18-year-old on drug money. And where were such declarations the night two teenagers were shot outside a Baltimore nightclub when guns turned an argument into the final solution?

Many factors influence our beliefs about social phenomena, but the media play a large role in how we perceive both problems and solutions. What are your perceptions of violence committed by youth, and how did you acquire such perceptions? What do you believe are the causes of youth violence? Many factors have been blamed for youth violence in American society, including the easy availability of guns, the use of weapons in movies and television, the moral decay of our nation, poor parenting, unaware teachers, school and class size, racial prejudice, teenage alienation, the Internet and the World Wide Web, anti-Semitism, rap and rock music, and the Goth culture. When trying to make sense out of the Littleton incident, President Bill Clinton talked about hate, prejudice, community policing, conflict resolution, parental responsibility, and violence in the culture. Charlton Heston, spokesman for the National Rifle Association, blamed the absence of armed security guards in schools, even though one was present in Littleton. Heston also blamed the parents and the school for allowing kids to wear black.

Each of you probably has your own ideas about what factors may be related to violence in general and youth violence in particular. However, the factors you believe are important in explaining a phenomenon may not always be the ones supported by empirical research. In fact, the factors often touted by politicians and the media to be related to violence are not always supported by empirical evidence. In the rest of this chapter, you will learn how the methods of social science research go beyond stories in the popular media to help us answer questions like "What are the causes of youth violence?" By the chapter's end, you should know what is scientific in criminal justice and criminology and appreciate how the methods of social science can help us understand and answer research questions in this discipline.

REASONING ABOUT THE SOCIAL WORLD

The story of just one murderous youth raises many questions. Take a few minutes to read each of the following questions and jot down your answers. Don't ruminate about the questions or worry about your responses. This is not a test; there are no wrong answers.

- How would you describe Eric Harris?
- Why do you think Eric Harris wanted to kill other students?
- Was Eric Harris typical of other murderers under 18 years of age?
- In general, why do people become murderers?
- How have you learned about youth violence?

Now let's consider the possible answers to some of these questions. The information about Eric Harris is somewhat inconsistent (Duggan, Shear, & Fisher, 1999). He was the 18-year-old son of middle-class professionals. He had an older brother who attended the University of Colorado. Harris apparently thought of himself as a white supremacist, but he also loved music by antiracist rock bands. On his Web page, he quoted from KMFDM, a German rock band whose song "Waste" includes these lyrics: "What I don't say I don't do. What I don't do I don't like. What I don't like I waste." Online, Harris referred to himself as "Darkness."

Do you have enough information now to understand why Eric went on a shooting rampage in his school?

A year before the shootings at Columbine High School, Harris was arrested on a felony count of breaking into a car. A juvenile court put him on probation, required him to perform community service and take criminal justice classes, and sent him to a school counseling program. He was described by one of his probation officers as a "very bright young man who is likely to succeed in life."

Now can you construct an adequate description of Eric Harris? Can you explain the reason for his murderous rampage? Or do you feel you need to know more about Eric Harris, about his friends and the family he grew up in? And how about his experiences in school and with the criminal justice system? We've attempted to investigate just one person's experiences, and already our investigation is spawning more and more questions.

Questions and Answers

When the questions concern not just one person but many people or general social processes, the possible questions and the alternative answers multiply. For example, consider the question of why incidents of school violence occur. Responses to a 1997 survey of mothers with children between the ages of 12 and 15 found that the majority of mothers considered the most important factors that contributed to school violence to be parents who did not teach children morals (84%), parents who supported aggressive behavior (78%), and gang/peer pressure (70%) (Kandakai et al., 1999). Compare these answers with

Exhibit 1.1   Mothers' Perceptions of the Factors Related to School Violence

	Percentage Who Said Factor Contributed a Great Deal
Parents who do not teach their kids right from wrong	87%
Parent support for aggressive behavior	78
Gang/peer pressure	70
Lack of family involvement	67
Sale of alcohol/cigarettes to children	61
Poor parent-teacher communication	60
Seeing violence in the community	53
Violent messages in rap music	47
Seeing violence in the media	44
Lack of a dress code	30

the opinion you recorded earlier. Was your idea about the causes of youth violence one of the more popular ones held by this sample of mothers?

We cannot avoid asking questions about the actions and attitudes of others. We all try to make sense of the social world, which is a very complex place, and to make sense of our position in it, in which we have quite a personal stake. In fact, the more that you begin to "think like a social scientist," the more questions will come to mind.

But why does each question have so many possible answers? Surely our perspective plays a role. One person may see a homicide offender as a victim of circumstance, and another person may see the same individual as inherently evil. Answers to questions we ask in the criminological sciences also vary because individual life experiences and circumstances vary. The study of mothers' perceptions conducted by Tina Kandakai, James Price, Susan Telljohann, and Carter Wilson (1999), summarized in Exhibit 1.1, gives some idea of how opinions about the causes and cures for school violence vary. Even though previous research has found that the general public believes school violence is worse in urban schools than in suburban and rural schools, only 14% of the mothers who had children in urban schools believed their child's school was more violent than other schools. However, a higher percentage of urban mothers (37%) than suburban mothers (17%) reported that their child had been involved in one or more fights at school. Somewhat surprisingly, even though these mothers perceived parental support for violence as a major contributor to school violence, 4 in 10 of them believed it was acceptable for their child to fight in certain situations.

Everyday Errors in Reasoning

People give different answers to research questions for yet another reason: It's simply too easy to make errors in logic, particularly when we are analyzing the social world in which we ourselves are conscious participants. We can call some of these everyday errors, because they occur so frequently in the nonscientific, unreflective discourse about the social world that we hear on a daily basis.

For evidence of everyday errors, just listen to your conversations or the conversations of others for one day. At some point in the day, it is inevitable that you or someone you are talking with will say something like "Well, I knew a person who did X and Y happened." From this one piece of information, you therefore draw a conclusion about the likelihood of Y. Four general errors in everyday reasoning can be made: overgeneralization, selective or inaccurate observation, illogical reasoning, and resistance to change.

Overgeneralization

Overgeneralization, an error in reasoning, occurs when we conclude that what we have observed or what we know to be true for some cases is true for all cases. We are always drawing conclusions about people and social processes from our own interactions with them, but sometimes we forget that our experiences are limited. The social (and natural) world is, after all, a complex place. We have the ability (and inclination) to interact with just a small fraction of the individuals who inhabit the social world, especially in a limited span of time.

Selective or Inaccurate Observation

Selective observation is choosing to look only at things that are in accordance with our preferences or beliefs. When we are inclined to criticize individuals or institutions, it is all too easy to notice their every failing. For example, if we are convinced in advance that all kids who are violent are unlikely to be rehabilitated and will go on to commit violent offenses in adulthood, we will probably find many confirming instances. But what about other youths who have become productive and stable citizens after engaging in violence as adolescents? Or the child who was physically or sexually abused and joined a gang to satisfy the need for a family surrogate? If we acknowledge only the instances that confirm our predispositions, we are victims of our own selective observation. Exhibit 1.2 depicts the difference between selective observation and overgeneralization.

Exhibit 1.2   The Difference Between Overgeneralization and Selective Observation

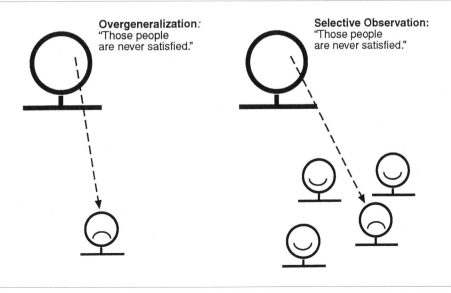

Exhibit 1.3   Anatomy of an Emotional Hijacking

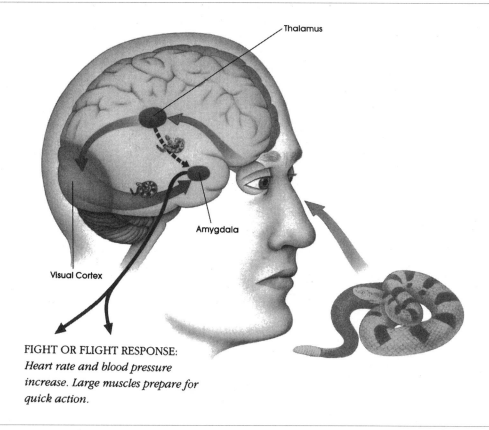

FIGHT OR FLIGHT RESPONSE:
*Heart rate and blood pressure
increase. Large muscles prepare for
quick action.*

Source: From Goleman, D., *Emotional Intelligence,* p. 19. Copyright © 1995. Used by permission of Bantam Books, a division of Bantam Doubleday Dell Publishing Group.

Recent research on cognitive functioning (how the brain works) helps to explain why our feelings so readily shape our perceptions (Seidman, 1997). Emotional responses to external stimuli travel a shorter circuit in the brain than do reasoned responses (see Exhibit 1.3). The result, according to some cognitive scientists, is that "what something reminds us of can be far more important than what it is" (Goleman, 1995:294–295). Our emotions can influence us even before we begin to reason about what we have observed.

Our observations also can simply be inaccurate. If a woman says she is *hungry* and we think she said she is *hunted,* we have made an **inaccurate observation.** If we think five people are standing on a street corner when seven actually are, we have made an inaccurate observation. Such errors occur often in casual conversation and in everyday observation of the world around us. In fact, our perceptions do not provide a direct window onto the world around us, for what we think we have sensed is not necessarily what we have seen (or heard, smelled, felt, or tasted). Even when our senses are functioning fully, our

Exhibit 1.4   An Optical Illusion

minds have to interpret what we have sensed (Humphrey, 1992). The optical illusion in Exhibit 1.4, which can be viewed as either two faces or a vase, should help you realize that perceptions involve interpretations. Different observers may perceive the same situation differently because they interpret it differently.

Illogical Reasoning

When we prematurely jump to conclusions or argue on the basis of invalid assumptions, we are using **illogical reasoning.** For example, it is not reasonable to propose that depictions of violence in media such as television and movies cause violence if evidence indicates that the majority of those who watch such programs do not become violent. However, it is also illogical to assume that media depictions of gratuitous violence have no effect on individuals. Of course, logic that seems impeccable to one person can seem twisted to another—the problem usually is reasoning from different assumptions rather than failing to "think straight."

Resistance to Change

Resistance to change, the reluctance to change our ideas in light of new information, may occur for several reasons:

Ego-based commitments. We all learn to greet with some skepticism the claims by leaders of companies, schools, agencies, and so on that people in their organization are happy, that revenues are growing, that services are being delivered in the best possible way, and so forth. We know how tempting it is to make statements about the social world that conform to our own needs rather than to the observable facts. It also can be difficult to admit that we were wrong once we have staked out a position on an issue.

Excessive devotion to tradition. Some degree of devotion to tradition is necessary for the predictable functioning of society. Social life can be richer and more meaningful if it is allowed to flow along the paths charted by those who have preceded us. But too much devotion to tradition can stifle adaptation to changing circumstances. When we distort our observations or alter our reasoning so that we can maintain beliefs that "were good enough for my grandfather, so they're good enough for me," we hinder our ability to accept new findings and develop new knowledge. The consequences can be deadly, as residents of Hamburg, Germany, might have realized in 1892 (Freedman, 1991). Until the last part of the 19th century, people believed that cholera, a potentially lethal disease, was due to minute, inanimate, airborne poison particles (miasmas). In 1850, English researcher John Snow demonstrated that cholera was, in fact, spread by contaminated water. When a cholera epidemic hit Hamburg in 1892, the authorities did what tradition deemed appropriate: digging up and carting away animal carcasses to prevent the generation of more miasmas. Despite their efforts, thousands died. New York City adopted a new approach based on Snow's discovery, which included boiling drinking water and disinfecting sewage. As a result, the death rate in New York City dropped to a tenth of what it had been in a previous epidemic.

Uncritical agreement with authority. If we do not have the courage to evaluate critically the ideas of those in positions of authority, we will have little basis for complaint if they exercise their authority over us in ways we don't like. And if we do not allow new discoveries to call our beliefs into question, our understanding of the social world will remain limited. An extreme example of this problem was the refusal of leaders in formerly Communist countries to acknowledge the decaying social and environmental fabric of their societies while they encouraged their followers to pay homage to the wisdom of Comrades Mao, Lenin, and Stalin. But we don't have to go so far afield to recognize that people often accept the beliefs of those in positions of authority without question.

Now take just a minute to reexamine the beliefs about youth violence that you recorded earlier. Did you grasp at a simple explanation even though reality was far more complex? Were your beliefs influenced by your own ego and feelings about your similarities to or differences from individuals prone to violence? Are your beliefs perhaps based on depictions of violence in the media or fiction? Did you weigh carefully the opinions of authority figures, including politicians, teachers, and even your parents, or just accept or reject those opinions out of hand? Could knowledge of research methods help to improve your own understanding of the factors related to violent behavior? By now, we hope that you will see some of the challenges faced by social scientists studying issues related to crime and the criminal justice system.

You don't have to be a scientist or use sophisticated research techniques to recognize and avoid these four errors in reasoning. If you recognize these errors for what they are and make a conscious effort to avoid them, you can improve your own reasoning. In the process, you will also be heeding the admonishments of your parents (or minister, teacher, or other adviser) to refrain from stereotyping people, to avoid jumping to conclusions, and to look at the big picture. These are the same errors that the methods of social science are designed to help criminologists avoid.

THE SOCIAL SCIENCE APPROACH

The social science approach to answering questions about the social world is designed to greatly reduce these potential sources of error in everyday reasoning. **Science** relies on logical and systematic methods to answer questions, and it does so in a way that allows others to inspect and evaluate its methods. In the realm of social research, these methods are not so unusual. After all, they involve asking questions, observing social groups, and counting people, which we often do in our everyday lives. However, social scientists develop, refine, apply, and report their understanding of the social world more systematically, or scientifically, than Joanna Q. Public:

- **Social science** research methods can reduce the likelihood of overgeneralization by using systematic procedures for selecting individuals or groups to study that are representative of the individuals or groups that we wish to generalize.
- Social science methods can reduce the risk of selective or inaccurate observation by requiring that we measure and sample phenomena systematically.
- To avoid illogical reasoning, social researchers use explicit criteria for identifying causes and for determining if these criteria are met in a particular instance.
- Because they require that we base our beliefs on evidence that can be examined and critiqued by others, scientific methods lessen the tendency to develop answers about the social world from ego-based commitments, excessive devotion to tradition, and/or unquestioning respect for authority.

Science   A set of logical, systematic, documented methods for investigating nature and natural processes; the knowledge produced by these investigations.

Social science   The use of scientific methods to investigate individuals, societies, and social processes, including questions related to criminology and criminal justice; the knowledge produced by these investigations.

Motives for Criminological Research

Like you, social scientists read stories about incidents of violence committed by youth, observe this violence occasionally in their lives, and try to make sense of what they see. For most, that's the end of it. But for some social scientists, the problem of youth violence has become a major research focus. The motivations for selecting this particular research focus, as with any social science topic, can be any or some combination of the following:

Policy motivations. Many social service agencies and elected officials seek better assessments and descriptions of youth violence so they can identify needs and allocate responsibility among agencies that could meet these needs. For example, federal agencies such as the U.S. Department of Justice and the Centers for Disease Control and Prevention want to identify the magnitude of youth violence, and many state and local officials use social research to guide development of their social service budgets. Programs designed to rehabilitate young offenders often use research to learn more about the needs of their clientele. These policy guidance and program management needs have resulted in numerous research projects.

Academic motivations. Young offenders have been a logical focus for researchers interested in a number of questions ranging from how an individual's connection to parents and peers influences their behavior to how the social conditions under which they live, such as poverty, affect their behavior. For example, social scientists have long been concerned with the impact that social disorganization has on individual behavior. Early in this century, researchers at the University of Chicago were interested in the effects that residential mobility and immigration had on levels of crime and delinquency in urban neighborhoods. Today researchers are exploring similar questions concerning the impact of disintegrating economic bases in central cities and their relationship to crime and violence. Other researchers have focused on individual-level explanations such as neurological damage. Those who study social policy also have sought to determine whether correctional programs such as boot camps and other forms of shock incarceration serve to decrease the probability of juveniles reoffending in the future.

Personal motivations. Many who conduct research on youth violence feel that by doing so they can help to prevent it and/or ameliorate the consequences of this violence when it occurs. Some social scientists first volunteered with at-risk youth in such organizations as Big Sisters and Big Brothers, and only later began to develop a research agenda based on their experiences.

Social Criminological Research in Practice

Of course, youth violence did not first appear in the United States in the 1980s. In fact, youth violence always has been a popular topic of social science research. However, the sharp increase in this violence in the United States that began in the late 1980s was unprecedented. Predictably, whenever a phenomenon is perceived as an epidemic, numerous explanations emerge to explain it. Unfortunately, most of these explanations are based on the media and popular culture, not on empirical research. Despite the anecdotal information floating around in the mass media about the factors that may have contributed to increases in youth violence, social scientists interested in this phenomenon have amassed a substantial body of findings that have refined knowledge about the problem and shaped social policy (Tonry & Moore, 1998). These studies fall into the four categories of purposes for social scientific research:

Descriptive research. Defining and describing social phenomena of interest is a part of almost any research investigation, but **descriptive research** is the primary focus of many studies of youth crime and violence. Some of the central questions used in these studies were: "How many people are victims of youth violence?" "How many youth are offenders?" "What are the most common crimes committed by youthful offenders?" and "How many youth are arrested and incarcerated each year for crime?" Measurement (the topic of Chapter 3) and sampling (Chapter 4) are central concerns in descriptive research.

Exploratory research. **Exploratory research** seeks to find out how people get along in the setting under question, what meanings they give to their actions, and what issues concern them. The goal is to answer the question "What is going on here?" and to investigate social phenomena without expectations. This purpose is associated with the use of methods that capture large amounts of relatively unstructured information. For example, researchers investigating the emergence of youth gangs in the 1980s were encountering a phenomenon with which they had no direct experience. Thus, an early goal was to find out what it was like to be a gang member and how gang members made sense of their situation. Exploratory research like this frequently involves qualitative methods, which are the focus of Chapter 8.

Explanatory research. Many people consider explanation to be the premier goal of any science. **Explanatory research** seeks to identify causes and effects of social phenomena, to predict how one phenomenon will change or vary in response to variation in some other phenomenon. Researchers adopted explanation as a goal when they began to ask such questions as "Why do people become offenders?" and "Does the unemployment rate influence the frequency of youth crime?" Methods with which to identify causes and effects are the focus of Chapter 5.

Evaluation research. **Evaluation research** seeks to determine the effects of a social program or other type of intervention. It is a type of explanatory research, because it deals with cause and effect. However, evaluation research differs from other forms of explanatory research because evaluation research considers the implementation and effects of social policies and programs. These issues may not be relevant in other types of explanatory research. The increase of youth violence in the 1980s spawned many new government programs and, with them, evaluation research to assess the impact of these programs. Some of these studies are reviewed in Chapter 5, which covers experimental design, and in Chapter 9, which covers evaluation research.

We will now summarize one study in each of these four areas to give you a feel for the projects motivated by these different concerns.

Description: What Is the Magnitude of Youth Violence?

One large research project undertaken to examine the magnitude of youth violence (along with other risk-taking behavior such as taking drugs and smoking) is called the Youth Risk Behavior Survey, which has been conducted every 2 years in the United States since 1990. Respondents to this survey are a national sample of approximately 16,000 high school students in Grades 9 through 12. To determine trends and patterns in violence-related behavior, Nancy Brener, Thomas Simon, Etienne G. Krug, and Richard Lowry examined the data for the years 1991 and 1997 and published their findings in the prestigious *Journal of the American Medical Association* (1999).

To measure the extent of youth violence, students were asked the following questions: "During the past 30 days, on how many days did you carry a weapon such as a gun, knife, or club?" "During the past 12 months, how many times were you in a physical fight?" "During the past 12 months, how many times were you in a physical fight in which you were injured and had to be seen by a doctor or nurse?" "During the past 30 days, how many times did you carry a weapon such as a gun, knife, or club on school property?" "During the past 12 months, how many times were you in a physical fight on school property?" and "During the past 12 months, how many times has someone threatened or injured you with a gun, knife, or club on school property?"

Before we tell you the results of this study, let's try a little experiment. You probably have your own ideas about the trends in youth violence and school-related violence, which may be based on your own experience or on media accounts. Do you believe that this violence increased or decreased from 1991 to 1997? Brener and her colleagues (1999) found that the number of all students who carried a weapon within the 30 days preceding the survey actually decreased by 30% from 1991 to 1997. Similarly, the number of students who engaged in a physical fight one or more times during the 12 months preceding the survey decreased 14%, and the number injured in a physical fight decreased 20%. Trends in violence occurring on school property also decreased during this time period. The number of students who carried a gun on school property on one or more of the 30 days preceding the survey decreased 28%, and the number of students who engaged in a physical fight on school property one or more times during the 12 months preceding the survey decreased 9%.

This research is consistent with other studies that have found that official rates of youth violence, and youth homicide in particular, peaked in the early 1990s and declined thereafter (Cook & Laub, 1998). What accounted for this unprecedented rise in youth violence during the late 1980s and early 1990s? To answer this question, explanatory research is necessary. However, after their in-depth descriptive analysis of youth violence during this time, Cook and Laub contend that the increasing homicide rates began with the introduction of crack cocaine and the conflict that surrounded its marketing. However, the primary factor postulated by Cook and Laub was the increased easy availability of firepower. "All of the increase in homicide rates was with guns, and it appears to be changing access [to] and use of guns, rather than a change in the character of the youths, that best accounts for their increased involvement in lethal violence" (Cook & Laub, 1998:60).

Exploration: How Do Schools Respond to Gun Violence?

Research that is exploratory in nature is generally concerned with uncovering detailed information about a given phenomenon—learning as much as possible about particular people and/or events. Kelly Asmussen and John Creswell (1995) were interested in the responses to school shooting incidents. Because school shootings are relatively rare and there was virtually no empirical literature that addressed the topic, Asmussen and Creswell performed an in-depth qualitative case study of a shooting incident that occurred at a large public university. The incident occurred in a senior-level actuarial science class when a male graduate student arrived early for the class one Monday morning armed with a vintage Korean War semiautomatic military rifle loaded with a 30-round clip of .30-caliber ammunition. He carried another 30-round clip in his pocket. Twenty of the 34 students in the class were already there, and most of them were quietly reading the student newspaper. The instructor was en route to class. The gunman pointed the rifle at the students, swept it across the room, and pulled the trigger. The gun jammed. Trying to unlock the rifle, he hit the butt of it on the desk and quickly tried firing it again. Again it did not fire. By this time, most students realized what was happening and dropped to the floor, overturned their desks, and tried to hide behind them. After about 20 seconds, one of the students shoved a desk into the gunman, and students ran past him out into the hall and out of the building.

The gunman hastily left the room and went out of the building to his parked car, which he had left running. He was captured by police within the hour.

Asmussen and Creswell (1995) were surprised to find that instead of seeking safety after leaving the classroom, all of the students had stood together just outside the building. Although a few were openly emotional and crying, many were kidding about the incident, as if it had posed no real danger. This denial response is noted by the mental health literature, which finds that feelings of fear and anger usually follow an initial response of denial and disbelief. The researchers found that many people in addition to the students who witnessed the incident were traumatized by the incident. In fact, three distinct groups of people sought counseling services during the weeks following the event. The first group had some direct involvement with the assailant, either by seeing him the day of the gun incident or because they had known him personally. The second group were the "silent connection," comprising individuals who were indirectly involved and yet emotionally traumatized. A large number of this group were parents. The third group included people who had previously experienced a trauma and whose fears were retriggered by this incident.

Because the assailant's future was in the hands of the criminal justice system, the importance of information from this system became critical to feelings of safety. Two combined debriefing sessions by mental health counselors, the campus police chief, and two county attorneys were held for all those interested.

Another phenomenon observed on the campus was an increase in the number of professors and staff who were concerned with disruptive students or students who exhibited aberrant behavior in class. To deal with this, the Student Judiciary Office advised departments on various methods of dealing with students who exhibited abnormal behavior in class. In addition, plainclothes police officers were sent to sit outside classrooms and offices whenever faculty and staff indicated concerns.

To their surprise, Asmussen and Creswell (1995) found that the campus did not establish a special unit to manage future incidents. The only structural change made was the installation of emergency phones throughout the campus. In addition, no discussion was reported about formal linkages with community agencies that might assist in the event of a future tragedy. In the end, Asmussen and Creswell's exploratory research illustrates the complexity involved in responding to a campus shooting.

Explanation: What Factors Are Related to Youth Delinquency and Violence?

Researchers Richard Felson, Allen Liska, Scott South, and Thomas McNulty (1994) sought to determine whether individual and group differences in beliefs and attitudes about violence were related to committing acts of delinquency and interpersonal violence. The theoretical argument they were attempting to test is actually termed the "subculture of violence" thesis (Wolfgang & Ferracuti, 1967). According to this thesis, some groups are more violent than others because they have a distinctive set of values that either support or tolerate violence.

Felson and his colleagues (1994) used a data set called the Youth in Transition data, which was a panel study of high school boys. The first interviews were conducted with sophomore boys attending 87 randomly selected public high schools. The second interview was collected 18 months later at the end of the boys' junior year in high school. The researchers measured each boy's adherence to a subculture of violence by asking him about situations in which he would approve of aggression as a legitimate expression of grievances and as an appropriate response to personal attack. For example, each boy was presented a series of personal values and asked whether each was a "good thing for people to do": (1) turning the other cheek and forgiving others when they harm you, (2) replying to anger with gentleness, and (3) being kind to people even if they do things against one's own beliefs. These items each focus on the approval of nonaggressive responses to some type of provocation. Agreement with these statements therefore suggests that respondents disapprove of aggressive responses to personal attacks and wrongdoing. Disagreement with these statements would result in a high score on the subculture of violence scale developed by Felson and his colleagues. To measure acts of interpersonal violence, each boy was asked the frequency with which he engaged in eight activities: got into a serious fight with a student in school, obtained something by telling a person something bad would happen to the person if he did not get what he wanted, hurt someone badly enough to need bandages or a doctor, hit a teacher, hit his father, hit his mother, took part in a group brawl in which his friends fought with another group, and used a knife or gun or some other thing to get something from a person. The respondents were also asked about other delinquent acts such as engaging in theft and vandalism.

The students' scores on the subculture of violence index were then used to predict scores on the interpersonal violence index, after controlling for the effects of other important variables such as socioeconomic status, race, attitudes toward academic achievement, and family stability. Felson and colleagues (1994) performed analyses using both individual and school-level data and found that in some schools, an aggressive response to a provocation was likely to meet with more peer approval than in other schools. They found that individuals who approved of aggressive responses to provocation were more likely to commit acts of interpersonal violence. In addition, individuals who went to schools where there was an atmosphere permissive of violence were more likely to act violently, a finding that remained true even after controlling for individual attitudes. Felson and colleagues attribute this to a social control process and explain, "If boys are expected to retaliate when provoked, it appears that they are more likely to engage in violence and other delinquent behavior, no matter what their personal values may be" (1994:164).

Evaluation: Do Violence Prevention Programs in Schools Work?

To reduce violence and create safer atmospheres at schools across the country, literally thousands of schools have adopted some form of violence prevention training (Powell, Muir-McClain, & Halasyamani, 1995). These programs generally provide cognitive-behavioral and social skills training on various topics using a variety of methods. Such programs are commonly referred to as *conflict resolution* and *peer mediation training*. Many of these prevention programs are designed to improve interpersonal problem-solving skills among children and adolescents by training children in cognitive processing, such as identifying the interpersonal problem and generating nonaggressive solutions. There is limited evidence, however, that such programs are actually effective in reducing violence.

David Grossman and his colleagues (1997) assessed the efficacy of one such program for children in elementary school called "The Second Step: A Violence Prevention Curriculum." The program involved 30 lessons, each lasting about 35 minutes, taught once or twice a week. Each lesson consisted of a photograph accompanied by a social scenario that formed the basis for discussion, role playing, and conceptual activities. Lessons were arranged in three units: (1) empathy training, in which students identified their own feelings and those of others; (2) impulse control, in which students were presented a problem-solving strategy and behavioral skills for effecting solutions (e.g., apologizing or dealing with peer pressure); and (3) anger management, in which students were presented a coping strategy and behavioral skills for tense situations.

Twelve elementary schools in King County, Washington, were paired according to three criteria: the school district, the proportion of students receiving free or reduced-cost lunch, and the proportion of minority enrollment. After pairing, schools in each pair were randomly assigned either to receive the Second Step program (experimental groups) or to receive no violence prevention curriculum (control groups). Random assignment was necessary so the researchers could be more confident that any differences observed in aggression and violent behavior between the two groups after the program could be attributed to the program alone and not to some other factor. Violent and aggressive behavior was measured in three ways: teacher ratings of each child's behavior, parent ratings, and direct observation of students by trained observers in the classroom, playground, and cafeteria. Measures of aggression were taken at three time periods: before the start of the curriculum (baseline), 2 weeks after the conclusion of the curriculum, and 6 months after the curriculum.

To determine the effectiveness of the Second Step program, researchers examined the change in aggression between scores measured at baseline and those from the second and third periods of data collection. Grossman and his colleagues found encouraging results: Observed physically aggressive behavior decreased significantly more among children who engaged in the curriculum than among children in the control group who were not exposed to the Second Step program. Moreover, prosocial behavior increased significantly among children in the Second Step program compared to the control group. The authors of the study concluded, "This violence prevention curriculum appears to lead to modest reductions in levels of aggressive behavior and increases in neutral/prosocial behavior in school among second and third graders" (Grossman et al., 1997:1608).

STRENGTHS AND LIMITATIONS OF SOCIAL RESEARCH

These case studies are only four of the dozens of studies investigating youth violence, but they illustrate some of the questions criminological research can address, several different methods social scientists studying these issues can use, and ways criminological research can inform public policy. Notice how each of the four studies was designed to reduce the errors common in everyday reasoning:

- The clear definition of the population of interest in each study and the selection of a broad, representative sample of that population in two studies increased the researchers' ability to draw conclusions without overgeneralizing findings to groups to which they did not apply.
- The use of surveys in which each respondent was asked the same set of questions reduced the risk of selective or inaccurate observation.

- The risk of illogical reasoning was reduced by carefully describing each stage of the research, clearly presenting the findings, and carefully testing the basis for cause-and-effect conclusions.
- Resistance to change was reduced by using an experimental design that randomly assigned classes to an experimental treatment (the Second Step program) and a control group to fairly evaluate the efficacy of the program.

Nevertheless, we would be less than honest if we implied that you enter the realm of beauty, truth, and light whenever you engage in research or whenever you base your opinions only on the best available social research. Research always has some limitations and some flaws (as does any human endeavor), and findings are always subject to differing interpretations. Social research permits you to see more, to observe with fewer distortions, and to describe more clearly to others what your opinions are based on, but it will not settle all arguments. Other people will always have differing opinions, and some of those others will be social scientists who have conducted their own studies and drawn different conclusions. Do other programs similar to Second Step reduce levels of aggression among students? Only a handful of studies have used randomized controlled designs to examine these programs, and the results of these studies have been mixed. Like the Grossman study, some researchers have found a reduction in aggressive behavior by children exposed to such social skills training programs, whereas others have not. Until more scientific research is conducted to evaluate these programs, it is difficult to determine whether the money poured into such programs by school districts is well spent.

But even in areas of research that are fraught with controversy, where social scientists differ in their interpretations of the evidence, the quest for new and more sophisticated research has value. What is most important for improving understanding of the social world and issues in criminology is *not* the result of any particular study but the accumulation of evidence from different studies of related issues. By designing new studies that focus on the weak points or controversial conclusions of prior research, social scientists contribute to a body of findings that gradually expands our knowledge about the social world and resolves some of the disagreements about it.

Social researchers investigating issues in criminal justice and criminology will always disagree somewhat because of their differing research opportunities, methodological approaches, and policy preferences. There are many heated debates in the criminological literature. For example, one issue that has recently received increased attention is how the availability of guns is related to overall levels of violence. Some research has found that greater gun availability is associated with more robberies, home burglaries, assaults, and homicides with guns. However, others have argued that gun ownership for self-defense can reduce robbery and home burglary completion rates, thus theoretically decreasing the rewards for these crimes and increasing the perceived risks to offenders. According to yet another view, someone who is planning an attack and fears that potential robbery and/or burglary victims are armed may simply decide to acquire superior firepower and carry out the attack regardless (see Reiss & Roth, 1993, for review). As you can see, much more research is required using a variety of methods to resolve this debate.

Whether you plan to conduct your own research projects, read others' research reports, or just think about and act in the social world, knowing about research methods has many benefits. This knowledge will give you greater confidence in your own opinions, improve your ability to evaluate others' opinions, and encourage you to refine your questions, answers, and methods of inquiry about the social world.

Of course, the methods of social science, as careful as they may be, cannot answer all questions of interest to criminologists. Should we do unto others what we would have them do unto us? That's a very important question that has been asked throughout history, but we must turn to religion or philosophy to answer questions about values. Social research on the consequences of forgiveness or the sources of interpersonal conflict may help us understand and implement our values, but even the best research cannot tell us which values should guide our lives.

TYPES OF RESEARCH METHODS

As you will see in this book, the data we utilize in criminological research are derived from many different sources, and the research methods we employ in criminology and criminal justice are very diverse.

An **experimental approach** is also used in criminological research, particularly when the efficacy of a program or policy is being evaluated. As we will see in Chapter 5, true experiments must have three things: two groups (one receiving the treatment or intervention and the other receiving no treatment or another form thereof); random assignment to these two groups; and an assessment of change in the outcome variable after the treatment or policy has been received. Quasi-experimental designs, experiments that lack one of these three ingredients, also are used in our discipline. Chapter 9 focuses exclusively on research designs used in evaluation research.

Asking people questions on **surveys** or **questionnaires** is another popular method used by criminological researchers, and is probably the most versatile. Most concepts about individuals can be defined in such a way that measurement with one or more questions becomes an option. These surveys can be self-administered by respondents (e.g., through the mail) or can be read by an interviewer (e.g., through a telephone survey).

Although in principle survey questions can be a straightforward and efficient means to measure individual characteristics, facts about events, level of knowledge, and opinions of any sort, in practice survey questions can result in misleading or inappropriate answers. All questions proposed for a survey must be screened carefully for their adherence to basic guidelines and then tested and revised until the researcher feels some confidence that they will be clear to the intended respondents (Fowler, 1995). Some variables may prove to be inappropriate for measurement with any type of question. We have to recognize that memories and perceptions of the events about which we might like to ask can be limited. Specific guidelines for writing questions and developing surveys are presented in Chapter 6.

In other cases, a researcher may want to make her presence known and directly participate in the activity being observed. Included in this type of research design is **participant observation,** which involves developing a sustained relationship with people while they go about their normal activities. In other instances, the subject matter of interest may not be amenable to a survey, or perhaps we want more detailed and in-depth information than questions with fixed formats can answer. In these cases, we turn to research techniques such as participant observation and **intensive interviewing**. These methods are preferred when we seek in-depth information on an individual's feelings, experiences, and perceptions. Chapter 7 shows how these methods and other field research techniques can uncover aspects of the social world that we are likely to miss in experiments and surveys.

Secondary data analysis (Riedel, 2000), which is the reanalysis of already existing data, is another method used by researchers. These data usually come from one of two places: from official sources such as local or federal agencies (e.g., rates of crime reported to police, information on incarcerated offenders from state correctional authorities, adjudication data from the courts), or from surveys sponsored by government agencies or conducted by other researchers. Virtually all of the data collected by government agencies and a great deal of survey data collected by independent researchers are made available to the public through the Inter-University Consortium for Political and Social Research (ICPSR), which is located at the University of Michigan. When documents from the past, such as correspondence, newspaper accounts, and trial transcripts, are analyzed, the research is generally termed *historical events research*. Another type of indirect measurement is called **content analysis.** In this type of study, a researcher studies representations of the research topic in such media forms as news articles, TV shows, and radio talk shows. An investigation of the drinking climate on campuses might include a count of the amount of space devoted to ads for alcoholic beverages in a sample of issues of the student newspaper. Campus publications also might be coded to indicate the number of times that statements discouraging substance abuse appear. Content analysis techniques also can be applied to legal opinions, historical documents, novels, songs, or other cultural productions. With the advent of computer technology, **crime mapping** also has become a popular method for examining the relationship between criminal behavior and other social indicators. Chapter 8 illustrates the importance of these unobtrusive research techniques in research in criminology and criminal justice.

Using available data, asking questions, making observations, and using indirect measures are interrelated measurement tools, each of which may include or be supplemented by the others. From people's answers to survey questions, the U.S. Bureau of the Census develops widely consulted census reports on people, firms, and geographic units in the United States. Data from employee surveys may be supplemented by information available in company records. Interviewers may record observations about those whom they question. Researchers may use insights gleaned from questioning participants to make sense of the social interaction they have observed. Unobtrusive indicators could be used to evaluate the honesty of survey responses. This multiple-method approach will be discussed in detail in Chapter 10.

Qualitative and Quantitative Methods

In general, research methods can be divided into two somewhat different domains called quantitative research methods and qualitative research methods. Did you notice the difference between the types of data the case studies discussed at the beginning of the chapter used? The data collected in the Youth Risk Behavior Survey were counts of the responses students gave on the survey. These data were numerical, so we say that this study used **quantitative methods.** Felson and his colleagues (1994) looked at the extent to which changes in attitudes toward violence also changed violent behavior; they examined this relationship with statistical methods like correlations and regression coefficients.

This, too, represents quantitative methods. In contrast, Asmussen and Creswell's (1995) exploratory study used in-depth interviews with people who had experienced the attempted school shooting. This methodology was designed to capture the social reality of the participants as they experienced it, in their own words rather than in predetermined categories. Because they focused on the participants' words rather than counts and numbers, we say that this study used **qualitative methods.**

Quantitative methods   Methods such as surveys and experiments that record variation in social life in terms of categories that vary in amount. Data that are treated as quantitative are either numbers or attributes that can be ordered in terms of magnitude.

Qualitative methods   Methods such as participant observation, intensive interviewing, and focus groups that are designed to capture social life as participants experience it, rather than in categories predetermined by the researcher. Data that are treated as qualitative are mostly written or spoken words or observations that do not have a direct numerical interpretation.

The distinction between quantitative and qualitative methods involves more than just the type of data collected. Quantitative methods are most often used when the motives for research are explanation, description, or evaluation. Exploration is the most common motive for using qualitative methods, although researchers also use these methods for descriptive and evaluative purposes. The goals of quantitative and qualitative researchers also may differ. Whereas quantitative researchers generally accept the goal of developing an understanding that correctly reflects what is actually happening in the real world, some qualitative researchers instead emphasize the goal of developing an "authentic" understanding of a social process or social setting (Gubrium & Holstein, 1997). An authentic understanding is one that reflects *fairly* the various perspectives of participants in that setting.

As important as it is, we don't want to place too much emphasis on the distinction between qualitative and quantitative methods because social scientists often combine these methods in order to enrich their research. For example, "qualitative knowing" about social settings can be essential for understanding patterns in quantitative data (Campbell & Russo, 1999:141). Qualitative data can be converted to quantitative data, for example, when we count the frequency of particular words or phrases in a text or measure the time elapsed between different behaviors that we have observed. Surveys that collect primarily quantitative data also may include questions asking for written responses, and these responses may be used in a qualitative, textual analysis. Researchers using quantitative methods may engage in some exploration in order to find unexpected patterns in their data. Qualitative researchers may test explicit explanations of social phenomena using textual or observational data. We will discuss qualitative methods in greater detail in Chapter 7, but we will highlight these "mixed method" approaches throughout the text, as well as in Chapter 10. Despite the use of mixed methods in criminological research, it is important to understand the different research philosophies that underlie the two categories of methods.

SOCIAL RESEARCH PHILOSOPHIES

What influences the choice of a research strategy? The motive for conducting research is critical: An explanatory or evaluative motive generally leads a researcher to use quantitative methods, whereas an exploratory motive often results in the use of qualitative methods. Of course, a descriptive motive means choosing a descriptive research strategy.

A researcher's philosophical perspective on reality and on the appropriate role of the researcher also will shape her methodological preferences. Researchers with a **positivist** philosophy believe that there is an objective reality that exists apart from the perceptions of those who observe it; the goal of science is to better understand this reality.

> Whatever nature "really" is, we assume that it presents itself in precisely the same way to the same human observer standing at different points in time and space. . . . We assume that it also presents itself in precisely the same way across different human observers standing at the same point in time and space. (Wallace, 1983:461)

This philosophy is traditionally associated with science (Weber, 1949:72), with the expectation that there are universal laws of human behavior, and with the belief that scientists must be objective and unbiased to see reality clearly.

Postpositivism is a philosophy of reality that is closely related to positivism. Postpositivists believe that there is an external, objective reality, but are very sensitive to the complexity of this reality and the limitations of the scientists who study it—and, for social scientists, the biases they bring to the study of social beings like themselves (Guba & Lincoln, 1994:109–111). As a result, they do not think scientists can ever be sure that their methods allow them to perceive objective reality; the goal of science can only be to achieve **intersubjective agreement** among scientists about the nature of reality (Wallace, 1983:461). For example, postpositivists may worry that researchers' predispositions may bias them in favor of deterrence theory. Therefore, they will remain somewhat skeptical of results that support predictions based on deterrence until a number of researchers feel that they have found supportive evidence. The postpositivist retains much more confidence in the ability of the community of social researchers to develop an unbiased account of reality than in the ability of any individual social scientist to do so (Campbell & Russo, 1999:144).

Qualitative research often is guided by a very different philosophy: **interpretivism**. Interpretive social scientists believe that social reality is socially constructed and that the goal of social scientists is to understand what meanings people give to reality, not to determine how reality works apart from these interpretations. This philosophy maintains that there is no concrete, objective reality that scientific methods help us to understand (Lynch & Bogen, 1997); instead, interpretivists (some call them constructivists) believe that scientists construct an image of reality based on their own preferences and prejudices and their interactions with others. From this standpoint, the goal of validity becomes meaningless: "Truth is a matter of the best-informed and most sophisticated construction on which there is consensus at a given time" (Schwandt, 1994:128).

> Searching for universally applicable social laws can distract from learning what people know and how they understand their lives. The interpretive social researcher examines

meanings that have been socially constructed. . . . There is not one reality out there to be measured; objects and events are understood by different people differently, and those perceptions are the reality—or realities—that social science should focus on. (Rubin & Rubin, 1995:35)

Positivism   The belief, shared by most scientists, that there is a reality that exists quite apart from our own perception of it, although our knowledge of this reality may never be complete.

Intersubjective agreement   An agreement by different observers on what is happening in the natural or social world.

Postpositivism   The belief that there is an empirical reality, but that our understanding of it is limited by its complexity and by the biases and other limitations of researchers.

Interpretivism   The belief that reality is socially constructed and that the goal of social scientists is to understand what meanings people give to that reality.

Which philosophy makes the most sense to you? Do you agree with positivists and postpositivists that scientific methods can help us understand the social world as it is, not just as we would like to think it is? Does the interpretivist focus on meanings sound like a good idea? Whatever your answers to these questions, you would probably agree that developing a valid understanding of the social world is not an easy task for social scientists. People are influenced by many other people and numerous events throughout their lives; we don't fully understand these influences until we know what meanings people attach to them, and we can't directly perceive these meanings.

VALIDITY: THE GOAL OF SOCIAL RESEARCH

A scientist seeks to develop an accurate understanding of empirical reality, the reality we encounter firsthand, by conducting research that leads to valid knowledge about the world. But when is knowledge valid? In general, we have reached the goal of **validity** when our statements or conclusions about empirical reality are correct. If you look out your window and observe that it is raining, this is probably a valid observation, if your eyes and ears are to be trusted. However, if you pick up the newspaper and read that the majority of Americans favor the death penalty, this conclusion is of questionable validity because it is probably based on an interpretation of a social survey. As you will see in Chapter 7, attitudes toward the death penalty vary substantially depending on the wording of the questions asked.

To some of you, the goal of validity may sound a bit far-fetched. After all, how can we really be sure our understandings of empirical phenomena are correct when we can perceive the world only through the filter of our own senses? You needn't worry. Such skepticism will help you remember the tenuousness of all knowledge and will keep you properly skeptical about new discoveries.

This book is about validity more than anything else—about how to conduct research that leads to valid interpretations of the social world. We will refer to validity repeatedly, and we ask you to register it in your brain now as the central goal of all the research conducted in our field. The goal of research conducted by social scientists investigating issues related to criminology and criminal justice is not to come up with conclusions that people will like or conclusions that suit their personal preferences. The goal is to determine the most valid answers through empirical research methods.

We must be concerned with three aspects of validity: **measurement validity, generalizability,** and **causal validity** (also known as internal validity). Each of these three aspects of validity is essential: Conclusions based on invalid measures, invalid generalizations, or invalid causal inferences will themselves be invalid.

Imagine that we survey a sample of 250 high school seniors and ask them two questions: "Do you have friends who have taken illegal drugs in the past 6 months? (the measure of peer behavior) and "Have you taken illegal drugs in the past 6 months?" (individual use measure). We then compare the frequency of illegal drug use between students who have friends who have used illegal drugs and those whose friends have not used illegal drugs. We find that students who have friends who have used illegal drugs in the last 6 months are more likely to have used drugs themselves, and we conclude that drug use is, in part, due to the influence of peers.

But did our questions indeed tell us the frequency with which the students and their peers took illegal drugs? If they did, we achieved measurement validity. Do our results hold true for the larger adolescent population to which our conclusion referred? If so, our conclusion would satisfy the criterion for generalizability. Did the likelihood of students taking drugs actually increase if they had friends who also took drugs? If so, our conclusion is causally valid.

Measurement validity   Exists when a measure measures what we think it measures.

Generalizability   Exists when a conclusion holds true for the population, group, setting, or event that we say it does, given the conditions that we specify.

Causal validity (internal validity)   Exists when a conclusion that A leads to or results in B is correct.

The goal in research is to achieve valid understandings of the social world by coming to conclusions that rest on valid measures and valid causal assertions and that are generalizable to the population of interest. Once we have learned how to develop studies that give us reasonably valid results and how to evaluate studies according to how well they meet this criterion, we will be well along on the road to becoming expert researchers. Chapters 3, 4, and 5 discuss these three aspects of validity and the specific techniques used to maximize the validity of our measures, our generalizations, and our causal assertions in greater detail.

CONCLUSION

We hope this first chapter has given you an idea of what to expect in the rest of this book. Our aim is to introduce you to social research methods by describing what social scientists have learned about issues in criminology and criminal justice as well as how they learned it. The substance of social science inevitably is more interesting than its methods, but the methods also become more interesting when they're not taught as isolated techniques. We have focused attention on research on youth violence and delinquency in this chapter; in subsequent chapters, we will introduce research examples from other areas.

Chapter 2 continues to build the foundation for our study of social research by reviewing the types of problems that criminologists study, the role of theory, the major steps in the research process, and other sources of information that may be used in social research. We stress the importance of considering scientific standards in social research and review generally accepted ethical guidelines. Throughout the chapter, we use several studies of domestic violence to illustrate the research process.

KEY TERMS

Causal validity (internal validity)
Content analysis
Crime mapping
Cross-population generalizability
Descriptive research
Evaluation research
Experimental approach
Explanatory research
Exploratory research
External validity
Generalizability
Illogical reasoning
Inaccurate observation
Intensive interviewing
Interpretivism
Intersubjective agreement

Measurement validity
Overgeneralization
Participant observation
Positivism
Postpositivism
Qualitative methods
Quantitative methods
Questionnaire
Resistance to change
Science
Secondary data analysis
Selective observation
Social science
Survey
Unobtrusive measures
Validity

HIGHLIGHTS

- Criminological research cannot resolve value questions or provide answers that will convince everyone and remain settled for all time.

- All empirically based methods of investigation are based on either direct experience or others' statements.

- Four common errors in reasoning are overgeneralization, selective or inaccurate observation, illogical reasoning, and resistance to change. Illogical reasoning is due to the complexity of the social world, self-interestedness, and human subjectivity. Resistance to change may be due to unquestioning acceptance of tradition or of those in positions of authority, or to self-interested resistance to admitting the need to change one's beliefs.

- Social science is the use of logical, systematic, documented methods to investigate individuals, societies, and social processes, as well as the knowledge produced by these investigations.

- Criminological research can be motivated by policy guidance and program management needs, academic concerns, and charitable impulses.

- Criminological research can be descriptive, exploratory, explanatory, or evaluative, or some combination of these.

- Quantitative methods record variation in social life in terms of categories that vary in amount. Qualitative methods are designed to capture social life as participants experience it, rather than in categories predetermined by the researcher.

- Positivism is the belief that there is a reality that exists quite apart from one's own perception of it that is amenable to observation.

- Intersubjective agreement is an agreement by different observers on what is happening in the natural or social world.

- Postpositivism is the belief that there is an empirical reality, but that our understanding of it is limited by its complexity and by the biases and other limitations of researchers.

- Interpretivism is the belief that reality is socially constructed and the goal of social science should be to understand what meanings people give to that reality.

- Valid knowledge is the central concern of scientific research. The three components of validity are measurement validity, generalizability (both from the sample to the population from which it was selected and from the sample to other populations), and causal (internal) validity.

EXERCISES

1. What criminological topic or issue would you focus on if you could design a research project without any concern for costs? What are your motives for studying this topic? List at least four of your beliefs about this phenomenon. Try to identify the sources of each belief—for example, the television, newspaper, parental influence.

2. Develop four research questions related to your chosen topic or issue, one for each of the four types of research (descriptive, exploratory, explanatory, and evaluative). Be specific.

3. Read the abstracts of each article in a recent issue of a major criminological journal. Identify the type of research conducted for each study.

DEVELOPING A RESEARCH PROPOSAL

Will you develop a research proposal in this course? If so, you should begin to consider your alternatives.

1. What topic would you focus on if you could design a social research project without any concern for costs? What are your motives for studying this topic?

2. Develop four questions that you might investigate about the topic you just selected. Each question should reflect a different research motive: description, exploration, explanation, or evaluation. Be specific.

3. Which question most interests you? Would you prefer to attempt to answer that question with quantitative or qualitative methods? Why?

WEB EXERCISES

1. You have been asked to prepare a brief presentation on a criminological topic or issue of interest to you. Go to the Bureau of Justice Statistics (BJS) Web site at www.ojp.usdoj.gov/bjs/. Browse the BJS publications for a topic that interests you. Write a short outline for a 5- to 10-minute presentation regarding your topic, including statistics and other relevant information.

2. Go to the Federal Bureau of Investigation (FBI) Web site at www.fbi.gov. Explore the types of programs and initiatives sponsored by the FBI. Discuss at least three of these programs or initiatives in terms of their purposes and goals. For each program or initiative examined, do you believe the program/initiative is effective? What are the major weaknesses? What changes would you propose the FBI make to more effectively meet the goals of the program or initiative?

SPSS EXERCISES

The SPSS exercises at the end of each chapter use the data sets included in the CD-ROM packaged with this book. In NCS91.POR, a sample of 503 robbery incidents from the 1991 National Crime Victimization Survey, variable V2089 identifies the metropolitan statistical area (MSA) status (urban, suburban, or rural) of each robbery incident included in the data set.

1. Create a bar chart of V2089 using the graph procedure to show the percentage of robbery incidents occurring in urban, suburban, and rural areas. Be sure to select "options" and indicate that you want to leave out the missing values.

2. Write four research questions, one for each type of social research (descriptive, exploratory, explanatory, and evaluative), regarding the distribution of robbery incidents by MSA status.

3. Discuss the possible reasons (policy, academic, or personal) for conducting research on the location of robbery incidents.

Chapter 2

THE PROCESS AND PROBLEMS OF CRIMINOLOGICAL RESEARCH

On July 4, 1997, the *Pathfinder* module landed on Mars after a 6-month trip from Earth. Within a day, a little vehicle was exploring Martian rocks and soil. Cameras were transmitting live pictures back to Earth, where millions of people were tuned in through their computers to special World Wide Web sites set up for the occasion. Once again, science was transforming our image of the universe and helping us transcend our natural physical and mental limits, just as computers, brain-imaging devices, and nuclear power had done before. It is no exaggeration to say that the physical and natural sciences have forever altered human life and continue to do so. Although social science has nothing like this impact, it does influence the design of social programs, the course of elections, the composition of juries, the strategies of business, and most important, our understanding of the social world.

Consider the impact of criminological research on the crime of domestic violence. Intimate partner violence (violence between spouses or intimates), sometimes referred to as domestic violence, is a major problem in our society, with police responding to between 2 million and 8 million complaints of assault by a spouse or lover yearly (Sherman, 1992:6). Moreover, it is estimated from victimization surveys that many of these assault are never reported to police (Bachman and Saltzman, 1995; Tjaden and Thoeness, 2000). Domestic violence is not just a frequent crime, it is also costly—not only in terms of the injuries suffered by the parties involved but also in terms of shattered families. What to do about this major social problem, then, is an important policy question. One thing the police could do would be to respond to incidents of domestic violence in such a way that the offender would be less likely to be violent in the future. That is, proper police response could possibly prevent some acts of domestic violence. But what is the proper police response?

In 1981, the Police Foundation and the Minneapolis Police Department began an experiment to determine whether arresting accused spouse abusers on the spot would deter future offending incidents. In responding to police calls for service in misdemeanor domestic cases, the responding officer randomly assigned the case to be resolved by either arresting or not arresting the suspect on the scene. The experimental treatment, then, was whether the suspect was arrested, and the researchers wanted to know whether arrest was better than not arresting the suspect in reducing recidivism (subsequent assaults against the same victim). The study's results, which were widely publicized, indicated that arrest did have a deterrent effect. Partly as a result of the reported results of this experiment, the percentage of urban police departments that made arrest the preferred response to complaints of domestic violence rose from 10% in 1984 to 90% in 1988 (Sherman, 1992:14). Six other cities then hosted studies like the Minneapolis experiment (collectively, this was called the Spouse Assault Replication Program—SARP), but the results were not always so clear-cut as in the original study (Buzawa & Buzawa, 1996; Hirschel, Hutchison, & Dean, 1992; Pate & Hamilton, 1992; Sherman, 1992; Sherman & Berk, 1984). In some cities (and for some people), arrest did seem to prevent future incidents of domestic assault; in other cities, it seemed only to make matters worse, contributing to additional assaults; and in still other cities, arrest seemed to have no discernable effect. After these replications of the original Minneapolis experiment, people wondered, "Just what is the effect of arrest in reducing domestic violence cases, and how should the police respond to such cases?" The answer was not clear. The Minneapolis Domestic Violence Experiment, the studies modeled after it, and the related controversies provide many examples for a systematic overview of the social research process.

The first concern in criminological research (indeed in any research) is deciding what to study. That is, how does one go about selecting an issue, problem, or question to address with research? As you will learn in the next section, one source of the motivation to do research is criminological theory. In criminology, as in any other science, theory plays an important role as a basis for formulating research questions and later understanding the larger implications of one's research results. Another motivation for research is one's personal interests. There is nothing wrong with researching those issues that you find fascinating or interesting. There are other motivational sources for research that we will explore in this chapter, including helping to answer questions illuminated by earlier research. In this chapter we use the Minneapolis experiment and the SARP replication research to illustrate the three main research strategies: deductive, inductive, and descriptive research. In all three, theory and data are inextricably linked. The chapter ends with scientific and ethical guidelines that should be adhered to no matter what the research strategy, and shows how the Minneapolis experiment followed these guidelines. By the chapter's end, you should be ready to formulate a criminological research question, design a general strategy for answering this question, and critique previous studies that addressed this question. You can think of Chapter 1 as having introduced the "why" of criminological research; Chapter 2 introduces the "how."

CRIMINOLOGICAL RESEARCH QUESTIONS

How does a criminologist decide what to study and research? A **criminological research question** is a question about some aspect of crime or criminals that you seek to answer through the collection and analysis of firsthand, verifiable, empirical data. The types of questions that can be asked are virtually limitless. For example, "Are children who are violent when young more likely than nonviolent children to use violence as adults?" "Does the race of the victim who is killed influence whether someone is sentenced to death rather than life imprisonment?" "Why do some kinds of neighborhoods have more crime than others? Is it due to the kinds of people who live there or characteristics of the neighborhood itself?" "Does community policing reduce the crime rate?" "Has the U.S. government's war on drugs done anything to reduce the use of illegal drugs?" So many research questions are possible in criminology that it is more of a challenge to specify what does *not* qualify as a social research question than to specify what does.

But that doesn't mean it is easy to specify a research question. In fact, formulating a good research question can be surprisingly difficult. We can break the process into three stages: identifying one or more questions for study, refining the questions, and then evaluating the questions.

Identifying Criminological Research Questions

Formulating a research question is often an intensely personal process in addition to being a scientific or professional one. Research questions may emerge from your "personal troubles," as C. Wright Mills (1959) put it, or your personal experiences. These troubles or experiences could range from how you felt when you were picked up by the police and perhaps arrested when you were a teenager for something you did not do, to the awareness you may have that crime is not randomly distributed within a city but that there seem to be "good" or safe parts of town and "bad" or unsafe areas. You may find yourself asking questions such as "Do the police sometimes make things worse for people when they arrest them—worse in the sense that they are more likely to commit crime in the future?" or "Does victimization change a person's trust in others?" or "Does involvement in crime vary by one's age, social class, gender, or racial/ethnic group?" Can you think of other possible research questions that flow from your own experiences in the world?

The experience of others is another fruitful source of research questions. Knowing a relative who was abused by a spouse, seeing a TV special about violence, or reading a gang member's autobiography can stimulate questions about general criminological processes. Can you draft a research question based on a relative's experiences, a TV show, or a book?

Other researchers may also pose interesting questions for you to study. Most research articles end with some suggestions for additional research that highlight unresolved issues. For example, Lawrence Sherman and Douglas Smith, with their colleagues, concluded an article on some of the replications of the Minneapolis experiment on police responses to spouse abuse by suggesting that "deterrence may be effective for a substantial segment of the offender population. . . . [H]owever, the underlying mechanisms remain obscure" (Sherman et al., 1992:706). A new study could focus on the mechanisms: Why or under what conditions does the arrest of offenders who are employed deter them from future criminal acts? Exactly what occurs when someone is arrested for domestic violence that may lead him or her not to be violent against a spouse in the future? Is it the brute fear of being arrested and having to go to jail? Is it the fear that one's employer may find out and fire him or her? Is it the fear that members of the community may learn about the arrest and the offender doesn't want to lose his or her good standing in the neighborhood? Is it all of these? Any issue of a journal in your field is likely to have comments that point toward unresolved issues.

The primary source of research questions for many criminologists is criminological theory. As you will soon learn, criminological theory provides an explanation as to why crime occurs, or occurs in some places and under some conditions but not others. Theory, then, is a very rich source of research ideas. Some researchers spend much of their careers conducting research intended to refine an answer to one central research question. For example, you may find rational choice theory to be a useful approach to understanding diverse forms of social behavior, like crime, because you think people do seem to make decisions on the basis of personal cost–benefit calculations. So you may ask whether rational choice theory can explain why some people commit crimes and others do not, or why some people decide to quit committing crimes while others continue their criminal ways.

Finally, some research questions have very pragmatic sources. You may focus on a research question posed by someone else because doing so seems to be to your professional or financial advantage. Some criminologists conduct research on specific questions posed by a funding source in what is termed a request for proposals (RFP). (Sometimes the acronym RFA is used, meaning request for applications.) Or you may learn that the public defenders in your city are curious as to whether they are more successful in getting their clients acquitted of a criminal charge than private lawyers.

Refining Criminological Research Questions

As you have perhaps surmised by now, the problem is not so much coming up with interesting criminological questions for research as it is focusing on a problem of manageable size. We are often interested in much more than we can reasonably investigate with our limited time and resources (or the limited resources of a funding agency). Researchers may worry about staking a research project (and thereby a grant) on a particular problem and so address several research questions at once, often in a jumbled fashion. It may also seem risky to focus on a research question that may lead to results discrepant with our own cherished assumptions about the social world. In addition, the prospective commitment of time and effort for some research questions may seem overwhelming, resulting in a certain degree of paralysis (not that the authors have any experience with this!).

The best way to avoid these problems is to develop the research question one bit at a time with a step-by-step strategy. Don't keep hoping that the perfect research question will just spring forth from your pen. Instead, develop a list of possible research questions as you go along. At the appropriate time, you can look through this list for the research questions that appear more than once. Narrow your list to the most interesting, most workable candidates. Repeat this process as long as it helps to improve your research questions. Keep in mind that the research you are currently working on will likely generate additional research questions for you to answer.

Evaluating Criminological Research Questions

In the third stage of selecting a criminological research question, you evaluate the best candidate against the criteria for good social research questions: feasibility given the time and resources available, social importance, and scientific relevance (King, Keohane, & Verba, 1994).

The research question in the Minneapolis Domestic Violence Experiment, "Does the formal sanction of police arrest versus non-arrest inhibit domestic violence?", certainly meets the criteria of social importance and scientific relevance, but it would not be a feasible question for a student project because it would require you to try to get the cooperation of a police department. You might instead ask the question "Do people (students) think that arrest will inhibit domestic violence?" This is a question that you could study with an on-campus survey. Or perhaps you could work out an arrangement with a local battered women's shelter to study the question "What leads some women to call the police when they are the victims of domestic violence, and why do they sometimes not call?" A review of the literature, however, might convince you that this and other questions may not be scientifically relevant because they have been studied enough.

Feasibility

You must be able to conduct any study within the time frame and resources you have. If time is short, questions that involve long-term change may not be feasible—for example, "If a state has recently changed its law so that it now permits capital punishment for those convicted of murder, does it eventually see a reduction in the homicide rate over time?" This is an interesting and important question, but one that requires years of data collection and research. Another issue is what people or groups you can expect to gain access to. Although well-experienced researchers may be granted access to police or correctional department files to do their research, less seasoned and well-known researchers or students may not be granted such access. It is also often difficult for even the most experienced of researchers to be given full access to the deliberations of a criminal jury. For someone interested in white-collar crime, recording the interactions that take place in corporate boardrooms may also be taboo.

Then you must consider whether you will have any additional resources, such as other researchers to collaborate with or research funds. Remember that there are severe limits on what one person can accomplish. On the other hand, you might work in an organization that collects data on employees, customers, or clients that are relevant to your research interests. Or you may be able to piggyback your research onto a larger research project.

You also must be prepared to handle large amounts of quantitative data. A computer and the skills to use it will be essential. Also take into account the constraints you face due to your schedule and other professional or personal commitments and obligations.

The Minneapolis Domestic Violence Experiment shows how ambitious social research questions can be when a team of seasoned researchers secures the backing of influential groups. The project required hundreds of thousands of dollars, the collaboration of many social scientists and criminal justice personnel, and the volunteer efforts of 41 Minneapolis police officers. But don't worry, many worthwhile research questions can be investigated with much more limited resources. You will read in subsequent chapters about studies that addressed important research questions with much fewer resources than the Minneapolis social scientists commanded.

Social Importance

Criminological research is not a simple undertaking, so you must focus on a substantive area that you feel is important and that is either important to the discipline or important for public policy. You also need to feel personally motivated to carry out the study; there is little point in trying to answer a question that doesn't interest you.

In addition, you should consider whether the research question is important to other people. Will an answer to the research question make a difference for society? Again, the Minneapolis Domestic Violence Experiment is an exemplary case. If that study showed that a certain type of police response to domestic violence reduced the risk of subsequent victimization, a great deal of future violence could be prevented. But clearly, criminology and criminal justice are not wanting for important research questions. Social scientists deal with such important issues as the effect of get-tough "three strikes" laws, whether strict supervision of those on parole and probation is more successful than less strict (and less costly) supervision, whether the death penalty deters criminals, whether gangs or the drug trade contributed to the rise in youth violence, whether crime is more prevalent in the United States than in European countries, whether gun control legislation reduces violence—we could go on and on. Many criminological questions deal with very important and troubling issues for our society.

Scientific Relevance

Every research question in criminology should be grounded in the existing empirical literature. By *grounded* we mean the research we do must be informed by what others before us have done on the topic. Whether you formulate a research question because you have been stimulated by an academic article or because you want to investigate a current public policy problem, you must turn to the criminological literature to find out what has already been learned about this question. (Appendix A explains how to find information about previous research, using both printed and computer-based resources.) Even if your research topic has already been investigated by someone else, that does not necessarily mean it would be a bad idea for you to do research on the issue. It would be unreasonable to think of any criminological research question as being settled for all time. You can be sure that some prior study is relevant to almost any research question you can think of, and you can also think of better ways to do research than have been done in the past.

For example, the Minneapolis experiment was built on a substantial body of contradictory theorizing about the impact of punishment on criminality (Sherman & Berk, 1984). Deterrence theory predicted that because it was a more severe penalty, arrest would better deter individuals from repeat offenses than not arresting them. Labeling theory, on the other hand, predicted that arrest would make repeat offenses more likely because it would stigmatize offenders. The researchers found one prior experimental study of this issue, but it was conducted with juveniles. Studies among adults and nonexperimental research had not yielded consistent findings about the effects of arrest on recidivism in domestic violence cases. Clearly, the Minneapolis researchers had good reason for another study. Prior research and theory also helped them develop the most effective research design.

THE ROLE OF CRIMINOLOGICAL THEORY

We have already pointed out that criminological **theory** can be a rich source of research questions. What deserves more attention at this point is the larger role of theory in research. Criminological theories do many things:

- They help us explain or understand things like why some people commit crimes or more crimes than others; why some people quit and others continue; and what the expected effect of good families, harsh punishment, or other factors on crime might be.
- They help us make predictions about the criminological world: "What would be the expected effect on the homicide rate if we employed capital punishment rather than life imprisonment?" "What would be the effect on the rate of property crimes if unemployment were to substantially increase?"
- They help us organize and make sense of empirical findings in a discipline.
- They help guide research.
- They help guide public policy: "What should we do to reduce the level of domestic violence?"

Social scientists, such as criminologists, who connect their work to theories in their discipline can generate better ideas about what to look for in a study and develop conclusions with more implications for other research. Building and evaluating theory is therefore one of the most important objectives of a social science like criminology.

> ***Theory***   A logically interrelated set of propositions about empirical reality. Examples of criminological theories are social learning, routine activities, labeling, general strain, and social disorganization theory.

For centuries, scholars have been interested in developing theories about crime and criminals. Sometimes these theories involve very fanciful ideas that are not well developed or organized, whereas at other times they strike us as being very compelling and well organized. Theories usually contain what are called **theoretical constructs.** In criminology, these theoretical constructs describe what is important to look at to understand, explain, predict, and "do something about" crime. For example, an important theoretical construct in differential association theory is the notion of "definitions favorable and unfavorable to the violation of law." Theories usually link one or more theoretical constructs to others in what are called *relationship statements*. Differential association theory, for example, would link the theoretical construct of favorable/unfavorable definitions to the theoretical construct of involvement in crime to argue: "As one is exposed to more definitions favorable to the violation of law relative to definitions unfavorable to the violation of law, the more one is at risk for criminal behavior." This is a relationship statement that links two theoretical constructs—it states that as exposure to definitions favorable to the law increase, the risk of crime also increases. This is essentially a hypothesis that the theory of differential association entertains—if the theory is true, then the expected relationship should be true. The purpose of much criminological research is to examine the truth value, or empirical validity, of such theoretical relationship statements or hypotheses. Some criminological theories reflect a substantial body of research and the thinking of many social scientists; others are formulated in the course of one investigation. A few have been widely accepted, at least for a time; others are the subject of vigorous controversy, with frequent changes and refinements in response to criticism and new research.

Most criminological research is guided by some theory, although the theory may be only partially developed in a particular study or may even be unrecognized by the researcher. When researchers are involved in conducting a research project or engrossed in writing a research report, they may easily lose sight of the larger picture. It is easy to focus on accumulating or clarifying particular findings rather than considering how the study's findings fit into a more general understanding of the social world. Furthermore, as we shall soon see, just as theory guides research, research findings also influence the development of theory.

We can use the studies of the police response to domestic assault to illustrate the value of theory for social research. Even in this very concrete and practical matter, we must draw on social theories to understand how people act and what should be done about those actions. Consider the three action options that police officers have when they confront a domestic assault suspect (Sherman & Berk, 1984:263). Fellow officers might urge forced separation to achieve short-term peace; police trainers might prefer mediation to resolve the underlying dispute; feminist groups might urge arrest to protect the victim. None of these recommendations is really a theory, but each suggests a different perspective on crime and legal sanctions. The traditional police perspective sees domestic violence as a family matter that should not be the object of formal legal action. The preference for mediation reflects the view that domestic violence involves a family crisis that can be solved with special counseling. The pro-arrest position views domestic violence as a crime as serious as that between strangers and favors arrest for its presumed deterrent effect.

You will encounter these different perspectives if you read much of the literature on domestic violence, or even if you talk with your friends about it. As Exhibit 2.1 shows, each perspective reflects different assumptions about gender roles, about the sources of crime, and about the impact of punishment. In turn, these assumptions reflect different experiences with family conflict, police actions, and the legal system. What we believe about one crime and the appropriate response to it relates to a great many other ideas we have about the social world. Recognizing these relationships is a first step toward becoming a theoretically guided social researcher and a theoretically informed consumer of social research.

Exhibit 2.1   Bases for Three Perspectives on Intimate Partner Violence

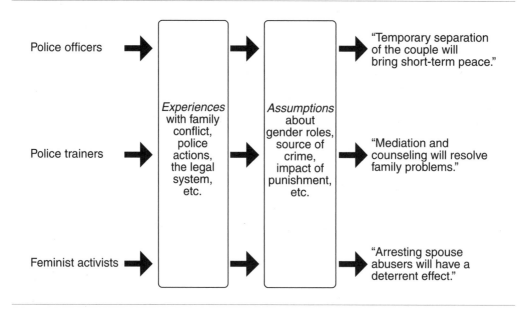

Remember, however, that social theories do not provide the answers to the questions we confront as we formulate topics for research. Instead, social theories suggest the areas on which we should focus and the propositions that we should consider for a test. That is, theories suggest testable hypotheses about things and research verifies whether those hypotheses are true. In fact, one of the most important requirements of theory is that it be testable, or what philosophers of science call **falsifiable**—theoretical statements must be capable of being proven wrong. If a body of thought cannot be empirically tested, it is more like philosophy than theory. For example, Sherman and Berk's (1984) domestic violence research was actually a test of predictions derived from two alternative theories of the impact of punishment on crime, deterrence theory and labeling theory:

Deterrence theory presumes that human beings are at least marginally rational beings who are responsive to the expected costs and benefits of their actions. Committing a crime nets certain benefits for offenders; therefore, if we want to inhibit crime there must be a compensating cost—one cost is the criminal sanction (arrest, conviction, punishment). Deterrence theory expects punishment to inhibit crime in two ways. General deterrence occurs when people see that crime results in undesirable punishments for others, that "crime doesn't pay." The persons who are punished serve as examples for those who have not yet committed an offense but might be thinking of what awaits them should they engage in proscribed acts. Specific deterrence occurs when persons who are punished decide not to commit another offense so they can avoid further punishment (Lempert & Sanders, 1986:86–87). Deterrence theory leads to the prediction that arresting spouse abusers will reduce the likelihood of their reoffending when compared with a less serious sanction (not being arrested but being warned or counseled).

Labeling theory distinguishes between primary deviance, the acts of individuals that lead to public sanction, and secondary deviance, the deviance that occurs in response to public sanction (Hagan, 1994:33). Arrest or some other public sanction for misdeeds labels the offender as deviant in the eyes of others. Once the offender is labeled, others will treat the offender as a deviant, and he or she is then more likely to act in a way that is consistent with the deviant label. Ironically, the act of punishment stimulates more of the very behavior that it was intended to eliminate (Tannenbaum, 1938). This theory suggests that persons arrested for intimate partner violence are more likely to reoffend than those who are caught but not punished because the formal sanction of arrest is more stigmatizing than being warned or counseled. This prediction about the effect of formal legal sanctions is the reverse of the deterrence theory prediction.

Theorizing about the logic behind formal legal punishment also can help us draw connections to more general theories about social processes. Deterrence theory reflects the assumptions of rational choice theory, which assumes behavior is shaped by practical calculations: People break the law if the benefits of doing so exceed the costs. If crime is a rational choice for some people, then increasing the certainty or severity of punishment for crime should shift the cost–benefit balance away from criminal behavior. Labeling theory is rooted in symbolic interactionism, which focuses on the symbolic meanings that people give to behavior (Hagan, 1994:40). Instead of assuming that some forms of behavior are deviant in and of themselves (Scull, 1988:678), symbolic interactionists would view deviance as a consequence of the application of rules and sanctions to an offender (Becker, 1963:9). Exhibit 2.2 summarizes how these general theories relate to the question of whether to arrest spouse abusers.

Exhibit 2.2   Two Social Theories and Their Predictions About the Effect of Arrest for Intimate Partner Assault

	Rational choice theory	**Symbolic interactionism**
Theoretical assumption	People's behavior is shaped by calculations of the costs and benefits of their actions.	People give symbolic meanings to objects, behaviors, and other people.
	⬇	⬇
Criminological component	Deterrence theory: People break the law if the benefits of doing so outweigh the costs.	Labeling theory: People label offenders as deviant, promoting further deviance.
	⬇	⬇
Prediction (effect of arrest for domestic assault)	Abusing spouse, having seen the costs of abuse (namely, arrest), decides not to abuse again.	Abusing spouse, having been labeled as "an abuser," abuses more often.

Does either deterrence theory or labeling theory make sense to you as an explanation for the impact of punishment? Do they seem consistent with your observations of social life? Over a decade after Sherman and Berk's study, Raymond Paternoster, Robert Brame, Ronet Bachman, and Lawrence Sherman (1997) decided to study punishment of domestic violence from a different perspective. They turned to a social psychological theory called procedural justice theory, which explains law-abidingness as resulting from a sense of duty or morality (Tyler, 1990). People obey the law from a sense of obligation that flows from seeing legal authorities as moral and legitimate. From this perspective, individuals who are arrested seem less likely to reoffend if they are treated fairly, irrespective of the outcome of their case, because fair treatment will enhance their view of legal authorities as moral and legitimate. Procedural justice theory expands our view of the punishment process by focusing attention on how police act and how authorities treat subjects, rather than just on the legal decisions they make. Thus, it gives us a sense of the larger importance of the research question.

Are you now less certain about the likely effect of arrest for intimate partner violence? Will arrest decrease abuse because abusers do not wish to suffer from legal sanctions again? Will it increase abuse because abusers feel stigmatized by being arrested and thus are more likely to act like criminals? Or will arrest reduce abuse only if the abusers feel they have been treated fairly by the legal authorities? By suggesting such questions, social theory makes us much more sensitive to the possibilities and so helps us to design better research. Before, during, and after a research investigation, we need to keep thinking theoretically.

SOCIAL RESEARCH STRATEGIES

All social research, including criminological research, is the effort to connect theory and empirical data, the evidence we find in the real world. As Exhibit 2.3 shows, theory and data have a two-way, mutually reinforcing relationship. Research that begins with a theory implying that certain data should be found involves **deductive reasoning,** which moves from general ideas (theory) to specific reality (data). In contrast, **inductive reasoning** moves from the specific to the general.

Both deductive reasoning and inductive reasoning are essential to criminologists. We cannot test an idea fairly unless we use deductive reasoning, stating our expectations in advance and setting up a test in which our idea could be shown to be wrong (falsified). A theory that has not survived these kinds of tests can be regarded only as very tentative. Yet theories, no matter how cherished, cannot make useful predictions for every social situation or research problem that we seek to investigate. Moreover, we may find unexpected patterns in the data we collect, called **serendipitous findings** or **anomalous findings.** In either situation, we should reason inductively, making whatever theoretical sense we can of our unanticipated findings. Then, if the new findings seem sufficiently important, we can return to deductive reasoning and plan a new study to formally test our new ideas.

The Research Circle

This process of conducting research, moving from theory to data and back again, or from data to theory and back again, can be characterized as a **research circle.** Exhibit 2.4

Exhibit 2.3   The Links Between Theory and Data

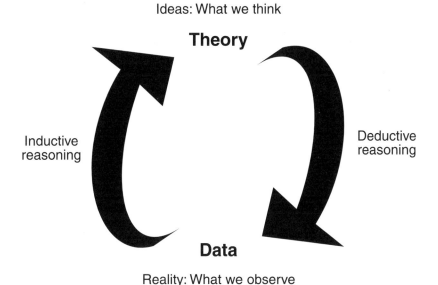

Ideas: What we think

Theory

Inductive
reasoning

Deductive
reasoning

Data

Reality: What we observe

depicts this circle. Note that it mirrors the relationship between theory and data shown in Exhibit 2.3 and that it comprises three main research strategies: deductive research, inductive research, and descriptive research.

Deductive Research

As Exhibit 2.4 shows, **deductive research** proceeds from theorizing to data collection and then back to theorizing. In essence, a specific expectation is deduced from a general premise and then tested.

Notice that a theory leads first to a **hypothesis,** which is a specific implication deduced from the more general theory. Researchers actually test a hypothesis, not the complete theory itself, because theories usually contain many hypotheses. As we stated earlier, a hypothesis proposes a relationship between two or more theoretical constructs or **variables.** Recall that a variable is a characteristic or property that can vary. A **constant** is a characteristic or a property that cannot vary. For example, if we were to conduct some research in a male adult penitentiary, the theoretical construct "type of crime committed" would be a variable because persons will have been incarcerated for different offenses (one person is in for armed robbery, another for rape, etc.). However, the theoretical construct "gender" would be a constant because every inmate in the penitentiary would be male—gender does not vary, it is constant. Would age be a variable or a constant in this group? Would "criminal status" (offender or nonoffender) be a variable or a constant?

Exhibit 2.4   The Research Circle

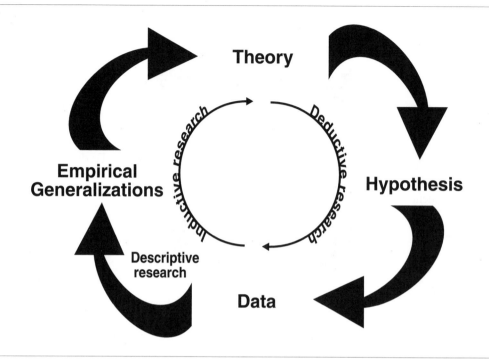

Hypothesis   A tentative statement about empirical reality, involving a relationship between two or more variables.

Example of a hypothesis: The higher the level of residential mobility in a community the higher its rate of crime.

Variable   A characteristic or property that can vary (take on different values or attributes).

Constant   A characteristic or property that does not vary but takes on only one value.

Variables are of critical importance in research because in a hypothesis, variation in one variable is proposed to predict, influence, or cause variation in the other variable. The proposed influence is the **independent variable;** its effect or consequence is the **dependent variable.** After the researchers formulate one or more hypotheses and develop research procedures, they collect data with which to test the hypothesis.

Independent variable   A variable that is hypothesized to cause, or lead to, variation in another variable.

Example of an independent variable: Residential mobility (residents moving in and out of the community).

Dependent variable   A variable that is hypothesized to vary depending on or under the influence of another variable.

Example of a dependent variable: The rate of crime in a community per 1,000 residents.

Hypotheses can be worded in several different ways, and identifying the independent and dependent variables is sometimes difficult. When in doubt, try to rephrase the hypothesis as an if-then statement: "If the independent variable increases (or decreases), then the dependent variable increases (or decreases)." Exhibit 2.5 presents several hypotheses with their independent and dependent variables and their if-then equivalents.

Exhibit 2.5 demonstrates another feature of hypotheses: **direction of association.** When researchers hypothesize that one variable increases as the other variable increases,

Exhibit 2.5   Examples of Hypotheses

Original Hypothesis	Independent Variable	Dependent Variable	If-Then Hypothesis
1. The greater the social disorganization in a community, the higher the rate of crime.	Social disorganization	Crime rate	If social disorganization is higher, then the crime rate is higher.
2. As one's self-control gets stronger, the fewer delinquent acts one commits.	Self-control	Self-reported delinquency	If self-control is higher, then the number of delinquent acts is lower.
3. As the unemployment rate in a community decreases, the community rate of property crime decreases.	Unemployment rate	Rate of property crime	If the unemployment rate is lower, then the rate of property crime is lower.
4. As the discrepancy between one's aspirations and expectations increases, one's level of strain increases.	Discrepancy between one's aspirations and expectations	Strain	If the discrepancy between one's aspirations and expectations is high, then the level of strain is high.
5. Crime is lower in those communities where the police patrol on foot.	Presence of foot patrols	Crime	If a community has police foot patrols, then the level of crime is lower.

the direction of the association is positive (hypotheses 1 and 4 in the exhibit); when one variable decreases as the other variable decreases, the direction of association is also positive (hypothesis 3). In positive relationships, then, the independent and dependent variables move in the same direction (as one increases, the other increases, or as one decreases, the other decreases). But when one variable increases as the other decreases, or vice versa, the direction of association is negative, or inverse (hypothesis 2). In a negative relationship, then, the independent and dependent variables move in opposite directions (as one increases, the other decreases, or as one decreases, the other increases). Hypothesis 5 is a special case, in which the independent variable is categorical. The independent variable cannot be said to increase or decrease. In this case, the concept of direction of association does not apply, and the hypothesis simply states that one category of the independent variable is associated with higher values on the dependent variable.

You can get a better sense of what the direction of a relationship means by looking at Exhibits 2.6 through 2.10, which correspond to the five hypotheses shown in Exhibit 2.5. In these graphs, the independent variable is displayed as the *x* or horizontal axis and the dependent variable is displayed as the *y* or vertical axis. Exhibit 2.6 illustrates the hypothesis that social disorganization and a community's crime rate are positively related. The positive association implies that as social disorganization (the independent variable) increases (moves from being low to being high), the expected change is that the dependent variable will also increase (move from being low to high). This is the same thing as saying that as the level of social disorganization in a community moves from low to high, the level of crime also moves from low to high. In other words, the more social disorganization the more crime. Notice that in a positive relationship the independent and dependent variables are moving in the same direction—as social disorganization increases, so does crime. This positive relationship is shown in Exhibit 2.6 as an upward sloping line in the graph.

Exhibit 2.7 illustrates a graph for a negative association. This graph shows that as one's self-control becomes high (where more self-control means greater restraint over

Exhibit 2.6   Relationship Between Social Disorganization and Crime

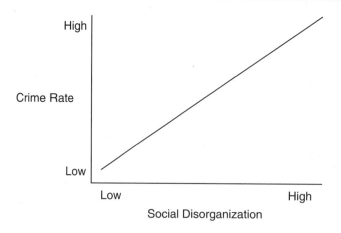

Exhibit 2.7 Relationship Between Self-Control and Number of Delinquent Acts

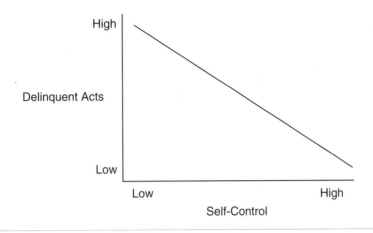

one's impulses), then the number of delinquent acts one commits declines or moves to low. This means that as self-control increases or strengthens, the frequency of delinquent behavior declines or decreases in number. Notice two things about this negative relationship. First, the independent and dependent variables move in opposite directions—as the independent variable (self-control) increases, the dependent variable (delinquency) decreases. Notice also that this negative relationship is shown as a downward sloping line in the graph.

Exhibit 2.8 illustrates a positive relationship but the hypothesis is stated differently. Hypothesis 3 in Exhibit 2.5 states that as the unemployment rate in a community decreases, the rate of property crime in that community is also expected to decrease. Now, this is a positive relationship because the two variables move in the same direction—as the

Exhibit 2.8 Relationship Between Unemployment and Property Crime

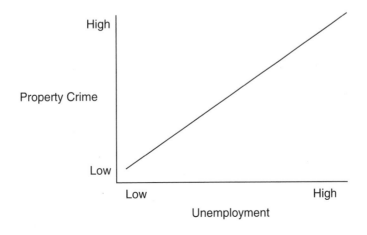

Exhibit 2.9   Relationship Between Aspirations/Expectations and Strain

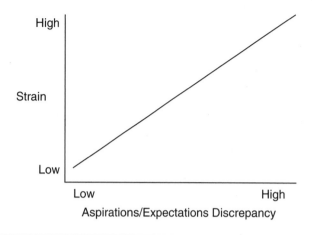

independent variable (unemployment) decreases, so does the dependent variable (the rate of property crime). As with Exhibit 2.6, this positive relationship is seen in an upward sloping line. Note that we could have expressed this hypothesis differently, and more similarly to the first hypothesis, by stating, "As the level of unemployment in a community increases the rate of property crime also increases." This, too, is a positive relationship, because the variables are again moving in the same direction.

Exhibit 2.9 corresponds to the fourth hypothesis in Exhibit 2.5, and illustrates another positive relationship. The hypothesis states that as the discrepancy between what one aspires to obtain and what one expects to obtain gets greater (moves from low to high), the level of strain the person feels also increases. Again, the independent and dependent variables move in the same direction, so the relationship or association between them is positive. Notice, we could have expressed this identical positive relationship slightly differently, by stating, "As the discrepancy between aspirations and expectations decreases, the level of strain decreases." Had we stated the hypothesis in this way, the graph would look exactly the same.

Finally, Exhibit 2.10 illustrates a relationship with a graph that is slightly different from Exhibits 2.6 through 2.9. Here, the hypothesis (hypothesis 5 in Exhibit 2.5) states that we expect to see lower crime in communities that have foot patrols compared with communities that do not have foot patrols. Unlike the other independent variables, the independent variable foot patrol does not vary from low to high: Either there are foot patrols in the community or there are not. If the hypothesis is true, what we should expect to see is that most of the communities that do not have foot patrols should have high rates of crime, whereas most of those communities that do have foot patrols should have lower rates of crime. This expectation is shown in Exhibit 2.10 with the clump of points (representing communities) for the "no foot patrol" communities at the high range of crime and the clump of points for the "yes foot patrol" communities at the low range of crime.

The motives for deductive research include both explanation and evaluation (as described in Chapter 1). An example of explanatory deductive research is the Minneapolis

Exhibit 2.10   Relationship Between Foot Patrols and Crime

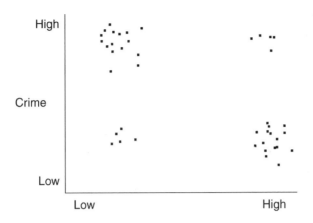

Domestic Violence Experiment, in which Sherman and Berk (1984) sought to explain what sort of response by the authorities might keep a spouse abuser from repeating the offense. The researchers deduced from deterrence theory the expectation that arrest would deter domestic violence. They then collected data to test this expectation.

An example of evaluative deductive research is the study of the Second Step violence prevention curriculum, by David Grossman and his colleagues (1997), that was discussed in Chapter 1. The developers of the Second Step program had deduced from previous research in the violence prevention literature that violence in children could be inhibited if they learned and had practice with empathy, impulse control, and anger management. Based on this trinity of approaches, Second Step was devised to reduce the expressed violence among those children in the program. Grossman and colleagues collected data to test this expectation. They did find that physically aggressive behavior was lower among those children in the program than among a comparable group not exposed to the curriculum. Even though they began not with an explicit theory of violence prevention but with a mass of previous research findings, the developers of the Second Step program did begin with some ideas about what would work in inhibiting the violent behavior of young children. The evaluation by Grossman and his colleagues confirmed those ideas.

In both explanatory and evaluative research, the statement of expectations for the findings and the design of the research to test these expectations strengthens the confidence we can place in the test. The deductive researcher shows her hand or states her expectations in advance and then designs a fair test of those expectations. Then "the chips fall where they may"; in other words, the researcher accepts the resulting data as a more or less objective picture of reality.

Inductive Research

In contrast to deductive research, **inductive research** begins at the bottom of the research circle and then works upward (see Exhibit 2.4). The inductive researcher begins with specific data, which are then used to develop (induce) a general explanation (a theory)

to account for the data. The patterns in the data are then summarized in one or more **empirical generalizations** that can be compared to the hypothesis. If the empirical generalizations are those stated in the hypothesis, then the theory from which the hypothesis was deduced is supported. If the empirical generalizations are inconsistent with the hypothesis, then the theory is not supported (Wallace, 1971:18).

The motive for inductive research is exploration. In Chapter 1, you read about an exploratory study of individuals' responses to an incident involving a school shooting (Asmussen & Creswell, 1995). The incident took place at a public university where a gunman tried to shoot the students in his class. Fortunately, the gun jammed, and all the students escaped uninjured. Because there was very little previous work in this area, Asmussen and Creswell conducted in-depth interviews with the students and tried to classify typical responses to the situation. Although the researchers did not develop a theory from their work, they did develop a classification scheme or taxonomy of different responses to traumatic events.

In strictly inductive research, the researcher already knows what he has found when he starts theorizing, or attempting to explain what accounts for these findings. The result can be new insights and provocative questions. But the adequacy of an explanation formulated after the fact is necessarily less certain than an explanation presented prior to the collection of data. Every phenomenon can always be explained in some way. Inductive explanations are thus more trustworthy if they are tested subsequently with deductive research.

A Qualitative Exploration of the Response to Domestic Violence

Qualitative research is often inductive: The researchers begin by observing social interaction or interviewing social actors in depth and then developing an explanation for what has been found. The researchers often ask questions like "What is going on here?" "How do people interpret these experiences?" or "Why do people do what they do?" Rather than testing a hypothesis, the researchers are trying to make sense of some social phenomenon. Lauren Bennett, Lisa Goodman, and Mary Ann Dutton (1999) used this approach to investigate one of the problems that emerge when police arrest domestic batterers: The victims often decide not to press charges. Bennett et al. (1999:762) did not set out to test hypotheses with qualitative interviews (there was another, hypothesis-testing component in their research), but sought, inductively, to "add the voice of the victim to the discussion" and present "themes that emerged from [the] interviews."

Research assistants interviewed 49 victims of domestic violence in one court; Lauren Bennett also worked in the same court as a victim advocate. The researchers were able to cull from their qualitative data four reasons why victims became reluctant to press charges: Some were confused by the court procedures, others were frustrated by the delay, some were paralyzed by fear of retribution, and others did not want to send the batterer to jail.

Explanations developed inductively from qualitative research can feel authentic because we have heard what people have to say "in their own words" and we have tried to see the social world "as they see it." One victim interviewed by Bennett (1999:768–769) felt that she "was doing time instead of the defendant"; another expressed her fear by saying that she would like "to keep him out of jail if that's what it takes to keep my kids safe." Explanations derived from qualitative research will be richer and more finely textured than those resulting from quantitative research, but they are likely to be based on fewer cases from a limited area. We cannot assume that the people studied in this setting are like others or that other researchers would develop explanations similar to ours to make sense of what was observed or heard. Because we do not initially set up a test of a hypothesis according to some specific rules, another researcher cannot come along and conduct just the same test.

Descriptive Research

You learned in Chapter 1 that description is one important motive for social research. Descriptive research can be considered a part of the research circle, even though such research does not involve connecting theory and data. As Exhibit 2.4 indicates, descriptive research starts with data and proceeds only to the stage of making empirical generalizations based on those data.

Valid description is important in its own right, but it is also critical in all research. Description of social phenomena can stimulate more ambitious deductive and inductive research. The Minneapolis Domestic Violence Experiment was motivated in part by a growing body of descriptive research indicating that spouse abuse is very common. You may recall from Chapter 1 that recent research on the magnitude of youth violence and other problem behaviors is heavily descriptive. The Youth Risk Behavior Survey is an ongoing study that attempts to measure the involvement of a national sample of youth in a wide sweep of antisocial behaviors. This descriptive work is valuable in documenting patterns and trends in violence by American youth throughout the 1990s. Theories will then be developed to account for these patterns and trends.

Domestic Violence and the Research Circle

The Sherman and Berk study of domestic violence that we have been discussing in this chapter is a good example of how the research circle works. In an attempt to determine ways to prevent the recurrence of spouse abuse, the researchers repeatedly linked theory and data, developing both hypotheses and empirical generalizations.

Phase 1: Deductive Research

The first phase of Sherman and Berk's study was designed to test a hypothesis. According to deterrence theory, punishment will reduce recidivism, or the propensity to commit further crimes. From this theory, Sherman and Berk deduced a specific hypothesis: "Arrest for spouse abuse reduces the risk of repeat offenses." In this hypothesis, arrest is the independent variable, and variation in the risk of repeat offenses is the dependent variable (it is hypothesized to depend on arrest).

Of course, in another study arrest might be the dependent variable in relation to some other independent variable. For example, in the hypothesis "The greater the rate of layoffs in a community, the higher the frequency of arrest," the dependent variable is frequency of arrest. Only within the context of a hypothesis, or a relationship between variables, does it make sense to refer to one variable as dependent and the other as independent.

Sherman and Berk tested their hypothesis by setting up an experiment in which the police responded to complaints of spouse abuse in one of three ways, one of which was to arrest the offender. When the researchers examined their data (police records for the persons in their experiment), they found that of those arrested for assaulting their spouse, only 13% repeated the offense, compared to a 26% recidivism rate for those who were

Exhibit 2.11   The Research Circle: Minneapolis Domestic Violence Experiment

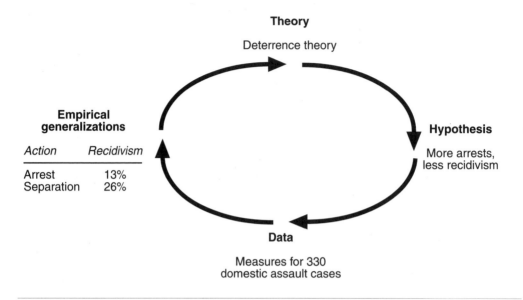

separated from their spouse by the police without any arrest. This pattern in the data, or empirical generalization, was consistent with the hypothesis that the researchers deduced from deterrence theory. The theory thus received support from the experiment (see Exhibit 2.11).

In designing their study, Sherman and Berk anticipated an important question: "How valid was the connection they [the researchers] were trying to make between theory and data?" The three dimensions of validity—measurement validity, generalizability, and causal validity—were at issue.

Determining whether spouses were assaulted after the initial police intervention was the key measurement concern. Official records of subsequent assaults by the suspect would provide one measure. But most spousal assaults are not reported to the police, and so research assistants also sought out the victims for interviews every 2 weeks during a 6-month follow-up period. Although fewer than half the victims completed all the follow-up interviews, the availability of the self-report measure allowed the researchers to shed some light on the validity of the official data. In general, the two measures yielded comparable results, although some discrepancies troubled critics.

The generalizability of the study's results was the researchers' greatest concern. Minneapolis is no more a typical U.S. city than any other, and we cannot assume that police policies that are effective in Minneapolis will be equally effective in cities with very different political histories, criminal justice agencies, and population characteristics. Sherman and Berk (1984:269) warned readers, "External validity will have to wait for replications"; that is, for repetitions of the study using the same research methods to answer the same research question.

Finally, Sherman and Berk's claims about the causal validity of their results rested primarily on the experimental design they used. The 330 domestic assault cases in the study were handled by the police in one of three ways: an arrest, an order that the offending spouse leave the house for 8 hours, or some type of verbal advice by the police officers. The officers were not allowed to choose which treatment to apply (except in extreme cases, such as when severe injury had occurred or when the spouse had demanded that an arrest be made). Instead, the treatments were carried out by police in random order, according to the color of the next report form on a pad that had been prepared by the researchers.

By insisting on the random assignment of cases to treatments, the researchers tried to ensure that police officers would not arrest just the toughest spouses or the spouses who seemed most obnoxious or the spouses they encountered late in the day. In other words, the random assignment procedure made it unlikely that arrested spouse abusers would differ, on average, from the other spouse abusers except for the fact that they were arrested (although, because of chance factors, the possibility of other differences cannot be completely ruled out). The researchers' conclusion that arrest caused a lower incidence of repeat offenses therefore seems valid.

Phase 2: Deductive Research

Because of their doubts about the generalizability of their results, Sherman, Berk, and new collaborators began to journey around the research circle again, with funding from the National Institute of Justice for **replications** (repetitions) of the experiment in six more cities. These replications used the same basic research approach but with some improvements. The random assignment process was tightened up in most of the cities so that police officers would be less likely to replace the assigned treatment with a treatment of their own choice. In addition, data were collected about repeat violence against other victims as well as against the original complainant. Some replications also examined different aspects of the arrest process, to see whether professional counseling helped and whether the length of time spent in jail after arrest mattered at all.

By the time results were reported from five of the cities in the new study, a problem was apparent. In three cities—Omaha, Nebraska; Charlotte, North Carolina; and Milwaukee, Wisconsin—researchers were finding long-term increases in domestic violence incidents among arrestees. But in Colorado Springs, Colorado, and Dade County, Florida, the predicted deterrent effects seemed to be occurring (Sherman, Smith, Schmidt, & Rogan, 1992).

Sherman and his colleagues had now traversed the research circle twice in an attempt to answer the original research question, first in Minneapolis and then in six other cities. But rather than leading to more confidence in deterrence theory, the research results were calling it into question. Deterrence theory now seemed inadequate to explain empirical reality, at least as the researchers had measured this reality. So the researchers began to reanalyze the follow-up data from several cities to try to explain the discrepant results, thereby starting around the research circle once again (Berk, Campbell, Klap, & Western, 1992; Pate & Hamilton, 1992; Sherman et al., 1992).

Phase 3: Inductive Research

At this point, the researchers' approach became more inductive, and they began trying to make sense of the differing patterns in the data collected in the different cities. Could systematic differences in the samples or in the implementation of arrest policies explain

Exhibit 2.12   The Research Spiral: Minneapolis Domestic Violence Experiment

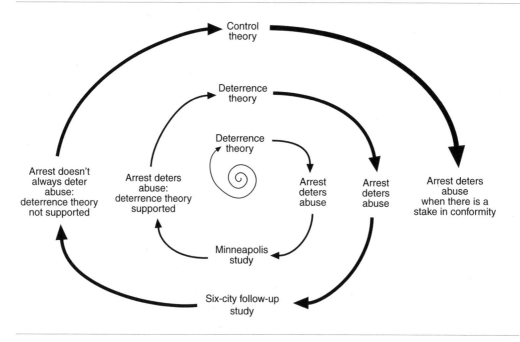

the differing outcomes? Or was the problem an inadequacy in the theoretical basis of their research? Was deterrence theory really the best way to explain the patterns in the data they were collecting?

Sherman and his colleagues now turned to control theory (Toby, 1957), yet another broad explanation for social behavior. It predicts that having a stake in conformity (resulting from inclusion in social networks at work or in the community) decreases a person's likelihood of committing crimes. The implication is that people who are employed and married are more likely to be deterred by the threat of arrest than those without such stakes in conformity. This is because an arrest for domestic violence could jeopardize one's job and one's marriage, thus making arrest more costly for the employed and married. This is indeed what a reexamination of the data revealed: Individuals who were married and employed were deterred from repeat offenses by arrest, but individuals who were unmarried and unemployed were actually more likely to commit repeat offenses if they were arrested. This was an important theoretical insight, for it suggested that one powerful way that formal sanctions work is that they can potentially trigger informal sanctions or costs (e.g., loss of respect from friends and family).

Now the researchers had traversed the research circle almost three times, a process perhaps better described as a spiral (see Exhibit 2.12). The first two times the researchers had traversed the research circle in a deductive, hypothesis-testing way: They started with theory and then deduced and tested hypotheses. The third time they traversed the research circle in a more inductive, exploratory way: They started with empirical generalizations from the data they had already obtained and then turned to a new theory to account for the unexpected patterns in the data. At this point they believed that deterrence theory makes correct predictions given certain conditions and that another theory, control theory, may specify what these conditions are.

After two and one-half cycles through the research circle, the picture became more complex but also conceptually richer. The researchers came closer to understanding how to inhibit domestic violence. But they cautioned us that their initial question—the research problem—was still not completely answered. Employment status and marital status alone do not measure the strength of social attachments; they also are related to how much people earn and the social standing of victims in court. So perhaps social ties are not really what make arrest an effective deterrent to domestic violence. The real deterrent may be cost–benefit calculations ("If I have a higher income, jail is more costly to me") or perceptions about the actions of authorities ("If I am a married woman, judges will treat my complaint more seriously"). More research was still needed (Berk et al., 1992).

Phase 4: Deductive Research

In 1997, Paternoster, Sherman, and two other criminologists reexamined data from the Milwaukee Domestic Violence Experiment to test hypotheses derived from yet another theory, procedural justice theory. As explained earlier in this chapter, procedural justice theory predicts that people will comply with the law out of a sense of duty and obligation if they are treated fairly by legal authorities. In the Milwaukee sample, arrest had a criminogenic effect: Those who were arrested were subsequently more likely to abuse their spouses than those who were simply warned. Paternoster and his colleagues thought that this effect might have been due to the way subjects were treated when they were arrested rather than simply to the fact that they were arrested. One of their hypotheses spells out the reasoning.

Among those persons arrested for spouse assault, those who perceive themselves as being treated in a procedurally unfair manner will be more likely to commit acts of spouse assault in the future than those arrested persons who perceive themselves as being treated in a procedurally fair manner, net of other determinants of violence. (Paternoster et al., 1997:173)

To carry out this study, Paternoster and his colleagues reexamined data collected earlier in Milwaukee, where the findings had seemed anomalous. However, this reanalysis of the data qualifies as deductive research, because the hypotheses were derived from theory and then tested with the data, rather than being induced by the data.

The procedural justice hypotheses were supported: Persons who were arrested in the Milwaukee experiment became more likely to reoffend only if they perceived that they had been treated unfairly by the police. Otherwise, their rate of rearrest was similar to that for the persons who were not arrested. Thus, another element was added to our understanding of the effects of the police response to domestic violence.

Clearly our understanding of effective responses to domestic violence will never truly be complete, but research to date has greatly improved our understanding of this social problem. The future should yield an even better understanding, even though at times it may be hard to make sense out of conflicting findings from different studies. Science is an ongoing enterprise in which findings cumulate and eventually yield greater understanding or even radical revisions in our understanding. Needless to say, researchers don't need to worry about running out of work to do.

GUIDELINES FOR CRIMINOLOGISTS

Any effort to understand the social world is plagued by pitfalls, including (as you learned in Chapter 1) such everyday errors in reasoning as overgeneralization, selective or inaccurate observation, illogical reasoning, and resistance to change. Social scientists, including criminologists, cannot avoid these problems entirely, but they try to minimize their impact by adhering to certain guidelines.

The guidelines followed by social researchers fall into two categories: those that help keep research scientific and those that help keep research ethical. Both types of guidelines are essential for a field of inquiry that seeks empirical generalizations about human society. To point out their value, we'll use some examples from the domestic violence research.

Scientific Guidelines

The following nine guidelines are applicable to any type of scientific research, but they are particularly useful to criminologists and to those who read about criminology and criminal justice. Adherence to these guidelines will reduce the temptation "to project on what is observed whatever [they] want the world to be for [their] own private purposes" (Hoover, 1980:131).

1. *Test ideas against empirical reality without becoming too personally invested in a particular outcome.* This testing approach is reflected in the research process and is implicit in the goal of validity. It contrasts markedly with our everyday methods of figuring things out, in which we typically just react to events as they happen, without paying much attention to whether we really are putting our ideas to a test. Empirical testing requires a neutral and open-minded approach: The scientists are personally disinterested in the outcome and not swayed by the popularity or the social status of those who would prefer other outcomes. This does not mean that the researchers are not personally involved or interested in the research—they must be—rather, the point is that they cannot have so much invested in a research project personally or professionally that they try in subtle or not-so-subtle ways to affect the outcome.

2. *Plan and carry out investigations systematically.* Social researchers have little hope of conducting a careful test of their ideas if they do not think through in advance how they should go about the test and then proceed accordingly. But a systematic approach is not always easy. For example, Sherman and Berk needed to ensure that spouse abusers were assigned to be either arrested or not on a random basis, rather than on the basis of the police officers' personal preferences. So the researchers devised an elaborate procedure using randomly sequenced report sheets in different colors. But the researchers found that police officers did not always follow this systematic procedure. Subsequently, in some replications of the study, the researchers ensured compliance with their research procedures by requiring police officers to call in to a central number to receive the experimentally determined treatment.

3. *Document all procedures, and disclose them publicly.* Social researchers who disclose the methods on which their conclusions rest allow others to evaluate for themselves the likely soundness of these conclusions. Such disclosure is a key feature of science. Again,

Sherman and Berk (1984) provide a compelling example. In their research report, after describing the formal research plan, they describe at length the apparent slippage from this plan, which occurred primarily because some police officers avoided implementing the random assignment procedure.

4. *Clarify assumptions.* No investigation is complete unto itself; whatever the researcher's method, the research rests on some background assumptions. Research to determine whether arrest has a deterrent effect assumes that potential law violators think rationally— that they calculate potential costs and benefits prior to committing crimes. When a researcher conducts an election poll, the assumption is that people actually vote for the candidate they say they will vote for. When government unemployment statistics are used to describe the state of the economy, the assumption is that those statistics reflect actual fluctuations in unemployment. By definition, research assumptions are not tested, so we do not know whether they are correct. In fact, researchers themselves do not always recognize the assumptions they are making. By taking the time to think about and to disclose their assumptions, researchers provide important information for those who seek to evaluate the validity of their conclusions.

5. *Specify the meaning of all terms.* Words often have multiple or unclear meanings. Strain, differential association, social disorganization, subculture of violence, problem-oriented policing, and so on can mean different things to different people. Thus the terms used in scientific research must be defined explicitly and used consistently. For example, Sherman and Berk (1984) identified their focus as misdemeanor domestic assault, not just wife beating. They specified that their work concerned those cases of domestic assault in which severe injury was not involved and both partners were present when police arrived.

6. *Maintain a skeptical stance toward current knowledge.* Scientists may feel very confident about interpretations of the social or natural world that have been supported by repeated investigations, but the results of any particular investigation must be examined critically. A general skepticism about current knowledge stimulates researchers to improve the validity of current research results and expand the frontier of knowledge. For example, in response to questions raised about the Sherman and Berk study, Lawrence Sherman and Ellen Cohn (1989) discussed 13 problems of the Minneapolis Domestic Violence Experiment in a published critique, weighing carefully the extent to which these problems might have affected its validity. This critique could then stimulate additional research designed to address the problematic aspects of the original research.

7. *Replicate research and accumulate knowledge.* No one study can be viewed as definitive in itself; usually at least some plausible threats to the validity of the conclusions exist. And no conclusion can be understood adequately apart from the larger body of knowledge to which the study is related. Scientific investigations may begin with a half-baked or off-the-wall idea, but a search of the literature for other relevant work must be conducted in short order. The other side of the coin is that the results of scientific research must be published, to serve as a foundation for others who seek to replicate or extend the research. Sherman (1992) reported that when he and his colleagues decided to attempt some replications of their own experiment, they found that another research team was

already planning to do so. The process of extending knowledge gained in the Minneapolis experiment had already begun.

8. *Maintain an interest in theory.* Theories organize the knowledge accumulated by numerous investigations into a coherent whole and serve as a guide to future inquiries. Even though much research is purely descriptive, this research can still serve as a basis for others to evaluate different theories. The Minneapolis Domestic Violence Experiment was devised initially as a test of the competing predictions of deterrence and labeling theory, but the researchers extended their attention to control theory to help them explain unanticipated findings. These theoretical connections make the research much more relevant to other criminologists working to understand different types of crime and social control.

9. *Search for regularities or patterns.* Science is concerned with classes rather than with individuals (except inasmuch as individuals are representatives of a class). Scientists assume that the natural world has some underlying order of relationships, and that every event and individual is not so unique that general principles cannot be discerned (Grinnell, 1992:27–29). Individuals are not unimportant to criminologists and other social scientists; Sherman (1992:162–164), for example, described the abuse histories of two men to provide greater insight into why arrest could have different effects for different people. But the goal of elaborating individual cases is to understand social patterns that characterize many individuals.

These general guidelines are only ideals for social research. No particular investigation is going to follow every guideline exactly. Real investigations by criminologists do not always include much attention to theory, specific definitions of all terms, and so forth. But any study that strays far from these guidelines cannot be considered scientific.

Ethical Guidelines

Every scientific investigation, whether in the natural sciences or in the social sciences, such as criminology and criminal justice, has an ethical dimension. First and foremost, the scientific concern with validity requires that scientists be honest and reveal their methods. (How else could we determine whether the requirement of honesty has been met?) Scientists also have to consider the uses to which their findings will be put. In addition, because criminological research deals with people, such as criminals, criminal suspects, and incarcerated inmates, and controversial topics (involvement in crime), criminologists have some unique ethical concerns.

Honesty and Openness

Research distorted by political or personal pressures to find particular outcomes or to achieve the most marketable results is unlikely to be carried out in an honest and open fashion or to achieve valid results. For example, noted English biologist Sir Cyril Burt published fabricated evidence in 1961 that purported to show intelligence is determined primarily by heredity. In the 35 years before Burt's deliberate falsification was exposed, his study influenced much social science theory and research (and was in part responsible for Burt's knighthood) (Kamin, 1974). Efforts to evaluate the influence of inherited characteristics on people were considerably set back by this fraud.

Being open about one's research is particularly important when the research is used or influential in public policy matters. For example, an economist, Isaac Ehrlich (1975), who was interested in the study of crime conducted a study that examined whether capital punishment deters murder. Using national data for the time period 1933–1969, Ehrlich concluded that each execution prevented or deterred 7–8 homicides—in other words, Ehrlich claimed that executions saved 7–8 innocent crime victims. This was one of a very few studies at the time to find a deterrent effect for capital punishment. In fact, his results were cited in a U.S. Supreme Court case (*Gregg v. Georgia*) as evidence in support of deterrence. His reported findings caused both a stir among proponents of capital punishment and skeptical hostility among its critics. Other researchers immediately wanted to reexamine Ehrlich's data to see how valid his results were. Unfortunately, Professor Ehrlich was not immediately forthcoming with his data. The controversy surrounding his findings grew when other researchers tried to duplicate his findings with data they collected and found that when they analyzed slightly different years, with slightly different variables and sometimes slightly different statistical strategies, the effect of executions changed. In some analyses, executions seemed to deter murder; in some others, it seemed to increase murders (what was called a brutalization effect); and in others it had no discernable effect at all. The controversy about Ehrlich's findings bubbled for years and might have been resolved much sooner had Professor Ehrlich been more open and forthcoming about his data.

Openness about research procedures and results goes hand in hand with honesty in research design. Openness is also essential if researchers are to learn from the work of others. In spite of this need for openness, some researchers may hesitate to disclose their procedures or results to prevent others from building on their ideas and taking some of the credit. You may have heard of the long legal battle between a U.S. researcher and a French researcher about how credit should be allocated for discovering the AIDS virus. Although such public disputes are unusual, concerns with priority of discovery are common. Scientists are like other people in their desire to be first. Enforcing standards of honesty and encouraging openness about research is the best solution for these problems.

The Uses of Science

Scientists must also consider the extent to which they should publicize their research and the uses to which it is put. Although many scientists believe that personal values should be left outside the laboratory, some argue that it is proper, even desirable, for scientists in their role as citizens to attempt to influence public policy. In other words, if their research has something to say about how things *should be* done, some scientists feel that they should actively promote their work. Sometimes, however, there is controversy on this point.

Throughout this chapter, we have been talking about one criminological experiment, the Minneapolis Domestic Violence Experiment, which found that arresting domestic violence suspects was more effective in reducing subsequent violence than not arresting them. Although the authors of the study, Professors Lawrence Sherman and Richard Berk, were generally cautious about the kinds of conclusions that should be drawn from their work, they were both active and passive in promoting their findings. Not only was their work published in scientific journals, but it also received widespread publicity in the national media—one of the authors and the Minneapolis chief of police wrote an editorial in the *Wall Street Journal* recommending that other jurisdictions pass laws similar to Minneapolis's, and one of the authors contracted with a Minneapolis television station to film a documentary on the research. In their published findings (1984:270), they concluded:

> [W]e favor a *presumption* of arrest: an arrest should be made unless there are good, clear reasons why an arrest would be counterproductive. We do not, however, favor *requiring* arrests in all misdemeanor domestic assault cases.

Sherman and Berk were criticized by other scholars on the basis that the findings of one study are not a sufficient empirical base on which to draw such an important public policy recommendation. In fact, Sherman and Berk did caution that their findings might not be replicated in other locations, and that their position is that police should be able to arrest domestic violence suspects, not that they should be required to. Nevertheless, because Sherman publicized the results of the research in the mass media, he was criticized by some social scientists for implicitly encouraging police departments to change their policies on the basis of preliminary evidence (the results of just one study in one city) (Binder & Meeker, 1993; Lempert, 1989). In part, the question was whether basing policy on partial information was preferable to waiting until the information was more complete (more studies conducted in different locations). Sherman (1992: 150–153) later pointed out that in the Omaha follow-up study, arrest warrants were very effective in reducing repeat offenses among spouse abusers who had already left the scene when police arrived at the time of the initial complaint. Absent offenders had not been included in the initial study, and because the Omaha finding was not publicized, it did not become known to police chiefs or battered women's groups. As a consequence, Sherman suggested, some domestic violence that might have been prevented was not prevented. How much publicity is warranted, and at what point in the research is it warranted? He also argued that public policy is better guided by partial knowledge than no knowledge at all.

Criminologists who conduct research on behalf of organizations and agencies may face additional difficulties. When an organization contracts with a researcher to evaluate a program, identify community needs, or explore product potential, usually the organization, not the researcher, controls the final report and the publicity it receives. If organizational leaders decide that particular research results are inconsistent with their funding requests, community image, or employee relations, they may refuse to release the results or require changes that the researcher deems unacceptable. In a situation like this, a researcher's desire to have findings used appropriately and reported fully can conflict with contractual obligations.

Researchers often can anticipate such dilemmas in advance and resolve them when the contract for research is negotiated, or decline a particular research opportunity altogether if acceptable terms cannot be worked out. But often these problems come up after a report has been drafted, when the researcher finds out that the report is unacceptable to a top-level administrator or executive whom the researcher does not even know. In addition, a researcher's need to have a job or to maintain particular personal relationships may make it difficult to act in what the researcher thinks is the most ethical manner. A way to minimize these possibilities is to acknowledge the source of research funding in reports and to carefully scrutinize those research reports funded by organizations or agencies with a stake in the outcome.

Research on People

In physics or chemistry, research subjects (objects and substances) may be treated to extreme conditions and then discarded when they are no longer useful. However, social (and medical) scientists must concern themselves with the way their human subjects are treated in the course of research. This treatment may involve manipulations and deceptions in laboratory experiments, sensitive questions in survey research, observations in field studies, or analyses of personal data. Here we will briefly review current ethical standards for the treatment of human subjects and dilemmas in their application. In the chapters on data collection, Chapters 5 through 9, we will examine the specific ethical problems that may arise in the course of using particular research methods.

Contemporary standards for the treatment of human subjects are set by the federal government, by professional associations, by special university review boards, and in some cases by ethics committees in other organizations. Federal regulations require that the proposals of researchers seeking federal funds for research on human subjects be reviewed by an **institutional review board (IRB)** before they are submitted for federal review. IRBs at universities and other agencies in turn apply ethics standards set by government agencies, like the National Institutes of Health, and may develop more specific guidelines of their own. The American Society of Criminology (ASC), one of criminology's professional organizations, is in the process of redrafting their code of ethics, but advises members to seek guidance from similar organizations including the American Sociological Association (ASA). The ASA's standards (ASA, 1997) concerning the treatment of human subjects include federal regulations and ethics guidelines emphasized by most professional social science organizations:

- Research should cause no harm to subjects.
- Participation in research should be voluntary, and therefore subjects must give their informed consent to participate in the research.
- Researchers should fully disclose their identity.
- Anonymity or confidentiality must be maintained for individual research participants, unless it is voluntarily and explicitly waived.
- The benefits of a research project should outweigh any foreseeable risks.

As simple as these guidelines may seem, they are difficult to interpret in specific cases and harder yet to define in a way agreeable to all criminologists. For example, how should we interpret the admonition that no harm should be done to subjects? Does it mean that subjects should not be at all harmed psychologically as well as physically? That they should feel no anxiety or distress during the study or only after their involvement ends? Should the possibility of any harm, no matter how remote, deter research?

Consider the question of possible harm to the subjects of a well-known prison simulation study (Haney, Banks, & Zimbardo, 1973). The study was designed to investigate the impact of social position on behavior, specifically, the impact of being either a guard or a prisoner in a prison, a total institution. The researchers selected 20 young men whom they judged to be the most stable and mature, and the least antisocial, of 75 applicants. The participants signed a contract agreeing to be either a guard or a prisoner in a simulated prison for 2 weeks, during which time they would be paid $15 daily and receive food, clothing, housing, and medical care. Some were randomly selected to be guards and were told to maintain order among the prisoners, who were then incarcerated in a makeshift basement prison. Within the first two days, marked differences in behavior emerged between the two groups. The prisoners acted passive and disorganized, and the guards became verbally and physically aggressive (although physical abuse was not allowed) and arbitrary. Five prisoners were soon released for depression, uncontrollable crying, fits of rage, and in one case a psychosomatic rash; on the sixth day the researchers terminated the experiment. Through discussions in special post-experiment encounter sessions, feelings of stress among the participants who played the role of prisoner seemed to be relieved; follow-up during the next year indicated no lasting negative effects on the participants and some benefits in the form of greater insight.

Would you ban such experiments because of the potential for harm to subjects? Does the fact that the experiment yielded significant insights into the effect of a situation on human behavior, insights that could be used to improve prisons, make any difference (Reynolds, 1979:133–139)? Do you believe that this benefit outweighed the foreseeable risks?

The requirement of informed consent is also more difficult to define than it first appears. To be informed, consent must be given by persons who are competent to consent, have consented voluntarily, are fully informed about the research, and have comprehended what they have been told (Reynolds, 1979). Can prisoners give informed consent? Can children or juveniles give their own consent? Can parents or guardians give consent on behalf of their children? Can students who are asked to participate in research by their professor give consent? Can participants in covert experiments do so?

Fully informed consent may also reduce participation in research and, because signing consent forms prior to participation may change participants' responses, produce biased results (Larson, 1993:114). In addition, there is always the problem that those persons who give their support in a research project may be quite different from those who do not. This differential selection of participants has implications for both the validity of the reported results and the generalizability of the study. Experimental researchers whose research design requires some type of subject deception try to get around this problem by withholding some information before the experiment begins but then debriefing subjects at the end. In the **debriefing,** the researcher explains to the subject what happened in the experiment and why. However, even though debriefing can be viewed as a substitute in some cases for securing fully informed consent prior to the experiment, if the debriefed subjects disclose the nature of the experiment to other participants, subsequent results may still be contaminated (Adair, Dushenko, & Lindsay, 1985).

Well-intentioned researchers also may fail to foresee all the potential problems. In the prison simulation, all the participants signed consent forms, but how could they have been fully informed in advance? The researchers themselves did not realize that the study participants would experience so much stress so quickly, that some prisoners would have to be released for severe negative reactions within the first few days, or that even those who were not severely stressed would soon be begging to be released from the mock prison. If this risk was not foreseeable, was it acceptable for the researchers to presume in advance that the benefits would outweigh the risks?

Maintaining confidentiality is another key ethical obligation. This standard, however, should be overridden if a health- or life-threatening situation arises and participants need to be alerted. Also, the standard of confidentiality does not apply to observation in public places and information available in public records.

The potential of withholding a beneficial treatment from some subjects is also cause for ethical concern. The Sherman and Berk experiment required the random assignment of subjects to treatment conditions and thus had the potential of causing harm to the victims of domestic violence whose batterers were not arrested. The justification for the study design, however, is quite persuasive: The researchers didn't know prior to the experiment which response to a domestic violence complaint would be most likely to deter future incidents (Sherman, 1992). The experiment provided clear evidence about the value of arrest, so it can be argued that the benefits outweighed the risks.

The evaluation of ethical issues in a research project should be based on a realistic assessment of the overall potential for harm to research subjects rather than an apparent inconsistency between any particular aspect of a research plan and a specific ethical guideline. For example, full disclosure of what is really going on in an experimental study is unnecessary if subjects are unlikely to be harmed. Nevertheless, researchers should make every effort to foresee all possible risks and to weigh the possible benefits of the research against these risks.

The extent to which ethical issues are a problem for researchers and their subjects varies dramatically with research design. Survey research, in particular, creates few ethical problems, unless the survey queries respondents about sensitive subject matter (e.g., victimization or offending experiences—see Chapter 6 for a more detailed discussion of this issue). In fact, researchers from Michigan's Institute for Survey Research interviewed a representative national sample of adults and found that 68% of those who participated in a survey were somewhat or very interested in participating in another; the more times respondents had been interviewed, the more willing they were to participate again. Presumably they would have felt differently if they had been treated unethically (Reynolds, 1979:56–57). On the other hand, some experimental studies in the social sciences that have put people in uncomfortable or embarrassing situations have generated vociferous complaints and years of debate about ethics (Reynolds, 1979; Sjoberg, 1967).

CONCLUSION

Criminological researchers can find many questions to study, but not all questions are equally worthy. The ones that warrant the expense and effort of social research are feasible, socially important, and scientifically relevant.

The simplicity of the research circle presented in this chapter belies the complexity of the social research process. In the following chapters, we will focus on particular aspects of that process. Chapter 3 examines the interrelated processes of conceptualization and measurement, arguably the most important part of research. Measurement validity is the foundation for the other two aspects of validity. Chapter 4 reviews the meaning of generalizability and the sampling strategies that help us to achieve this goal. Chapter 5 introduces causal validity, the third aspect of validity, and illustrates different methods for achieving causal validity, with particular emphasis on experimental designs. The following four chapters then introduce different approaches to data collection, including surveys, qualitative research methods, secondary data analysis, and evaluation research, that help us, in different ways, to achieve validity. Chapter 10 illustrates how the use of multiple methods can enhance our efforts to achieve validity.

As you encounter these specifics, don't lose sight of the basic guidelines that researchers need to follow to overcome the most common impediments to social research. Owning a large social science toolkit is no guarantee of making the right decisions about which tools to use and how to use them in the investigation of particular research problems. More important, our answers to research questions will never be complete or entirely certain. Thus, when we complete a research project, we should point out how the research could be extended and evaluate the confidence we have in our conclusions. Recall how the gradual elaboration of knowledge about the deterrence of domestic violence required sensitivity to research difficulties, careful weighing of the evidence, and identification of unanswered questions by several research teams.

Ethical issues also should be considered when evaluating research proposals and completed research studies. As the preceding examples show, ethical issues in social research are no less complex than the other issues that researchers confront. And it is inexcusable to jump into research on people without any attention to ethical considerations.

You are now forewarned about, and thus hopefully forearmed against, the difficulties that any scientists, but criminologists in particular, face in their work. We hope that you will return often to this chapter as you read the subsequent chapters, when you criticize the research literature, and when you design your own research projects. To be conscientious, thoughtful, and responsible—this is the mandate of every social scientist. If you formulate a feasible research problem, ask the right questions in advance, try to adhere to the research guidelines, and steer clear of the most common difficulties, you will be well along the road to fulfilling this mandate.

KEY TERMS

Anomalous finding
Constant
Criminological research question
Debriefing
Deductive reasoning
Deductive research
Dependent variable
Direction of association
Empirical generalization
Falsifiable statement
Hypothesis

Independent variable
Inductive reasoning
Inductive research
Institutional review board (IRB)
Replication
Research circle
Serendipitous finding
Theoretical construct
Theory
Variable

HIGHLIGHTS

• Research questions should be feasible (within the time and resources available), socially important, and scientifically relevant.

• Building criminological theory is a major objective of criminological research. Investigate relevant theories before starting criminological projects, and draw out the theoretical implications of research findings.

• The type of reasoning in most criminological research can be described as primarily deductive or inductive. Research based on deductive reasoning proceeds from general ideas, deduces specific expectations from these ideas, and then tests the ideas with empirical data. Research based on inductive reasoning begins with specific data and then develops general ideas or theories to explain patterns in the data.

- It may be possible to explain unanticipated research findings after the fact, but such explanations have less credibility than those that have been tested with data collected for the purpose of the study.

- The scientific process can be represented as circular, with connections from theory to hypotheses to data to empirical generalizations. Research investigations may begin at different points along the research circle and traverse different portions of it. Deductive research begins at the point of theory; inductive research begins with data but ends with theory. Descriptive research begins with data and ends with empirical generalizations.

- Replications of a study are essential to establish its generalizability in other situations. An ongoing line of research stemming from a particular research question should include a series of studies that, collectively, traverse the research circle multiple times.

- Criminologists, like all social and other scientists, should structure their research so that their own ideas can be proved wrong, should disclose their methods for others to critique, and should recognize the possibility of error. Nine specific guidelines are recommended.

- Scientific research should be conducted and reported in an honest and open fashion. Contemporary ethical standards also require that social research not place subjects in any jeopardy, that research subjects be forewarned of any risk to them, that participation be voluntary as expressed in informed consent, that researchers fully disclose their identity, and that researchers fully and honestly report their research findings and sources of financial support.

EXERCISES

1. State a problem for research related to a criminological topic or issue of interest to you. Write down as many questions as you can about this topic.
    a. Considering your interests, opportunities, and the work of others, which of your research questions does not seem feasible or interesting?
    b. Pick out one question that seems feasible and that your other coursework suggests has been the focus of prior research or theorizing. Write this research question in one sentence. Elaborate on your question in a single paragraph. List at least three reasons for why it is a good research question to investigate.

2. Search the scholarly literature on your topic of interest. Refer to Appendix A for guidance on conducting the search if necessary.
    a. Copy at least 10 citations to recent articles reporting research relevant to your research question.
    b. Look up at least three of these articles. Write a brief description of each article, and evaluate its relevance to your research question. What additions or changes to your thoughts about the research question are suggested by these sources?
    c. Would you characterize the findings of these articles as largely consistent or inconsistent? How would you explain discrepant findings?
    d. How well did the authors summarize their work in their abstracts for the articles you consulted? What important points would you have missed if you had relied on only the abstracts?

3. Using one of the research articles you consulted for Exercise 2, identify and look up one of the cited articles or Web sites. Compare the cited source to what was said about it in the original article or site. Was the discussion in the cited source accurate?

4. Using the same research article you focused on for Exercise 3, identify the stages of the research project corresponding to the points on the research circle. Did the research cover all four stages? Identify the theories and hypotheses underlying the study. What data were collected or utilized for the study? What were the findings (empirical generalizations)?

DEVELOPING A RESEARCH PROPOSAL

Now it's time to start writing the proposal. These next exercises are very critical first steps.

1. State a problem for research. If you have not already identified a problem for study, or if you need to evaluate whether your research problem is doable, a few suggestions should help to get the ball rolling and keep it on course:
    a. Jot down questions that have puzzled you in some area having to do with people and social relations, perhaps questions that have come to mind while reading textbooks or research articles or even while hearing news stories. Don't hesitate to jot down many questions, and don't bore yourself—try to identify questions that really interest you.
    b. Now take stock of your interests, your opportunities, and the work of others. Which of your research questions no longer seem feasible or interesting? What additional research questions come to mind? Pick out a question that is of interest and seems feasible and that your other coursework suggests has been the focus of some prior research or theorizing.
    c. Write out your research question in one sentence, and elaborate on it in one paragraph. List at least three reasons for why it is a good research question for you to investigate. Then present your proposal to your classmates and instructor for discussion and feedback.

2. Search the literature (and the Web) on the research question you identified. Refer to Appendix A for guidance on conducting the search. Copy down at least 10 citations to articles (with abstracts from *Soc Abstracts* or *Psych Abstracts*) and 5 Web sites reporting research that seems highly relevant to your research question; then look up at least 5 of these articles and 3 of the sites. Inspect the article bibliographies and the links in the Web site and identify at least one more relevant article and Web site from each source.

Write a brief description of each article and Web site you consulted and evaluate its relevance to your research question. What additions or changes to your thoughts about the research question are suggested by the sources?

3. Propose at least two hypotheses that pertain to your research question. Justify these hypotheses in terms of the literature you have read.

4. Which standards for the protection of human subjects might pose the most difficulty for researchers on your proposed topic? Explain your answers and suggest appropriate protection procedures for human subjects.

WEB EXERCISES

1. You have been assigned to write a paper on domestic violence and the law. To start, you would like to find out what the American Bar Association's stance is on the issue. Go to the American Bar Association Commission on Domestic Violence's Web site at www.abanet.org/domviol/mrdv/identify.html.

What is the American Bar Association's definition of domestic violence? How does it suggest one can identify a person as a victim of domestic violence? What does it identify as "basic warning signs"? Write your answers in a one- to two-page report.

2. Go to the Bureau of Justice Statistics (BJS) Web site at www.ojp.usdoj.gov/bjs/. Go to "Publications." Browse the list of publications for topics related to domestic violence. List the titles of all publications focusing on violence between intimate partners. Choose the most recent publication. How does the BJS define "intimate partners"? What are some of the characteristics of intimate partner violence? What trends are identified in the report?

SPSS EXERCISES

Browse the variables in YOUTH.POR, a survey of high school youth regarding attitudes toward delinquency and delinquent behavior.

1. From these variables (excluding sex of respondent), write two research questions about levels of delinquency (DELINQ1) among high school youth.

2. Create a bar chart for at least one of the variables you hypothesize to be associated with levels of delinquency.

3. Compare the distribution of your chosen variable across gender groups. Select all males (SEX = 1) and request a bar chart of your chosen variable; then select all females (SEX = 2) and generate the bar chart again.

4. Compare the distributions between the two bar charts and formulate a hypothesis as to the relationship between the two variables. Is there a relationship between SEX and your chosen variable?

5. From these results, what do you hypothesize is the relationship between gender and level of delinquency?

Chapter 3

CONCEPTUALIZATION AND MEASUREMENT

Substance abuse is a social problem of remarkable proportions. Alcohol is involved in about half of all fatal traffic crashes, and more than 1 million arrests are made annually for driving under the influence. As many as two-thirds of all persons arrested in urban areas test positive for drugs (Gruenewald, Treno, Taff, & Klitzner, 1997). College presidents rate alcohol abuse as the number-one campus problem (Wechsler, Davenport, Dowdall, Moeykens, & Castillo, 1994), and it is a factor in as many as two-thirds of on-campus sexual assaults (National Institute of Alcohol Abuse and Alcoholism [NIAAA], 1995). All told, the annual costs of prevention and treatment for alcohol and drug abuse exceed $4 billion (Gruenewald et al., 1997).

Whether your goal is to examine the factors related to criminal offending, to deliver useful services, or to design effective social policies, at some point you will probably need to read the research literature on substance abuse and perhaps even design your own study of it. Every time you begin to review or design relevant research, you will have to answer two questions: "What is meant by 'substance abuse' in this research?" (which concerns conceptualization) and "How was substance abuse measured?" (which concerns measurement). Both questions must be answered to evaluate the validity of substance abuse research. You cannot make sense of the results of a study until you know how the concepts were defined and measured. Nor are you ready to begin a research project until you have defined your concepts and constructed valid measures of them. Measurement validity is essential to successful research; in fact, without valid measures it is fruitless to attempt to achieve the other two aspects of validity—causal validity (Chapter 5) and generalizability (Chapter 4).

In this chapter, we first address the issue of conceptualization, using substance abuse and related concepts as examples. We then focus on measurement, reviewing first how measures of substance abuse have been constructed, using such operations as available data, questions, observations, and less direct and obtrusive measures. Then we explain how to assess the validity and reliability of these measures. The final topic is the level of measurement reflected in different measures. By the chapter's end, you should have a good understanding of measurement, the first of the three legs on which a research project's validity rests.

CONCEPTS

A May 1997 *New York Times* article (Johnson, 1997) reported that five U.S. colleges were participating in a pilot program to ban alcohol in their fraternities. Moreover, the article claimed that substance-free housing would soon become the norm on U.S. campuses. Do you know what the article means? Some of these **concepts**—*alcohol*, *colleges*, *campuses*, and *pilot program*—are widely understood and commonly used. However, do we all have the same thing in mind when we hear these terms? For example, are junior colleges subsumed within the term *college*? Does the concept of *on campus* extend to fraternity houses that are not physically on college property? Does *substance-free housing* mean banning tobacco products as well as alcohol?

Concept A mental image that summarizes a set of similar observations, feelings, or ideas.

Concepts such as *substance-free housing* require an explicit definition before they are used in research because we cannot be certain that all readers will share the same definition. It is even more important to define concepts that are somewhat abstract or unfamiliar. When we refer to concepts such as *poverty* or *social control* or *strain*, we cannot be certain that others know exactly what we mean.

Clarifying the meaning of such concepts doesn't just benefit those who are unfamiliar with them—even experts often disagree about their meaning. But we need not avoid using these concepts; we just have to specify clearly what we mean when we use them, and we must expect others to do the same.

Conceptualization in Practice

If we are to do an adequate job of **conceptualization,** we must do more than just think up some definition, any definition, for our concepts. We may need to distinguish subconcepts, or dimensions, of the concept. We also should ask how the concept's definition fits within the theoretical framework guiding the research and what assumptions underlie this framework.

Conceptualization   The process of specifying what we mean by a term. In deductive research, conceptualization helps to translate portions of an abstract theory into testable hypotheses involving specific variables. In inductive research, conceptualization is an important part of the process used to make sense of related observations.

Defining Substance Abuse

What observations or images should we associate with the concept *substance abuse*? Someone leaning against a building with a liquor bottle, barely able to speak coherently? College students drinking heavily at a party? Someone in an Alcoholics Anonymous group drinking one beer? A 10-year-old boy drinking a small glass of wine in an alley? A 10-year-old boy drinking a small glass of wine at the dinner table in France? Do all these images share something in common that we should define as substance abuse for the purposes of a particular research study? Do some of them? Should we take into account cultural differences? Social situations? Physical tolerance for alcohol? Individual standards?

Many researchers now use the definition of substance abuse contained in the *Diagnostic and Statistical Manual, IV* (*DSM-IV*) of the American Psychiatric Association (Mueser et al., 1990:33): "repeated use of a substance to the extent that it interferes with adequate social, vocational, or self-care functioning." In contrast, substance dependence is defined as "development of tolerance to a substance such that the person requires larger dosages to achieve the same psychoactive effect, and the experience of withdrawal symptoms and craving after a period of abstinence from the substance." Note that these definitions rely on behavioral and biological criteria rather than social expectations or cultural norms.

We cannot judge the *DSM-IV* definition of substance abuse as correct or incorrect. Each researcher has the right to conceptualize as he or she sees fit. However, we can say that the *DSM-IV* definition of substance abuse is useful, even good, in part because it has been very widely adopted. If we conceptualize substance abuse in the same way that the *DSM-IV* does, many others will share our definition and understand what we are talking about. This definition of substance abuse has two other attractive features: It is stated in clear and precise language that should minimize differences in interpretation and maximize understanding; and it can clearly be distinguished from the more specific concept of substance dependence.

One caution is in order. The definition of any one concept rests on a shared understanding of the terms used in the definition. So if our audience does not already have a shared understanding of terms such as *adequate social functioning*, *self-care functioning*, and *repeated use*, we must also define these terms before we are finished with the process of defining substance abuse.

Defining Poverty

Decisions about how to define a concept reflect the theoretical framework that guides the researchers. For example, the concept *poverty* has always been somewhat controversial, because different notions of what poverty is shape estimates of how prevalent it is and what can be done about it.

Most of the statistics that you see in the newspaper about the poverty rate reflect a conception of poverty that was formalized by Mollie Orshansky of the Social Security Administration in 1965 and subsequently adopted by the federal government and many researchers (Putnam, 1977). She defined poverty as an *absolute* standard, based on the amount of money required to purchase an emergency diet that is estimated to be nutritionally adequate for about 2 months. The idea is that people are truly poor if they can barely purchase the food they need and other essential goods. This poverty standard is adjusted for household size and composition (number of children and adults), and the minimal amount needed for food is multiplied by 3 because a 1955 survey indicated that poor families spend about one-third of their incomes on food (Orshansky, 1977).

Some social scientists disagree with the absolute standard and have instead urged adoption of a *relative* poverty standard or income inequality (Blau & Blau, 1982). The idea behind this relative conception is that poverty should be defined in terms of what is normal in a given society at a particular time.

Some social scientists prefer yet another conception of poverty. With the *subjective* approach, poverty is defined as what people think would be the minimal income they need to make ends meet. Of course, many have argued that this approach is influenced too much by the different standards that people use to estimate what they need (Ruggles, 1990:20–23).

Which do you think is a more reasonable approach to defining poverty—an absolute standard, a relative standard, or a subjective standard? Our understanding of the concept of poverty is sharpened when we consider the theoretical ramifications of these alternative definitions.

Defining Strain

Some concepts have multiple dimensions, bringing together several related concepts under a larger conceptual umbrella. One such concept is *strain*, first defined by Merton (1938) and later by Cloward and Ohlin (1960). In its simplest form, strain theory contends that delinquency and other forms of criminality and/or deviance are the result of frustrated needs or wants; this frustration is generally believed to result from a breakdown in the relationship between socially induced aspirations or goals and socially approved ways of achieving these goals. According to strain theory, delinquency is a response to actual or anticipated failure to achieve socially induced needs or goals (e.g., status, wealth, power, social acceptance). To determine the relationship between perceived strain and delinquency in a sample of 13- through 19-year-olds from the National Youth Survey (NYS), Delbert Elliott, David Huizinga, and Suzanne Ageton (1985) conceptualized strain as goal expectation discrepancies in both the home and school contexts. For example, strain would be increased at the individual level if being a good student was important to someone, but he or she did not perceive that teachers thought of him or her as a good student.

Relying on Merton's earlier conceptualization (1938), Steven Messner and Richard Rosenfeld (1994) utilized the macro-level analogue of strain called *anomie*. Anomie, in its most general formulation, is defined as a weakening in the normative regulation of behavior. Anomie theory posits that diminished normative regulation results from an overemphasis on cultural goals (e.g., wealth, prestige) relative to the legitimate means to achieve them (e.g., availability of a college education, high status jobs), or from the differential distribution of opportunities to achieve highly valued goals (some groups in society may not have the same opportunities to achieve these goals as others). According to Messner and Rosenfeld (1994), there are four cultural values within American society that contribute to anomie and therefore to crime in general: achievement, individualism, universalism, and materialism. To fully define anomie, Messner and Rosenfeld thus had to define these concepts. For example, to describe what they meant by the value of materialism, they state,

> . . . in American culture, success is signified in a profoundly significant way: by the accumulation of monetary rewards. Money is awarded special priority in American culture. . . . The point to emphasize here is not that Americans are uniquely materialistic, for a strong interest in material well-being can be found in most societies. Rather, the distinctive feature of American culture is the preeminent role of money as the "metric" of success. . . . Monetary success is inherently open-ended. It is always possible in principle to have more money. Hence, the American Dream offers no final stopping point. It requires never-ending achievement. The pressure to accumulate money is therefore relentless, which entices people to pursue their monetary goals by any means necessary. (Messner & Rosenfeld, 1994:71)

Concepts and Variables

After we define the concepts in a theory, we can identify variables corresponding to the concepts and develop procedures to measure them. This is an important step. Consider the concept of social control, which Donald Black (1984) defines as "all of the processes by which people define and respond to deviant behavior." What variables can represent this conceptualization of social control? Proportion of persons arrested in a community? Average length of sentences for crimes? Types of bystander reactions to public intoxication? Some combination of these?

Although we must proceed carefully to specify what we mean by a concept like social control, some concepts are represented well by the specific variables in the study and need not be defined so carefully. We may define binge drinking as heavy episodic drinking and measure it, as a variable, by asking people how many drinks they consumed in succession during some period (see Wechsler et al., 1994). That's pretty straightforward.

Be aware that not every concept in a study is represented by a variable. For example, if the term *tolerance of drinking* is defined as the absence of rules against drinking in a fraternity, it brings to mind a phenomenon that varies across different fraternities at different colleges. But if we study social life at only those fraternities that prohibit drinking, tolerance of drinking would not be a variable: All the fraternities studied have the same level of tolerance, and thus tolerance of drinking is a constant and not a variable. Of course, the concept of tolerance of drinking would still be important for understanding social life in the "dry" fraternities.

Exhibit 3.1   Concepts, Variables, and Indicators

Concepts	Variables	Indicators
Binge drinking	Frequency of heavy episodic drinking	"How often within the past two weeks did you consume five or more drinks containing alcohol in a row?"
Poverty	Subjective poverty	"Would you say you are poor?"
	Absolute poverty	Family income ÷ Poverty threshold
Social class	Income	
	Education	Income + Education + Prestige
	Occupational prestige	

MEASUREMENT OPERATIONS

After we have defined our concepts in the abstract—that is, after conceptualizing—and after we have specified the specific variables we want to measure, we must develop our measurement procedures. The goal is to devise **operations** that actually measure the concepts we intend to measure—in other words, to achieve measurement validity.

Operation   The procedure for actually measuring the concepts we intend to measure—identifying the value of a variable for each case.

Operationalization   The process of specifying the operations that will indicate the value of a variable for each case.

Exhibit 3.1 represents the **operationalization** process in three studies. The first researcher defines her concept (binge drinking) and chooses one variable (frequency of heavy episodic drinking) to represent it. This variable is then measured with responses to a single question, or indicator: "How often within the past two weeks did you consume five or more drinks containing alcohol in a row?" The second researcher defines her concept, poverty, as having two aspects or dimensions, subjective poverty and absolute poverty. Subjective poverty is measured with responses to a survey question: "Do you consider yourself poor?" Absolute poverty is measured by comparing family income to the poverty threshold. The third researcher decides that her concept, social class, can be indicated with three measured variables: income, education, and occupational prestige. The values of these three variables for each case studied are then combined into a single **indicator.**

Good conceptualization and operationalization can prevent confusion later in the research process. For example, a researcher may find that substance abusers who join a self-help group are less likely to drink again than those who receive hospital-based substance abuse treatment. But what is it about these treatment alternatives that is associated with successful abstinence? Level of peer support? Beliefs about the causes of alcoholism? Financial investment in the treatment? If the researcher had considered such aspects of the concept of substance abuse treatment before collecting her data, she might have been able to measure different aspects of treatment and so figure out which, if any, were associated with differences in abstinence rates. Because she did not measure these variables, she will not contribute as much as she might have to our understanding of substance abuse treatment.

Social researchers have many options for operationalizing their concepts. Measures can be based on activities as diverse as asking people questions, reading judicial opinions, observing social interactions, coding words in books, checking census data, enumerating the contents of trash receptacles, or drawing urine and blood samples. You will learn in later chapters that describe these research methods in detail that the particular measurement operations chosen for a study should be shaped by the research question. But before we embark on that adventure, it is first important to understand issues of measurement.

EVALUATION OF MEASURES

The issue of measurement error is very important. Do the operations developed to measure our concepts actually do so—are they valid? If we have weighed our measurement options, carefully constructed our questions and observational procedures, and carefully selected indicators from the available data, we should be on the right track. But we cannot have much confidence in a measure until we have empirically evaluated its validity.

Measurement Validity

We can consider **measurement validity** the first concern in establishing the validity of research results, because without having measured what we think we measured, we really don't know what we're talking about.

Measurement validity   The extent to which measures indicate what they are intended to measure.

As an example of measurement validity, consider the following question: "How prevalent is youth violence and delinquency in the United States; how many juveniles are involved in delinquency?" Data on the extent of juvenile delinquency come from two primary sources: official statistics and unofficial statistics. Official statistics are based on the aggregate records of juvenile offenders and offenses processed by agencies of the criminal justice system: police, courts, and corrections. One primary source of official statistics on juvenile delinquency is the *Uniform Crime Reports (UCR)*, produced by the Federal Bureau of Investigation (FBI). Unofficial statistics are data produced by people or agencies outside the criminal justice system such as victimization surveys and self-report studies. The validity of official statistics for measuring the extent of juvenile delinquency is a heated debate among criminologists. Although some researchers believe official reports are a valid measure of serious delinquency, others contend that UCR data say more about the behavior of the police than about delinquency. These criminologists think the police are predisposed against certain groups of people or certain types of crimes.

Unquestionably, official reports underestimate the actual amount of delinquency because a great deal of delinquent behavior never comes to the attention of police (Mosher, Miethe, & Phillips, 2002). Sometimes delinquent acts are committed and not observed; or they are observed and not reported. There is also evidence that the UCRs often reflect the political climate and police policies as much as they do criminal activity. Take the United States' "War on Drugs," which heated up in the 1980s. During this time, arrest rates for drug offenses soared, giving the illusion that drug use was increasing at an epidemic pace. However, self-report surveys that asked citizens directly about their drug use behavior during this same time period found that use of most illicit drugs was actually declining (Regoli & Hewitt, 1994). In your opinion, then, which measure of drug use, the UCR or self-report surveys, was more valid? Before you answer this question, let's continue with the delinquency example.

Despite the limitations of official statistics for measuring delinquency, these data were relied on by criminologists and used as a valid measure of the prevalence of delinquency for many decades. As such, delinquency and other violent offenses were thought to primarily involve minority populations and/or disadvantaged youth. In 1947, however, Wallerstein and Wyle (1947) surveyed a sample of 700 juveniles and found that 91% admitted to having committed at least one offense that was punishable by one or more years in prison, and 99% admitted to at least one offense for which they could have been arrested had they been caught. In 1958, James Short and F. Ivan Nye (1957–1958) reported the results from the first large-scale self-report study involving juveniles from a variety of locations. In their research, Short and Nye concluded that delinquency was widespread throughout the adolescent population and that youth from high-income families were just as likely to engage in delinquency as youth from low-income families. Contemporary studies using self-report data from the National Youth Survey (NYS) indicate that the actual amount of delinquency is much greater than that reported by the UCR and that unlike this official data, where nonwhites are overrepresented, self-report data indicate that white juveniles report nearly the identical number of delinquencies as nonwhites, but fewer of them are arrested (Elliott & Ageton, 1980). This is just one example of measurement validity and should convince you that we must be very careful in designing our measures and in subsequently evaluating how well they have performed.

The extent to which measures indicate what they are intended to measure can be assessed with one or more of four basic approaches: face validation, content validation, criterion validation, and construct validation. Whatever the approach to validation, no one measure is going to be valid for all times and places. For example, the validity of self-report measures of substance abuse varies with such factors as whether the respondents are sober or intoxicated at the time of the interview, whether the measure refers to recent or lifetime abuse, and whether the respondents see their responses as affecting their chances at receiving housing, treatment, or some other desired outcome (Babor, Stephens, & Marlatt, 1987). In addition, persons with severe mental illness are, in general, less likely to respond accurately (Corse, Hirschinger, & Zanis, 1995). These types of possibilities should always be considered when evaluating measurement validity.

Face Validity

Researchers apply the term **face validity** to the confidence gained from careful inspection of a concept to see if it is appropriate "on its face"—simply whether it appears to measure what it intends. For example, measuring people's favorite color seems unlikely on its face to tell us much about their alcohol consumption patterns. A measure with greater face validity would be a count of how many drinks they had consumed in the past week.

Although every measure should be inspected in this way, face validation in itself does not provide very convincing evidence of measurement validity. The question "How much beer or wine did you have to drink last week?" may look valid on its face as a measure of frequency of drinking, but people who drink heavily tend to underreport the amount they drink. So the question would be an invalid measure in a study that includes heavy drinkers.

Content Validity

Content validity establishes that the measure covers the full range of the concept's meaning. To determine that range of meaning, the researcher may solicit the opinions of experts and review literature that identifies the different aspects of the concept.

An example of a measure that covers a wide range of meaning is the Michigan Alcoholism Screening Test (MAST). The MAST includes 24 questions representing the following subscales: recognition of alcohol problems by self and others; legal, social, and work problems; help seeking; marital and family difficulties; and liver pathology (Skinner & Sheu, 1982). Many experts familiar with the direct consequences of substance abuse agree that these dimensions capture the full range of possibilities. Thus the MAST is believed to be valid from the standpoint of content validity.

Criterion Validity

When people drink an alcoholic beverage, the alcohol is absorbed into their blood and then gradually metabolized (broken down into other chemicals) in their liver (NIAAA, 1997). The alcohol that remains in their blood at any point, unmetabolized, impairs both thinking and behavior (NIAAA, 1994). As more alcohol is ingested, cognitive and behavioral consequences multiply. These biological processes can be identified with direct measures of alcohol concentration in the blood, urine, or breath. Questions about drinking behavior, on the other hand, can be viewed as attempts to measure indirectly what biochemical tests measure directly.

Criterion validity is established when the scores obtained on one measure can be accurately compared to those obtained with a more direct or already validated measure of the same phenomenon (the criterion). A measure of blood-alcohol concentration or a urine test could serve as the criterion for validating a self-report measure of drinking, as long as the questions we ask about drinking refer to the same period. Observations of substance use by friends or relatives could also, in some circumstances, serve as a criterion for validating self-report substance use measures.

Criterion validation studies of substance abuse measures have yielded inconsistent results. Self-reports of drug use agreed with urinalysis results for about 85% of the drug users who volunteered for a health study in several cities (Weatherby et al., 1994). On the other hand, the post-treatment drinking behavior self-reported by 100 male alcoholics was substantially less than the drinking behavior observed by the alcoholics' friends or relatives (Watson, Tilleskjor, Hoodecheck-Schow, Pucel, & Jacobs, 1984). Such inconsistent findings can occur because of differences in the adequacy of a measure across settings and populations. This underscores our point that you cannot assume that a measure that was validated in one study is also valid in another setting or with a different population.

An attempt at criterion validation is well worth the effort because it greatly increases confidence that the measure is measuring what was intended. However, often no other variable might reasonably be considered a criterion for feelings or beliefs or other subjective states. Even with variables for which a reasonable criterion exists, the researcher may not be able to gain access to the criterion, as would be the case with a tax return or employer document as a criterion for self-reported income.

Construct Validity

Measurement validity also can be established by showing that a measure is related to a variety of other measures as specified in a theory. This validation approach, known as **construct validity,** is commonly used in social research when no clear criterion exists for validation purposes. For example, in one study of the validity of the Addiction Severity Index (ASI), A. Thomas McLellan and his associates (1985) compared subject scores on the ASI to a number of indicators that they felt from prior research should be related to substance abuse: medical problems, employment problems, legal problems, family problems, and psychiatric problems. They could not use a criterion validation approach because they did not have a more direct measure of abuse, such as laboratory test scores or observer reports. However, their extensive research on the subject had given them confidence that these sorts of problems were all related to substance abuse, and thus their measures seemed to be valid from the standpoint of construct validity. Indeed, the researchers found that individuals with higher ASI ratings tended to have more problems in each of these areas, giving us more confidence in the ASI's validity as a measure.

A somewhat different approach to construct validation is termed **discriminant validity.** In this approach, scores on the measure to be validated are compared to scores on another measure of the same variable and to scores on variables that measure different but related concepts. Discriminant validity is achieved if the measure to be validated is related most strongly to its comparison measure and less so to the measures of other concepts. McLellan et al. (1985) found that the ASI passed this test, too: The ASI's measures of alcohol and drug problems were related more strongly to other measures of alcohol and drug problems than they were to measures of legal problems, family problems, medical problems, and the like.

The distinction between criterion and construct validation is not always clear. Opinions can differ about whether a particular indicator is indeed a criterion for the concept that is to be measured. For example, if you need to validate a question-based measure of sales ability for applicants to a sales position, few would object to using actual sales performance as a criterion. But what if you want to validate a question-based measure of the amount of social support that people receive from their friends? Should you just ask people about the social support they have received? Could friends' reports of the amount of support they provided serve as a criterion? Are verbal accounts of the amount of support provided adequate? What about observations of social support that people receive? Even if you could observe people in the act of counseling or otherwise supporting their friends, can an observer be sure that the interaction is indeed supportive? There isn't really a criterion here, just related concepts that could be used in a construct validation strategy. Even biochemical measures of substance abuse are questionable as criteria for validating self-reported substance use. Urine test results can be altered by ingesting certain substances, and blood tests vary in their sensitivity to the presence of drugs over a particular period of time.

What construct and criterion validation have in common is the comparison of scores on one measure to scores on other measures that are predicted to be related. It is not so important that researchers agree that a particular comparison measure is a criterion rather than a related construct. But it is very important to think critically about the quality of the comparison measure and whether it actually represents a different measure of the same phenomenon. For example, it is only a weak indication of measurement validity to find that scores on a new self-report measure of alcohol use are associated with scores on a previously used self-report measure of alcohol use.

Reliability

Reliability means that a measurement procedure yields consistent scores when the phenomenon being measured is not changing (or that the measured scores change in direct correspondence to actual changes in the phenomenon). If a measure is reliable, it is affected less by random error, or chance variation, than if it is unreliable. Reliability is a prerequisite for measurement validity; we cannot really measure a phenomenon if the measure we are using gives inconsistent results.

Reliability   A measure is reliable when it yields consistent scores or observations of a given phenomenon on different occasions. Reliability is a prerequisite for measurement validity.

There are four possible methods for measuring the reliability of a measure: test-retest reliability, interitem reliability, alternate-forms reliability, and interobserver reliability.

Test-Retest Reliability

When researchers measure a phenomenon that does not change between two points separated by an interval of time, the degree to which the two measurements yield comparable, if not identical, values is the **test-retest reliability** of the measure. If you take a test of your math ability and then retake the test 2 months later, the test is performing reliably if you receive a similar score both times, presuming that nothing happened during the 2 months to change your math ability. Of course, if events between the test and the retest have changed the variable being measured, then the difference between the test and retest scores should reflect that change.

When ratings by an observer, rather than ratings by the subjects themselves, are being assessed at two or more points in time, test-retest reliability is termed **intraobserver reliability** or **intrarater reliability.**

One example of how test-retest reliability may be assessed is a study by Linda Sobell and her associates (1988) of alcohol abusers' past drinking behavior (using the Lifetime Drinking History questionnaire) and life changes (using the Recent Life Changes questionnaire). All 69 subjects in the study were patients in an addiction treatment program. They had not been drinking prior to the interview (determined by a breath test). The two questionnaires were administered by different interviewers about 2 or 3 weeks apart, both times asking the subjects to recall events 8 years prior to the interviews. Reliability was high: 92% of the subjects reported the same life events both times, and at least 81% of the subjects were classified consistently at both interviews as having had an alcohol problem or not. When asked about their inconsistent answers, subjects reported that in the earlier interview they had simply dated an event incorrectly, misunderstood the question, evaluated the importance of an event differently, or forgotten an event. Answers to past drinking questions were less reliable when they were very specific, apparently because the questions exceeded subjects' capacities to remember accurately.

Interitem Reliability (Internal Consistency)

When researchers use multiple items to measure a single concept, they are concerned with **interitem reliability** (or internal consistency). For example, if we are to have confidence that a set of questions (such as those in Exhibit 3.2) reliably measures attitudes

Exhibit 3.2   Questions Used in the Violent Defensive Values Index

Would you approve of a man punching a stranger who had hit the man's child after the child accidentally damaged the stranger's car?

_____ No (0)
_____ I don't know or not sure (1)
_____ Yes (2)

Would you approve of a man punching a stranger who was beating up a woman and the man saw it?

_____ No (0)
_____ I don't know or not sure (1)
_____ Yes (2)

Would you approve of a man punching a stranger who had broken into the man's house?

_____ No (0)
_____ I don't know or not sure (1)
_____ Yes (2)

Source: Cao et al., 1997.

toward violence, the answers to the questions should be highly associated with one another. The stronger the association among the individual items, and the more items that are included, the higher the reliability of the index.

Alternate-Forms Reliability

Researchers are testing **alternate-forms reliability** when they compare subjects' answers to slightly different versions of survey questions (Litwin, 1995:13–21). A researcher may reverse the order of the response choices in an index or modify the question wording in minor ways and then readminister that index to subjects. If the two sets of responses are not too different, alternate-forms reliability is established.

A related test of reliability is the **split-halves reliability** approach. A survey sample is divided in two by flipping a coin or using some other random assignment method. These two halves of the sample are then administered the two forms of the questions. If the responses of the two halves of the sample are about the same, the measure's reliability is established.

Interobserver Reliability

When researchers use more than one observer to rate the same persons, events, or places, **interobserver reliability** is their goal. If observers are using the same instrument to rate the same thing, their ratings should be very similar. If they are similar, we can have much more confidence that the ratings reflect the phenomenon being assessed rather than the orientations of the observers.

Assessing interobserver reliability is most important when the rating task is complex. Consider a commonly used measure of mental health, the Global Assessment of Functioning Scale (GAFS), a bit of which is shown in Exhibit 3.3. The rating task seems straightforward, with clear descriptions of the subject characteristics that are supposed to lead to high or low GAFS scores. But in fact the judgments that the rater must make while using this scale are very complex. They are affected by a wide range of subject characteristics, attitudes, and behaviors as well as by the rater's reactions. As a result, interobserver agreement is often low on the GAFS, unless the raters are trained carefully.

Ways to Improve Reliability and Validity

We must always assess the reliability of a measure if we hope to be able to establish its validity. In fact, because it usually is easier to assess reliability than validity, you will see more evaluations of measurement reliability in research reports than evaluations of measurement validity.

Remember that a reliable measure is not necessarily a valid measure, as Exhibit 3.4 illustrates. This discrepancy is a common flaw of self-report measures of substance abuse. The multiple questions in self-report indexes of substance abuse are answered by most respondents in a consistent way, so the indexes are reliable. However, a number of respondents will not admit to drinking, even though they drink a lot. Their answers to the questions are consistent, but they are consistently misleading. So the indexes based on self-report are reliable but invalid. Such indexes are not useful and should be improved or discarded. Unfortunately, many measures are judged to be worthwhile on the basis only of a reliability test.

Exhibit 3.3   The Challenge of Interobserver Reliability: Excerpt from the Global Assessment
of Functioning Scale (GAFS)

Consider psychological, social, and occupational functioning on a hypothetical continuum of mental
health–illness. Do not include impairment in functioning due to physical (or environmental) limitations

Code   (**Note:** Use intermediate codes when appropriate, e.g., 45, 68, 72.)

100   **Superior functioning in a wide range of activities, life's problems never seem to get out of
hand, is sought by others because of his or her many positive qualities. No symptoms.**

91

90   **Absent or minimal symptoms** (e.g., mild anxiety before an exam), **good functioning in all areas,
interested and involved in a wide range of activities, socially effective, generally satisfied
with life, no more than everyday problems or concerns** (e.g., an occasional argument with
family members).

81

80   **If symptoms are present, they are transient and expectable reactions to psychosocial
stressors** (e.g., difficulty concentrating after family argument); **no more than slight impairment in
social, occupational, or school functioning** (e.g., temporarily falling behind in schoolwork).

71

70   **Some mild symptoms** (e.g., depressive mood and mild insomnia) **OR some difficulty in social,
occupational, or school functioning** (e.g., occasional truancy or theft within the household), **but
generally functioning pretty well, has some meaningful interpersonal relationships.**

61   .

60   **Moderate symptoms** (e.g., flat affect and circumstantial speech, occasional panic attacks) **OR
moderate difficulty in social, occupational, or school functioning** (e.g., few friends, conflicts
with peers or coworkers).

51

50   **Serious symptoms** (e.g., suicidal ideation, severe obsessional rituals, frequent shoplifting) **OR any
serious impairment in social, occupational, or school functioning** (e.g., no friend; unable to
keep a job).

41

40   **Some impairment in reality testing or communication** (e.g., speech is at times illogical, obscure,
or irrelevant) **OR major impairment in several areas, such as work or school, family relations,
judgment, thinking, or mood** (e.g., depressed man avoids friends, neglects family, and is unable
to work; child frequently beats up younger children, is defiant at home, and is failing at school).

31

30   **Behavior is considerably influenced by delusions or hallucinations OR serious impairment in
communication or judgment** (e.g., sometimes incoherent, acts grossly inappropriately, suicidal
preoccupation) **OR inability to function in almost all areas** (e.g., stays in bed all day, no job,
home, or friends).

21

20   **Some danger of hurting self or others** (e.g., suicide attempts without clear expectation of death,
frequently violent, manic excitement) **OR occasionally fails to maintain minimal personal
hygiene** (e.g., smears feces) **OR gross impairment in communication** (e.g., largely incoherent
or mute).

11

10   **Persistent danger of severely hurting self or others** (e.g., recurrent violence) **OR persistent
inability to maintain minimal personal hygiene OR serious suicidal act with clear expectation
of death.**

1

0   Inadequate information.

Source: Reprinted with permission from the *Diagnostic and Statistical Manual of Mental Disorders,
Fourth Edition.* Copyright © 1994 American Psychiatric Association.

Exhibit 3.4   The Difference Between Reliability and Validity: Drinking Behavior

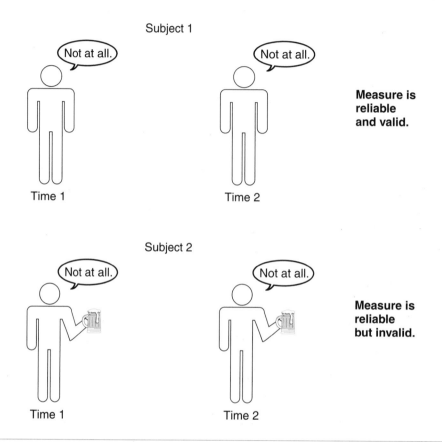

The reliability and validity of measures in any study must be tested after the fact to assess the quality of the information obtained. But then if it turns out that a measure cannot be considered reliable and valid, little can be done to save the study. Hence it is supremely important to select in the first place measures that are likely to be reliable and valid. In studies that use interviewers or observers, careful training is often essential to achieving a consistent approach. In most cases, however, the best strategy is to use measures that have been used before and whose reliability and validity have been established in other contexts. But the selection of "tried and true" measures still does not absolve researchers from the responsibility of testing the reliability and validity of the measure in their own studies.

When the population studied or the measurement context differs from that in previous research, instrument reliability and validity may be affected. So the researchers must take pains with the design of their study.

It may be possible to improve the reliability and validity of measures in a study that already has been conducted if multiple measures were used. For example, in our study of housing for homeless mentally ill persons, funded by the National Institute of Mental Health, we assessed substance abuse with several different sets of direct questions as well as with reports from subjects' case managers and others (Goldfinger et al., 1996). We found that the observational reports were often inconsistent with self-reports and that different self-report measures were not always in agreement and were thus unreliable. A more reliable measure of substance abuse was initial reports of lifetime substance abuse problems. This measure was extremely accurate in identifying all those who subsequently abused substances during the project. We concluded that the lifetime measure was a valid way to identify persons at risk for substance abuse problems.

If the research focuses on previously unmeasured concepts, new measures will have to be devised. Researchers can use one of three strategies to improve the likelihood that these new measures will be reliable and valid (Fowler, 1995):

- *Engage potential respondents in group discussions about the questions to be included in the survey.* This strategy allows researchers to check for consistent understanding of terms and to hear the range of events or experiences that people will report.
- *Conduct cognitive interviews.* Ask people test questions, and then probe with follow-up questions about how they understood the question and what their answer meant.
- *Audiotape test interviews during the pretest phase of a survey.* The researchers then review these audiotapes and systematically code them to identify problems in question wording or delivery.

Although these strategies have been developed for refining survey questions, they can also be used to refine observational procedures to improve reliability and validity.

LEVELS OF MEASUREMENT

When we know a variable's **level of measurement,** we can better understand how cases vary on that variable and so understand more fully what we have measured. Level of measurement also has important implications for the types of statistics that can be used with the variable, as you will learn in Chapter 11. There are four levels of measurement: nominal, ordinal, interval, and ratio. Exhibit 3.5 depicts the differences among these four levels.

Level of measurement   The complexity of the mathematical means that can be used to express the relationship between a variable's values. The nominal level of measurement, which is qualitative, has no mathematical interpretation; the quantitative levels of measurement (ordinal, interval, and ratio) are progressively more complex mathematically.

Nominal Level of Measurement

The **nominal level of measurement** (also called the categorical or qualitative level) identifies variables whose values have no mathematical interpretation; they vary in

Exhibit 3.5   Levels of Measurement

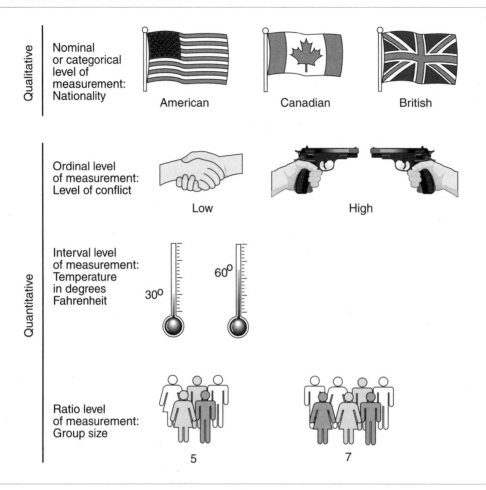

kind or quality but not in amount. In fact, it is conventional to refer to the values of nominal variables as attributes instead of values. Gender is one example. The variable "gender" has two attributes (or categories or qualities): male and female. We might indicate male with the value 1 and female with the value 2, but these numbers do not tell us anything about the difference between male and female except that they are different. Female is not one unit more of "gender" than male, nor is it twice as much "gender." Ethnicity, occupation, religious affiliation, and region of the country are also measured at the nominal level. A person may be Spanish or Portuguese, but one ethnic group does not represent more ethnicity than another, just a different ethnicity. A person may be a doctor or a truck driver, but one does not represent three units more occupation than the other.

Although the attributes of categorical variables do not have a mathematical meaning, they must be assigned to cases with great care. The attributes we use to measure, or categorize, cases must be mutually exclusive and exhaustive:

- A variable's attributes or values are **mutually exclusive attributes** if every case can have only one attribute.
- A variable's attributes or values are **exhaustive attributes** when every case can be classified into one of the categories.

When a variable's attributes are mutually exclusive and exhaustive, every case corresponds to one, and only one, attribute. Imagine the challenge of coming up with an exhaustive set of attributes when a large sample is being studied.

Ordinal Level of Measurement

The first of the three quantitative levels is the **ordinal level of measurement.** At this level, the numbers assigned to cases specify only the order of the cases, permitting greater-than and less-than distinctions; absolute mathematical distinctions cannot be made between categories. The Core Alcohol and Drug Survey (Core Institute, 1994) measures substance abuse with a series of questions that permit ordinal distinctions (see Exhibit 3.6). Although these categories may seem at first to be mathematically distinct, you can really only determine the extent to which a respondent who checks one category consumes more or less than another respondent.

The properties of variables measured at the ordinal level are illustrated in Exhibit 3.5 by the contrast between the level of conflict in two groups. The first group, symbolized by two people shaking hands, has a low level of conflict. The second group, symbolized by two persons using fists against each other, has a higher level of conflict. The third group,

Exhibit 3.6   Example of Ordinal Measures: Core Alcohol and Drug Survey

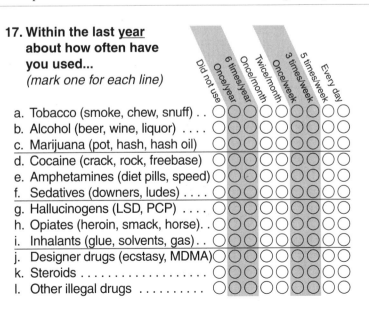

Source: Core Institute, 1994.

symbolized by two people pointing guns at each other, has an even higher level of conflict. To measure conflict, we would put the groups "in order" by assigning the number 1 to the low-conflict group, the number 2 to the group using fists, and the number 3 to the high-conflict group using guns. The numbers thus indicate only the relative position or order of the cases. Although low level of conflict is represented by the number 1, it is not mathematically two less units of conflict than the high level of conflict, which is represented by the number 3. These numbers really have no mathematical qualities—they are just used to represent relative rank in the measurement of conflict.

As with nominal variables, the different values of a variable measured at the ordinal level must be mutually exclusive and exhaustive. They must cover the range of observed values and allow each case to be assigned no more than one value.

Interval Level of Measurement

The numbers indicating the values of a variable at the **interval level of measurement** represent fixed measurement units but have no absolute, or fixed, zero point. This level of measurement is represented in Exhibit 3.5 by the difference between two Fahrenheit temperatures. Although 60 degrees is 30 degrees hotter than 30 degrees, 60 in this case is not twice as hot as 30. Why not? Because heat does not begin at 0 degrees on the Fahrenheit scale.

An interval-level measure is created by a scale that has fixed measurement units but no absolute, or fixed, zero point. The numbers can therefore be added and subtracted, but ratios are not meaningful. Again, the values must be mutually exclusive and exhaustive.

Social scientists often treat indexes that were created by combining responses to a series of variables measured at the ordinal level as interval-level measures. An index of this sort could be created with responses to the Core Institute's questions about friends' disapproval of substance use (see Exhibit 3.7). The survey has 13 questions on the topic, each of which has the same three response choices. If Don't disapprove is valued at 1, Disapprove is valued at 2, and Strongly disapprove is valued at 3, the summed index of disapproval would range from 12 to 36. The average could then be treated as a fixed unit of measurement. So a score of 20 could be treated as if it were 4 more units than a score of 16.

Ratio Level of Measurement

The numbers indicating the values of a variable at the **ratio level of measurement** represent fixed measuring units and an absolute zero point (zero means absolutely no amount of whatever the variable indicates). On a ratio scale, 10 is two points higher than 8 and is also two times greater than 5. Ratio numbers can be added and subtracted, and because the numbers begin at an absolute zero point, they can be multiplied and divided (so ratios can be formed between the numbers). For example, people's ages can be represented by values ranging from 0 years (or some fraction of a year) to 120 or more. A person who is 30 years old is 15 years older than someone who is 15 years old ($30 - 15 = 15$) and is twice as old as that person ($30/15 = 2$). Of course, the numbers also are mutually exclusive and exhaustive, so that every case can be assigned one and only one value.

Exhibit 3.7   Example of Interval-Level Measures: Core Alcohol and Drug Survey

**26. How do you think your
 close friends feel (or would
 feel) <u>about you</u>...**
(mark one for each line)

	Don't disapprove	Disapprove	Disapprove Strongly disapprove
a. Trying marijuana once or twice	○	○	○
b. Smoking marijuana occasionally	○	○	○
c. Smoking marijuana regularly	○	○	○
d. Trying cocaine once or twice	○	○	○
e. Taking cocaine regularly	○	○	○
f. Trying LSD once or twice	○	○	○
g. Taking LSD regularly	○	○	○
h. Trying amphetamines once or twice	○	○	○
i. Taking amphetamines regularly	○	○	○
j. Taking one or two drinks of an alcoholic beverage (beer, wine, liquor) nearly every day	○	○	○
k. Taking four or five drinks nearly every day	○	○	○
l. Having five or more drinks <u>in one sitting</u>	○	○	○
m. Taking steroids for body building or improved athletic performance	○	○	○

Source: Core Institute, 1994.

Exhibit 3.5 displays an example of a variable measured at the ratio level. The number of people in the first group is 5, and the number in the second group is 7. The ratio of the two groups' sizes is then 1.4, a number that mirrors the relationship between the sizes of the groups. Note that there does not actually have to be any group with a size of 0; what is important is that the numbering scheme begins at an absolute zero—in this case, the absence of any people.

The Case of Dichotomies

Dichotomies, variables having only two values, are a special case from the standpoint of levels of measurement. Although variables with only two categories are generally thought of as nominally measured, we can also think of a dichotomy as indicating the presence or absence of an attribute. Suppose, for example, we were interested in differences between individuals who had never used illegal drugs in the last year compared to those who had used at least one illegal drug in the last year. We could create a variable that indicated this dichotomous distinction by coding those individuals who said they did not use any of the substances listed as 0, and all others as 1. Viewed in this way, there is an inherent order to the two values: In one group the attribute of consuming illegal substances is absent (those coded 0), and in another it is present (those coded 1).

Exhibit 3.8   Properties of Measurement Levels

Examples of comparison statements	Appropriate math operations	Relevant level of measurement			
		Nominal	Ordinal	Interval	Ratio
A is equal to (not equal to) B	= (≠)	✓	✓	✓	✓
A is greater than (less than) B	> (<)		✓	✓	✓
A is three more than (less than) B	+ (−)			✓	✓
A is twice (half) as large as B	× (÷)				✓

Comparison of Levels of Measurement

Exhibit 3.8 summarizes the types of comparisons that can be made with different levels of measurement, as well as the mathematical operations that are legitimate. All four levels of measurement allow researchers to assign different values to different cases. All three quantitative measures allow researchers to rank cases in order.

An important thing to remember is that researchers *choose* levels of measurement in the process of operationalizing the variables; the level of measurement is not inherent in the variable itself. Many variables can be measured at different levels, with different procedures. For example, the Core Alcohol and Drug Survey (Core Institute, 1994) identifies binge drinking by asking students, "Think back over the last two weeks. How many times have you had five or more drinks at a sitting?" You might be ready to classify this as a ratio-level measure, but you must first examine the fixed response options given to respondents. This is a **closed-ended question,** and students are asked to indicate their answer by checking None, Once, Twice, 3 to 5 times, 6 to 9 times, or 10 or more times. Use of these categories makes the level of measurement ordinal. The distance between any two cases cannot be clearly determined. A student with a response in the "6 to 9 times" category could have binged just one more time than a student who responded 3 to 5 times, or they could have binged 4 more times. With these response categories, you cannot mathematically distinguish the number of times a student binged—only the relative amount of binging behavior.

The more information available, the more ways you have to compare cases. You also have more possibilities for statistical analysis with quantitative than with qualitative variables. Thus, it often is a good idea to try to measure variables at the highest level of measurement possible, if doing so does not distort the meaning of the concept that is to be measured. For example, measure age in years, if possible, rather than in categories. You can always recategorize the responses into categories that compare teenagers to young adults, but it is impossible to obtain the actual age in years when the question is asked using an ordinal response format.

Be aware, however, that other considerations may preclude measurement at a high level. For example, many people are very reluctant to report their exact incomes, even in anonymous questionnaires. So asking respondents to report their income in categories (such as under $10,000, $10,000–19,999, $20,000–29,999, etc.) will result in more responses, and thus more valid data, than asking respondents for their income in dollars.

CONCLUSION

Remember always that measurement validity is a necessary foundation for social research. Gathering data without careful conceptualization or conscientious efforts to operationalize key concepts often is a wasted effort.

The difficulties of achieving valid measurement vary with the concept being operationalized and the circumstances of the particular study. The examples in this chapter of difficulties in achieving valid measures of substance abuse should sensitize you to the need for caution, particularly when the concepts you wish to measure are socially stigmatized and/or illegal.

Planning ahead is the key to achieving valid measurement in your own research; careful evaluation is the key to sound decisions about the validity of measures in others' research. Statistical tests can help to determine whether a given measure is valid after data have been collected, but if it appears after the fact that a measure is invalid, little can be done to correct the situation. If you cannot tell how key concepts were operationalized when you read a research report, don't trust the findings. And if a researcher does not indicate the results of tests used to establish the reliability and validity of key measures, remain skeptical.

KEY TERMS

Alternate-forms reliability
Closed-ended question
Concept
Conceptualization
Construct validity
Content validity
Criterion validity
Dichotomy
Discriminant validity
Exhaustive attributes
Face validity
Indicator
Interitem reliability
Interobserver reliability

Interval level of measurement
Intraobserver reliability (intrarater reliability)
Level of measurement
Measurement validity
Mutually exclusive attributes
Nominal level of measurement
Operation
Operationalization
Ordinal level of measurement
Ratio level of measurement
Reliability
Split-halves reliability
Test-retest reliability

HIGHLIGHTS

- Conceptualization plays a critical role in research. In deductive research, conceptualization guides the operationalization of specific variables; in inductive research, it guides efforts to make sense of related observations.

- Concepts are operationalized in research by one or more indicators, or measures, which may derive from observation, self-report, available records or statistics, books and other written documents, clinical indicators, discarded materials, or some combination.

- The validity of measures should always be tested. There are four basic approaches: face validation, content validation, criterion validation, and construct validation. Criterion validation provides the strongest evidence of measurement validity, but there often is no criterion to use in validating social science measures.

- Measurement reliability is a prerequisite for measurement validity, although reliable measures are not necessarily valid. Reliability can be assessed through a test-retest procedure, in terms of interitem consistency, through a comparison of responses to alternate forms of the test, or in terms of consistency among observers.

- Level of measurement indicates the type of information obtained about a variable and the type of statistics that can be used to describe its variation. The four levels of measurement can be ordered by complexity of the mathematical operations they permit: nominal (least complex), ordinal, interval, ratio (most complex). The measurement level of a variable is determined by how the variable is operationalized. Dichotomies are a special case of measurement.

EXERCISES

1. Are important concepts in criminological research always defined clearly? Are they defined consistently? Search the literature for six articles that focus on "violent crime," "domestic violence," or some other concept suggested by your instructor. Is the concept defined clearly in each article? How similar are the definitions? Write what you have found in a short report.

2. What are some of the research questions you could attempt to answer with available statistical data? Visit your library and ask for an introduction to the government documents collection. Inspect the volumes from the Federal Bureau of Investigation (FBI) Uniform Crime Report (UCR) or the *Sourcebook for Criminal Justice Statistics,* both of which report statistics on crimes committed by offender characteristics. List 10 questions you could explore with such data.

3. Develop a plan for evaluating the validity of a measure. Your instructor will give you a copy of a questionnaire actually used in a study. Choose one question and define the concept that you believe it is intended to measure. Then develop a construct validation strategy involving other measures in the questionnaire that you think should be related to the question of interest—that is, if it measures what you think it measures.

DEVELOPING A RESEARCH PROPOSAL

At this point you can begin the processes of conceptualization and operationalization. You'll need to assume that your primary research method will be conducting a survey.

1. List at least 10 variables that will be measured in your research. No more than two of these should be sociodemographic indicators like race or age. The inclusion of each variable should be justified in terms of theory or prior research that suggests it would be an appropriate independent or dependent variable, or will have some relation to either of these.

2. Write a conceptual definition for each variable. Whenever possible, this definition should come from the existing literature—either a book you have read for a course or the research literature that you have been searching. Ask two class members for feedback on your definitions.

3. Develop measurement procedures for each variable. Several measures should be single questions and indexes that were used in prior research (search the Web and the journal literature in *Soc Abstracts* or *Psych Abstracts*). Make up a few questions and one index yourself. Ask classmates to answer these questions and give you feedback on their clarity.

4. Propose tests of reliability and validity for four of the measures.

WEB EXERCISES

1. Use the Web to find information regarding alcohol consumption and crime. Write a short report on your findings. How is "alcohol consumption" conceptualized and measured in the various sources you find?

2. How would you define "rape"? Write a brief definition. Based on this conceptualization, what circumstances constitute rape? Describe a method of measurement that would be valid for a study of rape (as you define it). Now go to the Rape Victim Advocates' Web site at www.RapeVictim Advocates.org. Go to "Myths & Facts." Discuss some facts about rape that you were previously unaware of or some myths you believed. Rewrite your definition of rape based on your new knowledge. What additional circumstances constitute rape based on your new conceptualization?

SPSS EXERCISES

HOMICIDE.POR contains a sample of homicide defendants from a sample of 33 U.S. counties for the year 1988.

Obtain a frequency distribution for the variables INTIMATE, NUMVICT, and PRITIME. At what levels (nominal/categorical, ordinal, interval, ratio) are each of these variables measured?

What conclusions do you make about the victim-offender relationship, number of victims, and length of sentence received based on these frequency distributions?

Chapter 4

SAMPLING

When a jury in Albany, New York, acquitted the four Caucasian police officers who had fired 41 bullets and killed a young African immigrant named Amadou Diallo, reporters went to the streets to uncover the public sentiment about the verdict. Reporters from the Associated Press went to the people gathered outside Diallo's Bronx home; reporters were also gathered to hear reaction from the rally at Reverend Al Sharpton's National Action Network headquarters in Harlem. Speakers at both rallies were not just average citizens but also politicians running for office or seeking reelection. For example, the Associated Press paraphrased U.S. Representative Charles Rangel's contention that officers never would have shot Diallo if he had been Caucasian. Other citizens' anger and frustration were revealed by these statements: "Murderers!" they shouted. "Racist cops!" "We want justice!" Providing quotations from individuals within news stories is a common technique in journalism. These quotes help to create a human face to go with the story.

The problem with these journalistic methods, however, is that we do not know whether the opinions selected to be printed by journalists represent the opinions of the larger population. For example, is the sentiment of Representative Rangel similar to all U.S. representatives from New York? All Democratic U.S. representatives? Do the quotes from citizens represent the opinion of everyone living in Harlem? How about the Bronx or New York City as a whole? In other words, we don't know how generalizable these comments are, and if we don't have confidence in their generalizability, their validity is suspect. In reality, of course, we have no idea whether these opinions are widely shared or quite unique.

In this chapter, we first review the rationale for using sampling in social research and consider two alternatives to sampling. We then turn to the topic of specific sampling methods and when they are most appropriate, using a variety of examples from the criminological research literature. We also briefly introduce the concept of a sampling distribution and explain how it helps in estimating our degree of confidence in statistical generalizations. By the chapter's end, you should know which questions you need to ask to evaluate the generalizability of a study as well as what choices you need to make to design a sampling strategy.

SAMPLE PLANNING

You have encountered the problem of generalizability in each of the studies you read about in this book. For example, Richard Felson, Allen Liska, Scott South, and Thomas McNulty (1994) generalized their sample-based explanation of adolescent aggression and violence to the population of high school students in the United States; Powell, Muir-McClain, and Halasyamani (1995) generalized their evaluation findings of violence prevention programs from an elementary school in King County, Washington, to all public elementary schools; and Lawrence Sherman and Richard Berk (1984) and others (Berk et al., 1992; Dunford, Huizinga, & Elliott, 1990; Garner, Fagan, & Maxwell, 1995; Hirschel, Hutchison, & Dean, 1992; Pate & Hamilton, 1992; Sherman et al., 1992) tried to determine the generalizability of findings from the original study of domestic violence in Minneapolis. Whether we, like these other researchers, are designing a sampling strategy or evaluating the generalizability of someone else's findings, we have to understand how and why researchers decide to sample. Sampling is very common in social research, but sometimes it isn't necessary.

Define Sample Components and the Population

Let's say that we are designing a study of a topic that involves a lot of people (or other entities such as cities, or countries), which are the elements in our study. We don't have the time or resources to study the entire **population**—all the elements in which we are interested—and so we resolve to study a **sample**, a subset of this population.

Population   The entire set of elements (e.g., individuals, cities, states, countries, prisons, schools) in which we are interested.

Sample   A subset of elements from the larger population.

We may collect our data directly from the elements in our sample. Some studies are not so simple, however. The entities we can easily reach to gather information are not the same as the entities about whom we really want information. So we may collect information about the elements from another set of entities called the **sampling units.** For example, if we interview mothers to learn about their families, the families are the elements and the mothers are the sampling units. If we survey prison wardens to learn about prisons, the prisons are the elements and the wardens are the sampling units.

A single-stage sample is a study in which individual people are sampled and are the focus of the study; the sampling units are the same as the elements. However, if a sample is selected in two or more stages, the units selected—let's say groups and individuals— at each stage within the groups are sampling units, but it may be that only one sampling unit is the study's element (see Exhibit 4.1). For example, a researcher might sample families for a survey about household theft victimizations and then interview only one adult representative of the family—such as a parent (a sample)—to obtain information about any victimizations. The families are the primary sampling units (and are the elements in the study), and the parents are secondary sampling units (but they are not elements, because they provide information about the family).

One key issue with selecting or evaluating sample components is understanding exactly what population they represent. In a survey of adult Americans, the general population may be reasonably construed as all residents of the United States who are at least 21 years old. But always be alert to ways the population may have been narrowed by the sample selection procedures. Perhaps only English-speaking adult residents of the continental United States were actually sampled. The population for a study is the aggregation of elements that we actually focus on and sample from, not a larger aggregation that we really wish we could have studied.

Some populations cannot be easily identified by a simple criterion such as a geographic boundary or an organizational membership. Let's say you were interested in victimizations experienced by the homeless population. In this case, a clear definition of the homeless population is difficult, but quite necessary. In research, anyone should be able to determine what population was actually studied. However, studies of homeless persons in the early 1980s "did not propose definitions, did not use screening questions to be sure that the people they interviewed were indeed homeless, and did not make major efforts to cover the universe of homeless people" (Burt, 1996:15). For example, some studies relied on homeless persons in only one shelter. The result was "a collection of studies that could not be compared" (Burt, 1996:15). Several studies of homeless persons in urban areas addressed the problem by employing a more explicit definition of the population: People are homeless if they have no home or permanent place to stay of their own (renting or owning) and no regular arrangement to stay at someone else's place (Burt, 1996).

Even this more explicit definition still leaves some questions unanswered: What is a regular arrangement? How permanent does a permanent place have to be? In a study of homeless persons in Chicago, Michael Sosin, Paul Colson, and Susan Grossman (1988) answered these questions in their definition of the population of interest:

We define the homeless as those currently residing for at least one day but for less than fourteen with a friend or relative, not paying rent, and not sure that the length of stay will surpass fourteen days; those currently residing in a shelter, whether overnight or

Exhibit 4.1   Sample Components in a Two-Stage Study

Sample of schools

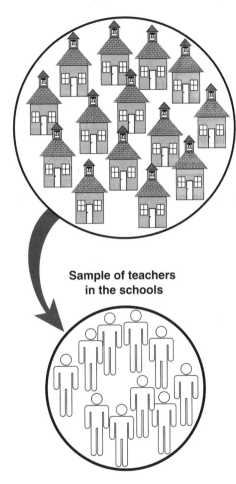

Schools are the elements and
the primary sampling unit.

**Sample of teachers
in the schools**

Teachers are the secondary sampling
units; they provide information
about the schools.

transitional; those currently without normal, acceptable shelter arrangements and thus sleeping on the street, in doorways, in abandoned buildings, in cars, in subway or bus stations, in alleys, and so forth; those residing in a treatment center for the indigent who have lived at the facility for less than 90 days and who claim that they have no place to go, when released. (p. 22)

This definition accurately reflects these researchers' concept of homelessness and allows researchers in other locations or at other times to develop procedures for studying a comparable population. The more complete and explicit the definition of the population from which a sample is selected, the more precise our generalizations from a sample to that population can be.

Evaluate Generalizability

After we clearly define the population we will sample, we need to determine the scope of the generalizations we will seek to make from our sample. Let's say we were interested in the extent to which high school youth are fearful of being attacked or harmed at school or going to and from their schools. It would be easy to go down to the local high school and hand out a survey asking students to report their levels of fear in these situations. But what if my local high school were located in a remote and rural area of Alaska? Would this sample reflect levels of fear perceived by suburban youth in California or urban youth in New York City? Obviously not. Oftentimes, regardless of the sample utilized, researchers will go on to talk about "this percentage of high school students are fearful" or "freshman students are more fearful than seniors," as if their study results represented all high school students. Many social researchers and criminologists (and most everyone else, for that matter) are eager to draw conclusions about all individuals they are interested in, not just their samples. Generalizations make their work (and opinions) sound more important. If every high school student were like every other one, generalizations based on observations of one high school student would be valid. But of course, that's not the case.

Generalizability has two aspects. **Sample generalizability** refers to the ability to generalize from a sample, or subset, of a larger population to that population itself. This is the most common meaning of generalizability. **Cross-population generalizability** refers to the ability to generalize from findings about one group, population, or setting to other groups, populations, or settings (see Exhibit 4.2). In this book, we use the term **external validity** to refer only to cross-population generalizability, not to sample generalizability.

Sample generalizability　Exists when a conclusion based on a sample, or subset, of a larger population holds true for that population.

Cross-population generalizability　Exists when findings about one group, population, or setting hold true for other groups, populations, or settings. Also called *external validity*.

Sample generalizability is a key concern in survey research, whether you are interested in measuring the extent of violent victimization, perceived levels of fear, or any other issue. A good example of the importance of sample generalizability comes from legitimate pollsters such as Gallup and Roper. Say we were interested in the likely winner of the next presidential election. To determine this, these pollsters might study a sample of likely voters, for example, and then generalize their findings to the entire population of likely voters. No one would be interested in the results of political polls if they represented only the tiny sample that actually was surveyed rather than the entire population.

Cross-population generalizability occurs to the extent that the results of a study hold true for multiple populations; these populations may not all have been sampled, or they may be represented as subgroups within the sample studied. For example, our cross-population generalizability would be called into question if we said all high school students perceived low levels of fear while going to and from school and we only had our rural Alaskan sample.

Generalizability is a key concern in research design. We rarely have the resources to study the entire population that is of interest to us, so we have to select cases to study that

---

Exhibit 4.2   Sample and Cross-Population Generalizability

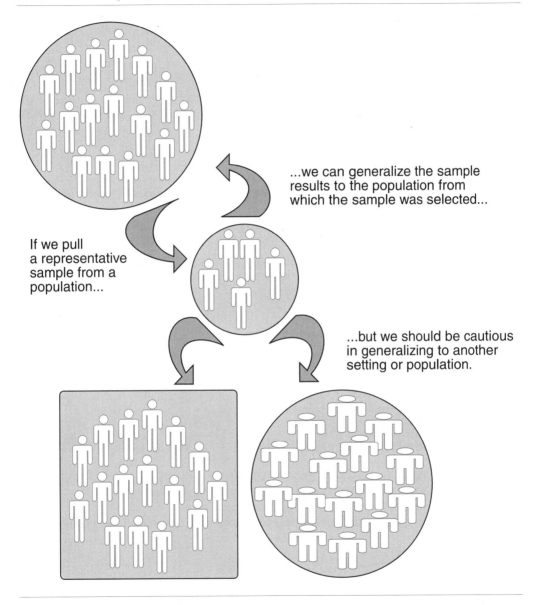

...we can generalize the sample results to the population from which the sample was selected...

If we pull a representative sample from a population...

...but we should be cautious in generalizing to another setting or population.

will allow our findings to be generalized to the population of interest. We can never be sure that our propositions will hold under all conditions, so we should be cautious in generalizing to populations that we did not actually sample.

This chapter primarily focuses on the problem of sample generalizability: Can findings from a sample be generalized to the population from which the sample was drawn? This is the most basic question to ask about a sample, and social research methods provide many tools to address it.

Sample generalizability depends on sample quality, which is determined by the amount of **sampling error.** Sampling error can generally be defined as the difference between the characteristics of a sample and the characteristics of the population from which it was selected. The larger the sampling error, the less representative the sample, and thus the less generalizable the findings. To assess sample quality when you are planning or evaluating a study, ask yourself these questions:

- From what population were the cases selected?
- What method was used to select cases from this population?
- Do the cases that were studied represent, in the aggregate, the population from which they were selected?

Sampling error   Any difference between the characteristics of a sample and the characteristics of the population from which it was drawn. The larger the sampling error, the less representative the sample is of the population.

In reality, researchers often project their theories onto groups or populations much larger than, or simply different from, those they have actually studied. The **target population** is a set of elements larger than or different from the population that was sampled, and to which the researcher would like to generalize any study findings. When we generalize findings to target populations, we must be somewhat speculative. We must carefully consider the claim that the findings can be applied to other groups, geographic areas, cultures, or times.

Because the validity of cross-population generalizations cannot be tested empirically, except by conducting more research in other settings, we do not focus much attention on this problem here. We'll return to the problem of cross-population generalizability in Chapter 5, which addresses experimental research.

Assess Population Diversity

Sampling is unnecessary if all the units in the population are identical. Physicists don't need to select a representative sample of atomic particles to learn about basic physical processes. They can study a single atomic particle, because it is identical to every other particle of its type. Similarly, biologists don't need to sample a particular type of plant to determine whether a given chemical has toxic effects on it. The idea is, "If you've seen one, you've seen 'em all."

What about people? Certainly all people are not identical; nor are animals in many respects. Nonetheless, if we are studying physical or psychological processes that are the same among all people, sampling is not needed to achieve generalizable findings. Psychologists and social psychologists often conduct experiments on college students to learn about processes that they think are identical for all individuals. They believe that most people will have the same reactions as the college students if they experience the same experimental conditions. Field researchers who observe group processes in a small community sometimes make the same assumption.

There is a potential problem with this assumption, however. There is no way to know if the processes being studied are identical for all people. In fact, experiments can give different results depending on the type of people studied or the conditions for the experiment.

Stanley Milgram's (1965) classic experiments on obedience to authority, among the most replicated experiments in the history of social psychological research, illustrate this point very well. The Milgram experiments tested the willingness of male volunteers in New Haven, Connecticut, to comply with instructions from an authority figure to give electric shocks to someone else, even when these shocks seemed to harm the person receiving them. In most cases, the volunteers complied. Milgram concluded that people are very obedient to authority.

Were these results generalizable to all men, to men in the United States, or to men in New Haven? Similar results were obtained in many replications of the Milgram experiments when the experimental conditions and subjects were similar to those studied by Milgram. Other studies, however, showed that some groups were less likely to react so obediently. Given certain conditions, such as another subject in the room who refused to administer the shocks, subjects were likely to resist authority.

So what do the experimental results tell us about how people will react to an authoritarian movement in the real world, when conditions are not so carefully controlled? In the real social world, people may be less likely to react obediently. Other individuals may argue against obedience to a particular leader's commands or people may see, on TV, the consequences of their actions. But alternatively, people may be even more obedient to authority than the experimental subjects, as they get swept up in mobs or are captivated by ideological fervor. Milgram's research gives us insight into human behavior, but there's no guarantee that what he found with particular groups in particular conditions can be generalized to the larger population (or to any particular population) in different settings.

Generalizing the results of experiments and of participant observation is risky, because such research often studies a small number of people who don't represent a particular population. Researchers may put aside concerns about generalizability when they observe the social dynamics of specific clubs, or college dorms, or a controlled experiment that tests the effect of, say, a violent movie on feelings for others. But we should be cautious about generalizing the results of such studies.

The important point is that social scientists rarely can skirt the problem of demonstrating the generalizability of their findings. If a small sample has been studied in an experiment or field research project, the study should be replicated in different settings or, preferably, with a **representative sample** of the population for which the generalizations are sought (see Exhibit 4.3).

The social world and the people in it are just too diverse to be considered identical units. Social psychological experiments and small field studies have produced good social science, but they need to be replicated in other settings, with other subjects, to claim any generalizability. Even when we believe that we have uncovered basic social processes in a laboratory experiment or field observation, we should be very concerned with seeking confirmation in other samples and other research.

Representative sample   A sample that looks like the population from which it was selected in all respects that are potentially relevant to the study. The distribution of characteristics among the elements of a representative sample is the same as the distribution of those characteristics among the total population. In an unrepresentative sample, some characteristics are overrepresented or underrepresented.

Exhibit 4.3   Representative and Unrepresentative Samples

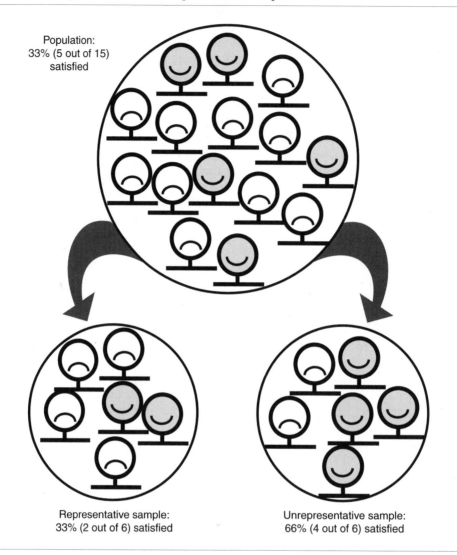

Population:
33% (5 out of 15)
satisfied

Representative sample:
33% (2 out of 6) satisfied

Unrepresentative sample:
66% (4 out of 6) satisfied

Consider a Census

In some circumstances, it may be feasible to skirt the issue of generalizability by conducting a **census** studying the entire population of interest rather than drawing a sample. The federal government tries to do this every 10 years with the U.S. Census. A census can also include studies of all the employees (or students) in small organizations (or universities), studies comparing all 50 states, and studies of the entire population of a particular type of organization in a particular area. However, in all of these instances, except for the U.S. Census, the population studied is relatively small.

The reason social scientists don't often attempt to collect data from all the members of some large population is simply that doing so would be too expensive and time-consuming. Some social scientists do conduct research with data from the U.S. Census, but it's the government that collects the data and your tax dollars that pay for the effort. For the 2000 census, the Bureau of the Census used half a million temporary workers just to follow up on the 34% of households that did not return their census form in the mail.

Even if the population of interest for a survey is a small town of 20,000 or students in a university of 10,000, researchers will have to sample. The costs of surveying just thousands of individuals far exceed the budgets for most research projects. In fact, even the U.S. Bureau of the Census cannot afford to have everyone answer all the questions that should be covered in the census. So it draws a sample. Every household must complete a short version of the census (it had 7 questions in 2000), and a sample consisting of one in six households must complete a long form (with 53 additional questions) (Rosenbaum, 2000).

Another costly fact is that it is hard to get people to complete a survey. Even the U.S. Bureau of the Census (1999) must make multiple efforts to increase the rate of response in spite of the federal law requiring all citizens to complete their census questionnaire. After spending $167 million on publicity (Forero, 2000), the Bureau still planned up to six attempts to contact each household that did not respond by mail (U.S. Bureau of the Census, 2000a). And then it planned an even more intensive sample survey to learn about the characteristics of those who still had not been contacted (U.S. Bureau of the Census, June 14, 2000b). Even relatively small rates of nonresponse in a survey can skew the results, so efforts to decrease nonresponse are essential. As the U.S. 2000 census progressed, concerns arose about under-representation of minority groups (Kershaw, 2000), impoverished cities (Zielbauer, 2000), well-to-do individuals in gated communities and luxury buildings (Langford, 2000), and even college students (Abel, 2000). The average survey has far less legal and financial backing, and so it is essential to limit the total number in the sample so there are more resources for follow-up procedures.

SAMPLING METHODS

As you can probably guess, the most important feature to know about a sample is whether it is truly representative of the population from which it was selected. The most important distinction made about samples is whether they are based on a probability or a nonprobability sampling method. Sampling methods that allow us to know in advance how likely it is that any element of a population will be selected for the sample are **probability sampling methods.** Sampling methods that do not let us know the likelihood in advance are **nonprobability sampling methods.**

Probability sampling methods rely on a random selection procedure. In principle, this is the same as flipping a coin to decide which person wins and which one loses. Heads and tails are equally likely to turn up in a coin toss, so both persons have an equal chance to win. That chance, their **probability of selection,** is 1 out of 2, or .5.

Probability of selection   The likelihood that an element will be selected from the population for inclusion in the sample. In a census of all the elements of a population, the probability that any particular element will be selected is 1.0 because everyone will be selected. If half the elements in the population are sampled on the basis of chance (say, by tossing a coin), the probability of selection for each element is one-half, or .5. When the size of the sample as a proportion of the population decreases, so does the probability of selection.

Flipping a coin is a fair way to select one of two people, because the selection process harbors no systematic bias. You might win or lose the coin toss, but you know that the outcome was due simply to chance, not to bias (unless your opponent tossed a two-headed coin!). For the same reason, rolling a six-sided die is a fair way to choose one of six possible outcomes (the odds of selection are 1 out of 6, or .17). Dealing out a hand after shuffling a deck of cards is a fair way to allocate sets of cards in a poker game (the odds of each person getting a particular outcome, such as a full house or a flush, are the same). Similarly, state lotteries use a random process to select winning numbers. Thus, the odds of winning a lottery, the probability of selection, are known even though they are very small (perhaps 1 out of 1 million) compared to the odds of winning a coin toss. As you can see, the fundamental strategy in probability sampling is the **random selection** of elements into the sample. When a sample is randomly selected from the population, every element has a known and independent chance of being selected into the sample.

Random selection   The fundamental element of probability samples. The essential characteristic of random selection is that every element of the population has a known and independent chance of being selected into the sample.

There is a natural tendency to confuse the concept of probability, in which cases are selected only on the basis of chance, with a haphazard method of sampling. On first impression, leaving things up to chance seems to imply not exerting control over the sampling method. But to ensure that nothing but chance influences the selection of cases, the researcher must proceed very methodically, leaving nothing to chance except the selection of the cases themselves. The researcher must carefully follow controlled procedures if a purely random process is to occur. In fact, when reading about sampling methods, do not assume that a random sample was obtained just because the researcher used a random selection method at some point in the sampling process. Look for these two particular problems: selecting elements from an incomplete list of the total population and failing to obtain an adequate response rate (say, only 45% of the people who were asked to participate actually agreed).

The list from which the elements of the population are selected is the **sampling frame.** If this list is incomplete, a sample selected randomly from the list will obviously not be a random sample of the population because not everyone in the population was represented on the list. Thus, you should always consider the adequacy of the sampling frame. Even for a simple population like a university's student body, the registrar's list is likely to be at least a bit out of date at any given time. For example, some students will have dropped out, but their status will not yet be officially recorded. Although you may judge the amount of error introduced in this particular situation to be negligible, the problems are greatly compounded for a larger population. The sampling frame for a city, state, or nation is always likely to be incomplete because of constant migration into and out of the area. Even unavoidable omissions from the sampling frame can bias a sample against particular groups within the population.

A very inclusive sampling frame may still yield systematic bias if many sample members cannot be contacted or refuse to participate. **Nonresponse** is a major hazard in survey research because individuals who do not respond to a survey are likely to differ systematically from those who take the time to participate. You should not assume that findings from a randomly selected sample will be generalizable to the population from which the sample was selected if the rate of nonresponse is considerable (certainly not if it is much above 30%).

Probability Sampling Methods

Probability sampling methods are those in which the probability of selection is known and is not zero (so there is some chance of selecting each element). These methods randomly select elements and therefore have no systematic bias; nothing but chance determines which elements are included in the sample. This feature of probability samples, sometimes referred to as random samples, makes them much more desirable than nonprobability samples when the goal is to generalize your findings to a larger population.

Even though a random sample has no systematic bias, it certainly will have some sampling error due to chance. The probability of selecting a head is .5 in a single toss of a coin, and in 20, 30, or however many tosses of a coin you like. But it is perfectly possible to toss a coin twice and get a head both times. The random sample of the two sides of the coin is selected in an unbiased fashion, but it still is unrepresentative. Imagine randomly selecting a sample of 10 people from a population comprising 50 men and 50 women. Just by chance, it is possible that your sample of 10 people will include 7 women and only 3 men. Fortunately, we can determine mathematically the likely degree of sampling error in an estimate based on a random sample (as you'll see later in this chapter), assuming that the sample's randomness has not been destroyed by a high rate of nonresponse or by poor control over the selection process.

In general, both the size of the sample and the homogeneity (sameness) of the population affect the degree of error due to chance; the proportion of the population that the sample represents does not. To elaborate:

The larger the sample, the more confidence we can have in the sample's representativeness of the population from which it was drawn. If we randomly pick five people to represent the entire population of our city, our sample is unlikely to be very representative of the entire population in terms of age, gender, race, attitudes, and so on. But if we randomly pick 100 people, the odds of having a representative sample are much better; with a random sample of 1,000, the odds become very good indeed.

The more homogeneous the population, the more confidence we can have in the representativeness of a sample of any particular size. Let's say we plan to draw samples of 50 from each of two communities to estimate mean family income. One community is very diverse, with family incomes ranging from $12,000 to $85,000. In the more homogeneous

Exhibit 4.4   Election Outcomes: Predicted[1] and Actual

Winner/Year	Polls	Result
Kennedy (1960)	51%	50%
Johnson (1964)	64%	61%
Nixon (1968)[2]	43%	43%
Nixon (1972)	62%	62%
Carter (1976)	48%	50%
Reagan (1980)[2]	47%	51%
Reagan (1984)	59%	59%
Bush (1988)	56%	54%
Clinton (1992)[2]	49%	43%
Clinton (1996)[2]	52%	50%
Bush, G. W. (2000)[2]	48%	50%

Source: Gallup Poll Accuracy Record, 12/13/00, www.gallup.com/poll/trends/ptaccuracy.asp.

[1] Final Gallup poll prior to the election.
[2] There was also a third-party candidate.

community, family incomes are concentrated in a narrower range, from $41,000 to $64,000. The estimated average family income based on the sample from the homogeneous community is more likely to be representative than is the estimate based on the sample from the more heterogeneous community. With less variation, fewer cases are needed to represent the homogeneous community.

The fraction of the total population that a sample contains does not affect the sample's representativeness, unless that fraction is large. We can regard any sampling fraction under 2% with about the same degree of confidence (Sudman, 1976:184). In fact, sample representativeness is not likely to increase much until the sampling fraction is quite a bit higher. Other things being equal, a sample of 1,000 from a population of 1 million (with a sampling fraction of 0.001, or 0.1%) is much better than a sample of 100 from a population of 10,000 (although the sampling fraction is 0.01, or 1%, which is 10 times higher). The size of a sample is what makes representativeness more likely, not the proportion of the whole that the sample represents.

Polls that predict presidential election outcomes illustrate both the value of random sampling and the problems that it cannot overcome. In most presidential elections, pollsters have accurately predicted the outcomes of the actual vote by using random sampling and, these days, phone interviewing to learn which candidate voters intend to choose. Exhibit 4.4 shows how close these sample-based predictions have been in the last 10 contests. The big exception was the 1980 election, when a third-party candidate had an unpredicted effect. Otherwise, the small discrepancies between the votes predicted through random sampling and the actual votes can be attributed to random error.

The Gallup poll did quite well in predicting the result of the remarkable 2000 presidential election. The final Gallup prediction was that George W. Bush would win with 48% (Al Gore was predicted to receive only 46%, and Green Party nominee Ralph

Nader was predicted to secure 4%). Although the race turned out much closer, with Gore actually winning the popular vote (before losing in the electoral college), Gallup accurately noted that there appeared to have been a late-breaking trend in favor of Gore (Newport, 2000).

Despite accurate sampling, election polls have produced some major errors in prediction. The reasons for these errors illustrate how unintentional systematic bias can influence sample results. In 1936, a *Literary Digest* poll predicted that Alfred M. Landon would defeat President Franklin Delano Roosevelt in a landslide, but instead Roosevelt took 63% of the popular vote. The problem? The *Digest* mailed out 10 million mock ballots to people listed in telephone directories, automobile registration records, voter lists, and so on. But in 1936, the middle of the Great Depression, only relatively wealthy people had phones and cars, and they were more likely to vote Republican. Furthermore, only 2,376,523 completed ballots were returned, creating a response rate of only 24%, which left much room for error. Of course, this poll was not designed as a random sample, so the appearance of systematic bias is not surprising. Gallup was able to predict the 1936 election results accurately with a randomly selected sample of just 3,000 (Bainbridge, 1989:43–44).

The year 1980 was the only year since 1948 that pollsters had the wrong prediction for the winner of a presidential election in the week prior to the election. With Jimmy Carter ahead of Ronald Reagan in the polls by 45% to 42%, Gallup predicted a race too close to call. The outcome: Reagan 51%, Carter 42%. The problem? A large bloc of undecided voters, an unusually late debate with a strong performance by Reagan, and the failure of many pollsters to call back voters whom interviewers had failed to reach on the first try (these harder-to-reach voters were more likely to be Republican-leaning) (Dolnick, 1984; Loth, 1992). In this case, the sample was systematically biased against voters who were harder to reach and those who were influenced by the final presidential debate. The presence of many undecided voters in the sample was apparently an accurate representation of sentiment in the general population, so the problem would not be considered sample bias; but it did make measuring voting preferences all the more difficult.

Because they do not disproportionately exclude or include particular groups within the population, random samples that are successfully implemented avoid systematic bias. Random sampling error can still be considerable, however, and different types of random samples vary in their ability to minimize it. The four most common methods for drawing random samples are simple random sampling, systematic random sampling, stratified random sampling, and cluster sampling.

Simple Random Sampling

Simple random sampling requires a procedure that generates numbers or identifies cases strictly on the basis of chance. As you know, flipping a coin and rolling a die can be used to identify cases strictly on the basis of chance, but these procedures are not very efficient tools for drawing a sample. A **random number table,** like the one in Appendix E, simplifies the process considerably. The researcher numbers all the elements in the sampling frame and then uses a systematic procedure for picking corresponding numbers from the random number table. (Exercise 2 at the end of the chapter explains the process step by step.) Alternatively, a researcher may use a lottery procedure. Each case number is written on a small card, and then the cards are mixed up and the sample selected from the cards.

When a large sample must be generated, these procedures are very cumbersome. Fortunately, a computer program can easily generate a random sample of any size. The researcher must first number all the elements to be sampled (the sampling frame) and then run the computer program to generate a random selection of the numbers within the desired range. The elements represented by these numbers are the sample.

Organizations that conduct phone surveys often draw random samples with another automated procedure called **random digit dialing.** A machine dials random numbers within the phone prefixes corresponding to the area in which the survey is to be conducted. Random digit dialing is particularly useful when a sampling frame is not available. The researcher simply replaces any inappropriate numbers (those no longer in service or for businesses, for example) with the next randomly generated phone number.

The probability of selection in a true simple random sample is equal for each element. If a sample of 500 is selected from a population of 17,000 (that is, a sampling frame of 17,000), then the probability of selection for each element is 500/17,000, or .03. Every element has an equal and independent chance of being selected, just like the odds in a toss of a coin (1/2) or a roll of a die (1/6). Thus simple random sampling is an equal probability of selection method (EPSEM).

Simple random sampling can be done either with or without replacement sampling. In **replacement sampling,** each element is returned to the sampling frame after it is selected so that it may be sampled again. In sampling without replacement, each element selected for the sample is then excluded from the sampling frame. In practice it makes no difference whether sampled elements are replaced after selection, as long as the population is large and the sample is to contain only a small fraction of the population.

Patricia Tjaden and Nancy Thoennes (2000) utilized simple random sampling when they sought to determine the magnitude of violent victimization in the United States using a telephone survey. They used random digit dialing to contact adult (18 years and older) residential household members in the continental United States and the District of Columbia; 72% of the females and 69% of the males selected for the sample participated in the survey. The final sample contained 8,000 adult men and 8,000 adult women. In their final report to the National Institute of Justice, Tjaden and Thoennes (2000) provide a comparison of demographic characteristics of men and women in their National Violence Against Men and Women Survey and men and women in the U.S. population as measured by the U.S. Bureau of the Census 1995 Current Population Survey of adult men and women. The two samples were remarkably similar. For example, an average of 48% of Tjaden's sample were between 30 and 49 years of age, compared to 43% of the U.S. Bureau of the Census sample; 10% of Tjaden's sample were African American compared to 11% of the Bureau of the Census sample; 8% of Tjaden's sample were of Hispanic origin compared to 9% of the U.S. Bureau of the Census sample; and 65% of Tjaden's sample was currently married compared to 61% of the U.S. Bureau of the Census sample.

How does this sample strike you? Let's assess sample quality using the questions posed earlier in the chapter:

- *From what population were the cases selected?* There is a clearly defined population—the adult residents of the continental United States (who live in households with phones).
- *What method was used to select cases from this population?* The case selection method is a random selection procedure, and there are no systematic biases in the sampling.

- *Do the cases that were studied represent, in the aggregate, the population from which they were selected?* The findings are very likely to represent the population sampled, because there were no biases in the sampling and a very large number of cases were selected. However, it must be remembered that an average of 30% of those selected for interviews could not be contacted or chose not to respond. This rate of non-response may have created a small bias in the sample for several characteristics.

We also must consider the issue of cross-population generalizability. Do findings from this sample have implications for any larger group beyond the population from which the sample was selected? Because a representative sample of the entire U.S. adult population was drawn, this question has to do with cross-national generalizations. Tjaden and Thoennes wisely do not make such generalizations because national cultures, norms, and social policies will undoubtedly be related to different rates of victimization.

Systematic Random Sampling

Systematic random sampling is a variant of simple random sampling and is a little less time consuming. When you systematically select a random sample, the first element is selected randomly from a list or from sequential files, and then every *n*th element is systematically selected thereafter. This is a convenient method for drawing a random sample when the population elements are arranged sequentially. It is particularly efficient when the elements are not actually printed (that is, there is no sampling frame) but instead are represented by folders in filing cabinets.

Systematic random sampling requires three steps:

1. The total number of cases in the population is divided by the number of cases required for the sample. This division yields the **sampling interval,** the number of cases from one sampled case to another. If 50 cases are to be selected out of 1,000, the sampling interval is 20 (1,000/50 = 20); every 20th case is selected.

2. A number from 1 to 20 (the sampling interval) is selected randomly. This number identifies the first case to be sampled, counting from the first case on the list or in the files.

3. After the first case is selected, every *n*th case is selected for the sample, where *n* is the sampling interval. If the sampling interval is not a whole number, the size of the sampling interval is systematically varied to yield the proper number of cases for the sample. For example, if the sampling interval is 30.5, the sampling interval alternates between 30 and 31.

In almost all sampling situations, systematic random sampling yields what is essentially a simple random sample. The exception is a situation in which the sequence of elements is affected by **periodicity**—that is, the sequence varies in some regular, periodic pattern. Thus, the list or folder device from which the elements are selected must be truly random. For example, we could not have a list of convicted felons sorted by offense type, age, or some other characteristic of the population. If the list is sorted in any meaningful way, this will introduce bias to the sampling process and the resulting sample is not likely to be representative of the population.

Stratified Random Sampling

Although all probability sampling methods use random sampling, some add steps to the sampling process to make sampling more efficient or easier. One sample is more efficient than another when it is easier to obtain without sacrificing confidence that the sample statistics are representative of the population. Samples are easier to collect when they require less time, money, or prior information.

Stratified random sampling uses information known about the total population prior to sampling to make the sampling process more efficient. First, all elements in the population (that is, in the sampling frame) are distinguished according to their value on some relevant characteristic, which forms the sampling strata. Next, elements are sampled randomly from within these strata. For example, race may be the basis for distinguishing individuals in some population of interest. Within each racial category selected for the strata, individuals are then sampled randomly.

Why is this method more efficient than drawing a simple random sample? Well, imagine that you plan to draw a sample of 500 from an ethnically diverse neighborhood. The neighborhood population is 15% African American, 10% Hispanic, 5% Asian, and 70% Caucasian. If you drew a simple random sample, you might end up with disproportionate numbers of each group. But if you created sampling strata based on race and ethnicity, you could randomly select cases from each stratum: 75 African Americans (15% of the sample), 50 Hispanics (10%), 25 Asians (5%), and 350 Caucasians (70%). By using **proportionate stratified sampling,** you would eliminate any possibility of error in the sample's distribution of ethnicity. Each stratum would be represented exactly in proportion to its size in the population from which the sample was drawn (see Exhibit 4.5).

In **disproportionate stratified sampling,** the proportion of each stratum that is included in the sample is intentionally varied from what it is in the population. In the case of the sample stratified by ethnicity, you might select equal numbers of cases from each racial or ethnic group: 125 African Americans (25% of the sample), 125 Hispanics (25%), 125 Asians (25%), and 125 Caucasians (25%). In this type of sample, the probability of selection of every case is known but unequal between strata. You know what the proportions are in the population, and so you can easily adjust your combined sample statistics to reflect these true proportions. For instance, if you want to combine the ethnic groups and estimate the average income of the total population, you would have to weight each case in the sample. The weight is a number you multiply by the value of each case based on the stratum it is in. For example, you would multiply the incomes of all African Americans in the sample by 0.6 (75/125), the incomes of all Hispanics by 0.4 (50/125), and so on. Weighting in this way reduces the influence of the oversampled strata and increases the influence of the undersampled strata to just what they would have been if pure probability sampling had been used.

Why would anyone select a sample that is so unrepresentative in the first place? The most common reason is to ensure that cases from smaller strata are included in the sample in sufficient numbers. Only then can separate statistical estimates and comparisons be made between strata (e.g., between African Americans and Caucasians). Remember that one determinant of sample quality is sample size. The same is true for subgroups within samples. If a key concern in a research project is to describe and compare the incomes of people from different racial and ethnic groups, then it is important that the researchers base the mean income of each group on enough cases to be a valid representation. If few

Exhibit 4.5   Stratified Random Sampling

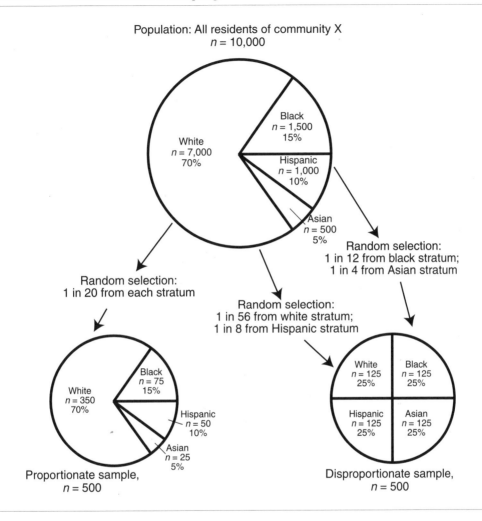

members of a particular minority group are in the population, they need to be oversampled. Such disproportionate sampling may also result in a more efficient sampling design if the costs of data collection differ markedly between strata or if the variability (heterogeneity) of the strata differs.

Cluster Sampling

Although stratified sampling requires more information than usual prior to sampling (about the size of strata in the population), cluster sampling requires less prior information. Specifically, **cluster sampling** can be useful when a sampling frame is not available, as often is the case for large populations spread across a wide geographic area or among many different organizations. In fact, if we wanted to obtain a sample from the entire U.S.

Exhibit 4.6 Cluster Sampling

Stage 1:	Stage 2:	Stage 3:	Stage 4:
Randomly select states	Randomly select cities, towns, and counties within those states	Randomly select schools within those cities and towns	Randomly select students within each school

population, there would be no list available. Yes, there are lists in telephone books of residents in various places who have telephones, lists of those who have registered to vote, lists of those who hold driver's licenses, and so on. However, all these lists are incomplete— some people do not list their phone number or do not have a telephone, some people are not registered to vote, and so on. Using incomplete lists such as these introduces bias into a sample.

In such cases, the sampling procedures become a little more complex. We usually end up working toward the sample we want through a series of steps—first by extracting a random sample of groups or clusters of elements that are available and then by randomly sampling the individual elements of interest from within these selected clusters. So what is a cluster? A **cluster** is a naturally occurring, mixed aggregate of elements of the population, with each element appearing in one and only one cluster. Schools could serve as clusters for sampling students, blocks could serve as clusters for sampling city residents, counties could serve as clusters for sampling the general population, and businesses could serve as clusters for sampling employees.

Drawing a cluster sample is at least a two-stage procedure. First, the researcher draws a random sample of clusters. A list of clusters should be much easier to obtain than a list of all the individuals in each cluster in the population. Next, the researcher draws a random sample of elements within each selected cluster. Because only a fraction of the total clusters are involved, obtaining the sampling frame at this stage should be much easier.

In a cluster sample of city residents, for example, blocks could be the first-stage clusters. A research assistant could walk around each selected block and record the addresses of all occupied dwelling units. Or in a cluster sample of students, a researcher could contact the schools selected in the first stage and make arrangements with the registrars to obtain lists of students at each school. Cluster samples often involve multiple stages (see Exhibit 4.6).

How many clusters and how many individuals within clusters should be selected? As a general rule, cases in the sample will be closer to the true population value if the researcher maximizes the number of clusters selected and minimizes the number of individuals within each cluster. Unfortunately, this strategy also maximizes the cost of the sample. The more clusters selected, the higher the travel costs. It also is important to take into account the homogeneity of the individuals within clusters; the more homogeneous the clusters, the fewer cases needed per cluster. This should make intuitive sense, as it is more likely that any selected element will represent other elements if they are alike. Although cluster sampling is a very popular method among survey researchers, it has one drawback: Sampling error is greater in a cluster sample than in a simple random sample. And as a general rule, this error increases as the number of clusters decreases.

Many professionally designed surveys use multistage cluster samples or even combinations of cluster and stratified probability sampling methods. For example, the U.S. Justice Department's National Crime Victimization Survey (NCVS) is an excellent example of a cluster sample. In the NCVS, the first stage of clusters selected are referred to as primary sampling units (PSUs), and represent a sample of rural counties and large metropolitan areas. From these PSUs, another stage of sampling involves the selection of geographic districts within each of the PSUs that have been listed by the U.S. Bureau of the Census population census. Finally, a probability sample of residential dwelling units is selected from these geographic districts. These dwelling units, or addresses, represent the final stage of the multistage sampling. Anyone who resides at a selected address who is 12 years of age or older and is a U.S. citizen is eligible for the NCVS sample. Approximately 50,500 housing units or other living quarters are designated for the NCVS each year and are selected in this manner.

How would we evaluate the NCVS sample, using the sample evaluation questions?

- *From what population were the cases selected?* The population was clearly defined for each cluster.
- *What method was used to select cases from this population?* The random selection method was carefully described.
- *Do the cases that were studied represent, in the aggregate, the population from which they were selected?* The unbiased selection procedures make us reasonably confident in the representativeness of the sample.

Nonprobability Sampling Methods

Unlike probability samples, when collecting a sample using nonprobability sampling techniques, elements within the population do not have a known probability of being selected into the sample. Thus, because the chance of any element being selected is unknown, we cannot be certain the selected sample actually represents our population. Why, you may be asking yourself right now, would we want to use such a sample if we cannot generalize our results to a larger population? Well, because these methods are useful for several purposes, including those situations in which we do not have a population list, when we are exploring a research question that does not concern a large population, or when we are doing a preliminary or exploratory study. Suppose, for example, that we were interested in the crime of shoplifting and wanted to investigate the rationalizations used by shoplifters. It would be hard to define a population in this case because we don't have a list of shoplifters from which to randomly select. There may be lists of convicted shoplifters, but of course, they only represent those shoplifters who were actually caught.

There are four nonprobability sampling methods frequently used in criminological research: availability sampling, quota sampling, purposive sampling, and snowball sampling.

Availability Sampling

The definition of **availability sampling** is straightforward—elements are selected because they're available or easy to find. Consequently, this sampling method is also known as haphazard, accidental, or convenience sampling. News reporters often use person-on-the-street interviews—availability samples—to inject a personal perspective into a news story and show what ordinary people may think of a given topic. Availability samples are also used by university professors and researchers all the time. Have you ever been asked to complete a questionnaire in one of your classes? If so, you have been selected for inclusion in an availability sample.

Even though they are not generalizable, availability samples are often appropriate in research; for example, when a field researcher is exploring a new setting and trying to get some sense of prevailing attitudes or when a survey researcher conducts a preliminary test of a questionnaire. There are a variety of ways to select elements for an availability sample—standing on street corners and talking to anyone walking by, asking questions of employees who come to pick up their paychecks at a personnel office, or distributing questionnaires to an available and captive audience such as a class or a group meeting. Availability samples are also frequently used in field work studies interested in obtaining detailed information about a particular group. For example, when Philippe Bourgois, Mark Lettiere, and James Quesada (1997) wanted to understand homeless heroin addicts, they immersed themselves in a community of addicts living in a public park in San Francisco. These addicts thus became the availability sample.

Another classic example of an availability sample used in research is found in John Irwin's *The Felon* (1970), a study of the post-prison careers of a group of California criminal felons. To conduct his study, Irwin did not take a simple or systematic random sample of all felons released from the California Department of Corrections. Instead, because he resided and worked in the San Francisco area, Irwin studied offenders released on parole from penal institutions in San Francisco and Oakland parole districts who volunteered for his study.

When such samples are used, it is necessary to explicitly describe the sampling procedures used in the methodology section of research reports to acknowledge the nonrepresentativeness of the sample. For example, in a study that one of the authors conducted to investigate the factors related to sexual assault offending, a sample of male college students was utilized. In a paper published from this research, we stated:

> The respondents in this study consisted of 94 male undergraduate students enrolled in introductory social science courses at a state university in New England. The students were given extra credit for their participation in the study, and were administered the data collection instrument during nonclass hours. (Bachman, Paternoster, & Ward, 1992, p. 412)

This availability sample was partially justified for two reasons: The study was exploratory in nature, and college women have been shown to be at extremely high risk of becoming the victims of sexual assault perpetrated by their male peers. However, it was still a large leap of faith to assume that the college males from one university used in this sample were representative of males in general, or even of male college students in general.

How do the answers to the sample evaluation questions differ for this type of sample from those obtained for probability samples? Well, there is no clearly definable population from which the respondents were drawn, and no systematic technique was used to select the respondents. Consequently, there is not much likelihood that the sample is representative of any target population—the problem is, we can never be sure.

Availability sampling often masquerades as a more rigorous form of research. Popular magazines and Internet sites periodically survey their readers by asking them to fill out questionnaires. Follow-up articles then appear in the magazine or on the site, displaying the results under such titles as "What You Think About the Death Penalty for Teenagers." If the magazine's circulation is large, a large sample can be achieved in this way. The problem is that usually only a tiny fraction of readers fill out the questionnaire, and these respondents are probably unlike other readers who did not have the interest or time to participate. So the survey is based on an availability sample. Even though the follow-up article may be interesting, we have no basis for thinking that the results describe the readership as a whole, much less the population at large. In fact, Richard Morin, a columnist for the *Washington Post*, implored his readers, "Promise me this: While I'm gone, please, oh please, don't take Internet polls seriously. For several years now, your Wiz has condemned those ghastly Web pseudo-surveys. But not everybody's paying attention" (Morin, 1999). Morin went on to chastise ABC's *Good Morning America* for grabbing a story based on a survey that Internet users filled out on ABC.com. Based on this survey, *Good Morning America,* and other journalists including those at the *Boston Herald,* ran stories stating that nearly 6% of Internet users were addicted to the Internet. Not only was the sample not selected randomly, but electronic surveys also remain very susceptible to electronic ballot stuffing; few sites restrict access, so you can answer the posted questions as many times as you want. The 6% estimate is obviously not generalizable to the population of all Internet users. Because of their nonscientific basis, many Internet sites that conduct such polls, including ABC.com, now add this disclaimer to the online poll's question of the day: "Not a scientific poll; for entertainment only."

Quota Sampling

Quota sampling is intended to overcome the most obvious flaw of availability sampling—that the sample will just consist of who or what is available, without any concern for its similarity to the population of interest. The distinguishing feature of a quota sample is that quotas are set to ensure that the sample represents certain characteristics in proportion to their prevalence in the population.

Quota samples are similar to stratified probability samples, but they are generally less rigorous and precise in their selection procedures. Quota sampling simply involves designating the population into proportions of some group that you want to be represented in your sample. Similar to stratified samples, in some cases, these proportions may actually represent the true proportions observed in the population. At other times, these quotas may represent predetermined proportions of subsets of people you deliberately want to oversample.

Suppose we were interested in investigating the crime of personal larceny with contact, which generally involves pocket picking and purse snatching. Because elderly citizens are disproportionately victimized by this crime, we would want to make sure we had enough elderly victims in our sample to make comparisons to their younger cohorts. For a study such as this, we may decide that we want 50% of the victims in our sample to consist of individuals 65 years of age or older and 50% to consist of those younger than 65 years of age. When these proportions are decided, they represent our *quotas*. Elements of the population are then collected until each quota is filled. In our example, we would select the sample until we have exactly 50% of the elements younger than 65 and 50% 65 years of age or older. Quota sampling may be more complex, in that we can add quotas to fill. For example, in addition to age, we may want to make sure that within each age group we have a certain proportion of African American men and women, a certain proportion of Hispanic men and women, and a certain proportion of Caucasian men and women.

In reality, researchers can set quotas for only a small fraction of the characteristics relevant to a study, so a quota sample is really not much better than an availability sample (although following careful, consistent procedures for selecting cases within the quota limits always helps). Thus, even though quota-sampling techniques range from the simple to the rigorous, all quota samples are still considered nonprobability samples.

Purposive or Judgment Sampling

In **purposive sampling,** each sample element is selected for a purpose, usually because of the unique position of the sample elements. It is sometimes referred to as *judgment sampling,* because the researcher uses his or her own judgment about whom to select into the sample, rather than drawing sample elements randomly. Purposive sampling may involve studying the entire population of some limited group (members of a street gang) or a subset of a population (juvenile parolees). Or a purposive sample may be a key informant survey, which targets individuals who are particularly knowledgeable about the issues under investigation.

Herbert Rubin and Irene Rubin (1995:66) suggest three guidelines for selecting informants when designing any purposive sampling strategy. Informants should be

- knowledgeable about the cultural arena or situation or experience being studied,
- willing to talk, and
- representative of the range of points of view.

In addition, Rubin and Rubin (1995) suggest continuing to select interviewees until you can pass two tests:

- *Completeness.* "What you hear provides an overall sense of the meaning of a concept, theme, or process" (p. 72).
- *Saturation.* "You gain confidence that you are learning little that is new from subsequent interview[s]" (p. 73).

Adhering to these guidelines will help to ensure that a purposive sample adequately represents the setting or issues being studied.

Of course, purposive sampling does not produce a sample that represents some larger population, but it can be exactly what is needed in a case study of an organization, community, or some other clearly defined and relatively limited group. For example, in their book *Crimes of the Middle Class,* Weisburd and his colleagues (1991) examined a sample of white-collar criminal offenders convicted in seven federal judicial districts. These judicial districts were not randomly selected from an exhaustive list of all federal districts, but were instead deliberately selected by the researchers because the seven districts were judged by them to provide a suitable amount of geographical diversity. They were also selected because they were believed to have a substantial proportion of white-collar crime cases. The cost of such nonprobability sampling, you should realize by now, is generalizability; we do not know if their findings hold true for white-collar crime in other areas of the country.

Snowball Sampling

For **snowball sampling,** you identify one member of the population and speak to him or her, then ask that person to identify others in the population and speak to them, then ask them to identify others, and so on. The sample thus snowballs in size. This technique is useful for hard-to-reach or hard-to-identify, interconnected populations where at least some members of the population know each other, such as drug dealers, prostitutes, practicing criminals, gang leaders, and informal organizational leaders.

In their study of juvenile gangs in St. Louis, Decker and Van Winkle (1996) utilized the technique of snowball sampling. Specifically, the snowball began with an earlier fieldwork project involving active residential burglars (Wright & Decker, 1994). The young members from this sample, along with contacts a field ethnographer had with several active street criminals, started the referral process. The initial interviewees then nominated other gang members as potential interview subjects.

One problem with this technique is that the initial contacts may shape the entire sample and foreclose access to some members of the population of interest. Because Decker and Van Winkle (1996) wanted to interview members from several gangs, they had to restart the snowball sampling procedure many times to gain access to a large number of gangs. One problem, of course, was validating whether individuals claiming to be gang members, so-called wannabes, actually were legitimate members. Over 500 contacts were made before the final sample of 99 was complete.

More systematic versions of snowball sampling can also reduce the potential for bias. The most sophisticated version, *respondent-driven sampling,* gives financial incentives, also called gratuities, to respondents to recruit peers (Heckathorn, 1997). Limitations on the number of incentives that any one respondent can receive increase the sample's diversity. Targeted incentives can steer the sample to include specific subgroups. When the sampling is repeated through several waves, with new respondents bringing in more peers, the composition of the sample converges on a more representative mix of characteristics. Exhibit 4.7 shows how the sample spreads out through successive recruitment waves to an increasingly diverse pool (Heckathorn, 1997:178). As with all nonprobability sampling techniques, however, researchers using even the most systematic versions of snowball sampling cannot be confident that their sample is representative of the population of interest.

Lessons About Sample Quality

Some lessons are implicit in our evaluations of the samples in this chapter:

- We can't evaluate the quality of a sample if we don't know what population it is supposed to represent. If the population is unspecified because the researchers were never clear about just what population they were trying to sample, then we can safely conclude that the sample itself is no good.

Exhibit 4.7   Respondent-Driven Sampling—A Version of Snowball Sampling

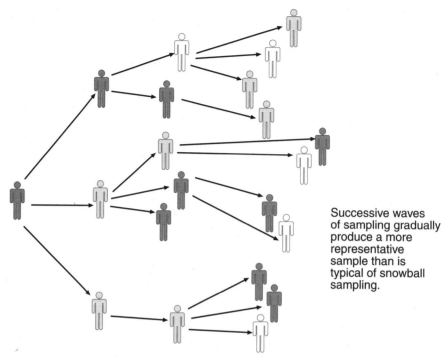

Successive waves of sampling gradually produce a more representative sample than is typical of snowball sampling.

Instructions to respondents:
"We'll pay you $5 each for up to three names, but only one of those names can be somebody from your own town. The others have to be from somewhere else."

- We can't evaluate the quality of a sample if we don't know exactly how cases in the sample were selected from the population. If the method was specified, we then need to know whether cases were selected in a systematic fashion or on the basis of chance. In any case, we know that a haphazard method of sampling (as in person-on-the-street interviews) undermines generalizability.

- Sample quality is determined by the sample actually obtained, not just by the sampling method itself. If many of the people (or other elements) selected for our sample do not respond or participate in the study, even though they have been selected for the sample, the quality of our sample is undermined even if we chose the sample in the best possible way.

- We need to be aware that even researchers who obtain very good samples may talk about the implications of their findings for some group that is larger than or just different from the population they actually sampled. For example, findings from a representative sample of students in one university often are discussed as if they tell us about university students in general. And maybe they do; the problem is we just don't know.

SAMPLING DISTRIBUTIONS

A well-designed probability sample is one that is likely to be representative of the population from which it was selected. But as you've seen, random samples still are subject to sampling error due only to chance. To deal with that problem, social researchers take into account the properties of a **sampling distribution,** a hypothetical distribution of a statistic across an infinite number of random samples that could be drawn from a population. Any single random sample can be thought of as just one of an infinite number of random samples that, in theory, could have been selected from the population. If we had the finances of Bill Gates and the patience of Job, and were able to draw an infinite number of samples, and we calculated the same type of statistic (e.g., percentage of those in favor of the three strikes laws) for each of these samples, we would then have a sampling distribution. Understanding sampling distributions is the foundation for understanding how researchers can estimate sampling error.

Sampling distribution A hypothetical distribution of a statistic (e.g., proportion, mean, etc.) across an infinite number of random samples that could be drawn from a population.

What does a sampling distribution look like? Because a sampling distribution is based on some statistic calculated for different samples, we need to choose a statistic. Let's focus on the arithmetic average, or mean. We will explain the calculation of the mean in Chapter 11, but you may already be familiar with it: It is simply the arithmetic average of a variable distribution and is obtained by adding up the values of all the cases and then dividing this sum by the total number of cases. Let's say you draw a random sample of 500 families and find that their average (mean) family income is $36,239. This $36,239 would be the sample statistic for this one sample. But imagine that you then drew another random sample, and another, and another, and so on, and calculated the mean from each of these samples. Then imagine marking these means on graph paper. The resulting graph would be a sampling distribution of the mean.

Exhibit 4.8 demonstrates what happens when we do something very similar to what we just described. We did not take an infinite number of samples from a large population, but used the 1996 General Social Survey (GSS) sample as if it were a population. We first drew 50 different random samples, each consisting of 30 cases, from the 1996 GSS. (The standard notation for the number of cases in each sample is $n = 30$.) Then we calculated for each random sample the approximate mean family income (approximate because the GSS does not record actual income in dollars). We then graphed the means of the 50 samples. Each column in Exhibit 4.8 shows how many samples had a particular family income. The mean for the population (the total sample) is $38,249, and you can see that the sampling distribution clusters around this value. Also notice, however, that although many of our selected sample means are close to the population mean, some are quite far from it. If you had calculated the mean from only one sample, it could have fallen anywhere in this distribution, from the low of $25,000 to the high of $47,000. From probability theory, however, we know that the one mean we actually obtain from our sample is unlikely to be far from the true population mean if, in fact, we have drawn a true random sample.

Exhibit 4.8 Partial Sampling Distribution: Mean Family Income

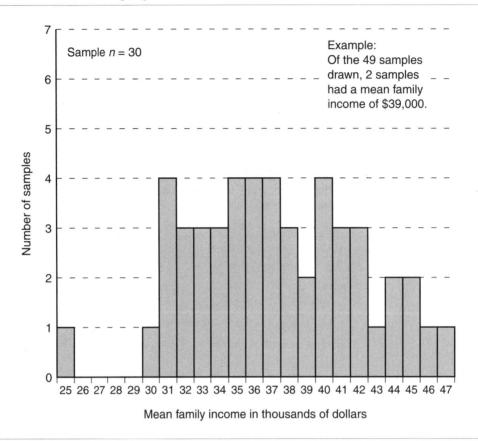

Mean family income in thousands of dollars

Estimating Sampling Error

In reality, we don't actually observe sampling distributions in real research; it would take too much time and money. Instead, researchers just draw the best sample they can. (Now you understand why it is important to have a sample that is representative of the population!). A sampling distribution usually remains hypothetical or a theoretical distribution. We can use the properties of sampling distributions, however, to calculate the amount of sampling error that was likely with the random sample used in a study. The tools for calculating sampling error are called **inferential statistics.**

> *Inferential statistics*   Mathematical tools for estimating how likely it is that a statistical result based on data from a random sample is representative of the population from which the sample was selected.

Sampling distributions for many statistics, including the mean, have a normal shape. A graph of a **normal distribution** looks like a bell, with one hump in the middle, centered

Exhibit 4.9   Normal Sampling Distribution: Mean Family Income

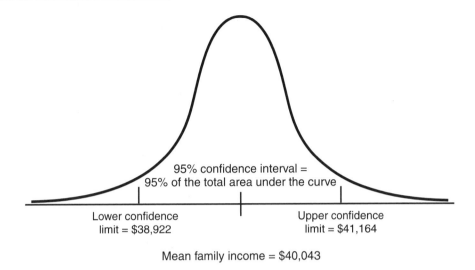

95% confidence interval =
95% of the total area under the curve

Lower confidence
limit = $38,922

Upper confidence
limit = $41,164

Mean family income = $40,043

around the population mean, and the number of cases tapering off on both sides of the mean. Note that a normal distribution is symmetrical: If you fold it in half at its center (at the population mean), the two halves will match perfectly. This shape is produced by **random sampling error.** The value of the statistic varies from sample to sample because of chance, so higher and lower values are equally likely. A good example of a normally shaped distribution is the grades that will be received in the class for which you are reading this text. The majority of students in the class will receive C's, fewer will receive B's and D's, and fewer still will receive A's and F's.

The partial sampling distribution in Exhibit 4.8 does not have a completely normal shape because it involves only a small number of samples (50), each of which has only 30 cases. Exhibit 4.9 shows what the sampling distribution of family incomes would look like if it formed a perfectly normal distribution if, rather than 50 random samples, we had selected thousands of random samples.

Systematic sampling error   Overrepresentation or underrepresentation of some population characteristics in a sample due to the method used to select the sample. A sample shaped by systematic sampling error is a biased sample.

Random sampling error   Differences between the population and the sample that are due only to chance factors (random error), not to systematic sampling error. Random sampling error may or may not result in an unrepresentative sample. The magnitude of sampling error due to chance factors can be estimated statistically.

As we have stated earlier, in research our goal is to generalize what we observe in our sample to the population of interest. In statistical terminology, a **sample statistic** is an estimate of the **population parameter** we want to estimate. The properties of a sampling distribution facilitate this process of statistical inference. In the sampling distribution, the most frequent value of the sample statistic (such as the mean) computed from sample data is identical to the population parameter—the statistic computed for the entire population. In other words, we can have a lot of confidence that the value at the peak of the bell curve represents the norm for the entire population.

Sample statistic   An estimated statistic (e.g., proportion, mean, etc.) from the one sample we actually selected from a population.

In a normal distribution, a predictable proportion of cases also falls within certain ranges under the curve. Inferential statistics take advantage of this feature and allow us to estimate how likely it is that, given a particular sample, the true population value will be within some range around the statistic. For example, a statistician might conclude from a sample of 30 families that we can be 95% confident that the true mean family income in the total population is between $23,012 and $38,120. The interval from $23,012 to $38,120 would then be called the **confidence interval** for the mean. The upper ($38,120) and lower ($23,012) bounds of this interval are the **confidence limits.** Exhibit 4.9 marks such confidence limits, indicating the range that encompasses 95% of the area under the normal curve; in theory, then, 95% of all sample statistics would fall within this range.

Although all normal distributions have these same basic features, they differ in the extent to which they cluster around the mean. A sampling distribution is more compact when it is based on larger samples. Stated another way, we can be more confident in estimates based on larger random samples because we know that a larger sample creates a more compact sampling distribution. This should make intuitive sense. If you want to estimate the average family income of residents in New York City and you only select a sample of 30 families, the mean you estimate from this sample of 30 is less likely to reflect New York City residents' annual family income compared to a sample of, say, 3,000.

Let us illustrate the importance of sample size for you. Compare the two sampling distributions of mean family income in Exhibit 4.10. Both depict the results for 50 samples. However, in one study each sample comprised 100 families, and in the other study each sample comprised only 5 families. Clearly, the larger samples ($n = 100$) result in a sampling distribution that is much more tightly clustered around the true mean of the population compared to the smaller samples ($n = 5$). The 95% confidence interval for mean family income for the entire GSS sample of 1,368 cases was $29,421 to $31,711, an interval only about $2,300 wide. But the 95% confidence interval for the mean family income in one GSS subsample of 100 cases was much wider, with limits of $25,733 and $35,399. And for a subsample of only 5 cases, the 95% confidence interval was very broad: $14,104 to $47,028. This wide interval reflects the fact that we are less confident in this sample estimate. Because the confidence we have in statistics obtained from such small samples is so low, they give us very little useful information about the population.

In most social science disciplines, including ours, researchers typically rely on 95% or 99% confidence intervals. In fact, every time you read the results of an opinion poll in the newspaper or hear about one on a news broadcast, you are really being given a confidence interval. For example, when a newscaster reports that 30% of high school seniors have used marijuana in the past 6 months, the reporter will also usually add the phrase "plus or

Exhibit 4.10   The Effect of Sampling Size on Sample Distribution

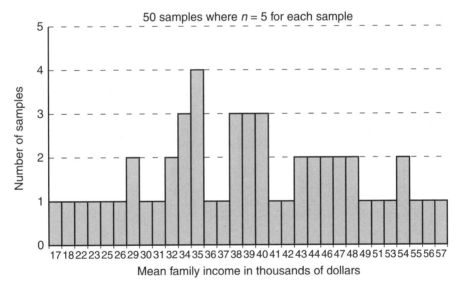

minus 4 percentage points." This is a confidence interval. These conventional confidence limits reflect the conservatism inherent in classical statistical inference. As researchers, we can't make an inferential statement (e.g., the population does or believes such and such) unless we are very confident (at least 95% confident) that it is correct.

Even though we have not explained how to calculate confidence intervals, all of this discussion about theoretical sampling distributions and inferential statistics may have left you a little confused. We hope we have achieved our goal, however, and that you now have a sense of how researchers make inferences from a random sample to a population.

Now that you understand that more confidence can be placed in statistics obtained from large samples, you may wonder why researchers don't obtain large random samples all the time. The primary answer to this question is, "Bucks!" Researchers often cannot afford to sample a large number of cases from their population of interest. They therefore try to determine during the design phase of their study how large a sample they must have to achieve their research purpose. This is usually done through a method called statistical power analysis (Kraemer & Thiemann, 1987), which is a mathematical way to determine the sample size needed to find relationships between a given set of variables. Researchers also obtain some general guidance about sample sizes from the current practices of social scientists. For professional studies of the national population in which only a simple description is desired, professional social science studies typically use a sample size of 1,000 to 3,000 individuals. Studies of local or regional populations often sample only a few hundred people, in part because these studies lack sufficient funding to draw larger samples. The sampling error in these smaller studies, of course, is considerably larger than in a typical national study (Sudman, 1976:87).

UNITS OF ANALYSIS AND ERRORS IN CAUSAL REASONING

In criminological research, we obtain samples from many different units, including individuals, groups, cities, prisons, countries, and so on. When we make generalizations from a sample to the population, it is very important to keep in mind the units under study, which are referred to as the **units of analysis.** These units of analysis are the level of social life on which the research question is focused, such as individuals, groups, towns, or nations.

Individual and Group Units of Analysis

In most of social science research, including criminological studies, the units of analysis are individuals. The researcher may collect survey data from individuals, analyze the data, and then report on how many individuals felt socially isolated and whether substance abuse by individuals related to their feelings of social isolation. Data are collected from individuals, and the focus of analysis is on the individual.

In other instances, however, the units of analysis may instead be groups, such as families, schools, prisons, towns, states, or countries. For example, a researcher may collect data from town and police records on the number of accidents in which drivers were intoxicated, and the presence or absence of a server liability law, which makes those who serve liquor liable for accidents caused by those they served. The researcher can then analyze the relationship between server liability laws and the frequency of accidents due to drunk driving (perhaps also taking into account town population). Because the data describe the towns, towns are the units of analysis.

In some studies, groups are the units of analysis but data are collected from individuals. For example, Robert Sampson, Stephen W. Raudenbush, and Felton Earls (1997) studied influences on violent crime in Chicago neighborhoods. Collective efficacy was one variable they hypothesized as an influence on the neighborhood crime rate. This variable was a characteristic of the neighborhood residents who were likely to help other residents and were trusted by other residents. However, they measured this variable in a survey of individuals. The responses of individual residents about their perceptions of their neighbors' helpfulness and trustworthiness were averaged to create a collective efficacy score for each neighborhood. It was this neighborhood measure of collective efficacy that was used to explain variation in the rate of violent crime between neighborhoods. The data were collected from individuals and were about individuals, but they were combined (aggregated) so as to describe neighborhoods. The units of analysis were thus groups (neighborhoods).

In a study like Sampson's, we can distinguish the concept of units of analysis from the units of observation. Data were collected from individuals, the **units of observation,** and then the data were aggregated and analyzed at the group level. In some studies, the units of observation and the units of analysis are the same. The important point is to know when this is true. A conclusion that crime increases with joblessness could imply that individuals who lose their jobs are more likely to commit a crime, that a community with a high unemployment rate is likely to have a high crime rate, or both. Whether we are drawing conclusions from data or interpreting others' conclusions, we have to be clear about which relationship is referenced.

To interpret statistics appropriately, we also have to know the units of analysis. Measures of association tend to be stronger for group-level than for individual-level data because measurement errors at the individual level tend to cancel out at the group level (Bridges & Weis, 1989:29–31).

The Ecological Fallacy and Reductionism

Researchers should make sure that their conclusions reflect the units of analysis in their study. Conclusions about processes at the individual level should be based on individual-level data; conclusions about group-level processes should be based on data collected about groups. In most cases, violation of this rule creates one more reason to suspect the validity of the causal conclusions.

A researcher who draws conclusions about individual-level processes from group-level data is making an **ecological fallacy** (see Exhibit 4.11). The conclusions may or may not be correct, but we must recognize that group-level data do not describe individual-level processes. For example, a researcher may examine prison employee records and find that the higher the percentage of correctional workers without college education in prisons, the higher the rate of inmate complaints of brutality by officers in prisons. But the researcher would commit an ecological fallacy if she then concluded that individual correctional officers without a college education were more likely to engage in acts of brutality against inmates. This conclusion is about an individual-level causal process (the relationship between the education and criminal propensities of individuals), even though the data describe groups (prisons). It could actually be that college-educated officers are the ones more likely to commit acts of brutality. If more officers in prison are not college educated, perhaps the college-educated officers feel they won't be suspected.

Bear in mind that conclusions about individual processes based on group-level data are not necessarily wrong. The data simply do not provide information about processes at the individual level. Suppose we find that communities with higher average incomes have lower crime rates. The only thing special about these communities may be that they have

Exhibit 4.11   Errors in Causal Conclusions

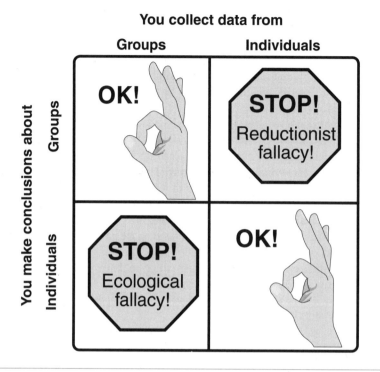

more individuals with higher incomes, who tend to commit fewer crimes. Even though we collected data at the group level and analyzed them at the group level, they reflect a causal process at the individual level (Sampson & Lauritsen, 1994:80–83).

When data about individuals are used to make inferences about group-level processes, a problem occurs that can be thought of as the mirror image of the ecological fallacy: the **reductionist fallacy**, or **reductionism** (see Exhibit 4.11). For example, William Wilson (1987:58) notes that we can be misled into concluding from individual-level data that race has a causal effect on violence. However, community-level data reveal that almost 40% of poor African Americans lived in extremely poor areas in 1980, compared to only 7% of poor Caucasians. The concentration of African Americans in poverty areas, not the race or other characteristics of the individuals in these areas, may be the cause of higher rates of violence. Explaining violence in this case requires community-level data.

The fact that errors in causal reasoning can be made should not deter you from conducting research with aggregate data nor make you unduly critical of researchers who make inferences about individuals on the basis of aggregate data. When considered broadly, many research questions point to relationships that could be manifested in many ways and on many levels. Sampson et al.'s (1987) study of urban violence is a case in point. Their analysis involved only aggregate data about cities, and they explained their research approach as, in part, a response to the failure of other researchers to examine this problem at the structural, aggregate level. Moreover, Sampson and colleagues argued that the rates of joblessness and family disruption in communities influence community social processes, not just the behavior of the specific individuals who are unemployed or who grew up without two parents. Yet Sampson et al. suggest that the experience of joblessness and poverty is what tends to reduce the propensity of individual men to marry and that the experience of growing up in a home without two parents in turn increases the propensity of individual juveniles to commit crimes. These conclusions about the behavior of individuals seem consistent with the patterns Sampson et al. found in their aggregate, city-level data; so it seems unlikely that they are committing an ecological fallacy.

The solution is to know what the units of analysis and units of observation were in a study, and to take these into account when weighing the credibility of the researcher's conclusions. The goal is not to reject conclusions that refer to a level of analysis different from what was actually studied. Instead, the goal is to consider the likelihood that an ecological fallacy or a reductionist fallacy has been made when estimating the causal validity of the conclusions.

CONCLUSION

Sampling is the fundamental starting point in criminological research. Probability sampling methods allow a researcher to use the laws of chance, or probability, to draw samples from population parameters that can be estimated with a high degree of confidence. A sample of just 1,000 or 1,500 individuals can be used to reliably estimate the characteristics of the population of a nation comprising millions of individuals.

But researchers do not come by representative samples easily. Well-designed samples require careful planning, some advance knowledge about the population to be sampled, and adherence to systematic selection procedures so that the selection procedures are not biased. And even after the sample data are collected, the researcher's ability to generalize from the sample findings to the population is not completely certain. The best the researcher can do is to perform additional calculations that state the degree of confidence that can be placed in the sample statistic.

The alternatives to random, or probability-based, sampling methods are almost always much less palatable, even though they typically are much cheaper. Without a method of selecting cases likely to represent the population in which the researcher is interested, research findings will have to be carefully qualified. Unrepresentative samples may help researchers understand which aspects of a social phenomenon are important, but questions about the generalizability of this understanding are left unanswered.

Social scientists often seek to generalize their conclusions from the population that they studied to some larger target population. The validity of generalizations of this type is necessarily uncertain, for having a representative sample of a particular population does not at all ensure that what we find will hold true in other populations. Nonetheless, the accumulation of findings from studies based on local or otherwise unrepresentative populations can provide important information about broader populations.

KEY TERMS

Availability sampling
Census
Cluster

Cluster sampling
Confidence interval
Confidence limits

Cross-population generalizability
Disproportionate stratified sampling
Ecological fallacy
External validity
Inferential statistics
Nonprobability sampling method
Nonresponse
Normal distribution
Periodicity
Population
Population parameter
Probability of selection
Probability sampling method
Proportionate stratified sampling
Purposive sampling
Quota sampling
Random digit dialing
Random number table
Random sampling error
Random selection

Reductionist fallacy (reductionism)
Replacement sampling
Representative sample
Sample
Sample generalizability
Sample statistic
Sampling distribution
Sampling error
Sampling frame
Sampling interval
Sampling unit
Simple random sampling
Snowball sampling
Stratified random sampling
Systematic random sampling
Systematic sampling error
Target population
Units of analysis
Units of observation

HIGHLIGHTS

• Sampling theory focuses on the generalizability of descriptive findings to the population from which the sample was drawn. It also considers whether statements can be generalized from one population to another.

• Sampling is usually necessary except in two conditions: (1) when the elements that would be sampled are identical, which is almost never the case, and (2) when you have the option of conducting a complete census of a population.

• Nonresponse undermines sample quality: It is the obtained sample, not the desired sample, that determines sample quality.

• Probability sampling methods rely on a random selection procedure to ensure there is no systematic bias in the selection of elements. In a probability sample, the odds of selecting elements are independent, equal, and known, and the method of selection is carefully controlled.

• A sampling frame (a list of elements in the population) is required in most probability sampling methods. The adequacy of the sampling frame is an important determinant of sample quality.

• Simple random sampling and systematic random sampling are equivalent probability sampling methods in most situations. However, systematic random sampling is inappropriate for sampling from lists of elements that have a regular, periodic structure.

• Stratified random sampling uses prior information about a population to make sampling more efficient. Stratified sampling may be either proportionate or disproportionate. Disproportionate stratified sampling is useful when a research question focuses on a stratum or on strata that make up a small proportion of the population.

• Cluster sampling is less efficient than simple random sampling but is useful when a sampling frame is unavailable. It is also useful for large populations spread out across a wide area or among many organizations.

• Nonprobability sampling methods can be useful when random sampling is not possible, when a research question does not concern a larger population, and when a preliminary exploratory study is appropriate. However, the representativeness of nonprobability samples cannot be determined.

• The likely degree of error in an estimate of a population characteristic based on a probability sample decreases as the size of the sample increases. Sampling error also decreases if the population from which the sample was selected is homogeneous. Sampling error is not affected by the proportion of the population that is sampled, except when that proportion is large. The degree of sampling error affecting a sample statistic can be estimated from the characteristics of the sample and knowledge of the properties of sampling distributions. Through these inferential statistics, we can estimate the degree of confidence we have in our findings.

• Invalid generalizations about causal relationships may occur when relationships between variables measured at the group level are assumed to apply at the individual level (the ecological fallacy) and when relationships between variables measured at the level of individuals are assumed to apply at the group level (the reductionist fallacy). Nonetheless, many research questions point to relationships at multiple levels and may profitably be answered by studying different units of analysis.

EXERCISES

1. Locate one or more newspaper articles reporting the prevalence of crime or drugs/alcohol. What information does the article provide on the sample that was selected? What additional information do you need to determine whether the sample was a representative one?

2. Select a random sample using the table of random numbers in Appendix E. Compute a statistic based on your sample, and compare it to the corresponding figure for the entire population. Here's how to proceed:

   a. First, select the crime statistics of your choice at the city or state level from the most recent FBI Uniform Crime Report (UCR).

   b. Next, create your sampling frame, a numbered list of all the elements in the population. If you are using a complete listing of all elements, such as state-level crime statistics, the sampling frame is the same as the list. Just number the elements (states). If your population is composed of cities, your sampling frame will be those cities that meet certain criteria (e.g., all cities with a population of 250,000 or greater); you may need to refer to another source, such as the U.S. Bureau of the Census, to determine which cities meet your criteria. Identify these cities, and then number them sequentially, starting with 1.

   c. Decide on a method of picking numbers out of the random number table in Appendix E, such as taking every number in each row, row by row, or by moving down or diagonally across the columns. Use only the first (or last) digit in each number if you need to select 1 to 9 cases; select the first (or last) two digits if you want fewer than 100 cases.

   d. Pick a starting location in the random number table. It's important to pick a starting point in an unbiased way, perhaps by closing your eyes and then pointing to some part of the page.

   e. Record the numbers you encounter as you move from the starting location in the direction you decided in advance, until you have recorded as many random numbers as the number of cases you need in the sample. If you are selecting states, 10 might be a good number. Ignore numbers that are too large (or small) for the range of numbers used to identify the elements in the population. Discard duplicate numbers.

   f. Calculate the mean value (mathematical average) in your sample for the crime statistic you selected. Calculate the mean by adding up the values of all the elements in the sample and dividing by the number of elements in the sample.

   g. Go back to the sampling frame and calculate this same average for all the elements in the list. How close is the sample average to the population average?

3. Select five scholarly journal articles that describe criminological research using a sample drawn from some population. Identify the type of sample used in each study, and note any strong and weak points in how the sample was actually drawn. Did the researchers have a problem due to non-response? Considering the sample, how confident are you in the validity of generalizations about the population based on the sample? Do you need any additional information to evaluate the sample? Do you think a different sampling strategy would have been preferable? What larger population were the findings generalized to? Do you think these generalizations were warranted? Why or why not?

DEVELOPING A RESEARCH PROPOSAL

Consider the possibilities for sampling.

1. Propose a sampling design that would be appropriate if you were to survey students on your campus only. Define the population, identify the sampling frame(s), and specify the elements and any other units at different stages. Indicate the exact procedure for selecting people to be included in the sample.

2. Propose a different sampling design for conducting your survey in a larger population, such as your city, state, or the entire nation.

WEB EXERCISES

1. What can you learn about sampling on the Web? Conduct a search on "sampling" and "population" and select a few of these sites. List a few new points that you learn about sampling.

2. Go to the INFOMINE Scholarly Internet Resource Collections Web site at http:/ lib-www.ucr.edu. Search for five sources of information on crime or victimization. Briefly describe your sources and list the Web sites where they can be found. How do these sources of information differ in their approaches to collecting information? Do they report the sampling information? What statistics do they present? Do they report the sampling method used in the studies from which they obtained these statistics? What sampling methods were used? Evaluate the sampling methods in terms of representativeness and generalizability. How would you improve on the sampling methods to increase the representativeness and generalizability of the data? If no sampling methods are mentioned, propose one that would have been appropriate to obtain the statistics.

SPSS EXERCISES

In NCS91.POR, the V2089 variable measures the location (urban, suburban, rural) of each robbery incident.

1. Create a frequency distribution for this variable, and record the valid percentage for each category.

2. Select a random sample of approximately 5% of all cases. Create a second frequency distribution for the robbery location, and record the valid percentage for each category.

3. Select a random sample containing approximately 1% of all cases. Create a third frequency distribution, and record the valid percentage for each category.

4. Compare the three frequency distributions. How does sample size influence the results? Does the sample size affect the reliability or validity of where robbery is most likely to occur?

Chapter 5

CAUSATION AND EXPERIMENTAL DESIGNS

T he Bureau of Justice Statistics recently released a report demonstrating that criminal victimization in the United States had fallen 10% in 2001, continuing a trend observed since 1994 (Bureau of Justice Statistics, 2002). Based on information obtained from the National Crime Victimization Survey (NCVS), the report noted that during the last 7 years, the annual violent crime rate had decreased by about 50%. In fact, both violent and property crime victimization rates were the lowest recorded since the NCVS began in 1973. Is this news too good to be true? If it is true, will the trend last? Who should get the credit for this heartening trend? To answer these questions, we need to investigate the causes of crime.

There are many candidates for cause, according to the following news articles. Geoffrey Canada, president of Harlem's Rheedlen Centers for Children and Families, states in one article that changing attitudes toward violence among young people have been key (Butterfield, 1996a). Frank A. Camino, a Manhattan realtor, feels safer because of a decline in the crack-cocaine market (Krauss, 1996). Former Attorney General Janet Reno highlights law-enforcement strategies (Butterfield, 1996a). Sarah Brady points to the Brady bill's requirement of a waiting period to buy a hand gun (Butterfield, 1996b). Chicago detective Sergeant Tom Keane stresses tougher prison sentences (Butterfield, 1996a), and Cleveland's Sergeant Kaminski suggests the decline in bars and hence in barroom brawls (Butterfield, 1996a). Boston Police Commissioner Paul Evans (Radin, 1997:B7) touts the benefits of community policing strategies but cautions that "anyone who comes into a city like this and looks for one central cause just doesn't get it."

Identifying causes—figuring out why things happen—is the goal of most social science research, as well as a critical interest of newspaper reporters, government officials, and ordinary citizens (Larson & Garrett, 1996:222–251). Unfortunately, valid explanations for the causes of social phenomena, including crime, do not come easily. Research must be designed carefully if we are to draw causal conclusions. Even researchers who proceed with care often encounter obstacles to achieving causal validity.

This chapter considers the definitions of causation and the criteria proposed for achieving causally valid explanations. We will review three general types of research design used for identifying causal effects, and then focus on research design used to identify whether the cause truly precedes the effect. This is one of the critical issues involved in achieving causal validity. Then, using examples of recent experiments from the literature, this chapter examines experimental methodology in more detail. And finally, we examine how non-experimental research designs such as cross-sectional designs and longitudinal designs attempt to determine causality. You will learn to distinguish the different experimental designs, evaluate the utility of particular designs for reaching causally valid conclusions, and consider ethical problems in experimentation.

CAUSAL EXPLANATION

In the movie *Money Train*, two men spray the inside of a subway token booth with a flammable liquid, blowing up the toll booth and killing the collector. In 1995, while the movie was still showing in theaters, a similar incident actually occurred in a New York City subway. The toll collector was hospitalized with widespread third-degree burns. The media violence, it was soon alleged, had caused the crime.

How would you evaluate this claim? What evidence do we need to develop a valid conclusion about a hypothesized causal effect? First we must distinguish two separate causal questions that are suggested by the toll booth crime. The more general research question is, "Does media violence result in or cause actual violence?"

Most social scientists think of a **causal effect** as an explanation for events or for some characteristics, attitudes, or behaviors of groups, types of individuals, or other entities such as families, organizations, or states. For example, a researcher may seek to determine whether exposure to media violence leads people to commit violent behavior.

More specifically, a causal effect is said to occur if variation in the independent variable is followed by variation in the dependent variable, when all other things are equal (***ceteris paribus***). Of course, you can legitimately argue that "all" other things can't literally be equal: We will not be able to compare the same people at the same time in exactly the same circumstances except for the variation in the independent variable (King, Keohane, & Verba, 1994). However, you will see that we can design research to create conditions that are very comparable, so that we can isolate the impact of the independent variable on the dependent variable.

Causal effect   The finding that change in one variable leads to change in another variable, *ceteris paribus* (other things being equal).

Example of a causal effect: Individuals exposed to media violence are more likely to engage in violent behavior than similar individuals who have not been exposed to media violence.

CRITERIA FOR CAUSAL EXPLANATION

Imagine a friend saying, after reading about the *Money Train* incident, "See, media violence causes people to commit crimes." Of course, after reading Chapter 1 you wouldn't be so quick to jump to such a conclusion. "Don't overgeneralize," you would remind yourself. When your friend insists, "But I recall that type of thing happening before," you might even suspect selective observation. As a blossoming criminological researcher, you now know that if we want to have confidence in the validity of our causal statements, we must meet a higher standard.

Specifically, we need to consider five criteria for deciding whether a causal connection exists. Three of these criteria—empirical association, appropriate time order, and nonspuriousness—are widely accepted as the basis for identifying a causal effect. The other two criteria—identifying a causal mechanism and specifying the context in which the effect occurs—can also considerably strengthen causal explanations.

Conditions Necessary for Determining Causality

1. Empirical association

2. Appropriate time order

3. Nonspuriousness

Conditions Important in Specifying Causal Relationships

1. Mechanism

2. Context

Brad Bushman's (1995) experiment on media violence and aggression illustrates well the five criteria for establishing causal relationships. Bushman's study focused in part on this specific research question: Do individuals who view a violent videotape act more aggressively than individuals who view a nonviolent videotape?

Undergraduate psychology students were recruited to watch a 15-minute videotape in a screening room, one student at a time. Half of the students watched a movie excerpt that was violent (from *Karate Kid III*), and half watched a nonviolent movie excerpt (from *Gorillas in the Mist*). After viewing the videotape, the students were told that they were to compete with another student, in a different room, on a reaction-time task. When the students saw a light cue, they were to react by trying to click a computer mouse faster than their opponent. On a computer screen, the students set a level of radio static that their opponents would hear when the opponents reacted more slowly. The students themselves heard this same type of noise when they reacted more slowly than their opponents, at the intensity level supposedly set by their opponents.

Each student in the study participated in 25 trials, or competitions, with the unseen opponent. Their aggressiveness was operationalized as the intensity of noise that they set for their opponents over the course of the 25 trials. The louder the noise level they set, the more aggressively they were considered to be behaving toward their opponents. The question that we will focus on first is whether students who watched the violent video behaved more aggressively than those who watched the nonviolent video.

Association

The results of Bushman's experiment are represented in Exhibit 5.1. The average intensity of noise administered to the opponent was indeed higher for students who watched the violent videotape than for those who watched the nonviolent videotape. But is Bushman justified in concluding from these results that viewing a violent videotape increased aggressive behavior in his subjects? Would this conclusion have any greater claim to causal validity than the statement that your friend made in response to the *Money Train* incident? Perhaps it would.

If for no other reason, we can have greater confidence in Bushman's conclusion because he did not observe just one student who watched a violent video and then acted aggressively, as was true in the *Money Train* incident. Instead, Bushman observed a number of students, some of whom watched a violent video and some of whom did not. So his conclusion is based on finding an **association** between the independent variable (viewing of a violent videotape) and the dependent variable (likelihood of aggressive behavior).

Exhibit 5.1 Association: Noise Intensity for Two Groups in an Experiment

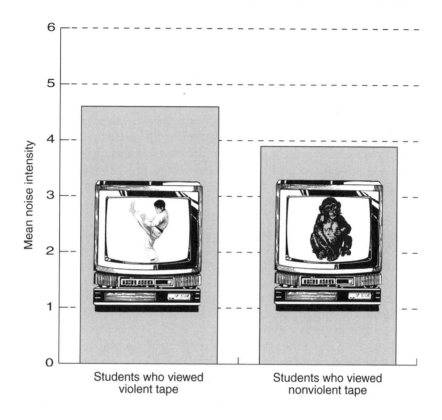

Source: Adapted from Bushman, 1995.

Time Order

Association is a necessary criterion for establishing a causal effect, but it is not sufficient. Suppose you find in a survey that most people who have committed violent crimes have also watched the movie *Money Train,* and that most people who have not committed violent crimes have not watched the movie. You believe you have found an association between watching the movie and committing violent crimes. But imagine you learn that the movie was released after the crimes were committed. Thus, those people in your survey who said they had seen the movie had actually committed their crimes before the movie characters committed their crimes. Watching the movie, then, could not possibly have led to the crimes. Perhaps the criminals watched the movie because committing violent crimes made them interested in violent movies.

This discussion points to the importance of the criterion of **time order.** To conclude that causation was involved, we must see that cases were exposed to variation in the independent variable *before* variation in the dependent variable. Bushman's experiment satisfied this criterion because he controlled the variation in the independent variable: All the students saw the videotape excerpts (which varied in violent content) before their level of aggressiveness was measured.

Nonspuriousness

Even when research establishes that two variables are associated and that variation in the independent variable precedes variation in the dependent variable, we cannot be sure we identified a causal relationship between the two variables. Have you heard the old adage "Correlation does not prove causation"? It is meant to remind us that an association between two variables might be caused by something else. If we measure children's shoe sizes and their academic knowledge, for example, we will find a positive association. However, the association results from the fact that older children have larger feet as well as more academic knowledge. Shoe size does not cause knowledge or vice versa.

Before we conclude that variation in an independent variable causes variation in a dependent variable, we must have reason to believe that the relationship is nonspurious. **Nonspuriousness** is a relationship between two variables that is not due to variation in a third variable. When this third variable, an **extraneous variable,** causes the variation, it is said to have created a **spurious relationship** between the independent and dependent variables. We must design our research so that we can see what happens to the dependent variable when only the independent variable varies. If we cannot do this, there are other statistical methods we must use to control the effects of other variables we also believe are related to our dependent variable. (You will be relieved to know that a discussion of these statistical techniques is way beyond the scope of this text!)

In reality, then, the fact that someone blew up a toll booth after seeing the movie *Money Train* might be related to the fact that he was already feeling enraged against society. This led him to seek out a violent movie for entertainment purposes (see Exhibit 5.2). Thus, seeing the violent movie itself in no way led him to commit the crime. We must be sure that all three conditions of association, time order, and nonspuriousness are met before we make such claims.

Does Bushman's claim of a causal effect rest on any stronger ground? To evaluate nonspuriousness, you need to know about one more feature of his experiment. He assigned students to watch either the violent video or the nonviolent video randomly, that is, by the toss of a coin. Because he used **random assignment,** the characteristics and attitudes that students already possessed when they were recruited for the experiment could not influence either of the two videos they watched. As a result, the students' characteristics and attitudes could not explain why one group reacted differently from the other after watching the videos. In fact, because Bushman used 296 students in his experiment, it is highly unlikely that the violent video group and the nonviolent video group differed in any relevant way at the outset, even on the basis of chance. This experimental research design meets the criterion of nonspuriousness. Bushman's conclusion that viewing video violence causes aggressive behavior thus rests on firm ground indeed.

Causal (internal) validity is achieved by meeting the criteria of association, time order, and nonspuriousness. Others, however, believe that two additional criteria should also be considered: mechanism and context.

Exhibit 5.2   A Spurious Relationship

Spurious relationship

**The extraneous variable creates
the spurious relationship**

Mechanism

Confidence in a conclusion that two variables have a causal connection will be strengthened if a **mechanism**—some discernable means of creating a connection—can be identified (Cook & Campbell, 1979:35; Marini & Singer, 1988). Many social scientists (and scientists in other fields) argue that a causal explanation is not adequate until a causal mechanism is identified. What process or mechanism actually is responsible for the relationship between the independent and dependent variables?

Bushman did not empirically identify a causal mechanism in his experiment, but he did suggest a possible causal mechanism for the effect of watching violent videos. Before we can explain this causal mechanism, we have to tell you about one more aspect of his research. He wasn't just interested in whether viewing violent films resulted in aggressive behavior. Actually, his primary hypothesis was that individuals who are predisposed to aggression before the study began would be more influenced by a violent film than individuals who were not aggressive at the outset. And that is what happened: Individuals who were predisposed to aggression became more aggressive after watching Bushman's violent video, but individuals who were not predisposed to aggression did not become more aggressive.

After the experiment, Bushman proposed a causal mechanism to explain why aggressive individuals became even more aggressive after watching the film:

[H]igh trait aggressive individuals [people predisposed to aggression] are more susceptible to the effects of violent media than are low trait aggressive individuals because they possess a relatively large network of aggressive associations that can be activated by violent cues. Habitual exposure to television violence might be partially responsible. (Bushman, 1995:959)

Note that this explanation relies more on speculation than on the actual empirical evidence from this particular experiment. Nonetheless, by proposing a reasonable causal mechanism that connects the variation in the independent and dependent variables, Bushman strengthens the argument for the causal validity of his conclusions.

It is often possible to go beyond speculation by designing research to test one or more possible causal mechanisms. Perhaps other researchers will design a new study to measure directly the size of individuals' networks of aggressive associations that Bushman contends are part of the mechanism by which video violence influences aggressive behavior.

Context

In the social world, it is virtually impossible to claim that one and only one independent variable is responsible for causing or effecting a dependent variable. Stated another way, no cause can be separated from the larger **context** in which it occurs. A cause is really only one of a set of interrelated factors required for the effect (Hage & Meeker, 1988; Papineau, 1978). Some researchers argue that we do not fully understand the causal effect of media violence on behavioral aggression unless we have identified these other related factors. As we have just seen, Bushman (1995) proposed at the outset of his research at least one other condition: Media violence would increase aggression only among individuals who were already predisposed to aggression.

Identification of the context in which a causal effect occurs is not a criterion for a valid causal conclusion. Some contextual factors may not turn out to be causes of the effect being investigated. The question for researchers is, "How many contexts should we investigate?" In a classic study of children's aggressive behavior in response to media violence, Albert Bandura, Dorothea Ross, and Sheila Ross (1963) examined several contextual factors. They found that effects varied with the children's gender and with the gender of the opponent toward whom they acted aggressively, but not with whether they saw a real (acted) or filmed violent incident. For example, children reacted more aggressively after observing men committing violent acts than after observing women committing these same acts. But Bandura and his colleagues did not address the role of violence within the children's families or the role of participation in sports or many other factors that could be involved in children's responses to media violence. Bandura et al. strengthened their conclusions by focusing on a few likely contextual factors.

Specifying the context for a causal effect helps us to understand that effect, but it is a process that can never really be complete. We can always ask what else might be important: In which country is the study conducted? What are the ages of the study participants? We need to carefully review the results of prior research and the implications of relevant theory to determine what contextual factors are likely to be important in a causal relationship. Our confidence in causal conclusions will be stronger when we know these factors are taken into account.

In summary, before researchers can infer a causal relationship between two variables, three criteria are essential: empirical association, appropriate time order, and nonspuriousness. After these three conditions have been met, two other criteria are also important: causal mechanism and context.

EXPERIMENTAL DESIGN AND THE CRITERIA FOR CAUSATION

The criteria for establishing causal effects are met to different degrees by different research designs. The experimental design provides the most powerful design for testing causal hypotheses about the effect of a treatment or some other variable whose values can be manipulated by the researchers. It is so powerful for testing causal hypotheses because it allows us to establish the three criteria for causality with a great deal of confidence.

True experiments must have at least three things:

1. Two comparison groups—one receiving the experimental condition (e.g., treatment or intervention) and the other receiving no treatment/intervention or another form thereof.

2. Random assignment to the two (or more) comparison groups.

3. Assessment of change in the dependent variable for both groups after the experimental condition has been received.

The combination of these features permits us to have much greater confidence in the validity of causal conclusions than is possible in other research designs. Confidence in the validity of an experiment's findings is further enhanced by identification of the causal mechanism and control over the context of an experiment.

Throughout the remainder of this chapter, you will learn more about each of these key features of experimental design. To help you understand the variability across different experimental designs, we will incorporate the use of simple diagrams. These diagrams also show at a glance just how well suited any experiment is to identifying causal relations, by indicating whether it has a comparison group, a pretest and a posttest, and random assignment.

Experimental and Comparison Groups

True experiments must have at least one **experimental group** (subjects who receive some treatment) and at least one **control/comparison group** (subjects to whom the experimental group can be compared). The control group differs from the experimental group by one or more independent variables, whose effects are being tested. In other words, the difference between the two groups is that the experimental group receives the treatment or condition we are interested in, whereas the comparison group does not.

Experimental group   In an experiment, the group of subjects that receives the treatment or experimental manipulation.

Control/comparison group   The group of subjects that is either exposed to a different treatment from the experimental group or that receives no treatment at all.

An experiment can have more than one experimental group if the goal is to test several versions of the **treatment** (the independent variable) or several combinations of different treatments. An experiment also may have more than one comparison group, as when outcome scores for the treatment group need to be compared to more than one comparison group.

Pretest and Posttest Measures

All true experiments have a **posttest**—that is, measurement of the outcome in both groups after the experimental group has received the treatment. In fact, we might say that any hypothesis-testing research involves a posttest. The dependent variable is measured after the independent variable has had its effect, if any. True experiments also may have **pretests** that measure the dependent variable prior to the experimental intervention. A pretest is exactly the same as the posttest, just administered before the treatment. Strictly speaking, however, an experiment does not require a pretest. When researchers use random assignment, the groups' initial scores on the dependent variable and on all other variables will most likely be similar—we can be confident in this because of the random assignment. Any difference in outcome between the experimental group and the comparison group is likely caused by only the intervention or experimental condition.

Having pretest scores, however, has many advantages. They provide a direct measure of how much the experimental and comparison groups changed over time. They allow the researcher to verify that randomization was successful (that chance factors did not lead to an initial difference between the groups). In addition, by identifying subjects' initial scores on the dependent variable, a pretest provides a more complete picture of the conditions in which the intervention had (or did not have) an effect (Mohr, 1992:46–48).

An experiment may have multiple posttests and perhaps even multiple pretests. Multiple posttests can identify just when the treatment has its effect and for how long. They are particularly important for treatments delivered over time (Rossi & Freeman, 1989:289–290).

Random Assignment

Random assignment, sometimes referred to as randomization, is what makes the comparison group in a true experiment such a powerful tool for identifying the effects of the treatment. If subjects are randomly assigned to either the experimental group or the comparison group, then a researcher can assume that the only difference between the two groups is that the experimental group received the treatment or intervention and the comparison group did not. Thus, a randomly assigned comparison group can provide a good estimate of the **counterfactual**—the outcome that would have occurred if the subjects had not been exposed to the treatment but had otherwise equal experiences (Mohr, 1992:3; Rossi & Freeman, 1989:229). If the comparison group differed from the experimental group in any way besides not receiving the treatment (or receiving a different treatment), a researcher would not be able to determine the unique effects of the treatment.

Assigning subjects randomly to the experimental and comparison groups ensures that systematic bias does not affect the assignment of subjects to groups. But of course random assignment cannot guarantee that the groups are perfectly identical at the start of the experiment. Similar to random selection in sampling, random assignment removes bias

Exhibit 5.3   Random Sampling Versus Random Assignment

Random sampling (a tool for ensuring generalizability):
Individuals are randomly selected from a population to participate in a study.

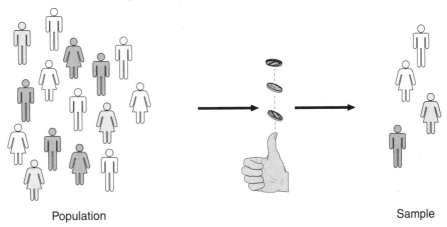

Population   Sample

Random assignment, or randomization (a tool for ensuring internal validity):
Individuals who are to participate in a study are randomly divided into an
experimental group and a comparison group.

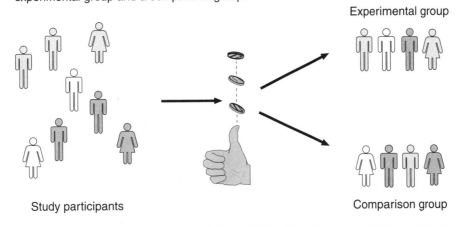

Experimental group

Study participants   Comparison group

from the assignment process but only by relying on chance, which itself can result in some intergroup differences. Fortunately, researchers can use statistical methods to determine the odds of ending up with groups that differ on the basis of chance alone; these odds are low even for groups of moderate size.

   Although similar in procedure, it is important to note here that random assignment of subjects to experimental and comparison groups is not the same as random sampling of individuals from a larger population (see Exhibit 5.3). In fact, random assignment (randomization) does not help to ensure that the research subjects are representative of some larger population; that is the goal of random sampling. What random assignment does by creating two or more equivalent groups is useful for ensuring internal validity, not generalizability.

Random assignment does share with random sampling the use of a chance selection method. In random assignment, a random procedure is used to determine the group into which each subject is placed. In random sampling, a random procedure is used to determine which cases are selected for the sample. The random procedure of tossing a coin, using a random number table, or generating random numbers with a computer can be similar in both random assignment and random sampling.

Matching is another procedure sometimes used to equate experimental and comparison groups, but by itself it is a poor substitute for randomization. Matching of individuals in a treatment group with those in a comparison group might involve pairing persons on the basis of similarity of gender, age, year in school, or some other characteristic. The basic problem is that, as a practical matter, individuals can be matched on only a few characteristics; unmatched differences between the experimental and comparison groups may still influence outcomes. However, matching combined with randomization can reduce the possibility of differences due to chance. For example, if individuals are matched by gender and age, then the members of each matched pair are randomly assigned to the experimental and comparison groups and the possibility of differences due to chance in the gender and age composition of the groups is eliminated (see Exhibit 5.4). Matching is also used in some quasi-experimental designs when randomization is not possible, as you will see later in this chapter.

We have already discussed two true experimental designs in this text: the Bushman (1995) experiment on media violence and the Sherman and Berk (1984) experiment on the effects of arrest on intimate partner violence. Both are graphically displayed for you now in Exhibit 5.5. As you can see, in the Bushman experiment of media violence and

Exhibit 5.4 Experimental Design Combining Matching and Random Assignment

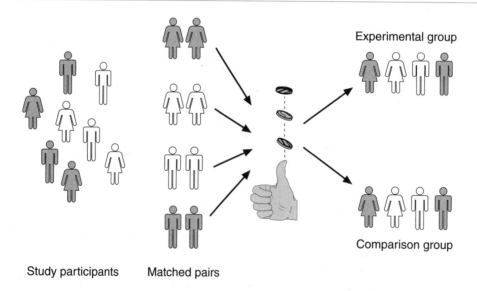

Study participants   Matched pairs

Exhibit 5.5   Experimental Designs Used in the Bushman (1995) and Sherman and Berk (1984) Research

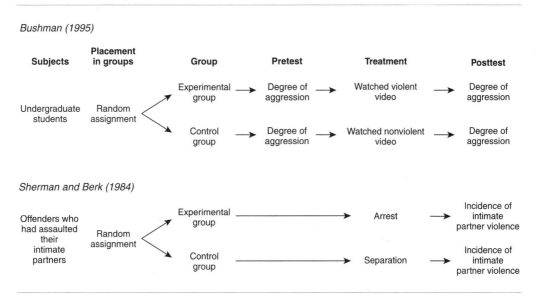

Bushman (1995)

Sherman and Berk (1984)

aggression, the experimental design included a pretest. In this experiment, undergraduate college students were randomly assigned to experimental and control groups.

Subjects in both groups were required to perform a learning task with a fake partner. In the task, subjects were to administer noises as a form of punishment to their partners when their partners gave an incorrect answer. The noise level was the operationalization of aggression for the experiment. The louder the noises administered, the higher the aggression score. Both experimental and control group subjects thus received a pretest score on their aggressiveness.

Subjects in both groups then watched a videotape—experimental group subjects watched a violent video while control group subjects watched a nonviolent video. After viewing the tapes, aggression levels were then similarly measured in the posttests. Using this design, Bushman was not only able to measure differences in aggression after the treatment (viewing the videotapes), but he was also able to determine whether aggression levels for the experimental and control subjects differentially changed from pretest to posttest. This illustrates the advantage of utilizing pretest measures in an experimental design.

The bottom panel of Exhibit 5.5 depicts the Sherman and Berk (1984) experiment. The subjects for the Sherman and Berk experiment were all reported offenders of misdemeanor intimate-partner assault in Minneapolis during the time of the experiment. The experimental treatment was arrest and the control treatment was separation and no arrest. The key to this experimental design was that incidents were randomly assigned to the arrest and nonarrest conditions. That is, when an officer arrived at the scene, he or she randomly assigned offenders to the treatment based on a randomly color-coded police record sheet. For example, if they arrived at the scene and the next sheet in their book was pink, they would make an arrest; if the sheet was white, they would not make an arrest. The posttest measurement was recidivism. If those offenders who were arrested were less likely than nonarrested offenders to have assaulted their partners 6 months after the incident, this decreased rate of assault could be attributed to the treatment of arrest. This, of course, is what happened.

To help you understand the procedures involved in true experimental designs, we will describe an experiment conducted by Richard Nisbett and Dov Cohen (1996), which investigated individuals' violent responses to personal insults.

Experiment on Violent Responses to Insults

Using historical evidence and contemporary homicide rates, some researchers contend that people residing in the southern region of the United States are more violent than those residing in the north. Nisbett and Cohen examined one hypothesized cause of male violence related to regional differences, namely a male's reputation for strength and toughness. What does this have to do with geographic regions? Well, along with other researchers, Nisbett and Cohen contend that the South has developed what has been termed a culture of honor. One property of this culture is the necessity for men to appear strong and unwilling to tolerate an insult. They state (1996:xv), "[an individual] must constantly be on guard against affronts that could be construed by others as disrespect. When someone allows himself to be insulted, he risks giving the impression that he lacks the strength to protect what is his."

Nisbett and Cohen (1996) developed an experiment that would determine whether southerners became more upset by insults and affronts and therefore would be more likely to take aggressive action than would northerners. In this experiment, one group of southern students and one group of northern students were brought to a laboratory and told they would be participating in a study concerning the effect of response-time constraints on judgment. After an initial introduction to the study, the subjects were asked to fill out a brief demographic questionnaire and take it to a table at the end of a long, narrow hallway. Subjects from both southern and northern groups were randomly assigned to a control and an experimental condition. In the control condition, nothing happened as the subject returned the questionnaire. However, in the experimental condition, as the subject walked down the hall, a confederate of the experimenter walked out of a door marked "Photo Lab" and began working at a file cabinet in the hall. The confederate had to push the file drawer in to allow the subject to pass by him and drop his paper off at the table. As the subject returned seconds later and walked down the hall toward the experiment room, the confederate, who had just reopened the file drawer, slammed it shut on seeing the subject approach, bumped into him with his shoulder, and called the subject an asshole. The confederate then walked back into the photo lab. Exhibit 5.6 illustrates this experiment.

Two observers, who appeared to be working on homework, were stationed in the hall to monitor the subjects' verbal, nonverbal, and/or physical response to the insult. When the subjects returned to the laboratory they were asked to conduct several tasks, including a word completion task in which they were given a string of letters (e.g., _ight or gu_) that they could complete in either a hostile way (fight or gun) or a nonhostile way (light or gum). The subjects were also asked to do a scenario completion task in which the subjects were required to fill in the beginning or ending of a story. One story was neutral, in which a man was rescued by an ambulance; the other story was presented as clearly confrontational, in which a woman at a party is telling her boyfriend that another man has made several passes at her and even attempted to kiss her.

Exhibit 5.6   Experimental and Control Groups in One of Nisbett and Cohen's (1996)
Experiments on Hostile Responses to an Insult

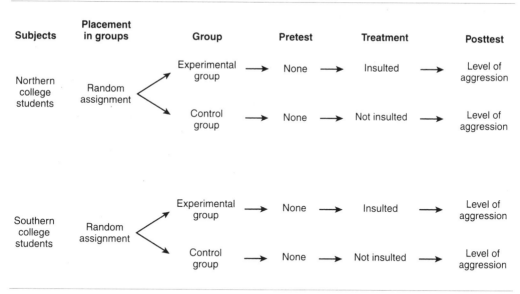

Ratings by the staged observers revealed that for northerners, the overwhelmingly
dominant emotional reaction to the insult was to show more amusement than anger. Conversely, the overwhelmingly dominant reaction for southerners was to show as much or
more anger than amusement. For the word-completion task and story completion of the
neutral scenario (involving the man and the ambulance), Nisbett and Cohen found no differences between northerners and southerners in their hostile responses. However, for the
scenario describing the attempted pass at the girlfriend, the southerners who were insulted
in the hall were much more likely to end this scenario with violence than were northerners
who were also insulted.

The three experiments we have discussed so far in this text, the Sherman and Berk
experiment on arrest and domestic assault, the Bushman experiment on media violence,
and the Nisbett and Cohen experiment on reactions to insults are all true experiments. Take
a minute now and think about how these studies meet the criteria necessary for determining
causality.

A prerequisite for meeting each of the three criteria to identify causal relations
is maintaining control over the conditions subjects are exposed to after they are
assigned to the experimental and comparison groups. If these conditions begin to differ, the variation between the experimental and comparison groups will not be what
was intended. Even a subsequent difference in the distribution of cases on the dependent variable will not provide clear evidence of the effect of the independent variable.
Such unintended variation is often not much of a problem in laboratory experiments
where the researcher has almost complete control over the conditions and can ensure
that these conditions are nearly identical for both groups. But control over conditions
can become a very big concern for experiments that are conducted in the field in

real-world settings, such as Sherman and Berk's study of the deterrent effects of arrest on intimate partner assaults.

Experimental designs do not, however, help researchers identify the causal mechanisms by which treatments or conditions have their effects. In fact, this question of causal mechanism often is not addressed in experimental research. The hypothesis test itself does not require an analysis of mechanism, and if the experiment is conducted under carefully controlled conditions during a limited span of time, the causal effect (if any) may seem to be quite direct. But attention to causal mechanisms can obviously augment experimental findings.

Let's examine how well true experiments meet the criteria necessary for establishing causality in greater detail:

Association between the hypothesized independent and dependent variables. As you have seen, experiments can provide unambiguous evidence of association by randomly assigning subjects to experimental and comparison groups.

Time order of effects of one variable on the others. Unquestionably, the independent variable (treatment of condition) preceded the posttest measures in each of the experiments described so far. For example, arrest for partner abuse preceded recidivism in the Sherman and Berk (1984) study, and the exposure to media violence preceded the aggression in the Bushman (1995) experiment. In experiments with a pretest, time order can be established by comparing posttest to pretest scores. In experiments with random assignment of subjects to the experimental and comparison groups, time order can be established by comparison of posttest scores only.

Nonspurious relationships between variables. Nonspuriousness is difficult to establish; some would say it is impossible to establish in nonexperimental designs. The random assignment of subjects to experimental and comparison groups makes true experiments powerful designs for testing causal hypotheses. Randomization controls the host of possible extraneous influences that can create misleading, spurious relationships in both experimental and nonexperimental data. If we determine that a design has used randomization successfully, we can be much more confident in the causal conclusions.

Mechanism that creates the causal effect. The features of a true experiment do not, in themselves, allow identification of causal mechanisms; as a result there can be some ambiguity about how the independent variable influenced the dependent variable and the causal conclusions.

Context in which change occurs. Control over conditions is more feasible in many experimental designs than it is in nonexperimental designs, but it is often difficult to control conditions in field experiments. Later in this chapter, you will learn how the lack of control over experimental conditions can threaten internal validity.

QUASI-EXPERIMENTS

Testing a hypothesis with a true experimental design often is not feasible with the desired subjects and in the desired setting. Such a test may be too costly, take too long to carry out, be inappropriate for the particular research problem, or presume ability to manipulate an intervention that already has occurred. To overcome these problems, yet still benefit from the logic of the experimental method, researchers may use designs that retain several components of experimental design but differ in other important details.

Usually the best alternative to an experimental design is a **quasi-experimental design,** maximizing internal validity. Although not defined consistently by all experts, in a quasi-experimental design the comparison group is predetermined to be comparable to the treatment group in critical ways, such as eligibility for the same services or attendance at the same school cohort (Rossi & Freeman, 1989:313). However, because subjects are not randomly assigned to the comparison and experimental groups, these research designs are "quasi"-experimental. In other quasi-experimental designs, there may be just one group that is monitored before and after a treatment is delivered and no comparison group. In both cases we cannot be as confident in their causal conclusions as we can with true experimental designs.

The following are the three major types of quasi-experimental designs (others can be found in Cook & Campbell, 1979; Mohr, 1992):

- **Nonequivalent control group designs** have experimental and comparison groups designated before the treatment occurs and are not created by random assignment.
- **Before-and-after designs** have a pretest and posttest but no comparison group. In other words, the subjects exposed to the treatment served, at an earlier time, as their own controls.
- **Ex post facto control group designs,** like nonequivalent control group designs, have experimental and comparison groups that are not created by random assignment. But unlike the groups in nonequivalent control group designs, the groups in ex post facto designs are designated after the treatment or intervention has occurred. For this reason, some researchers consider this design to be nonexperimental, not even quasi-experimental.

Nonequivalent Control Group Designs

In this type of quasi-experimental design, a comparison group is selected to be as comparable as possible to the treatment group. Two selection methods can be used:

Individual matching. Individual cases in the treatment group are matched with similar individuals in the comparison group. A Mexican American male about 20 years old who is assigned to the treatment group may be matched with another Mexican American male about 20 years old who is assigned to the comparison group. The problem with this method is determining in advance which variables should be used for matching. It is also unlikely that a match can be found for all cases. However, in some situations matching can create a comparison group that is very similar to the experimental group. For example, some studies of the effect of Head Start, the government program that prepares disadvantaged toddlers for school, used participants' siblings as the comparison group. Therefore, they were similar to the experimental group.

Aggregate matching. A comparison group is identified that matches the treatment group in the aggregate rather than trying to match individual cases. In most situations when random assignment is not possible, this method of matching makes sense. Matching in the aggregate means finding a group with similar distributions on key variables such as the same average age, the same percentage of females, and so on. For this design to be considered even quasi-experimental, individuals cannot choose which group to join or where to seek services. In other words, the subjects cannot opt for or against the experimental treatment.

Roy Watson's (1986) study of the deterrent effect of police action on violations of a seat-belt law illustrates a quasi-experimental nonequivalent control group design. Watson's quasi-experimental design is diagrammed in Exhibit 5.7. This study used aggregate matching and a pretest. It was conducted in British Columbia, Canada, where a mandatory seat-belt law had been enacted but had not elicited high rates of compliance. Watson selected two communities of comparable size where police enforcement of the seat-belt law was low. The units of analysis in the study were the drivers, and seat-belt usage was the dependent variable.

In a pretest, Watson measured seat-belt usage in both communities. Then, in the experimental community, he instituted a media campaign to increase seat-belt usage, followed by increased police enforcement of the seat-belt law. A posttest followed both the media campaign and the increased police enforcement. In the comparison community, one posttest was conducted at about the same time as a final posttest was conducted in the experimental community. Because the two communities were geographically distant and in different media markets, it seemed unlikely that the experiment in one community would have affected the other community while the study was in progress. As Exhibit 5.8 shows, the experimental program had a marked effect on seat-belt use.

Exhibit 5.7   Quasi-Experimental Design

Nonequivalent control group design:
Police enforcement of seat-belt laws (Watson, 1986)

Experimental group:	O_1	X	O_2
Comparison group:	O_1		O_2

	O_1	X	O_2
Experimental community	*Pretest:* Percentage using seat belts	Police enforcement of seat-belt law	*Posttest:* Percentage using seat belts
Comparison community	*Pretest:* Percentage using seat belts		*Posttest:* Percentage using seat belts

---

Key: O = Observation (pretest or posttest)
        X = Experimental treatment

Exhibit 5.8   Driver Use of Seat Belts in Two Communities

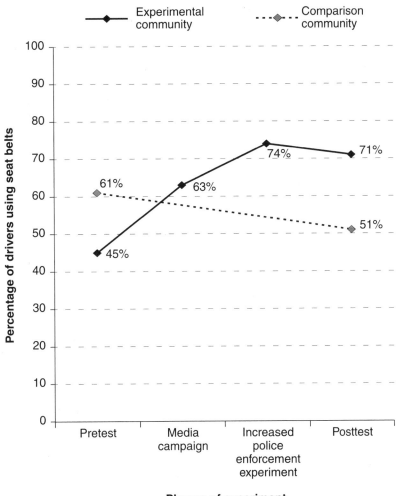

Source: Watson, 1986.

Before-and-After Designs

The common feature of before-and-after designs is the absence of a comparison group. All cases are exposed to only the experimental treatment. The basis for comparison is provided by the pretreatment measures in the experimental group. These designs are useful for studies of interventions that are experienced by virtually every element in some population.

The simplest type of before-and-after design is the fixed-sample panel design. A panel design involves only one pretest and one posttest. It does not qualify as a quasi-experimental design because comparing subjects to themselves at only one earlier point in time does not provide an adequate comparison group. Many influences other than the experimental treatment may affect a subject following the pretest. Consequently, if there is a change in the dependent variable from pre- to post-measures, we cannot be certain that the treatment itself is the sole cause of this change.

Julie Horney and Cassia Spohn's (1991) study of the effect of rape law reforms on the number of actual rapes reported to police and processed in six urban jurisdictions illustrates a more powerful before-and-after design sometimes called a **time series design** or a **repeated measures panel design.** This design typically includes many pretest and posttest observations that allow the researcher to study the process by which an intervention or treatment has an impact over time. Horney and Spohn identified six urban jurisdictions that implemented some type of rape reform legislation—Detroit, Chicago, Philadelphia, Atlanta, Houston, and Washington, D.C. The overall purpose of the reforms was to treat rape like other crimes, focusing not on the behavior and reputation of the victim but on the unlawful acts of the offender. Advocates of the reformed laws anticipated that by improving the treatment of rape victims, the reforms would lead to an increase in the number of reports of rape to police. Advocates also expected the reforms to remove legal barriers to effective prosecution and would make arrest, prosecution, and conviction for rape more likely. Horney and Spohn tracked several dependent variables thought to measure the success of these reforms, including reports of rape to police. These data were monitored for several years before and after reforms were implemented in each jurisdiction. An example of this design for one jurisdiction is presented in Exhibit 5.9.

Horney and Spohn (1991) performed experiments for three different variables for each of the six jurisdictions. As you can see, this design allows researchers to determine the magnitude of change in a given variable before and after an intervention or event (in this case rape law reform) has taken place. It appears from Exhibit 5.9 that reports of rape to police did increase in the post-reform time period as compared to the time period before rape reform legislation was implemented. Of course, special statistics are required to analyze time series data. The intent is to identify a trend in the dependent variable up to the date of the intervention or event whose effect is being studied and then to project the trend into the postintervention period. This projected trend is then compared to the actual trend of the dependent variable after the intervention. A substantial disparity between the actual trend and the projected trend is evidence that the intervention or event had an impact (Rossi & Freeman, 1989:260–261, 358–363). This time series design is particularly useful for studying the impact of new laws or social programs that affect everyone and can be readily assessed by ongoing measurement.

Ex Post Facto Control Group Designs

A design in which the treatment and comparison groups are designated after the treatment is administered is an ex post facto (after the fact) control group design. This design perhaps should be considered nonexperimental rather than quasi-experimental, because the comparison group may not be comparable to the treatment group. Carefully designed ex post facto studies, however, can result in comparisons between the treatment and control groups that give us almost as much confidence in the validity of their causal

Exhibit 5.9   A Repeated Measures Panel Design Used to Examine the Efficacy
of Rape Law Reforms

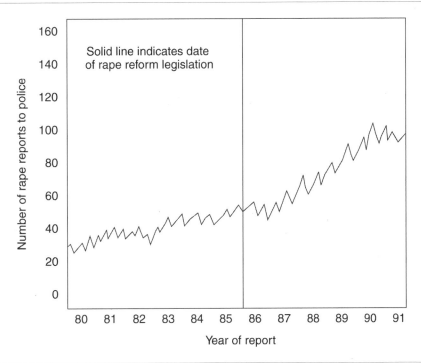

Source: Horney & Spohn, 1991.

conclusions as we can have in the causal conclusions from a quasi-experimental design (Rossi & Freeman, 1989:343–344).

David Farrington's (1977) classic study of the deviance amplification process is an excellent example of an ex post facto control group design. Farrington was interested in testing the main hypothesis about deviance amplification from labeling theory. Becker (1963:31) describes deviance amplification thus: "One of the most crucial steps in the process of building a stable pattern of deviant behavior is likely to be the experience of being caught and publicly labeled as deviant." Accordingly, Farrington tested the hypothesis that individuals who were publicly labeled as deviant would increase their deviant behavior compared to those who were not so labeled. To measure the process of being publicly labeled, he used the criteria of whether individuals had been found guilty of a delinquent act in court.

To use a true experimental design to test this hypothesis, individuals who engaged in criminal behavior would have to be randomly assigned to either a group found guilty in court or a group not taken to court. It would then be possible to conclude that any subsequent differences between the groups resulted from the presence or absence of public labeling (being convicted), and did not reflect pre-existing differences or the influence of any other factor. Because of ethical considerations, of course, such an experiment is difficult to carry out.

Instead, Farrington used the Cambridge Study of Delinquent Development that interviewed adolescents from London at three different ages—14, 16, and 18. (The Cambridge

Exhibit 5.10 Ex Post Facto Control Group Design: Farrington's (1977) Test of Deviance Amplification

Study in Delinquent Development actually maintained intermittent contact with 400 London working-class youths from ages 8 to 18. In this study, only the interviews at ages 14, 16, and 18 were used.) At all three times, the youth were asked about their participation in delinquency. For example, the questionnaire given at age 18 included seven delinquent acts: breaking and entering, stealing from vehicles, stealing from slot machines, shoplifting, joy-riding, damaging property, and buying stolen goods. The dependent variable, then, was the youth's self-reported delinquency score. The treatment or intervention was whether the youth was convicted of an offense by the Criminal Record Office. Pretest measures of self-reported delinquency were taken at age 14, and posttest scores were taken at age 18. Individuals convicted of an offense between the times of these interviews were considered the experimental publicly labeled group. Individuals who were not convicted were considered the control group (Exhibit 5.10).

Farrington actually conducted many hypothesis tests with these data, trying to rule out the effects of other variables and to investigate the intervening processes or causal mechanisms linking public labeling and deviant acts. In conclusion, Farrington appropriately included a caveat about his methodology along with directions for future research:

> The results obtained with the quasi-experimental matching design, although less conclusive than would have been the case in a true experiment, were in agreement with the hypothesis that public labeling (measured by criminal convictions) increases deviant behavior (measured by self-reported delinquency scores). As a next step, it would be useful to establish the generality of this finding by investigating whether deviance amplification still occurred with different operational definitions of public labeling and deviant behavior, and with different samples of people in different places and at different times. (1977:123)

VALIDITY IN EXPERIMENTS

Like any research design, experimental designs must be evaluated for their ability to yield valid conclusions. True experiments are particularly well suited to producing valid conclusions about causality (internal validity), but they are less likely to fare well in achieving generalizability. Quasi-experiments may provide more generalizable results than true experiments, but they are more prone to problems of internal invalidity (although some allow the researcher to rule out almost as many potential sources of internal invalidity as does a true experiment). Measurement validity is also a central concern, but an experimental design does not in itself offer any special tools or particular advantages or disadvantages in measurement. In this section you will learn more about the ways in which experiments help (or don't help) to resolve potential problems of internal validity and generalizability.

Causal (Internal) Validity

An experiment's ability to yield valid conclusions about causal effects is determined by the comparability of its experimental and comparison groups. First, of course, a comparison group must be created. Second, this comparison group must be so similar to the experimental group that it will show what the experimental group would be like if it did not receive the experimental treatment—if the independent variable was not varied. For example, the only difference between the two groups in Bushman's (1995) study was that one group watched a violent movie and the other group did not.

There are five basic sources of internal invalidity:

1. *Selection bias.* When characteristics of the experimental and comparison group subjects differ.

2. *Endogenous change.* When the subjects develop or change during the experiment as part of an ongoing process independent of the experimental treatment.

3. *External events/history effects.* When something occurs during the experiment, other than the treatment, that influences outcome scores.

4. *Contamination.* When either the experimental group or the comparison group is aware of the other group and is influenced in the posttest as a result (Mohr, 1992).

5. *Treatment misidentification.* When variation in the independent variable (the treatment) is associated with variation in the observed outcome, but the change occurs through a process that the researcher has not identified.

Selection Bias

You may already realize that the composition of the experimental and comparison groups in a true experiment is unlikely to be affected by their difference. If it were affected, it would cause **selection bias.** Random assignment equates the groups' characteristics, though with some possibility for error due to chance. The likelihood of difference due to chance can be identified with appropriate statistics.

But in field experiments, what is planned as a random assignment process may deteriorate when it is delegated to front-line program staff. The staff may not always follow the process guidelines. This problem occurred in the Sherman and Berk domestic violence experiment in Minneapolis. Police officers sometimes violated the random assignment plan because they thought the circumstances warranted arresting a suspect who had been randomly assigned to receive only a warning. In several of the follow-up studies, the researchers maintained closer control over the assignment process so the randomization could be maintained.

Even when the random assignment plan works, the groups can differ over time because of **differential attrition,** or what can be thought of as deselection. That is, the groups become different because for various reasons subjects are more likely to drop out of groups. This is not a likely problem for a laboratory experiment that occurs in one session, but for laboratory experiments that occur over time, differential attrition may become a problem.

Differential attrition is quite common in field experiments that evaluate the impact of social programs (Cook & Campbell, 1979:359–366). Subjects who receive some advantageous program benefit are more likely to stay in the experiment (making themselves available for measurement in the posttest); subjects who do not receive program benefits are more likely to drop out. Another possibility is that individuals who may be more in need of a program, such as severe alcoholics in a detoxification study, are more likely to drop out (Rossi & Freeman, 1989:236). The problem this creates is that the two groups are no longer equivalent, despite the fact that subjects were originally randomly assigned.

In evaluation research that monitors program impact over an extended period, the possibility of differential attrition can be very high. When the treatment group is receiving some service or benefit that the control group is not, the individuals in the control group will be more likely to drop out of the study.

When subjects are not randomly assigned to treatment and comparison groups, as in nonequivalent control group designs, there is a serious threat of selection bias. Even if the researcher selects a comparison group that matches the treatment group on important variables, there is no guarantee that the groups were similar initially in terms of the dependent variable or another characteristic that ultimately influences posttest scores. However, a pretest helps the researchers to determine whether selection bias exists and to control for it. Most variables that might influence outcome scores will also influence scores on the pretest. Statistically controlling for the pretest scores also serves to control for unmeasured variables that influence the pretest scores.

Endogenous Change

The type of problem considered an **endogenous change** occurs when natural developments in the subjects, independent of the experimental treatment, account for some or all of the observed change between pretest and posttest. Endogenous change includes three specific threats to internal validity:

Testing. Taking the pretest can in itself influence posttest scores. Subjects may learn something or be sensitized to an issue by the pretest and as a result, respond differently when they are asked the same questions in the posttest.

Maturation. Changes in outcome scores during experiments that involve a lengthy treatment period may be due to maturation. Subjects may age, or gain experience in school, or grow in knowledge, all as part of a natural maturational experience and thus respond differently on the posttest from the way they responded on the pretest.

Regression. People experience cyclical or episodic changes that result in different posttest scores, a phenomenon known as a **regression effect.** Subjects who are chosen for a study because they received very low scores on a test may show improvement in the posttest, on average, simply because some of the low scorers were having a bad day. On the other hand, individuals selected for an experiment because they are suffering from tooth decay will not show improvement in the posttest because a decaying tooth is not likely to improve in the natural course of things. It is hard, in many cases, to know whether a phenomenon is subject to naturally occurring fluctuations, so the possibility of regression effects should be considered whenever subjects are selected because of their extremely high or low values on the outcome variable (Mohr, 1992:56, 71–79).

Testing, maturation, and regression effects are generally not a problem in true experiments. Both the experimental group and the comparison group take the pretest, so even if this experience itself leads to a change in posttest scores, the comparison between the experimental and comparison groups will not be affected. Of course, in experiments with no pretest, testing effects are not a problem. Similarly, both the experimental and comparison groups are equally subject to maturation and regression, since they are the same at the outset (unless chance factors led to a difference). These endogenous changes may affect outcome scores for both groups, but both groups should be equally affected. As a result, the estimates of treatment effects should not be biased.

Endogenous change is, however, a major problem with quasi-experimental designs, particularly before-and-after designs. In panel designs with a single pretest and a single posttest, any change may be due to testing, maturation, or regression. But a study that is completed within a short time would have little concern with maturation effects, and use of a diverse subject group will reassure those concerned about regression effects. Unfortunately, the possibility of endogenous change accounting for pretest–posttest change cannot be eliminated with before-and-after designs. Repeated-measures panel studies and time series designs are more effective because they allow the researcher to trace the pattern of change or stability in the dependent variable up to and after the treatment. Ongoing effects of maturation and regression can thus be identified and taken into account.

External Events

External events, sometimes referred to as the **history effect** during the experiment— things that happen outside the experiment—can also change the subjects' outcome scores. An example of this is a newsworthy event that has to do with the focus of an experiment and the major disasters to which subjects are exposed. What if researchers were evaluating the effectiveness of a mandatory arrest policy in decreasing incidents of intimate partner assault, and an event such as the murder trial of O. J. Simpson occurred during the experiment? This would clearly be a historical event that might compromise the results. The media were obsessed with the trial of O. J. Simpson, and as a result, intimate partner assault and homicide were given a tremendous amount of media attention. Because of this increased awareness, many victims of intimate partner violence reported their victimizations during this time—police agencies and women's shelters were flooded with calls. If a researcher had been using calls to police in a particular jurisdiction as an indicator of the incidence of intimate partner assault, this historical event would have seriously jeopardized the internal validity of his or her results. Why? Because the increase in police calls would have had more to do with the trial than with any recent change in arrest policies.

Causal conclusions can be invalid in true experiments because of the influence of external events, but not every experiment is affected by them. The specific features of an experiment must be considered carefully to evaluate the possibility of problems due to external events. For example, in an experiment in which subjects go to a particular location for the treatment and the control group subjects do not, something at the location unrelated to the treatment could influence the experimental subjects.

The more carefully controlled the conditions for experimental and comparison groups, the less likely external events will invalidate the causal conclusions of an experiment. External events seldom affect laboratory experiments. In addition, when using nonequivalent control group designs, a comparison group can minimize the effect of external events if the two groups are exposed to the same environment during the experiment. For example, the relatively constant level of seat-belt use in the comparison community in the Watson study suggests that a national series of TV announcements to encourage compliance is not what resulted in the changes in seat-belt use observed in the experimental community (Watson, 1986:294).

Before-and-after designs are much less prone to problems of external events, and become quasi-experimental when the researchers make multiple before-and-after comparisons or when they apply multiple pretest and posttest measures to the same group in successive time intervals. If **multiple-group before-and-after designs** yield comparable results, the observed pretest–posttest change is less likely to be due to unique external events that would have affected only some of the comparisons.

Contamination

Contamination occurs in an experiment when the comparison group is in some way affected by, or affects, the treatment group. This problem basically arises from failure to adequately control the conditions of the experiment. When comparison group members become aware that they are being denied some advantage, they may increase their efforts to compensate, creating a problem called **compensatory rivalry,** or the **John Henry effect** (Cook & Campbell, 1979:55). (Saretsky [1972] coined the term *John Henry effect* in honor of the steel driver who, when he learned that his output was to be compared to that of a steam drill, worked so hard that he outperformed the drill and died of overexertion.)

On the other hand, comparison group members may become demoralized if they feel that they have been left out of some valuable treatment and may perform worse than they would have outside the experiment. The treatment may seem, in comparison, to have a more beneficial effect than it actually did. Both compensatory rivalry and demoralization thus distort the impact of the experimental treatment. Similar problems could occur if members of the experimental group become aware of the control group and feel differently as a result.

Although the components of a true experiment guard against internal invalidity due to history and selection, the threat of contamination is always present. Careful inspection of the research design can determine whether contamination is likely to be a problem in a particular experiment. If the experiment is conducted in a laboratory, if members of the experimental group and the comparison group have no contact while the study is in progress, and if the treatment is relatively brief, contamination is not likely to be a problem. To the degree that these conditions are not met, the likelihood of contamination will increase.

The threat of contamination is not necessarily any different in a quasi-experimental design than it is in a true experiment. Some nonequivalent control group designs minimize the threat of contamination by using a comparison group whose members will have no contact with the treatment group or awareness of the treatment. For example, Watson chose two communities for his seat-belt compliance study that were far enough apart to be in different media markets.

Treatment Misidentification

Treatment misidentification occurs when the treatment itself does not cause the outcome but does cause some intervening process the researcher is not aware of and has not identified. This term can also refer to unknown concomitants or consequences for subjects in the control group that have to do with the experimental manipulation. In either case, the subjects experienced something other than, or in addition to, what the researchers believed they would experience. Treatment misidentification has at least three sources:

1. *Expectancies of experimental staff.* Change among experimental subjects may be due to the positive **expectancies of the experimental staff** who are delivering the treatment rather than due to the treatment itself. This type of treatment misidentification can occur even in randomized experiments when well-trained staff convey their enthusiasm for an experimental program to the subjects in subtle ways. Such positive staff expectations create a self-fulfilling prophecy. Because social programs are delivered by human beings, such expectancy effects can be very difficult to control in field experiments. However, in experiments on the effects of treatments such as medical drugs, **double-blind procedures** can be used. Staff will deliver the treatments without knowing which subjects are getting the treatment and which are receiving a placebo, something that looks like the treatment but has no effect.

2. *Placebo effect.* Treatment misidentification may occur when subjects receive a treatment that they consider likely to be beneficial, then improve because of that expectation rather than the treatment itself. In medical research the placebo is often a chemically inert substance that looks like the experimental drug but actually has no medical effect. Research indicates that the **placebo effect** produces positive health effects in two-thirds of patients suffering from relatively mild medical problems (Goleman, 1993a:C3). Placebo effects can also occur in social science research. The only way to reduce this threat to internal validity is to treat the comparison group with something similar.

3. *Hawthorne effect.* Members of the treatment group may change in terms of the dependent variable because their participation in the study makes them feel special. This problem can occur when treatment group members compare their situation to that of the control group members, who are not receiving the treatment. In this case, this is a type of

contamination effect. But experimental group members could feel special simply because they are in the experiment. The **Hawthorne effect** is named after a famous productivity experiment at the Hawthorne electric plant outside Chicago. Workers were moved to a special room for a study of the effects of lighting intensity and other work conditions on their productivity. After this move, the workers began to increase their output no matter what change was made in their working conditions, even when the conditions became worse. The researchers concluded that the workers felt they should work harder because they were part of a special experiment. By the time the study was over, the researchers were convinced that it was social interaction among workers, not physical arrangements, that largely determined their output. Most management historians believe that the human relations school of management began with this insight.

In a **process analysis,** periodic measures are taken throughout the experiment to assess whether the treatment is being delivered as planned. To avoid treatment misidentification, field researchers are now using process analysis more often than in the past. Process analysis is also a necessary component of evaluation studies, when researchers need to be very confident that the effects they observe are caused by the policy or program change they are studying (Hunt, 1985:272–274).

Generalizability

The need for generalizable findings can be thought of as the Achilles heel of the true experimental design. The design components that are essential for a true experiment and minimize the threats to causal (internal) validity make it more difficult to achieve sample generalizability—the ability to apply the findings to a clearly defined, larger population. In contrast, cross-population generalizability is no more or less achievable with experiments than with other research designs. As you learned in Chapter 1, the extent to which treatment effects can be generalized across subgroups and to other populations and settings is external validity.

Sample Generalizability

Subjects who can be recruited for a laboratory experiment, randomly assigned to a group, and kept under carefully controlled conditions for the study's duration are unlikely to be a representative sample of any large population of interest to social scientists. In fact, most are recruited from college populations. Can they be expected to react to the experimental treatment in the same way as members of the larger population? The more artificial the experimental arrangements, the greater the problem (Campbell & Stanley, 1966:20–21). As you learned in Chapter 4, randomly selecting a sample from a population is the best way to ensure sample generalizability (this has nothing to do with randomly assigning the sample to the control or experimental groups). A large percentage of laboratory experiments, including those performed by Nisbett and Cohen (1996), utilize availability samples such as college students. As Nisbett and Cohen clearly state:

When we refer to northerners and southerners who participated in the experiments, we use those words as a shorthand way of referring to male students from the North and the South attending the University of Michigan who are Caucasian, non-Hispanic, and non-Jewish. Our sample is certainly not a representative one—even of Caucasian, non-Hispanic, non-Jewish males. On average, the students came from families that were financially well-off, with the median income for northerners about $85,000 and for southerners, $95,000. The southerners might also be unusual in that they chose to leave the South at least temporarily and come to school in the North. (1996:41–42)

It is not only the characteristics of the subjects themselves that determine the generalizability of the experimental results. The generalizability of the treatment and of the setting for the experiment also must be considered (Cook & Campbell, 1979:73–74). However, researchers can take steps both before and after an experiment to increase a study's generalizability. Field experiments are likely to yield findings that are more generalizable to broader populations than are laboratory experiments, using subjects who must volunteer. Sherman and Berk's experimental study of arrest and domestic violence and Watson's quasi-experimental study of seat-belt use were both conducted with people and police engaged in their normal activities in real communities, greatly increasing our confidence in the studies' generalizability.

In a few field experiments, participants can be randomly selected from the population of interest, so the researchers can achieve results generalizable to that population. The Sherman and Berk arrest study did not use random selection. Because it was to include all actual domestic assault cases processed by police in two Minneapolis precincts during a certain period, the resulting sample of cases should represent at least the two precincts.

But in most experiments, neither random selection from the population nor selection of the entire population is possible. Potential subjects must make a conscious decision to participate. This undoubtedly increases the possibility that the resulting sample is an unrepresentative pool of volunteers. Even in the Sherman and Berk study, many police officers did not participate, so the attempt to include all domestic assault cases that met study criteria did not succeed. The results of the study may not have been generalizable even to the two precincts.

When random selection is not feasible, the researchers may be able to increase generalizability by selecting several sites for conducting the experiments that offer obvious contrasts in the key variables of the population. The follow-up studies to Sherman and Berk's work, for example, were conducted in cities that differed from Minneapolis, the original site, in social class and ethnic composition. As a result, although the findings are not statistically generalizable to a larger population, they do give some indication of the study's general applicability (Cook & Campbell, 1979:76–77).

External Validity

Researchers are often interested in determining whether the treatment effects identified in an experiment hold true for subgroups of subjects or across different populations. Of course, determining that a relationship between the treatment and the outcome variable holds true for certain subgroups does not establish that the same relationship also holds true for these subgroups in the larger population, but it does suggest that the relationship might be **externally valid.**

External validity   The applicability of a treatment effect (or noneffect) across subgroups within an experiment and/or across different populations, times, or settings.

Example: Sherman and Berk (1984) found that arrest reduced repeat offenses for employed subjects but not for unemployed subjects. The effect of arrest thus varied with employment status, so a conclusion that arrest deters recidivism would not be externally valid.

Imagine a field experiment in which subjects were randomly sampled from the population of interest but in which the treatment effect occurred only for some subgroups. Suppose, for example, that you conduct an experiment on the effects of alcohol on violent behavior and find that alcohol increases the probability for males to act violently, but not females. The finding about the overall effect of alcohol, then, would not apply to all groups within the population. In this instance, the external validity of the conclusions would be equivalent to their cross-population generalizability.

Ultimately, the external validity of experimental results will increase with the success of replications taking place at different times and places, using different forms of the treatment. As indicated by the replications of the Sherman and Berk study of arrest for domestic violence, the result may be a more detailed, nuanced understanding of the hypothesized effect.

Interaction of Testing and Treatment

A variation of the problem of external validity occurs when the experimental treatment is effective only when particular conditions created by the experiment occur. For example, if subjects have had a pretest it may sensitize them to a particular issue, so when they are exposed to the treatment, their reaction is different from what it would have been if they had not taken the pretest. In other words, testing and treatment interact to produce the outcome.

Suppose you were interested in the effects of a diversity training film on prejudicial attitudes. After answering questions in a pretest about their attitudes on various topics related to diversity (e.g., racial or sexual prejudice), the subjects generally became more sensitive to the issue of prejudice without seeing the training film. On the posttest, then, their attitudes may be different from pretest attitudes simply because they have become sensitized to the issue of diversity through pretesting. In this situation, the treatment may actually have an effect, but it would be difficult to determine how much of the effect was attributable to the sensitizing pretest and how much was due to seeing the film.

Researchers sometimes deliberately take advantage of the interaction of testing and treatment to increase external validity. One design for doing so, the **Solomon four-group design,** randomly assigns subjects to at least two experimental groups and at least two comparison groups. One experimental group and one comparison group will have a pretest, and the other two groups will not have a pretest (see Exhibit 5.11). If testing and treatment do interact, the difference in outcome scores between the experimental and comparison groups will differ between subjects who took the pretest and those who did not.

Exhibit 5.11 Solomon Four-Group Design Testing the Interaction of Pretesting and Treatment

Experimental group:	R	O_1	X	O_2
Comparison group:	R	O_1		O_2
Experimental group:	R		X	O_2
Comparison group:	R			O_2

Key: R = Random assignment
     O = Observation (pretest or posttest)
     X = Experimental treatment

NONEXPERIMENTAL RESEARCH AND CAUSATION

The **nonexperimental approach to establishing causality** (sometimes called the descriptive or observational approach) involves studying naturally occurring variation in the dependent and independent variables, without intervention by researchers or anyone else. Instead, the researchers equate cases prior to exposure to the independent variable. Survey research (the subject of Chapter 6) is the primary type of nonexperimental research design.

Nonexperimental research designs can be either cross-sectional or longitudinal. In a **cross-sectional research design,** all data are collected at one point in time. Identifying the time order of effects can be an insurmountable problem with this design. In a **longitudinal research design,** data are collected at two or more points in time, so identifying the time order of effects can be quite simple.

Cross-Sectional Research Designs

A cross-sectional research design is one in which all data are collected at one point in time. With a cross-sectional design, a researcher can easily determine whether two variables are associated. Sampson's (1987) study of the association among male joblessness, family disruption, and violence is a good example of a cross-sectional design. However, it can be difficult, and sometimes impossible, to determine time order with cross-sectional data. If you need to know whether variation in the independent variable occurred prior to variation in the dependent variable, you usually need to measure the independent variable at some time before you measure the dependent variable.

In the following four circumstances, cross-sectional data can reasonably be used to infer the time order of effects. In these circumstances, the data provide measures of variables in earlier periods. In effect, they are longitudinal, because they can be ordered in time (Campbell, 1992).

1. *The independent variable is fixed at some point prior to the variation in the dependent variable.* Demographic variables determined at birth, such as sex, race, and age, are fixed in this way. So are variables such as education and marital status if we know when the value of cases on these variables was established, and if we know that the value of cases on the dependent variable was set some time later. For example, suppose we hypothesize that education influences the type of job individuals have. If we know that respondents

completed their education before taking their current jobs, we would satisfy the time order requirement even if we were to measure education at the same time we measure the type of job. However, if some respondents went back to school as a benefit of their current job, the time order requirement would not be satisfied.

2. *We believe that respondents can give us reliable reports of what happened to them or what they thought at some earlier point in time.* Julie Horney, D. Wayne Osgood, and Ineke Haen Marshall (1995) provide an interesting example of the use of such retrospective data. The researchers wanted to identify how criminal activity varies in response to changes in life circumstances. They interviewed 658 newly convicted male offenders sentenced to a Nebraska state prison. In a 45- to 90-minute interview, they recorded each inmate's report of his life circumstances and his criminal activities for the preceding 2 to 3 years. They found that criminal involvement was related strongly to adverse changes in life circumstances, such as marital separation or drug use. Retrospective data are often inadequate for measuring variation in past psychological states or behaviors, because what we recall about our feelings or actions in the past is likely to be influenced by what we feel in the present. For example, retrospective reports by both adult alcoholics and their parents appear to greatly overestimate the frequency of childhood problems (Vaillant, 1995). People cannot reliably report the frequency and timing of many past events, from hospitalization to hours worked. However, retrospective data tend to be reliable when they concern major, persistent experiences in the past, such as what type of school someone attended, or how a person's family was structured (Campbell, 1992).

3. *Our measures are based on records that contain information on cases in earlier periods.* Government, agency, and organizational records are an excellent source of time-ordered data after the fact. However, sloppy record keeping and changes in data-collection policies can lead to inconsistencies, which must be taken into account. Another weakness of such archival data is that they usually contain measures of only a fraction of the variables that we think are important.

4. *We know that cases were equivalent on the dependent variable prior to the treatment or intervention.* For example, we may hypothesize that compared to a traditional correctional facility, a training program such as a boot camp (independent variable) decreases the likelihood that young, nonviolent offenders will reoffend in the future (dependent variable). Because all of the individuals were sent to either the boot camp or prison, we can be confident that any subsequent variation in their offending did not precede exposure to the training program. This is one way that traditional experiments establish time order: Two or more equivalent groups are formed prior to exposing one of them to some treatment.

Longitudinal Research Designs

Except in the special cases just noted (which can themselves be considered types of longitudinal designs), it is risky to draw conclusions about causality on the basis of cross-sectional data. In longitudinal research, data are collected that can be ordered in time. By measuring the value of cases on an independent variable and a dependent variable at each of these different times, the researcher can determine whether variation in the independent variable preceded variation in the dependent variable.

Many versions of longitudinal designs exist (Campbell, 1992). In some longitudinal designs, the same sample, called a panel, is followed over time. In other designs, sample members are rotated or completely replaced. The population from which the sample is selected may be broadly defined, as when conducting a longitudinal survey of the general population. Or the population may be narrowly defined, as when members of a specific age group are sampled at multiple points in time. The frequency of follow-up measurement can vary, ranging from a before-and-after design with just one follow-up to studies with various indicators that are measured every month for many years.

Certainly it is more difficult to collect data at two or more points in time than at only one time. Quite frequently researchers simply cannot, or are unwilling to, delay completion of a study for even 1 year to collect follow-up data. But think of the many research questions that really should involve a much longer follow-up period: What is the impact of job training on recidivism? Do social skills training programs in grade school reduce the likelihood of aggressive behavior in adolescence? Under what conditions do traumatic experiences in childhood result in such things as mental illness and/or violent offending? It is safe to say we will never have enough longitudinal data to answer many important research questions. The value of longitudinal data is so great that every effort should be made to develop longitudinal research designs when they are appropriate. The following discussion of three types of longitudinal designs will give you a sense of the possibilities.

Repeated Cross-Sectional Designs

Repeated cross-sectional designs, also known as trend studies, are commonly used in the political arena around election time. Particularly during presidential election years, we are all accustomed to reading weekly, even daily, reports on the percentage of the population that supports each candidate. Similar polls are conducted to track sentiment on many other social issues. For example, a 1993 poll reported that 52% of adult Americans supported a ban on the possession of handguns, compared to 41% in a similar poll conducted in 1991. According to pollster Louis Harris, this increase indicated a "sea of change" in public attitudes (Barringer, 1993). Another researcher said, "It shows that people are responding to their experience [of an increase in handgun-related killings]" (Barringer, 1993:1).

Repeated cross-sectional design   A type of longitudinal study in which data are collected at two or more points in time from different samples of the same population.

Repeated cross-sectional designs allow identification of change in general attitudes and behavior for a defined population, but not for the same people. Repeated cross-sectional surveys are conducted as follows:

1. A sample is drawn from a population at Time 1, and data are collected from the sample.

2. As time passes, some people leave the population and others enter it.

3. At Time 2, a different sample is drawn from this population.

These features indicate that the repeated cross-sectional design is appropriate to use when the goal is to determine whether a population has changed over time. Has racial tolerance increased among Americans in the past 20 years? Have attitudes toward the death penalty changed since the 1970s? These questions concern changes in the population as a whole, not changes in individuals within the population. We want to know whether racial tolerance increased in society, not whether this change was due to migration that brought more racially tolerant people into the country or to individual U.S. citizens becoming more tolerant. For questions concerning specific individuals in the population, we must use a panel design.

Fixed-Sample Panel Designs

Panel designs allow identification of changes in individuals, groups, or any selection we are studying. **Fixed-sample panel designs** are conducted as follows:

1. A sample (called a panel) is drawn from a population at Time 1, and data are collected from the sample.

2. As time passes, some panel members become unavailable for follow-up, and the population changes.

3. At Time 2, data are collected from the same people as at Time 1 (the panel), except for those people who cannot be located.

Fixed-sample panel design A type of longitudinal study in which data are collected from the same individuals on the panel at two or more points in time. In other types of panel design, panel members who leave are replaced with other members.

Because a panel design follows the same individuals, it is better than a repeated cross-sectional design for testing causal hypotheses. For example, Sampson and Laub (1990) used a fixed-sample panel design to investigate the effect of childhood deviance on adult crime. They studied a sample of Caucasian males in Boston when the subjects were between 10 and 17 years old and then followed up when the subjects were adults. Data were collected from multiple sources, including the subjects themselves and criminal justice records. Sampson and Laub (1990:614) found that children committed to a correctional school for persistent delinquency were much more likely to commit crimes as adults: 61% were arrested between the ages of 25 and 32, compared to 14% of children who had not been in correctional schools. In this study, juvenile delinquency unquestionably occurred before adult criminality. If the researchers had used a cross-sectional design to study the past of adults, the juvenile delinquency measure may have been biased by memory lapses, self-serving recollections about behavior as juveniles, or loss of agency records.

If you now wonder why every longitudinal study isn't designed as a panel study, you've understood the advantages of panel designs. However, remember that this design does not in itself establish causality. Variation in both the independent variable and the dependent variables may be due to some other variable, even to earlier variation in what is considered the dependent variable. In the example in Exhibit 5.12 there is a hypothesized association between delinquency in the 11th grade and grades obtained in the 12th grade (the dependent variable). The time order is clear. However, both variables are consequences of grades

Exhibit 5.12 Causality in Panel Studies

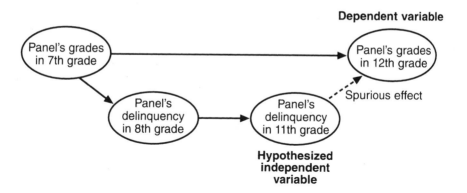

Although delinquency in the 11th grade and grades in the 12th grade are clearly associated and the time order is clear, causality cannot be determined. In reality, grades in the 7th grade also play a role.

obtained in the 7th grade. The apparent effect of 11th-grade delinquency on 12th-grade grades is spurious because of variation in the dependent variable (grades) at an earlier time.

One way to more accurately control the effects of extraneous variables is to add a control group to a panel design. Cathy Spatz Widom (2000) conducted one of the most comprehensive studies of this nature. In her study, Widom attempted to determine the long-term effects of childhood abuse and neglect. To establish a group of neglected and/or abused children, Widom obtained cases of children from county juvenile and adult criminal court records in a metropolitan area of the Midwest between 1967 and 1971. The children were age 11 or younger at the time of the incident. To create a control group, another group of children who had not been victimized but were similar to the study subjects in other respects (age, sex, race, socioeconomic background, etc.) were selected from elementary school records. Beginning in 1986, the criminal histories of the individuals in both groups were traced to determine the extent to which they had become involved in delinquency and crime. Official juvenile and adult criminal histories were searched for all subjects (at the local, state, and federal levels). In 1989, more than 20 years after the original victimization, 1,196 of the original 1,575 individuals in the study were interviewed. As you can see, this methodology is similar to an experimental design. However, because it was not possible to randomly assign individuals to the abused versus nonabused group, it does not constitute a true experiment. The addition of a control group into the panel design did allow Widom and her colleagues to sort out the effects of childhood victimization from other potential effects traceable to causes such as socioeconomic conditions.

Panel designs are powerful but they are a challenge to implement successfully. Often these designs are not even attempted, because of two categories of difficulty:

Expense and attrition. It can be difficult, and very expensive, to keep track of individuals over a long period. Inevitably, the proportion of panel members who can be located for follow-up will decline over time. Panel studies often lose more than one-quarter of their members through attrition (Miller, 1991:170). However, subject attrition can be reduced substantially if sufficient staff can be used to keep track of panel members. In their panel study, Sampson and Laub (1990) lost only 12% of the juveniles in the original sample (8% if you do not count those who died). The Widom sample lost 25% of the original sample, but this is still remarkably low considering the study spanned 20 years. The consequences of a high rate of subject attrition are that the follow-up sample may no longer be representative of the population from which it was drawn and may no longer provide a sound basis for estimating change. Subjects who were lost to follow-up may have been those who changed the most, or the least, over time. It does help to compare the baseline characteristics of those who are interviewed at follow-up with characteristics of those lost to follow-up. If these two groups of panel members are not very different, it is less likely that changes had anything to do with characteristics of the missing panel members.

Subject fatigue. Panel members may grow weary of repeated interviews and drop out of the study, or they may become so used to answering the standard questions in the survey that they start giving stock answers rather than actually thinking about their current feelings or actions (Campbell, 1992). This is called the problem of **subject fatigue.**

Because panel studies are so useful, social researchers have developed increasingly effective techniques for keeping track of individuals and overcoming subject fatigue. But when resources do not permit use of these techniques to maintain an adequate panel, repeated cross-sectional designs can usually be employed at a cost not much higher than a one-time cross-sectional study. The payoff in explanatory power should be well worth the cost.

Event- or Cohort-Based Designs

An **event- or cohort-based design,** often called a *cohort study,* is like the repeated cross-sectional design but with one important exception: The follow-up samples (at one or more times) are not selected from the whole population, but are selected from the same **cohort**—people who have experienced a similar event. A cohort consists of individuals or groups with a common starting point. Examples include:

- *Birth cohorts.* Those who share a common period of birth (born in the 1940s, 1950s, 1960s, and so on).
- *Seniority cohorts.* Those who have worked at the same place for about 5 years, about 10 years, and so on.
- *School cohorts.* Those who are freshmen, sophomores, juniors, or seniors.

Event- or cohort-based design   A type of longitudinal study in which data are collected at two or more points in time from individuals in a population defined by a common starting point or event (or cohort).

Examples of cohorts: College class of 2000, people who graduated from high school in the 1980s, police officers who started work between 1990 and the year 2000, people who were born in the late 1940s or the 1950s (the baby boom generation).

An event-based design can be a type of repeated cross-sectional design or a type of panel design. In an event-based, repeated cross-sectional design, separate samples are drawn from the same cohort at two or more different times. In an event-based panel design, the same individuals from the same cohort are studied at two or more different times.

We can see the value of event-based research in a comparison of two studies that estimated the impact of public and private schooling on high school students' achievement test scores. In a cross-sectional study, James Coleman, Thomas Hoffer, and Sally Kilgore (1982) compared standardized achievement test scores of high school sophomores and seniors in public, Catholic, and other private schools. They found that test scores were higher in the private high schools (both Catholic and other) than in the public high schools. But was this difference a causal effect of private schooling? Perhaps the parents of higher-performing children were choosing to send them to private rather than to public schools. In other words, the achievement levels of private school students might be higher before they start high school and not increased as a result of their high school education.

The researchers tried to reduce the impact of this problem by statistically controlling for a range of family background variables: family income, parents' education, race, number of siblings, number of rooms in the home, number of parents present, mother working, and other indicators of a family oriented to education. But some critics pointed out that even with all these controls for family background, the cross-sectional study did not ensure that the students had been comparable in achievement when they started high school.

So James Coleman and Thomas Hoffer (1987) went back to the high schools and studied the test scores of the former sophomores two years later, when they were seniors. These researchers used an event-based panel design. This time they found that the verbal and math achievement test scores for the Catholic school students had increased more over the 2 years than had the scores of the public school students. It was not clear whether the scores of the other private school students had increased. Irrespective of students' initial achievement test scores, the Catholic schools seemed to do more for their students than did the public schools. This finding continued to be true even when dropouts were also studied. The researchers' causal conclusion rested on much stronger ground because they used an event-based design.

Comparison of Experimental and Nonexperimental Designs

How well do the research designs just described satisfy the criteria necessary to determine causality? Although it is relatively easy to establish that an empirical association exists between an independent and dependent variable in these designs, the other criteria are much more difficult to assess.

Let us first illustrate the importance of time order. Robert Sampson (1987) studied urban African American violence with the specific hypothesis that higher rates of African American family disruption (the percentage of African American, single-mother households with children) resulted in more violence. He found that family disruption was indeed associated with higher rates of African American male violence, but he also found similar relationships among Caucasians. Does this finding establish that family disruption causes violence among urban African American males? Or, as Sampson correctly asked, does violent crime lead to family disruption, because women are unlikely to marry or remain married to men who are incarcerated? Because Sampson collected his data on family disruption and violence at the same point in time, this alternative time order cannot definitively be ruled out.

Another concern with nonexperimental research is meeting the criterion of nonspuriousness. In nonexperimental research, unlike experimental research, cases cannot be randomly assigned to receive one or another value of the independent variable, so it is hard to determine whether variation in the dependent variable is due to variation in the independent variable, or something else altogether. Consider the relationship Sampson found between family disruption and the homicide rate. The two variables may be correlated, but they may have had no causal relationship. Perhaps an extraneous third variable, say joblessness, led to both family disruption and greater likelihood of violence (see Exhibit 5.13). If joblessness is the result of the association between the two original variables, then the apparent causal relationship between family disruption and the homicide rate is spurious; they are merely correlated.

To reduce the risk of spuriousness, nonexperimental researchers use the technique of **statistical control**. Exhibit 5.14 represents the important concept of statistical control with a hypothetical study of the relationship between attending a boot camp in prison (a highly regimented, discipline-focused rehabilitation program) and the likelihood of committing crimes after prison (the recidivism rate). In Exhibit 5.14, the data for all prisoners show that prisoners who attended boot camp were less likely to return to committing crimes after they left prison. However, as the more detailed data show, more female prisoners attended boot camp than male prisoners, so gender may have played a significant role in recidivism. The researchers, however, reduced the risk of spuriousness by using two statistical control methods: They examined the association between attending boot camp and postprison criminality for men and for women. After doing this, researchers determined that boot

Exhibit 5.13   Extraneous Variables in Nonexperimental Research: Family Disruption and the Homicide Rate

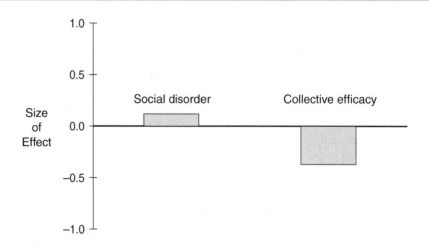

Source: Sampson, 1987.

Exhibit 5.14 The Use of Statistical Control to Reduce Spuriousness

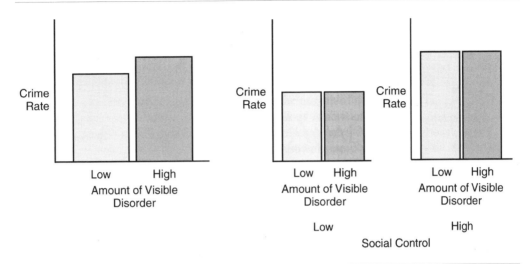

camp did not reduce recidivism. It just appeared to do so, because women were more likely to attend boot camp and less likely to commit crimes after prison, regardless of whether they attended boot camp.

Similarly, Sampson (1987) used statistical control for variation in joblessness when he tested for a relationship between rates of family disruption and violence. In effect, he compared family disruption and rates of violence for cities with similar levels of joblessness. Because the relationship between family disruption and violence still held after joblessness was controlled, our confidence is considerably strengthened that the hypothesized association was not spurious and due to the extraneous influence of joblessness.

Statistical control A technique used in nonexperimental research to reduce the risk of spuriousness. One variable is held constant so the relationship between two or more other variables can be assessed without the influence of variation in the control variable.

Example of statistical control: Sampson (1987) found that the relationship between rates of family disruption and violent crimes held true for cities with similar levels of joblessness (the control variable). So the rate of joblessness could not have caused the association between family disruption and violent crime.

Our confidence in causal conclusions based on nonexperimental research also increases with identification of a causal mechanism. These mechanisms are **intervening variables** in nonexperimental research, and help us to understand how variation in the independent variable results in variation in the dependent variable. For example, Robert Sampson and John Laub (1993) found that people who were delinquent as juveniles were more likely to commit crimes as adults. They also found, as Exhibit 5.15 shows, that juvenile

Exhibit 5.15   Intervening Variables in Nonexperimental Research: Juvenile Delinquency and Adult Criminality

Source: Sampson & Laub, 1993.

delinquency was followed in later years by lower levels of job stability, career aspirations, and marital attachment. These low levels were associated with higher rates of adult criminality. The identification of causal mechanisms in this research was particularly important because it also indicated how juvenile delinquents might be prevented from becoming adult criminals. Sampson and Laub (1993) found that juvenile delinquents who achieved stable jobs, developed career aspirations, and became committed to a spouse were less likely to commit crimes as adults.

Identification of one or more intervening variables does not end the possibilities for clarifying the causal mechanisms. You might ask why juvenile delinquency tends to result in lower career aspirations or why career aspirations influence adult criminality. You could then conduct research to identify the mechanisms that link juvenile delinquency and career aspirations. Perhaps schoolteachers tell delinquents that they will never get ahead, so the juveniles' aspirations decline. Or perhaps delinquents decide that committing crimes is more fun or more lucrative than working in a regular job. This process could go on and on. The point is that identification of a mechanism through which the independent variable influences the dependent variable increases our confidence in the conclusion that a causal connection does indeed exist.

When you think about the role of variables in causal relationships, don't confuse variables that cause spurious relationships with variables that intervene in causal relationships, even though both are third variables that do not appear in the initial hypothesis. In Exhibit 5.13 the extraneous variable, joblessness, creates a spurious relationship. By contrast, in Exhibit 5.15, the three intervening variables are part of the process that links the independent variable and the dependent variable. Intervening variables help explain the relationship between the independent variable (juvenile delinquency) and the dependent variable (adult criminality).

Nonexperimental research can be a very effective tool for exploring the context in which causal effects occur. Administering surveys in many different settings and to different types of individuals is usually much easier than administering various experiments.

Given the differences in their approaches to establishing causality, how similar are the results of experimental and nonexperimental hypothesis tests? Not enough attention has been given to answering this question, but the existing evidence is not very encouraging. For example, one experimental study found that youth earnings increased as a result of participation in a supported work program, but nonexperimental studies tended to show a decrease in earnings due to program participation. In general, the extent of the differences in results depended on which specific comparison group was selected and which variables were statistically controlled (Fraker & Maynard, 1987; LaLonde, 1986). Unfortunately, researchers using nonexperimental methods usually have no way of knowing exactly which variables to control to meet the criterion of nonspuriousness or which comparison group to select to most closely approximate the results that would be obtained with an experimental design.

The difficulty of establishing nonspuriousness does not rule out using nonexperimental data to evaluate causal hypotheses. In fact, when enough nonexperimental data are collected to allow tests of multiple implications of the same causal hypothesis, the results can be very convincing (Freedman, 1991).

In any case, nonexperimental tests of causal hypotheses will continue to be popular because practical and ethical problems in randomly assigning people to different conditions preclude the test of many important hypotheses with an experimental design. Just remember to carefully consider possible sources of spuriousness and other problems when evaluating causal claims based on individual nonexperimental studies. In general, conclusions about causal effects based on nonexperimental studies are more likely to be valid if the comparison group is very similar to the group receiving the treatment of interest or if many potentially important variables are statistically controlled.

ETHICAL ISSUES IN EXPERIMENTAL RESEARCH

Social science experiments often involve subject deception. Primarily due to this, some experiments have prompted contentious debates about research ethics. Experimental evaluations of social programs also pose ethical dilemmas because they require researchers to withhold possibly beneficial treatment from some subjects who are selected on the basis of chance. In this section we weigh the ethical problems posed by experimental research and discuss the two primary ethical dilemmas: deception and selective distribution of benefits.

Deception

In the most general sense, deception occurs whenever subjects in an experiment are misled about the procedures or treatment they will receive. Deception, of course, is necessary in many instances to determine how subjects will react to the treatment if they are not research subjects. As such, deception is a critical component of many social experiments, in part due to the difficulty of simulating real-world stresses and dilemmas in a laboratory setting. Virtually all of the experiments we have discussed in this text involve some type of deception.

Although the American Society of Criminology's (ASC) and the American Sociological Association's Codes of Ethics do not discuss experimentation explicitly, both codes highlight the ethical dilemma posed by deceptive research. For example, an early version of the ASC code stated:

The process of criminological research must not expose respondents to substantial risk of personal harm. Investigators must make every effort to ensure the safety and security of respondents and project staff. Informed consent must be obtained when the risks of research are greater than the risks of everyday life. All research must meet the human subjects requirements of educational institutions and funding sources. (1997)

Does informed consent mean that subjects must be told exactly what they will be experiencing and why? When are the risks of research greater than those of everyday life?

Although many experiments involve deceiving subjects, some social science laboratory experiments obviously involve much more deception and an apparent greater risk of harm to subjects. Needless to say, these experiments stimulate many questions about research ethics. Stanley Milgram's (1965) experiments on obedience to authority raise most of the relevant issues. Milgram's research was stimulated by the success of Germany's Nazi regime of the 1930s and 1940s in enlisting the participation of ordinary citizens in unconscionable acts of terror and genocide. Milgram set out to identify through laboratory experiments the conditions under which ordinary citizens will be obedient to authority figures' instructions to inflict pain on others. He operationalized this obedience by asking subjects to deliver electric shocks (fake, of course) to students supposedly learning a memory task. Subjects ("teachers") were told to administer a shock to the learner each time he gave a wrong response and to move one level higher on the shock generator each time an incorrect response was given.

Can you imagine your reaction if you volunteered for such an experiment and were forced to inflict pain on another human being? Much to the surprise of Milgram and others, the great majority of subjects administered shocks beyond the danger level, even though the actor being shocked begged (fake begging, of course) the subjects to stop, complained about a heart condition, and/or banged on the wall in feigned pain. The teacher–subjects were not oblivious to the pain they were supposedly causing—they trembled, groaned, broke into nervous laughter, and generally did not seem to want to go on. But in many cases they did go on. A narrative of one subject objecting to administering the shocks should illuminate the stress subjects were under:

Subject: I can't stand it. I'm not going to kill that man in there. You hear him hollering?

Experimenter: As I told you before, the shocks may be painful, but—

Subject: But he's hollering. He can't stand it. What's going to happen to him?

Experimenter: The experiment requires that you continue, Teacher.

Subject: Aaah, but, unh, I'm not going to get that man sick in there . . . know what I mean?

Experimenter: Whether the learner likes it or not, we must go on, through all the word pairs.

Subject: I refuse to take the responsibility. He's in there hollering!

Milgram's research was an empirical success. He identified at least some of the conditions in which ordinary people will resist authority. But was the research ethical?

Thorough **debriefing** of each participant was used to lessen the probability of harm to subjects. All subjects were told the victim did not receive dangerous electric shocks, and each subject had a friendly reconciliation with the unharmed learner and an extended discussion about the experiment's purposes and methods with the experimenter. Obedient subjects were assured that their behavior was entirely normal and that their feelings of conflict or tension were shared by other participants. To determine long-term trauma, participants were also interviewed after one year. No evidence of lingering trauma was uncovered, and almost all participants said they strongly supported the research.

Paul Reynolds (1979:130–133) makes several additional points about Milgram's classic experiment:

- The knowledge resulting from these experiments could be of substantial benefit to the general public if it were used to reduce conflict in organizations and to encourage individuals to question authority. On the other hand, there was some risk that organizational leaders might use the knowledge to manipulate members.
- The research had no direct major benefits to participants while clearly producing stress for individuals during the experiment and possibly some self-doubt afterward. However, the follow-up interviews indicated that research subjects interpreted the experiment in a way that avoided a harmful level of self-blame.
- The research subjects were not a disadvantaged group, and their rights and welfare were taken adequately into account through careful monitoring of the experiment (it was stopped for subjects in extreme stress), full debriefing, and follow-up interviews.

Overall, Reynolds suggests, the costs of the research were minor relative to its benefits:

The effects for the individuals cannot be considered benign: they suffered extreme stress. . . . But participants appeared to have received no lasting negative effects. . . . The value of the project can be judged only on the basis of its contribution to knowledge and possible contributions to the improvement of society. (1979:132–133)

Today researchers must usually follow more stringent standards set by current federal ethical guidelines and administered by institutional review boards (IRBs). It is unlikely an experiment like Milgram's would pass the requirements of an IRB today. At minimum, the current guidelines would require informed consent to be obtained from the subjects. Informed consent, in turn, would require subjects to be told that another human being would not be harmed in the experiment. And since the experimental design required deceiving subjects about this precise point, informed consent could not have been carried out. Clearly, the need to adhere to ethical standards can conflict with the investigation of important social issues.

Selective Distribution of Benefits

Although all experiments, whether conducted in the laboratory or in the field, can involve issues of informed consent (Hunt, 1985:275–276), one ethical issue somewhat unique to field experiments is the **distribution of benefits.** How much are subjects harmed by the way benefits are distributed as part of an experiment? This issue is particularly salient for treatments that may hold some positive benefit for the experimental subjects and deny the same benefits to subjects in the control group. Although this issue poses more ethical dilemmas for medical research investigating the effectiveness of new drugs, it is also important for many social and criminological experiments. For example, Sherman and Berk's experiment, and its successors, required police to make arrests in domestic violence cases primarily on the basis of a random process. When arrests were not made, did the subjects' abused spouses suffer?

Is it ethical to give some potentially advantageous or disadvantageous treatment to people on a random basis? As a general rule, random distribution of benefits is justified when the researchers do not know whether some treatment actually is beneficial or not and, of course, it is the goal of the experiment to find out. In this case, random assignment is the only way to assess whether one treatment is more beneficial than another or than no treatment at all. Also, if insufficient resources are available to fully fund a benefit for every eligible person, distribution of the benefit on the basis of chance to equally needy persons is ethically defensible.

Let's examine the experiment of Sherman and Berk (1984). Victims who called police to report an incident of misdemeanor assault perpetrated by an intimate during the course of the experiment (and who did not insist on arrest) did not know they were in a research study and had no choice about whether their assailants were arrested or received a warning. Perhaps it seems unreasonable to let a random procedure determine how police resolve cases of domestic violence. And indeed it would be unreasonable if this procedure were regular police practice. The Sherman and Berk experiment and its successors do pass ethical muster, however, when seen for what they were—a way of learning how to increase the effectiveness of police response to this all-too-common crime. The initial Sherman and Berk findings encouraged police departments to make many more arrests for these crimes, and the follow-up studies resulted in a better understanding of when arrests are not likely to be effective. The implications of this research may be complex and difficult to implement, but the research provides a much stronger factual basis for policy development.

CONCLUSION

True experiments play two critical roles in criminological research. First, they are the best research design for testing causal hypotheses. Even when conditions preclude the use of a true experimental design, many research designs can be improved by adding experimental components. Second, true experiments provide a comparison point for evaluating the ability of other research designs to achieve causally valid results.

In spite of their obvious strengths, true experiments are used infrequently to study many research problems related to criminology and criminal justice. There are three basic reasons for this:

1. The experiments required to test many important hypotheses require more resources than most social scientists can access.

2. Most research problems of interest to social scientists simply are not amenable to experimental designs, for reasons ranging from ethical considerations to the limited possibilities for randomly assigning people to different conditions in the real world.

3. The requirements of experimental design usually preclude large-scale studies and so limit generalizability to a degree that is unacceptable to many social scientists.

And just because it is possible to test a hypothesis with an experiment, it may not always be desirable to do so. When a program is first developed and its elements are in flux, it is not a good idea to begin a large evaluation study that cannot possibly succeed unless the program design remains constant. Researchers should wait until the program design stabilizes somewhat. It also does not make sense for evaluation researchers to test the impact of programs that cannot actually be implemented or that are unlikely to be implemented in the real world due to financial or political problems (Rossi & Freeman, 1989:304–307).

Even laboratory experiments are inadvisable when they do not test the real hypothesis of interest but instead test a limited version amenable to laboratory manipulation. The intersecting complexity of societies, social relationships, and social beings of people and the groups to which they belong is so great that it often defies reduction to the simplicity of a laboratory or restriction to the requirements of experimental design. Yet the virtues of experimental designs indicate they should always be considered when explanatory research is planned.

When a true experimental design is not feasible, researchers may instead use a quasi-experimental design, including nonequivalent control group designs, before-and-after designs, and ex post facto control group designs. These research designs are termed "quasi"-experimental because the units under study are not randomly assigned to the comparison and experimental groups. As a result, we cannot be as confident in the comparability of the groups in these designs. However, there are several steps that can be taken, such as matching certain individual or group characteristics across the two groups, that allow us to have more confidence in the results of quasi-experimental research.

KEY TERMS

Association
Before-and-after design
Causal effect
Ceteris paribus
Cohort
Compensatory rivalry (John Henry effect)
Contamination
Context
Control/comparison group
Cross-sectional research design
Debriefing
Differential attrition
Distribution of benefits
Double-blind procedure
Endogenous change
Evaluation research
Event- or cohort-based design
Ex post facto control group design
Expectancies of the experimental staff
Experimental group
External event
External validity
Extraneous variable
Fixed-sample panel design

Hawthorne effect
History effect
Intervening variables
Longitudinal research design
Matching
Mechanism
Multiple-group before-and-after design
Nonequivalent control group design
Nonexperimental approach to establishing
  causality
Nonspuriousness
Placebo effect
Posttest
Pretest
Process analysis
Quasi-experimental design
Random assignment
Regression effect
Repeated cross-sectional design
Repeated measures panel design
Selection bias
Self-fulfilling prophecy
Solomon four-group design
Spurious relationship

Statistical control
Subject fatigue
Time order
Time series design (repeated measures
   panel design)

Treatment
Treatment misidentification
True experiment

HIGHLIGHTS

- Three criteria are generally viewed as necessary for identifying a causal relationship: association between the variables, proper time order, and nonspuriousness of the association. In addition, the basis for concluding that a causal relationship exists is strengthened by identification of a causal mechanism and the context.

- The independent variable in an experiment is represented by a treatment or other intervention. Experiments have a comparison group that represents what subjects are like on the dependent variable without the treatment. In true experiments, subjects are randomly assigned to comparison and experimental groups.

- Experimental research designs have three essential components: use of at least two groups of subjects for comparison, measurement of the change that occurs as a result of the experimental treatment, and use of random assignment. In addition, experiments may include identification of a causal mechanism and control over experimental conditions.

- Random assignment of subjects to experimental and comparison groups eliminates systematic bias in group assignment. The odds of a difference between the experimental and comparison groups on the basis of chance can be calculated. They become very small for experiments with at least 30 subjects per group.

- Random assignment and random sampling both rely on a chance selection procedure, but their purposes differ. Random assignment involves placing predesignated subjects into two or more groups on the basis of chance; random sampling involves selecting subjects out of a larger population on the basis of chance. Matching cases in the experimental and comparison groups is a poor substitute for randomization because it is not possible to identify in advance all important variables to use for the match. However, matching can improve the comparability of groups when it is used to supplement randomization.

- Causal conclusions derived from experiments can be invalid due to selection bias, endogenous change, the effects of external events, cross-group contamination, or treatment misidentification. In true experiments, randomization should eliminate selection bias and bias due to endogenous change. External events, cross-group contamination, and treatment misidentification can threaten the validity of causal conclusions in both true experiments and quasi-experiments.

- Process analysis can be used in experiments to identify how the treatment had (or didn't have) its effect—a matter of particular concern in field experiments. Treatment misidentification is less likely when process analysis is used.

- The generalizability of experimental results declines if the study conditions are artificial and the experimental subjects are unique. Field experiments are likely to produce more generalizable results than experiments conducted in the laboratory.

- Causal conclusions can be considered externally valid if they apply to all the subgroups in a study. When causal conclusions do not apply to all the subgroups, they are not generalizable to corresponding subgroups in the population and are not externally valid. Causal conclusions can also be considered externally invalid when they occur only under the experimental conditions.

- Nonexperimental designs use statistical controls to reduce the risk of spuriousness. A variable is controlled when it is held constant so that the association between the independent and dependent variables can be assessed without being influenced by the control variable.

- Longitudinal designs are usually preferable to cross-sectional designs for establishing the time order of effects. Longitudinal designs vary even when the same persons are measured at different times, and depend on how the population of interest is defined and how frequently follow-up measurements are taken. Fixed-sample panel designs provide the strongest test for the time order of effects, but they can be difficult to carry out successfully because of their expense and the attrition and fatigue of subjects.

- Subject deception is common in laboratory experiments and poses unique ethical issues. Researchers must weigh the potential harm to subjects and debrief subjects who have been deceived. In field experiments, a common ethical problem is selective distribution of benefits. Random assignment may be the fairest way of allocating treatment when treatment openings are insufficient for all eligible individuals and when the efficacy of the treatment is unknown.

EXERCISES

1. Read the original article reporting one of the experiments described in this chapter. Critique the article, using as your guide the article review questions presented in Appendix B. Focus on the extent to which experimental conditions were controlled and the causal mechanism was identified. Did inadequate control over conditions or inadequate identification of the causal mechanism make you feel uncertain about the causal conclusions?

2. Design a laboratory experiment to determine whether alcohol consumption leads to increased violent attitudes or actions. Describe how your design incorporates the three components of experiments. Evaluate how well your design meets the criteria for identifying causality.

3. Select a true experiment, from the *Journal of Experimental and Social Psychology,* the *Journal of Personality and Social Psychology,* or sources suggested by your instructor. Diagram the experiment using the Exhibits 5.1 and 5.5 in this chapter as models. Discuss the extent to which experimental conditions were controlled and the causal mechanism was identified. How confident can you be in the causal conclusions from the study, based on review of the threats to internal validity discussed in this chapter: selection bias, endogenous change, external events, contamination, and treatment misidentification?

4. Repeat Exercise 3 with a quasi-experiment.

5. Critique the ethics of one of the articles from Exercise 3 or 4. What specific rules do you think should guide researchers' decisions about subject deception and the selective distribution of benefits?

DEVELOPING A RESEARCH PROPOSAL

1. Design a laboratory experiment to text one of your hypotheses from Chapter 5 or a related hypothesis. Describe the experimental design, commenting on each component of a true experiment. Specify clearly how the independent variable will be manipulated and how the dependent variable will be measured.

2. Assume that your experiment will be conducted on campus. Formulate recruitment and randomization procedures.

3. Discuss the extent to which each source of internal validity is a problem in the study. Propose procedures like process analysis to cope with these sources of invalidity.

4. How generalizable would you expect the study's findings to be? What can be done to increase generalizability?

5. Develop appropriate procedures for the protection of human subjects in your experiment, including a consent form. Give particular attention to any aspects of the study that are likely to raise ethical concerns.

WEB EXERCISES

1. Go to Sociosite at www.pscw.uva.nl/sociosite. Choose "Subject Areas." Choose "Crime" or "Criminology." Find an example of research that has been done using experimental methods. Explain the experiment. Choose at least five of the key terms listed at the end of this chapter that are relevant to and incorporated in the research experiment you have located on the Web. Explain how each of the five key terms you have chosen plays a role in the research example you have found on the Web.

2. Go to the Stanford Prison Experiment Web site at www.prisonexp.org. Read the information provided about the Stanford Prison Experiment.
   a. Write a brief essay on the study, including the purpose of the study, the type of experiment, the participant selection process, the problems encountered during the study, and the results.
   b. Go to the discussion questions provided on the Web site. Answer the questions listed. What conclusions do you make about the Stanford Prison Experiment?

SPSS EXERCISES

1. How do homicide offender characteristics influence length of sentence? You can test various hypotheses by comparing means across categories for the characteristics of interest using HOMICIDE.POR.
   a. Obtain frequency distributions for whether or not the defendant knew the victim (KNOWN), race of the defendant (RACE), and sex of the defendant (SEX).
   b. Pose at least three hypotheses about the relationship between homicide defendant characteristics and length of sentence.
   c. Test these hypotheses by comparing the mean sentence length in days received by defendants (PRITIME) between categories of the independent variables listed in Part a. Which of your hypotheses appear to be supported? What do you theorize the cause of these findings to be?

2. Do prior convictions influence the number of days to which homicide defendants are sentenced?
   a. Obtain a frequency distribution for the variable PRCONV (prior convictions). According to the data, do homicide defendants frequently have prior convictions? What do you hypothesize is the relationship between prior convictions and sentence length? Why?
   b. Compare the mean sentence length in days received by defendants against their number of prior convictions. For example, do defendants who had no prior convictions receive a shorter sentence length compared to those with at least one prior conviction? Do the data support your hypothesis? Do any of the categories deviate from what you hypothesized? Explain.
   c. Recode the PRCONV variable into a new dichotomous variable, measuring whether the homicide defendant had prior convictions or no prior convictions. If necessary, reword your hypothesis to reflect the dichotomous nature of the new variable.
   d. Test your hypothesis by comparing the mean sentence length in days received by defendants with prior convictions and those with no prior convictions. What conclusions do you make about the relationship between prior convictions and sentence length of homicide defendants?

Chapter 6

SURVEY RESEARCH

Despite over two decades of research, the magnitude of intimate-perpetrated violence against men and women is still frequently disputed. For many reasons, including the historical stigma attached to intimate partner violence (IPV), fear of retaliation from their perpetrators, and other safety concerns, estimating incidence rates of this violence has always been a difficult task. The most enduring source of statistical information about violent crime in the United States is the Uniform Crime Report (UCR) Program compiled by the Federal Bureau of Investigation (FBI). The UCR collects information about criminal incidents of violence that are reported to the police. However, using police reports to estimate incidence rates of violence between intimates and family members is problematic for several reasons. Perhaps foremost is the fact that a large percentage of these crimes are never reported to police. Based on comparisons with national survey data, it is estimated that only 40–50% of crimes become known to police, and the percentage may be much lower for crimes committed by intimates and other family members (Reiss & Roth, 1993). In addition, except for the crime of homicide, the current UCR program does not include information on the relationship between the victim and the offender.

Due to the weaknesses of the UCR program in estimating rates of violence within families, random sample surveys of the population are now being used as a social science tool for uncovering incidents of violence within families. However, as can be expected, surveys employing diverse methodologies and different definitions of violence result in tremendously diverse estimates. For example, studies show that the number of women who experience violence by an intimate partner annually range from 9.3 per 1,000 women (Bachman & Saltzman, 1995) to 116 per 1,000 women (Straus & Gelles, 1990). Further, the methodological differences among random survey methodologies often preclude any direct comparisons.

To increase our understanding of violent victimization, the National Institute of Justice and the Centers for Disease Control and Prevention cosponsored a national telephone survey called the National Violence Against Men and Women (NVAMW) Survey, conducted by the Center for Policy Research in 1995 (Tjaden & Thoennes, 2000). Respondents to the NVAMW Survey were asked about a number of health and safety issues, including physical assault they experienced as children by adult caretakers, physical assault they experienced as adults by any type of perpetrator, and forcible rape or stalking they experienced at any time in their life by any type of perpetrator. In this chapter, we will use this project along with the U.S. Justice Department's National Crime Victimization Survey (NCVS) to illustrate some key features of survey research. After an initial review of the reasons for using survey methods, we explain the major steps in questionnaire design and then consider the features of four types of surveys, highlighting the unique problems of each and suggesting possible solutions. Important ethical issues are discussed in the final section. By the chapter's end, you should be well on your way to becoming an informed consumer of survey reports and a knowledgeable developer of survey designs. In addition, you will become a more informed student of the methodological issues surrounding the measurement of violent victimization in the United States.

SURVEY RESEARCH IN THE SOCIAL SCIENCES

Survey research involves the collection of information from a sample of individuals through their responses to questions. In addition to social scientists, many newspaper editors, political pundits, and marketing gurus have turned to survey research because it is an efficient method for systematically collecting data from a broad spectrum of individuals and social settings. The results of surveys are broadcast daily on most network news programs. In fact, surveys have become such a vital part of our nation's social fabric that we cannot assess much of what we read in the newspaper or see on TV without having some understanding of this method of data collection (Converse, 1984).

Modern survey research methods were developed in the early and middle years of the 20th century (Lazarsfeld & Oberschall, 1965; Oberschall, 1972). Beginning in the 1920s, psychologists used surveys to test the abilities of students, employees, and army recruits. For their part, sociologists conducted a few ambitious attitude surveys of the general population, such as Emory S. Bogardus's study of race relations, which had a sample of 1,725 respondents (Converse, 1984). Industrial psychologists began to rely on surveys to study employee morale and other attitudes. Psychologist Paul F. Lazarsfeld studied consumers' reactions to particular products before moving into sociology and becoming one of the discipline's leading survey proponents (Converse, 1984).

Political demands also stimulated the growth of survey research. Professional polling became a regular fixture after the 1936 presidential election. Professional polling firms such as the one operated by George Gallup correctly predicted that President Franklin Delano Roosevelt would win reelection, whereas the poorly designed *Literary Digest* poll led to an infamous forecast that challenger Alfred M. Landon would win (see Chapter 4). The U.S. Bureau of the Census began to supplement its 10-year census with more frequent surveys of population samples to monitor respondents' income and other economic variables. And in 1973, the U.S. Department of Justice implemented the National Crime Survey to capture incidents of crime victimization not reported to police.

Since the early days of survey research, professional survey organizations have provided a base of support for social science researchers affiliated with universities. The development of electronic computers also aided the growth of survey research, allowing great increases in the speed and accuracy for processing and reporting data. Surveys soon became the most popular research method in the social sciences.

Attractive Features of Survey Research

Regardless of its scope, survey research owes its continuing popularity to three features: versatility, efficiency, and generalizability.

Versatility

The first and foremost reason for the popularity of survey methods is their versatility. Although a survey is not the ideal method for testing all hypotheses or learning about every social process, a well-designed survey can enhance our understanding of just about any social issue. In fact, there is hardly any topic of interest to social scientists that has not been studied at some time with survey methods. Politicians campaigning for election use surveys, as do businesses marketing a product, governments assessing community needs, agencies monitoring program effectiveness, and lawyers seeking to buttress claims of discrimination or select favorable juries.

Efficiency

Surveys also are popular because data can be collected from many people at relatively low cost and, depending on the survey design, relatively quickly. For the NVAMW Survey, Patricia Tjaden and Nancy Thoennes contracted with Schulman, Ronca, and Bucuvalas, Inc. (SRBI) to conduct the telephone survey, primarily because SRBI had conducted nationally representative sample surveys before on sensitive subject matters such as victimization. Surveys were conducted from November 1995 to May 1996 with an average cost of $30 per respondent. Large, mailed surveys are less expensive, at $10 to $15 per potential respondent, but the costs can increase greatly when intensive follow-up efforts are made. Surveys of the general population using personal interviews are much more expensive, with costs ranging from $100 per potential respondent for studies in a limited geographical area to $300 or more when lengthy travel or repeat visits are needed to connect with respondents (Floyd J. Fowler, personal communication, January 7, 1998, Center for Survey Research, University of Massachusetts–Boston; see also Dillman, 1982; Groves & Kahn, 1979). As you would expect, phone surveys are the quickest survey method, which accounts for their popularity in political polling.

Surveys are efficient research methods because many variables can be measured without substantially increasing the time or cost. Mailed questionnaires can include up to 10 pages of questions before respondents lose interest (and before more postage must be added). The maximum time limit for phone surveys seems to be about 45 minutes. In-person interviews can last much longer, taking more than an hour. For example, the 1991 General Social Survey (GSS) included 196 questions, many with multiple parts, and was 75 pages long.

Of course, the efficiency of the surveys can be attained only in a place with a reliable communications infrastructure (Labaw, 1980:xiii–xiv). A reliable postal service, required for mail surveys, has generally been available in the United States, and phone surveys can be effective in the United States because 95% of its households have phones (Czaja & Blair, 1995). Also important to efficiency are the services of the many survey organizations that provide the trained staff and the proper equipment for conducting high-quality surveys.

Generalizability

Survey methods lend themselves to probability sampling from large populations. Thus, survey research is very appealing when sample generalizability is a central research goal. In fact, survey research is often the only means available for developing a representative picture of the attitudes and characteristics of a large population.

Surveys also are the research method of choice when cross-population generalizability is a primary concern. They allow a range of social contexts and subgroups to be sampled, and the consistency of relationships can be examined across the various subgroups.

The Omnibus Survey

Most surveys are directed at a specific research question. In contrast, an **omnibus survey** covers a range of topics of interest to different social scientists. It has multiple sponsors or is designed to generate data useful to a broad segment of the social science community rather than answer one particular research question.

One of the most successful omnibus surveys is the General Social Survey (GSS) of the National Opinion Research Center at the University of Chicago. After taking a teaching position at Dartmouth College, James A. Davis, who worked at the National Opinion Research Center for 10 years, was dismayed to discover how difficult it was for faculty in small schools to obtain worthwhile survey data. Starting in 1972, the National Science Foundation agreed to fund the GSS as an annual, publicly available national survey on topics of general interest to sociologists. In 1992, the GSS changed to a biennial schedule.

Today, the GSS is administered every 2 years as a 90-minute interview to a probability sample of almost 3,000 Americans. It includes more than 500 questions about background characteristics and opinions, with an emphasis on social stratification, race relations, family issues, law and social control, and morale. It explores political views, work experiences, social ties, news sources, and views on law, health, and religion. Questions and topic areas are chosen by a board of overseers drawn from the best survey researchers.

The core of the GSS is the set of questions asked in every survey. Other questions are repeated only in alternating surveys, and some questions are added in single or multiyear supplements paid for by special grants. Since 1988, most of the questions have been asked in each survey, but many of them have been asked of only a randomly selected subset of respondents. This **split-ballot design** allows the inclusion of more questions without increasing the survey's cost. The split-ballot design also allows for experiments on the effect of question wording—different phrasings of the same question are included in the split-ballot subsets.

What is most remarkable about the GSS is its availability. The survey data sets are distributed at cost to any interested individual (only $95 for a single year's data set), and most universities obtain the GSS each year. The data are then available to faculty and students free of charge. By 1992, over 2,800 articles, scholarly papers, books, and dissertations had used GSS data. Many instructors use GSS data in methods, statistics, and other courses (Davis & Smith, 1992; National Opinion Research Center, 1992).

Although the NVAMW Survey is not exactly an omnibus survey, it was developed to obtain detailed information on a number of phenomena related to victimization. For example, because the Centers for Disease Control and Prevention was a co-sponsor of the survey, many questions were added to obtain detailed information on a respondent's history of health and injuries in addition to injuries resulting from victimization.

Most survey data sets sponsored by the federal government are made available for use by scholars through the Inter-University Consortium for Political and Social Research (ICPSR—more details about this are in Chapter 8). For example, all of the data sets produced by the Bureau of Justice Statistics, including the NCVS, the National Prison Survey, and many others, can be obtained almost instantaneously from the ICPSR Web (www.icpsr.umich.edu).

The deficiency of the omnibus approach is the limited depth that can be achieved in any one substantive area. In some years, the GSS avoids this problem by going into greater depth in one particular area. But the best way to get survey data about one particular topic is still the survey developed around that topic alone. The surveys we are going to highlight in this chapter were all developed to measure one topic, victimization.

QUESTIONNAIRE DEVELOPMENT AND ASSESSMENT

The **questionnaire** (or **interview schedule,** as it's often called in interview-based studies) is the central feature of the survey process. Without a well-designed questionnaire tailored to the study's purposes, survey researchers have little hope of achieving their research goals.

Questionnaire The survey instrument containing the questions for a self-administered survey.

Interview schedule The survey instrument containing the questions asked by the interviewer for an in-person interview or phone survey.

The correct design of a questionnaire varies with the specific survey method used and the other particulars of a survey project. There is no precise formula for a well-designed questionnaire. Nonetheless, some key principles should guide the design of any questionnaire, and some systematic procedures should be considered for refining it.

Maintain Consistent Focus

A survey (with the exception of an omnibus survey) should be guided by a clear conception of the research problem under investigation and the population to be sampled. Does the study seek to describe some phenomenon in detail, explain some behavior, or explore some type of social relationship? Until the research objective is clearly formulated, survey design cannot begin. Throughout the process of questionnaire design, this objective should be the primary basis for making decisions about what to include and exclude, and what to emphasize or treat in a cursory fashion. Moreover, the questionnaire should be viewed as an integrated whole, in which each section and every question serves a clear purpose related to the study's objective and is a complement to other sections or questions.

Surveys often include too many irrelevant questions and fail to include questions that the researchers realize later are crucial. One way to ensure that all possibly relevant questions are asked is to use questions suggested by prior research, theory, or experience, or by experts (including participants) who are knowledgeable about the setting under investigation. Of course, even the best researcher cannot anticipate every question that could be worthwhile, nor those that are worthless.

Build on Existing Instruments

When another researcher already has designed a set of questions to measure a key concept in your study, that existing set of questions can be called a survey instrument. If evidence from previous surveys indicates that these questions provide a good measure of the concept or behaviors you are interested in, then why reinvent the wheel? To measure incidents of physical assault, Tjaden and Thoennes (2000) modified an instrument that had already been widely used in the literature: the Conflict Tactics Scale (CTS)

Exhibit 6.1   Rape Screening Questions Used by the NVAMW Survey and by the NCVS
Survey

National Violence Against Men and Women (NVAMW) Survey

[For females only] *Regardless of how long ago it happened, has a man or boy ever made you have sex by using force or threatening to harm you or someone close to you? Just so there is no mistake, by sex we mean putting a penis in your vagina.*

[For males and females] *Has anyone, male or female, ever made you have oral sex by using force or threat of harm? Just so there is no mistake, by oral sex we mean that a man or boy put his penis in your mouth or someone, male or female, penetrated your vagina or anus with their mouth or tongue.*

[For males and females] *Has anyone ever made you have anal sex by using force or threat of harm? Just so there is no mistake, by anal sex we mean that a man or boy put his penis in your anus.*

[For males and females] *Has anyone, male or female, ever put fingers or objects in your vagina or anus against your will by using force or threats?*

[For males and females] *Has anyone, male or female, ever attempted to make you have vaginal, oral, or anal sex against your will, but intercourse or penetration did not occur?*

National Crime Victimization Survey (NCVS)

Incidents involving forced or unwanted sexual acts are often difficult to talk about. Have you been forced or coerced to engage in unwanted sexual activity by—
   a. Someone you didn't know before
   b. A casual acquaintance OR
   c. Someone you know well

(Straus, 1979). To measure incidents of rape and sexual victimization, Tjaden and Thoennes (2000) utilized questions that had already been used by Kilpatrick and his colleagues at the University of South Carolina in the National Women's Study (National Victim Center, 1992). As you can see in Exhibit 6.1, these questions were very specific in nature and covered all behaviors that are legally defined as rape or sexual assault in most states. In contrast, you will also see in Exhibit 6.1 that the screening questions used by the NCVS to uncover incidents of rape and sexual assault are not as specific about behavior.

Respondents to the NVAMW Survey who answered yes to any of these screening questions were asked many specific questions about the nature of the victimization, including information about the offender, injuries sustained, and reports to police. Respondents to the NCVS who answered yes to their screening questions were further queried, "Do you mean forced or coerced sexual intercourse?" Only if respondents answered yes to this question were they counted as rape victims; the others were classified as other sexual assault victims. In the end, both surveys purport to measure incidents of rape in the United States, but which methodology is most appropriate? In the next section, we will provide you with some specific guidelines for writing questions and you will see that the answer to this question is not so clear-cut.

QUESTION CONSTRUCTION

Asking people questions is the most common operation for measuring social variables, and probably the most versatile. In principle, survey questions can be a straightforward and efficient means of measuring individual characteristics, facts about events, levels of knowledge, and opinions of any sort. In practice, however, survey questions can result in misleading or inappropriate answers. All questions proposed for a survey must be screened carefully for their adherence to basic guidelines and then tested and revised until the researcher feels confident they will be clear to the intended respondents (Fowler, 1995). Some variables may prove to be inappropriate for measurement with any type of question. We have to recognize that memories and perceptions of the events we might like to ask about can be limited.

Structurally, questions on surveys generally fall into two categories: those with and those without explicit response choices. The **open-ended questions** are those without explicit response choices. This type of question is usually used only for explorative purposes when there is little knowledge about a particular topic and you want to uncover as much about it as possible without restricting responses. For example, if you are investigating the perceptions of residents regarding a new community policing program instituted in the neighborhood, open-ended questions such as the following one could be very informative:

```
"In your opinion, what have been the benefits of the community
policing program in your neighborhood?"
```

The information obtained from open-ended questions such as this could then be used as the basis for questions with fixed responses in future studies that evaluate the efficacy of community policing.

Open-ended questions are also excellent tools for obtaining respondents' interpretations in greater detail and can often illuminate flaws in other questions. A survey researcher can also try to understand what respondents mean by their responses after the fact by including additional open-ended questions in the survey. Adding such **interpretive questions** after key survey questions is always a good idea, but it is of utmost importance when the questions in a survey have not been pretested. An example from a study of people with motor-vehicle driving violations illustrates the importance of interpretive questions:

> When asked whether their emotional state affected their driving at all, respondents would reply that their emotions had very little effect on their driving habits. Then, when asked to describe the circumstances surrounding their last traffic violation, respondents typically replied, "I was mad at my girlfriend," or "I had a quarrel with my wife," or "We had a family quarrel," or "I was angry with my boss." (Labaw, 1980:71)

Were these respondents lying in response to the first question? Probably not. More likely, they simply didn't interpret their own behavior in terms of a general concept such as "emotional state." But their responses to the first question were likely to be misinterpreted without the further detail provided by answers to the second.

In summary, one strength of open-ended questions is the wealth of information they provide. This wealth of information, however, is exactly why many researchers do not use them. The verbatim text narratives obtained from open-ended questions take a great deal of time and energy to organize and summarize. In addition, many respondents may feel overwhelmed about writing a lengthy essay. If you want to ask a large number of open-ended questions, it is perhaps best to consider an in-person interview or phone interview instead of a questionnaire (both of which are discussed later in this chapter).

When respondents are offered explicit responses to choose from, this type of question is referred to as a **fixed-choice question.** For example, in the NVAMW Survey, respondents were asked:

```
Overall, would you say that personal safety in this country has
improved since you were a child, gotten worse since you were a
child, or stayed about the same?
```

□ Improved

□ Gotten worse

□ Stayed about the same

Most surveys of a large number of people primarily contain fixed-choice questions, which are easy to process with computers and analyze with statistics. With fixed-choice questions, respondents are also more likely to answer the question that researchers want them to answer. By including the response choices, the survey reduces ambiguity. However, fixed-choice questions can obscure what people really think unless the choices are carefully designed to match the range of all possible responses to the question.

Regardless of the format used for questions, there are several rules to follow and pitfalls to avoid that will maximize the validity of your survey instrument. We will highlight these in the next section.

Write Clear and Meaningful Questions

All hope for achieving measurement validity is lost unless survey questions are clear and convey the intended meaning to respondents. You may be thinking that you ask people questions all the time and have no trouble understanding the answers you receive, so it may seem that writing clear and meaningful questions would not be difficult. But consider just a few of the differences between everyday conversations and standardized surveys:

- Survey questions must be asked of many people, not one person.
- The same survey questions must be used with each person, not tailored to the specifics of a given conversation.
- Survey questions must be understood in the same way by people who differ in many ways.
- You will not be able to rephrase a survey question if someone doesn't understand it.
- Survey respondents don't know you and can't be expected to catch the nuances of expression that your friends would know.

These features make a survey very different from natural conversation and make question writing a challenging and important task for survey researchers.

Questions must be very clear and specific about what is being asked of respondents. Note the differences in specificity between the rape screening questions used by the

NVAMW Survey and the NCVS displayed in Exhibit 6.1. It is logical that these multiple, behaviorally specific questions will be associated with greater disclosure by survey respondents compared to the one question about sexual intercourse posed by the NCVS. In fact, results of the two surveys indicate that the NVAMW Survey uncovers about four times as many rapes as does the NCVS (Bachman, 2000).

Another powerful illustration of the effect of questions on responses comes from the redesign of the NCVS itself. The NCVS was implemented in 1972 to complement what was known about crime from police reporting data from the UCR. In the 1980s, the survey's sponsor, the Bureau of Justice Statistics (BJS), redesigned the screening instrument used by the NCVS to more accurately measure incidents of violent crime, particularly those perpetrated by known offenders such as intimates and other family members (Bachman & Taylor, 1994). Among the most important changes to the questionnaire were: (1) additional cues to help survey respondents recall incidents, (2) questions encouraging respondents to report victimizations that they themselves may not define as crimes, (3) more direct questions on rape and sexual assault, and (4) new questions to encourage disclosure of victimizations by nonstrangers.

Exhibit 6.2 displays the old screening questions of the NCVS along with the redesigned violent crime screen questions that were implemented into a small percentage of the total NCVS sample beginning in 1989; by 1992 the entire sample was asked these questions. As you can see, not only are there more questions in the redesigned instrument, but the questions also are much more behaviorally specific than those in the old questionnaire. In fact, note that the old questionnaire did not contain a specific question about rape. Prior to the redesign, only those respondents who said they were "attacked some other way" and who self-reported that attack as a rape were classified as rape victims.

In 1994, the BJS began publishing the results of the redesigned survey. Not surprisingly to survey methodologists, rates of violent crime such as rape, intimate perpetrated assault, and other family violence increased dramatically. Exhibit 6.3 displays the rate changes for various types of violent crime against men and women. Do these dramatic increases from 1991 to 1992 actually reflect increases in victimizations? Obviously not. The increase is due primarily to the new screening questionnaire. The more specific questions increased the extent to which respondents disclosed their victimizations. As you might imagine, BJS had to educate the media and public about this methodology before these rates were released, to avoid headlines such as "The Justice Department Finds Rates of Family Violence Skyrocketing."

In addition to writing clear and meaningful questions, there are several other rules to follow and pitfalls to avoid that we will highlight in the next section.

Avoid Confusing Phrasing

Good grammar is a basic requirement for clear questions. Clearly and simply phrased questions are most likely to have the same meaning for different respondents. So be brief and to the point.

Avoid Vagueness

Virtually all questions about behavior and feelings will be more reliable if they refer to specific times or events (Turner & Martin, 1984:300). Without a **reference period,**

Exhibit 6.2   Comparison of the Redesigned and Old Screener Questions Used by the National Crime Victimization Survey

Screener questions for violent crimes
New (beginning January 1992)

1. Has anyone attacked or threatened you in any of these ways—
   a. With any weapon, for instance, a gun or knife—
   b. With anything like a baseball bat, frying pan, scissors, or stick—
   c. By something thrown, such as a rock or bottle—
   d. Include any grabbing, punching, or choking,
   e. Any rape, attempted rape, or other type of sexual assault—
   f. Any face to face threats—
      OR
   g. Any attack or threat or use of force by anyone at all? Please mention it even if you were not certain it was a crime.
2. Incidents involving forced or unwanted sexual acts are often difficult to talk about. Have you been forced or coerced to engage in unwanted sexual activity by—
   a. Someone you didn't know before
   b. A casual acquaintance OR
   c. Someone you know well.

Old (1972–1992)

1. Did anyone take something directly from you by using force, such as by a stickup, mugging, or threat?
2. Did anyone TRY to rob you by using force or threatening to harm you?
3. Did anyone beat you up, attack you, or hit you with something, such as a rock or bottle?
4. Were you knifed, shot at, or attacked with some other weapon by anyone at all?
5. Did anyone THREATEN to beat you up or THREATEN you with a knife, gun, or some other weapon, NOT including telephone threats?
6. Did anyone TRY to attack you in some other way?
*During 1992 half of the sampled households responded to the old questionnaire, and half to the redesigned survey.

Screener questions for all types of crimes
New

1. Were you attacked or threatened OR did you have something stolen from you—
   a. At home including the porch or yard—
   b. At or near a friend's relative's, or neighbor's home—
   c. At work or school—
   d. In place such as a storage shed or laundry room a shopping mall, restaurant, bank or airport—
   e. While riding in any vehicle—
   f. On the street or in a parking lot—
   g. At such places as a party, theater, gym, picnic area, bowling lanes, or while fishing or hunting.
      OR
   h. Did anyone ATTEMPT to attack or attempt to steal anything belonging to you from any of these places?
2. People often don't think of incidents committed by someone they know. Did you have something stolen from you OR were you attacked or threatened by—
   a. Someone at work or school—
   b. A neighbor or friend—
   c. A relative or family member—
   d. Any other person you've met or known?
3. Did you call the police to report something that happened to YOU which you thought was a crime?
4. Did anything happen to you which you thought was a crime, but did NOT report to the police?

Old

1. Was anything stolen from you while you were away from home, for instance, at work, in a theater or restaurant, or while traveling?
2. Did you call the police to report something that happened to YOU that you thought was a crime?
3. Did anything happen to YOU that you thought was a crime, but did NOT report to the police?

Exhibit 6.3 Comparison of Violent Crime Rates per 1,000 Males and Females by Victim-Offender Relationship Obtained by the Redesigned Screener and the Older Screener of the NCVS

Relationship	Female Rate	Male Rate
Older Questionnaire		
Intimate	5.4	.5
Other relative	1.1	.7
Acquaintance/friend	7.6	13.0
Stranger	5.4	12.2
Redesigned Questionnaire		
Intimate	9.3	1.4
Other relative	2.8	1.2
Acquaintance/friend	12.9	17.2
Stranger	7.4	19.0

Source: R. Bachman & L. Saltzman. 1995. *Violence Against Women: Estimates from the Redesigned Survey (NCJ-154348)*, Appendix Table. Washington, DC: Bureau of Journal Statistics, U.S. Department of Labor.

a researcher will not know how to interpret an answer. For example, the question "How often do you carry a method of self-protection such as pepper spray?" will produce answers that have no common reference period and can therefore not be reliably compared to answers from other respondents. A more specific way to ask the question is "In the last month, how many days did you carry a method of self-protection such as pepper spray?"

In general, research shows that the longer the reference period, the greater the underreporting of a given behavior (Cantor, 1984, 1985; Kobelarcik, Alexander, Singh, & Shapiro, 1983). For example, one survey asked, "During the past 12 months, about how many times did you see or talk to a medical doctor?" When official records were checked, respondents forgot about 60% of their doctor visits (Goleman, 1993b:C11). In general, when information about mundane or day-to-day activities are solicited, reference periods should be no longer than "in the past month." However, when rare events are being measured, such as experiences with victimizations, "the last 6 months," as utilized by the NVAMW Survey, or "the past 12 months," as used by the NCVS, are both acceptable.

Avoid Negatives and Double Negatives

Picture yourself answering the following question: "Do you disagree that juveniles should not be tried as adults if they commit murder?" It probably took a long time for you to figure out if you would actually agree or disagree with this statement, because it is written as a **double-negative question.** For example, if you think juveniles who commit murder should be tried as adults, you would actually agree with this statement. Even questions that are written with a single negative are usually difficult to answer. For example, suppose you were asked to respond to "I can't stop thinking about the terrorist attacks on 9-11" using a five-point response set of "very rarely" to "very often." A person who marks "very rarely" is actually saying "I very rarely can't stop thinking about the incident at

Columbine High School." Confusing, isn't it? Even the most experienced survey researchers can unintentionally make this mistake, perhaps while trying to avoid some other wording problem. For instance, in a survey commissioned by the American Jewish Committee, the Roper polling organization wrote a question about the Holocaust that was carefully worded to be neutral and value-free: "Does it seem possible or does it seem impossible to you that the Nazi extermination of the Jews never happened?" Among a representative sample of adult Americans, 22% answered it was possible the extermination never happened (Kifner, 1994:A12). Many Jewish leaders and politicians were stunned, wondering how one in five Americans could be so misinformed. But a careful reading of the question reveals how confusing it is: Choosing "possible," the seemingly positive response, means that you don't believe the Holocaust happened. In fact, the Gallup organization then rephrased the question to avoid the double negative, giving a brief definition of the Holocaust and then asking, "Do you doubt that the Holocaust actually happened or not?" Only 9% responded that they doubted it happened. When a wider range of response choices was given, only 2.9% said that the Holocaust "definitely" or "probably" did not happen. This should convince you that it is best to avoid negative statements altogether. If you feel you must use a negative in a statement, be certain it stands out with boldface type or italics so that it is clear exactly what you are asking.

Avoid Double-Barreled Questions

When a question is really asking more than one question it is called a **double-barreled question.** For example, the statement, "I believe we should stop spending so much money building prisons and put it into building more schools," is really asking respondents two different questions. Some respondents may believe we should stop building so many prisons but may not want the revenue to go into building more schools. Double-barreled questions can also show up in the response categories. For example, the item below is really asking two questions and would be better stated as such:

```
Do you know anyone who has ever used cocaine?

___Yes ___No ___I have used cocaine
```

Additional Guidelines for Fixed-Response Questions

Creating questions that are clear and meaningful is only half of the formula to creating a good survey instrument. The choices you provide respondents in fixed-choice questions are also important. In this section, we provide you with several rules that will help to ensure that the response choices you provide to your questions will also be clear and concise.

Response Choices Should Be Mutually Exclusive

When you want respondents to make only one choice, the fixed-response categories must not overlap. For example, if you were interested in the ways foot patrol officers spent their time while working, you might ask the following question:

On average, how much time do you spend on the job each week taking care of traffic violations?

☐ ____ Less than 1 hour

☐ ____ 1-3 hours

☐ ____ 3-6 hours

☐ ____ 6-10 hours

☐ ____ 10 hours or more

The choices provided for respondents in this question are not **mutually exclusive responses,** because they overlap. Which choice would an officer select if he or she spent an hour a week on traffic violations? Choices that are mutually exclusive would look like this:

____ Less than 1 hour

____ 2-3 hours

____ 4-6 hours

____ 7-10 hours

____ 11 hours or more

Make the Response Categories Exhaustive

In addition to mutual exclusivity, fixed-response categories must also allow all respondents to select an option. Consider the same research question about foot patrol officers. Suppose we asked a question such as this:

In what activity do you spend the most time in an average week on the job?

____ Traffic violations

____ Disturbance-related issues

____ Felony arrests

____ Misdemeanor arrests

Regardless of how exhaustive we think the response categories are, there must always be an option for respondents who require another choice. Response categories can easily be made **exhaustive** if respondents are provided with a choice labeled:

____ Other, please specify:_____

Note, however, that "Other" should be used only after you have included all options that you believe to be relevant. Otherwise, a large percentage of respondents will select the "Other" category and you will have to spend time coding their responses.

Utilize Likert-Type Response Categories

Likert-type responses generally ask respondents to indicate the extent to which they agree or disagree with statements. Why the name? Well, this format is generally believed to have been developed by Rensis Likert back in the 1930s. Likert-type response categories list choices for respondents to select their level of agreement with a statement and may look something like this:

```
I think "three-strikes" laws that increase penalties for individ-
uals convicted of three or more felonies will help to decrease the
crime rate.
```

```
1                        2                   3                   4
Strongly                 Agree               Disagree            Strongly
Agree                                                            Disagree
```

Minimize Fence-Sitting and Floating

Two related problems in question writing stem from the respondent's desire to choose an acceptable or socially desirable answer. There is no uniformly correct solution to these problems, so you must carefully select an alternative.

Fence-sitters are people who see themselves as neutral in their attitudes toward a particular issue. If you are truly interested in those who do not have strong feelings on an issue, one alternative is to provide a neutral or undecided response option. The disadvantage to these options is that they may encourage some respondents to take the easy way out rather than really thinking about their feelings. They may also provide an out for respondents who don't want to reveal how they truly feel about an issue. On the other hand, not providing respondents who really have no opinion on an issue with an option such as "undecided" can be very frustrating and may encourage them to leave the item blank. Whatever you decide, it is generally a good idea to provide respondents with instructions that ask them to "select the choice in each item that most closely reflects your opinion." This should help make all respondents feel more comfortable about their answers, particularly those who only slightly feel one way or the other.

Floaters are respondents who choose a substantive answer even when they don't know anything about a particular question. For example, research has shown that a third of the public will provide an opinion on a proposed law they know nothing about if they are not provided with a "don't know" option (Schuman & Presser, 1981). Of course, providing a "don't know" option has the same disadvantage as providing a neutral response option; its inclusion leads some people who do have an opinion to take the easy way out and choose "don't know."

If you are really interested in informed opinions about an issue, it is best to provide detailed information about that issue when asking a question. For example, let's say we were interested in attitudes about the treatment of juvenile offenders by the criminal justice system. Suppose we asked respondents to provide their opinion to the following statement: "The Juvenile Justice Bill before Congress will help reduce crime committed by juveniles." Do you know what the Juvenile Justice Bill is? If we did not provide a "don't know" option, respondents who knew nothing about the Juvenile Justice Bill would be forced to select a response that would not be meaningful and may bias the results of the entire survey. Instead of a "don't know" option, another way to handle the problem is to provide details of the issue you are interested in. For example, you could tell respondents that one component of the bill encourages states to adjudicate all juvenile homicide offenders 13 years of age or older as adults and then ask respondents their opinion about this particular issue. If you are truly interested in the extent to which respondents have knowledge about a particular issue and you want to include a "don't know" response, it should be set apart from the other choices so that respondents don't mistake it as a neutral or undecided choice. Of course, as with all questions, there should be clear instructions about what the response options actually mean. For example, if you wanted to examine citizens' knowledge and opinion about the Independent Counsel statute, you could ask:

Instructions: For each statement, check the box that best indicates your agreement about the statement. If you do not have enough information about a statement to determine your level of agreement, leave the boxes blank and put an X on the diamond next to "Don't Know."

☐ I think the Independent Counsel Law should remain as it is.

☐ Strongly Agree

☐ Agree

☐ Disagree

☐ Strongly Disagree

☐ Don't Know

Utilize Filter Questions

The use of filter questions is important to ensure that questions are asked only of relevant respondents. For example, if you are interested in the utilization of police services by robbery victims, you would first need to establish victimization with a **filter question.** These filter questions create **skip patterns.** For example, respondents who answer no to one question are directed to skip ahead to another question, but respondents who answer yes go on to the **contingent question** or questions. Skip patterns should be indicated clearly with arrows or other directions in the questionnaire, as demonstrated in Exhibit 6.4.

Single or Multiple Questions?

Measuring variables with single questions is very popular. Public opinion polls based on answers to single questions are reported frequently in newspaper articles and TV newscasts: "Do you favor or oppose U.S. policy in . . . ?" "If you had to vote today, for which candidate would you vote?" The primary problem with using a single question is that if respondents misunderstand the question or have some other problem with the phrasing, there is no way to tell. Single questions are prone to this **idiosyncratic variation,** which occurs when individuals' responses vary because of their reactions to particular words or ideas in the question. Differences in respondents' backgrounds, knowledge, and beliefs almost guarantee that they will understand the same question differently. If some respondents do not know some of the words in a question, we will not know what the respondents' answers mean—if they answer at all. If a question is too complex, respondents may focus on different parts of the question. If prior experiences or culturally biased orientations lead different groups to interpret questions differently, answers will not have a consistent meaning.

Exhibit 6.4   Filter Questions and Skip Patterns

14. In the past 6 months, has anyone taken something from you by force or the threat of force?
    ❏ Yes (If yes, please answer question 15 through 16)
    ❏ No (If no, please skip to question 17)

15. What was the approximate monetary value of the items taken?
    ❏ Under $50
    ❏ $51 to $99
    ❏ $100 to $299
    ❏ $300 to $500
    ❏ Over $500

16. Was the incident reported to police?
    ❏ Yes
    ❏ No

17. How fearful are you of walking alone at night in your neighborhood?
    ❏ Extremely Afraid   ❏ Afraid   ❏ Unafraid
    ❏ Extremely Unafraid

If just one question is used to measure a variable, the researcher may not realize respondents had trouble with a particular word or phrase in the question. Although writing carefully worded questions will help reduce idiosyncratic variation, the best option is to devise multiple rather than single questions to measure concepts.

When several questions are used to measure one concept, the responses may be combined by taking the sum or average of the responses. A composite measure based on this type of sum or average is called an **index** or **scale.** The idea is that idiosyncratic variation in response to single questions will average out, so the main influence on the combined measure will be the concept focused on by the questions. In addition, the index can be considered a more complete measure of the concept than can any one of the component questions.

Creating an index, however, is not just a matter of writing a few questions that seem to focus on one concept. Questions that seem to you to measure a common concept might seem to respondents to concern several different issues. The only way to know that a given set of questions does, in fact, form an index is to administer the questions to people similar to those you plan to study. If a common concept is being measured, people's responses to the different questions should display some consistency. Special statistics called **reliability measures** help researchers decide whether responses are consistent. Most respondent attitudes are complex and consist of many elements.

Be aware of response sets when constructing an index measuring attitudes. For example, some people tend to agree with almost everything asked of them, whereas others tend to disagree. Still others are prone to answer neutrally to everything if given the option. To decrease the likelihood of this happening, it is a good idea to make some statements favorable to a particular attitude and some unfavorable. In this way, respondents are forced to be more careful in their responses to individual items. Exhibit 6.5 displays a hypothetical set of questions designed to solicit respondent's attitudes toward police in their community.

Exhibit 6.5   Items in an "Attitude Toward Police" Index

1. I think police officers are generally fair to all people regardless of their race or ethnicity.
   ____ Strongly Agree   ____ Agree   ____ Disagree   ____ Strongly Disagree

2. Police officers are given too much freedom to stop and frisk community residents.
   ____ Strongly Agree   ____ Agree   ____ Disagree   ____ Strongly Disagree

3. I think if someone resisted arrest, even a little, most police officers would become assaultive if they thought they could get away with it.
   ____ Strongly Agree   ____ Agree   ____ Disagree   ____ Strongly Disagree

4. Police officers put their lives on the line every day trying to make it safe for residents of this community.
   ____ Strongly Agree   ____ Agree   ____ Disagree   ____ Strongly Disagree

5. I think the majority of police officers have lied under oath at least once.
   ____ Strongly Agree   ____ Agree   ____ Disagree   ____ Strongly Disagree

6. The majority of police officers are honest and fair.
   ____ Strongly Agree   ____ Agree   ____ Disagree   ____ Strongly Disagree

When scoring indexes and scales are made up of both favorable and unfavorable statements, you must remember to reverse code the unfavorable items. For example, marking "strongly agree" to the first item in Exhibit 6.5 should not be scored the same as a "strongly agree" response to the second item.

Due to the popularity of survey research, indexes already have been developed to measure many concepts, and some of these indexes have proved to be reliable in a range of studies. It usually is much better to use these indexes to measure concepts than to try to devise new questions to form a new index. As noted earlier in this chapter, the use of a preexisting measure both simplifies the work involved in designing a study and facilitates a comparison of findings to those obtained in previous studies.

One index available in the NCVS is designed to measure what is referred to in criminological literature as *routine activities*. To explain crime victimization, the Routine Activities Theory focuses on the circumstances in which crimes are committed rather than on the circumstances of the offender. According to Lawrence Cohen and Marcus Felson (1979), each criminal act requires the convergence of three elements: likely and motivated offenders, suitable targets, and an absence of capable guardians to prevent the would-be offender from committing the crime. Thus, the routine patterns of work, play, and leisure time affect the convergence in time and place of the motivated offenders, the suitable targets, and the absence of guardians. To measure the extent to which respondents engage in routine activities away from the home, the NCVS asks three questions that are displayed in Exhibit 6.6 These questions measure different types of activities people routinely engage in away from the home and, when combined, create a better measure of an individual's activities away from the home than would a single question.

Exhibit 6.6   Example of an Index: NCVS Questions Used to Make Up an Index of Routine
Activities Away from the Home

Before we get to the crime questions, I'd like to ask you about
some of YOUR usual activities. We have found that people with
different lifestyles may be more or less likely to become victims
of crime.

30. On average, during the last 6 months, that is since _____, 20___,
    how often have YOU gone shopping? For example, at drug, clothing,
    grocery, hardware, and convenience stores. (Read answer categories
    until respondent answers yes.)
    ____ Almost every day (or more frequently)
    ____ At least once a week
    ____ At least once a month
    ____ Less often
    ____ Never
    ____ Don't know

31. On average, during the last 6 months, how often have you spent the
    evening out away from home for work, school, or entertainment?
    (Read answer categories until respondent answers yes.)
    ____ Almost every day (or more frequently)
    ____ At least once a week
    ____ At least once a month
    ____ Less often
    ____ Never
    ____ Don't know

32. On average, during the last 6 months, how often have you ridden
    public transportation? Do not include school buses. (Read answer
    categories until respondent answers yes.)
    ____ Almost every day (or more frequently)
    ____ At least once a week
    ____ At least once a month
    ____ Less often
    ____ Never
    ____ Don't know

Another example of an index is that used to measure student perceptions of tolerance
for substance abuse on college campuses (Core Institute, 1994). An excerpt from this is
shown in Exhibit 6.7. Alone, no single question would be sufficient to capture the overall
tolerance of substance abuse on campus. A person's total response to these questions is
likely to provide a more accurate indication of tolerance for substance abuse than would a
single, general question such as "Do students on this campus feel that drinking or using
drugs is OK?"

The advantages of using indexes rather than single questions to measure important
concepts are very clear. Surveys often include sets of multiple-item questions, and the
following are four cautions to consider:

Exhibit 6.7 Example of an Index: Excerpt from the Index of Student Tolerance of Substance Abuse

37. During the past 30 days, to what extent have you engaged in any of the following behaviors?
(mark one for each line)

Response options (right to left): Zero times, One time, Two times, 3–5 times, 6–9 times, 10 or more times

a. Refused an offer of alcohol or other drugs . . . . ○○○○○○

b. Bragged about your alcohol or other drug use . . . . ○○○○○○

c. Heard someone else brag about his/her alcohol or other drug use ○○○○○○

d. Carried a weapon such as a gun, knife, etc. (do not count hunting situations or weapons used as part of your job) . . . . . . ○○○○○○

e. Experienced peer pressure to drink or use drugs . . . . ○○○○○○

f. Held a drink to have people stop bothering you about why you weren't drinking. . . . . ○○○○○○

g. Thought a sexual partner was not attractive because he/she was drunk . . . . ○○○○○○

h. Told a sexual partner that he/she was not attractive because he/she was drunk. . . . . ○○○○○○

Source: Core Institute, 1994.

Our presupposition that each component question is indeed measuring the same concept may be mistaken. Although we may include multiple questions in a survey to measure one concept, we may find that answers to the questions are not related to one another, and so the index cannot be created. Alternatively, we may find that answers to just a few of the questions are not related to the answers given to most of the other questions. We may therefore decide to discard these particular questions before computing the average that comprises the index.

Combining responses to specific questions can obscure important differences in meaning among the questions. One of the authors' research projects on the impact of AIDS prevention education in shelters for the homeless provides an example. In this research, Schutt asked a series of questions to ascertain respondents' knowledge about HIV risk factors and about methods of preventing exposure to those risk factors. After combining the responses into an overall knowledge index, he was surprised to find that the knowledge index scores were no higher in a shelter with an AIDS education program than in a shelter without such a program. Further analysis, however, showed that respondents in the shelter with an AIDS education program were more knowledgeable than the other respondents about the specific ways to prevent AIDS, which were in fact the primary focus of the program. Combining the

Exhibit 6.8   Life-Events Indicators in the 1982 State Stress Index (SSI)

Economic Stressors

Business failures per 1 million population, 1982
Unemployment claims per 100K adults age 18 and over, 1982
Striking workers per 100K adults age 18 and over, 1981
Bankruptcy cases per 100K population, 1982
Mortgage foreclosures per 100K population, 1982

Family Stressors

Divorces per 1K population, 1982
Abortions per 100K population, 1982
Illegitimate births per 100K population age 14 and over, 1982
Infant deaths per 1K live births, 1982
Fetal deaths per 1K live births, 1982

Community Stressors

Disaster assistance per 100K population, 1982
Percentage residing in state less than 5 years, 1980
New housing units per 1K population, 1982
New welfare recipients per 100K population, 1982
High school dropouts per 100K population, 1982

Source: Linsky, Bachman, and Straus, 1995.

responses to these questions with the other responses about general knowledge of HIV risk factors obscured this important finding (Schutt, Gunston, & O'Brien, 1992).

The questions in an index may cluster together in subsets. All the questions may measure the intended concept, but we may conclude that the concept actually has several different aspects. A multidimensional index has then been obtained. This conclusion can in turn help us refine our understanding of the original concept. For example, over two decades of work have culminated in the development of a multidimensional index of stress at the state level. Research has found that this index, the State Stress Index (SSI), is related to a number of aggressive behaviors also measured at the state level such as state rates of homicide and rape (Linsky, Bachman, & Straus, 1995). The SSI is based on the life-events theory of stress, which holds that the more events such as divorce or the movement to a new community individuals must adapt to, the greater risk they have of not being able to cope. The administration and scoring of life-event measures of stressors experienced by an individual are straightforward. Respondents are asked to indicate events on the list they experienced in the recent past. The number of life events is then added to provide a score that indicates the extent to which the respondent has experienced these stressful events. The SSI is a translation of the life-events approach from the original individual level to the macro or societal level. The basic strategy was to measure the rate at which these events occurred in each state to evaluate the stressfulness of living in each state. What developed was a multidimensional index composed of 15 indicators that statistically fell into three categories: economic stressors, family stressors, and community stressors. The specific variables used to make up the SSI are presented in Exhibit 6.8.

Exhibit 6.9   Question on Income from the NVAMW Survey

Including income from all sources, such as work, child support, and AFDC, how much income did you personally receive in 1995 before taxes? Stop me when I get to the category that applies.
Was it . . .

01 Less than $5,000
02 $5001, to $10,000
03 $10,001 to $15,000
04 $15,001 to $20,000
05 $20,001 to $25,000
06 $25,001 to $35,000
07 $35,001 to $50,000
08 $50,001 to $80,000
09 $80,001 to $100,000
10 Over $100,001
11 (Volunteer) None
12 (Volunteer) Don't Know
13 (Volunteer) Refused

Source: Tjaden & Thoennes, 2000.

Sometimes particular questions are counted, or weighted, more than others in the calculation of the index. Some questions may be more central to the concept being measured than others, and so may be given greater weight in the index score. It is difficult to justify this approach without extensive testing, but some well-established indexes do involve differential weighting.

Demographic Questions

Almost all questionnaires include a section on demographic information such as sex, age, race/ethnicity, income, and religion. For many research studies, these questions are important independent variables. For example, research has shown that all four of these factors are related to the probability of victimization. Many researchers, however, include demographic questions that are not necessary for purposes of their research. Try to avoid this, particularly for questions on income because it makes the questionnaire more intrusive than necessary. In fact, many respondents feel that questions about their income invade their privacy. If you believe income is an essential variable for your study, providing fixed responses that include a range of values to select from is less intrusive than asking respondents for specific annual incomes. This format was utilized by the NVAMW Survey, as shown in Exhibit 6.9.

Care should also be taken when writing questions about race and ethnicity. Many people are justifiably sensitive to these questions. Even the U.S. Bureau of the Census has been struggling with appropriate categories to offer respondents. In fact, the bureau still utilizes two questions, one for race and one for respondent ethnicity (Hispanic/NonHispanic), which is obviously problematic. Most survey researchers now include questions such as the following:

Which of the following best describes your racial or ethnic
background? Please check one.

☐ Asian

☐ Black/African American

☐ White/Caucasian

☐ Hispanic (may be of any race)

☐ Native American

☐ Of Mixed Race/Ethnicity

☐ Other (Please specify:_____)

Deciding which categories to include remains difficult. Some researchers still prefer to exclude the Mixed category, because they believe most respondents will identify primarily with one race.

Questions on marital status can also be tricky to compose. The traditional categories of married, single, divorced, and widowed, still used by unsavvy researchers, can be interpreted very differently by respondents. Why? Well, isn't someone currently divorced also single? And what about someone not officially divorced but separated? To avoid confusing respondents, the U.S. Bureau of the Census adopted the following response categories: Married, Separated, Widowed, Divorced, and Never Married.

Because demographic questions are usually perceived as private by respondents, some researchers place them in a section at the end of the questionnaire with an introduction reassuring respondents that the information will remain confidential. However, when the information being gathered in the rest of the questionnaire is even more sensitive, such as violence respondents may have experienced at the hands of a family member or intimate partner, some researchers opt to keep demographic questions near the beginning of the questionnaire. For example, the NVAMW Survey asked demographic questions after the first section, which asked respondents about their general perceptions of fear and safety.

Don't Forget to Pretest!

Adhering to the preceding question-writing guidelines will go a long way toward producing a useful questionnaire. However, simply asking what appear to be clear questions does not ensure that people have a consistent understanding of what you are asking. You need some external feedback, and the more of it the better.

No questionnaire should be considered ready for use until it has been **pretested.** Try answering the questionnaire yourself, and then revise it. Try it out on some colleagues or other friends, and then revise it. Then select a small sample of individuals from the population you are studying or one very similar to it, and try out the questionnaire on them. Audiotape the test interviews for later review, or for a written questionnaire, include in the pretest version some space for individuals to add comments on each key question.

The NVAMW Survey was pretested in *four* different trials on a total of 107 respondents. Yes, four! The pretests were used to assess the effectiveness of the interview introduction, identify confusion and awkwardness in question wording and response categories, and evaluate the flow and length of the interview. Once the fourth pretest established that the instrument was workable, it was then fielded to replicate samples of 500, 1,000, or 2,000 completed interviews. This additional pretesting allowed Tjaden and Thoennes (2000) to determine whether they should retain, drop, or revise particular questions.

Another important form of feedback results from simply discussing the questionnaire content with others. Persons to consult should include other researchers, key figures in the locale or organization to be surveyed (such as elected representatives, company presidents, and community leaders), and some individuals from the population to be sampled. If you find you have to explain a particular question in detail, you probably need to rewrite it. Run your list of variables and specific questions by such figures whenever you have a chance. Reviewing the relevant literature to find results obtained with similar surveys and comparable questions is also an important step to take. Of course, you should have already conducted such a review before writing your questions!

Another increasingly popular form of feedback comes from guided discussions among potential respondents, called focus groups, to check for consistent understanding of terms and to identify the range of events or experiences about which people will be asked to report. By listening and observing the focus group discussions, researchers can validate their assumptions about what level of vocabulary is appropriate and what people are going to be reporting (Fowler, 1995).

Professional survey researchers have also developed a technique for evaluating questions called the **cognitive interview** (Fowler, 1995). Although the specifics vary, the basic approach is to ask people test questions, then probe with follow-up questions to learn how they understood the question and what their answers mean.

Review the distribution of responses to each question, listen to the audiotapes, or read all the comments, and then code what you heard or read to identify problems in question wording or delivery. Revise any questions that respondents do not seem to interpret as you had intended or that are not working well for other reasons.

To create a good questionnaire takes several drafts. By the time you have gone through just a couple of drafts, you may not be scanning the instrument as clearly as you think. A very honest illustration of this is provided by Don Dillman, the Director of the Social and Economic Sciences Research Center at Washington State University. His research team was about ready to mail a questionnaire with the following response categories:

What is your opinion?

Strongly Oppose	Oppose	Neither	Favor	Strongly Oppose

This Likert-type response format not only slipped by Dillman, but by his typist, a research assistant, and another person working on the project. He explains:

> By the time a would-be surveyor has reached the final draft, he or she is often scanning the questionnaire for errors but not absorbing the detail. . . . All of us were looking for other things, such as spacing, punctuation, and content. The uniform appearance of the response categories looked right to all of us. (Seltzer, 1996: p. 98)

A careful scrutiny of your questionnaire using the procedures outlined in this section will help you detect these and other problems.

ORGANIZATION OF THE QUESTIONNAIRE

Once the basic topics and specific variables for a questionnaire have been identified, they can be sorted into categories (which may become separate sections) and listed in tentative order. Throughout the question-writing process, the grouping of variables into sections and the ordering of questions within sections should be adjusted. These adjustments will in turn require changes in the specific questions, in an iterative process that leads to a polished, coherent questionnaire.

The first thing needed is a descriptive title for the questionnaire that indicates the overall topic. The title is essential because it sets the context for the entire survey. For example, the NCVS and the NVAMW Survey are both interested in measuring the magnitude of crime victimization in the United States. The NVAMW Survey, however, was presented as a survey interested in a number of personal safety–related issues, including tactics used in conflict resolution. The NCVS is named a crime survey and is a survey interested in obtaining information only about crimes. Unfortunately, some survey participants still may not view assaults by intimates and other family members as criminal acts.

Even though many of the behaviors conveyed in the screening instruments (e.g., kicking and punching) are the same for both surveys, the context in which these questions are asked must inevitably play a role in the candor respondents are willing to provide. The contextual message of crime may take precedence over the questions and may discourage respondents from reporting incidents they do not perceive as crimes. Lynch (1996) illuminates the importance of context by citing a study undertaken by BJS in 1975 when a fear-of-crime supplement was asked of a subsample of the NCVS prior to the screening interview. Reports of victimization in the subsample that received the fear of crime supplement increased significantly; this finding was attributed to a warm-up effect of the fear supplement, such that the additional questions about fear of crime stimulated recall of crime events.

In addition to the title, question order is important because this also can influence responses. Consider the issue of capital punishment. For nearly a decade after the 1976 Supreme Court case of *Gregg v. Georgia,* which made capital punishment constitutional under guided discretion statutes, proponents of the death penalty were quick to note public sentiment favoring the use of capital punishment. But refined public opinion polls reveal how this sentiment can change dramatically when respondents are given other choices. For example, a 1986 Gallup poll (Gallup, 1986) revealed that 70% of those surveyed approved of the death penalty for murder. However, when respondents were given the alternative punishment of life imprisonment without the possibility of parole, the support declined to 55%. This suggests that public opinion questions that simply ask whether the person approves of capital punishment for convicted murderers are a misleading indicator of the strength of support for the death penalty. As Paternoster (1991:30) explains:

> These questions, which have been asked since the 1930s, have formed the basis of a folklore that Americans mandate capital punishment. This folklore has informed the attitudes of both state legislatures and Supreme Court justices who are led by these opinion polls into believing that this represents "the will of the people." What Americans may be expressing, however, is a desire for protection against dangerous

criminals, not a desire for capital punishment. More sophisticated polling questions indicate that the public does not necessarily want to repay one life with another, but wants the murderer to be unable to offend again, and to ease the hardship and loss for those left behind.

A similar phenomenon has been observed with questions about abortion. When a sample of the general public was asked, "Do you think it should be possible for a pregnant woman to obtain a legal abortion if she is married and does not want any more children?" Of the respondents, 58% said yes. However, when this abortion question was preceded by one asking whether the respondent would allow abortion of a damaged fetus, only 40% said yes to the more permissive question. Clearly the first question altered the respondents' frame of reference, perhaps by making abortion as a simple way to avoid having more children seem frivolous compared to the problem of having a damaged fetus (Turner & Martin, 1984:135). The point to take away from these cases is that question order is extremely important. As Schuman and Presser acknowledge:

> Both examples illustrate the potential impact of question order on the respondents' answers. This potential is greatest when two or more questions concern the same issue or closely related issues so that asking one question affects reactions to the next question. The impact of question order also tends to be greatest for general summary-type questions (Schuman & Presser, 1981:23).

There is no real cure for this potential problem, although the split-ballot technique may help the problem to at least be identified when the question order is reversed on a subset of the questionnaires. What is most important is to be aware of the potential for problems due to question order and carefully evaluate the likelihood of their occurrence in any particular questionnaire. Those who report survey results should mention, at least in a footnote, the order in which key questions were asked when more than one such question was used (Labaw, 1980). Questionnaires should conform to several other organizational guidelines as well:

- Major topic divisions within the questionnaire should be organized in separate sections, and each section introduced with a brief statement. This helps respondents understand the organization of the questionnaire.
- Instructions should be used liberally to minimize respondent confusion. Instructions should explain how each type of question is to be answered (such as circling a number or writing a response) in a neutral way that isn't likely to influence responses. This type of instruction is particularly important with groups of questions that have standard answers laid out in a matrix format. The same set of response choices appear next to each question, because many respondents do not realize that they should circle one response on each line. Instructions also should route respondents through skip patterns.
- Instructions may also be used to clarify for respondents why some information is included in the questionnaire (such as the implicit instruction to skip a set-off box of lines that are "For coding purposes only").
- The questionnaire should look attractive, be easy to complete, and have substantial open space. Resist the temptation to cram as many questions as possible onto one

page. Response choices should be printed in a font or format and location different from the questions (such as in all capital letters down the middle of the page).

- Response choices should be designated by numbers to facilitate coding and data entry after the questionnaire is completed.

There were several sections in the NVAMW Survey, including sections on fear of violence and accommodation behavior, previous relationships, current partner (spouse, boy/girlfriend) characteristics, sexual victimization, physical victimization, stalking victimization, violence in current relationships, and threat victimization. Exhibit 6.10 presents the introduction and a portion of the section on stalking victimization given to female respondents. Even though this questionnaire was given over the phone by professional interviewers, notice the specific instructions provided throughout.

The **cover letter** for a mailed questionnaire and the introductory statement read by interviewers in telephone or in-person interviews are critical to the survey's success. Similar to the context set by the title of the survey, the initial statement of the cover letter sets the tone for the entire questionnaire. For example, the first thing interviewers said to respondents of the NVAMW Survey was, "Hello, I'm _____ from SRBI, the national research organization. We are conducting a national survey on personal safety for the Center for Policy Research, under a grant from the federal government." Notice that even though the survey's primary purpose was to uncover incidents of victimization, it was presented to respondents as a survey interested in issues of personal safety. This was done to increase the probability of respondents disclosing incidents of victimization even if they did not perceive them as crimes. Also note that the introductory statement disclosed the researcher's affiliation and the project sponsor. In addition, the purposes of the survey should also be briefly described and a contact number for those who wish to ask questions or register complaints should be included.

A carefully prepared cover letter or initial statement should increase the response rate and result in more honest and complete answers to the survey questions; a poorly prepared cover letter or initial statement can have the reverse effects. There is no opportunity to clarify misunderstandings.

The cover letter or introductory statement must have the following characteristics:

Credible. The letter should establish that the research is conducted by a researcher or organization the respondent is likely to accept as a credible, unbiased authority. Research conducted by government agencies, university personnel, and recognized research organizations (such as Gallup or RAND) is usually considered credible. On the other hand, a questionnaire from an animal rights group on the topic of animal rights will probably be viewed as biased.

Personalized. The cover letter should include a personalized salutation (not just "Dear Student"), refer to the respondent in the second person ("Your participation . . ."), and close with the researcher's signature.

Interesting. The statement should interest the respondent in the contents of the questionnaire. Never make the mistake of assuming that what interests you will also interest your respondents. Try to put yourself in their shoes before composing the statement, and then test your appeal with a variety of potential respondents.

Exhibit 6.10 Section of the NVAMW Survey on Stalking Victimizations Given to Female Respondents

SECTION H: STALKING VICTIMIZATION

H1. Now I'd like to ask you some questions about following or harassment you may have experienced on more than one occasion by strangers, friends, relatives, or even husbands and partners. Not including bill collectors, telephone solicitors or other sales people, has anyone, male or female, ever . . . MARK ALL THAT APPLY

01 Followed you or spied on you?

02 Sent you unsolicited letters or written correspondence?

03 Made unsolicited phone calls to you?

04 Stood outside your home, school, or workplace?

05 Showed up at places you were even though he or she had no business being there?

06 Left unwanted items for you to find?

07 Tried to communicate with you in other ways against your will?

08 Vandalized your property or destroyed something you loved?

09 (Volunteered) Don't Know	GO TO SECTION I
10 (Volunteered) Refused	GO TO SECTION I
11 (Volunteered) None	GO TO SECTION I

H2. If H1 = ANY OF 1-8 (RESPONDENT HAS BEEN STALKED) GO TO H3, ELSE GO TO SECTION I.

H3. Has anyone ever done any of these things to you on more than one occasion?

1 Yes	
2 No	GO TO SECTION I
3 (Volunteered) Don't Know	GO TO SECTION I
4 (Volunteered) Refused	GO TO SECTION I

H4. How many different people have ever done this to you on more than one occasion?

____ Number of people [RANGE IS 1-97]

98 (Volunteered) Don't Know	GO TO SECTION I
99 (Volunteered) Refused	GO TO SECTION I

H5. Was this person/these persons . . . MARK ALL THAT APPLY

01 Your current spouse?

02 An ex-spouse?

03 A male live-in partner?

04 A female live-in partner?

05 A relative?

06 Someone else you know?

07 A stranger?

08 (Volunteered) Don't Know

09 (Volunteered) Refused

Source: Tjaden & Thoennes, 2000.

Responsible. Reassure the respondent that the information you obtain will be treated confidentially, and include a phone number the respondent can use if her or she has questions or would like a summary of the final report. Point out that the respondent's participation is completely voluntary (Dillman, 1978:165–172). For example, in the NVAMW Survey, respondents were told, "I will be asking you about your personal experiences and opinions. You don't have to answer any questions you don't want to. All of your answers will be treated as strictly confidential. Your participation is completely voluntary, but very important to the study. You can confirm the authenticity of the survey by calling our 800 number and asking for the Women's Safety Survey Coordinator."

SURVEY DESIGNS

The five basic survey designs are the mailed survey, group-administered survey, phone survey, in-person survey, and electronic survey. Each survey has some unique advantages and disadvantages:

Manner of administration. The five survey designs differ in the manner in which the questionnaire is administered. Mailed, group, and electronic surveys are completed by the respondents themselves. During phone and in-person interviews, however, the researcher or a staff person asks the questions and records the respondent's answers.

Questionnaire structure. Survey designs also differ in the extent to which the content and order of questions are structured in advance by the researcher. Most mailed, group, phone, and electronic surveys are highly structured, fixing in advance the content and order of questions and response choices. Some of these types of surveys, particularly mailed surveys, may include some open-ended questions (respondents write in their answers rather than checking off one of several response choices). In-person interviews are often highly structured, but they may include many questions without fixed response choices. Moreover, some interviews may proceed from an interview guide rather than a fixed set of questions. In these relatively unstructured interviews, the interviewer covers the same topics with respondents but varies questions according to the respondent's answers to previous questions. Extra questions are added as needed to clarify or explore answers to the most important questions.

Setting. Most surveys are conducted in settings where only one respondent completes the survey at a time; most mail and electronic questionnaires and phone interviews are intended for completion by only one respondent. The same is usually true of in-person interviews, although sometimes researchers interview several family members at once. On the other hand, a variant of the standard survey is a questionnaire distributed simultaneously to a group of respondents, who complete the survey while the researcher (or assistant) waits. Students in classrooms are typically the group involved, although this type of group distribution also occurs in surveys of employees and members of voluntary groups.

Cost. As mentioned earlier, in-person interviews are the most expensive type of survey. Phone interviews are much less expensive, but surveying by mail is cheaper yet. Electronic surveys are now the least expensive method because there are no interviewer costs, no

Exhibit 6.11   Typical Features of the Four Survey Designs

Design	Setting	Manner of Administration	Questionnaire Structure
Mailed survey	Individual	Self	Mostly structured
Group survey	Group	Self	Structured
Phone survey	Individual	Professional	Structured
In-person interview	Individual	Professional	Structured or unstructured
Electronic survey	Individual	Self	Mostly structured

mailing costs, and, for many designs, almost no costs for data entry. Of course extra staff time and expertise is required to prepare an electronic questionnaire.

Exhibit 6.11 summarizes the typical features of the five different survey designs. Because of their different features, the five designs vary in the types of errors to which they are most prone and the situations in which they are most appropriate. The rest of this section focuses on the unique advantages and disadvantages of each design.

Mailed, Self-Administered Surveys

A **mailed (self-administered) survey** is conducted by mailing a questionnaire to respondents, who then administer the survey themselves. The central concern in this method of survey administration is maximizing the response rate. The final response rate is unlikely to be much above 80%, and almost surely will be below 70% unless procedures to maximize the response rate are precisely followed. A response rate below 60% is a disaster, and even a 70% response rate is not much more than minimally acceptable. It is hard to justify the representativeness of the sample if more than a third of those surveyed fail to respond.

Some ways to maximize the response rate (Fowler, 1988:99–106; Mangione, 1995:79–82; Miller, 1991:144) include the following:

- Make the questionnaire attractive, with plenty of white space.
- Use contingent questions and skip patterns infrequently. When they are necessary, guide respondents visually through the pattern.
- Make individual questions clear and understandable to all the respondents. No interviewers will be on hand to clarify the meaning of the questions or probe for additional details.
- Use no more than a few open-ended questions. Respondents are likely to be put off by the idea of having to write out answers.
- Include a personalized and professional cover letter. Using an altruistic appeal (informing respondents that their response will do some good) seems to produce a response rate 7% higher than indicating that respondents will receive something for their participation.
- Have a credible research sponsor. According to one investigation, a sponsor known to respondents may increase the rate of response by as much as 17%. The next most

credible sponsors are the state headquarters of an organization and then other people in a similar field. Publishing firms, college professors or students, and private associations elicit the lowest response rates.

- Write an identifying number on the questionnaire so you can determine the nonrespondents.
- A small incentive can help. Even a coupon or ticket worth $1 can be enough to increase the response rate.
- Include a stamped, self-addressed return envelope with the questionnaire.

Most important, use follow-up mailings to encourage initial nonrespondents to return a completed questionnaire. Don Dillman (1978) recommends a standard procedure for follow-up mailings:

1. Send a reminder postcard, thanking respondents and reminding nonrespondents, to all sample members 2 weeks after the initial mailing.

2. Send a replacement questionnaire with a new cover letter only to nonrespondents about 3 or 4 weeks after the initial mailing.

3. Send another replacement questionnaire with a new cover letter 8 weeks after the initial mailing by certified mail if possible (it's pretty expensive). If enough time and resources are available for telephone contacts or in-person visits for interviews, they will also help.

If Dillman's procedures are followed, and the guidelines for cover letters and questionnaire design are followed, the response rate is almost certain to approach 70%. One review of studies using Dillman's method to survey the general population indicates that the average response to a first mailing will be about 24%; the response rate will rise to 42% after the postcard follow-up, to 50% after the first replacement questionnaire, and to 72% after a second replacement questionnaire is sent by certified mail (Dillman, Christenson, Carpenter, & Brooks, 1974).

The response rate may be higher with particular populations surveyed on topics of interest to them, and it may be lower with surveys of populations that do not have much interest in the topic. When a survey has many nonrespondents, getting some ideas about who they are by comparing late respondents to early respondents can help to determine the likelihood of bias due to the low rate of response. If the early respondents are more educated or more interested in the topic of the questionnaire, the sample may be biased; if the respondents are not more educated or more interested than nonrespondents, the sample will be more credible.

Related to the threat of nonresponse in mailed surveys is the hazard of incomplete response. Some respondents may skip some questions or just stop answering questions at some point in the questionnaire. Fortunately, this problem does not often occur with well-designed questionnaires. Potential respondents who decide to participate in the survey will usually complete it. But there are many exceptions to this observation, since questions that are poorly written, too complex, or about sensitive personal issues simply turn off some respondents. Revising or eliminating such questions during the design phase should minimize the problem.

Group-Administered Surveys

A **group-administered survey** is completed by individual respondents assembled in a group. The response rate is not usually a concern in surveys that are distributed and collected in a group setting because most group members will participate. The difficulty with this method is that assembling a group is seldom feasible because it requires a captive audience. Individuals going about their daily activities are usually not amenable to group-administered surveys. With the exception of students, employees, members of the armed forces, and some institutionalized populations, most populations cannot be sampled in such a setting.

One issue of special concern with group-administered surveys is the possibility that respondents will feel coerced to participate and as a result will be less likely to answer questions honestly. Also, because administering a survey to a group requires approval of the group's administrators and this sponsorship is made quite obvious by the fact that the survey is conducted on the organization's premises, respondents may infer that the researcher is not at all independent of the sponsor. No complete solution to this problem exists, but it helps to make an introductory statement that emphasizes the researcher's independence and gives participants a chance to ask questions about the survey. The sponsor should also understand the need to keep a low profile and to allow the researcher both control over the data and autonomy in report writing.

Surveys by Telephone

In a **phone survey,** interviewers question respondents over the phone and then record respondents' answers. Phone interviewing has become a very popular method of conducting surveys in the United States because almost all families have phones. But two matters may undermine the validity of a phone survey—not reaching the proper sampling units and not getting enough complete responses to make the results generalizable.

Reaching Sampling Units

Today, drawing a random sample is easier than ever due to random digit dialing (Lavrakas, 1987). A machine calls random phone numbers within designated exchanges, regardless of whether the numbers are published. When the machine reaches an inappropriate household (such as a business in a survey directed to the general population), the phone number is simply replaced with another.

The NVAMW Survey collected a national probability sample of 8,000 English- and Spanish-speaking women and 8,000 English- and Spanish-speaking men 18 years of age and older residing in households throughout the United States through random digit dialing (RDD). The generation of the NVAMW Survey sample is described below:

The geographic frame for the sample was the fifty states and the District of Columbia. Within this geographic frame SRBI systematically selected household telephone bands and conducted a random digit dialing (RDD) sampling screen for gender and age eligible respondents. In households with more than one eligible respondent a designated respondent was randomly selected using the "most recent birthday method." If the interviewer encountered a language barrier, either with the person answering the phone or with the designated respondent, the interviewer thanked the person and terminated the call. If a case was designated as Spanish language, it was turned over to a Spanish-speaking interviewer.

However households are contacted, the interviewers must always ask a series of questions at the start of the survey to ensure that they are speaking to the appropriate member of the household. Exhibit 6.12 displays the beginning of the phone interview schedule utilized by the NVAMW Survey. This example shows how to distinguish appropriate and inappropriate households in a phone survey, so the interviewer is guided to the correct respondent.

Maximizing Response to Phone Surveys

Three issues require special attention in phone surveys. First, because people often are not home, multiple call-backs will be necessary for many sample members. The failure to call people back was one reason for the discrepancy between poll predictions and actual votes in the 1988 presidential race between George Bush and Michael Dukakis. Kohut (1988) found that if pollsters in one Gallup poll had stopped attempting to contact unavailable respondents after one call, a 6-percentage-point margin for Bush would have been replaced by a 2-point margin for Dukakis. Those with more money and education are more likely to be away from home, and more likely to vote Republican.

In addition, interviewers must be prepared for distractions if the respondent is interrupted by other household members. Sprinkling interesting questions throughout the questionnaire may help to maintain respondent interest. In general, rapport between the interviewer and the respondent is likely to be lower with phone surveys than in-person interviews, as respondents may tire and refuse to answer all the questions (Miller, 1991:166).

Phone surveys also must cope with difficulties due to the impersonal nature of phone contact. Visual aids cannot be used, so the interviewer must be able to verbally convey all information about response choices and skip patterns. With phone surveys, instructions for the interviewer must clarify how to ask each question, and the response choices must be short.

Careful interviewer training is essential for phone surveys. Below is a brief description of how SRBI interviewers were trained before conducting the NVAMW Survey:

Because of the complexity of the survey, only the most experienced SRBI interviewers worked on the survey. Before fielding the survey, interviewers received specialized training on the general principles of survey research and the requirements of the study at hand. Interviewers were also trained to recognize and respond appropriately to cues that the respondent may have been concerned about being overheard. Telephone numbers of local support services (e.g., domestic violence shelters, rape crisis hotlines, child protective services) were offered to respondents who disclosed current abuse or appeared in distress.

Procedures can be standardized more effectively, quality control maintained, and processing speed maximized when phone interviewers are assisted by computers. This

Exhibit 6.12   Phone Interview Procedures for Respondent Designation in the NVAMW Survey

CONTROL FORM

Respondent Number:

        ID   **1:1-6**

Interview Date:

        MO   **1:7-8**
        DAY   **1:9-10**
        YEAR   **1:11-12**

Telephone Number:

        PHONE   **1:13-22**

Interviewer Gender: 1 Male   2 Female

        IGENDER   **1:23**

Respondent Gender: 1 Male   2 Female

        RGENDER   **1:24**

Zip Code:

        ZIP   **1:25-29**

FIPS Code:

        FIPS   **1:30-34**

State Code:

01	Alabama		27	Montana
02	Alaska		28	Nebraska
03	Arizona		29	Nevada
04	Arkansas		30	New Hampshire
05	California		31	New Jersey
06	Colorado		32	New Mexico
07	Connecticut		33	New York
08	Delaware		34	North Carolina
09	District of Columbia		35	North Dakota
10	Florida		36	Ohio
11	Georgia		37	Oklahoma
12	Hawaii		38	Oregon
13	Idaho		39	Pennsylvania
14	Illinois		40	Rhode Island
15	Indiana		41	South Carolina
16	Iowa		42	South Dakota
17	Kansas		43	Tennessee
18	Kentucky		44	Texas
19	Louisiana		45	Utah
20	Maine		46	Vermont
21	Maryland		47	Virginia
22	Massachusetts		48	Washington
23	Michigan		49	West Virginia
24	Minnesota		50	Wisconsin
25	Mississippi		51	Wyoming
26	Missouri			

STATE   **1:35-36**

Region Code:

01	New England	06	ESC
02	Mid-Atlantic	07	WSC
03	ENC	08	Mountain
04	WNC	09	Pacific
05	South Atlantic		

REGION   **1:37-38**

Survey Wave:

1	Cf/m	4	Ff/m
2	Df/m	5	Af
3	Ef/m	6	Bf

WAVE   **1:39**

CF2   How many persons, age 18 and older, live in this household?
      [RANGE IS 0-20, 21=Don't know; 22=Refused]

PERS18   **1:40-41**

CF3   How many of these adults are:

A   Women [RANGE IS 0-99]
B   Men [RANGE IS 0-99]in household
C   Refused [1=Don't know/refused; O = Other]

WOMEN18   **1:42-43**
MEN18   **1:44-45**
REF18   **1:46-47**

Source: Tjaden and Thoennes, 2000.

computer-assisted telephone interview has become known as CATI, and most large surveys are now performed in this way. There are several advantages to using CATI, but perhaps the foremost advantage is that data collection and data entry can occur concurrently. Second, the CATI system has several machine edit features that help to minimize data entry error. For example, by automatically assigning single-punch fields of appropriate width for each data item in the questionnaire, the CATI system eliminates the possibility of over-punching and the possibility of including blanks as legitimate values. Third, by programming the skip patterns into its data entry program, the CATI system ensures that the aggregated database is comprehensive and accurate.

In summary, phone surveying is the best method to use for relatively short surveys of the general population. Response rates in phone surveys tend to be very high, often above 80%, because few individuals will hang up on a polite caller or refuse to stop answering questions (at least within the first 30 minutes or so). The NVAMW Survey obtained a response rate of 72% in the female survey and 69% in the male survey.

In-Person Interviews

What is unique to the **in-person interview,** compared to the other survey designs, is the face-to-face social interaction between interviewer and respondent. If money is no object, in-person interviewing is often the best survey design.

In-person interviewing has several advantages. Response rates are higher for this survey design than with any other, when potential respondents are approached by a courteous interviewer. For example, respondents for the NCVS actually stay in the sample for 3 years. The first of these surveys is performed in person. This is one reason the NCVS obtains a very high response rate of approximately 95%. In addition, in-person interviews can be much longer than mailed or phone surveys; the questionnaire can be complex, with both open-ended and closed-ended questions and frequent branching patterns; the order in which questions are read and answered can be controlled by the interviewer; the physical and social circumstances of the interview can be monitored; and respondents' interpretations of questions can be probed and clarified.

Researchers must be alert to some special hazards due to the presence of an interviewer. Respondents should experience the interview process as a personalized interaction with an interviewer who is very interested in the respondent's experiences and opinions. At the same time, however, every respondent should have the same interview experience and be asked the same questions in the same way by the same type of person, who reacts similarly to the answers. Therein lies the researcher's challenge: to plan an interview process that will be personal, engaging, consistent, and nonreactive and to hire interviewers who can carry out the plan. Without a personalized approach, the rate of response will be lower and answers will be less thoughtful and potentially less valid. Without a consistent approach, information obtained from different respondents will not be comparable because it is less reliable and less valid.

Balancing Rapport and Control

Adherence to some basic guidelines for interacting with respondents can help interviewers maintain an appropriate balance between personalization and standardization:

- Project a professional image in the interview, that of someone who is sympathetic to the respondent but nonetheless has a job to do.
- Establish rapport at the outset by explaining what the interview is about and how it will work and by reading the consent form. Ask the respondent if he or she has any questions or concerns, and respond to these honestly and fully. Emphasize that everything the respondent says is confidential.
- During the interview, ask questions at a close but not intimate distance. Stay focused on the respondent, and be certain your posture conveys interest. Maintain eye contact, respond with appropriate facial expressions, and speak in a conversational tone of voice.
- Be sure to maintain a consistent approach; deliver each question as written and in the same tone of voice. Listen empathically, but avoid self-expression or loaded reactions.
- Repeat questions if the respondent is confused. Use nondirective probes such as "Can you tell me more about that?" for open-ended questions.

As with phone interviewing, computers can be used to increase control of the in-person interview. In a computer-assisted personal interviewing (CAPI) project, interviewers carry a laptop computer programmed to display the interview questions and process the responses that the interviewer types in, as well as to check that these responses fall within the allowed ranges. Interviewers seem to like CAPI, and the data obtained are at least as good quality as a noncomputerized interview (Shepherd, Hill, Bristor, & Montalvan, 1996).

The presence of an interviewer may make it more difficult for respondents to give honest answers to questions about sensitive personal matters. For this reason, interviewers may hand respondents a separate, self-administered questionnaire containing the more sensitive questions. After answering these questions, the respondent then seals the separate questionnaire in an envelope so that the interviewer does not know the answers.

Although in-person interview procedures are typically designed with the expectation that the interview will involve only the interviewer and the respondent, one or more other household members are often within earshot. This is particularly problematic if you are asking respondents about issues related to other family members, such as victimizations by family members. Although the NVAMW Survey only interviewed one member of each household, the NCVS interviews all members of a selected household. Thus, all family members are asked the same set of screening questions regarding their victimization experiences with both known and unknown offenders. Even though respondents are instructed to reschedule a telephone or personal interview for a more convenient time (e.g., when others are not present), this situation may nevertheless prevent some respondents from disclosing incidents of violence to interviewers, particularly those incidents perpetrated by intimate partners within the household.

Maximizing Response to Interviews

Even if the right balance is struck between maintaining control over interviews and achieving good rapport with respondents, in-person interviews can still have a problem. Due to the difficulty of catching all the members of a sample, response rates may suffer.

Exhibit 6.13   Reasons for Nonresponse in Personal Interviews (1990 General Social Survey)

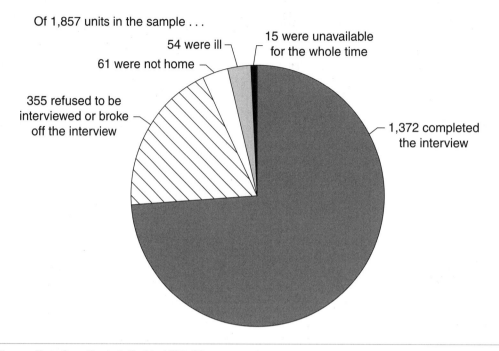

Of 1,857 units in the sample . . .

54 were ill

15 were unavailable for the whole time

61 were not home

355 refused to be interviewed or broke off the interview

1,372 completed the interview

Source: Data from Davis & Smith, 1992: 54.

Exhibit 6.13 displays the breakdown of nonrespondents to the 1990 General Social Survey. From the total original sample of 2,165, only 86% (1,857) were determined to be valid selections of dwelling units with potentially eligible respondents. Among these potentially eligible respondents, the response rate was 74%. The GSS is a well-designed survey using carefully trained and supervised interviewers, so this response rate indicates the difficulty of securing respondents from a sample of the general population even when everything is done "by the book."

Several factors affect the response rate in interview studies. Contact rates tend to be lower in city centers, in part because of difficulties in finding people at home and gaining access to high-rise apartments and in part because of interviewer reluctance to visit some areas at night, when people are more likely to be home (Fowler, 1988:45–60). Households with young children or elderly adults tend to be easier to contact, whereas single-person households are more difficult to reach (Groves & Couper, 1998:119–154).

Refusal rates vary with some respondent characteristics. People with less education participate somewhat less in surveys of political issues (perhaps because they are less aware of current political issues). Less education is also associated with higher rates of "don't know" responses (Groves, 1989). High-income persons tend to participate less in surveys about income and economic behavior (perhaps because they are suspicious about why others want to know about their situation). Unusual strains and disillusionment in a society can also undermine the general credibility of research efforts and the ability of interviewers to achieve an acceptable response rate. These problems can be lessened with an advance letter introducing the survey project and by multiple contact attempts throughout the day and evening, but they cannot entirely be avoided (Fowler, 1988:52–53; Groves & Couper, 1998).

Electronic Surveys

The widespread use of personal computers and the growth of the Internet have created new possibilities for survey research. In 1999, 43% of American households were connected to the Internet and another 22% had personal computers without Internet connections (Nie & Erbring, 2000). These percentages are growing rapidly; it is not unreasonable to think that use of the Internet will soon become comparable to the use of telephones. As the proportion of the population that is connected increases, the Internet will become the preferred medium for survey research on many topics.

Electronic surveys can be prepared in two ways (Dillman, 2000:352–354). **E-mail surveys** can be sent as messages to respondent e-mail addresses. Respondents then mark their answers in the message and send them back to the researcher. This approach is easy for researchers to develop and for respondents to use. However, this approach is cumbersome for surveys that are more than four or five pages in length. By contrast, **Web surveys** are designed on a server controlled by the researcher; respondents are then asked to visit the Web site and respond to the Web questionnaire by checking answers. This approach requires more programming by the researcher and in many cases requires more skill on the part of the respondent. However, Web surveys can be quite long, with questions that are inapplicable to a given respondent hidden from them so that the survey may actually seem much shorter than it is.

Web surveys are becoming the more popular form of Internet survey because they are so flexible. The design of the questionnaire can include many types of graphic and typographic features. Respondents can view definitions of words or instructions for answering questions by clicking on linked terms. Lengthy sets of response choices can be presented with pull-down menus. Pictures and audio segments can be added when they are useful. Because answers are recorded directly in the researcher's database, data entry errors are almost eliminated and results can be reported quickly.

The most important drawback to either Internet survey approach is the large fraction of households that are not yet connected to the Internet. For special populations with high rates of Internet use, though, the technology makes possible fast and effective surveys. Another problem researchers must try their best to avoid is creating survey formats that are so complicated that some computers cannot read them or would display them in a way that differs from what the researchers intended. Also, access to a Web survey must be limited to the sample members, perhaps by requiring use of a personal identification number (PIN) (Dillman, 2000:353–401).

Computerized **interactive voice response (IVR)** systems already allow the ease of Internet surveys to be achieved with a telephone-based system. In IVR surveys, respondents receive automated calls and answer questions by pressing numbers on their touchtone phones or speaking numbers that are interpreted by computerized voice recognition software. These surveys can also record verbal responses to open-ended questions for later transcription. Although they present some difficulties when many answer choices must be used or skip patterns must be followed, IVR surveys have been used successfully with short questionnaires and when respondents are highly motivated to participate (Dillman, 2000:402–411). When these conditions are not met, potential respondents may be put off by the impersonality of this computer-driven approach.

Mixed-Mode Surveys

Survey researchers increasingly are combining different survey designs. **Mixed-mode surveys** allow the strengths of one survey design to compensate for the weaknesses of another and can maximize the likelihood of securing data from different types of respondents. For example, a survey may be sent electronically to sample members who have e-mail addresses and mailed to those who don't. Alternatively, nonrespondents in a mailed survey may be interviewed in person or over the phone. As noted previously, an interviewer may use a self-administered questionnaire to present sensitive questions to a respondent.

Mixing survey designs like this makes it possible that respondents will give different answers to different questions because of the mode in which they are asked, rather than because they actually have different opinions. However, use of what Dillman (2000: 232–240) calls "unimode design" reduces this possibility substantially. A unimode design uses questions and response choices that are least likely to yield different answers according to the survey mode that is used. Unimode design principles include use of the same question structures, response choices, and skip instructions across modes, as well as using a small number of response choices for each question.

A Comparison of Survey Designs

Which survey design should be used when? Group-administered surveys are similar in most respects to mailed surveys, except they require the unusual circumstance of having access to the sample in a group setting. We therefore don't need to consider this survey design by itself; what applies to mailed survey designs applies to group-administered survey designs, with the exception of sampling issues. Thus, we can focus our comparison on the four survey designs that involve the use of a questionnaire with individuals sampled from a larger population—mailed surveys, phone surveys, in-person surveys, and electronic surveys. Exhibit 6.14 summarizes their strong and weak points.

The most important consideration in comparing the advantages and disadvantages of the four survey designs is the likely response rate they will generate. Because of the great weakness of mailed surveys in this respect, they must be considered the least preferred survey design from a sampling standpoint. However, researchers may still prefer a mailed survey when they have to reach a widely dispersed population and don't have enough financial resources to hire and train an interview staff or to contract with a survey organization that already has an interview staff available in many locations.

Contracting with an established survey research organization for a phone survey is often the best alternative to a mailed survey. The persistent follow-up attempts necessary to secure an adequate response rate are much easier over the phone than in person. But the process is not simple:

Initial telephone contact with households was attempted during hours of the day and days of the week which had the greatest probability of respondent contact (between 5:30 P.M. and 10:00 P.M. on weekdays, between 9:00 A.M. and 10:00 P.M. on Saturdays,

Exhibit 6.14 Advantages and Disadvantages of Four Survey Designs

Characteristics of Design	In-Person Survey	Mail Survey	Phone Survey	Electronic Survey
Representative sample				
Opportunity for inclusion is known				
For completely listed populations	High	High	High	Medium
For incompletely listed populations	High	Medium	Medium	Low
Selection within sampling units is controlled	High	Medium	High	Low
(e.g., specific family members must respond)				
Respondents are likely to be located	Medium	High	High	Low
If samples are heterogeneous	High	Medium	High	Low
If samples are homogeneous				
and specialized	High	High	High	High
Questionnaire construction and question design				
Allowable length of questionnaire	High	Medium	Medium	Medium
Ability to include				
Complex questions	Medium	Low	High	High
Open questions	Low	High	High	Medium
Screening questions	Low	Low	High	
Tedious, boring questions	High	High	High	High
Ability to control question sequence	Low	High	High	High
Ability to ensure questionnaire completion	Medium	High	High	Low
Distortion of answers				
Odds of avoiding social desirability bias	High	Medium	Low	High
Odds of avoiding interviewer distortion	Low	High	Medium	
Odds of avoiding contamination by others	High	Medium	Medium	Medium
Administrative goals				
Odds of meeting personnel requirements	High	High	Low	Medium
Odds of implementing quickly	Low	High	Low	High
Odds of keeping costs low	High	Medium	Low	High

Source: Adapted from Dillman, 1978:74–75. *Mail and Telephone Surveys: The Total Design Method.* Copyright © 1978 Don A. Dillman. Reprinted by permission of John Wiley & Sons, Inc.

and between 10:00 A.M. and 10:00 P.M. on Sundays). Interviewers made five attempts to ringing unanswered telephones on different days and at different times over a period of at least three weeks in order to obtain the highest possible response rate. If the interview could not be conducted or completed at the time of the initial contact, the interviewer rescheduled the interview at a time convenient to the respondent. (From a description of the NVAMW Survey)

In-person surveys are clearly preferable in terms of the possible length and complexity of the questionnaire itself, as well as the researcher's ability to monitor conditions while the questionnaire is being completed. Mailed surveys often are preferable for asking sensitive questions, although this problem can be lessened in an interview by giving respondents a separate sheet to fill out on their own. Although interviewers may themselves distort results, either by changing the wording of questions or failing to record answers properly, this problem can be lessened by careful training, monitoring, and tape-recording the answers.

A phone survey limits the length and complexity of the questionnaire but offers the possibility of very carefully monitoring interviewers (Dillman, 1978; Fowler, 1988:61–73). For the NVAMW Survey, SRBI assured quality control over its interviews in the following manner:

> Throughout the project, interviewers were silently monitored by a supervisor at least twice during each of their interviewing shifts to evaluate the manner in which interviewers were conducting the interview and the accuracy with which they were entering responses.

The advantages and disadvantages of electronic surveys must be weighed in light of the capabilities at the time that the survey is to be conducted. At this time, too many people lack Internet connections for general use of Internet surveying, and too many people who have computers lack adequate computer capacity for displaying complex Web pages.

These various points about the different survey designs lead to two general conclusions. First, in-person interviews are the strongest design and generally preferable when sufficient resources and a trained interview staff are available; telephone surveys have many of the advantages of in-person interviews at a much lower cost. Second, a decision about the best survey design for any particular study must take into account the unique features and goals of the study.

ETHICAL ISSUES IN SURVEY RESEARCH

Survey research usually poses fewer ethical dilemmas than do experimental or field research designs. Potential respondents to a survey can easily decline to participate, and a cover letter or introductory statement that identifies the sponsors of and motivations for the survey gives them the information required to make this decision. The methods of data collection are quite obvious in a survey, so little is concealed from the respondents. The primary ethical issue in survey research involves protecting respondents.

Protection of Respondents

If the survey could possibly have any harmful effects for the respondents, these should be disclosed fully in the cover letter or introductory statement. The procedures used to reduce such effects should also be delineated, including how the researcher is going to keep interviews confidential and anonymous. In addition, surveys such as the NVAMW Survey and NCVS that attempt to measure sensitive subject matter such as rape and intimate-perpetrated assault should also have other protections in place. Holly Johnson (1996:52) has stated the most important of these succinctly: "Researchers must never lose sight of the possibility that with every telephone call, respondent[s] could be living with an abusive [partner] and that their safety could be jeopardized should they learn of the content of the survey." In addition, by asking respondents to recall incidents of abuse and violence, there is always the possibility of causing victims serious emotional trauma. How can researchers ameliorate the negative consequences that responding to these surveys may have? What responsibility do researchers have in providing respondents safety should they need it? We believe these important questions have received far too little attention. For the most part, the NCVS has done nothing to protect the safety of its respondents or offer guidance in finding emotional support should they need it. In contrast, respondents in the NVAMW Survey were given a toll-free number they could call if they needed to suddenly hang up during the course of the interview (e.g., if they felt in danger). In addition, interviewers of the NVAMW Survey were instructed to contact an attending supervisor at the first sign a respondent was becoming upset or emotionally distraught. These supervisors were provided with a source book from the National Domestic Violence Coalition that listed rape crisis and domestic violence hotline numbers from around the country.

Confidentiality

Do any of the questions have the potential to embarrass respondents or otherwise subject them to adverse consequences such as legal sanctions? If the answer to this question is no, and it often is in surveys about general social issues, other ethical problems are unlikely. But if the questionnaire includes questions about attitudes or behaviors that are socially stigmatized or generally considered to be private or questions about actions that are illegal, the researcher must proceed carefully and ensure that respondents' rights are protected.

The first step to take with potentially troublesome questions is to consider omitting or modifying them. Researchers often include some questions in surveys just out of curiosity or out of a suspicion that the questions might prove to be important. If sensitive questions fall into this category, they probably should be omitted. There is no point in asking, "Have you ever been convicted of a felony?" if the answers are unlikely to be used in the analysis of survey results.

Many surveys do include some essential questions that might prove damaging to the subjects if their answers were disclosed, particularly surveys interested in delinquent or criminal offending behavior. To prevent any possibility of harm to subjects due to disclosure of such information, it is critical to preserve subject confidentiality. No one other than research personnel should have access to information that could be used to link respondents to their responses, and even that access should be limited to what is necessary for specific research purposes. Only numbers should be used to identify respondents on their questionnaires, and the researcher should keep the names that correspond to these numbers in a safe, private location, unavailable to staff and others who might otherwise come across them. Follow-up mailings or contact attempts that require linking the ID numbers with names and addresses should be carried out by trustworthy assistants under close supervision.

Only if no identifying information about respondents is obtained can surveys provide true **anonymity** to respondents. In this way, no identifying information is ever recorded to link respondents with their responses. However, the main problem with anonymous surveys is that they preclude follow-up attempts to encourage participation by initial non-respondents, and they prevent panel designs, which measure change through repeated surveys of the same individuals. In-person surveys rarely can be anonymous because an interviewer must in almost all cases know the name and address of the interviewee. However, phone surveys that are meant only to sample opinion at one point in time, as in political polls, can safely be completely anonymous. When no follow-up is desired, group-administered surveys also can be anonymous. To provide anonymity in a mail survey, the researcher should omit identifying codes from the questionnaire but could include a self-addressed, stamped postcard so the respondent can notify the researcher that the questionnaire has been returned, without being linked to the questionnaire itself (Mangione, 1995:69).

Any survey can allow anonymous responses to a subset of particularly sensitive questions. A tear-off sheet containing these questions and a separate return envelope, without identifying information, can be included with a mailed survey. In an in-person interview, this special section can be left with the respondent to be completed later and returned by mail. Of course, a response obtained in this way cannot be linked with the response of the same subject to the same question in some later follow-up survey. But if it increases the response rate, this method can provide more valid results for the initial survey.

CONCLUSION

Survey research is an exceptionally efficient and productive method for investigating a wide array of social research questions. In addition to the potential benefits for social science, considerations of time and expense frequently make a survey the preferred data-collection method. One or more of the four survey designs reviewed in this chapter can be applied to almost any research question. It is no wonder that surveys have become the most popular research method in sociology and that they frequently influence discussion and planning about important social and political questions.

The relative ease of conducting at least some types of survey research leads many people to imagine that no particular training or systematic procedures are required. Nothing could be further from the truth. As a result of this widespread misconception, you will encounter a great many nearly worthless survey results. You must be prepared to carefully examine the procedures used in any survey before accepting its findings as credible. And if you decide to conduct a survey, you must be prepared to invest the time and effort required to follow proper procedures.

KEY TERMS

Anonymity
Cognitive interview
Contingent question
Cover letter
Double-barreled question
Double-negative question
Electronic survey
E-mail survey
Exhaustive responses
Fence-sitter
Filter question
Fixed-choice question
Floater

Group-administered survey
Idiosyncratic variation
Index (scale)
In-person interview
Interactive voice response (IVR)
Interpretive question
Interview schedule
Likert-type responses
Mailed (self-administered) survey
Mixed-mode survey
Mutually exclusive responses
Omnibus survey
Open-ended question

Phone survey

Pretest

Questionnaire (interview schedule)

Reference period

Reliability measures

Scale

Skip pattern

Split-ballot design

Survey research

Web survey

HIGHLIGHTS

• Surveys are the most popular form of social research because of their versatility, efficiency, and generalizability. Many survey data sets, such as the General Social Survey (GSS), are available for social scientists to use in teaching and research.

• Surveys can fail to produce useful results due to problems in sampling, measurement, and overall survey design. Political polling can produce inconsistent results because of rapid changes in popular sentiment.

• A survey questionnaire or interview schedule should be designed as an integrated whole, with each question and section serving some clear purpose and complementing the others.

• Questions must be worded carefully to avoid confusing the respondents or encouraging a less-than-honest response. Inclusion of "don't know" choices and neutral responses may help, but the presence of such options also affects the distribution of answers. Open-ended questions can be used to determine the meaning that respondents attach to their answers. Answers to any survey questions may be affected by the questions that precede them in a questionnaire or interview schedule.

• Every questionnaire and interview schedule should be pretested on a small sample that is like the sample to be surveyed.

• The cover letter for a mailed questionnaire and the introductory statement for an interview should be credible, personalized, interesting, and responsible.

• Response rates in mailed surveys are typically well below 70% unless multiple mailings are made to nonrespondents and the questionnaire and cover letter are attractive, interesting, and carefully planned. Response rates for group-administered surveys are usually much higher.

• Phone interviews using random digit dialing allow fast turnaround and efficient sampling. Multiple call-backs may be required, but once the people are contacted, most can be interviewed by phone for 30 to 45 minutes.

• In-person interviews have several advantages over other types of surveys: They allow longer and more complex interview schedules, monitoring of the conditions when the questions are answered, probing for respondents' understanding of the questions, and high response rates.

• Electronic surveys may be e-mailed or posted on the Web. Interactive voice-response systems using the telephone are another option. At this time, use of the Internet is not sufficiently widespread to allow e-mail or Web surveys of the general population, but these approaches can be fast and efficient for populations with high rates of computer use.

• Mixed-mode surveys allow the strengths of one survey design to compensate for the weaknesses of another. However, questions and procedures must be designed carefully, using "unimode design" principles, to reduce the possibility that responses to the same question will vary as a result of the mode of delivery.

• Most survey research poses few ethical problems because respondents are able to decline to participate. This option should be stated clearly in the cover letter or introductory statement. Special care must be taken when questionnaires are administered in group settings (to captive audiences) and when sensitive personal questions are to be asked; subject confidentiality should always be preserved.

EXERCISES

1. Read the original article reporting one of the surveys described in this book (check the text of the chapters for ideas). Critique the article using the questions presented in Appendix B as your guide. Focus particular attention on sampling, measurement, and survey design.

2. Write 8 to 10 questions for a one-page questionnaire on fear of crime among students. Include some questions to measure characteristics (such as income or year in school) that might help to explain the attitudes. Make all but one of your questions closed-ended.

3. By interviewing two students, conduct a preliminary pretest of the questionnaire you wrote for Exercise 2. Follow up the closed-ended questions with open-ended questions that ask the students what they meant by each response or what came to mind when they were asked each question. Take account of these answers when you revise your questions.

4. Make any necessary revisions to the questionnaire you wrote in Exercise 2. Write a cover letter that presumes the survey will be administered to students in a class at your school. Submit the questionnaire and cover letter to your instructor for comment and evaluation.

DEVELOPING A RESEARCH PROPOSAL

1. Write 10 questions for a one-page questionnaire that concerns your proposed research question. Your questions should operationalize at least three of the variables on which you have focused, including at least one independent and one dependent variable (you may have multiple questions to measure some variables). Make all but one of your questions closed-ended. If you completed the "research proposal" exercises in Chapter 3, you can select your questions from the ones you developed for those exercises.

2. Conduct a preliminary pretest of the questionnaire by conducting cognitive interviews with two students or other persons like those to whom the survey is directed. Follow up the closed-ended questions with open-ended probes that ask the students what they meant by each response or what came to mind when they were asked each question. Take account of the feedback you receive when you revise your questions.

3. Polish up the organization and layout of the questionnaire, following the guidelines in this chapter. Prepare a rationale for the order of questions in your questionnaire. Write a cover letter directed to the appropriate population that contains appropriate statements about research ethics (human subjects issues).

WEB EXERCISES

1. Go to the Social Science Information Gateway (SOSIG) at http://sosig.esrc.bris.ac.uk. Search SOSIG for electronic journal articles that use surveys to collect information on crime, criminal behavior, or criminal victimization. Find at least five articles and briefly describe each.

2. Go to the Council of European Social Science Data Archives (CESSDA) at www.nsd. uib.no/cessda/index.html. Go to "The Map." View the type of data provided by various European data banks. Browse the publications list or conduct a search at the site for at least three countries for studies that use surveys to collect information on crime, criminal behavior, or criminal victimization.

What type of information did you find? If possible, do a cross-national comparison between the studies reviewed in Exercise 1 and the studies found in this exercise.

SPSS EXERCISES

Injuries are often sustained by victims of violent crime. Using NCS93.POR, a sample of incidents of violent crime for female victims from the National Crime Victimization Survey in 1993, you can explore what factors most often lead to injury for female victims of rape, robbery, and assault.

1. Browse the variables in the data set. What factors do you think are related to whether or not a victim of rape, robbery, or assault is injured?

2. Choose at least three of these variables, and state your hypotheses about the relationship between each of these variables and injury.

3. Generate crosstabulations of your chosen variables and INJURY. (If you have had a statistics course, you may want to request the CHI-SQUARE statistic for each of the crosstabulations.)

4. Describe the relationships you have found, noting the difference in the distribution of the dependent (row) variables between the categories of each independent (column) variables.

5. Do these relationships vary for the type of violent crime committed? Add the variable measuring the type of violent crime committed (TOC) as a CONTROL variable in your cross-tabulation request. Describe your results.

Chapter 7

Qualitative Methods

"It's more like a family away from home. You're with your friends, you all stick together. They ain't going to let nothing happen to you, you ain't going to let nothing happen to them." This was one youth's reason for joining a gang. Such specific narrative information would not be easy to obtain from a structured survey. Thus, in an attempt to situate the origin, structure, and practices of street gangs within the social organizational context of the family and the larger community, Scott Decker and Barrik Van Winkle (1996) obtained this information by conducting 3 years of fieldwork and interviews with 99 active gang members and 24 of their family members. As you will see, experimental or survey methodologies would be ill suited to examine the unique institutional and cultural contexts of gang values and activities such as those uncovered by Decker and Van Winkle.

In this chapter you will learn how qualitative methods were used to illuminate the relationships, both individually and collectively, that gang members have with other social institutions (Decker & Van Winkle, 1996). You will also get an inside look at community policing in action (Miller, 1999). Throughout the chapter, you will learn, from a variety of other examples, that some of our greatest insights into social processes can result from what appear to be very ordinary activities—observing, participating, listening, and talking.

But you will also learn that qualitative research is much more than just doing what comes naturally in social situations. Qualitative researchers must keenly observe respondents, sensitively plan their participation, systematically take notes, and strategically question respondents. They must also prepare to spend more time and invest more of their whole selves than often occurs with experiments or surveys. Moreover, if we are to have any confidence in the validity of a qualitative study's conclusions, each element of its design must be reviewed as carefully as the elements of an experiment or survey.

The chapter begins with an overview of the major features of qualitative research, as reflected in Venkatesh's (1997) study of Blackstone (the fictitious name given to the residential area). The next section discusses the various approaches to participant observation research, which is the most distinctive qualitative method, and reviews the stages of research using participant observation. We then review, in some detail, the issues involved in intensive interviewing, before briefly explaining focus groups, an increasingly popular qualitative method. The last two sections cover issues that are of concern in any type of qualitative research project—analyzing the data collected and making ethical decisions. By the chapter's end, you should appreciate the hard work required to translate "doing what comes naturally" into systematic research, be able to recognize strong and weak points in qualitative studies, and be ready to do some research yourself.

FUNDAMENTALS OF QUALITATIVE METHODS

Qualitative methods can often be used to enrich experiments and surveys, and refer to three distinctive research designs: **participant observation, intensive interviewing,** and **focus groups.** Participant observation and intensive interviewing are often used in the same project; focus groups combine some elements of these two approaches into a unique data-collection strategy.

Participant observation   A qualitative method for gathering data that involves developing a sustained relationship with people while they go about their normal activities.

Intensive interviewing   A qualitative method that involves open-ended, relatively unstructured questioning in which the interviewer seeks in-depth information on the interviewee's feelings, experiences, and perceptions (Lofland & Lofland, 1984:12).

Focus groups   A qualitative method that involves unstructured group interviews in which the focus group leader actively encourages discussion among participants on the topics of interest.

Although these three qualitative designs differ in many respects, they share several features that distinguish them from experimental and survey research designs (Denzin & Lincoln, 1994; Maxwell, 1996; Wolcott, 1995). These features are:

Collection primarily of qualitative rather than quantitative data. Any research design may collect both qualitative and quantitative data, but qualitative methods emphasize observations about natural behavior and artifacts that capture social life as it is experienced by the participants rather than in categories predetermined by the researcher.

Exploratory research questions, with a commitment to inductive reasoning. Qualitative researchers typically begin their projects seeking not to test preformulated hypotheses but to discover what people think and how and why they act in certain social settings. Only after many observations do qualitative researchers try to develop general principles to account for their observations.

A focus on previously unstudied processes and unanticipated phenomena. Previously unstudied attitudes and actions can't adequately be understood with a structured set of questions or within a highly controlled experiment. Therefore, qualitative methods have their greatest appeal when we need to explore new issues, investigate hard-to-study groups, or determine the meaning people give to their lives and actions.

An orientation to social context, to the interconnections between social phenomena rather than to their discrete features. The context of concern may be a program, an organization, a case study, or a broader social context. For example, in Venkatesh's analysis of the social space occupied by a street gang, he observed:

> The result of their [Saint's street gang] corporatization was the emergence of a novel social space in Blackstone, that is, a new orientation to local geography in which the symbolic distinctions of local street gangs challenged the building-centered distinctions that had previously underwritten the power of the Councils. (Venkatesh, 1997:7)

A focus on human subjectivity, on the meanings that participants attach to events and people give to their lives. "Through life stories, people account for their lives. . . . [T]he themes people create are the means by which they interpret and evaluate their life experiences and attempt to integrate these experiences to form a self-concept" (Kaufman, 1986:24–25).

A focus on the events leading up to a particular event or outcome instead of general causal explanations. With its focus on particular actors and situations and the processes that connect them, qualitative research tends to identify causes as particular events embedded within an unfolding, interconnected action sequence (Maxwell, 1996:20–21). The language of variables and hypotheses appears only rarely in the qualitative literature.

Reflexive research design. The design develops as the research progresses:

> Each component of the design may need to be reconsidered or modified in response to new developments or to changes in some other component. . . . The activities of

collecting and analyzing data, developing and modifying theory, elaborating or refocusing the research questions, and identifying and eliminating validity threats are usually all going on more or less simultaneously, each influencing all of the others. (Maxwell, 1996:2–3)

Sensitivity to the subjective role of the researcher. Little pretense is made of achieving an objective perspective on social phenomena. One qualitative researcher studying young girls observed:

I felt closer to the girls not only through memories of my own past, but also because I knew more about their gender-typed interactions. I had once played games like jump rope and statue buyer, but I had never ridden a skateboard and had barely tried sports like basketball and soccer. . . . Were my moments of remembering, the times when I felt like a ten-year-old girl, a source of distortion or insight? (Thorne, 1993:26)

Origins of Qualitative Research

Anthropologists and sociologists laid the foundation for modern qualitative methods while doing **field research** in the early decades of the twentieth century. Dissatisfied with studies of native peoples that relied on second-hand accounts and inspection of artifacts, anthropologists Franz Boas and Bronislaw Malinowski went to live in or near the communities they studied. Boas visited Native American villages in the American Northwest; Malinowski lived among New Guinea natives. Neither truly participated in the ongoing social life of those they studied (Boas collected artifacts and original texts, and Malinowski reputedly lived as something of a noble among the natives he studied), but both helped to establish the value of intimate familiarity with the community of interest and thus laid the basis for modern anthropology (Emerson, 1983:2–5).

Many of sociology's field research pioneers were former social workers and reformers. Some brought their missionary concern with the spread of civic virtue among new immigrants to the Department of Sociology and Anthropology at the University of Chicago. Their successors continued to focus on sources of community cohesion and urban strain but came to view the city as a social science laboratory rather than as a focus for reform. They adopted the fieldwork methods of anthropology for studying the "natural areas" of the city and the social life of small towns (Vidich & Lyman, 1994). By the 1930s, 1940s, and 1950s, qualitative researchers were emphasizing the value of direct participation in community life and sharing in subjects' perceptions and interpretations of events (Emerson, 1983:6–13).

Case Study: Life in the Gang

The use of fieldwork techniques to study gangs has a long tradition in a variety of cities, including Frederic Thrasher's classic study of gangs in Chicago (1927), and others, including Whyte (1943), Hagedorn (1988), Vigil (1988), Padilla (1992), Sanchez-Jankowski (1991), and Joan Moore (1978, 1991), who spent over two decades studying the "homeboys" of Hispanic barrios all over the country. All of these researchers employed a fieldwork approach to the study of gangs rather than the more structured approaches offered by quantitative methods.

You can get a better feel for qualitative methods by reading the following excerpts from Scott Decker and Barrik Van Winkle's book about gangs, *Life in the Gang: Family, Friends, and Violence* (1996), and by reasoning inductively from their observations. See if you can induce from these particulars some of the general features of field research. Ask yourself, "What were the research questions?" "How were the issues of generalizability, measurement, and causation approached?" "How did social factors influence the research?"

One of the first issues Decker and Van Winkle were challenged with was precisely defining a gang. After all, the term *gang* could refer to many groups of youth, including high school Debate Society or the Young Republicans. After reviewing the literature, Decker and Van Winkle developed a working definition of a gang as an "age-graded peer group that exhibits some permanence, engages in criminal activity, and has some symbolic representation of membership" (1996:31). To operationalize who was a gang member, they relied on self-identification. "Are you claiming . . . ." was a key screening question that was also verified, as often as possible, with other gang members.

There were several questions that Decker and Van Winkle were interested in:

Our study revolved around a number of activities, both gang and nongang related, that our subjects were likely to engage in. First, we were interested in motivations to join gangs, the process of joining the gang, the symbols of gang membership, the strength of associational ties, the structure or hierarchy within the gang, motivations to stay (or leave) the gang, and how this generation of St. Louis gangs began. The second set of issues concerned the activities gang members engaged in. These included such things as turf protection, drug sales and use, and violence, as well as conventional activities. An accurate picture of gang members must portray both the nature of their gang involvement and the legal status of their activities. . . . A unique feature of our work is its focus on families. There has been little research examining specifically the links between gang members and their family members. For this reason, we have separated the family from our analysis of other social institutions and devote special attention to this relationship. (Decker & Van Winkle, 1996:54–55)

With these research questions in mind, Decker and Van Winkle explain why they chose a fieldwork approach: "A single premise guided our study; the best information about gangs and gang activity would come from gang members contacted directly in the field" (1996:27). As stated earlier, Decker and Van Winkle combined two methods of qualitative data collection. With the help of a field ethnographer who spent the majority of each day "on the streets," direct observation was conducted along with the intensive interviewing conducted by Decker and Van Winkle.

The data in Decker and Van Winkle's (1996) study were obtained from the observations in the field and from the intensive interviews. As they state,

Learning about gangs and gang members can be best accomplished by hearing the gang member's story directly from the individuals involved. . . . We went to great lengths to ensure that each person we interviewed felt they had received the opportunity to "tell their story in their own words." (Decker & Van Winkle, 1996:45)

Because they did not rely on structured questionnaires with fixed-response formats, their data are primarily qualitative rather than quantitative.

As for their method, it was inductive. First they gathered data. Then, as data collection continued, they figured out how to interpret the data—how to make sense of the social situations they were studying. Their analytic categories ultimately came not from social theory but from the categories by which the gang members themselves described one another and their activities and how they made sense of their social world.

To summarize, Decker and Van Winkle's research began with exploratory questions and proceeded inductively throughout, developing general concepts to make sense of specific observations. Although the researchers were not gang members themselves, with observational data collected on the streets and transcripts from intensive interviews, Decker and Van Winkle were able to share many gang members' experiences and perspectives. They provided the field of criminology with in-depth descriptions and idiographic connections of sequences of events that could not have been obtained through other methodologies. They successfully used field research to explore human experiences in depth, carefully analyzing the social contexts in which the experiences occurred.

PARTICIPANT OBSERVATION

Other researchers have utilized a more direct observational strategy for studying gangs. For example, to illuminate the nuances and complexities of the role of a street gang in community social life, Sudhir Alladi Venkatesh (1997) conducted intensive participant observation in Blackstone, a midsize public housing development located in a poor ghetto of a large midwestern city. As Venkatesh describes, "Having befriended these gang members, I moved into their world, accompanying them into Blackstone and other spaces where they were actively involved in illicit economic activities, member recruitment, and the general expansion of their street-based organization" (1997:4). As this quote eloquently depicts, participant observation, called fieldwork in anthropology, is a method of studying natural social processes as they happen (in the field rather than in the laboratory) and leaving them relatively undisturbed. It is the seminal field research method, a means for seeing the social world as the research subjects see it, in its totality, and for understanding subjects' interpretations of that world (Wolcott, 1995:66). By observing people and interacting with them in the course of their normal activities, participant observers seek to avoid the artificiality of experimental designs and the unnatural structured questioning of survey research (Koegel, 1987:8).

The term *participant observer* actually represents a continuum of roles (see Exhibit 7.1), ranging from being a complete observer who does not participate in group activities and is publicly defined as a researcher, to being a covert participant who acts just like other group members and does not disclose his or her research role. Many field researchers develop a role between these extremes, publicly acknowledging being a researcher but nonetheless participating in group activities. In some settings, it also is possible to observe covertly, without acknowledging being a researcher or participating.

Choosing a Role

The first concerns of all participant observers is to decide what balance to strike between observing and participating and whether to reveal their role as researchers. These

Exhibit 7.1   The Observational Continuum

To study a political activist group...

You could take the role of complete observer:

You could take the role of participant and observer:

You could take the role of covert participant:

decisions must take into account the specifics of the social situation being studied, the researcher's own background and personality, the larger sociopolitical context, and ethical concerns. The balance of participating and observing that is most appropriate also changes during most projects, often many times. And the researcher's ability to maintain either a covert or an overt role will be challenged many times.

Complete Observation

Susan Miller (1999) adopted the role of a complete observer when she conducted research on community policing. Community policing, as most of you probably know, is a new approach to policing that emphasizes building closer ties between police and members of the community. Miller was particularly interested in how gender affected the attitudes and behavior of neighborhood police officers (NPOs). She states:

I was curious as to whether the interpersonal dynamics I observed with Officer Terry [a female officer] would be like those when a male NPO was involved. I wanted to delve into the heads and hearts of the NPOs, to see for myself what worked in community policing and to see what they felt did not. I wanted to examine how such a paradigm shift in the theory and practice of policing would affect the officers who desire street action, and how they would assess their new "walk and talk" colleagues. (Miller, 1999:x)

In **complete observation**, researchers try to see things as they happen, without disrupting the participants. Along with intensive interviews with police officers, Miller also observed police officers on their daily shifts:

Both neighborhood and patrol officers' shifts were observed, either on foot with neighborhood officers, or in squad cars with patrol officers. This component of the project also permitted gathering some observational information about citizens' reactions to police delivery of services. . . . Typically, we tried to work the same shifts as the neighborhood police officers, and we shadowed the NPO and each corresponding patrol officer during the same shift. Eight-hour shifts were evenly divided into four-hour blocks of walking in the neighborhood with the neighborhood officer and four-hour blocks of riding in the squad car with the patrol officer assigned to the same neighborhood. Shadowing both permitted a cross-check of how neighborhood officers perceived the role of patrol officers and of how patrol officers saw their role in conjunction with, or opposition to, the neighborhood policing concept. (Miller, 1999:232–233)

As clearly depicted in this quote, the "shadowing" is visible. Thus, the researcher's very presence as an observer alters the social situation being observed. It is not natural in most social situations to have an observer present, one who will record at some point her or his observations for research and publication purposes. The observer thus sees what individuals do when they are being observed, which is not necessarily what they would do without an observer. This is called a **reactive effect,** and the extent to which it can be a problem varies with the situation. In Miller's study, her long tenure as an observer made her presence commonplace, thereby serving to decrease the problem of reactive effects. She states:

Since I had spent so many hours over eighteen months with the Jackson City Police Department [fictional name], I had grown to be a familiar face; this, I believe, decreased respondents' tendencies toward social desirability. Officers took my presence for granted in the briefing room, the hallways, the interview rooms, and in the field, including me in jokes and informal conversation in the coffee shop. (Miller, 1999:235)

In general, in social settings involving many people, where observing while standing or sitting does not attract attention, the complete observer is unlikely to have much effect on the social processes. On the other hand, when the social setting involves few people and observing is unlike the usual activities in the setting, or when the observer differs in obvious respects from the participants, the complete observer is more likely to have an impact.

Participation and Observation

Most field researchers adopt a role that involves some active participation in the setting. Usually they inform at least some group members of their research interests, but then they participate in enough group activities to develop rapport with members and to gain a direct sense of what group members experience. This is not an easy balancing act, but

> the key to participant observation as a fieldwork strategy is to take seriously the challenge it poses to participate more, and to play the role of the aloof observer less. Do not think of yourself as someone who needs to wear a white lab coat and carry a clipboard to learn about how humans go about their everyday lives. (Wolcott, 1995:100)

In his classic study of corner gangs and other social organizations in a poor Boston community he called Cornerville, William Foote Whyte (1943) spent a large part of nearly 4 years trying to be accepted by the community and seen as a good fellow. He describes his efforts:

> My aim was to gain an intimate view of Cornerville life. My first problem, therefore, was to establish myself as a participant in the society so that I would have a position from which to observe. I began by going to live in Cornerville, finding a room with an Italian family. . . . It was not enough simply to make the acquaintance of various groups of people. The sort of information that I sought required that I establish intimate social relations, and that presented special problems. Since illegal activities are prevalent in Cornerville, every newcomer is under suspicion. . . . I put in a great deal of time simply hanging around with them [the men] and participating in their various activities. . . . This active participation gave me something in common with them so that we had other things to talk about besides the weather. It broke down the social barriers and made it possible for me to be taken into the intimate life of the group. (Whyte, 1943:v–vii)

Because of the great deal of time he spent with each gang and social organization he was studying, Whyte became accepted into each group and the community. The result was his famous book, *Street Corner Society* (1943).

Participating and observing have two clear ethical advantages. Because group members know the researcher's real role in the group, they can choose to keep some information or attitudes hidden. By the same token, the researcher can decline to participate in unethical or dangerous activities without fear of exposing his or her identity.

Most field researchers who opt for disclosure get the feeling that, after they have become known and at least somewhat trusted figures in the group, their presence does not have a palpable effect on members' actions. The major influences on individual actions and attitudes are past experiences, personality, group structure, and so on, and these continue to exert their influence even when an outside observer is present. The participant observer can presumably be ethical about identity disclosure and still observe the natural social world. Of course, the argument is less persuasive when the behavior to be observed is illegal or stigmatized, giving participants reason to fear the consequences of disclosure to any outsider. In practice it can be difficult to maintain a fully open research role even in a setting without these special characteristics.

Even when researchers maintain a public identity as researchers, the ethical dilemmas arising from participation in group activities do not go away. In fact, researchers may have to prove themselves to group members by joining in some of their questionable activities. For example, police officers gave John Van Maanen (1982) a nonstandard and technically prohibited pistol to carry on police patrols. Harold Pepinsky (1980) witnessed police harassment of a citizen but did not intervene when the citizen was arrested. Trying to strengthen his ties with a local political figure in Cornerville, William Foote Whyte (1943) illegally voted multiple times in a local election.

Experienced participant observers try to lessen some of the problems of identity disclosure by evaluating both their effect on others in the setting and the effect of others on the observers. The observers must write about these effects throughout the time they are in the field and as they analyze their data. While in the field they must preserve some regular time when they can concentrate on their research and schedule occasional meetings with other researchers to review the fieldwork. Participant observers modify their role as circumstances seem to require, perhaps not always disclosing their research role at casual social gatherings or group outings but always informing new members of their role.

Covert Participation

To lessen the potential for reactive effects and to gain entry to otherwise inaccessible settings, some field researchers have adopted the role of covert participant. By doing so they keep their research secret and try their best to act like other participants in a social setting or group. **Covert participation** is also known as *complete participation*. Laud Humphreys (1970) served as a "watch queen" so that he could learn about men engaging in homosexual acts in a public restroom. Randall Alfred (1976) joined a group of Satanists to investigate group members and their interaction. Erving Goffman (1961) worked as a state hospital assistant while studying the treatment of psychiatric patients.

Although the role of covert participant lessens some of the reactive effects encountered by the complete observer, covert participants confront other problems. The following are a few examples:

- Covert participants cannot openly take notes or use any obvious recording devices. They must write up notes based solely on memory and must do so at times when it is natural for them to be away from group members.
- Covert participants cannot ask questions that will arouse suspicion. Thus they often have trouble clarifying the meaning of other participants' attitudes or actions.
- Covert participants have a difficult role to play successfully, because covert participants will not know how regular participants act in every situation in which the researchers find themselves. Regular participants enter the observed situation with social backgrounds and goals different from the researchers, whose spontaneous reactions to every event are unlikely to be consistent with those of the regular participants. Suspicion that researchers are not "one of us" may then have reactive effects, obviating the value of complete participation (Erikson, 1967). In his study of the Satanists, for example, Alfred (1976) pretended to be a regular group participant until he completed his research, at which time he informed the group leader of his covert role. Rather than act surprised, the leader told Alfred that he had long considered Alfred to be strange, not like the others. We will never be certain how Alfred's observations were affected.

- Covert participants must keep up the act at all times while in the setting under study. Researchers may experience enormous psychological strain, particularly in situations where they are expected to choose sides in intragroup conflict or to participate in criminal or other acts. Of course, some covert observers may become so wrapped up in their role that they adopt not just the mannerisms but also the perspectives and goals of the regular participants—they "go native." At this point, they abandon research goals and cease to critically evaluate their observations.

Ethical issues have been at the forefront of debate over the strategy of covert participation. Kai Erikson (1967) argues that covert participation is by its very nature unethical and should not be allowed except in public settings. Covert researchers cannot anticipate the unintended consequences of their actions for research subjects, Erikson points out. If others suspect the researcher's identity or if the researcher contributes to, or impedes, group action, these consequences can be adverse. In addition, other social research is harmed when covert research is disclosed—either during the research or upon its publication—because distrust of social scientists increases and access to research opportunities may decrease.

But a total ban on covert participation would "kill many a project stone dead" (Punch, 1994:90). Studies of unusual religious or sexual practices and of institutional malpractice would rarely be possible. "The crux of the matter is that some deception, passive or active, enables you to get at data not obtainable by other means" (Punch, 1994:91). Therefore, some field researchers argue that covert participation is legitimate in some settings. If the researcher maintains the confidentiality of others, keeps commitments to others, and does not directly lie to others, some degree of deception may be justified in exchange for the knowledge gained (Punch, 1994:90).

Entering the Field

Entering the field—the setting under investigation—is a critical stage in a participant observation project because it can shape many subsequent experiences. Some background work is necessary before entering the field—at least enough to develop a clear understanding of what the research questions are likely to be and to review one's personal stance toward the people and problems likely to be encountered. With participant observation, researchers must also learn in advance about the participants' dress and their typical activities to avoid being caught completely unprepared.

Entering the field even required Whyte to learn a new language:

Since the mother and father of the family spoke no English, I began studying Italian. Conversations with them and practice with the Linguaphone enabled me to learn enough to talk fairly fluently with the older generation. As I became largely concerned with the second-generation men, who conducted their activities in English, Italian was not essential to me; but the fact that I made the effort to learn the language was important, since it gave the impression that I had a sincere and sympathetic interest in Cornerville people. (Whyte, 1943:v)

Many field researchers avoid systematic study and extensive reading about a setting for fear that it will bias their first impressions, but entering without a sense of the social norms can lead to disaster. Whyte came close to such disaster when he despaired about not making social contacts in Cornerville and decided to try an unconventional entry approach (unconventional for a field researcher, that is). He describes what happened when he went to a hotel bar in search of women to talk with:

> I looked around me again and now noticed a threesome: one man and two women. It occurred to me that here was a maldistribution of females which I might be able to rectify. I approached the group and opened with something like this: "Pardon me. Would you mind if I joined you?" There was a moment of silence while the man stared at me. He then offered to throw me downstairs. I assured him that this would not be necessary and demonstrated as much by walking right out of there without any assistance. (Whyte, 1943:289)

Developing trust with at least one member of the research setting is a necessity in qualitative research. Such a person can become a valuable informant throughout the project, and most participant observers make a point of developing trust with at least one informant in a group under study. The entry gambit that finally worked for Whyte was to rely on a local community leader for introductions. A helpful social worker at the local settlement house introduced Whyte to "Doc," who agreed to help:

> Well, any nights you want to see anything, I'll take you around. I can take you to the joints—gambling joints—I can take you around to the street corners. Just remember that you're my friend. That's all they need to know [so they won't bother you]. (Whyte, 1943:291)

Miller (1999) gained access to the police department she studied through a chief of police who was extremely open to research. She also had two friends on the police force at the time of her study, as she describes:

> Both of my friends were well-liked on the force and had great credibility with their colleagues. They vouched for me to others, tracked down retired officers for me to interview, helped with scheduling, answered my questions, and provided clarification and other assistance as the need arose. . . . Whenever I encountered scheduling snafus or any reluctance by a police offer to schedule an interview or a walk-along, my friends on the force would make a call and easily arrange the time I needed with other officers. (Miller, 1999:230)

In short, field researchers must be very sensitive to the impression they make and the ties they establish when entering the field. This stage of research lays the groundwork for collecting data from people who have different perspectives and for developing relationships that the researcher can use to surmount the problems that inevitably arise in the field.

Developing and Maintaining Relationships

Researchers must be careful to manage their relationships in the research setting so they can continue to observe and interview diverse members of the social setting throughout the long period typical of participant observation (Maxwell, 1996:66). Every action the researcher takes can develop or undermine this relationship. As Decker and Van Winkle describe,

> There are a number of groups and individuals with whom field relationships must be maintained. Doing so effectively often involves balancing the competing demands of confidentiality, trust, and danger that emerge in a field study of individuals actively engaged in offending. (1996:45)

Maintaining trust is the cornerstone to successful research engagement, as Decker and Van Winkle further elaborate:

> We were able to maintain good field relations with our subjects by strictly observing our own commitment to the confidentiality of their statements. Since we interviewed many individuals from the same gang, it was often the case that one member would want to know what an earlier participant had told us. We refused to honor such inquiries, reminding them that the same confidentiality that applied to their own answers also covered those of their fellow gang members. We received numerous requests from gang members to sit in on the interview of a fellow member. These requests were declined as well. The strict confidentiality we were committed to was respected by our subjects, and appeared to enhance our own credibility as "solid" in their eyes. (1996:46)

Whyte (1943) used what was in retrospect a sophisticated two-part strategy to develop and maintain relationships with the Cornerville street-corner men. The first part of Whyte's strategy was to maintain good relations with Doc and, through Doc, stay on good terms with the others. The less obvious part of Whyte's strategy was a consequence of his decision to move into Cornerville, a move he decided was necessary to really understand and be accepted in the community. The room he rented in a local family's home became his base of operations. In some respects, this family became an important dimension of Whyte's immersion in the community. But he also recognized that he needed a place to unwind after his days of constant alertness in the field, so he made a conscious decision not to include the family as an object of study. Living in this family's home became a means for Whyte to maintain standing as a community insider without becoming totally immersed in the demands of research (Whyte, 1943:294–297).

Experienced participant observers (Whyte, 1943:300–306; Wolcott, 1995:91–95) have developed some sound advice for others seeking to maintain relationships in the field:

- Develop a plausible (and honest) explanation for yourself and your study.
- Maintain the support of key individuals in groups or organizations under study.
- Don't be too aggressive in questioning others (for example, don't violate implicit norms that preclude discussion of illegal activity with outsiders). Being a researcher requires that you not simultaneously try to be the guardian of law and order.
- Don't fake social similarity with your subjects. Taking a friendly interest in them should be an adequate basis for developing trust.
- Avoid giving and receiving monetary or other tangible gifts, but do not violate norms of reciprocity. Living with other people, taking others' time for conversations, and going out for a social evening all create expectations and incur social obligations. You can't be an active participant without occasionally helping others. But you will

lose your ability to function as a researcher if you are seen as someone who gives away money or other favors. Such small forms of assistance as an occasional ride to the store or advice on applying to college may strike the right balance.

- Be prepared for special difficulties and tensions if multiple groups are involved. It is hard to avoid taking sides or being used in situations of intergroup conflict.

Sampling People and Events

Decisions to study one setting or several settings and to pay attention to specific people and events will shape field researchers' ability to generalize about what they have found as well as the confidence that others can place in the results of their study. Limiting a particular study to a single setting allows a more intensive portrait of actors and activities in that setting, but also makes generalization of the findings questionable.

We may be reassured by information indicating that a typical case was selected for study or that the case selected was appropriate in some way for the research question. We also must keep in mind that many of the most insightful participant observation studies were conducted in only one setting and draw their credibility precisely from the researcher's thorough understanding of that setting. Nonetheless, studying more than one case or setting almost always strengthens the causal conclusions and makes the findings more generalizable (King, Keohane, & Verba, 1994).

Decker and Van Winkle utilized the technique of snowball sampling. In addition, they chose to contact gang members directly, without the intervention of social service or criminal justice agencies for several reasons, including their concern that they would be identified with law enforcement. To make their findings more generalizable, they interviewed members of several different gangs. Specifically, the snowball began with an earlier fieldwork project on active residential burglars (Wright & Decker, 1994). The young members from this sample, along with contacts the field ethnographer had with several active street criminals, started the referral process. The initial interviewees then nominated other gang members as potential interview subjects. Because they wanted to interview members from several gangs, they had to restart the snowball sampling procedure many times to gain access to a large number of gangs. One problem, of course, was validating whether individuals claiming to be gang members, so-called "wannabes," actually were legitimate members. Over 500 contacts were made before the final sample of 99 was complete.

Another sampling issue Decker and Van Winkle dealt with was representing within their sample various subgroups such as race, sex, or type of gang. To do this, they used a systematic strategy for sampling in participant observation studies, called **theoretical sampling** (Glaser & Strauss, 1967). When field researchers discover in an investigation that particular processes seem to be important, implying that certain comparisons should be made or that similar instances should be checked, the researchers then choose new settings or individuals to study as well, as diagrammed in Exhibit 7.2 (Ragin, 1994:98–101). Based on the existing literature and anecdotal knowledge, Decker and Van Winkle knew that not all gang members were young minority-group males. They describe their strategy to obtain a full range of gang members as follows:

We aggressively pursued leads for female gangs and gang members as well as opportunities to locate older and nonblack gang members. These leads were more difficult to find and often caused us to miss chances to interview other gang members. Despite

Exhibit 7.2   Theoretical Sampling

Original cases interviewed in a study of cocaine users:

Realization: Some cocaine users are businesspeople.
Add businesspeople to sample:

Realization: Sample is low on women.
Add women to sample:

Realization: Some female cocaine users are mothers of young children.
Add mothers to sample:

these "missed opportunities," our sample is strengthened in that it more accurately represents the diverse nature of gangs and gang members in St. Louis. (Decker & Van Winkle, 1996:43)

The resulting sample of gang members in Decker and Van Winkle's study represented 29 different gangs; 16 were affiliated with the Crips and 13 were affiliated with the Bloods. Thus, Decker and Van Winkle's ability to draw from different gangs in developing conclusions gives us greater confidence in their studies' generalizability.

You already learned in Chapter 4 about nonprobability sampling methods, which can also be used to develop a more representative range of opinions and events in a field setting. Purposive sampling, which is a type of theoretical sampling, can be used to identify opinion leaders and representatives of different roles. With snowball sampling, field researchers learn from participants about who represents different subgroups in a setting. Quota sampling also may be employed to ensure the representation of particular categories of participants. Using some type of intentional sampling strategy within a particular setting can allow tests of some hypotheses that would otherwise have to wait until comparative data could be collected from several settings (King, Keohane, & Verba, 1994).

When field studies do not require ongoing, intensive involvement by researchers in the setting, the **experience sampling method (ESM)** can be used. The experiences, thoughts, and feelings of a number of people are randomly sampled as they go about their daily activities. Participants in an ESM study carry an electronic pager and fill out reports when they are beeped. For example, 107 adults carried pagers in Robert Kubey's (1990) ESM study of television habits and family quality of life. Participants' reports indicated that heavy TV viewers were less active during non-TV family activities, although heavy TV viewers also spent more time with their families. They felt as positively toward other family members as did those who watched less TV. Although ESM is a powerful tool for field research, it is still limited by the need to recruit people to carry pagers. Ultimately, the generalizability of ESM findings relies on the representativeness, and reliability, of the persons who cooperate in the research.

Taking Notes

Written **field notes** are the primary means of recording participant observation data (Emerson, Fretz, & Shaw, 1995). Of course, written no longer means handwritten; many field researchers jot down partial notes while observing and then retreat to their computers to write up more complete notes on a daily basis. The computerized text can then be inspected and organized after it is printed out, or it can be marked up and organized for analysis using one of several computer programs designed especially for the task.

It is almost always a mistake to try to take comprehensive notes while engaged in the field—the process of writing extensively is just too disruptive. The usual procedure (see Exhibit 7.3) is to jot down brief notes about the highlights of the observation period. These brief notes then serve as memory joggers when writing the actual field notes at a later time. With the aid of the brief notes and some practice, researchers usually remember a great

Exhibit 7.3   The Note-Taking Process

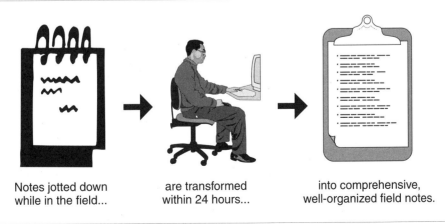

Notes jotted down
while in the field...   are transformed
within 24 hours...   into comprehensive,
well-organized field notes.

deal of what happened, as long as the comprehensive field notes are written within the next 24 hours—that night or upon arising the next day.

In her study of community policing, Miller describes how her research team monitored what they observed and heard on ride- and walk-alongs:

Before beginning, the researchers were trained to follow Lofland and Lofland's field-work steps (1995:89–98): during the period of observation, take notes to aid memory and to let respondents know that they are being taken seriously; convert these to full field-notes at the end of each shift to minimize the time between observation and writing so that crucial material is not lost; write up observations fully before the next trip to the field; and, when additional information is recalled, add it to the written notes. For the research team, fieldnotes were a "running description of events, people, things heard and overheard, conversations among people, conversations with people. Each new physical setting and person encountered merit[ed] a description" (Lofland & Lofland, 1995:93). Investigators distinguished between the respondents' verbatim accounts and their own paraphrasing and general recall. The researchers also recorded their private emotional responses, based on Lofland and Lofland's admonition (1995:95) that their "emotional experience, even if not shared by others in the setting, may still suggest important analytical leads." (Miller, 1999)

Usually, writing up notes takes as long as making the observations. Field notes must be as complete, detailed, and true to what was observed and heard as possible. Quotes should be clearly distinguished from the researcher's observations and phrased in the local vernacular; pauses and interruptions should be indicated. The surrounding context should receive as much attention as possible, and a map of the setting always should be included, with indications of where individuals were at different times.

Careful note-taking yields a big payoff for the researcher. On page after page, field notes will suggest new concepts, causal connections, and theoretical propositions. Social processes and settings can be described in rich detail, with ample illustrations. Exhibit 7.4, for example, contains field notes recorded by Susan Miller (1999) for her study of community police officers. The notes include observations of the setting, the questions Miller asked and the answers she received, and her analytic thoughts about one of the police officers. What can be learned from just this one page of field notes? You can vividly visualize the neighborhood patrolled on the evening described. Key concepts and phrases are identified in the notes, such as "the hole," which refers to the worst apartment houses in the city ("absent landlords, repairs unattended"), and "jackets," which are tiny bags used to sell crack. The notes depict the nature and tone of the interactions between the patrol officer and several residents, with the officer knowing most of the residents by name and asking about other family members. From such notes, researchers can develop a theoretical framework for understanding the setting and a set of concepts and questions to inform subsequent observations.

Complete field notes must provide more than only a record of what was observed or heard. Notes also should include descriptions of the methodology—where researchers were standing while observing, how they chose people for conversation or observation, and what counts of people or events they made and why. Sprinkled throughout the notes also should be a record of the researchers' feelings and thoughts while observing—when they were disgusted by some statement or act, when they felt threatened or intimidated,

Exhibit 7.4   Field Notes from Susan Miller's Study of Community Policing

(7-6-95, Officer P, NBH #4)
Once the sergeant arrived, we walked around in groups for
high visibility in the 1900 block, "the hole" (worst apartment
houses—absent landlords, repairs unattended, no background check for
tenants). Planned to search some of the basements for drugs. Several
officers commented that "Linc" was seen hanging around the hole more
frequently than usual—could indicate increased drug activity. We drove
towards the hole. When we got within a block, Officer P. slowed down
and asked over radio if everybody was ready. In we went. We parked by
the other police mini-station in case anyone wanted sodas later. P.
noticed that the windows had been broken, with rocks around. A white
woman (early 30s) from the apt across the street came over and said it
happened Wed night, and she had already reported it to the other
neighborhood officers. Unclear if break happened after incidents on
Wed·or even if they were related. P. felt they were related since they
picked police windows to break. She was very friendly and cooperative,
as were her kid (white 12 years old) and her boyfriend (black). We
started to walk up to the building on the way to 1900 block. Kids came
up to us to say hi to P. Adults (mostly black) asked P. how he was
doing and how things were since the mini-riot last night. Residents
seemed to know him, and they answered his questions with ease, some
volunteering more information than others. P. knew many by name and
often asked about other family members. Easy rapport. At each
building, P. would knock on the door of one of the ground floor
apartments to ask for a basement key. Women always answered and were
friendly and cooperative. Before P. got to the door with a key, one of
the private security guards had already forced it open with a knife.
The women, upon seeing this, complained to P. that everyone got in
that way. (All women are African American unless otherwise noted.)
One woman ran after P. asking him to get the landlord to fix the lock
on the basement door. P. whipped out his cell phone and dialed right
there in front of her (she was happy about that). In the basements,
officers poked at the insulation where the walls met ceilings. Last
week, they found a gun hidden there, and often find stashes of drugs.
Our search found two different baggies full of "jackets," which is a
way to sell crack (tiny bags) and a bag of pot. Corners of baggies
used to sell crack in $20 quantities on the street. P. documented
all of this to show the absent landlord. Back outside (around 8:10),
several officers and squad cars surrounding a bunch of on-lookers as
well as 3 young males (2 black, 1 white, in 20s) being frisked.
They were spotted going from their car into an apartment where they
don't live—a known apt where people went to do heroin. One of the
bystanders (black, mid 20s) took P. aside to talk about getting some
of his personal items back from jail (P. had visited him earlier in
jail to get his version of the mini-riot). Search revealed a rock
of cocaine.

Source: From personal communication with Susan Miller; used with permission.

why their attention shifted from one group to another. Notes like these provide a foundation for later review of the likelihood of bias or of inattention to some salient features of the situation.

Managing the Personal Dimensions

Our overview of participant observation is not complete without considering its personal dimensions. Because field researchers become a part of the social situation they are studying, they cannot help but be affected on a personal, emotional level. At the same time, those being studied react to researchers not just as researchers but as personal acquaintances—often as friends, sometimes as personal rivals. Managing and learning from this personal side of field research is an important part of any project.

The impact of personal issues varies with the depth of researchers' involvement in the setting. The more involved researchers are in multiple aspects of the ongoing social situation, the more important personal issues become and the greater the risk of "going native." Even when researchers acknowledge their role, "increased contact brings sympathy, and sympathy in its turn dulls the edge of criticism" (Fenno, 1978:277). To study the social life of "corner boys," however, Whyte could not stay so disengaged. Recall that he moved into an apartment with a Cornerville family and lived for about 4 years in the community he was investigating:

> The researcher, like his informants, is a social animal. He has a role to play, and he has his own personality needs that must be met in some degree if he is to function success-fully. Where the researcher operates out of a university, just going into the field for a few hours at a time, he can keep his personal social life separate from field activity. His problem of role is not quite so complicated. If, on the other hand, the researcher is living for an extended period in the community he is studying, his personal life is inex-tricably mixed with his research. (Whyte, 1943:279)

The correspondence between researchers' social attributes—age, sex, race, and so on—and those of their subjects also shapes personal relationships, as Miller noted:

> In the face-to-face interviews with neighborhood police officers it was my sense that being a woman facilitated the conversation. In fact, other investigators who have con-sidered how the researcher's gender could impede or enhance rapport with respondents have found that women interviewing men may facilitate the subjects' ability to talk openly about their feelings. Men may be more comfortable speaking of intimate topics with women than with other men (Williams & Heikes, 1993:281). . . . It made sense to the police that a female researcher would ask them about gender issues and that, as a criminologist, I would ask these questions in the context of community policing. Thus, I was able to examine gendered behavior and assumptions of masculinity and femininity within community policing with greater ease. (Miller, 1999:232)

There is no formula for successfully managing the personal dimension of field research. It is much more art than science and flows more from the researcher's own personality and natural approach to other people than from formal training. Novice field researchers often neglect to consider how they will manage personal relationships when they plan and carry out their projects. Then suddenly they find themselves doing something they don't believe they should, just to stay in the good graces of research subjects, or juggling the emotions resulting from conflict within the group. As Whyte noted:

> The field worker cannot afford to think only of learning to live with others in the field. He has to continue living with himself. If the participant observer finds himself engaging in behavior that he has learned to think of as immoral, then he is likely to begin to wonder what sort of a person he is after all. Unless the field worker can carry with him a reasonably consistent picture of himself, he is likely to run into difficulties. (Whyte, 1943:317)

These issues are even more salient when researchers place themselves in potentially dangerous situations. As Decker and Van Winkle explain:

> In part, gang members were of interest to us because of their involvement in violence. Because of this, we took steps to insure our own safety. One of the guiding principles was to limit the number of people being separately interviewed at the same time and location. In addition, we steadfastly avoided interviewing members of rival gangs at the same time. The field ethnographer carried a portable phone with him at all times, to insure that he could check in with us and we with him. Despite our best efforts, there were occasions when these precautions did not work. The field ethnographer witnessed several drive-by shootings while on the way to pick up interview subjects, and on one occasion, he saw three of our subjects shot while waiting to be picked up for an interview. . . . Not all exposure to risk of physical danger comes through such obvious means; however, during one interview, when asked whether he owned any guns, a gang member reached into his coat pocket and pulled out a .32 caliber pistol. We assured him that we would have taken his word for it. (Decker & Van Winkle, 1996:46)

If you plan a field research project, there are some general guidelines to follow:

- Take the time to consider how you want to relate to your potential subjects as people.
- Speculate about what personal problems might arise and how you will respond to them.
- Keep in touch with other researchers and personal friends outside the research setting.
- Maintain standards of conduct that make you comfortable as a person and that respect the integrity of your subjects. (Whyte, 1943:300–317)

When you evaluate participant observers' reports, pay attention to how they defined their role in the setting and dealt with personal problems. Don't place too much confidence in such research unless the report provides this information.

INTENSIVE INTERVIEWING

Asking questions is part of almost all participant observation (Wolcott, 1995:102–105). Many qualitative researchers employ intensive interviewing exclusively, without systematic observation of respondents in their natural setting. Unlike the more structured interviewing that may be used in survey research (discussed in Chapter 6), intensive interviewing relies on open-ended questions. Qualitative researchers do not presume to know the range of answers that respondents might give and they seek to hear these answers in the respondents' own words. Rather than asking standard questions in a fixed order, intensive interviewers allow the specific content and order of questions to vary from one interviewee to another.

What distinguishes intensive interviewing from less structured forms of questioning is consistency and thoroughness. The goal is to develop a comprehensive picture of the interviewees' background, attitudes, and actions, in their own terms; to "listen to people as they describe how they understand the worlds in which they live and work" (Rubin & Rubin, 1995:3). For example, even though Decker and Van Winkle had an interview guide, they encouraged elaboration on the part of their respondents and "went to great lengths to insure that each person we interviewed felt they had received the opportunity to tell their story in their own words" (1996:45).

Intensive interview studies do not directly reveal the social context in which action is taken and opinions are formed. Similar to participant observation studies, intensive interviewing engages researchers more actively with their subjects than does standard survey research. The researchers must listen to lengthy explanations, ask follow-up questions tailored to the preceding answers, and seek to learn about interrelated belief systems or personal approaches to things rather than measure a limited set of variables. As a result, intensive interviews are often much longer than standardized interviews, sometimes as long as 15 hours, conducted in several different sessions (Kaufman, 1986:22).

The intensive interview becomes more like a conversation between partners than between a researcher and a subject. Intensive interviewers actively try to probe understandings and engage interviewees in a dialogue about the intended meaning of their comments. The interview typically follows a preplanned outline of topics, which often are asked of selected group members or other participants in a reasonably consistent manner. Some projects may use relatively structured interviews, particularly when the focus is on developing knowledge about prior events or some narrowly defined topic. But more exploratory projects, particularly those aimed at learning the interviewees' interpretations of the world, may let each interview flow in a unique direction in response to the interviewee's experiences and interests (Kvale, 1996:3–5; Rubin & Rubin, 1995:6; Wolcott, 1995:113–114). In either case, qualitative interviewers must nimbly adapt throughout the interview, paying attention to nonverbal cues, expressions with symbolic value, and the ebb and flow of the interviewee's feelings and interests. "You have to be free to follow your data where they lead" (Rubin & Rubin, 1995:64).

Random selection is rarely used to select respondents for intensive interviews, but the selection method still must be carefully considered. If interviewees are selected in a haphazard manner, as by speaking just to those who happen to be available at the time that the researcher is on site, the interviews are likely to be of less value than when a more purposive selection strategy is used. Researchers should try to select interviewees who are knowledgeable about the subject of the interview, who are open to talking, and who represent the range of perspectives (Rubin & Rubin, 1995:65–92). Selection of new interviewees should continue, if possible, at least until the **saturation point** is reached, the point when new interviews seem to yield little additional information (see Exhibit 7.5). As new issues are uncovered, additional interviewees may be selected to represent different opinions about these issues.

Exhibit 7.5   The Saturation Point in Intensive Interviewing

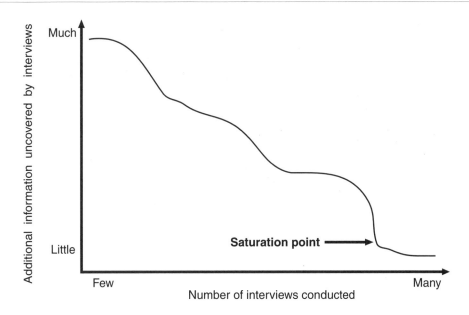

A recent book written by Benjamin Fleury-Steiner that examines the thoughts and emotions of jurors in death penalty cases is an excellent illustration of the tremendous insights that can be uncovered through intensive interviewing. In *Jurors' Stories of Death* (2003), Fleury-Steiner reports on his work with the Capital Jury Project (CJP), which was a national study of the experiences of citizens who served as jurors on death penalty cases. To encourage respondents to tell stories about their experiences, the CJP survey explicitly asked jurors to tell interviewers about important moments during the trial and deliberations, and their impressions of the defendant. Fleury-Steiner states, "The goal of these questions was to facilitate jurors to construct their responses in their own ways. . . . Given the leeway to answer as they saw fit, in many instances jurors' stories emerged when I least expected them to" (Fleury-Steiner, 2003:44).

The inductive analytic process of generating theory and making conclusions based on intensive interview narratives is often a time-consuming process. Fleury-Steiner explains,

Through numerous rounds of retranscribing and revising, I was able to clarify my interpretations of jurors' stories. . . . Expanding beyond a literal interpretation of what was on the page, I began to notice consistencies in the way jurors made sense in their stories, including the taken for granted normative grammars of both speaker and listener. By privileging the "telling" of jurors' stories, I was able to make subsequent analytical interpretations. Indeed, the more I returned to the data, the more I began to connect the particularities of jurors' stories to broader sociohistorical, cultural, and institutional interpretations of identity, morality, and punishment. (Fleury-Steiner, 2003:47)

Establishing and Maintaining a Partnership

Because intensive interviewing does not engage researchers as participants in subjects' daily affairs, the problems of entering the field are much reduced. However, the logistics of arranging long periods for personal interviews can still be fairly complicated. It is important to establish rapport with subjects by considering in advance how they will react to the interview arrangements and by developing an approach that does not violate their standards for social behavior. Interviewees should be treated with respect, as knowledgeable partners whose time is valued. (In other words, avoid coming late for appointments.) A commitment to confidentiality should be stated and honored (Rubin & Rubin, 1995).

But the intensive interviewer's relationship with the interviewee is not an equal partnership, for the researcher seeks to gain certain types of information and strategizes throughout to maintain an appropriate relationship (Kvale, 1996:6). In the first few minutes of the interview, the goal is to show interest in the interviewee and to clearly explain the purpose of the interview (Kvale, 1996:128). During the interview, the interviewer should maintain an appropriate distance from the interviewee, one that doesn't violate cultural norms; the interviewer should maintain eye contact and not engage in distracting behavior. An appropriate pace is also important; pause to allow the interviewee to reflect, elaborate, and generally not feel rushed (Gordon, 1992). When an interview covers emotional or otherwise stressful topics, at the end the interviewer should give the interviewee an opportunity to unwind (Rubin & Rubin, 1995:138).

Asking Questions and Recording Answers

Intensive interviewers must plan their main questions around an outline of the interview topic. The questions should generally be short and to the point. More details can then be elicited through nondirective probes (such as "Can you tell me more about that?"), and follow-up questions can be tailored to answers to the main questions. Interviewers should strategize throughout an interview about how best to achieve their objectives while taking into account interviewees' answers.

Decker and Van Winkle's interview narratives illustrate this well:

Nearly half of the gang members identified leaders as persons who could provide material advantages, thus ascribing a functional character to leadership within the gang. Since half of our sample was in their early teens, someone with the ability to procure cars, drugs, guns, or alcohol could play a valuable role in the gang. Consequently, it was no surprise to find that over half of gang members identified leaders as persons who could "deliver." Because of the situational nature of leadership, persons moved in and out of this role. This was especially true in the case of being able to provide drugs in large quantities for street sales:

Q: Does someone have more juice in the gang?

A: Yeah, you always got someone that got more juice.

Q: What is the type of person who usually have more juice?

A: The one who got the connection with the drugs.

Q: Who has the most juice?

A: Dude named T-Loc.

Q: Why does he have more juice than everybody else?

A: Cause he travels a lot. Gets the good stuff.

Q: What's the good stuff?

A: Like guns, cocaine, weed.

Q: What gives him the juice? (Decker & Van Winkle, 1996:97–98)

Do you see how the interviewer actively encouraged the subject to elaborate on answers? More important, intensive interviews can also uncover true meanings that questions utilizing fixed formats would surely miss. For example, during an interview with a female gang member, Decker and Van Winkle discovered that some gang members were actually confused about what marijuana (weed) actually was:

Q: What drugs are being sold?

A: Coke, crack, marijuana.

Q: Anything else?

A: Weed, that's all.

Q: Weed is marijuana?

A: No.

Q: What is marijuana then?

A: I don't know.

Q: What is weed?

A: Stuff you smoke.

Tape recorders commonly are used to record intensive interviews. Most researchers who have tape-recorded interviews feel that they do not inhibit most interviewees and, in fact, are routinely ignored. The occasional respondent who is very concerned with his or her public image may speak "for the tape recorder," but such individuals are unlikely to speak frankly in any research interview. In any case, constant note-taking during an interview prevents adequate displays of interest and appreciation by the interviewer and hinders the degree of concentration that results in the best interviews.

Of course, there are exceptions to every rule. Fenno presents a compelling argument for avoiding the tape recorder when interviewing public figures who are concerned with their public image:

My belief is that the only chance to get a nonroutine, nonreflexive interview [from many of the members of Congress] is to converse casually, pursuing targets of opportunity without the presence of a recording instrument other than myself. If [worse] comes to worst, they can always deny what they have said in person; on tape they leave themselves no room for escape. I believe they are not unaware of the difference. (Fenno, 1978:280)

Combining Participant Observation and Intensive Interviewing

Many large research projects aimed at uncovering detailed information about a particular phenomenon often combine the qualitative research techniques of participant observation and intensive interviewing. As we have already seen, Decker and Van Winkle (1996) utilized this double strategy. Susan Miller also combined participant observation with intensive interviewing in her study of community policing (1999). The information obtained from both methodologies was vital to her conclusions. For example, the observational component of Miller's research revealed how traditional patrol officers' perceptions and experiences differ from those of neighborhood patrol officers. Her observations also uncovered how rarely the paths of patrol officers crossed with their community policing counterparts. These limited interactions contributed, Miller believed, to patrol officers' misconceptions about community policing. Patrol officers believed that neighborhood police officers (NPOs) did not do real police work and spent too much time responding to residents and political needs, not to crime-fighting goals.

Through both methods, Miller also uncovered differences in what was observed in group settings compared to what was revealed in one-on-one interviews with the officers. On ride-alongs with patrol officers, Miller observed that it was customary to gather during the shift at a predetermined place for dinner or in an uncrowded parking lot. She observed that although these meetings involved both women and men, the discussions usually revolved around "guy stuff," such as joking about guns, and pretending to pull out a gun. Miller describes:

> Their language was full of expletives, with some version of "f—k" being the most common. . . . Common topics of conversation were upcoming shooting competitions, physical training, qualifications, and similar physical activities. The men tended to tell us, the researchers, what kind of exercise regimens they followed, and which officers helped with running, training, and weight lifting at the police academy. These topics reinforced the tough, masculine, crime-fighting image of policing. Patrolwomen who were part of these "jawing" sessions engaged in the conversation with equal heartiness. (1999:175–176)

If Miller had only performed this observation, she would not have discovered the more gendered nature of the patrol officers' perceptions and experiences that was uncovered in her intensive interviews:

> Even though the patrolwomen joined in the banter and told their share of crime-fighting war stories, it became clear during one-on-one conversations with them they dropped their aggressive facade when their actions were less visible to other patrol officers. The women were more than superficially involved in some of the local people's lives, particularly with the children. (Miller, 1999:176)

FOCUS GROUPS

Focus groups are groups of unrelated individuals that are formed by a researcher and then led in group discussion of a topic. The researcher asks specific questions and guides the discussion to ensure that group members address these questions, but the resulting information is qualitative and relatively unstructured. Unlike most other survey designs, focus groups do not involve representative samples; instead, a few individuals are recruited for the group who have the time to participate and who share key characteristics with the target population.

Focus groups have their roots in the interviewing techniques developed in the 1930s by sociologists and psychologists who were dissatisfied with traditional surveys. Traditionally, in a questionnaire survey, subjects are directed to consider certain issues and particular response options in a predetermined order. The spontaneous exchange and development of ideas that characterize social life outside the survey situation are lost—and with them, some social scientists feared, the prospects for validity.

Focus groups were used by the military in World War II to investigate morale and then were popularized by the great American sociologist Robert K. Merton and two collaborators, Marjorie Fiske and Patricia Kendall in *The Focused Interview* (1956). But marketing researchers were the first to adopt focus groups as a widespread methodology. Marketing researchers use focus groups to investigate likely popular reactions to possible advertising themes and techniques. Their success has prompted other social scientists to use focus groups to evaluate social programs and to assess social needs (Krueger, 1988:18–22).

Most focus groups involve 7 to 10 people, a number that facilitates discussion by all in attendance. Although participants usually do not know one another, they are chosen so that they are relatively homogeneous, which tends to reduce their inhibitions in discussion. (Some researchers conduct discussions among groups of people who know one another, which may further reduce inhibitions.) Of course, the characteristics of individuals that determine their inclusion are based on the researcher's conception of the target population for the study. Focus group leaders must begin the discussion by creating the expectation that all will participate and that the researcher will not favor any particular perspective or participant.

Focus groups are interviewed to collect qualitative data using open-ended questions posed by the researcher (or group leader). Thus a focused discussion mimics the natural process of forming and expressing opinions—and may give some sense of validity. The researcher may also want to conduct a more traditional survey, asking a representative sample of the target population to answer closed-ended questions, to weigh the validity of data obtained from the focus group. No formal procedure exists for determining the generalizability of focus group answers, but the careful researcher should conduct at least several focus groups on the same topic and check for consistency in the findings as a partial test of generalizability.

Tina Kandakai and her colleagues' (1999) study of mothers' perceptions of violence in schools provides a good example of the effective use of focus groups in research. Recall from Chapter 1 that this research involved survey methodology and examined the reasons mothers most often gave for school violence. Before Kandakai and her colleagues designed their questionnaire, however, they conducted focus groups with mothers to identify in a more detailed manner their perceptions of the causes of school violence. Specifically, four focus groups of six to eight mothers of junior high school students from both urban and suburban areas were conducted to ascertain mothers' most salient beliefs regarding school violence. Responses that were given at least three times during a focus group were then added to the final questionnaire. For example, if during the course of a focus group, at least three mothers mentioned that the lack of supervision in schools was an important factor related to school violence, then this reason was included as a response choice in the questionnaire.

Focus group methods share with other field research techniques an emphasis on discovering unanticipated findings and exploring hidden meanings. Although they do not provide a means for developing reliable, generalizable results (the traditional strong suits of survey research), focus groups can be an indispensable aid for developing hypotheses and survey questions, for investigating the meaning of survey results, and for quickly assessing the range of opinion about an issue.

ANALYSIS OF QUALITATIVE DATA

The data for a qualitative study most often are notes jotted down in the field or during an interview. From these notes the original comments are reconstructed or the text is transcribed from an audio tape. The procedure used by Miller's (1999:233) research team is typical: "Each observer carried a tiny notebook on shift, and transcribed notes from it into longer, more descriptive typed versions within twenty-four hours of the shift's completion."

Many projects have slowed to a halt because a novice researcher becomes overwhelmed by the quantity of information that has been collected. A 1-hour interview can generate 20 to 25 pages of single-spaced text (Kvale, 1996:169). Analysis is less daunting, however, if the process is broken into smaller steps.

The Phases of Analysis

The analysis of qualitative research notes typically proceeds sequentially, with the researcher first identifying problems and concepts that appear likely to help in understanding the situation. This phase of the analysis should begin while the researcher is still engaged in the field or conducting interviews, so analytic insights can be tested against new observations. Miller's research team met weekly to go over field notes and resolve any points of confusion. In addition, Miller brought in other researchers who were not involved in the project but who were skilled with qualitative data analysis to help uncover emerging concepts. She describes:

> The fieldwork team met weekly to talk about situations that were unclear and to troubleshoot any problems. We also made use of peer-debriefing techniques. Here, multiple colleagues, who were familiar with qualitative data analysis but not involved in our research, participated in preliminary analysis of our findings. (Miller, 1999:233)

Development of theory continually occurs in qualitative research and explicitly occurs in interaction with analysis of the data (Coffey & Atkinson, 1996:23). The goal of many qualitative researchers is to create **grounded theory**—that is, to inductively build up a

Exhibit 7.6   The Development of Grounded Theory

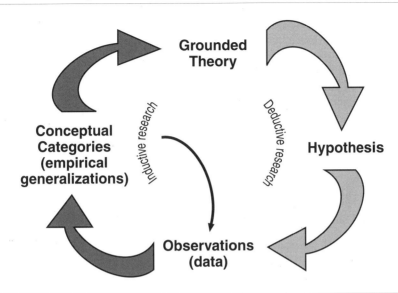

systematic theory "grounded" in, or based on, the observations. The observations are summarized into conceptual categories, which are tested directly in the research setting with more observations. Over time, as the conceptual categories are refined and linked, a theory evolves (Glaser & Strauss, 1967; Huberman & Miles, 1994:436). Exhibit 7.6 diagrams this process. Notice that it corresponds to the inductive portion of the research circle, which was introduced in Chapter 2 (see Exhibit 2.4).

Simply reading the notes or transcripts is an important step in the analytic process. Researchers should make frequent notes in the margins to identify important statements and to propose ways of coding the data: "husband–wife conflict," perhaps, or "tension reduction strategy." An interim stage may consist of listing the concepts reflected in the notes and diagramming the relationships among concepts (Maxwell, 1996:78–81).

As observation, interviewing, and reflection continue, researchers refine their definitions of problems and concepts and select indicators. They can then check the frequency and distribution of phenomena. How many people made a particular type of comment? How often did social interaction lead to arguments? Social system models may be developed, which specify the relationships among different phenomena. These models are modified as researchers gain experience in the setting. For the final analysis, the researchers check their models carefully against their notes and make a concerted attempt to discover negative evidence that might suggest the model is incorrect.

Finally, the researchers should add a natural history of the development of the evidence so that others can evaluate their findings. After the intensive interview data with police officers revealed that most officers perceived community neighborhood patrol officers (NPOs) as "pansy police" or "social workers," Miller reveals her thought process, which illustrates this final element of the analysis:

The interview data raised a question: If the neighborhood officer position was a "feminized" aspect of macho policing, how would men manage their masculinity? In the interviews and fieldwork, both women and men addressed the issue by giving information that demonstrated their competency. Data that I gathered on career histories demonstrated that the men who requested an NPO position had a background in traditional, "macho" police work. Most of the men who were former or serving neighborhood officers had previous (or ongoing) experience with elite law enforcement units, such as the SWAT team, drug and gang squads, undercover detail, and hostage negotiation team. These specialty positions were very well known, and the male officers were eager to tell me and members of the research team about this part of their background, often before we asked for the information. (Miller, 1999:106)

Use of Computers

The analysis process can be enhanced in various ways by using a computer. Programs designed for qualitative data can speed up the analysis process, make it easier for researchers to experiment with different codes, test different hypotheses about relationships, and facilitate diagrams of emerging theories and preparation of research reports (Coffey & Atkinson, 1996; Richards & Richards, 1994). The steps involved in computer-based qualitative analysis parallel those used traditionally to analyze such text as notes, documents, or interview transcripts: preparation, coding, analysis, and reporting. We use two of the most popular programs to illustrate these steps: HyperRESEARCH and QSR NVivo. The latter is one of two programs in the NUD*IST software for Non-Numerical Unstructured Data Indexing, Searching, and Theorizing. (See Appendix F for an extended exercise introducing HyperRESEARCH.)

Text preparation begins with typing or scanning text in a word processor or, alternatively, directly into NVivo's rich text editor. NVivo will create or import a rich text file. HyperRESEARCH requires that your text be saved as a text file (as "ASCII" in most word processors) before you transfer it into the analysis program. HyperRESEARCH expects your text data to be stored in separate files corresponding to each unique case, such as an interview with one subject.

Coding the text involves categorizing particular text segments. This is the foundation of much qualitative analysis. Either program allows you to assign a code to any segment of text (in NVivo, you drag through the characters to select them; in HyperRESEARCH, click on the first and last words to select text). You can make up codes as you go through a document or assign codes that you have already developed to text segments. Exhibit 7.7 shows the screens that appear in the two programs at the coding stage, when a particular text segment is being labeled. You can also have the programs "autocode" text by identifying a word or phrase that should always receive the same code, or, in NVivo, by coding each section identified by the style of the rich text document—for example, each question or speaker (of course, you should check carefully the results of autocoding). Both programs also let you examine the coded text "in context"—embedded in its place in the original document.

In qualitative data analysis, coding is not a one-time-only or one-code-only procedure. Both HyperRESEARCH and NVivo allow you to be inductive and holistic in your coding: You can revise codes as you go along, assign multiple codes to text segments, and link your own comments ("memos") to text segments. In NVivo you can work "live" with

Exhibit 7.7a HyperRESEARCH Coding Stage

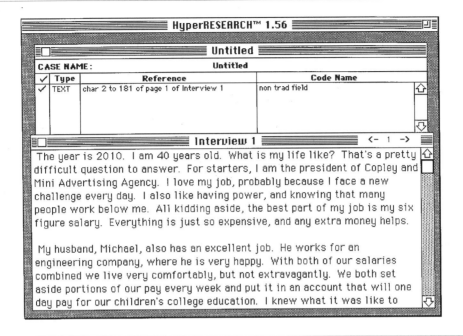

Exhibit 7.7b NVivo Coding Stage

Exhibit 7.8   A Free-Form Model in NVivo

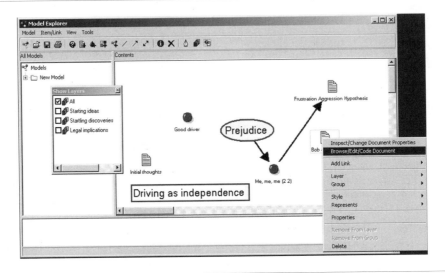

the coded text to alter coding or create new, more subtle categories. You can also place hyperlinks to other documents in the project or any multimedia files outside it.

Analysis focuses on reviewing cases or text segments with similar codes and examining relationships among different codes. You may decide to combine codes into larger concepts. You may specify additional codes to capture more fully the variation among cases. You can test hypotheses about relationships among codes. NVivo allows development of an indexing system to facilitate thinking about the relationships among concepts and the overarching structure of these relationships. It will also allow you to draw more free-form models (Exhibit 7.8). In HyperRESEARCH, you can specify combinations of codes that identify cases that you want to examine.

Reports from both programs can include text to illustrate the cases, codes, and relationships that you specify. You can also generate counts of code frequencies and then import these counts into a statistical program for quantitative analysis. However, the many types of analyses and reports that can be developed with qualitative analysis software do not lessen the need for a careful evaluation of the quality of the data on which conclusions are based.

In reality, using a qualitative data analysis computer program is not always as straightforward as it appears. As Decker and Van Winkle (1996:53–54) describe:

> The software we used is essentially a text retrieval package and allows the use of boolean operators to retrieve, link, and print various segments of an interview. One of the dilemmas faced in the use of such software is whether to employ a coding scheme within the interviews or simply to leave them as unmarked text. We chose the first alternative, embedding conceptual tags at the appropriate points in the text. An example illustrates this process. One of the activities we were concerned with was drug sales. Our first chore (after a thorough reading of all the transcripts) was to use the software to "isolate" all of

the transcript sections dealing with drug sales. One way to do this would be to search the transcripts for every instance in which the word "drugs" was used. However, such a strategy would have the disadvantages of providing information of too general a character while often missing important statements about drugs. Searching on the word "drugs" would have produced a file including every time the word was used, whether it was in reference to drug sales, drug use, or drug availability, clearly more information than we were interested in. However, such a search would have failed to find all of the slang used to refer to drugs ("boy" for heroin, "Casper" for crack cocaine) as well as the more common descriptions of drugs, especially rock or crack cocaine.

Decker and Van Winkle solved this problem by parenthetically inserting "conceptual tags" in the text whenever talk of "drug sales" was found. This process allowed them to examine all of the statements made by gang members about a single concept (drug sales). As you can imagine, however, this still left the researchers with many pages of transcript material to analyze.

Evaluation of Conclusions

No set standards exist for evaluating the validity of conclusions in a qualitative study, but the need to carefully consider the evidence and methods on which conclusions are based is just as great as with other types of research. Individual items of information can be assessed in terms of at least three criteria (Becker, 1958):

1. *How credible was the informant?* Were statements made by someone with whom the researcher had a relationship of trust, or by someone the researcher had just met? Did the informant have reason to lie? If the statements do not seem to be trustworthy as indicators of actual events, can they at least be used to help understand the informant's perspective?

2. *Were statements made in response to the researcher's questions, or were they spontaneous?* Spontaneous statements are more likely to indicate what would have been said had the researcher not been present.

3. *How does the presence or absence of the researcher or the researcher's informant influence the actions and statements of other group members?* Reactivity to being observed can never be ruled out as a possible explanation for some directly observed social phenomenon. However, if the researcher carefully compares what the informant says with what goes on when the researcher is not present, what the researcher observes directly, and what other group members say about their normal practices, the extent of reactivity can be assessed to some extent.

A qualitative researcher's conclusions should also be assessed by her or his ability to provide a credible explanation for some aspect of social life. That explanation should capture the group members' tacit knowledge of the social processes that were observed, not just their verbal statements about these processes. **Tacit knowledge**—"the largely unarticulated, contextual understanding that is often manifested in nods, silences, humor, and naughty nuances"—is reflected in participants' actions as well as their words and in what they fail to state but nonetheless feel deeply and even take for granted

(Altheide & Johnson, 1994:492–493). These features are evident in Whyte's analysis of Cornerville social patterns:

> The corner-gang structure arises out of the habitual association of the members over a long period of time. The nuclei of most gangs can be traced back to early boyhood. . . . Home plays a very small role in the group activities of the corner boy.
>
> . . . The life of the corner boy proceeds along regular and narrowly circumscribed channels. . . . Out of [social interaction within the group] arises a system of mutual obligations which is fundamental to group cohesion. . . . The code of the corner boy requires him to help his friends when he can and to refrain from doing anything to harm them. When life in the group runs smoothly, the obligations binding members to one another are not explicitly recognized. (Whyte, 1943:255–257)

Conclusions drawn from qualitative research are also strengthened if they are consistent with other research from related projects. For example, Miller (1999) found the narratives used my male NPOs to affirm their masculinity and heterosexuality were similar to those found by researchers who studies males in other traditionally female jobs such as nursing:

> In part, male NPOs construct an exaggerated masculinity so that they are not seen as feminine as they carry out the social-work functions of policing. Related to this is the almost defiant expression of heterosexuality, so that the men's sexual orientation can never truly be doubted even if their gender roles are contested. Male patrol officers' language—such as their use of terms like "pansy police" to connote neighborhood police officers—served to affirm their own heterosexuality. . . . In addition, the male officers, but not the women, deliberately wove their heterosexual status into conversations, explicitly mentioning their female domestic partner or spouse and their children. This finding is consistent with research conducted in the occupational field. The studies reveal that men in female-dominated occupations, such as teachers, librarians, and pediatricians, over-reference their heterosexual status to ensure that others will not think they are gay. (Miller, 1999:222)

Confidence in the conclusions from a field research study is also strengthened by an honest and informative account about how the researcher interacted with subjects in the field, what problems he or she encountered, and how these problems were or were not resolved. Such an account is important first and foremost because of the evolving and variable nature of field research. To an important extent, the researcher makes up the method in the context of a particular investigation rather than applying standard procedures that are specified before the investigation begins.

In recent years, qualitative researchers also have become increasingly sensitive to the idea that a social situation or process is interpreted from a particular background and values and not simply from the situation itself (Altheide & Johnson, 1994). Researchers are only human, after all, and must rely on their own senses and process all information through their own minds. By reporting how and why they think they did what they did, they can help others determine whether, or how, the researchers' perspectives influenced their conclusions: "There should be clear tracks indicating the attempt [to show the hand of the ethnographer] has been made" (Altheide & Johnson, 1994:493).

Can the participant observer truly gain access to the minds and behaviors of other people? Can participant observation really lead to insights into the social world? Most field researchers now believe that no outsider can really see the world just as an insider does. We all filter our observations through a subjective mental apparatus. But certainly the qualitative methodologies used by Decker and Van Winkle and by Miller seem to get us closer to the reality of ongoing social life than would a survey or experiment.

In general, the usual approach to the analysis of qualitative data contrasts markedly with the procedures used to analyze quantitative data collected in experimental and survey research. Qualitative researchers seek to maximize the validity of their understanding of the social world by learning as much as possible about how it works and why people think as they do. They return again and again to the field to explore new ideas as old ideas are elaborated or rejected on the basis of previously collected data. This inductive approach is quite different from the deductive, hypothesis-testing logic that guides the analysis of quantitative data. But just as experimental and survey researchers engage in exploratory analyses to gain insights into social patterns, so qualitative researchers sometimes develop quantitative indicators from their data and formally test hypotheses. Qualitative analysis software facilitates the process of blending qualitative with more quantitative approaches to data analysis. The two approaches are complementary, and understanding their advantages and disadvantages enhances our ability to fit our methods to the problems we investigate.

ETHICAL ISSUES IN QUALITATIVE RESEARCH

Qualitative research can raise some complex ethical issues. No matter how hard the field researcher strives to study the social world naturally, leaving no traces, the very act of research itself imposes something unnatural on the situation. It is up to the researchers to identify and take responsibility for the consequences of their involvement. Four main ethical issues arise: voluntary participation, subject well-being, identity disclosure, and confidentiality.

Voluntary Participation

Ensuring that subjects are participating in a study voluntarily is not often a problem with intensive interviewing and focus group research, but it is often a point of contention in participant observation studies. Few researchers or institutional review boards are willing to condone covert participation because it does not offer a way to ensure that participation by the subjects is voluntary. Even when the researcher's role is more open, interpreting the standard of voluntary participation still can be difficult. Practically, much field research would be impossible if the participant observer were required to request permission of everyone having some contact, no matter how minimal, with a group or setting being observed. And should the requirement of voluntary participation apply equally to every member of an organization being observed? What if the manager consents, the workers are ambivalent, and the union says no? Requiring everyone's consent would limit participant observation research only to settings without serious conflicts of interest.

The issue of voluntary participation is particularly important when interviewing or observing minors. At what age can individuals validly give their voluntary consent to participate in a project? It is customary for human subjects committees to want the consent of parents when their children are participating in research. This requirement poses a problem for research that may be investigating issues that parents or guardians may not want uncovered, such as abuse or neglect. In other instances, alerting parents or guardians about the nature of the study may compromise the confidentiality of the participants. For example, if Decker and Van Winkle had been forced to obtain parental approval for their gang member interviews, it would have violated the confidentiality they tried to provide to their respondents. To assure the human subjects committee that their participants understood their rights, Decker and Van Winkle obtained an advocate for each juvenile member of their sample. This advocate was responsible for making sure that the juveniles each understood their right to refuse or quit the interview at any time without penalty, and the confidential nature of the project. Only after these issues were carefully explained did the participant sign a consent form.

Subject Well-Being

Before beginning a project, every field researcher should carefully consider how to avoid harm to subjects. It is not possible to avoid every theoretical possibility of harm nor to be sure that any project will not cause adverse consequences to any individual. Some of the Cornerville men read Whyte's book and felt discomfited by it (others found it enlightening). Some police accused Van Maanen of damaging their reputations with his studies. But such consequences could follow from any research, even from any public discourse. Direct harm to the reputations or feelings of particular individuals is what researchers must carefully avoid. They can do so in part by maintaining the confidentiality of research subjects. They must also avoid adversely affecting the course of events while engaged in a setting. Whyte (1943:335–337) found himself regretting having recommended that a particular politician be allowed to speak to a social club he was observing because the speech led to serious dissension in the club and strains between Whyte and some club members. These problems are rare in intensive interviewing and focus groups, but even there, researchers should try to identify negative feelings and help distressed subjects cope with their feelings through debriefing or referrals for professional help.

Identity Disclosure

We already have considered the problems of identity disclosure, particularly in the case of covert participation. But how much disclosure about the study is necessary, and how hard should researchers try to make sure that their research purposes are understood? Less-educated subjects may not readily comprehend what a researcher is or be able to weigh the possible consequences of the research for themselves. Should researchers inform subjects if the study's interests and foci change while it is in progress? Current ethical standards require informed consent of research subjects; can this standard be met in any meaningful way if researchers do not fully disclose their identity? But isn't some degree of dissimulation a natural part of social life (Punch, 1994:91)? Can a balance be struck between the disclosure of critical facts and a coherent research strategy?

Confidentiality

Field researchers normally use fictitious names for the characters in their reports, but doing so does not always guarantee confidentiality to their research subjects. Individuals in the setting studied may be able to identify those whose actions are described and may thus become privy to some knowledge about their colleagues or neighbors that had formerly been kept from them. Researchers should thus make every effort to expunge possible identifying material from published information and to alter unimportant aspects of a description when necessary to prevent identity disclosure. In any case, no field research project should begin if some participants clearly will suffer serious harm by being identified in project publications.

Confidentiality is particularly important if the research is uncovering deviant or illegal behavior. In research such as Decker and Van Winkle's, it was almost inevitable their information about illegal activity would be revealed during the course of observing or interviewing. Because they had promised confidentiality to their interviewees, Decker and Van Winkle did not use specific information they gained about past crimes—they would only refer to this activity in an aggregate form to describe the activities of gang members in general. They state, "had we violated this promise [of confidentiality], we would have placed the lives of several individuals (including the field-worker) in jeopardy." In addition, Decker and Van Winkle told their subjects that they did not want to know about information concerning future crimes, as this information would not be protected by their pledge of confidentiality.

These ethical issues cannot be evaluated independently. The final decision to proceed must be made after weighing the relative benefits and risks to participants. Few qualitative research projects will be barred by consideration of these ethical issues, except for those involving covert participation. The more important concern for researchers is to identify the ethically troublesome aspects of their proposed research, resolve them before the project begins, and act on new ethical issues as they come up during the project. Combining methods is often the best strategy.

CONCLUSION

Qualitative research allows the careful investigator to obtain a richer and more intimate view of the social world than can be achieved with more structured methods. It is not hard to understand why so many qualitative studies have become classics in the literature. And the emphases in qualitative research on inductive reasoning and incremental understanding help to stimulate and inform other research approaches. Exploratory research to chart the dimensions of previously unstudied social settings and intensive investigations of the subjective meanings that motivate individual action are particularly well served by the techniques of participant observation, intensive interviewing, and focus groups.

The very characteristics that make qualitative research techniques so appealing restrict their use to a limited set of research problems. It is not possible to draw representative samples for study using participant observation, and for this reason the generalizability of any particular field study's results cannot really be known. Only the accumulation of findings from numerous qualitative studies permits confident generalization, but here again the time and effort required to collect and analyze the data make it unlikely that many particular field research studies will be replicated.

Even if qualitative researchers made more of an effort to replicate key studies, their notion of developing and grounding explanations inductively in the observations made in a particular setting would hamper comparison of findings. Measurement reliability is thereby hindered, as are systematic tests for the validity of key indicators and formal tests for causal connections.

In the final analysis, qualitative research involves a mode of thinking and investigating different from that used in experimental and survey research. Qualitative research is inductive and idiographic; experiments and surveys tend to be conducted in a deductive, quantitative framework. Both approaches can help social scientists learn about the social world; the proficient researcher must be ready to use either. Qualitative data are often supplemented with many quantitative characteristics or activities. And as you have already seen, quantitative data are often enriched with written comments and observations, and focus groups have become a common tool of survey researchers seeking to develop their questionnaires. Thus the distinction between qualitative and quantitative research techniques is not always clear-cut.

KEY TERMS

Complete observation	Intensive interviewing
Covert (complete) participation	Participant observation
Experience sampling method (ESM)	Qualitative methods
Field notes	Reactive effect
Field research	Saturation point
Focus group	Tacit knowledge
Grounded theory	Theoretical sampling

HIGHLIGHTS

- Qualitative methods are most useful in exploring new issues, investigating hard-to-study groups, and determining the meaning people give to their lives and actions. In addition, most social research projects can be improved in some respects by taking advantage of qualitative techniques.

- Qualitative researchers tend to develop ideas inductively, try to understand the social context and sequential nature of attitudes and actions, and explore the subjective meanings that participants attach to events. They rely primarily on participant observation, intensive interviewing, and in recent years, focus groups.

- Participant observers may adopt one of several roles for a particular research project. Each role represents a different balance between observing and participating, which may or may not include public acknowledgment of the researcher's real identity. Many field researchers prefer a moderate role, participating as well as observing in a group but publicly acknowledging the researcher role. Such a role avoids the ethical issues posed by covert participation while still allowing the customary insights into the social world derived from directly participating in it. The role that the participant observer chooses should be based on an evaluation of the problems likely to arise from reactive effects, the ethical dilemmas of covert observation, and the consequences of identity disclosure in the particular setting.

- Field researchers must develop strategies for entering the field, developing and maintaining relations in the field, sampling, and recording and analyzing data. Sampling techniques commonly used in field research include theoretical sampling, purposive sampling, snowball sampling, quota sampling, and in special circumstances, random selection with the experience sampling method.

- Recording and analyzing notes is a crucial step in field research. Detailed notes should be recorded and analyzed daily to refine methods and to develop concepts, indicators, and models of the social system observed.

- Intensive interviews involve open-ended questions and follow-up probes, with specific question content and order varying from one interview to another. Intensive interviews can supplement participant observation data.

- Focus groups combine elements of participant observation and intensive interviewing. They can increase the validity of attitude measurement by revealing what people say when presenting their opinions in a group context.

- The four main ethical issues in field research concern voluntary participation, subject well-being, identity disclosure, and confidentiality.

EXERCISES

1. Review the experiments and surveys described in previous chapters. Choose one and propose a field research design that would focus on the same research question but with participant observation techniques in a local setting. Propose the role that you would play in the setting, along the participant observation continuum, and explain why you would favor this role. Describe the stages of your field research study, including your plans for entering the field, developing and maintaining relationships, sampling, and recording and analyzing data. Then discuss what you would expect your study to add to the findings resulting from the study described in the book.

2. Review Appendix F and explore a qualitative project using the software HyperRESEARCH and your own data. Conduct a brief observational study in a public location on campus where students congregate. A cafeteria, a building lobby, or a lounge would be ideal. You can sit and observe, taking occasional notes unobtrusively, without violating any expectations of privacy. Observe for 30 minutes. Write up field notes, being sure to include a description of the setting and a commentary on your own behavior and your reactions to what you observed. Then load the demonstration copy of HyperRESEARCH, and make your own project.

3. Develop an interview guide that focuses on a research question addressed in one of the studies in this book. Using this guide, conduct an intensive interview with one person who is involved with the topic in some way. Take only brief notes during the interview, and then write as complete a record of the interview as you can immediately afterward. Turn in an evaluation of your performance as an interviewer and note-taker, together with your notes.

4. Read about focus groups in one of the references cited in this chapter and then devise a plan for using a focus group to explore and explain student perspectives about crime on campus. How would you recruit students for the group? What types of students would you try to include? How would you introduce the topic and the method to the group? What questions would you ask? What problems would you anticipate (e.g., discord between focus group members or digressions from the chosen topic)? How would you respond to these problems?

5. Read and summarize one of the qualitative studies discussed in this chapter or another classic study recommended by your instructor. Review and critique the study using the article review questions presented in Appendix B. What questions are answered by the study? What questions are raised for further investigation?

DEVELOPING A RESEARCH PROPOSAL

Add a qualitative component to your proposed study. You can choose to do this with a participant observation project or intensive interviewing. Pick the method that seems most likely to help answer the research question for the overall survey project.

1. For a participant observation component, propose an observational plan that would complement the overall survey project. Present in your proposal the following information about your plan: (a) choose a site and justify its selection in terms of its likely value for the research; (b) choose a role along the participation–observation continuum and justify your choice; (c) describe access procedures and note any likely problems; (d) discuss how you will develop and maintain relations in the site; (e) review any sampling issues; (f) present an overview of the way in which you will analyze the data you collect.

2. For an intensive interview component, propose a focus for the intensive interviews that you believe will add the most to findings from the survey project. Present in your proposal the following information about your plan: (a) present and justify a method for selecting individuals to interview; (b) write out three introductory biographical questions and five "grand tour" questions for your interview schedule; (c) list at least six different probes you may use; (d) present and justify at least two follow-up questions for one of your grand tour questions; (e) explain what you expect this intensive interview component to add to your overall survey project.

WEB EXERCISES

1. Go to the *Annual Review of Sociology*'s Web site by following the publication link at http://soc.AnnualReviews.org. Search for articles that use field research as the primary method of gathering data on gangs or delinquency. Find at least three articles and report on the specific method of field research used in each.

2. Search the Web for information on focus groups (previous, upcoming, or ongoing) involving victims, offenders, fear of crime, crime prevention, or another criminological topic. List the Web sites you found, and write a paragraph about the purpose of each focus group and the sample involved. How might these focus groups be used to influence public policy?

SPSS EXERCISES

The YOUTH.POR data set includes some questions on opinions regarding friends' attitudes toward delinquent acts and the extent to which getting caught for committing a crime would negatively effect the respondent's life.

1. Describe the opinions about friends' attitudes and personal misfortune based on the frequencies for these variables (V77; V79; V109; V119).

2. What explanation can you develop (inductively) for these attitudes? Do you believe that either friends' attitudes toward delinquent acts or getting caught for committing a crime would influence behavior? Explain.

3. Propose a participant observation, a focus group, or an intensive interview study to explore these attitudes further. Identify the sample for the study, and describe how you would carry out your observations, focus groups, or interviews.

Chapter 8

SECONDARY DATA ANALYSIS

The research methods we have examined so far have relied on researchers collecting the data or information themselves. Increasingly, however, those interested in criminological research questions are relying on data previously collected by other investigators (Riedel, 2000). As we noted in Chapter 1, this is referred to as secondary data analysis. Secondary data analysis is simply the act of collecting or analyzing data that was originally collected for another purpose (Riedel, 2001). Thus, if a researcher goes to a police department and personally compiles information from police reports to examine a research question, she is still engaging in secondary data analysis because the police records were originally collected for another purpose.

Secondary data analysis has a long history. Since the late seventeenth century, people have been monitoring the state of their localities by examining rates of population, mortality, marriage, disease, climate, and crime. Adolphe Quételet, an ambitious Belgian mathematician, was one of the first to show that the annual number of murders reported in France from 1826 to 1831 was relatively constant and, further, that the proportion of murders committed with guns, swords, knives, stones, kicks and punches, and strangulation was also relatively constant. He concluded that although we may not know who will kill whom by what means, we do know, with a high degree of probability, that a certain number of murders of a certain type will happen every year in France (Menand, 2001). This was one of the first attempts to apply the methods of science to social phenomena. You are also probably familiar with Emile Durkheim's use of official statistics on suicide rates in different areas to examine the relationship between religion and suicide (Durkheim, 1897).

In this chapter, we will tell you about a number of data sets including surveys and official records that are publicly available for research purposes. Then, we examine several research methods that rely on secondary data including historical events research, cross-cultural research, content analysis, and crime mapping. Because using data originally gathered for other purposes poses unique concerns for a researcher, we spend the latter part of the chapter highlighting these methodological issues.

ANALYZING SECONDARY DATA

In general, there are four major types of secondary data—surveys, official statistics, official records, and other historical documents. Although a data set can be obtained by an agreement between two or more researchers, many researchers obtain data through the Inter-University Consortium for Political and Social Research (ICPSR) (www.icpsr. umich.edu). Data stored at ICPSR primarily include surveys, official records, and official statistics. ICPSR stores data and information for nearly 5,000 sources and studies, including those conducted independently and those conducted by the U.S. government. Marc Riedel (2000) has documented the majority of data sets that are available from the ICPSR and that are appropriate for crime research, including the following:

Census enumerations: historical and contemporary population characteristics. The most well-known data sets within this category are the surveys conducted every decade by the Bureau of the Census. Linking information from this data set (e.g., neighborhood characteristics including such things as poverty and residential mobility) to crime data at the same level (e.g., census block, county) has provided researchers with a rich source of data to test theories of crime.

The National Archive of Criminal Justice Data (NACJD). The Bureau of Justice Statistics and National Institute of Justice co-sponsored NACJD, which provides more than 600 criminal justice data collections to the public. A sample of these data sets include:

- Capital Punishment in the United States
- Expenditure and Employment Data for the Criminal Justice System
- Gang Involvement in Rock Cocaine Trafficking in Los Angeles, 1984–1985
- Criminal Careers and Crime Control in Massachusetts
- Longitudinal Research Design, Phase I, 1940–1965.

- Changing Patterns of Drug Use and Criminality Among Crack Cocaine Users
- In New York City: Criminal Histories and CJ Processing, 1983–84, 1986
- The National Crime Victimization Survey, ongoing
- National Jail Census
- National Judicial Reporting Program
- National Survey of Jails
- Survey of Adults on Probation
- Survey of Inmates of Federal Correctional Facilities
- Survey of Inmates of Local Jails
- Survey of Inmates of State Correctional Facilities
- FBI Uniform Crime Reporting Program (UCR) data, including the Supplementary Homicide Reports (SHR)

Social indicators and behavior. There are a series of annual surveys under this heading including the General Social Survey, which has been conducted annually by the National Opinion Research Center since 1972. In addition, Monitoring the Future: A Continuing Study of the Lifestyles and Values of Youth is a survey of a nationally representative sample of high school seniors that asks them many things including self-reports of drug and alcohol use and their attitudes toward a number of issues. The National Youth Survey Series (1976–1980 and 1983) is another survey available at ICPSR that examines factors related to delinquency.

Case Study: Gender and Violent Offending

As you can see, the research possibilities are almost limitless with the wealth of data already made available to researchers interested in issues of criminology and criminal justice. For example, Karen Heimer and Stacy De Coster (1999) used the National Youth Survey to examine the mechanisms explaining variation in violent delinquency between male and female youth. Generally, studies of self-reported violent delinquency find gender ratios (self-reports of delinquency of males to females) ranging from approximately 1.1 to 5.3, depending on the specific aggressive offense being measured. These ratios show that although males generally commit more violent acts than females, young females do engage in violence.

One of the primary mechanisms related to violent offending that Heimer and De Coster examined was "cultural definitions of violence." Specifically, according to differential association theory, interactions with others and social structural context are important because they shape the learning of violent definitions, which in turn affects the likelihood that youths engage in violent delinquency. Heimer and De Coster believed that one factor affecting the violent offending disparities between young males and females was that, on average, boys tend to acquire more violent definitions than girls. In addition, the "gender definitions" held by boys and girls are different; femininity often is equated with a high capacity for nurturance and a tendency toward passivity rather than aggressiveness. In contrast, masculinity tends to be equated with competitiveness, independence, rationality, and strength. Heimer and De Coster tested many hypotheses including the following:

Hypothesis: Higher levels of violent definitions among boys than girls will explain part of the gender gap in violent offending.

Hypothesis: Learning traditional gender definitions will reduce the chances of violent delinquency among females and increase the chances of violent delinquency among males.

To operationalize the concepts of violent definitions and gender definitions, Heimer and De Coster (1999) used several questions in the National Youth Survey (NYS), which are displayed in Exhibit 8.1 along with the questions used to uncover incidents of violent offending. After statistically controlling for other important factors proven to be related to violent offending, such as socioeconomic status, age, prior violent delinquency, association with aggressive friends, and attachments to family, the results of the analyses of the NYS data provided support for both hypotheses. The authors concluded,

In sum, girls are less violent than boys mainly because they are influenced more strongly by bonds to family, learn fewer violent definitions, and are taught that violence is inconsistent with the meaning of being female. These mechanisms appear to be so effective among girls, that direct, overt controls like supervision and coercive discipline contribute little to the explanation of variation in female violence, while they are important for explaining variation in male violence. (Heimer & De Coster, 1999:303)

HISTORICAL EVENTS RESEARCH

The central insight behind historical methods is that we can improve our understanding of social processes when we make comparisons to other times and places. Although there are no rules for determining how far in the past the focus of research must be in order for it to be considered historical, in practice, research tends to be considered historical when it focuses on a period prior to the experience of most of those conducting research (Abbott, 1994).

Historical research in the social sciences differs from traditional historical research because researchers seek to develop general theoretical explanations of historical events and processes instead of just detailed, "fact-centered" descriptions of them (Monkkonen, 1994:8). Social scientists do not ignore the details of historical events; rather, they "unravel" unique events to identify general patterns (Abrams, 1982:200). However, as in traditional history, the focus on the past presents special methodological challenges. Documents and other evidence may have been lost or damaged and what evidence there is may represent a sample biased toward those who were more newsworthy figures or who were more prone to writing. The feelings of individuals involved in past events may be hard, if not impossible, to reconstruct. Nonetheless, in many situations the historical record may support very systematic research on what occurred in the past.

When research on past events does not follow processes for a long period of time—when it is basically cross-sectional—it is usually referred to as **historical events research.** Investigations of past events may be motivated by the belief that they had a critical impact on subsequent developments or because they provide opportunities for testing the implications of a general theory (Kohn, 1987).

Exhibit 8.1   Questions from the National Youth Survey Used to Measure Violent Definitions, Gender Definitions, and Violent Delinquent Offending

Violent Delinquency

The below items were coded 1 = never; 2 = once or twice a year; 3 = once or twice every 2-3 months; 4 = once a month; 5 = once every 2-3 weeks; 6 = once a week; 7 = 2-3 times a week; 8 = once a day; 9 = 2-3 times a day.
   How may times in the past year have you........

   a) carried a hidden weapon other than a plain pocket knife?
   b) attacked someone with the idea of seriously hurting or killing them?
   c) been involved in gang fights?
   d) hit or threatened to hit a teacher or other adult at school?
   e) hit or threatened to hit your parents?
   f) hit or threatened to hit other students?
   g) had or tried to have sexual relations with someone against their will?
   h) used force (strong-arm methods) to get money or things from other students?
   i) used force (strong-arm methods) to get money or things from a teacher or adult at school?
   j) used force (strong-arm methods) to get money or things from other people (not teachers or students)?

Violent Definitions

The following questions were coded 1 = strongly disagree; 2 = disagree; 3 = neither agree or disagree; 4 = agree; 5 = strong agree.

   a) In order to gain respect from your friends, it is sometimes necessary to beat up on other kids.
   b) It is alright to beat up another person if he/she called you a dirty name.
   c) It is alright to beat up another person if he/she started the fight.
   d) Hitting another person is an acceptable way to get him/her to do what you want.

Gender Definitions

   a) In general, the father should have greater authority than the mother in the bringing up of children.
   b) Women with children should not work outside the home unless there is no one else to support the family.
   c) In a marriage, it is the woman's responsibility to care for any children and take care of the home.
   d) Women are too emotional to solve problems well.
   e) Women are physically and emotionally weaker than men and therefore need male protection and support.

Source: Heimer & De Coster, 1999.

Case Study: The Martinsville Seven

In *The Martinsville Seven: Race, Rape, and Capital Punishment*, Eric Rise (1995) offers an in-depth example of historical events research. On January 8, 1949, a 32-year-old white woman in Martinsville, Virginia, accused seven young black men of violently raping her. These men became known as the "Martinsville Seven." Within two days of the allegation, state and local police had arrested and obtained confessions from each of the suspects. In a rapid succession of brief trials held over the course of 11 days, six separate juries convicted the defendants of rape and sentenced each to death. During the first week of February 1951, each of the "Martinsville Seven" died in the electric chair of the Virginia State Penitentiary. At a time when African Americans were beginning to assert their civil rights vigorously, the executions provided a stark reminder of the harsh treatment reserved for blacks who violated southern racial codes.

In his analysis of the case, Rise examined a wealth of historical documents, including

1. Legal papers that the lawyers involved in the case made available to such archives as the Virginia State Library and Archives, the Archives and Rare Books Division of the Schomburg Center for Research in Black Culture at the New York Public Library, the Truman Library, the Margaret I. King Library at the University of Kentucky, and the United States National Archive

2. Official transcripts of the cases from the Clerk's Office in Martinsville, Virginia

3. Briefs and petitions to the Virginia State Supreme Court

4. Related case law from the Supreme Court

5. Annual reports from the Virginia Department of Corrections, 1946–1951

6. Newspaper accounts of the event from 16 local and national newspapers including the *Martinsville Bulletin*, the *New York Times*, and the *Washington Post*.

The large number of defendants, the rapid pace of the trials, and the specter of multiple executions attracted the attention of two national organizations, the National Association for the Advancement of Colored People (NAACP) and the Civil Rights Congress (CRC). In addition to the discriminatory nature of the jury's harsh sentences, Rise also found that another factor that obstructed justice in this case was the escalating tensions and antagonisms between these two organizations. Ironically, both were trying to obtain justice for the Martinsville Seven.

The CRC was a radical communist organization, and during this time of domestic tension and extreme anticommunist sentiments, most civil rights organizations, including the NAACP, did not want to appear aligned with them. Rise's analysis of historical documents and correspondence revealed extreme conflict between the two organizations while they were both vying for top billing in representing the Martinsville Seven. The inherent goal of the CRC, of course, was not so much to seek justice for the seven men, but to "reveal the capitalist conspiracy of racial and economic oppression in America. The divergent manner in which each organization proposed to handle the cases highlighted fundamental disagreements over strategy, ingrained suspicions of motive, and fierce competition for membership" (Rise, 1995:68). Because cooperation was never established through the appeals process, both organizations continued to pursue the cases in a manner consistent with their own ideological and institutional interests. The result, of course, was deadly. As Rise notes, "Never before had a state executed so many men for a single rape incident, nor had a lynching of that magnitude for men accused of rape ever been reported" (Rise, 1995:3)

Rise's analysis revealed the critical effect that this historical event had on subsequent developments. The revelation that capital sentencing disparities existed between white and African American defendants during the appeals process of the Martinsville Seven was significant for modern jurisprudence. Specifically, the Martinsville case was the first time attorneys presented in court equal protection arguments that challenged the racial disparity of death sentences for rape. Subsequent to the Martinsville case, civil rights lawyers have not only used the equal protection strategy in the pursuit of equal justice for African Americans, but they also have used it as evidence for the abolition of the death penalty.

COMPARATIVE METHODS

The limitations of examining data from a single location have encouraged many social scientists to turn to comparisons among many geographical entities. Although comparative methods are often associated with cross-national comparisons, research examining smaller aggregates such as states and cities can also be subsumed under the comparative research umbrella. **Comparative research** methods allow for a broader vision about social relations than is possible with cross-sectional research limited to one country or one location.

Case Study: The Comparative Crime Data File

One of the largest comparative research projects undertaken in criminology was the development of the Comparative Crime Data File (CCDF), which was created by Dane Archer and Rosemary Gartner (1984). Archer and Gartner articulated the need for comparative research in the field succinctly:

> The need for cross-national comparisons seems particularly acute for research on crime and violence since national differences on these phenomena are of a remarkable magnitude. In some societies, homicide is an hourly, highly visible, and therefore somewhat unexceptional cause of death. In other nations, homicides are so infrequent that, when they do occur, they receive national attention and lasting notoriety. (1984:4)

The CCDF continues to be updated, but originally contained crime and violence data from 110 nations and 44 major international cities covering the period from approximately 1900 to 1970.

Without investigating the patterns and correlates of crime and violence across different societies, Archer and Gartner (1984) contend that criminological research has five major problems:

- *Generalization.* It has been impossible to test the generality of a finding based on single-society research by means of replication in a sample of several societies.
- *Controlled comparison.* The absence of a sufficient number of cases (e.g., nations or cities) has hindered rigorous comparisons between those cases affected by some social change and control cases unaffected by the same change.

- *Causal inference.* With longitudinal data unavailable, researchers have not been able to satisfy one of the classic requirements for making causal inferences—the correct temporal relationship among the variables under study.
- *Mediation and intervening variables.* Without a reasonably large sample of nations, it is impossible to discover whether certain variables may mediate the effects of a social change. Without a large sample of societies, a general pattern that explains or orders these different outcomes will never be seen.
- *Methodological uncertainty.* Without an archive of broadly comparative and longitudinal crime data, some key methodological issues have been largely uninvestigable. For example, it would not be possible to assess the reliability of different crime indicators like the number of offenses known or the number of arrests using data from a number of societies.

In their work, Archer and Gartner examined many research questions using the CCDF. One of these questions is related to the idea that war might increase the level of postwar homicide within nations involved in wars. There are several theoretical models that speculate about the possible effects of wars on postwar violence within a nation. For example, the social solidarity model posits a wartime *decrease* in violence because of the increase in social solidarity among a nation's citizenry. At a more individual level, the violent veteran model predicts that postwar levels of violence within a nation will *increase* as a result of the violent acts of returning war veterans. At a societal level, the legitimization of violence model postulates that during a war, a society reverses its prohibitions against killing and instead honors acts of violence that would be regarded as murderous in peacetime. This social approval or legitimation of violence, this model predicts, may produce a lasting reduction of inhibitions against taking human life, even after the war, thereby increasing levels of violence within nations.

To empirically examine the effects of war on postwar violence, Archer and Gartner compared national rates of homicide before and after many wars, both small and large, including the two World Wars. Exhibit 8.2 displays the increase or decrease of homicide rates in combatant nations and a sample of control nations that were not involved in World War I and World War II. The researchers also controlled for a number of other factors related to war, including the number of combat deaths in war, whether nations were victorious or defeated, and whether the nation's postwar economies were improved or worsened, and for several types of homicide offenses committed by both men and women. The researchers found that most combatant nations in their analysis experienced substantial postwar increases in their rates of homicide after both small and large wars. Archer and Gartner concluded,

> The one model that appears to be fully consistent with the evidence is the legitimation of violence model, which suggests that the presence of authorized or sanctioned killing during war has a residual effect on the level of homicide in peacetime society. (Archer & Gartner, 1984:96)

CONTENT ANALYSIS

Content analysis is a research method for systematically analyzing and making inferences from text (Weber, 1985:9). You can think of a content analysis as a survey of documents

Exhibit 8.2   Homicide Rate Changes in Combatant and Control Nations After World War I and World War II

Combatant Nations

Rates Decreased	Rates Remained Unchanged	Rates Increased
Australia (I)	England (I)	Belgium
Canada (I)	France (I)	Bulgaria
Hungary (I)	S. Africa (I)	Germany
Finland (II)	Canada (II)	Italy (I)
N. Ireland (II)		Japan (I)
U.S. (II)		Portugal (I)
		Scotland (I)
		U.S. (I)
		Australia (II)
		Denmark (II)
		England (II)
		France (II)
		Italy (II)
		Japan (II)
		Netherlands (II)
		New Zealand (II)
		Norway (II)
		Scotland (II)
		S. Africa (II)

Control Nations

Rates Decreased	Rates Remained Unchanged	Rates Increased
Norway (I)	Ceylon (I)	Finland (I)
Ceylon (II)	Chile (I)	Thailand (I)
Chile (II)	Netherlands (I)	Colombia (II)
El Salvador (II)		Sweden (II
Ireland (II)		Turkey (II)
Switzerland (II)		
Thailand (II)		

Source: Archer & Gartner, 1984, Table 4.1.

or other records of prior communication. This method was first applied to the study of newspaper content and then to the analysis of Nazi propaganda broadcasts in World War II, but it can also be used to study historical documents, records of speeches, and other "voices from the past."

The units that are surveyed in a content analysis can range from newspapers, books, or TV shows to persons referred to in other communications, themes expressed in documents, or propositions made in different statements. Words or other features of these units are then coded in order to measure the variables involved in the research question. The content analysis proceeds through several stages (Weber, 1985):

Identify a population of documents or other textual sources for study. This population should be selected so that it is appropriate to the research question of interest. Perhaps the population will be all newspapers published in the United States, college student newspapers, nomination speeches at political party conventions, or "state of the nation" speeches by national leaders.

Determine the units of analysis. These could be newspaper articles, whole newspapers, speeches, or political conventions.

Select a sample of units from the population. The simplest strategy might be a simple random sample of documents. However, a stratified sample might be needed to ensure adequate representation of community newspapers in large and small cities, or of weekday and Sunday papers, or of political speeches during election years and in off years (see Chapter 4).

Design coding procedures for the variables to be measured. This requires deciding what unit of text to code, such as words, sentences, themes, or paragraphs. Then the categories into which the text units are to be coded must be defined. These categories may be broad, such as "supports democracy," or narrow, such as "supports universal suffrage."

Test and refine the coding procedures. Clear instructions and careful training of coders are essential.

Base statistical analyses on counting occurrences of particular items. These could be words, themes, or phrases. You will also need to test relations between different variables.

Developing reliable and valid coding procedures is not an easy task. The meaning of words and phrases is often ambiguous. Homographs (words such as *mine* that have different meanings in different contexts) create special problems, as do many phrases that have special meanings (such as "point of no return") (Weber, 1985:30). As a result, coding procedures cannot simply categorize and count words; text segments in which the words are embedded must also be inspected before codes are finalized. Because different coders may perceive different meanings in the same text segments, explicit coding rules are required to ensure coding consistency. Special dictionaries can be developed to keep track of how the categories of interest are defined in the study (Weber, 1985:24–34).

After coding procedures are developed, their reliability should be assessed by comparing different coders' codes for the same variables. Computer programs for content analysis can be used to enhance reliability (Weber, 1985). Whatever rules the computer is programmed to use to code text will be applied consistently. Validity can be assessed with a construct validation approach by determining the extent to which theoretically predicted relationships occur (see Chapter 3).

Case Study: Media Representations of Crime

Researchers interested in the media and crime have used content analysis in a number of ways. For example, scholars analyzing crime depictions presented in the media often conclude that newspaper and television coverage of crime is frequently inaccurate and misleading; stories disproportionately report violent crimes and reporters tend to focus attention on sensational matters such as the capture of a criminal or high status offenders.

One type of television program presents vignettes depicting actual crimes in which theories of crime are dramatized. These dramatizations feature actors, actual photographs or film footage, and interviews conducted with participants and the police. Viewers are urged to call the police or program representatives with information related to the crime, and police officers are on standby in the television studio to take these calls. Two such programs are *America's Most Wanted* (AMW) and *Unsolved Mysteries* (UM).

To analyze the images these programs were sending to viewers, Gray Cavender and Lisa Bond-Maupin (2000) conducted a content analysis of AMW and UM programs that aired between January 25 and May 31, 1989. All programs that aired during this time period were videotaped and a subsample of 16 episodes were randomly selected that contained 77 crime vignettes. The crime vignettes served as the study's units of analysis. The coding protocol used for data collection was focused on three aspects of the programs:

1. *Demographics.* Types of crime and general information on the crime, criminals, and victims;

2. *Characterizations.* Specific depictions of crime, criminals, and victims, such as brutality, dangerousness, or a victim's vulnerability; and

3. *Worldview.* The relative safety of people and places, the terror and randomness of crime, and what the audience should do about crime.

Exhibit 8.3 presents the percentage of program vignettes that depicted offense types for both AMW and UM. Consistent with previous research, Cavender and Bond-Maupin (2000) found that these shows focused a majority of their attention on violent crime directed at persons. Corporate and political criminals were notably absent from the vignettes.

Exhibit 8.3   Number and Percentage of Vignettes Depicted by the Programs *Unsolved Mysteries and America's Most Wanted*

	%	n
Murder	52	40
Theft/Fraud Extortion	13	10
Escape	12	9
Bank robbery/Armed Robbery	10	8
Illegal Arms/Terrorism	3	2
Unexplained death/missing	7	5
Rape	5	4
Kidnapping	5	4
Child molestation	5	4
Attempted Murder	3	2
Drug Dealing	3	2
Other	7	5

Source: Adapted from Cavender & Bond Maupin, 2000.

Cavender and Bond-Maupin concluded that the overwhelming majority of criminals on these shows were depicted as dangerous people who were beyond the help of social control or rehabilitation. In addition, both shows regularly featured criminals who were characterized with deviant psychological labels such as a "crazed killer, a psycho, a maniac," schizophrenic, emotionally disturbed, or showing no emotion. Other criminals were portrayed as Satanists, gang members, and drug dealers. On the other hand, victims were usually presented as upstanding citizens who you would like to have as a neighbor. The camera most often took the victims' perspective as well, achieving what Cavender and Bond-Maupin called the "good/evil dichotomy," with the victim and the audience aligned against the criminal.

Cavender and Bond-Maupin were particularly interested in how the shows cinemato-graphic techniques were used to make the dramas entertaining. They found that in a majority of the violent crimes, graphic details of the incident were depicted, including the number and location of a victim's wounds. For example, one victim was stabbed 30 times through the heart, and another victim was shot five times and ultimately died of massive bleeding. To sensationalize these acts, in some vignettes the film speed was reduced to slow motion to capture the muzzle flash as a criminal drew a gun and shot the victim. What the authors called "fear cues" were also frequently employed by the shows to capture the attention of viewers. For example, in one vignette, the host emerges from the night on a deserted road and makes reference to a common fear of driving on a lonely stretch of high-way where one's cries for help would go unheeded. In sum, Cavender and Bond-Maupin concluded that the messages sent to viewers by both programs was that danger lurks every-where, awaiting the victim, and by implication, the viewer.

CRIME MAPPING

The image of crime mapping most of you probably have in your head is one of a large map on a police precinct wall with push pins stuck all over it identifying the location of crime incidents. Although applied crime mapping like this has been used for over 100 years in policing, the type of crime mapping we will discuss here is related to mapping techniques used for traditional research purposes (e.g., testing theory about the causes of crime), not for investigative purposes.

Case Study: Social Disorganization and the Chicago School

Crime mapping for general research purposes has a long history in criminological research. **Crime mapping** for research purposes is generally used to identify the spatial distribution of crime along with the social indicators such as poverty and social disorga-nization that are similarly distributed across areas (e.g., neighborhood, census tracks). Although they were not the first researchers to use crime mapping, Shaw and McKay (1942) conducted a landmark analysis in criminology on juvenile delinquency in Chicago neighborhoods back in the 1930s. These researchers mapped thousands of incidents of juvenile delinquency and analyzed relationships between delinquency and various social conditions such as social disorganization. After analyzing rates of police arrests for delin-quency, using police records to determine the names and addresses of those arrested in

Exhibit 8.4   Zone rates of Police Arrests in Chicago, 1931

B. Zone rates of police arrests, 1927

Source: Shaw & McKay, 1984.

Chicago between 1927 and 1935, Shaw and McKay observed a striking pattern that persisted over the years.

   Exhibit 8.4 displays one of the maps Shaw and McKay created that illuminates the spatial distribution of delinquency within concentric circles of Chicago that spread out to the suburbs from the city's center. As noted in the exhibit, there is a linear decrease in rates of delinquency as the distance from the Loop (city center) increases. When rates of other community characteristics were similarly mapped (e.g., infant mortality, tuberculosis cases, percentage of families who own their own homes, percentage of foreign born residents, percentage of families on relief), the conclusions were obvious. Shaw and McKay concluded,

> It may be observed, in the first instance, that the variations in rates of officially recorded delinquents in communities of the city correspond very closely with variations in economic status. The communities with the highest rates of delinquents are occupied by these segments of the population whose position is most disadvantageous in relation to the distribution of economic, social, and cultural values. Of all the communities in the city, these have the fewest facilities for acquiring the economic goods indicative of status and success in our conventional culture. . . . In the low-income areas, where there is the greatest deprivation and frustration, where, in the history of the city, immigrant and migrant groups have brought together the widest variety of divergent cultural traditions and institutions, and where there exists the greatest disparity between the social values to which the people aspire and the availability of facilities for acquiring these values in conventional ways, the development of crime as an organized way of life is most marked. (1984:318–319)

Case Study: Gang Homicides in St. Louis

Contemporary researchers interested in issues related to crime and criminology have access to more sophisticated computer technology that allows the creation of more enhanced crime maps. The purpose of crime maps, however, remains the same: to illuminate the relationship between some category of crime and corresponding characteristics such as poverty and disorganization across given locations. Richard Rosenfeld, Timothy Bray, and Arlen Egley (1999) recently examined the mechanisms through which gangs facilitate violent offending in St. Louis, Missouri. The primary purpose of this research was to examine whether gang membership impels members to engage in violence or merely exposes them to violent persons and situations. Rosenfeld and his colleagues compared gang-affiliated, gang-motivated, and nongang youth homicides occurring in St. Louis between 1985 and 1995. In one part of their analysis, they examined the spatial distribution of gang and nongang youth homicide in relation to attributes of the neighborhood context (e.g., economic deprivation) in which the incidents occurred.

Rosenfeld and his colleagues did not rely on the police classification of homicides as gang-related; they coded homicide reports themselves. Operationally, a homicide was coded gang-motivated if it resulted from gang behavior or relationships, such as an initiation ritual, the "throwing" of gang signs, or a gang fight. A case was coded as gang-affiliated if the homicide involved a suspect or victim identified in the police report as a gang member but did not arise from gang activity. For example, an incident in which a gang member was killed during a robbery would be gang-affiliated but not gang-motivated. A youth homicide was coded as nongang related if no indication of gang activity or affiliation was present in the case file, and the suspect was between 10 and 24 years of age. To examine the spatial relationship between these three types of homicides and the relationship they had to neighborhood disadvantage (such as economic deprivation or social disorganization) and instability (such as residents moving in and out of neighborhood), the researchers used the census block group as their units of analysis. Exhibit 8.5 displays the map of block

Exhibit 8.5 Neighborhoods in St. Louis Where Gang-Affiliated and Gang-Motivated Homicides Occurred

Source: Rosenfeld et al., 1999.

groups where gang-affiliated and gang-motivated homicides occurred, along with the extent of neighborhood disadvantage in each block for 1990–1995 (Rosenfeld et al., 1999). Exhibit 8.6 displays this same information for nongang youth homicides.

Exhibit 8.6   Neighborhoods in St. Louis Where Nongang Homicides Occurred

Legend:

8   **Non-Gang Youth Homicides**
St. Louis Block Groups
  Not Disadvantaged
  Disadvantaged
  Very Disadvantaged

2   0   2   4 **Miles**

N

Source: Rosenfeld et al., 1999.

From these maps, you can see that both gang and nongang homicides were concentrated in disadvantaged areas. Other maps revealed a similar finding with regard to neighborhood instability; homicides were concentrated in neighborhoods with moderate levels of instability regardless of whether they were gang-affiliated, gang-motivated, or nongang related. Rosenfeld and his colleagues conclude,

Our results offer powerful evidence of the clustering of both gang and nongang youth homicides in areas characterized by high levels of social-economic disadvantage and racial isolation. Although the accumulated evidence for gang facilitation of violence is quite compelling, our results serve as a reminder that concentrated disadvantage and racial isolation remain the fundamental sources of lethal violence in urban areas. (Rosenfeld et al, 1999:514)

These conclusions echo those made over a half century earlier by Shaw and McKay. As such, we are compelled to note Ernest W. Burgess' words in the introduction of Shaw and McKay's original work (1942:xiii),

We must realize that the brightest hope in reformation is in changing the neighborhood and in control of the gang in which the boy moves, lives, and has his being and to which he returns after his institutional treatment. . . . we must reaffirm our faith in prevention, which is so much easier, cheaper, and more effective than cure and which begins with the home, the play group, the local school, the church, and the neighborhood.

METHODOLOGICAL ISSUES WHEN USING SECONDARY DATA ANALYSIS

Each of the methods we have discussed in this chapter presents unique methodological challenges. For example, in historical events research and comparative research, small numbers of cases, spotty historical records, variable cross-national record-keeping practices, and different cultural and linguistic contexts limit the confidence that can be placed in measures, samples, and causal conclusions. Just to identify many of the potential problems for a comparative historical research project requires detailed knowledge of the times and of the nations or other units investigated (Kohn, 1987). This requirement often serves as a barrier to in-depth historical research and to comparisons between nations.

Analysis of secondary data presents several challenges, ranging from uncertainty about the methods of data collection to the lack of maximal fit between the concepts that the primary study measured and each of the concepts that are the focus of the current investigation. Responsible use of secondary data requires a good understanding of the primary data source. The researcher should be able to answer the following questions (most of which were adapted from Riedel, 2000:55–69; Stewart, 1984:23–30):

1. What were the agency's goals in collecting the data? If the primary data were obtained in a research project, what were the project's purposes?

2. Who was responsible for data collection, and what were their qualifications? Are they available to answer questions about the data? Each step in the data-collection process should be charted and the personnel involved identified.

3. What data were collected, and what were they intended to measure?

4. When was the information collected?

5. What methods were used for data collection? Copies of the forms used for data collection should be obtained and the way in which these data are processed by the agency/agencies should be reviewed.

6. How is the information organized (by date, event, etc.)? Are there identifiers that are used to identify the different types of data available on the same case? In what form are the data available (computer tapes, disks, paper files)? Answers to these questions can have a major bearing on the work that will be needed to carry out the study.

7. How consistent are the data with data available from other sources?

8. What is known about the success of the data-collection effort? How are missing data indicated? What kind of documentation is available?

Answering these questions helps to ensure that the researcher is familiar with the data he or she will analyze and can help to identify any problems with it.

Data quality is always a concern with secondary data, even when the data are collected by an official government agency. The need for concern is much greater in research across national boundaries, because different data-collection systems and definitions of key variables may have been used (Glover, 1996). Census counts can be distorted by incorrect answers to census questions as well as by inadequate coverage of the entire population (see Chapter 4; Rives & Serow, 1988:32–35). Social and political pressures may influence the success of a census in different ways in different countries. These influences on records are particularly acute for crime data. For example, Archer and Gartner note, "It is possible, of course, that many other nations also try to use crime rate fluctuations for domestic political purposes—to use 'good' trends to justify the current administration or 'bad' trends to provide a mandate for the next" (1984:16).

Researchers who rely on secondary data inevitably make trade-offs between their ability to use a particular data set and the specific hypotheses they can test. If a concept that is critical to a hypothesis was not measured adequately in a secondary data source, the study might have to be abandoned until a more adequate source of data can be found. Alternatively, hypotheses or even the research question itself may be modified in order to match the analytic possibilities presented by the available data (Riedel, 2000:53).

Measuring Across Contexts

One problem that historical and comparative research projects often confront is the lack of data from some historical periods or geographical units (Rueschemeyer, Stephens, & Stephens, 1992:4; Walters, James, & McCammon, 1997). The widely used U.S. Uniform Crime Reporting System did not begin until 1930 (Rosen, 1995). Missing data prevented Susan Olzak, Suzanne Shanahan, and Elizabeth McEneaney (1996:598) from including more than 55 out of a total of 212 standard metropolitan statistical areas (SMSAs) in their analysis of race riots. Sometimes alternative sources of documents or estimates for missing quantitative data can fill in gaps (Zaret, 1996), but even when measures can be created for key concepts, multiple measures of the same concepts are likely to be out of the question; as a result, tests of reliability and validity may not be feasible. Whatever the situation, researchers must assess the problem honestly and openly (Bollen, Entwisle, & Alderson, 1993).

Those measures that are available are not always adequate. What remains in the historical archives may be an unrepresentative selection of materials that still remain from the past. At various times, some documents could have been discarded, lost, or transferred elsewhere for a variety of reasons. "Original" documents may be transcriptions of spoken words or handwritten pages and could have been modified slightly in the process; they could also be outright distortions (Erikson, 1966:172, 209–210; Zaret, 1996). When relevant data are obtained from previous publications, it is easy to overlook problems of data quality, but this simply makes it all the more important to evaluate the primary sources. Developing a systematic plan for identifying relevant documents and evaluating them is very important.

A somewhat more subtle measurement problem is that of establishing measurement equivalence. The meaning of concepts and the operational definitions of variables may change over time and between nations or regions (Erikson, 1966:xi). The concept of being a "good son or daughter" refers to a much broader range of behaviors in China than in most Western countries (Ho, 1996). Individuals in different cultures may respond differently to the same questions (Martin & Kinsella, 1995:385). Alternatively, different measures may have been used for the same concepts in different nations and the equivalence of these measures may be unknown (van de Vijver & Leung, 1997:9).

The value of statistics for particular geographic units like counties may vary over time simply due to changes in the boundaries of these units (Walters, James, & McCammon, 1997). As Archer and Gartner note,

> These comparative crime data were recorded across the moving history of changing societies. In some cases, this history spanned gradual changes in the political and social conditions of a nation. In other cases, it encompassed transformations so acute that it seems arguable whether the same nation existed before and after. (1984:15)

Such possibilities should be considered, and any available opportunity should be taken to test for their effects.

A different measurement concern can arise as a consequence of the simplifications made to facilitate comparative analysis. In many qualitative comparative analyses, the values of continuous variables are dichotomized. For example, nations may be coded as "democratic" or "authoritarian." This introduces an imprecise and arbitrary element into the analysis (Lieberson, 1991). On the other hand, for some comparisons, qualitative distinctions such as "simple majority rule" or "unanimity required" may capture the important differences between cases better than quantitative distinctions. It is essential to inspect carefully the categorization rules for any such analysis and to consider what form of measurement is both feasible and appropriate for the research question being investigated (King, Keohane, & Verba, 1994:158–163).

Sampling Across Time and Place

The simplest type of sample is the selection of one case for a historical study. Although a great deal can be learned from the intensive focus on one nation or other unit, the lack of a comparative element shapes the type of explanations that are developed. Explanations for change within one nation are likely to focus on factors that have changed within it, such as the decisions of a political leader, rather than factors like political systems that vary between nations (Rueschemeyer, Stephens, & Stephens, 1992:31–36). However, comparisons between nations may reveal that differences in political systems are much more important than voluntary decisions by individual political leaders. It is only when the political system changes over time within one nation that its impact can be evaluated empirically (Rueschemeyer, Stephens, & Stephens, 1992:29).

Qualitative comparative historical studies are likely to rely on availability samples or purposive samples of cases. In an availability sample, researchers study a case or multiple cases simply because they are familiar with or have access to them. When using a purposive sampling strategy, researchers select cases because they reflect theoretically important distinctions. Quantitative historical comparative researchers often select entire populations of cases for which the appropriate measures can be obtained.

When geographic units like nations are sampled for comparative purposes, it is assumed that the nations are independent of each other in terms of the variables examined. Each nation can then be treated as a separate case for identifying possible chains of causes and effects. However, in a very interdependent world, this assumption may be misplaced—nations may develop as they do because of how other nations are developing (and the same can be said of cities and other units). As a result, comparing the particular histories of different nations may overlook the influence of global culture, international organizations, or economic dependency. These common international influences may cause the same pattern of changes to emerge in different nations; looking within the history of these nations for the explanatory influences that would lead to spurious conclusions. The possibility of such complex interrelations should always be considered when evaluating the plausibility of a causal argument based on a comparison between two apparently independent cases (Jervis, 1996).

Identifying Causes

The restriction of historical research to one setting in the past limits possibilities for testing causal connections, because explanations applied to these events can seem arbitrary (Skocpol, 1984:365). The researcher can reduce this problem by making some comparisons to other events in the past or present. However, the interdependence of sampled units (noted in the previous section) may mean that several cases available for comparison should be treated as just one larger case. There may also be too many possible combinations of causal factors to test and not enough cases to test them with.

The inductive approach taken by many qualitative comparative researchers can also make it seem that whatever the causal explanation developed, it has been tailored to fit the particulars of the historical record and so is unlikely to be confirmed by other cases (Rueschemeyer, Stephens, & Stephens, 1992:30).

Some comparative researchers use a systematic method for identifying causes, developed by the English philosopher John Stuart Mill (1872), called the **method of agreement** (Exhibit 8.7). The core of this approach is the comparison of nations (*cases*) in terms of similarities and differences on potential causal variables and the phenomenon to be explained. For example, suppose three nations that have all developed democratic political systems are compared in terms of four socioeconomic variables hypothesized by different theories to influence violent crime. If the nations differ in terms of three of the variables but are similar in terms of the fourth, this is evidence that the fourth variable influences violent crime.

Exhibit 8.7   John Stuart Mill's Method of Agreement

Variable	Case 1	Case 2	Case 3
A	Different	Different	Different
B	Different	Same	Same
C	Different	Different	Different
D*	Same	Same	Same
Outcome	Same	Same	Same

Source: Adapted from Skocpol, 1984:379.
* *D* is considered the cause of the outcome

The features of the cases selected for comparison have a large impact on the ability to identify influences using the method of agreement. Cases should be chosen for their difference in terms of key factors hypothesized to influence the outcome of interest and their similarity on other, possibly confounding, factors (Skocpol, 1984:383). For example, in order to understand how unemployment influences violent crime, you would need to select cases for comparison that differ in unemployment rates, so that you could then see if they differ in rates of violence (King, Keohane, & Verba, 1994:148–152).

This **deterministic causal approach** (Ragin, 1987:44–52) requires that there be no deviations from the combination of factors that are identified as determining the outcome for each nation. Yet there are likely to be exceptions to any explanatory rule that we establish (Lieberson, 1991). A careful analyst will evaluate the extent to which exceptions should be allowed in particular analyses.

With these cautions in mind, the combination of historical and comparative methods allows for rich descriptions of social and political processes in different nations or regions as well as for causal inferences that reflect a systematic, defensible weighing of the evidence. Data of increasingly good quality are available on a rapidly expanding number of nations, creating many opportunities for comparative research. We cannot expect one study comparing the histories of a few nations to control adequately for every plausible alternative causal influence, but repeated investigations can refine our understanding and lead to increasingly accurate causal conclusions (King, Keohane, & Verba, 1994:33).

ETHICAL ISSUES IN SECONDARY DATA ANALYSIS

Analysis of historical documents or quantitative data collected by others does not create the potential for harm to human subjects that can be a concern when collecting primary data. It is still important to be honest and responsible in working out arrangements for data access when data must be obtained from designated officials or data archivists, but of course many data are easily accessed in libraries or on the Web. Researchers who conclude that they are being denied access to public records of the federal government may be able to obtain the data by filing a Freedom of Information Act request. The FOIA stipulates that all persons have a right to access all federal agency records unless the records are specifically exempted (Riedel, 2000:130–131). Researchers who review historical or government documents must also try to avoid embarrassing or otherwise harming named individuals or their descendants by disclosing sensitive information.

Ethical concerns are multiplied when surveys are conducted or other data are collected in other countries. If the outside researcher lacks much knowledge of local norms, values, and routine activities, the potential for inadvertently harming subjects is substantial. For this reason, cross-cultural researchers should spend time learning about each of the countries in which they plan to collect primary data and strike up collaborations with researchers in those countries (Hantrais & Mangen, 1996). Local advisory groups may also be formed in each country so that a broader range of opinion is solicited when key decisions must be made. Such collaboration can also be invaluable when designing instruments, collecting data, and interpreting results.

CONCLUSION

Historical and comparative social science investigations use a variety of techniques that range from narrative histories having much in common with qualitative methods to analyses of secondary data that in many respects are like traditional survey research. Each of these methods can help researchers gain new insights into processes like democratization. They encourage intimate familiarity with the course of development of the nations studied and thereby stimulate inductive reasoning about the interrelations among different historical events. Systematic historical and comparative techniques can be used to test deductive hypotheses concerning international differences as well as historical events.

Most historical and comparative methods encourage causal reasoning. They require the researcher to consider systematically the causal mechanism, or historical sequences of events, by which earlier events influence later outcomes. They also encourage attention to causal context, with a particular focus on the ways in which different cultures and social structures may result in different effects of other variables. There is much to be gained by continuing to use and develop these methods.

KEY TERMS

Comparative research	Deterministic causal approach
Content analysis	Historical events research
Crime mapping	Method of agreement

HIGHLIGHTS

• Secondary data analysis is the act of collecting or analyzing data that was originally collected for another purpose.

• In general, there are four major types of secondary data: surveys, official statistics, official records, and other historical documents including written text or media representations (e.g., trial transcripts, newspaper articles, television shows).

• The central insight behind historical and comparative methods is that we can improve our understanding of social processes when we make comparisons to other times and places.

• When research on past events does not follow processes for some long period of time, when it is basically cross-sectional, then it is usually referred to as historical events research.

- Content analysis is a tool for systematic analysis of documents and other textual data. It requires careful testing and control of coding procedures to achieve reliable measures.

- Counterfactual thought experiments are a systematic method for adding a comparative element to studies of single historical cases. They involve trying to answer a "what if" question.

- Crime mapping for research purposes is generally used to identify the spatial distribution of crime along with the social indicators such as poverty and social disorganization that are similarly distributed across areas (e.g., neighborhoods, census tracks).

- Secondary data for historical and comparative research are available from many sources. The Inter-University Consortium for Political and Social Research (ICPSR) provides the most comprehensive data archive.

EXERCISES

1. Read the original article reporting one of the studies described in this chapter. Critique the article, using the article review questions presented in Appendix B as your guide. Focus particular attention on procedures for measurement, sampling, and establishing causal relations.

2. What historical events have had a major influence on social patterns in the nation? The possible answers are too numerous to list, ranging from any of the wars to major internal political conflicts, economic booms and busts, scientific discoveries, and legal changes. Pick one such event in your own nation for this exercise. Find one historical book on this event and list the sources of evidence used. What additional evidence would you suggest for a social science investigation of the event?

3. Using your library's government documents collection or the U.S. Census site on the Web (www.census.gov), select one report by the U.S. Bureau of the Census about the population of the United States or some segment of it. Outline the report and list all of the tables included in it. Summarize the report in two paragraphs. Suggest a historical or comparative study for which this report would be useful.

4. Review the survey data sets available through the Inter-University Consortium for Political and Social Research (ICPSR), using either its published directory or its Internet site (www.icpsr.umich.edu). Select two data sets that might be used to study a research question in which you are interested. Use the information ICPSR reports about them to answer Questions 1–5 in the section "Methodological Issues When Using Secondary Data" earlier in this chapter. Is the information adequate to answer these questions? What are the advantages and disadvantages of using one of these data sets to answer your research question compared to designing a new study?

5. Find a magazine or newspaper report on a demographic issue, such as population change or migration. Explain how one of the key demographic concepts could be used or was used to improve understanding of this issue.

6. Select a current social or political topic that has been the focus of news articles. Propose a content analysis strategy for this topic, using newspaper articles or editorials as your units of analysis. Your strategy should include a definition of the population, selection of the units of analysis, a sampling plan, and coding procedures for key variables. Now find an article on this topic and use it to develop your coding procedures. Test and refine your coding procedures with another article on the same topic.

DEVELOPING A RESEARCH PROPOSAL

Add a historical or comparative dimension to your proposed study.

1. Consider which of the four types of comparative-historical methods would be most suited to an investigation of your research question. Think of possibilities for qualitative and quantitative research

on your topic with the method you prefer. Will you conduct a variable-oriented or case-oriented study? Write a brief statement justifying the approach you choose.

2. Review the possible sources of data for your comparative-historical project. Search the Web and relevant government, historical, and international organization sites or publications. Search the social science literature for similar studies and read about the data sources that they used.

3. Specify the hypotheses you will test or the causal sequences you will investigate. Describe what your cases will be (nations, regions, years, etc.). Explain how you will select cases. List the sources of your measures and describe the specific type of data you expect to obtain for each measure.

4. Review the list of potential problems in comparative-historical research and discuss those that you believe will be most troublesome in your proposed investigation. Explain your reasoning.

WEB EXERCISES

1. The Bureau of Justice Statistics (BJS) home page can be found at www.ojp.usdoj.gov/bjs. The site contains an extensive list of reports published by the BJS along with links to the data used in the reports. You can access tables of data that display phenomena over time and across various geographical locations.

   a. Using data and/or reports available from the National Crime Victimization Survey, conduct an analysis of the rates of violent victimization from 1993 until the most recent date the data is available. What do you conclude about the trends of violent victimization?

   b. Find a report available on the site that makes cross-national comparisons. Summarize the methods by which the data were collected. Now summarize the findings of the report.

2. The National Institute of Justice has a wealth of information on crime mapping located at www.nicrs.org. Search the site for information on "crime mapping" and you will find that the site contains a multitude of information, including the latest technological advances in crime mapping strategies for police departments as well as full-text articles discussing recent research that uses crime mapping techniques. Select a report available online and summarize its findings.

3. The World Bank offers numerous resources that are useful for comparative research. Visit the World Bank Web site at www.worldbank.org. You will find data listed by countries; select a random sample of countries along with social indicators of your choice. Now summarize the differences and similarities you have identified between the countries.

4. The U.S. Bureau of Labor Statistics (BLS) provides extensive economic indicator data on the Web for regions, states, and cities. Go to the BLS Web page, which offers statistics by location: http://stats.bls.gov/eag/. Click on a region and explore the types of data that are available. Write out a description of the steps you would have to take to conduct a comparative analysis using the data available from the BLS Web site.

5. The U.S. Census Bureau's home page can be found at www.census.gov. This site contains extensive reporting of census data including population data, economic indicators, and other information acquired through the U.S. Census. This Web site allows you to collect information on numerous subjects and topics, which can be used to make comparisons between different states or cities. Find the "State and County Quick Facts" option and choose your own state. Now pick the county in which you live and copy down several statistics of interest. Repeat this process for other counties in your state. Use the data you have collected to compare your county with other counties in the state. Write a one-page report summarizing your findings.

6. Go to the International Association of Law Enforcement Intelligence Analysts Web site at www.ialeia.org. On the site you can download papers and information regarding numerous topics, including crime mapping. Provide a review of at least one of these applications. You can also link

to the IALEIA's journal (Hank Brightman, Saint Peter's College, The Jesuit College of New Jersey, Editor) to read the latest publications in this area.

SPSS EXERCISES

1. Using the data set STATE2000, examine the rates of violence and murder across the four regions of the country (REGION). The best procedure to use for this is called MEANS. You can access this under ANALYZE, then COMPARE MEANS, then click on MEANS. In the Mean dialog box, place the rate of violence you wish to compare first (VIOLENT or MURDER) in the dependent variables box and REGION in the independent variable box. Summarize your findings.

Now, using this same procedure, examine whether there are similar differences across regions for rates of poverty, which are often found to be associated with rates of violence. That is, geographical locations that have higher rates of poverty and overdeprivation also tend to have higher rates of violence. What do you conclude?

2. Because the GSS file is cross-sectional, we cannot use it to conduct historical research. However, we can develop some interesting historical questions by examining differences in the attitudes of Americans in different birth cohorts.
   a. Inspect the distributions of the same set of variables. Would you expect any of these attitudes and behaviors to have changed over the twentieth century? State your expectations in the form of hypotheses.
   b. Request a crosstabulation of these variables by birth COHORT.
   c. What appear to be the differences among the cohorts? Which differences do you think are due to historical change, and which do you think are due to the aging process? Which attitudes and behaviors would you expect to still differentiate the baby-boom generation and the post-Vietnam generation in 20 years?

Chapter 9

EVALUATION RESEARCH IN CRIMINOLOGY AND CRIMINAL JUSTICE

In the beginning, God created the heaven and the earth. And God saw everything that he made. "Behold," God said, "it is very good." . . . And on the seventh day God rested from all His work. His archangel came then unto Him asking, "God, how do you know that what you have created is 'very good'? What are your criteria? On what data do you base your judgment. . . . And aren't you a little close to the situation to make a fair and unbiased evaluation?"

God thought about these questions all that day and His rest was greatly disturbed. On the eighth day God said, "Lucifer, go to hell." Thus was evaluation born in a blaze of glory.

—Halcolm, the evaluation sage, a.k.a.
Michael Quinn Patton (1997:1)

Every year, the U.S. Department of Justice (DOJ) spends an average of $3 billion in grants to help state and local law enforcement and communities prevent and ameliorate the consequences of crime. But similar to virtually every government agency, very little money has been allocated by the DOJ to determine whether these prevention programs actually work. In 1996, Congress required the attorney general to provide a "comprehensive evaluation of the effectiveness" of the programs that had been implemented with this money. Do not be alarmed if you think $3 billion is too much money to spend on prevention. By definition, virtually every aspect of the criminal justice system as well as other government and private institutions are considered preventive in nature. Not only does the money go for such stereotypical prevention programs as after-school recreation programs, but it also supports such efforts as community-oriented policing, drug raids, prisoner rehabilitation, boot camps, home confinement and electronic monitoring, job corps and vocational training for prison inmates, preschool education programs, and other programs too numerous to mention. Most of the Department of Justice money set aside for prevention, however, is allocated most heavily in police and prisons, with very little support for prevention programs in other institutions (Sherman et al., 1997).

As the mandate from Congress suggests, evaluation plays an increasingly important role in the fields of criminology and criminal justice. Despite the increased attention given to evaluation research in the field, the results of evaluation studies have always influenced decisions made by criminal justice policy makers. The Manhattan Bail Project, for example, is a frequently cited example of how evaluation research led to massive policy change in the criminal justice system (Botein, 1965). The Manhattan Bail Project was an experiment designed by the Vera Institute of Justice in New York City in 1961 to determine whether certain kinds of defendants could be released without bail and still be counted on to appear for their trials. The project was primarily undertaken because of the inequity many believed existed in the pretrial release of defendants—defendants with financial means were able to post bail to secure pretrial release, whereas indigent defendants who could not afford bail had to remain in custody. This, of course, is not fair. It was hypothesized by researchers that those with strong ties to the community (e.g., those married with children and stable employment) could be released without bail and still be expected to show up for future adjudication. To investigate this hypothesis, the Vera Institute identified a sample of defendants who had strong community ties and then randomly divided this group into a group recommended for release without bail (experimental group) and a group in which no recommendation was made (control group). The results of the initial study found that over 99% of those released without bail appeared in court for trial at the appropriate time. This was an even higher compliance rate than those who were released on bail. Thus, the results suggested that releasing a person on the basis of verified information such as marital and employment status more effectively guaranteed appearance in court than did money bail. As a result of this study and research like it, almost every major jurisdiction in the nation today now allows eligible defendants to be released on their own recognizance (ROR) without bail.

In this chapter, we will provide you with an overview of evaluation research in the field of criminology and criminal justice. Although all the research we have discussed in this text is ultimately useful, evaluation research is inherently so because the results generally have an impact on policy choices in the immediate future. As such, evaluation research is often referred to as *applied research* because the findings can immediately be utilized and applied. We will first provide you with a brief history of evaluation research. Then, after describing the different types of evaluation research, we will provide you with case studies that illustrate the various methodologies used to assess the impacts of programs and policies in criminology and criminal justice.

A BRIEF HISTORY OF EVALUATION RESEARCH

Evaluation research is not a method of data collection, like survey research or experiments, nor is it a unique component of research designs, like sampling or measurement. Instead, evaluation research is social research that is conducted for a distinctive purpose: to investigate social programs (such as substance abuse treatment programs, welfare programs, criminal justice programs, or employment and training programs). For each project, an evaluation researcher must select a research design and method of data collection that are useful for answering the particular research questions posed and appropriate for the particular program investigated.

You can see why we placed this chapter after most of the others in the text: When you review or plan evaluation research, you have to think about the research process as a whole and how different parts of that process can best be combined.

Although scientific research methods had been used prior to the 1950s (in fact as early as the 1700s) to evaluate outcomes of particular social experiments and programs, it was not until the end of the 1950s that social research became immersed in the workings of government with the common goal of improving society. As Carole Weiss observed, social science was expected to bring rationality to the untidy world of government:

> It would provide hard data for planning and give cause-and-effect theories for policy making, so that statesmen would know which variables to alter in order to affect the desired outcomes. . . . And once policies were in operation, it would provide objective evaluation of their effectiveness so that necessary modifications could be made to improve performance. (1977:4)

During the 1960s, the practice of evaluation research increased dramatically not only in the United States but also around the world. One of the main initiatives that spawned this growth of evaluation research in the United States was the so-called War on Poverty that was part of the Great Society legislation of the 1960s. When the federal government began to take a major role in alleviating poverty and the social problems it left behind, such as delinquency and crime, the public wanted accountability for the tax dollars spent on such programs. Were these programs actually having their intended effects? Did the benefits outweigh the costs? During this time, the methods of social science were utilized like never before to evaluate this proliferation of new programs.

In 1967, Edward Suchman put forth his seminal definition of evaluation research as the application of social research techniques to the study of large-scale human service programs. In fact, a version of this definition is still utilized by some scholars today. For example, Rossi and Freeman (1989:18) encompass his definition in their more recent version: "Evaluation research is the systematic application of social research procedures for assessing the conceptualization, design, implementation, and utility of social intervention programs." What exactly does *systematic* mean? Well, regardless of what treatment or program is being examined, evaluations are systematic because they employ social research approaches to gathering valid and reliable data. Note the plural *approaches* instead of the singular *approach*. Evaluation research covers the spectrum of research methods that we have discussed in this text.

By the mid-1970s, evaluators were called on not only to assess the overall effectiveness of programs, but also to determine whether programs were being implemented as intended and to provide feedback to help solve programming problems as well. As an indication of the growth of evaluation research during this time, several professional organizations emerged to assist in the dissemination of ideas from the burgeoning number of social scientists engaged in this type of research in the United States, along with similar organizations in other countries (Patton, 1997).

Of course, despite the programs implemented by Presidents Kennedy and Johnson in the 1960s, poverty and its requisite social problems did not go away. By the 1990s, the public wanted even more accountability. Unfortunately, clear answers were not readily available. Few social programs could provide hard data on results achieved and outcomes obtained. Of course, government bureaucrats had produced a wealth of data on other things, including exactly how funds in particular programs were spent, for whom this money was spent, and for how many. However, these data primarily measured whether government staff were following the rules and regulations, not whether the desired results were being achieved. Instead of being rewarded for making their programs produce the intended outcomes (e.g., more jobs, fewer delinquents), the bureaucracy of government had made it enough simply to do the required paperwork of program monitoring. The results of evaluations that were conducted rarely saw the light of day. This, in turn, was interpreted by many politicians and individual citizens alike as "nothing works."

Professional evaluation researchers soon realized that it was not enough simply to perform rigorous experiments to determine program efficacy—they must also be responsible for making sure their results could be understood and utilized by the practitioners (e.g., government officials, corporations, and nonprofit agencies) to make decisions about scrapping or modifying existing programs. In addition, there was increased concern in the field regarding fiscal accountability—documenting the worth of social program expenditures in relation to their costs.

It was in this context that professional evaluators began discussing standards for the field of evaluation research. In 1981, a Joint Committee on Standards published the list of features all evaluations should have. These standards still exist today (Joint Committee, 1994, as cited in Patton, 1997:17):

Utility: The utility standards are intended to ensure that an evaluation will serve the practical information needs of intended users.

Feasibility: The feasibility standards are intended to ensure that an evaluation will be realistic, prudent, diplomatic, and frugal.

Propriety: The propriety standards are intended to ensure that an evaluation will be conducted legally, ethically, and with due regard for the welfare of those involved in the evaluation, as well as those affected by its results.

Accuracy: The accuracy standards are intended to ensure that an evaluation will reveal and convey technically adequate information about the features that determine worth or merit of the program being evaluated.

To the surprise of many in the field, utility was at the top of the list. This conveyed the idea that an evaluation only met the standards if, in fact, it served the needs of intended users. Professionals in the field responded accordingly. For example, Michael Quinn Patton (1997) developed the practice of and coined the term "utilization-focused evaluation" as a way to fulfill the utility standard. Utilization-focused evaluation offered both a philosophy of evaluation and a practical framework for designing and conducting evaluations. The primary premise of this method was that evaluations should be judged by their utility and actual use. Use concerned how real people in the real world applied evaluation findings and experienced the evaluation process. As such, the focus in utilization-focused evaluation was on intended use by intended users. Like the field as a whole, utilization-focused evaluation does not advocate any particular evaluation content, model, method, or theory. Rather, it stresses an interactive process between an evaluator and primary intended users to select the most appropriate content, model, and methods for their particular situation. To stress this process, Patton (1997:23) offers the following definition of program evaluation:

> Program evaluation is the systematic collection of information about the activities, characteristics, and outcomes of programs to make judgments about the program, improve program effectiveness, and/or inform decisions about future programming. Utilization-focused evaluation (as opposed to program evaluation in general) is evaluation done for and with specific, intended primary users for specific, intended uses.

Setting the Stage

The process of evaluation research can be viewed as a simple systems model. First, clients, customers, students or some other persons or units—cases—enter the program, as **inputs.** Students may begin a new school program, welfare recipients may enroll in a new job training program, crime victims may be sent to a victim advocate. Resources and staff required by a program are also program inputs.

Inputs   Resources, raw materials, clients, and staff that go into a program.

Next, some service or treatment is provided to the cases. This may be attendance in a class, assistance with a health problem, residence in new housing, or receipt of special cash benefits. The process of service delivery (**program process**) may be simple or complicated, short or long, but it is designed to have some impact on the cases, as inputs are consumed and outputs are produced.

Program process   The complete treatment or service delivered by the program.

The direct product of the program's service delivery process is its **output.** Program outputs may include clients served, case managers trained, food parcels delivered, or arrests made. The program outputs may be desirable in themselves, but they primarily serve to indicate that the program is operating.

Outputs   The services delivered or new products produced by the program process.

Program **outcomes** indicate the impact of the program on the cases that have been processed. Outcomes can range from improved test scores or higher rates of job retention to fewer criminal offenses and lower rates of poverty. There are likely to be multiple outcomes of any social program, some intended and some unintended, some positive and others that are viewed as negative.

Outcomes   The impact of the program process on the cases processed.

Variation in both outputs and outcomes in turn influence the inputs to the program through a **feedback** process. If not enough clients are being served, recruitment of new clients may increase. If too many negative side effects result from a trial medication, the trials may be limited or terminated. If a program does not appear to lead to improved outcomes, clients may go elsewhere.

Feedback   Information about service delivery system outputs, outcomes, or operations that is available to any program inputs.

Evaluation research enters into this picture as a more systematic approach to feedback that strengthens the feedback loop through credible analyses of program operations and outcomes. Evaluation research also broadens this loop to include connections to parties outside of the program itself. A funding agency or political authority may mandate the research, outside experts may be brought in to conduct the research, and the evaluation research findings may be released to the public, or at least funders, in a formal report.

The evaluation process as a whole, and the feedback process in particular, can only be understood in relation to the interests and perspectives of program stakeholders. **Stakeholders** are those individuals and groups who have some basis of concern with the program. They might be clients, staff, managers, funders, or the public. The board of a program or agency, the parents or spouses of clients, the foundations that award program grants, the auditors who monitor program spending, the members of Congress—each is a potential program stakeholder, and each has an interest in the outcome of any program evaluation. Some may fund the evaluation, some may provide research data, some may review, even approve, the research report (Martin & Kettner, 1996:3). Who the program stakeholders are and what role they play in the program evaluation will have tremendous consequences for the research.

Stakeholders   Individuals and groups who have some basis of concern with the program.

Can you see the difference between evaluation research and traditional social science research? Unlike explanatory social science research, evaluation research is not designed to test the implications of a social theory; the basic issue is often just, "What is the program's impact?" Process evaluation often uses qualitative methods, but unlike traditional exploratory research, the goal is not to create a broad theoretical explanation for what is discovered; instead, the question is, "How does the program do what it does?" Unlike social science research, the researchers cannot design evaluation studies simply in accord with the highest scientific standards and the most important research questions; instead, it is program stakeholders who set the agenda. But there is no sharp boundary between the two: In their attempt to explain how and why the program has an impact, and whether the program is needed, evaluation researchers often bring social theories into their projects.

Evaluation Alternatives

Today, the field of evaluation research remains somewhat of a dichotomy. There are those who conduct evaluation research for the sake of knowledge alone (the more general evaluation research, such as the research performed by Horney and Spohn, discussed in Chapter 5), whereas others strive to make their products useful for some action (the more specific program evaluation research, such as that performed by Sherman and Berk, discussed in Chapter 2). Regardless of the emphasis, however, all evaluation is empirical and data-driven. Both program evaluation and evaluation research in general offer empirical answers to questions of policy and policy effectiveness. Objective and empirical assessments of policies and programs are the cornerstone of the evaluation field. Because there will never be an infinite amount of financial resources to fund all the programs we think will work, social scientists will always have work to do. As Patton (1997:11) so eloquently states, "As not everything can be done, there must be a basis for deciding which things are worth doing. Enter evaluation."

Entire manuscripts have been devoted to delineating the various theories and methodologies utilized in evaluation research. Because this is a methods text, we are going to concentrate on the research methodologies most often utilized in criminology for evaluation purposes. Methods are always driven by research questions, however, so it is important to say something about the types of questions addressed by evaluation research. Patton (1997) distinguishes these three general question types:

Judgment-oriented evaluation. Evaluations aimed at determining the overall merit, worth, or value of something are **judgment-oriented evaluations.** Merit refers to the intrinsic value of a program. Questions addressed in this type of research include "How effective is the program in meeting the needs of those it is intended to help?" and "Does the program have the desired outcomes?"

Improvement-oriented evaluation. Using evaluation results to improve a program turns out, in practice, to be fundamentally different from rendering judgment about overall effectiveness, merit, or worth. **Improvement-oriented evaluation** focuses on making things better, rather than just rendering summative judgment. Although the questions addressed in this research are similar to those addressed in a judgment-oriented study, they are somewhat different: "What are the program's strengths and weaknesses?" and "To what extent are participants progressing toward the desired outcomes (e.g., are there any barriers to overcome in the delivery of services)?"

Knowledge-oriented evaluation. Contrary to the instrumental use of results of both judgment- and improvement-oriented evaluations, **knowledge-oriented evaluation** is used to influence thinking about issues in a general way. This knowledge can be as specific as clarifying a program's model, testing a theory, or figuring out how to measure outcomes. Academic researchers often initiate this type of an evaluation simply because the knowledge gained may fill a gap or add significantly to a particular research literature. For example, when Sherman and Berk (1984) began their experiment that examined the effect of arrest on recidivism rates of men who had assaulted their partners, they were not only concerned with the specific effect of arrest, but also with testing some basic tenets of deterrence theory such as "Are would-be offenders really deterred by the threat of formal sanctions like arrest and imprisonment?" and "Does the severity of the sanction effect the deterrent effect of formal sanctions?"

As these questions illustrate, evaluation research may be undertaken for a variety of reasons: for management and administrative purposes, to test hypotheses derived from theory, to identify ways to improve the delivery of services, or to decide whether to continue, cut, or modify a particular program. The goal of evaluation research, however, is primarily the same as the goal for all social science research—to design and implement a study that is objective and grounded in the rules of scientific methodology. These methods span the gamut of the methods we have discussed in this text. They can range from the strictly quantitative experimental and quasi-experimental designs to the qualitative methodologies of observation and intensive interviewing.

There are generally four types of evaluation research:

- the evaluation of need;
- the evaluation of process, sometimes referred to as *program monitoring;*
- the evaluation of impact or outcomes;
- the evaluation of efficiency.

We will next provide a brief discussion of each type of evaluation research.

The Evaluation of Need

The initial impetus for implementing programs to alleviate social problems and other societal ailments typically comes from a variety of sources, including advocacy groups, moral leaders, community advocates, and political figures. Before a program is designed and implemented, however, it is essential to obtain reliable information on the nature and the scope of the problem, and the target population in need of the intervention. Evaluation researchers often contribute to these efforts by applying research tools to answer such questions as "What is the magnitude of this problem in this community?" "How many people in this community are in need of this program?" "What are the demographic characteristics of these people (e.g., age, gender, race/ethnicity)?" and "Is the proposed program/intervention appropriate for this population?"

Rossi and Freeman (1989) provide several examples of the problems encountered in program implementation when these questions are not adequately answered. For example, during the early 1990s, when juvenile crime and delinquency were increasing, a suburban community in the Midwest implemented a program designed to prevent adolescent criminal behavior. However, after the program was started, it was discovered that there was virtually no juvenile crime in that particular community to begin with. The community planners had wrongly assumed that because juvenile delinquency was a social problem nationally, it was a problem in their community as well. Consequently, a lot of time, effort, and financial resources were wasted.

An empirical assessment by a social researcher of the community's needs in this area could have avoided this costly mistake. This research could have taken several forms, including doing an in-depth records search of local police agencies to determine the extent of crime and delinquency committed by juveniles in the area. A survey is another appropriate method used to determine the incidence rates of crime among juveniles in the community. For example, questionnaires could have been distributed in the schools to determine whether the rate of juvenile offending was serious enough in the community to warrant allocating the financial resources for the prevention programs.

The Evaluation of Process (Program Monitoring)

Once a program has been started, evaluators are often called on to document the extent to which implementation has taken place, whether the program is reaching the target individuals or groups, whether the program is actually operating as expected, and what resources are being expended (e.g., bucks spent!) in the conduct of the program. Rossi and Freeman define program monitoring as the

> systematic attempt by evaluation researchers to examine program coverage and delivery. Assessing program coverage consists of estimating the extent to which a program is reaching its intended target population; evaluating program delivery consists of measuring the degree of congruence between the plan for providing services and treatments and the ways they actually are provided. (1989:170)

Process evaluations are extremely important primarily because there is no way to reliably determine whether the intended outcomes have occurred without being certain the program is working according to plan. For example, imagine you are responsible for determining whether an anti-bullying curriculum given in a school has been successful in decreasing the amount of bullying behavior by the students. You conduct a survey of the students both before and after the curriculum was given and determine that rates of bullying have not significantly changed in the school since the curriculum was given. After you write your report, however, you find out that instead of being given in a 5-day series of 1-hour sessions as intended, the curriculum was actually crammed into a 2-hour format delivered on a Friday afternoon. A process evaluation would have revealed this implementation problem. If a program has not been implemented as intended, there is obviously no need to ask whether it had the intended outcomes.

A process evaluation can take many forms. Because most government and private organizations inherently monitor their activities through such things as application forms, receipts, and stock inventories, it should be relatively easy to obtain quantitative data for monitoring the delivery of services. This information can be summarized to describe things such as the clients served and the services provided. In addition to this quantitative information, a process evaluation will also likely benefit from qualitative methodologies such as unstructured interviews with people using the service or program. Interviews can also be conducted with staff to illuminate what they perceive to be obstacles to their delivery of services. As Posavac and Carey (1997:8) state, "Such qualitative information often provides points of view that neither evaluators nor service providers had considered."

The Evaluation of Impact or Outcomes

If a process study shows that the implementation of the program has been delivered to the target population as planned, the next role for an evaluator is to assess the extent to which the program achieved its goals. "Did the program have the intended consequences?" This question should by now be familiar to you; stated more like a research question we are used to, "Did the treatment or program (independent variable) affect change in the dependent variable?" It all comes back to the issue of causality.

The bulk of the published evaluation studies in our field are devoted to some type of impact assessment. Have new seat-belt laws increased rates of seat-belt usage? Have rape reform statutes increased the willingness of rape victims to report their victimizations to police? Are boot camps more likely to reduce recidivism among juveniles compared to more traditional juvenile detention settings? Have mandatory minimum sentencing guidelines decreased the probability that extra legal factors such as sex and race will affect an individual's sentence? The list could go on and on. Because impact evaluations comprise the bulk of the published literature, we will concentrate on highlighting the methods used for this type of evaluation research in the latter part of the chapter.

The Evaluation of Efficiency

Even when research shows that a program has helped the target population, policy makers must still deal with the question of costs. Being able to relate program outcomes to program costs is becoming increasingly important to policy makers. The evaluation of efficiency can involve two types of analyses. The first is a **cost-benefit analysis,** in which both program expenditures (e.g., staff wages, material costs) and outcomes (e.g., dollars saved by fewer crimes committed) are estimated in monetary terms. The second is a **cost-effectiveness analysis,** in which inputs are estimated in monetary terms while outcomes are estimated in terms of actual impacts (e.g., number of lives saved).

The goal of most policy makers, of course, is to offer services that will justify the investment of funds. In a business, these cost-benefit analyses are relatively straightforward. When delivering human services, however, the evaluation of efficiency is a bit more tricky, because the benefits are usually hard to convert into a dollar figure. The procedures involved in these types of analyses are highly technical and, as such, are beyond the scope of this book. It is important, however, to understand the concept of efficiency analysis. Larry Sherman (1997:11) succinctly describes the importance of this type of evaluation:

Even though scientific evaluation results are a key part of rational policy analysis, those results cannot automatically select the best policy. This is due not just to the scientific limitations of generalizing results from one setting to the next. Another reason is that evaluations often omit key data on cost-benefit ratios; the fact that a program is "effective" may be irrelevant if the financial or social costs are too high.

Exhibit 9.1   The Cost-Benefit Analysis of Police Helicopter Patrols in Reducing
Rates of Burglary

	Total	Per Day
Cost of the program	$3,032	$126
Cost of the burglaries without helicopter patrols	$27,171	$494
Cost of burglaries with helicopter patrols	$3,853	$161
Benefits of program	$8,004	$333
Benefit-to-cost ratio	$333/126 = 2.6	

Source: Reprinted with permission. From Schnelle, et al. (1978) "Police Evaluation Research: An
Experimental and Cost-Benefit Analysis of a Helicopter Patrol in a High Crime Area." *Journal of Applied
Behavior Analysis,* 11, 11–21, as cited by Posavac & Carey, 1997.

An early study by Schnelle and his colleagues (1978, as cited in Posavac & Carey, 1997) provides a good example of a cost-benefit analysis in criminal justice. Schnelle's research team was interested in estimating the benefits of helicopter patrol in preventing burglaries. In the neighborhood studied, most burglaries were done in the daylight hours by local juvenile offenders. Because a police officer in a helicopter could repeatedly observe large areas, policy makers believed that helicopter patrols would decrease the rate of burglary compared to traditional car patrols. The dependent variable in the study was the burglary rate during the 9 A.M. to 5 P.M police shift. Results indicated that the average daily burglary rate with regular patrol in force was 1.02, whereas the rate when the helicopter patrol supplemented the ground patrols was only .33. The next question to be addressed was "Did this reduction in burglaries justify the extra cost of helicopter patrol?"

The cost-benefit analysis performed by Schnelle and his colleagues was really a bit crude. For example, because the helicopter, pilot, and hanger were already part of the police department, these costs were not incorporated. The only additional costs estimated for the helicopter patrols were for fuel and maintenance. The benefits were defined as the value of the goods not stolen, which was estimated from insurance company material. Exhibit 9.1 summarizes the calculation of the benefit-to-cost ratio. The fact that the benefit-to-cost ratio was 2.6 indicates that the benefits exceeded the cost; the value of the goods not stolen exceeded the cost of the additional helicopter patrol.

As noted earlier, the majority of the published evaluation research in criminology and criminal justice concentrates on the evaluation of impacts or outcomes. The remainder of the chapter will offer several case studies from the literature, which serve to illustrate the primary methods that have been utilized by evaluation researchers. Because we have already examined most of these research methods in detail, we will concentrate on the application of different methods for evaluation purposes. The strengths and weakness of each method, however, should be immediately apparent to you. We will start with an evaluation study that utilized the strongest method for determining causality (internal validity). If you guessed a true experimental design, you were correct!

TRUE RANDOMIZED EXPERIMENTAL DESIGNS

Recall from Chapter 5 that true **experimental designs** must have three things:

1. Two comparison groups—one receiving the experimental condition (e.g., treatment or intervention) and the other one receiving no treatment/intervention or another form thereof.

2. Random assignment to these two (or more) comparison groups.

3. An assessment of change in the dependent variable for both groups after the experimental condition has been received.

The combination of these features permits us to have much greater confidence in the validity of causal conclusions than is possible in other research designs. As such, the randomized controlled experiment is the strongest research design for assessing the impacts and outcomes of programs and other interventions. As you can imagine, it is often difficult and sometimes impossible to use a true experimental design in a field setting. Nevertheless, many social researchers studying the effects of criminal justice policies and programs have been successful with their use. Moreover, understanding why these designs are superior for evaluation research seeking to examine program impacts is important so that you can better judge the strengths and weaknesses of other designs.

In this section, we will highlight two evaluation studies that have utilized a true randomized experiment to examine the effectiveness of policies and programs in obtaining their desired outcomes. The first evaluation examines the effects of using problem-oriented policing strategies to reduce violent crime in crime-ridden neighborhoods. The second example is taken from an evaluation of the Children at Risk program that was designed to prevent drug use and delinquency in adolescents 11 to 13 years of age. In each of these studies, only one program or policy was tested for impact. Keep in mind, however, that experimental designs can involve the simultaneous testing of several alternative interventions or different combinations of interventions (Chapter 5).

Case Study: Problem-Oriented Policing in Violent Crime Areas—A Randomized Controlled Experiment

Several studies have found that over half of all crimes in a city are committed at a few criminogenic places within communities. These places have been called "hot spots" by some criminologists (Sherman, Gartin, & Buerger, 1989; Weisburd, Maher, & Sherman, 1992). Even within the most crime-ridden neighborhoods, it has been found that crime clusters at a few discrete locations while other areas remain relatively crime-free. The clustering of violent crime at particular locations suggests that there are important features or dynamics at these locations that give rise to violent situations. As such, focused crime prevention efforts should be able to modify these criminogenic conditions and reduce violence.

Problem-oriented policing strategies are increasingly utilized by urban jurisdictions to reduce crime in these high-activity crime places. Problem-oriented policing challenges officers to identify and analyze the causes of problems behind a string of criminal incidents. Once the underlying conditions that give rise to crime problems are known, police officers can then develop and implement appropriate responses. Despite the increasing use of problem-oriented policing strategies, however, there has been very little evaluation research conducted to determine whether such strategies are actually effective in decreasing crime rates.

Anthony Braga and David Weisburd, and their colleagues Elin Waring, Lorraine Green Mazerolle, William Spelman, and Francis Gajewski (1999), created a novel experiment designed to determine the effectiveness of problem-oriented policing to decrease the incidence of violent street crime in Jersey City, New Jersey. The methodology they employed for their study was a true randomized experimental design. Recall from Chapter 5 that this design allows researchers to assume that the only systematic difference between a control and an experimental group is the presence of the intervention—in this case, the presence or absence of problem-oriented policing strategies.

To determine which places would receive the problem-oriented strategies and which places would not, Braga and his colleagues used computerized mapping technologies to analyze all 1993 robbery and assault incidents and emergency citizen calls for services in Jersey City, New Jersey. These incidents were then matched to intersection areas (the intersection and its four adjoining street segments) and counted. Braga and his colleagues then identified 56 discrete high-activity violent crime places. These 56 places were then matched into 28 pairs. Matching was done on a number of variables, including the primary offenses in each place (e.g., places with lower numbers of robberies and higher numbers of assaults were grouped together), types of problems at a place (e.g., robberies of commuters versus robberies of convenience stores), known dynamics of the place (e.g., the presence of active drug markets), and physical characteristics (e.g., presence of a park or school). A coin was flipped by the researchers to randomly determine which of the places within the pair would receive the problem-oriented policing treatment (experimental places). Remember that a key feature of true experimental designs is this **random assignment.** The places that were not selected from the flip in each pair did not receive the new policing strategies (control places). The design of this experimental evaluation is illustrated in Exhibit 9.2.

In each of the experimental places, police officers from the Violent Crime Unit (VCU) of the Jersey City police department established networks consistent with problem-oriented policing. For example, community members were used as information sources to discuss the nature of the problems the community faced, the possible effectiveness of

Exhibit 9.2   Randomized Experimental Design Used to Evaluate Problem-Oriented Policing Strategies

Source: Braga et al., 1999.

proposed responses, and the assessment of implemented responses. In most places, the VCU officers believed that the violence that distinguished these places from other areas of the city was closely related to the disorder of the place. Although specific tactics varied from place to place, most attempts to control violence in these places were actually targeted at the social disorder problems. For example, some tactics included cleaning up the environment of the place through aggressive order maintenance and making physical improvements such as securing vacant lots or removing trash from the street. Other tactics included aggressive interventions to control the social disorder of a place, such as repeat foot and radio car patrols, dispersing groups of loiterers, and stop-and-frisks of suspicious persons. In addition, in places where drug markets were located, VCU officers increased their investigations to disrupt both the selling and the consumption of illicit drugs. The independent variable or treatment, then, was the use of problem-oriented policing, which comprised a number of specific tactics implemented by police officers to control the physical and social disorder at experimental violent places. In contrast, control places did not receive these problem-solving efforts; they received traditional policing strategies such as arbitrary patrol interventions and routine follow-up investigations by detectives. No problem-oriented strategies were employed.

Braga and his colleagues examined the efficacy of these problem-oriented policing strategies by using three separate dependent variables. The first two were traditional indicators of crime—incident report data and citizen emergency calls for service within each place. The third variable was a physical observation of each place during the pretest and posttest periods. This variable was used to indicate changes in both physical incivilities at places such as vacant lots, trash, graffiti, or broken windows and social incivilities such as drinking in public and loitering. These variables were measured for 6-month preintervention and postintervention periods. If the problem-oriented policing approach was effective, then Braga and his colleagues should have seen a decrease in incidents and emergency calls for service in the experimental areas in the posttest compared to the control areas. They should also have seen decreased signs of physical and social incivilities in the experimental areas compared to the control areas.

Statistical results indicated that the total number of criminal incidents and the total number of citizen calls for service were significantly reduced at the experimental places relative to the control places. This effect was true for most specific crime types examined as well. Examination of the observational data indicated that both physical and social disorder was reduced in 91% of the experimental places compared to the control places. Thus, the problem-oriented policing strategies examined in this evaluation research appear to have had a great deal of success in controlling and preventing crime.

Recall from Chapter 5 that although randomized experiments do allow us to determine whether the independent variable had an effect on the dependent variable, they do not tell us why. That is, they do not provide us with information about the causal **mechanisms** that may be producing this effect. Braga and his colleagues, however, utilized several theories to speculate on how these problem-oriented strategies may have changed the dynamics of a place in ways that resulted in a decrease in crime. For example, based on rational choice theory, which asserts that offenders consider risks, effort, and rewards when contemplating criminal acts, the researchers speculated that the increased presence and order maintenance activities at the experimental places may have served as a powerful deterrent by communicating to offenders that disorderly behavior would no longer be tolerated. Braga and his colleagues correctly pointed out, however, that the study did not gather data to determine the specific causal mechanisms responsible for the reductions found in crime. To do this, other forms of research would be necessary, such as interviewing offenders to determine their perceptions regarding their decisions to offend or to desist from offending in particular places.

What is certain from this research is that problem-oriented policing strategies are more effective in reducing both incidents of violent crime and citizen calls for emergency service than traditional policing strategies. The authors concluded (Braga et al., 1999:571):

> Law enforcement agencies interested in controlling violence should consider implementing problem-oriented policing programs that focus on the places where violence clusters by developing tailored interventions addressing the underlying conditions and dynamics that give rise to violent situations.

Case Study: Children at Risk Program

One of the most innovative drug and delinquency prevention programs implemented to date is the Children at Risk (CAR) program. In general, this program intervenes in the lives of high-risk adolescents 11 to 13 years of age who live in severely distressed neighborhoods (e.g., extreme poverty, high incidence of substance abuse and drug trafficking). The strategy behind the CAR program is to prevent drug use and delinquency in at-risk youths by reducing the number of risk factors to which they are exposed. The goal of the intervention is to deliver a broad range of services to at-risk youths and their families, involving the close collaboration of police, school administrators, case managers, and other service providers such as nonprofit groups like Big Brothers/Big Sisters. The CAR program generally provides several service components that target neighborhood, peer group, family, and individual risk factors. These services include case management, which assesses the needs of participating youths and their families and develops and implements plans to meet those needs; family services such as therapeutic services and skills training to help families and adult caregivers function better; after-school and summer activities that offer youths alternatives to hanging out without adult supervision in neighborhoods rife with gangs and drug dealers; education services such as tutoring and homework assistance; incentives including monetary rewards to both youth and their families for participation; and community and problem-oriented policing strategies in the community.

Adele Harrell of the Urban Institute was the principal investigator for the research team that conducted an evaluation of the CAR program in five cities: Austin, Texas; Bridgeport, Connecticut; Memphis, Tennessee; Savannah, Georgia; and Seattle, Washington (Harrell, Cavanagh, & Sridharan, 1999). Their research design combined true and quasi-experimental techniques and is illustrated in Exhibit 9.3.

In each of the five cities, at-risk adolescents in troubled neighborhoods were randomly assigned to participate in the CAR program (experimental group) or not (control group). In addition, a quasi-experimental comparison group of subjects from matched high-risk neighborhoods, who did not participate in CAR, was also monitored. This component makes it a **quasi-experimental design,** of course, because the youths were not randomly assigned to this last group. The addition of this group, however, lends a great deal of confidence in Harrell and her colleagues' findings.

For participants in all groups, interviews were conducted in the home at baseline (between recruitment and the start of services) and at the end of the program period. A follow-up survey with the youths was also conducted one year after the end of the

Exhibit 9.3   Randomized Experimental Design Used to Evaluate Children at Risk (CAR) Program

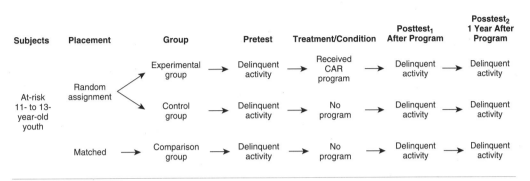

Source: Harrell, Cavanagh, & Sridharan, 1999.

program. The interview and survey were designed to measure a number of things, including the presence of both risk and protective factors related to delinquency and drug use (e.g., nature of peer groups, family conflict, lack of parental supervision). They also measured youths' self-reported involvement in delinquency and drug use. Thus there were one pretest and two posttests in this design. In addition to the dependent variables measured in the survey, pretest and posttest data were also obtained from officially recorded criminal activity (police records) and school performance and attendance (school records). Harrell and her colleagues sought to answer three primary questions:

- Did CAR youths and families participate in more services and prosocial activities during the program than youths and families in the control and comparison groups?
- Did CAR youths and caregivers have fewer risk factors and/or protective factors than youths and caregivers in the control and comparison groups one year after the program ended?
- Were CAR youths less likely to exhibit problem behaviors in the year following the end of the program than high risk youths in the control group who did not receive CAR services?

Regarding the first question, Harrell found that compared with youths in the **control group** and **comparison group,** CAR youths participated in a significantly higher number of positive activities, such as sports, school clubs, religious groups, and community-organized programs during the program period. They also were more likely to report attending a drug or alcohol prevention program. CAR caregivers also participated in more kinds of positive activities, such as religious, community, and recreational activities than did control group caregivers. Despite the fact that CAR nearly doubled the youths' chances of participating in mentoring and tutoring programs, however, fewer than half of the CAR families reported receiving these services. This was consistent with the process evaluation component performed by Harrell and her colleagues, which revealed the difficulties encountered in getting youths to participate voluntarily in tutoring programs and establishing stable mentoring relationships.

Did CAR reduce risk factors or enhance protective factors? The data revealed mixed findings. One year after the program ended, CAR youths had more positive peer support and associated less often with delinquent peers than youths in the control group. However, no significant differences were found between the groups in self-esteem, alienation, feeling sad and lonely, or risk taking. In school performance, the CAR youth were more likely to have been promoted in school than youths in the control groups. However, their attachment to school, school attendance, and educational and job expectations resembled their peers who did not receive CAR services. Similarly, there was no indication of lower family risk factors among CAR youths compared to the other groups. This, too, was echoed by the process evaluation, which documented substantial problems in engaging these multiproblem families in services.

Did CAR reduce or prevent problem behaviors like drug use and delinquency? The results of the evaluation were more positive regarding this question. Compared with youths in the control group one year after the end of the program, CAR youths were less likely to have used drugs or to have sold drugs in the past month. In addition, CAR youths committed fewer violent crimes, but not fewer property crimes, than the youths who did not receive the CAR program.

Was the program a success? As with many evaluations, the authors concede that conclusions may be premature. Harrell and her colleagues are appropriately cautious in their conclusion:

> The answer to whether the substantial investment in this effort pays long-term dividends must await follow-up. If, as some studies suggest, increased rates of school promotion, reduced involvement in drug use during early adolescence, and positive peer influence result in high rates of high school graduation and reduced involvement in the adult criminal justice system, then the investment may have long-term benefits that outweigh the short-term costs. (1999:9)

Strengths of Randomized Experimental Designs

The research designs used by Braga et al. and Harrell et al. meet all three criteria for a true experimental design. First, they used at least two comparison groups. In the Braga research, some communities received the problem-oriented patrol strategies (experimental groups) while the other comparison communities received traditional police patrol (control groups). In Harrell's research, some adolescents received the CAR program (experimental group) while the others did not. Second, the units in each group (communities in Braga's research and adolescents in Harrell's study) were randomly assigned to each condition. And finally, the assessments of change in the dependent variables used in their studies were performed after the experimental condition (problem-oriented strategies or CAR program) had been delivered.

Recall that the three criteria necessary for establishing a causal relationship between independent and dependent variables are:

1. Association between the independent and dependent variables

2. Correct time order (independent variable precedes the dependent)

3. Nonspuriousness (rule out influence of other variables)

Data obtained from a true experimental design is the best way to determine that all three of these criteria have been met.

Because the communities in Braga's study were randomly assigned to receive either problem-oriented or traditional patrol strategies, the relationship found between these strategies (independent variable) and the dependent variables (incidents of crime, etc.) are unambiguous. Braga and his colleagues monitored their dependent variables both before and after the different policing strategies were implemented, so there is also no question that the strategies came before the change in the dependent variable. Finally, the random assignment of the communities to either the problem-oriented or traditional police conditions controlled for a host of possible extraneous influences that may have created spurious relationships. The same is true for Harrell's evaluation of the CAR program.

The extent to which the findings of these studies can be generalized to the larger population, however, is another issue. Can Braga's findings be generalized to the larger population in New Jersey (sample generalizability) or to other states and communities (external validity)? Can Harrell's findings be generalized to other at-risk adolescent populations? Issues of sample generalizability, you will recall, are related to selecting a random sample from the population in the first place (random selection), not random assignment. However, because Braga's study utilized several experimental and control communities and Harrell added another comparison group, this increases the likelihood that their findings are generalizable to their respective populations. In addition, because both Braga's and Harrell's studies were performed in the field (i.e., real world) and not in a laboratory, their findings are more likely to be generalizable to the larger population.

QUASI-EXPERIMENTAL DESIGNS IN EVALUATION RESEARCH

We have already learned that many research questions or situations are not amenable to a true experimental design. The same is true in evaluation research. There are many reasons why it may be impossible to use randomized experiments to evaluate the impacts of programs and policies. The primary reason why randomization is not possible in evaluation research is that the program is usually outside the control of the evaluator. As Rossi and Freeman state (1989:313), "for political, human subject or other considerations, program staff, sponsors, or other powerful stakeholders resist randomization." Obtaining the cooperation of the program staff and sponsors is often an obstacle in evaluation research. In fact, when there are several locations implementing similar programs, the sites included in an evaluation study may be selected based primarily on the cooperation of the staff and sponsors. For example, in their evaluation study of Treatment Alternatives to Street Crime (TASC), Anglin and his associates (1999:172) state, "The program's ability to negotiate successfully with local officials to ensure their cooperation with evaluation activities was also a condition of study inclusion."

In general, quasi-experimental designs are the most powerful alternatives to true randomized experimental designs. The more alike the experimental and control groups are to each other, particularly on characteristics thought to be related to the intervention or treatment, the more confident we can be in a study's findings. In this section, we are going to discuss two types of quasi-experimental designs that are often utilized in criminology and criminal justice to determine the impacts of programs. To illustrate the first type, a **nonequivalent control group design,** we will use research that has been done to evaluate whether boot camps are more likely to reduce recidivism after release compared to traditional incarceration. The second type of quasi-experimental design we will highlight is the **time series design.** To illustrate this design, we will use a study that evaluated the impact of mandatory sentences for gun crimes.

Case Study: Boot Camps

Since their beginning in 1983 in Georgia, the use of correctional boot camps, sometimes called shock incarceration programs, has skyrocketed in both state and federal prison systems. For politicians and citizens alike, the notion of a strict, military-style punishment as an alternative to extended incarceration is attractive. Many questions remain, however, about the value of boot camps. Do they work? Because there are so many different types of boot camps (e.g., some have military-style atmospheres whereas others do not) there is no easy answer to this question. Moreover, despite their increased popularity, there have been only a few systematic attempts to evaluate their efficacy in reducing recidivism.

In 1990, Doris MacKenzie was the principal investigator of a National Institute of Justice (NIJ) grant, which funded evaluation of boot camp program efficacy in eight states—Florida, Georgia, Illinois, Louisiana, New York, Oklahoma, South Carolina, and Texas. These sites were selected because they incorporated the core elements of boot camp programs, including (1) strict rules, discipline, and a military boot camp–like atmosphere; (2) mandatory participation in military drills and physical training; and (3) separation of program participants from other prison inmates.

The evaluation was extensive and resulted in many publications (Brame & MacKenzie, 1996; MacKenzie, 1994; MacKenzie, Brame, McDowall, & Souryal, 1995; MacKenzie & Piquero, 1994; MacKenzie & Souryal, 1995). Rather than focusing on one measure of program success, such as recidivism reduction, MacKenzie and her colleagues developed five different components to their evaluation—a process evaluation of the programs based on interviews with staff and inmates, official program materials, and observation; a study of inmate attitudinal change during incarceration; a study of offender recidivism; a study of positive adjustment during community supervision; and a study of prison bed-space savings.

We will highlight the results of the impact assessments for recidivism here. To determine whether boot camps were more likely than traditional prison time to reduce recidivism after release, MacKenzie and her colleagues utilized a quasi-experimental design. In each state, a sample of male boot camp program graduates was used as the experimental condition. Two other offender samples were used as comparison groups and usually included regular prison parolees, probationers, and boot camp dropouts. The individuals from all samples, however, met the eligibility requirements for the boot camp programs. This nonequivalent control group design is illustrated for you in Exhibit 9.4.

After being sentenced to probation or released from boot camps and prison, subjects were tracked for a follow-up period of up to 2 years of community supervision. Recidivism was measured by arrests and revocations for new crimes and/or for technical violations.

Were boot camps successful in meeting their goals? Well, in five states (Florida, Georgia, Oklahoma, South Carolina, and Texas), MacKenzie's findings suggest that boot camp graduates appeared to recidivate at about the same rate as those from the comparison

Exhibit 9.4   Nonequivalent Control Group Design Used to Evaluate Boot Camps

Subjects	Group	Treatment/ Condition	Posttest
Boot camp-eligible offenders	Experimental group $\longrightarrow$	Boot camp $\longrightarrow$	Recidivism
	Comparison $\longrightarrow$	Prison $\longrightarrow$	Recidivism
	Comparison $\longrightarrow$	Probation $\longrightarrow$	Recidivism

Source: Brame & MacKenzie, 1996.

groups. In Illinois, Louisiana, and New York, however, boot camp graduates had lower recidivism rates on particular recidivism measures. Graduates in Illinois and Louisiana, for example, were less likely to have their supervision status revoked as a result of a new crime revocation than were comparison samples. And although they did not differ from the comparison sample on other measures of recidivism, New York boot camp graduates were less likely to be returned to prison as a result of a technical violation.

The weakness of this quasi-experimental design is that MacKenzie was not able to randomly assign offenders to the boot camps or the comparison treatments. Therefore, there is less confidence in the findings, primarily because there is no assurance that the offenders were equivalent before they received the treatments. To control for these differences, MacKenzie and her colleagues utilized strong statistical techniques that served to increase the internal validity of their findings.

In addition, even for the modest effects found in the three states, there is still some ambiguity about how the independent variable, in this case the type of incarceration, influenced the dependent variable (recidivism). Because this evaluation was not performed using a true experimental design with random assignment to the boot camps, prison, or probation, there is even more ambiguity regarding the extent to which boot camps actually affected recidivism rates. MacKenzie does, however, speculate about the reasons why the Illinois, Louisiana, and New York programs showed reduced recidivism rates compared to their respective comparison programs. In fact, she contends that one of the reasons may have had little to do with the boot camps themselves (MacKenzie & Souryal, 1996:293):

> These programs stand out as the only boot camps in the study that have developed an intensive supervision phase for boot camp graduates. It is therefore very likely that differences in recidivism rates in these states were due to the type of community supervision provided to graduates, not in-prison programming.

In addition, these boot camps also devoted a considerable amount of time per day to rehabilitative activities such as drug treatment services.

In summary, MacKenzie's results were not very favorable for boot camps. She states,

Results clearly show that the core elements of boot camp programs—military-style discipline, hard labor, and physical training—by themselves did not reduce offender recidivism—but it is likely that some mixture of rehabilitation and intensive follow-up supervision plays an important role. (1996:65)

Case Study: Mandatory Sentencing Laws

In this era of "get tough on crime" policies, the use of mandatory and enhanced sentences at both the federal and state levels has dramatically increased. The effects of most of these policies, however, remain unevaluated (this is becoming a theme, huh?). The most obvious impact they have had, particularly those policies related to the use and sale of drugs, is to increase the prison population in the United States to the highest levels in history.

One category of mandatory sentences that has received research attention is the mandatory sentence enhancements for gun crimes. By providing stiff and certain penalties when a gun is involved in an offense, sentence enhancement laws are meant to reduce the use of firearms by criminals. The most comprehensive evaluation of these laws to date was performed by David McDowall, Colin Loftin, and Brian Wiersema (1992). These researchers conducted a time series analysis based on six cities that had enacted similar mandatory sentence enhancements for gun crimes: Detroit, Jacksonville, Tampa, Miami, Philadelphia, and Pittsburgh. The key features of the law were the same in each city: (1) judges were required to impose a specified sentence on defendants convicted of an offense that involved a gun; (2) probation, suspended sentences, and parole under these sentences were prohibited; and (3) all areas used advertising campaigns involving radio and television commercials, posters, bumper stickers, and billboards to communicate the message that offenders would receive additional punishment if they used a gun to commit a crime.

McDowall and his colleagues examined the law's effects in each city separately and in a pooled analysis to obtain an overall estimate of the effect of the statutes on three types of violent crimes: homicide, robbery, and assault. We will summarize the findings from the combined study here. The statistical methods used in this analysis were quite complex, so we won't burden you with them—those of you who are interested can go right to the source! In general, what McDowall did was examine rates of gun-related violent crime both before (pretest) and after (posttest) the mandatory sentencing laws were implemented. If the laws were effective in reducing firearm crimes, the number of gun offenses should decrease during the posttest period. The dependent variables monitored were monthly rates of various violent crimes.

To enhance the research design, the researchers did not just examine a few months before and after statute implementation. McDowall and his colleagues examined many months of data (up to 150 depending on data availability in each city) both before and after implementation of the law. Recall that this is similar to the research design used by Horney and Spohn that evaluated the impacts of rape reform legislation (Chapter 5).

Were the sentencing enhancements effective in reducing violent crime? Well, the results were somewhat mixed. The only crimes for which the laws had a consistent impact across all cities were homicides committed with guns. For example, McDowall et al. offer a statistical illustration of the law's efficacy in Detroit:

Consider Detroit, a city with a pre-intervention mean of forty gun homicides per month and a standard deviation of eight. Here, a decrease of .69 standard deviation units represents an average of 5.5 lives saved each month, a fourteen percent reduction. (1992:386)

The analyses of gun-related assaults and armed robberies, however, were not so positive. The only city in which gun assaults significantly decreased was Jacksonville. Although gun assaults also decreased in Detroit, Miami, Philadelphia, and Pittsburgh, the decrease was not significantly different from zero (no decrease at all). Further, gun assaults actually increased in Tampa. Armed robberies (armed with any weapon) did not significantly decrease in any city and only showed small decreases in two cities. Tampa and Miami, however, showed large and significant increases in unarmed robbery follow-ing the laws' adoption. The researchers argue that this may illustrate that enhanced sentencing laws may have prevented armed robberies from increasing in the same way as unarmed robberies.

So, you may be asking yourself, what did they conclude about the effects of the laws? McDowall and his colleagues were confident in their results regarding the benefits of the sentence enhancements in reducing gun homicides. In fact, they state,

> The consistency of the effects on gun homicide virtually rules out the possibility that factors confounded with mandatory sentencing could account for the reductions in this crime. . . . There is clear and convincing evidence of preventive effects for homicide. (1992: 389)

However, the researchers remained appropriately hesitant about conclusions for the other types of violent crime.

NONEXPERIMENTAL DESIGNS

Much research that is conducted to evaluate the effectiveness of programs or policies uses a **nonexperimental design** in which a single group is studied only once, after the treat-ment or program has been delivered. Unfortunately, such studies have absolutely no form of control or comparison. As such, they are "of almost no scientific value" (Campbell & Stanley, 1966:6). Nevertheless, because they are so common in evaluation research, we provide an illustration of their use.

Case Study: Vocational Education for Serious Juvenile Offenders—A One-Shot Design

Some of the earliest programs for crime reduction have been those that provide legiti-mate employment or employment skills to offenders or at-risk individuals. Most of these programs target adolescents. One of the myriad programs to provide vocational education for juvenile offenders is New Pride, Inc. This program has been providing vocational services to serious young offenders (14 through 18 years of age) for almost two decades. Designed as an alternative to institutionalization in state correctional facilities, New Pride

Exhibit 9.5   One-Shot Design Used to Evaluate the New Pride Program

	Subjects	Treatment/ Condition		Posttest
	Serious young offenders (14–18 years old)	Received New Pride program	→	Recidivism and school placement

Source: James & Granville, 1984.

uses a holistic approach and provides a wide array of services, including diagnostic and needs assessment, intensive supervision in the community, individual and family counseling, prevocational training (e.g., basic academic and social interactional skills), vocational training and job placement, structured recreation, and cultural education. Based on results of the diagnostic and needs assessment, services are individualized to meet the specific needs of each youth and are integrated into a single treatment plan.

The planners of New Pride, understandably, have a lot of faith in their program. Unfortunately, there have been few systematic attempts to evaluate the effectiveness of this program and others like it in either increasing employment or reducing recidivism (Bushway & Reuter, 1997). For example, the results of the **one-shot design** methodology evaluation performed by Thomas James and Jeanne Granville (1984) of the New Pride program are too scientifically deficient to be of value. This methodology is displayed in Exhibit 9.5.

Basically, a one-shot design measures the dependent variable after the treatment has been delivered for only those who received the treatment. James and Granville found that over 70% of those who completed the New Pride program were successfully reintegrated into the public school system, continued part-time employment, and were not rearrested within 6 months of program completion. Unfortunately, because there was no random assignment to another comparison group—in fact, no comparison group whatsoever—these results tell us very little. This type of design is vulnerable to all the confounding effects described in Chapter 5 including selection bias, endogenous change, and history effects. Perhaps the results would have been the same for youths who had received no vocational training. The problem is, we can never be sure when a one-shot design such as this is used.

QUALITATIVE AND QUANTITATIVE METHODS

Because we have been concentrating on the evaluation of impacts, our focus has been primarily on quantitative methods. Do children who received the Children at Risk program have lower rates of delinquency compared to those children who did not receive the program? Do young offenders incarcerated in boot camps fair better after release compared to those offenders sent to traditional correctional institutions? It's fair to say that when there's an interest in comparing outcomes between an experimental and a control group, or tracking change over time in a systematic manner, quantitative methods are favored.

But qualitative methods can add much to quantitative evaluation research studies, including more depth, detail, nuance, and exemplary case studies (Patton, 1997). Perhaps the greatest contribution qualitative methods can make in many evaluation studies is investigating program process—finding out what is "inside the black box." Although it is possible, even recommended, to track the process of service delivery with quantitative measures like staff contact hours, frequency of complaints, and the like, the goal of finding out what is happening to program clients and how clients experience the program can often best be achieved by observing program activities and interviewing staff and clients intensively.

Another good reason for using qualitative methods in evaluation research is the importance of learning how different individuals react to the treatment. For example, a quantitative evaluation of student reactions to an adult basic skills program for new immigrants relied heavily on the students' initial statements of their goals. However, qualitative interviews revealed that most new immigrants lacked sufficient experience in America to set meaningful goals; their initial goal statements simply reflected their eagerness to agree with their counselors' suggestions (Patton, 1997:177–181).

Qualitative methods can also help in understanding how social programs actually operate. Complex social programs have many different features, and it is not always clear whether it is the combination of those features or some particular features that are responsible for the program's effect—or for the absence of an effect. Lisbeth B.Schorr, director of the Harvard Project on Effective Interventions, and Daniel Yankelovich, president of Public Agenda, put it this way: "Social programs are sprawling efforts with multiple components requiring constant mid-course corrections, the involvement of committed human beings, and flexible adaptation to local circumstances"(Schorr & Yankelovich, 2000).

The more complex the social program, the more value that qualitative methods can add to the evaluation process. Schorr and Yankelovich (2000) point to the Ten Point Coalition, an alliance of African American ministers who helped to reduce gang warfare in Boston through multiple initiatives, "ranging from neighborhood probation patrols to safe havens for recreation." Qualitative methods would help to describe a complex, multifaced program like this.

For the most part, the strengths and weaknesses of methodologies used in evaluation research are those of the methods we have already discussed throughout this text. As Patton contends, "There are no perfect [evaluation] studies. And there cannot be, for there is no agreement on what constitutes perfection" (Patton, 1997:23). There are, however, methods that are better able to infer cause and effect. Because the basic question of most impact evaluations is "Does a program (cause) have its intended consequences (effect)?" there are basic methodological criteria we can use to judge the methods discussed in this chapter.

In their review of the crime prevention evaluation literature, Larry Sherman and his colleagues (1997) adopted a way to judge the "methodological rigor" of evaluation studies using a 5-point scale. The researchers gave each study examined in their review a "scientific methods score" of 1 to 5, with 5 being the strongest scientific evidence. Studies were assigned a score based on the following criteria:

1. Correlation between a crime prevention program and its intended outcome (e.g., a measure of crime or crime risk factors)

2. Temporal sequence between the program and the crime or risk outcome clearly observed (e.g., program before outcome), or a comparison group present without demonstrated comparability to the treatment group

3. A comparison between two or more groups or units, one with and one without the program and/or a long time series analysis

4. A comparison between multiple groups or units with and without the program, controlling for other factors, or a nonequivalent comparison group that has only minor differences evident between the groups

5. Random assignment to program (experimental group) and comparison groups (control groups)

As you can see, a study with a score of 1 simply demonstrated a correlation between a crime prevention program and its intended outcome. But as you learned in Chapter 5, correlation does not mean causation. Hence the low rating of 1 for studies only demonstrating correlation. To reach level 3, a study had to employ some kind of control or comparison group to determine what would have happened without the prevention program. If that comparison group consisted of a large number of matched or almost randomized cases, the study could achieve a score of 4. If the comparison was to a large number of comparable units selected at random to receive the program or not, the study received the highest score of 5 because, as Sherman et al. state (1997:18), "Random assignment offers the most effective means available of eliminating competing explanations for whatever outcome is observed."

Despite the fact that a randomized experiment is the best way to determine the impacts of a program, it is also important to remember that the methodology selected for an evaluation project should be relevant to the policy makers and planners who intend to use the results. Also, as you will see in Chapter 10, using multiple methods to answer one research question is always advantageous (e.g., combining a quantitative analysis of recidivism rates with interviews with offenders who received treatment). Although some researchers vehemently contend that only a randomized experimental design can provide reliable information on the impacts of a program, others just as vehemently disagree. For example, in his utilization-focused method of evaluation, Patton (1997) believes that when making evaluation methods decisions, the primary focus should be on getting the best possible data to answer primary users' questions. This cannot be done without involving them in the decision-making process to begin with. For methods decisions, the emphasis is on the appropriateness of the method to answer the practitioner's questions. Patton (1997) contends that only when these decisions are made in collaboration with the primary users will they be perceived as credible and, thus, more likely to be used.

It should also be noted that evaluation research faces obstacles not faced by general social research. We have already highlighted a few of these including the obstacle of obtaining support and cooperation from program staff and sponsors. In their review of evaluation research on crime prevention programs, Sherman and his colleagues (1997) delineate several other obstacles. For example, one obstacle noted is the structural separation of research and program funding. In everyday life, this often means that an evaluator is brought in after a program has been implemented and asked to assess its consequences. This, of course, leads to several problems. How can the consequences be accurately assessed if the evaluator did not have the opportunity to monitor the dependent variable (outcomes) before the program was started? How can the consequences be accurately assessed if the evaluator had no chance to obtain a comparison group by randomly assigning some units (e.g., individuals or communities) to the program/treatment condition and others elsewhere? To ameliorate this problem, Sherman recommends that Congress produce financial incentives for partnerships to be created between local agencies implementing programs and researchers evaluating them.

CONCLUSION

In recent years, the field of evaluation research has become an increasingly popular and active research specialty within the fields of criminology and criminal justice. Many social scientists find special appeal in evaluation research because of its utility.

The research methods applied to evaluation research are not different from those covered elsewhere in this text; they can range from qualitative intensive interviews to rigorous randomized experimental designs. In process evaluations, qualitative methodologies can be particularly advantageous. However, the best method for determining cause and effect, or for determining whether a program had its intended consequences (impacts), is the randomized experimental design. Although this may not always be possible in the field, it is the "gold standard" with which to compare methodologies used to assess the impacts of all programs and/or policies.

KEY TERMS

Accuracy

Comparison group

Control group

Cost-benefit analysis

Cost-effectiveness analysis

Evaluation of efficiency

Evaluation of impact

Evaluation of need

Evaluation of process

Experimental designs

Feasibility

Feedback

Improvement-oriented evaluation

Inputs

Judgment-oriented evaluation

Knowledge-oriented evaluation

Mechanisms

Nonequivalent control group design

Nonexperimental design

One-shot design

Outcomes

Outputs

Program process

Propriety

Quasi-experimental design

Random assignment

Stakeholders

Time series design

Utility

HIGHLIGHTS

- Whenever people implement a program for a specific purpose, they pay attention to the consequences of it, even if this attention is not in the form of rigorous scientific methods. Evaluation research, however, has become increasingly used to assess the impacts of programs and policies since the 1950s.

- The evaluation of need generally aims to describe the nature and scope of the problem along with the target population in need of services.

- The evaluation of process determines the extent to which implementation has taken place, whether the program is reaching the target population, whether the program is actually operating as expected, and what resources are being expended.

- Impact evaluations determine whether the program or policy produced the desired outcomes.

- The evaluation of efficiency relates program outcomes to program costs.

- True randomized experiments are the most appropriate method for determining cause and effect, and as such, for determining the impacts of programs and policies.

- When randomized experiments are not possible, the best alternatives are quasi-experimental designs such as the nonequivalent control group design or multiple time series analyses.

- One-shot designs in which the group that received the treatment is monitored only after the treatment has been delivered have little scientific merit.

- Although the evaluation of impacts remains largely a quantitative endeavor, the addition of qualitative methods to any evaluation can add invaluable information.

EXERCISES

1. Read one of the articles reviewed in this chapter. Fill in the answers to the article review questions (Appendix B) not covered in the chapter. Do you agree with the answers to the other questions discussed in the chapter? Could you add some points to the critique provided by the author of the text, or to the lessons on research designs drawn from these critiques?

2. Evaluate the ethics of one of the studies reviewed in which human subjects were used. Sherman and Berk's (1984) study of domestic violence raises some interesting ethical issues, but there are also points to consider in most of the other studies. Which ethical guidelines (see Chapter 2) seem most difficult to adhere to? Where do you think the line should be drawn between not taking any risks at all with research participants and developing valid scientific knowledge? Be sure to consider various costs and benefits of the research.

DEVELOPING A RESEARCH PROPOSAL

Imagine that you are submitting a proposal to the U.S. Justice Department to evaluate the efficacy of a new treatment program for substance abusers within federal correctional institutions.

1. What would your research question be if you proposed a process evaluation component to your research?

2. For the outcome evaluation, what is your independent variable and what would your dependent variable be? How would you operationalize both?

3. What type of research design would you propose to answer both the process evaluation and outcome evaluation components in your proposal?

WEB EXERCISES

1. Go to the American Evaluation Association Web site at www.eval.org. Choose "Publications" and then "Guiding Principles for Evaluators." What are the five guiding principles discussed in this document? Provide a summary of each principle.

2. How adequate are juvenile court records? Go to the Bureau of Justice Statistics Web site at http://blackstone.ojp.usdoj.gov/bjs/pub/ascii/pjjr.txt.
   a. Read the report and write a brief summary.
   b. The Bureau of Justice Statistics would like to find out if any improvements have been made in the collection and maintenance of juvenile records. Propose a research project to evaluate

the adequacy of the juvenile justice system in the collection and maintenance of juvenile law enforcement records and/or juvenile court records.

4. Describe the resources available for evaluation researchers at one of the following three Web sites:

www.wmich.edu/evalctr/

www.stanford.edu/~davidf/empowermentevaluation.html

www.worldbank.org/oed/

SPSS EXERCISES

Do hospitals provide equal treatment across race and social class? Although the data available do not provide enough information for an in-depth evaluation of hospital procedures or quality of care, NCS93.POR enables you to explore the relationship between the total amount of medical expenses incurred as a result of injuries sustained from rape, robbery, or assault (MEDEXP) and the victim's family income (INCOME), race/ethnicity (PPRACE), and coverage by any medical insurance or other type of health benefits program (INSURANC).

1. Write at least three hypotheses about the relationship between medical expenses incurred from rape, robbery, or assault across race and social class based on the variables discussed above.

2. Obtain a frequency distribution for INCOME. Recode INCOME to measure victim's family income into three or four categories.

3. Select all cases in which the victim sustained injuries (YES = 1). Compare the mean amount of expenses incurred as a result of the victim's injuries across categories of each independent variable. Describe the results; be sure to note the number of victims for each category when interpreting your results.

4. Were your hypotheses supported? What conclusions do you make about these relationships? Can you determine whether hospitals provide equal treatment across race and social class based on these data? Explain.

Chapter 10

MULTIPLE METHODS IN CONTEXT: INTEGRATION AND REVIEW

Designing research means deciding how to measure empirical phenomena, how to identify causal connections, and how to generalize findings not as separate decisions, but in tandem, with each decision having implications for the others. A research design is an integrated whole involving both fruitful conjunctions and necessary compromises. The carefully controlled laboratory conditions that increased the causal validity of Bushman's (1995) experiments on media violence decreased the generalizability of his conclusions (Chapter 5). The representative sampling plan that increased the generalizability of Tjaden and Thoennes (2000) national study of violent victimization limited their options for estimating causal effects (Chapter 6). The observations that underlay Decker and Van

Winkle's (1996) descriptions of gang members would not be feasible in a national sample of gang members (Chapter 7).

The goals of this chapter are to deepen your understanding of research designs and their consequences for achieving valid results and to alert you to the value of using multiple methods within a single research project. First, we evaluate the various research designs discussed in this book by reviewing their strengths and weaknesses. Later in the chapter we discuss the value of using multiple methods and give examples of combined designs. We will also see how social science research designs can be extended to take account of context and to identify the influence of natural processes. The chapter concludes with a case study of meta-analysis.

EVALUATING AND
COMPARING RESEARCH DESIGNS

It is not enough to ask of a study you critique, or one that you plan, such questions as, "Were the measures valid?" and "Were the causal conclusions justified?" You must also consider how the measurement approach might have affected the causal validity of the researcher's conclusions and how the sampling strategy might have altered the quality of measures. In fact, you must be concerned with how each component of the research design influenced the other components.

In the real world of social and criminological research, the boundaries separating different methods of data collection often overlap: experiments may be conducted in the field; surveys may involve some intensive open-ended questioning; field research may utilize quantitative counts of phenomena or random samples of events. The central features of experiments, surveys, and qualitative methods provide distinct perspectives even when used to study the same social processes. Comparing subjects randomly assigned to a treatment and a comparison group, asking standard questions of the members of a random sample, and observing while participating in a natural social setting involve markedly different decisions about measurement, causality, and generalizability. As you can see in Exhibit 10.1, not one of these methods can reasonably be graded as superior to the others, and each varies in its suitability to different research questions and goals.

In general, experimental designs are strongest for testing causal hypotheses and most appropriate for studies of treatment (see Chapter 5). Because random assignment reduces the possibility of preexisting differences between treatment and comparison groups to small, specifiable, chance levels, many of the variables are controlled that might otherwise create a spurious association. But in spite of this clear advantage, experimental designs require a degree of control that cannot always be achieved outside of the laboratory (see Chapter 5). It can be difficult to ensure in real-world settings that a treatment was delivered as intended and that other influences did not intrude. As a result, what appears to be a treatment effect or noneffect may be something else altogether. Field experiments thus require careful monitoring of the treatment process.

Laboratory experiments permit much more control over conditions, but at the cost of less generalizable findings. People must volunteer for most laboratory experiments, and so there is a good possibility that experimental subjects differ from those who do not volunteer. The problem of generalizability in an experiment using volunteers lessens only when

Exhibit 10.1 Comparison of Research Methods

Design	Measurement Validity	Generalizability	Causal Validity
Experiments	+	−	+
Surveys	+	+	−/+ [a]
Participant observation	−/+ [b]	−	−

a. Surveys are a weaker design for identifying causal effects than true experiments, but use of statistical controls can strengthen causal arguments.
b. Reliability is low compared to surveys, and systematic evaulation of measurement validity is often not possible. However, direct observations may lead to great confidence in the validity of measures.

the object of investigation is an orientation, a behavior, or a social process that is relatively invariable among people.

Both surveys and experiments typically use standardized, quantitative measures of attitudes, behaviors, or social processes. Closed-ended questions are most common and are well suited for the reliable measurement of variables that have been studied in the past and whose meaning is well understood (see Chapter 3). Of course, surveys often include measures of many more variables than are included in an experiment, but this quality is not inherent in either design. Phone surveys may be quite short, and some experiments can involve very lengthy sets of measures (see Chapter 6).

Most social science surveys rely on random sampling for their selection of cases from a larger population, and it is this feature that makes them preferable for maximizing generalizability (see Chapter 4). When description of a particular large population is a key concern, survey research is likely to be the method of choice. Surveys are also often used to investigate hypothesized causal relationships, because many variables can be measured within a given survey, and repeated measurements are possible over time. If variables that might create spurious relations are included in the survey, they can be controlled statistically in the analysis, thus strengthening the evidence for or against a hypothesized causal relationship.

Qualitative methods presume an intensive measurement approach in which indicators of concepts are drawn from direct observation or in-depth commentary (see Chapter 7). This approach is most appropriate when it is not clear what meaning people attach to a concept or what sense they might make of particular questions about it. Qualitative methods are also admirably suited to the exploration of new or poorly understood social settings, when it is not even clear what concepts would help to understand the situation. For these reasons, qualitative methods tend to be preferred when exploratory research questions are posed. But, of course, intensive measurement necessarily hampers the study of large numbers of cases or situations, resulting in the limitation of many field research efforts to small numbers of people or unique social settings.

When qualitative methods are used to study several individuals or settings that provide marked contrasts in a presumed independent variable, it becomes possible to evaluate causal hypotheses with these methods. However, for hypotheses testing, the impossibility of taking into account many possible extraneous influences in such limited comparisons makes qualitative methods a weak approach. Qualitative methods are more suited to the elucidation of causal mechanisms, and can be used to identify the multiple successive events that might have led to some outcome.

Historical and comparative methods range from cross-national quantitative surveys to qualitative comparisons of social features and political events (see Chapter 8). Their suitability for exploration, description, explanation, and evaluation varies in relation to the particular method used, but they are essential for research on historical processes and national differences. If the same methods are used to study multiple eras or nations rather than just one nation at one time, the results are likely to be enhanced generalizability and causal validity.

In reality, none of these methods of data collection provides a foolproof means for achieving measurement validity, causal validity, or generalizability. Each will have some liabilities in a specific research application, and all can benefit from combination with one or more other methods (Sechrest & Sidani, 1995). To benefit from this multiple-method approach, researchers have been using a triangulated methodology, that is, combining different methods in the same project to reveal different dimensions of the same phenomenon. It is to this subject that we now turn.

TRIANGULATING RESEARCH DESIGNS

The use of multiple methods to study one research question is called **triangulation.** The term suggests that a researcher can get a clearer picture of the social reality being studied by viewing it from several different perspectives. The term is actually derived from land surveying, where knowing a single landmark allows you to locate yourself only somewhere along a line in a single direction from the landmark. However, with two landmarks you can take bearings on both and locate yourself at their intersection.

Triangulation The use of multiple methods to study one research question.

Triangulation in Action: American Indian Homicide

When studying the social causes of homicide and other violence within contemporary American Indian communities, one of your authors used triangulation (Bachman, 1992). To examine the social causes of homicide within this population, she conducted in-depth interviews with American Indian homicide offenders who were incarcerated in state prisons in two states. In addition, she conducted national-, state-, and reservation-level statistical analyses to determine the social factors, such as levels of poverty and social disorganization, that were related to American Indian homicide rates at the aggregate level. When she focused her attention on intimate partner violence within American Indian families, she performed intensive interviews with the staff and residents of three battered women's shelters located on reservations. She also performed a statistical analysis of data obtained from the National Family Violence Survey (NFVS) (Straus & Gelles, 1990).

To illustrate triangulation, let's take a closer look at the process of Bachman's work on American Indian homicide offending. Bachman found that compared to all other racial/ethnic groups, American Indians had some of the highest rates of homicide, sometimes reaching over 100 per 100,000 population on some reservations (e.g., Douglas,

Nevada, 103.5; Harney, Oregon, 127.5). Although other researchers had noted high rates of American Indian homicide, virtually no attempts were made to explore the factors that contributed to such high rates. Are the causal mechanisms that create these high rates the same as those that were documented in the population in general? Or are the social forces that were identified as increasing both African American and white homicide rates different from those forces that contribute to American Indian homicide? Because there was virtually no research examining the etiology of American Indian homicide, Bachman first wanted to gain some insight into and understanding of the structural and cultural conditions that may contribute to lethal violence at the individual level. Accordingly, she selected the qualitative method of intensive interviewing as her first method.

Bachman conducted face-to-face interviews with homicide offenders at three midwestern state prisons. Offenders responded to a lengthy set of open-ended questions and probes concerning the circumstances surrounding their crime, their life before the crime, and their attitudes about crime in general. Bachman (1992:32) characterized the interview process as

> a conversation between two people getting to know one another rather than a rigid structure in which questions were formally addressed. An interview was usually ended not because there was nothing left to talk about, but because there was another interview scheduled or because the prisoner had to return to his cell for count.

Thus Bachman started with inductive research, beginning with qualitative interview data, which were then used to develop (induce) a general explanation (a theory) to account for the data. The theoretical model that emerged from her interview data is displayed in Exhibit 10.2. The model combines the causal forces of social disorganization, economic deprivation, a culture of honor/violence, and the psychological mechanisms of culture conflict and perceived powerlessness with the intervening variable of alcohol/drug abuse. Also included in the theoretical guide is the antecedent variable to each of these concepts,

Exhibit 10.2   Theoretical Model for American Indian Homicide That Emerged From Bachman's Qualitative Interviews with American Indian Homicide Offenders

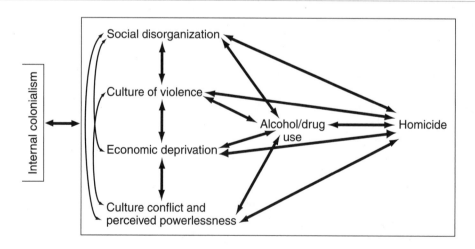

internal colonialism. Although this concept was not explicitly derived from the qualitative analysis, Bachman explained (1992:36), "No model explaining any phenomenon with regard to American Indians would be complete without acknowledgment of the colonization process to which our government has subjected this population."

This model assisted Bachman in subsequent quantitative analysis by providing a theoretical framework from which to start. Using this model as a guide along with the other relevant literature on the etiology of homicide, Bachman then performed deductive research in which she obtained American Indian homicide rates (dependent variable) and indicators of some of these theoretical constructs (independent variables) at the state and reservation levels to test three hypotheses:

1. The higher the level of social disorganization within a reservation community, the higher the rate of homicide.

2. The higher the level of economic deprivation within a reservation community, the higher the rate of homicide.

3. The more traditional and integrated a reservation community, the lower the rate of homicide.

Results indicated that American Indian communities with higher levels of both social disorganization and economic deprivation also had higher rates of homicide. She did not find support in her data for the third hypothesis. In addition to guiding her deductive research, the qualitative interview data also provided Bachman's research with a wealth of narratives that added meaning and depth to the statistical relationships that were found at the aggregate level. For example, many homicide offenders revealed what conditions of social disorganization and economic deprivation were like in their own lives. One offender talked about the reality of his disorganized childhood, being placed in multiple foster homes:

I was pretty much living in foster homes since I was about two. I guess my parents weren't doing too good—you know, drinking and partying. My brother got put into a different foster home, but my sister and I got in the same one. After several moves, we all eventually got placed in the same home. We moved around quite a bit. (Bachman, 1992:38)

Another talked about his existence living on a reservation without a job:

Without a job, you sit in your house day after day—nothing to do. You listen to that same car drive by your house again and again, and pretty soon you hate those people in that car. Kids go running through your yard—back and forth and back and forth—and pretty soon you hate those kids. Pretty soon you want to hurt somebody. (Bachman, 1992:50)

As you can see, using triangulation in which both quantitative and qualitative methods are used to investigate the same research question has many advantages. In addition, finding support for relationships between independent and dependent variables at two different levels—the individual level and the community level—also provided validity to

Bachman's conclusions that social disorganization and economic deprivation are both related to homicide in American Indian communities. Campbell and Fiske (1959:82) explain the validity-enhancing qualities of triangulation:

> If a hypothesis can survive the confrontation of a series of complementary methods of testing, it contains a degree of validity unattainable by one tested within the more constricted framework of a single method. . . . Findings from this latter approach must always be subject to the suspicion that they are method-bound: Will the comparison totter when exposed to an equally prudent but different testing method?

Adding Qualitative Data to Official Records or Experiments

It makes sense to use official records to study the treatment of juveniles accused of illegal acts because these records document the critical decisions to arrest, to convict, or to release (Dannefer & Schutt, 1982). Research based on official records can be only as good as the records themselves. In contrast to the interview process in a research study, there is no guarantee that officials' acts and decisions were recorded in a careful and unbiased manner.

Case Study: Juvenile Court Records

Research on official records can be strengthened by interviewing officials who create the records or by observing them while they record information. A participant observation study of how probation officers screened cases in two New York juvenile court intake units shows how important such information can be (Needleman, 1981). As indicated in Exhibit 10.3, Needleman found that the concepts most researchers believe they are measuring with official records differ markedly from the meaning attached to these records by probation officers.

Researchers assume that sending a juvenile case to court indicates a more severe disposition than retaining a case in the intake unit, but probation officers often diverted cases

Exhibit 10.3   Researchers' and Juvenile Court Workers' Discrepant Assumptions

Researchers' Assumptions	Intake Workers' Assumptions
Being sent to court is a harsher sanction that diversion from court.	Being sent to court often results in more lenient and less effective treatment.
Screening involves judgments about individual juveniles.	Screening centers on the juvenile's social situation.
Official records accurately capture case facts.	Records are manipulated to achieve the desired outcome.

Source: From Needleman, C., "Discrepant Assumptions in Empirical Research." *Social Problems*, 28, No. 1, pp. 71–93. Copyright © 1991 by the Society for the Study of Social Problems. Used with permission.

from court because they thought the court would be too lenient. Researchers assume that probation officers evaluate juveniles as individuals, but in these settings probation officers often base their decisions on juveniles' current social situations (whether they were living in a stable home, for example), without learning about the individual juvenile. Perhaps most troubling for research using case records, Needleman (1981) found that probation officers decided how to handle cases first and then created an official record that appeared to justify their decisions.

This one example certainly does not call into question all legal records or all other types of official records, but it does highlight the value of using multiple methods, particularly when the primary method of data collection is analysis of records generated by **street-level bureaucrats**—officials who serve clients and have a high degree of discretion (Lipsky, 1980). When officials make decisions and record the bases for their decisions without much supervision, records may diverge considerably from the decisions they are supposed to reflect. More generally, Needleman's (1981) research indicates how important it is to learn how people make sense of the social world when we want to describe their circumstances and explain their behavior (see Chapter 7).

Case Study: Decision Making in Delinquency Cases

Although the juvenile justice system was established to rehabilitate rather than punish, there has been a growing tension between these two alternatives in juvenile courts today. If rehabilitation is the primary goal of the juvenile justice system, then indicators of potential for rehabilitation should be important factors in the decisions of judges and probation officers. Specifically, if rehabilitation is important, then juveniles' acceptance of responsibility and motivation to accept intervention should predict the decisions in the juvenile justice system. One indicator of the juvenile's motivation to accept intervention is admitting the crime. This admission can be seen as an indication that the youth accepts responsibility for the act and feels remorse. In addition, an admission of guilt can be seen as an indication of rehabilitative potential (e.g., that treatment may actually be effective) and might lead to less punishment. On the other hand, denial of guilt could possibly lead to less punishment because it requires an evidentiary hearing, and prosecutors in crowded juvenile courts might dismiss rather than pursue a case that could be lost at the adjudication stage without an admission of guilt.

To investigate how admissions of guilt affect adjudication and disposition decisions in juvenile cases, R. Barry Ruback and Paula Vardaman (1997) utilized a triangulated methodology. They first conducted a statistical analysis of juvenile court records in which adjudication and disposition decisions were treated as the dependent variable along with several independent variables, including whether the juvenile admitted or denied guilt, prior juvenile record, the type of offense committed, and the juvenile's race. Second, they conducted a survey of judges, probation officers, and court service workers in which respondents to the survey were asked to make adjudication and disposition decisions to fictitious juvenile case scenarios. In these scenarios, several factors were manipulated, including whether the juvenile admitted or denied the offense. For example, some respondents were asked to make an adjudication decision for a juvenile depicted in a scenario who had been accused of motor vehicle theft and who did not admit to the crime, while other respondents made an adjudication decision for a similar juvenile who did admit guilt.

Analysis of the court records to examine the adjudication decision indicated that juveniles who admitted to the crime were more likely to be declared delinquent compared to juveniles who did not admit to it. Similarly, juveniles who admitted to their offense received harsher punishments (e.g., assigned to residential commitment instead of probation) compared to those who denied their offense.

Survey data from the court personnel supported these findings: Judges, probation officers, and case workers all more severely adjudicated the fictitious juveniles who admitted their guilt, compared to the fictitious juveniles who denied their guilt. However, admission of guilt did not affect the levels of punishment given to the fictitious scenario youth. The only variables that affected the level of punishment received were prior record and type of crime; fictitious juveniles with prior records received more severe dispositions than juveniles with no prior record. Drug offenses were generally treated more severely than the other two offenses depicted in the scenarios, battery and theft.

Using both types of methodology (analysis of court records and a survey of court personnel), Ruback and Vardaman (1997) thus found a consistent effect of a juvenile's reaction to his or her crime (admission or denial) and the adjudication outcome. In both methodologies, an admission of guilt by a juvenile was more likely to receive an official "delinquent" status than a less serious outcome (e.g., dismissal). Only in the court records, however, did the admission of guilt similarly increase the severity of the penalty.

Case Study: Obedience to Authority

Even the results of laboratory experiments can be enriched by incorporating qualitative methodology to a study. For example, recall from Chapter 5 Stanley Milgram's (1974) study of obedience to authority. Many subjects obeyed the authority in the study (the experimenter), even when their obedience involved administering potentially lethal shocks to another person. Before Milgram performed his experiment, however, he obtained qualitative data on the expected outcome of the experiment from several different groups of people. Using a group of psychiatrists, college students, and middle-class adults, Milgram set up the study by asking each group of respondents to come and hear a lecture on the topic of obedience to authority. The experiment that was to be carried out (learning a task, with subjects administering fake shocks to the learner) was described in detail. All audience members were provided with a schematic diagram of the shock generator, showing verbal and voltage designations. The respondents were then asked to reflect on the experiment and privately record in detail how they would perform in it.

Milgram used these qualitative data as a benchmark to compare with the actual outcomes of the experiment. It is interesting to note that, unlike many of the subjects in the actual experiment, the respondents in this exploratory component of Milgram's research predicted that they would disobey the experimenter at some point in the command series. Typical explanations offered to justify their disobedience are illuminating:

". . . I myself am scared stiff of shocks and I couldn't give shocks to people that were protesting because I was causing the pain. I couldn't deliberately hurt a perfect stranger."

"I do not think any experiment is worth inflicting strong shock on another human being. The fact that the subject responded as he did indicates to me that he was suffering from severe discomfort. I could not be the one to inflict this pain on him. The moment the subject insists he wants to leave the experiment, I respect his judgment."

". . . since the subject volunteered, and I volunteered, and since the experimenter has no physical authority over me, the subject should be released when he is at such a point that he asks to be released, and I would release him." (Milgram, 1974:28)

Milgram interpreted these qualitative data as a validation to his contention that placing people in a situation and instructing them to harm another nonthreatening person would inherently compel most to disobey rather than obey. This disobedience, Milgram believed, would flow from empathy, compassion, and a sense of justice. Of course, as you learned in Chapter 5, when people are placed in an experimental condition and instructed to obey the experimenter, results can be very different.

This was not the only qualitative component to Milgram's research. You will recall that he also tape-recorded all experimental sessions. These verbatim transcripts are testimony to the fact that the experimental subjects actually believed that they were harming someone:

150 volts delivered.   You want me to keep going?

165 volts delivered.   That guy is hollering in there. There's a lot of them here. He's liable to have a heart condition. You want me to go on?

180 volts delivered.   He can't stand it! I'm not going to kill that man in there! You hear him hollering? He's hollering. He can't stand it. . . . I mean who is going to take responsibility if anything happens to that gentleman?

[The experimenter accepts responsibility.]   All right.

195 volts delivered.   You see he's hollering. Hear that. Gee, I don't know. *[The experimenter says: "The experiment requires that you go on."]* I know it does, sir, but I mean—uhh—he don't know what he's in for. He's up to 195 volts. (Milgram, 1974:67)

In this experiment, as in each of the studies discussed in this chapter, utilizing more than one methodology to investigate the same research question resulted in a better understanding of social processes. To reiterate Bachman's praise for triangulation,

This methodology proved invaluable. The qualitative fieldwork I conducted assisted my subsequent quantitative analyses by providing a theoretical framework from which to start. It also allowed me to add meaning and depth to the statistical relationships that were found at the aggregate level. In using this triangulate methodology, it was my goal to make the findings of this research more cumulative and unequivocal, while at the same time more adequately controlling the bias that I, as a researcher, may have brought along with me. (Bachman, 1992:9)

QUANTIFYING OBSERVATIONAL DATA

We already have studied some of the possibilities for enriching qualitative research with quantitative methods. The experience sampling method added a survey sampling component to field research methods (Chapter 7); some quasi-experimental designs combine elements of survey research with experimental methods (Chapter 5); and comparative studies often use survey data collected from multiple nations (Chapter 7). In each case, quantitative data allow more systematic comparisons and more confident generalizations.

Case Study: Systematic Observation of Public Spaces

Informal social control networks are factors that control individual behavior that are not related to the criminal justice or legal system, such as family, peers, and educational institutions. Robert Sampson and Stephen Raudenbush (1999) observed neighborhoods in Chicago to determine whether neighborhood measures of informal social control were related to the crime rates within neighborhoods in addition to the general signs of disorder within neighborhoods, like graffiti and abandoned buildings. To measure the crime rate within neighborhoods, a survey of residents was conducted along with data from official police records. The level of neighborhood informal social control was also measured with the average resident responses.

The observational component to measure neighborhood disorder involved a stratified probability (random) sample of 196 Chicago census tracts. A specially equipped sport utility vehicle was driven down each street in these tracts at the rate of 5 miles per hour. Two video recorders taped the blocks on both sides of the street, while two observers peered out the van windows and recorded their observations in logs. The result was an observational record of 23,816 face blocks (the block on one side of the street is a face block). The observers recorded in their logs codes that indicated land use, traffic, physical conditions, and evidence of physical disorder. The videotapes were sampled and then coded for 126 variables, including housing characteristics, businesses, and social interactions. Physical disorder was measured by counting such features as cigarettes or cigars in the street, garbage, empty beer bottles, graffiti, condoms, and syringes. Indicators of social disorder included adults loitering, drinking alcohol in public, fighting, and selling drugs. To check for reliability, a different set of coders recoded the videos for 10% of the blocks. The repeat codes achieved 98% agreement with the original codes.

The combination of data from these sources allowed a test of the relative impact on the crime rate of informal social control efforts by residents and of the appearance of social and physical disorder. The data for all neighborhoods showed that neighborhoods with much visible disorder had higher crime rates than those with less visible disorder. However, when the relationship between visible disorder and neighborhood crime rates were examined separately for neighborhoods with high and low levels of informal social control (when they "statistically controlled for social control level"), the crime rate no longer varied with visible disorder. Therefore, Sampson and Raudenbush concluded that the apparent effect of "broken windows" was spurious due to level of informal social control. Neighborhoods with low levels of social control were more likely to have high levels of visible social and physical disorder, and they were also more likely to have a high crime rate, but the visible disorder itself did not alter the crime rate.

This ambitious multiple methods investigation combined observational research, survey research, and archival research. This study illustrates both the value of multiple methods and the technique of recording observations in a form from which quantitative data can be obtained.

CONDUCTING FACTORIAL SURVEYS

Factorial surveys combine the features of true experiments that maximize causal validity with the features of surveys that maximize generalizability. In the simplest type of factorial survey, randomly selected subsets of survey respondents are asked different questions. These different questions represent, in effect, different experimental treatments; the goal is to determine the impact of these questions on answers to other questions. For example, Howard Schuman and Stanley Presser (1981) used factorial surveys to assess how different wording of survey questions influenced respondents' answers. In another type of factorial survey, respondents are asked for their likely responses to one or more vignettes about hypothetical situations. The content of these vignettes is varied randomly among survey respondents to create "treatment groups" that differ in terms of particular variables reflected in the vignettes.

Case Study: Wrongdoing in Japan and Detroit

V. Lee Hamilton and Joseph Sanders (1983) conducted a factorial survey in Japan and Detroit to test the effect of people's deeds and social roles on judgments of wrongdoing. For example, one set of vignettes involved friends who get into a fight and are in what is called the equal/status condition—they are in equal positions of authority and have a status relation to each other rather than a contractual relation.

> In the *equal/status* story two twin brothers are playing baseball with a friend. Either Billy, the protagonist, or the friend . . . decides that it is Billy's turn to bat. Billy grabs the bat and the brothers begin fighting. The brother is then hit with the bat; the hit is described as accidental in the low mental state condition, and done out of anger in the high condition. Billy has either often or rarely gotten into fights before (past pattern). The consequence is a large bump on the head or a head injury requiring a hospital visit. (Hamilton & Sanders, 1983:201–202)

The variations of this vignette allowed Hamilton and Sanders to test a hypothesis about how aspects of the deed at the focus of the dispute influenced judgments of responsibility.

> We hypothesize that Japanese respondents, like their American counterparts, use information about an actor's mental state in determining responsibility for wrongdoing [whether the injury was accidental or not and whether the actor had a history of bad behavior] but make little, if any, use of information about consequence severity [whether the fight resulted in an injury requiring a hospital visit]. (Hamilton & Sanders, 1983:202)

This hypothesis was supported in both Japan and Detroit.

Another set of vignettes allowed a test of the same hypothesis for people in a social relationship called authority/contract. This relationship involved a foreman and a worker, two individuals of unequal authority whose social roles are defined by contract.

> In the *authority/contract* story, Joe is a foreman on an assembly line. The company is trying to fill a large order and Joe either does not want to stop the line, or is told by his

supervisor not to let the line stop. . . . Joe is described as always being careful about safety procedure in the past or sometimes being careless (past pattern) . . . a worker suffers a bruised hand or loses two fingers. (Hamilton & Sanders, 1983:202)

As in the baseball field fight, evaluations by respondents of who was responsible in this story provided support for the importance of the actor's (the foreman's) mental state but indicated that little importance was placed on the severity of the action's consequence. By comparing responses to these two sets of vignettes, Hamilton and Sanders were also able to test hypotheses about the importance of role variables:

Concerning hierarchy: Authorities are held more responsible than equals because authority positions carry with them greater social obligations. . . . Concerning solidarity: More responsibility is assigned to wrongdoing in contract relations than status relations. (Hamilton & Sanders, 1983:202)

The findings indicated that in both Japan and Detroit, as hypothesized, people in positions of authority were judged as more responsible than were equals, whereas actors tied by contract were seen as more responsible than actors related by status (friends or family). Because the research was based on random samples from cities in both countries, the findings are generalizable to those populations (except for the possibility of sampling error).

There is still an important limitation to the generalizability of factorial surveys—they only indicate what respondents say they would do in situations that have been described to them. If these individuals had to make decisions in comparable real-life situations, we cannot be sure that they would act in accord with their stated intentions. So factorial surveys do not completely resolve the problems caused by the difficulty of conducting true experiments with representative samples. Nonetheless, by combining some of the advantages of experimental and survey designs, factorial surveys can provide stronger tests of causal relations than surveys and more generalizable findings than experiments.

EXTENDING SOCIAL SCIENCE INVESTIGATIONS

Even when an individual study combines multiple methods, focusing on people and processes in one setting can obscure or distort important social processes. Concluding, on the basis of one study, that arrest deters partner abuse is very different from concluding, after several studies, that arrest deters partner abuse only if the abuser is employed. Taking social context into account not only will improve our understanding of important concepts and causal processes but also will identify the limits to our generalizations. We also need to consider the possibility of influence from the natural world in which social life takes place. Are there biological processes or ecological relationships that influence particular social processes? New quantitative procedures give us techniques for analyzing the impact of context and other factors across many studies.

Taking Context into Account

Do the processes we are interested in vary across neighborhoods or communities? Among organizations? Across regions? These are the types of questions we seek to answer by taking social context into account. When relationships among variables differ across geographic units such as counties or across other contexts, researchers say there is a **contextual effect.**

Case Study: Juvenile Justice

Robert Sampson and John Laub (1993) drew a large sample of 538,000 juvenile justice cases from 322 counties across the United States. They then matched these case data from official records with census data on county social characteristics. They hypothesized that juvenile justice would be harsher in areas characterized by racial poverty and a large underclass (see Chapter 3). Statistical analysis of their data supported the hypothesis: In counties with a relatively large underclass and poverty concentrated among minorities, juvenile cases were more likely to be treated harshly. These relationships occurred for both African American and white juveniles, but were particularly strong for African Americans. Because counties' average income levels and criminal justice system resources were not related to juvenile justice case processing, it seems that racial polarization and underclass poverty, rather than the overall affluence of the county, were critical.

The results of this research suggest the importance of taking social context into account when examining criminal justice processes. Studies limited to one social context would not be generalizable to the entire country and would seriously misrepresent the role of race and other factors. Awareness of contextual differences helps to make sense of the discrepant findings from many purely local studies of juvenile justice case processing.

Recognizing Natural Processes

Although the social world is sufficiently complex to challenge the most able researcher, features of the natural world must also be taken into account in order to explain some social phenomena. The natural environment in which people live and the biology of the human body influence the social world in many ways. Recall from Chapter 5 the experiment conducted by Nisbett and Cohen (1996) that investigated northern and southern responses to an insult. In the next section, we will illustrate a second experiment by this research team that examined whether these responses were accompanied by physiological changes of a sort that might mediate real behavioral aggression.

Case Study: Physiological Reactions to an Insult

Let us refresh your memory about the procedures of Nisbett and Cohen's (1996) experiment. These researchers were testing propositions derived from a theory called the "culture of honor" in which they examined regional differences (individuals from the South and from the North) in violent/aggressive reactions to an insult. Unlike the first experiment (described in detail in Chapter 5) in which the experimental subjects encountered a confederate in the hall who called each of them an asshole, Nisbett and Cohen set up two additional scenarios in the second experiment. The northern and southern students were met in the laboratory by an experimenter, who explained that the study concerned people's performance on tasks under various conditions. The experimenter said that she would be measuring the subject's blood sugar levels throughout the experiment by taking saliva samples. To get a baseline measurement, the subject was given a piece of sugarless gum to generate saliva, a test tube to fill to the 5 ml level, and a brief questionnaire to fill out as he provided the first sample.

After the saliva sample was given, the subject was sent down the hall to drop off his questionnaire. Control subjects were not bumped or insulted at all. In the experimental conditions, however, subjects were either bumped and insulted (called an asshole) publicly with two male witnesses to the insult or bumped and insulted privately with no witnesses. After a few minutes, all subjects and two confederates were called to the experimental room. In the public condition, the confederates were the same two men who had seen the subject get insulted. The experimenter then explained that the subjects would be performing mechanical aptitude tasks and she asked them to give another saliva sample. Subjects were then given questionnaires that had a number of scenarios that were ambiguous about whether an insult had been delivered. For example, in one scenario, one character cuts another off as they are driving down the road. For each scenario, subjects were asked to guess the likelihood of a physical fight or verbal argument occurring. After the questionnaire was finished, another saliva sample was obtained.

As you might guess, the real data the researchers wanted were chemical readings from the saliva samples. Nisbett and Cohen (1996) were investigating whether southern and northern students who had been insulted differed in two hormones thought to be physiological measures of stress: cortisol and testosterone. Cortisol is a hormone associated with high levels of stress, anxiety, and arousal in humans and in animals. If southerners were more upset by the acute stress of the insult, they should show a rise in cortisol levels after the insult (post measures of saliva) compared to both northern experimental subjects and southern and northern control subjects. Testosterone is a hormone associated with aggression and dominance behavior in animals and humans. Research suggests that testosterone plays a role in preparing participants for competitions or dominance contests, perhaps by facilitating the aggressive behaviors and display of dominance cues that make one act and even look tougher. If southerners responded to the insult as a challenge and prepared themselves for future aggression or dominance contests, their testosterone levels should increase after the bump and insult compared to both northern subjects who had been similarly bumped and all control subjects.

As expected, results indicated that insulted southerners showed larger increases in both cortisol and testosterone levels after the bump and insult than did northern subjects. Nisbett and Cohen interpreted this as another indication that regional differences exist in the extent to which individuals interpret affronts to their honor. They state (1996:48),

> [These findings] show that the insult produces effects in the southerner that go far beyond mere cognitive changes. Southerners are put into a physiological state that should not merely affect interpretations of subsequently encountered affronts but could also be expected to impel aggressive action.

Research such as this that traces the relationships between biological and social processes only begins to identify the many ways the natural world provides the context for social life. Microorganisms that spread disease, pollutants that stunt growth, and rivers that power electric generators all shape the context of social life in ways too numerous to list. Research in collaboration with scientists who study the natural world can often generate insights into these connections and is itself another form of triangulation (Janesick, 1994:215).

Performing Meta-Analyses

We also can gain insights into the impact of social context and the consequences of particular methodologies with meta-analysis. A **meta-analysis** is a quantitative method for identifying patterns in findings across multiple studies of the same research question. Unlike a traditional literature review, which verbally describes previous research studies, meta-analyses treat previous studies as cases whose features are measured as variables and then analyzed statistically. Whereas a macrolevel analysis like Sampson and Laub's (1993) shows how social processes vary across social contexts, meta-analysis shows how evidence about social processes varies across research studies. If the methods used in these studies varied, then meta-analysis can describe how this variation affected study findings. If social contexts varied across the studies, then meta-analysis will indicate how social context affected study findings.

Meta-analysis can be used when a number of studies have attempted to answer the same research question with some quantitative method, most often experiments. Once a research problem is formulated about the findings of such research, the literature must be searched systematically to identify the entire population of relevant studies. Typically, multiple bibliographic databases are used; some researchers also search for relevant dissertations and conference papers. After the studies are identified, their findings, methods, and other features are coded (for example, sample size, location of sample, strength of the association between the independent and dependent variables). Statistics are then calculated to identify the average effect of the independent variable on the dependent variable, as well as the effect of methodological and other features of the studies (Cooper & Hedges, 1994).

The meta-analysis approach to synthesizing research results can result in much more generalizable findings than those obtained with just one study. Methodological weaknesses in the studies included in the meta-analysis are still a problem, however; it is only when other studies without particular methodological weaknesses are included that we can estimate effects with some confidence. Before we can place any confidence in the results of a meta-analysis, we must be confident that all (or almost all) relevant studies were included and that the information we need to analyze was included in all (or most) of the studies (Matt & Cook, 1994).

Case Study: Broken Homes and Delinquency

Many studies have tested the hypothesis that juveniles from broken homes have higher rates of delinquency than those from homes with intact families, but findings have been inconclusive. L. Edward Wells and Joseph Rankin (1991) were able to find 50 studies that tested this hypothesis, with estimates of the increase in delinquency among juveniles from broken homes ranging from 1% to 50%. In order to explain this variation, Wells and Rankin coded key characteristics of the research studies, such as did the research sample the general population? A specific age range? They also coded the measures used: Did researchers take account of stepparents? Did they measure juveniles' relations with the absent parent? Was delinquency measured with official records or by self-report? What types of delinquency were measured?

The average effect of broken homes across the studies was to increase the likelihood of delinquency by about 10 to 15% (see Exhibit 10.4), but effects varied with the studies' substantive features and methods. Juveniles from broken homes were more likely to be

Exhibit 10.4   Delinquency by Broken Homes

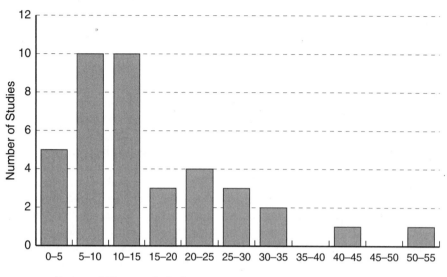

Source: Adapted from Wells & Rankin, 1991:80.

involved in status offenses (such as truancy and running away) and drug offenses but were no more likely to commit crimes involving theft or violence than were juveniles from intact homes. Juveniles' race, sex, age, and whether a stepparent was present did not have consistent effects. On the other hand, differences in methods accounted for much of the variation among the studies in the estimated effect of broken homes. The effect of broken homes on delinquency tended to be greater in studies using official records rather than surveys and in studies of smaller special populations rather than of the general population. In general, the differences in estimates of the association between broken homes and delinquency were due primarily to the differences in study methods and only secondarily to differences in the social characteristics of the people studied.

Meta-analyses like the Wells and Rankin study make us aware of how hazardous it is to base understanding of social processes on single studies that are limited in time, location, and measurement. Although one study may not support the hypothesis that we deduced from what seemed to be a compelling theory, this is not a sufficient basis for discarding the theory, nor for assuming that the hypothesis is no longer worthy of consideration in future research. You can see that a meta-analysis that combines the results of many studies may identify conditions when the hypothesis is supported and others when it is not.

Of course we need to have our wits about us when we read reports of meta-analytic studies. It is not a good idea to assume that a meta-analysis is the definitive word on a research question just because it cumulates the results of multiple studies. Fink (1998:215–237) suggests evaluating meta-analytic studies in terms of the following seven criteria:

Clear statement of the analytic objectives. The study's methods cannot be evaluated without knowledge of the objectives they were intended to achieve. Meta-analyses are most appropriate for summarizing research conducted to identify the effect of some type of treatment or some other readily identifiable individual characteristic.

Explicit inclusion and exclusion criteria. On what basis were research reports included in the analysis? Were high-quality studies distinguished from low-quality studies? If low-quality studies were included, were they analyzed separately, so that effects could be identified separately for only the population of high-quality studies?

Satisfactory search strategies. Both electronic and written reference sources should be searched. Was some method used to find studies that were conducted but not published? It may be necessary to write directly to researchers in the field and to consult lists of papers presented at conferences.

A standardized protocol for screening the literature. Screening involves rating the quality of the study and its relevance to the research question. This screening should be carried out with a simple rating form.

A standardized protocol for collecting data. It is best to have two reviewers use a standard form for coding the characteristics of the reported research. The level of agreement between these reviewers should be assessed.

Complete explanation of the method of combining results. Some checks should be conducted to determine where variable study features influenced the size of the treatment effect.

Report of results, conclusions, and limitations. This seems obvious, but it's easy for a researcher to skirt over study limitations or some aspects of the findings.

CONCLUSION

Choice of a data-collection method should be guided in part by the aspect of validity that is of most concern, but each aspect of validity must be considered in attempting to answer every research question. Experiments may be the preferred method when causal validity is a paramount concern, and surveys may be the natural choice if generalizability is critical. But generalizability must still be a concern when assessing the results of an experiment, and causal validity is a key concern in most social science surveys. Field research has unique value for measuring social processes as they happen, but the causal validity and generalizability of field research results are often open to question. A researcher should always consider whether data of another type should be collected in what is basically a single-method study and whether additional research using different methods is needed before the research question can be answered with sufficient confidence.

The ability to apply diverse techniques to address different aspects of a complex research question is one mark of a sophisticated social researcher. Awareness that one study's findings must be understood in the context of a larger body of research, and the ability to speculate on how the use of different methods might alter a study's findings are prerequisites for informed criticism of social research. As social research methods and substantive findings continue to grow in number, these insights should stimulate more ambitious efforts to combine research methods and integrate many studies' findings.

But the potential for integrating methods and combining findings does not decrease the importance of single studies using just one method of data collection. The findings from well-designed studies in carefully researched settings are the necessary foundation for broader, more integrative methods. There is little point in combining methods that are poorly implemented or in merging studies that produced invalid results. Whatever the research question, consider the full range of methodological possibilities, make an informed and feasible choice, and then carefully carry out your strategy.

Finally, realistic assessment of the weaknesses as well as the strengths of each method of data collection should help you to remember that humility is a virtue in science. Advancement of knowledge and clear answers to specific research questions are attainable with the tools you now have in your methodological toolbox. Perfection, however, is not a realistic goal. No matter what research method we use, our mental concepts cannot reflect exactly what we measured, our notions of causation cannot reveal a tangible causal force, and our generalizations cannot always extend beyond the cases that were actually studied. This is not cause for disillusionment, but it should keep us from being excessively confident in our own interpretations or unreasonably resistant to change. Final answers to every research question we pose cannot be achieved; what we seek are new, ever more sophisticated questions for research and additional propositions for social theory.

KEY TERMS

Contextual effect   Street-level bureaucrats
Factorial survey   Triangulation
Meta-analysis

HIGHLIGHTS

- The three dimensions of validity (measurement, causality, and generalizability) must be considered as an integrated whole when evaluating and planning research projects. Decisions about each dimension have implications for the others. Because quantitative and qualitative research methods both have unique strengths and weaknesses, using a combination of these methods to address the same research question will inevitably increase at least two types of validity.

- Triangulation is the use of multiple methods to study one research question. Research on most topics can be improved by using mixed methods.

- Factorial surveys combine features of experimental design with survey research methods. Variation of hypothetical vignettes or particular questions across randomly assigned survey subgroups can strengthen the validity of conclusions about causal processes if these processes can be modeled with vignettes or questions.

- Researchers can statistically test for patterns across multiple studies with meta-analysis. This technique can be used only in areas of research in which there have been many prior studies using comparable methods.

- Understanding of many social processes can be enriched by taking into account related biological and physical processes.

EXERCISES

1. Read the original article reporting one of the studies described in this chapter. Critique the article, using the article review questions presented in Appendix B as your guide. Focus particular attention on procedures for measurement, sampling, and establishing causal relationships.

2. What is the value of mixed methods? In a professional journal, find two research articles that use different methods of data collection to study the same research question. Review the articles, using the questions in Appendix B as a guide. See whether you can identify some differences in the conclusions that may have reflected the different methods.

DEVELOPING A RESEARCH PROPOSAL

1. Add a component involving a second method to your research proposal. If you already developed alternative approaches in answer to the exercises in earlier chapters, just write a justification for these additions that points out the potential benefits.

2. Consider the possible influences of social context and biological factors on the variables pertinent to your research question. Write a rationale for including a test for contextual or biological influences in your proposed research.

3. Describe a method for studying the contextual or biological influences in Question 2.

WEB EXERCISES

1. You've been asked to be a research assistant for a professor in your criminology department who is doing a cross-sectional comparative study of homicide. She has asked you to get information regarding homicide from at least 10 countries. A good place to find international crime statistics is the Web site for the International Police Organization, INTERPOL, at www.interpol.com. Go to the location for international statistics and collect this homicide data. To find out about how these countries rank according to other social indicators such as poverty and urbanicity, you can go to the United Nations web site at www.unstats.un.org. How do these countries rank on both homicide and other social data? Write a short report about your findings.

2. How do law-enforcement agencies define gang activity? Go to www.fbi.gov and search the site for publications and narratives about gangs. Another site that has a great deal of information on gangs is the National Criminal Justice Reference Service, www.ncjrs.org. Based on everything you have read about gangs from these two sites, how could you study gangs with qualitative methods? What would this study add to the statistical information included in the reports on these sites? What indicators could you use to differentiate the types of gangs? Do you think the distinction among the types of gangs is conceptually useful?

SPSS EXERCISES

1. Are there regional differences in rates of homicide across the United States? Using STATE.POR, a data set containing state-level homicide rates and other demographic variables, you can conduct a cross-sectional comparative analysis of the homicide rates in the different regions of the country (Northeast, Midwest, South, and West).
   a. Would you expect homicide rates to vary among the four U.S. regions? Write at least one hypothesis to indicate your expectations.
   b. Test your hypothesis by comparing the mean total homicide rate per 100,000 population (R8TOT) across the four regions of the United States (REGION).

   c. Describe the results. Was your hypothesis supported?
   d. What explanations can you develop (inductively) to explain these differences?

   2. Repeat Exercise 1 using the family homicide rate (R8V10), acquaintance homicide rate (R8V11), and stranger homicide rate (R8V12).

   3. Focusing on the results of Exercises 1 and 2 from this chapter, explain what level of analysis is the most informative and why.

DATA ANALYSIS

"Oh no, not data analysis and statistics!" Perhaps most of you have been sailing along in this textbook understanding almost everything you have been reading and studying, if not immediately, then at least after a second reading or a classroom lecture. You probably feel somewhat confident that you can design your own criminological research project, develop a measuring instrument, and collect your own data. Now, however, you hit the chapter that you may have been fearing all along—the chapter on data analysis and the use of statistics. This chapter describes what you need to do after your data have been collected. You now need to analyze what you have found, interpret it, and decide how to present your data so that you can most clearly make the points you wish to make.

What you probably dread about this chapter is something that you either sense or know from a previous course: The studying of data analysis and statistics will lead you into that feared world of mathematics. You may not be too crazy about this if you lack confidence in your mathematical abilities. You may, therefore, be going into this chapter with a great deal of apprehension. We would like to state at the beginning, however, that you have relatively little to fear. The kind of mathematics required to perform the data analysis tasks in this chapter are minimal. If you can add, subtract, multiply, and divide, and are willing to put some effort into carefully reading the chapter, you will do well in the statistical analysis of your data. In fact, it is our position that the analysis of your data will require more in the way of careful and logical thought than in mathematical skill. One helpful way to think of statistics is that it consists of a set of tools that you will use to examine your data to help you answer the questions that motivated your research in the first place. Right now, the toolbox that holds your statistical tools is fairly empty (or completely empty). In the course of this chapter, we will add some fundamental tools to that toolbox. We would also like to note at the beginning that the kinds of statistics you will use on criminological data are very much the same as those used by economists, psychologists, political scientists, sociologists, and other social scientists. In other words, statistical tools are statistical tools, and all that changes is the nature of the problem to which those tools are applied.

This chapter will introduce several common statistics in social research and highlight the factors that must be considered in using and interpreting statistics. Think of it as a review of fundamental social statistics, if you have already studied them, or as an introductory overview, if you have not.

Two preliminary sections lay the foundation for studying statistics. In the first we will discuss the role of statistics in the research process, returning to themes and techniques you already know. In the second preliminary section, we will outline the process of acquiring data for statistical analysis. In the rest of the chapter, we will explain how to describe the distribution of single variables and the relationship between variables. Along the way, we will address ethical issues related to data analysis. This chapter will be successful if it encourages you to use statistics responsibly and evaluate them critically, and gives you the confidence necessary to seek opportunities for extending your statistical knowledge.

It should be noted that in this chapter we focus primarily on the use of statistics for descriptive purposes. Those of you seeking a more advanced discussion of statistical methods used in criminal justice and criminology should seek other textbooks (see, for example, Bachman & Paternoster, 2003).

INTRODUCING STATISTICS

Statistics play a key role in achieving valid research results, in terms of measurement, causal validity, and generalizability. Some statistics are useful primarily to describe the results of measuring single variables and to construct and evaluate multi-item scales. These statistics include frequency distributions, graphs, measures of central tendency and variation, and reliability tests. Other statistics are useful primarily in achieving causal validity, by helping us describe the association among variables and to control for, or otherwise take into account, other variables. Crosstabulation is one technique for measuring association and controlling other variables and is introduced in this chapter. All of these statistics are called **descriptive statistics** because they are used to describe the distribution of and relationship among variables.

You learned in Chapter 4 that it is possible to estimate the degree of confidence that can be placed in generalizations for a sample and for the population from which the sample was selected. The statistics used in making these estimates are called **inferential statistics,** and they include confidence intervals, to which you were exposed in Chapter 4. In this chapter we will refer only briefly to inferential statistics, but we will emphasize later in the chapter their importance for testing hypotheses involving sample data.

Criminological theory and the results of prior research should guide our statistical plan or analytical strategy, as they guide the choice of other research methods. In other words, we want to use the statistical strategy that will best answer our research question. There are so many particular statistics and so many ways for them to be used in data analysis that even the best statistician can become lost in a sea of numbers if she is not using prior research and theorizing to develop a coherent analysis plan. It is also important for an analysis to choose statistics that are appropriate to the level of measurement of the variables to be analyzed. As you learned in Chapter 3, numbers used to represent the values of variables may not actually signify different quantities, meaning that many statistical techniques will be inapplicable. Some statistics, for example, will only be appropriate when the variable you are examining is measured at the nominal level. Other kinds of statistics will require interval-level measurement. To use the right statistic, then, you must be very familiar with the measurement properties of your variables (and you thought that stuff would go away!).

Case Study: The Causes of Delinquency

In this chapter we will use research on the causes of delinquency for our examples. More specifically, our data will be a subset of a much larger study of a sample of approximately 1,200 high school students selected from the metropolitan and suburban high schools of a city in South Carolina. These students, all of whom were in the tenth grade, completed a questionnaire that asked about such things as how they spent their spare time; how they got along with their parents, teachers, and friends; their attitudes about delinquency; whether their friends committed delinquent acts; and their own involvement in delinquency. The original research study was designed to test specific hypotheses about the factors that influence delinquency. It was predicted that delinquent behavior would be affected by such things as the level of supervision provided by parents, the students' own moral beliefs about delinquency, their involvement in conventional activities such as studying and watching TV, their fear of getting caught, their friends' involvement in crime, and whether these friends provided verbal support for delinquent acts. All of these hypotheses were derived from extant criminological theory—theories we have referred to throughout this book. One specific hypothesis, derived from deterrence theory, predicts that youths who believe they are likely to get caught by the police for committing delinquent acts are less likely to commit delinquency than others. This hypothesis is shown in Exhibit 11.1. The variables from this study that we will use in our chapter examples are displayed in Exhibit 11.2.

Exhibit 11.1 Perceived Fear of Punishment and Delinquency

Fear of getting $\longrightarrow$ Delinquency
caught by police

Exhibit 11.2 List of Variables for Class Examples of Causes of Delinquency

Variable	SPSS Variable Name	Description
Gender	V1	Sex of respondent.
Age	V2	Age of respondent.
TV	V21	Number of hours per week the respondent watches TV.
Study	V22	Number of hours per week the respondent spends studying.
Supervision	V63	Do parents know where respondent is when he/she is away from home?
Friends think theft wrong	V77	How wrong respondents' best friends think it is to commit petty theft.
Friends think drinking wrong	V79	How wrong respondents' best friends think it is to drink liquor under age.
Punishment for drinking	V109	If respondent was caught drinking liquor under age and taken to court, how much of a problem it would be.
Cost of vandalism	V119	How much would respondent's chances of having good friends be hurt if he/she was arrested for petty theft.
Parental supervision	PARSUPER	Added scale from items that ask respondent if parents know where he/she is and who he/she is with when away from home. A high score means more supervision.
Friend's opinion	FROPINON	Added scale that asks respondent if his/her best friend thought that committing various delinquent acts was all right. A high score means more support for delinquency from friends.
Friend's behavior	FRBEHAVE	Added scale that asks respondent how many of his/her best friends committed delinquent acts. A high score means more friends commit delinquent acts.
Certainty of punishment	CERTAIN	Added scale that measures how likely respondent thinks it is that he/she will be caught by police if he/she were to commit delinquent acts. A high score means more fear of getting caught.
Morality	MORAL	Added scale that measures how morally wrong respondent thinks it is to commit diverse delinquent acts. A high score means strong moral inhibitions against committing delinquency.
Delinquency	DELINQ1	An additive scale that counts the number of times respondent admits to committing a number of different delinquent acts in the past year. The higher the score, the more delinquent acts committed.

PREPARING DATA FOR ANALYSIS

Our analysis of the causes of delinquency in this chapter is an example of **secondary data analysis.** As we described in Chapter 8, it is secondary because we received the data secondhand; we did not design the data-collection instrument ourselves. Using secondary data in this way has a major disadvantage—if you did not design the study yourself, it is unlikely that all the variables you think should have been included actually were included, and that they were measured in the way that you prefer. In addition, the sample may not represent the population in which you are interested, and the study design may be only partially appropriate to your research question. For example, this particular study was completed before recent theoretical work in criminology on self-control. It also contains only self-reported delinquency and no measures as to whether these delinquent acts resulted in an arrest or juvenile court appearance. Further, because it is a survey of individuals, the study has no measures of the kinds of communities within which the students lived; for example, the level of crime in the community or measures of informal community control. Because the survey sample is selected only from one city in South Carolina, we cannot make generalizations to youths in other cities or in other states.

Although it comes with many disadvantages, there is one important advantage of secondary data—they are readily available. It is the availability of secondary data that makes their use preferable for many purposes. A great many high-quality data sets (such as the data set on delinquency we are using) are available for reanalysis from the Inter-University Consortium for Political and Social Research (ICPSR) at the University of Michigan. Other data sets for secondary data analysis can be obtained from the government, individual researchers, and other research organizations. Most of these data sets are stored on computer disks or CD-ROMs, ready for use without any further effort. Therefore, for a great many research problems, a researcher should first check what data sets on the question already are available. An enormous savings in time and resources may be the result.

If you have conducted your own survey or experiment, your quantitative data must be prepared in a format suitable for computer entry. You learned in Chapter 6 that questionnaires and interview schedules can be precoded to facilitate data entry by representing each response with a unique number (see Exhibit 11.3). This method allows direct entry of the precoded responses into a computer file, after responses are checked to ensure that only one valid answer code has been circled (extra written answers can be assigned their own numerical codes). Most survey research organizations now use a database management program to control data entry. The program prompts the data entry clerk for each response, checks the response to ensure that it is a valid response for that variable, and then saves the response in the data file. Exhibit 11.4 is an example of a computer data entry screen. Not all studies have used precoded data entry, however, and individual researchers must enter the data themselves. This is an arduous and time-consuming task, but not for us if we use secondary data. After all, we get the data only after they have been coded and computerized.

Of course, numbers stored in a computer file are not yet numbers that can be analyzed with statistics. After the data are entered, they must be checked carefully for errors—a process called **data cleaning.** If a data entry program has been used and programmed to flag invalid values, the cleaning process is much easier. If data are read in from a text file, a computer program must be written that defines which variables are coded in which columns, attaches meaningful labels to the codes, and distinguishes values representing

Exhibit 11.3   Section of the National Violence Against Men and Women Survey on Stalking Victimizations Given to Female Respondents

```
SECTION H: STALKING VICTIMIZATION

H1. Now I'd like to ask you some questions about following or
    harassment you may have experienced on more than one occasion by
    strangers, friends, relatives, or even husbands and partners. Not
    including bill collectors, telephone solicitors or other sales
    people, has anyone, male or female, ever . . . MARK ALL THAT
    APPLY
    01 Followed you or spied on you?
    02 Sent you unsolicited letters or written correspondence?
    03 Made unsolicited phone calls to you?
    04 Stood outside your home, school, or workplace?
    05 Showed up at places you were even though he or she had no
       business being there?
    06 Left unwanted items for you to find?
    07 Tried to communicate with you in other ways against your
       will?
    08 Vandalized your property or destroyed something you loved?
    09 (Volunteered) Don't Know                  GO TO SECTION I
    10 (Volunteered) Refused                      GO TO SECTION I
    11 (Volunteered) None                         GO TO SECTION I

H2. If H1 = ANY OF 1-8 (RESPONDENT HAS BEEN STALKED) GO TO H3,
    ELSE GO TO SECTION I.

H3. Has anyone ever done any of these things to you on more than one
    occasion?
    1  Yes
    2  No                                         GO TO SECTION I
    3  (Volunteered) Don't Know                   GO TO SECTION I
    4  (Volunteered) Refused                      GO TO SECTION I

H4. How many different people have ever done this to you on more
    than one occasion?
    ___ Number of people [RANGE IS 1-97]
    98 (Volunteered) Don't Know                   GO TO SECTION I
    99 (Volunteered) Refused                      GO TO SECTION I

H5. Was this person/these persons . . . MARK ALL THAT APPLY
    01 Your current spouse?
    02 An ex-spouse?
    03 A male live-in partner?
    04 A female live-in partner?
    05 A relative?
    06 Someone else you know?
    07 A stranger?
    08 (Volunteered) Don't Know
    09 (Volunteered) Refused
```

Source: Tjaden & Thoennes, 2000.

Exhibit 11.4   An Example of a Data Entry Screen from SPSS

missing data. The procedures for doing so vary with each specific statistical package. We used the Windows version of the Statistical Package for the Social Sciences (SPSS) for the analysis in this chapter; you will find examples of SPSS commands required to define and analyze data in Appendix D. More detailed information on using SPSS is contained in SPSS manuals and in the Pine Forge Press book *Adventures in Social Research: Data Analysis Using SPSS v. 9.0 and 10.0 for Windows 95/98*® by Earl Babbie, Fred Halley, and Jeanne Zaino (2000).

DISPLAYING UNIVARIATE DISTRIBUTIONS

The first step in data analysis is usually to display the variation in each variable of interest in what are called *univariate frequency distributions.* For many descriptive purposes, the analysis may go no further. Frequency distributions and graphs of frequency distributions are the two most popular approaches for displaying variation; both allow the analyst to display the distribution of cases across the value categories of a variable. Graphs have the advantage over numerically displayed frequency distributions because they provide a picture that is easier to comprehend. Frequency distributions are preferable when exact numbers of cases with particular values must be reported, and when many distributions must be displayed in a compact form.

No matter which type of display is used, the primary concern of the data analyst is to accurately display the distribution's shape; that is, to show how cases are distributed across the values of the variable. Three features of the shape of a distribution are important: **central tendency, variability,** and **skewness** (lack of symmetry). All three of these features can be represented in a graph or in a frequency distribution.

Central tendency   The most common value (for variables measured at the nominal level) or the value around which cases tend to center (for a quantitative variable).

Variability   The extent to which cases are spread out through the distribution or clustered in just one location.

Skewness   The extent to which cases are clustered more at one or the other end of the distribution of a quantitative variable, rather than in a symmetric pattern around the center. Skew can be positive (a "right skew") with the number of cases tapering off in the positive direction, or negative (a "left skew"), with the number of cases tapering off in the negative direction.

These features of a distribution's shape can be interpreted in several different ways, and they are not all appropriate for describing every variable. In fact, all three features of a distribution can be distorted if graphs, frequency distributions, or summary statistics are used inappropriately.

A variable's level of measurement is the most important determinant of the appropriateness of particular statistics. For example, we cannot talk about the skewness (lack of symmetry) of a qualitative variable (measured at the nominal level). If the values of a variable cannot be ordered from lowest to highest—if the ordering of the values is arbitrary—we cannot say whether the distribution is symmetric because we could just reorder the values to make the distribution more (or less) symmetric. Some measures of central tendency and variability are also inappropriate for qualitative variables.

The distinction between variables measured at the ordinal level and those measured at the interval or ratio level should also be considered when selecting statistics to use, but social researchers differ on just how much importance they attach to this distinction. Many social researchers think of ordinal variables as imperfectly measured interval-level variables, and believe that in most circumstances statistics developed for interval-level variables also provide useful summaries for ordinal variables. Other social researchers believe that variation in ordinal variables will often be distorted by statistics that assume an interval level of measurement. We will touch on some of the details of these issues in the following sections on particular statistical techniques.

We will now examine graphs and frequency distributions that illustrate these three features of shape. Summary statistics used to measure specific aspects of central tendency and variability will be presented in a separate section. There is a summary statistic for the measurement of skewness, but it is used only rarely in published research reports and will not be presented here.

Graphs

A picture often is worth some unmeasurable quantity of words. Even for the statistically uninitiated, graphs can be easy to read, and they very nicely highlight a distribution's shape. They are particularly useful for exploring data because they show the full range of variation and identify data anomalies that might be in need of further study. And good, professional-looking graphs can now be produced relatively easily with software available for personal computers. There are many types of graphs, but the most common and most useful are bar charts, histograms, and frequency polygons. Each has two axes, the vertical axis (y-axis) and the horizontal axis (x-axis), and labels to identify the variables and the values with tick marks showing where each indicated value falls along the axis. The vertical y-axis of a graph is usually in frequency or percent units, whereas the horizontal x-axis displays the values of the variable being graphed. There are different kinds of graphs you can use to descriptively display your data, depending upon the level of measurement of the variable.

A **bar chart** contains solid bars separated by spaces. It is a good tool for displaying the distribution of variables measured at the nominal level and other discrete categorical variables because there is, in effect, a gap between each of the categories. In our delinquency data, one of the questions asked of respondents was if their parents knew where they were when they were away from home. We graphed the responses to this question in a bar chart, which is shown in Exhibit 11.5. In this bar chart we report both the frequency count for each value and the percentage of the total that each value represents. The bar chart in Exhibit 11.5 indicates that very few of the respondents (only 16 or 1.3%) reported that their parents "never" knew where they were when they were not at home. Almost one-half (563 or 44.3%) of the youths reported that their parents "usually" knew where they were. What you can also see by noticing the height of the bars above "usually" and "always" is

Exhibit 11.5 Bar Chart Showing Youths' Responses on Parents Knowing Where They Are

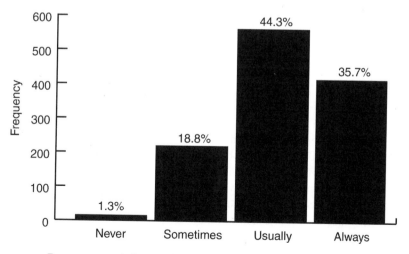

Do your parents know where you are when you are away from home?

Exhibit 11.6   Bar Chart Showing Youths' Responses on Underage Drinking

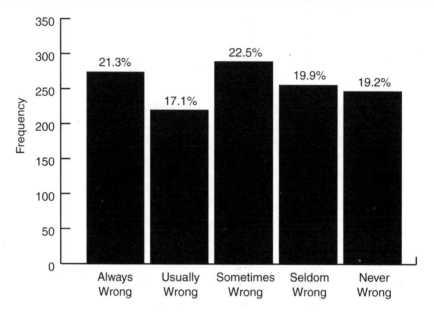

How wrong do your best friends think it is to drink liquor under age?

that most youths report that their parents provide very adequate supervision. You can also see that the most frequent response was "usually" and the least frequent was "never." Because the response "usually" is the most frequent value, it is called the **mode** or modal response. With ordinal data like these, the mode is the most appropriate measure of central tendency. (More about this later.)

Notice that the cases tend to cluster in the two values of "usually" and "always"; in fact, about 80% of all cases are found in those two categories. There is not much variability in this distribution, then. In Exhibit 11.6 we show another bar chart from the delinquency data. In this example, the variable is the attitude of one's friends toward drinking under age. Respondents were asked how wrong their best friends thought it was to drink liquor under age. As you can see, unlike the case in Exhibit 11.5, the frequencies are more evenly spread out across the various values (the height of the bars don't differ as much in this bar chart), so there is more variability in this variable than for the one shown in Exhibit 11.5.

A **histogram** is like a bar chart, but it has bars that are adjacent, or right next to each other, with no gaps. This is done to indicate that data displayed in a histogram, unlike the data in a bar chart, are quantitative variables that vary along a continuum (see the discussion of levels of measurement for variables in Chapter 3). Exhibit 11.7 shows a histogram from the delinquency data set we are using. The variable being graphed is the number of hours per week the respondent reported to be studying. Notice that the cases cluster at the low end of the values. In other words, there are a lot of youths who spend between 0 and 15 hours per week studying. After that, there are only a few cases at each different value with a "spike" occurring at 25, 30, 38, and 40 hours studied. This distribution is clearly not

Exhibit 11.7 Histogram

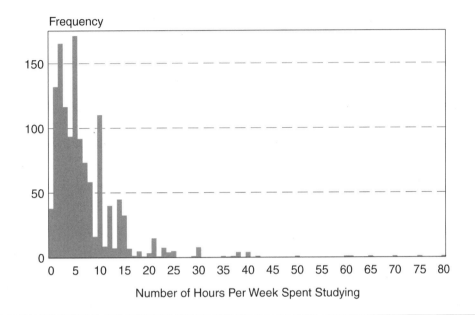

symmetric. In a symmetric distribution there is a lump of cases or a "spike" with an equal number of cases to the left and right of that spike. In the distribution shown in Exhibit 11.7, most of the cases are at the left end of the distribution (i.e., at low values) and the distribution trails off on the right side. The ends of a histogram like this are often called the *tail* of a distribution. In a symmetric distribution, the left and right tails are approximately the same length. As you can clearly see in Exhibit 11.7, however, the right tail is much longer than the left tail. When the tails of the distribution are uneven the distribution is said to be asymmetrical or skewed. A skew is either positive or negative. When the cases cluster to the left and the right tail of the distribution is longer than the left, as in Exhibit 11.7, our variable distribution is **positively skewed.** When the cases cluster to the right side and the left tail of the distribution is long, our variable distribution is **negatively skewed.**

In a **frequency polygon,** a continuous line connects the points representing the number or percentage of cases with each value. The frequency polygon is an alternative to the histogram when the distribution of a quantitative, continuous variable must be displayed; this alternative is particularly useful when the variable has a wide range of values. We used the same number of hours studying data shown in Exhibit 11.7 to make the frequency polygon in Exhibit 11.8. Notice that the frequency polygon is constructed by making a point or dot to represent the frequency of each value and then drawing a line by connecting the dots. The frequency polygon gives us the same impression of the data as the histogram. These data cluster near the low values (representing fewer hours studied), and there are only a very few respondents who report studying more than 25 hours per week. Because the right tail is long, relative to the left tail of the distribution, we have a positive skew. We could have easily constructed both the histogram and the frequency polygon with percentages rather than raw frequencies.

Exhibit 11.8 Frequency Polygon

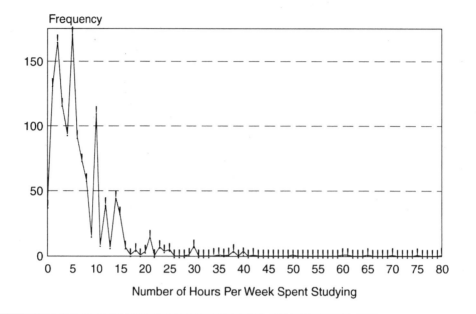

If graphs are misused, they can distort, rather than display, the shape of a distribution. Compare, for example, the two graphs in Exhibit 11.9. The first graph shows that high school seniors reported relatively stable rates of lifetime use of cocaine between 1980 and 1985. The second graph, using exactly the same numbers, appeared in a 1986 *Newsweek* article on the coke plague (Orcutt & Turner, 1993). To look at this graph, you would think that the rate of cocaine usage among high school seniors increased dramatically during this period. But, in fact, the difference between the two graphs is due simply to changes in how the graphs are drawn. In the "plague" graph (B), the percentage scale on the vertical axis begins at 15 rather than 0, making what was about a one-percentage point increase look very big indeed. In addition, omission from the plague graph of the more rapid increase in reported usage between 1975 and 1980 makes it look as if the tiny increase in 1985 were a new, and thus more newsworthy, crisis.

Adherence to several guidelines (Tufte, 1983) will help you to spot these problems and to avoid them in your own work:

- The difference between bars can be exaggerated by cutting off the bottom of the vertical axis and displaying less than the full height of the bars. Instead, begin the graph of a quantitative variable at 0 on both axes. It may at times be reasonable to violate this guideline, as when an age distribution is presented for a sample of adults, but in this case be sure to mark the break clearly on the axis.
- Bars of unequal width, including pictures instead of bars, can make particular values look as if they carry more weight than their frequency warrants. Always use bars of equal width.

Exhibit 11.9 Two Graphs of Cocaine Usage

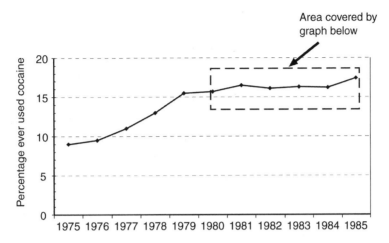

A. University of Michigan Institute for Social Research,
Time Series for Lifetime Prevalence of Cocaine Use

B. Final Stages of Construction

Source: James D. Orcutt and J. Blake Turner, 1993. "Shocking Numbers and Graphic Accounts." *Social Problems,* Vol. 49, No. 2, pp. 190–206. © 1993 by the Society for the Study of Social Problems. Reprinted by permission.

- Either shortening or lengthening the vertical axis will obscure or accentuate the differences in the number of cases between values. The two axes usually should be of approximately equal length.
- Avoid chart junk that can confuse the reader and obscure the distribution's shape (a lot of verbiage, numerous marks, lines, lots of crosshatching, etc.).

Exhibit 11.10 Frequency Distribution

How much of a problem would it be if you went to court for drinking liquor under age?

Value	Frequency(f)	Percentage (%)
No problem at all	14	1.1
Hardly any problem	53	4.2
A little problem	196	15.4
A big problem	421	33.1
A very big problem	588	46.2
Total	1,272	100.0

Frequency Distributions

A **frequency distribution** displays the number, the **percentage** (the relative frequencies), or both for cases corresponding to each of a variable's values or group of values. The components of the frequency distribution should be clearly labeled, with a title, a stub (labels for the values of the variable), a caption (identifying whether the distribution includes frequencies, percentages, or both), and perhaps the number of missing cases. If percentages are presented rather than frequencies (sometimes both are included), the total number of cases in the distribution (the **base** N) should be indicated (see Exhibit 11.10). Remember that a percentage is simply a relative frequency. A percentage shows the frequency of a given value relative to the total number of cases times 100.

Ungrouped Data

Constructing and reading frequency distributions for variables with few values is not difficult. In Exhibit 11.10, we created the frequency distribution from the variable "Punishment for Drinking" found in the delinquency data set (see Exhibit 11.2). This variable asked the youths to respond to the following question, "How much of a problem would it be if you went to court for drinking liquor under age?" The frequency distribution in Exhibit 11.10 shows the frequency for each value and its corresponding percentage.

As another example of calculating the frequencies and percentages, suppose we had a sample of 25 youths and asked them their gender. From this group of 25 youths, 13 were male and 12 were female. The frequency of males (symbolized here by f) would be 13 and the frequency of females would be 12. The percentage of males would be 52% , calculated by f/the total number of cases x 100 (13/25 x 100 = 52%). The percentage of females would be 12/25 x 100 = 48%.

In the frequency distribution shown in Exhibit 11.10, you can see that only a very small number (14 out of 1,272) of youths thought that they would experience "no problem" if they were caught and taken to court for drinking liquor under age. You can see that most, in fact 1,009 of these youths or 79.3% of them, thought that they would have either "a big problem" or "a very big problem" with this. If you compare Exhibit 11.10 to Exhibit 11.5, you can see that a frequency distribution (Exhibit 11.10) can provide much of the same information as a graph about the number and percentage of cases in a variable's categories. Often, however, it is easier to see the shape of a distribution when it is graphed. When the goal of a presentation is to convey a general sense of a variable's distribution, particularly when the presentation is to an audience not trained in statistics, the advantages of a graph outweigh those of a frequency distribution.

Exhibit 11.10 is a frequency distribution of an ordinal-level variable—it has a very small number of discrete categories. In Exhibit 11.11, we provide an illustration of a frequency distribution with a continuous quantitative variable. This variable is one we have already looked at and graphed from the delinquency data—the number of hours per week the respondent spent studying. Notice that this variable, like many continuous variables in criminological research, has a large number of values. Although this is a reasonable frequency distribution to construct—you can, for example, still see that the cases tend to cluster in the low end of the distribution and are strung way out at the upper end—it is a little difficult to get a good sense of the distribution of the cases. The problem is that there are too many values to easily comprehend. It would be nice if we could simplify distributions like these that have a large number of different values. Well, we can. We can construct what is called a **grouped frequency distribution.**

Grouped Data

Many frequency distributions, such as those in Exhibit 11.11, and many graphs require grouping of some values after the data are collected. There are two reasons for grouping:

1. There are more than 15–20 values to begin with, a number too large to be displayed in an easily readable table.

2. The distribution of the variable will be clearer or more meaningful if some of the values are combined.

Inspection of Exhibit 11.11 should clarify these reasons. In this distribution it is very difficult to discern any shape, much less the central tendency. What we would like to now do to make the features of the data more visible is change the values into intervals of values, or a range of values. For example, rather than having five separate values of 0, 1, 2, 3, 4 hours studied per week, we can have a range of values or an interval for the first value, such as 0–4 hours studied. Then we can get a count or frequency of the number of cases (and percentage of the total) that fall within that interval.

Once we decide to group values, or categories, we have to be sure that in doing so we do not distort the distribution. Adhering to the following guidelines for combining values in a frequency distribution will prevent many problems:

- Categories should be logically defensible and preserve the distribution's shape.
- Categories should be mutually exclusive and exhaustive, so every case is classifiable in one and only one category.
- The first interval must contain the lowest value and the last interval must contain the highest value in the distribution.
- Each interval width, the number of values that fall within each interval, should be the same size.

Exhibit 11.11   Frequency Distribution with Continuous Quantitative Data:
Hours Studied per Week

Value	Frequency (f)	Percentage (%)
0	38	3.0
1	132	10.4
2	165	13.0
3	116	9.1
4	94	7.4
5	171	13.4
6	92	7.2
7	73	5.7
8	58	4.6
9	16	1.3
10	110	8.6
11	9	.7
12	40	3.1
13	7	.6
14	45	3.5
15	32	2.5
16	7	.6
17	5	.4
18	4	.3
19	1	.1
20	15	1.2
21	8	.6
22	1	.1
23	1	.1
24	4	.3
25	5	.4
29	1	.1
30	8	.6
35	1	.1
37	1	.1
40	4	.3
42	1	.1
50	1	.1
60	1	.1
61	1	.1
65	1	.1
70	1	.1
75	1	.1
80	1	.1
Total	1,272	100.0

- There should be between 7 and 13 intervals. This is a tough rule to follow. The key is not to have so few intervals that your data are clumped or clustered into only a few intervals (you will lose too much information about your distribution) and not to have so many intervals that the data are not much clearer than an ungrouped frequency distribution.

Let's use the data in Exhibit 11.11 on the number of hours studied by these youths to create a grouped frequency distribution. We will follow a number of explicit steps:

Step 1. Determine the number of intervals you think you want. This decision is arbitrary, but try to keep the number of intervals you have in the 7–13 range. For our example, let's say we initially decided we wanted to have 10 intervals. (Note, if you do your frequency distribution and it looks too clustered or there are too many intervals, redo your distribution with a different number of intervals.) Don't worry, there are no hard and fast rules for the correct number of intervals, and constructing a grouped frequency distribution is as much art as science. Just remember that the frequency distribution you make is supposed to convey information about the shape and central tendency of your data.

Step 2. Decide on the width of the interval (symbolized by w_i). The interval width is the number of different values that falls into your interval. For example, an interval width of 5 has five different values that fall into it, say, the values 0, 1, 2, 3, or 4 hours studied. There is a simple formula to approximate what your interval width should be given the number of intervals you decided on in the first step—determine the range of the data, where the range is simply the highest score in the distribution minus the lowest score. In our data, with the number of hours studied, the range is 80 because the high score is 80 and the low score is 0, so range = 80 – 0 = 80. Then determine the width of the interval by dividing the range by the number of intervals you want from Step 1. We wanted 10 intervals, so our interval width would be $w_i = 80/10 = 8$. We should therefore have an interval width of 8. If you use this simple formula for determining your interval width and you end up with a decimal, say 8.2 or 8.6, then simply round up or down to an integer.

Step 3. Make your first interval so that the lowest value falls into it. Our lowest value is 0 (for studied 0 hours per week), so our first interval begins with the value 0. Now, if the beginning of our first interval is 0 and we want an interval width of 8, is the last value of our interval 7 (with a first interval of 0–7 hours), or is the last value of our interval 8 (with a first interval of 0–8 hours)? One easy way to make a grouped frequency distribution is to do the following: Take the beginning value of your first interval (in our case, it is 0), and add the interval width to that value (8). This new value is the first value of your next interval. What we now know, then, is that the first value of our first interval is 0, and the first value of our second interval is 8: (0–?, 8–?). This must mean that the last value to be included in our first interval is one less than 8, or 7. Our first interval, therefore, includes the range of values 0–7. If you count the number of different values in this interval you will find that it includes eight different values (0, 1, 2, 3, 4, 5, 6, 7). This is our interval width of 8.

Step 4. After your first interval is determined, the next intervals are easy. They must be the same width and not overlap (mutually exclusive). You must make enough intervals to include the last value in your variable distribution. The highest value in our data is 80 hours per week, so we construct the grouped frequency distribution as follows:

0–7	48–55
8–15	56–63
16–23	64–71
24–31	72–79
32–39	80–87
40–47	

Notice that in order to include the highest value in our data (80 hours) we had to make 11 intervals instead of the 10 we originally decided upon in Step 1. No problem. Remember, the number of intervals is arbitrary and this is as much art as science.

Step 5. Count the number or frequency of cases that appear in each interval and their percentage of the total.

The completed grouped frequency distribution is shown in Exhibit 11.12. Notice that this grouped frequency distribution conveys the important features of the distribution of this data. Most of the data cluster at the low end of the number of hours studied. In fact, more than two-thirds of these youths studied fewer than 8 hours per week. Notice also that the frequency of cases thins out at each successive interval. In other words, there is a long right tail to this distribution indicating a positive skew because fewer youths studied a high number of hours. Notice also that the distribution was created in such a way that the interval widths are all the same and each case falls into one and only one interval (i.e., the

Exhibit 11.12 Example of a Grouped Frequency Distribution from Hours Studied

Value	Frequency (f)	Percentage (%)
0–7	881	69.26
8–15	317	24.92
16–23	42	3.30
24–31	18	1.42
32–39	2	.16
40–47	5	.39
48–55	1	.08
56–63	2	.16
64–71	2	.16
72–79	1	.08
80–87	1	.08
Total	1,272	100.00*

*May not sum exactly to 100.0%, due to rounding error.

intervals are exhaustive and mutually exclusive). We would have run into trouble if we had two intervals like 0–7 and 7–14 because we would not know where to place those youths who spent 7 hours a week studying. Should we put them in the first or second interval? If the intervals are mutually exclusive, as they are here, you will not run into these problems.

SUMMARIZING UNIVARIATE DISTRIBUTIONS

Summary statistics focus attention on particular aspects of a distribution and facilitate comparison among distributions. For example, suppose you wanted to report the rate of violent crimes for each city in the United States with over 100,000 in population. You could report each city's violent crime rate, but it is unlikely that two cities would have the same rate and you would have to report approximately 200 rates, one for each city. This would be a frequency distribution that many, if not most, people would find difficult to comprehend. One way to interpret your data for your audience would be to provide a summary measure that indicates what the average violent crime rate is in large U.S. cities. That is the purpose of the set of summary statistics called *measures of central tendency.* You would also want to provide another summary measure that shows the variability or heterogeneity in your data. In other words, a measure that shows how different the scores are from each other or from the central tendency. That is the purpose of the set of summary statistics called *measures of variation or dispersion.* We will discuss each type of measurement in turn.

Measures of Central Tendency

Central tendency is usually summarized with one of three statistics: the mode, the median, or the mean. For any particular application, one of these statistics may be preferable, but each has a role to play in data analysis. To choose an appropriate measure of central tendency, the analyst must consider a variable's level of measurement, the skewness of a quantitative variable's distribution, and the purpose for which the statistic is used. In addition, the analyst's personal experiences and preferences inevitably will play a role.

Mode

The mode is the most frequent value in a distribution. For example, refer to the data in Exhibit 11.12, which shows the grouped frequency distribution for the number of hours studied. The value with the greatest frequency in that data is the interval 0–7 hours; this is the mode of that distribution. Notice that the mode is the most frequently occurring value; it is not the frequency of that value. In other words, the mode in Exhibit 11.12 is 0–7 hours, the mode is not 881, which is the frequency of the modal category. To show how the mode can also be thought of as the value with the highest probability, refer again to Exhibit 11.12. Suppose you had this grouped frequency distribution, but knew nothing else about each of the 1,272 youths in the study. If you were to pick a case at random from the distribution of 1,272 youths, and were asked how many hours they studied per week, what would your best guess be? Well, since 881 of the 1,272 youths fall into the first interval of 0–7 hours studied, the probability that a randomly selected youth studied from 0 to 7 hours would be .696 (881/1,272). This is higher than the probability of any other interval. It is the interval with the highest probability because it is the interval with the greatest

Exhibit 11.13   Frequency Distribution of Offense Convicted for 1,000 Offenders

Offense	Frequency (f)
Violent	125
Drug	210
Property	480
Public order	100
Other	85
Total	1,000

frequency or mode of the distribution. When a variable distribution has one case or interval that occurs more often than the others, it is called a **unimodal** distribution.

Sometimes a distribution has more than one mode because there are two values that have the highest frequency. This distribution would be called **bimodal.** Some distributions are trimodal in that there are three distinctively high frequency values. And some distributions have no mode. Look back at the graph of the frequency distribution in Exhibit 11.6. There is no one value with a frequency much higher than another. In fact, if you calculate the probability of a randomly selected person falling into each of the different values, they would not be all that different. In other words, the outcomes are equiprobable, or there is no mode. In saying that there is no mode, though, you are communicating something very important about the data: that no case is more common than the others. Another potential problem with the mode is that it might happen to fall far from the main clustering of cases in a distribution. It would be misleading in this case, then, to say simply that the variable's central tendency was the same as the modal value.

Nevertheless, there are occasions when the mode is very appropriate. Most important, the mode is the only measure of central tendency that can be used to characterize the central tendency of variables measured at the nominal level. In Exhibit 11.13 we have the frequency distribution of the conviction offense for 1,000 offenders convicted in a criminal court. The central tendency of the distribution is property offense, because more of the 1,000 offenders were convicted of a property crime than any other crime. For the variable "type of offense convicted of," the most common value is property crime. The mode also is often referred to in descriptions of the shape of a distribution. The terms *unimodal* and *bimodal* appear frequently, as do descriptive statements such as "The typical (most probable) respondent was in her 30s." Of course, when the issue is determining the most probable value, the mode is the appropriate statistic.

Median

The **median** is the score in the middle of a rank-ordered distribution. It is, then, the score or point that divides the distribution in half (the 50th percentile). The median is inappropriate for variables measured at the nominal level because their values cannot be put in ranked order (remember, there is no "order" to nominal-level data), and so there is no meaningful middle position. To determine the median we simply need to do the following. First, rank-order the values from lowest to highest. If there is an odd number of scores then you can find the position of the median in the rank order of scores by using the following simple formula:

$$\text{Median position} = \frac{N+1}{2}$$

where N is equal to the total number of cases. If there is an even number of scores, then you can find the position of the median in the rank order of scores by finding the midpoint of the scores in the following two positions:

$$\text{Position 1} = \frac{N}{2}$$

$$\text{Position 2} = \frac{N+2}{2}$$

The midpoint of the two scores can be found by adding the scores in the two positions and dividing by 2. Please note that in both formulas you use the formula to find the position of the median; the formula does not give you the value of the median. Let's do an example.

In Exhibit 11.14, we first list a sample of nine U.S. cities and their rate of violent crime in 1994. In the bottom panel of Exhibit 11.14, we drop one of the cities (San Francisco) and have eight cities.

Exhibit 11.14   Rate of Violent Crime for Selected U.S. Cities

City	Number of Violent Crimes per 100,000
Atlanta	3,571
Boston	1,916
Cleveland	1,530
Dallas	1,589
Los Angeles	2,059
New Orleans	1,887
New York	1,861
Philadelphia	1,322
San Francisco	1,461
Atlanta	3,571
Boston	1,916
Cleveland	1,530
Dallas	1,589
Los Angeles	2,059
New Orleans	1,887
New York	1,861
Philadelphia	1,322

Let's determine the median for both lists. First, we rank-order the violent crime rates for the first list:

Rank	Crime Rate
1	1,322
2	1,461
3	1,530
4	1,589
5	1,861
6	1,887
7	1,916
8	2,059
9	3,571

Because we have an odd number of scores ($N = 9$), the position of the median is determined by $(9 + 1)/2 = 10/2 = 5$. The median violent crime rate, then, is in the fifth position in this rank order. Starting either at the top of the scores and counting down to the fifth position or the bottom and counting up, we find that in the fifth position is the score 1,891 violent crimes per 100,000, which is the median violent crime rate for these nine U.S. cities.

Now let's find the median in the second list. We first rank-order these eight scores:

Rank	Crime Rate
1	1,322
2	1,530
3	1,589
4	1,861
5	1,887
6	1,916
7	2,059
8	3,571

Because we now have an even number of scores (notice that the violent crime rate for San Francisco is missing from this list), we know that the median position is the midpoint in between the fourth ($8/2 = 4$) and fifth ($[8 + 2]/2$) positions. The score at the fourth position is 1,861 and at the fifth is 1,887. The value of the median can now be found by adding these two scores and dividing by two. The median rate of violent crime is equal to $(1,861 + 1,887)/2 = 1,874$ violent crimes per 100,000 population.

The median is the score at the 50th percentile, so in a frequency distribution it is determined by identifying the value corresponding to a cumulative percentage of 50. We show you how do to this in Exhibit 11.15. These data are a repeat of the data in Exhibit 11.11 and show the number of hours studied for the youths in the delinquency data set. To find the 50th percentile, we simply added a new column to these data, labeled cumulative percentage. Cumulative percentages are found by taking the percentage of the interval percentage plus all others below it. So the first value (3.0%) would be entered as the first cumulative percentage because there are no other intervals below the first. This cumulative percentage simply means that 3% of the youths studied for 0 hours per week. Then we add the percentage in the next value (10.4%) to this to arrive at a cumulative percentage of 13.4%. This means that 13.4% of the youths studied for 1 hour per week or less. This becomes the second entry in the cumulative percentage column. We continue adding each

Exhibit 11.15   Frequency Distribution with Continuous Quantitative Data:
Hours Studied per Week

Value	Frequency (f)	Percentage (%)	Cumulative Percentage
0	38	3.0	3.0
1	132	10.4	13.4
2	165	13.0	26.4
3	116	9.1	35.5
4	94	7.4	42.9
5	171	13.4	56.3 ⌀ 50th percentile
6	92	7.2	
7	73	5.7	
8	58	4.6	
9	16	1.3	
10	110	8.6	
11	9	.7	
12	40	3.1	
13	7	.6	
14	45	3.5	
15	32	2.5	
16	7	.6	
17	5	.4	
18	4	.3	
19	1	.1	
20	15	1.2	
21	8	.6	
22	1	.1	
23	1	.1	
24	4	.3	
25	5	.4	
29	1	.1	
30	8	.6	
35	1	.1	
37	1	.1	
40	4	.3	
42	1	.1	
50	1	.1	
60	1	.1	
61	1	.1	
65	1	.1	
70	1	.1	
75	1	.1	
80	1	.1	
Total	1,272	100.0	

adjacent percentage value until we reach 50%. There is a cumulative percentage of 56.3% at the value of 5 hours per week. The median number of hours studied per week, then, is 5 hours. Of the respondents, 50% studied less than 5 hours per week, and 50% studied more than 5 hours per week.

Mean

The **mean** is simply the arithmetic average of all scores in a distribution. It is computed by adding up the value of all the cases and dividing by the total number of cases, thereby taking into account the value of each case in the distribution:

Mean = Sum of value of all cases/Number of cases

The symbol for the mean is $\bar{x}$ (pronounced "x-bar"). In algebraic notation, the equation is:

$$\bar{x} = \frac{\sum_{1}^{N} x_i}{N}$$

where x_i is a symbol for each ith score and i's go from 1 to N; N is the total number of cases. What the algebraic equation says to do is to sum all scores, starting at the first score and continuing until the last, or Nth, score; then divide this sum by the total number of cases (N).

We will calculate the mean rate of violent crime for the nine U.S. cities listed in Exhibit 11.14:

$$\bar{x} = \frac{(3,571 + 1,916 + 1,530 + 1,589 + 2,059 + 1,887 + 1,861 + 1,332 + 1,461)}{9}$$

$$= 1,910.7$$

The mean rate of violent crime for these nine U.S. cities, then, is 1,910.7 violent crimes per 100,000 population. Notice that in calculating the mean we do not have to first rank-order the scores. The mean takes every score into account, so it does not matter if we add 3,571 first, in the middle, or last.

Computing the mean requires adding up the values of the cases, so it makes sense to compute a mean only if the values of the cases can be treated as actual quantities, that is, if they reflect an interval or ratio level of measurement, or if they are ordinal and we assume that ordinal measures can be treated as interval. It would make no sense, however, to calculate the mean for the variable racial/ethnic status. Imagine a group of four people in which there were two Caucasians, one African American, and one Hispanic. To calculate the mean you would need to solve the equation (Caucasian + Caucasian + African American + Hispanic)/4 = ?. Even if you decide that Caucasian = 1, African American = 2, and Hispanic = 3 for data entry purposes, it still doesn't make sense to add these numbers because they don't represent real numerical quantities. In other words, just because you code Caucasian as "1" and African American as "2," that does not mean that African Americans possess twice the race/ethnicity as Caucasians. To see how numerically silly this is, note that we could just as easily have coded African Americans as "1" and Caucasians as "2." Now, with one arbitrary flip of our coding scheme Caucasians have twice the race/ethnicity as African Americans. Thus both the median and the mean are inappropriate measures of central tendency for variables measured at the nominal level.

Median or Mean?

Both the median and the mean are used to summarize the central tendency of quantitative variables, but their suitability for a particular application must be carefully assessed. The key issues to be considered in this assessment are the variable's level of measurement, the shape of its distribution, and the purpose of the statistical summary. Consideration of these issues will sometimes result in a decision to use both the median and the mean, and will sometimes result in neither measure being seen as preferable. But in many other situations, the choice between the mean and the median will be clear-cut as soon as the researcher takes the time to consider these three issues.

Level of measurement is a key concern because to calculate the mean, we must add up the values of all the cases, a procedure that assumes the variable is measured at the interval or ratio level. So even though we know that coding Agree as 2 and Disagree as 3 does not really mean that Disagree is one unit more of disagreement than Agree, the mean assumes this evaluation to be true. Calculation of the median requires only that we order the values of cases, so we do not have to make this assumption. Technically speaking, then, the mean is simply an inappropriate statistic for variables measured at the ordinal level (and you already know that it is completely meaningless for nominal variables). In practice, however, many social researchers use the mean to describe the central tendency of variables measured at the ordinal level, for the reasons outlined earlier.

The shape of a variable's distribution should also be taken into account when deciding whether to use the median or the mean. When a distribution is perfectly symmetric (i.e., when the distribution is bell shaped), the distribution of values below the median is a mirror image of the distribution of values above the median, and the mean and median will be the same. But the values of the mean and median are affected differently by skewness, or the presence of cases with extreme values on one side of the distribution but not the other side. The median takes into account only the number of cases above and below the median point, not the value of these cases, so it is not affected in any way by extreme values. The mean is based on adding the value of all the cases, so it will be pulled in the direction of exceptionally high (or low) values. When the value of the mean is larger than the median, we know that the distribution is skewed in a positive direction, with proportionately more cases with higher than lower values. When the mean is smaller than the median, the distribution is skewed in a negative direction.

This differential impact of skewness on the median and mean is illustrated in Exhibit 11.16. We show in the first list the crime rate per 1,000 residents for seven neighborhoods in a hypothetical city. The crime rates range from a low of 51.7 per 1,000 to 135.3 per 1,000. When we calculate the mean crime rate for these seven neighborhoods we find that it is 94.8 crimes per 1,000; the median is 98.7 crimes per 1,000. Notice that this is a relatively symmetrical distribution, with the values of the mean and the median very comparable to each other. With these data both the mean and the median provide an accurate description of the central tendency.

Exhibit 11.16   Rates of Crime in Selected Neighborhoods

Community	Crime Rate per 1,000
Valley View	51.7
Glen Commons	63.1
Springdale	75.3
Green Acres	98.7
Oceanside	113.4
Meadowbrook	125.9
King's Crossing	135.3
Valley View	51.7
Glen Commons	63.1
Springdale	75.3
Green Acres	98.7
Oceanside	113.4
Meadowbrook	125.9
West Chester	697.5
Pleasantville	5.3
Glen Commons	63.1
Springdale	75.3
Green Acres	98.7
Oceanside	113.4
Meadowbrook	125.9
King's Crossing	135.3

In the second list of neighborhoods we replace the neighborhood that had the highest crime rate (King's Crossing), with West Chester, which has a substantially higher crime rate—697.5 per 1,000. It is, then, an unusually high score. When we calculate the mean for these data, we find that it is 175.1 per 1,000—it has increased from its previous value of 94.8. The median, however, remains the same; it is still 98.7 crimes per 1,000. When an unusually high score is added to a distribution, then, the mean gets inflated relative to the median. In distributions that are positively skewed, the mean is of greater magnitude than the median. Notice also that with this unusually high crime rate added, the median is still an accurate picture of the central tendency, whereas the mean of 175.1 is no longer accurate.

In the third list of neighborhoods we replace the neighborhood that has the lowest crime rate (Valley View) with another, Pleasantville, which has a substantially lower crime rate—5.3 per 1,000. It is, then, an unusually low score. When we calculate the mean for these data, we find that it is 88.1 per 1,000—it has decreased from the value in the first list, which was 94.8. The median, however, remains the same; it is still 98.7 crimes per 1,000. When an unusually low score is added to a distribution, then, the mean gets deflated relative to the median. In distributions that are negatively skewed, the mean is less than the median. Notice also that even with this unusually low crime rate added, the median is still an accurate picture of the central tendency, whereas the mean of 88.1 is no longer as accurate.

This example illustrates one of the problems with using the mean as a measure of central tendency. If the data are skewed (either positively or negatively), then the mean will be affected by the extreme scores in the distribution and will not give as accurate an estimate of the central tendency of the data as the median. The lesson is that one should probably report both the mean and the median. In general, the mean is the most commonly used measure of central tendency for quantitative variables, because it takes into account the value of all cases in the distribution and it is the foundation for many other more advanced statistics. However, the mean's very popularity results in its use in situations for which it is inappropriate. Keep an eye out for this problem.

Measures of Variation

You have learned that central tendency is only one aspect of the shape of a distribution. Although the measure of center is the most important aspect for many purposes, it is still just a piece of the total picture. A summary of distributions based only on their central tendency can be very incomplete, even misleading. For example, three towns might have the same mean and median crime rate but still be very different in their social character due to the shape of the crime distributions. We show three distributions of community crime rates for three different towns in Exhibit 11.17. If you calculate the mean and median crime rate for each town, you will find that the mean and median crime rate is the same for all three. In terms of its crime rate, then, each community has the same central tendency. As you can see, however, there is something very different about these towns. Town A is a very heterogeneous town; crime rates in its neighborhoods are neither very homogeneous nor clustered at either the low or high end. Rather, the crime rates in its communities are spread out from one another. Crime rates in these neighborhoods are, then, very diverse. Town B is characterized by neighborhoods with very homogeneous crime rates; there are no real high or low crime areas because each neighborhood is not far from the overall mean of 62.4 crimes per 1,000. Town C is characterized by neighborhoods with either very low crime rates or very high crime rates. Crime rates in the first four neighborhoods are much lower than the mean (62.4 crimes per 1,000), whereas the last four neighborhoods are much higher than the mean. Although they share identical measures of central tendency, these three towns have neighborhood crime rates that are very different.

Exhibit 11.17   Neighborhood Crime Rates in Three Different Towns

Town A	Town B	Town C
19.5	58.1	8.9
28.2	59.7	15.4
35.7	60.1	18.3
41.9	62.7	21.9
63.2	63.2	63.2
75.8	63.9	103.5
92.0	64.2	104.2
95.7	64.5	110.7
109.4	65.0	115.3

The way to capture these differences is with statistical measures of variation. Four popular measures of variation are the range, the interquartile range, the variance, and the standard deviation (which is the most popular measure of variability). To calculate each of these measures, the variable must be at the interval or ratio level. Statistical measures of variation are used infrequently with qualitative variables, so these measures will not be presented here.

Range

The **range** is a simple measure of variation, calculated as the highest value in a distribution minus the lowest value:

$$\text{Range} = \text{Highest value} - \text{Lowest value}$$

It often is important to report the range of a distribution, to identify the whole range of possible values that might be encountered. However, because the range can be drastically altered by just one exceptionally high or low value (called an **outlier**), it does not do an adequate job of summarizing the extent of variability in a distribution. For our three towns in Exhibit 11.17, the range in crime rates for Town A is 89.9 (109.4 – 19.5), for Town B it is 6.9 (65.0 – 58.1), and for Town C it is 106.4 (115.3 – 8.9).

Interquartile Range

A version of the range statistic, the **interquartile range,** avoids the problem created by unusually high or low scores in a distribution. It is the difference between the scores at the first quartile and the third quartile. **Quartiles** are the points in a distribution corresponding to the first 25% of the cases (the first quartile), the first 50% of the cases (the second quartile), and the first 75% of the cases (the third quartile). You already know how to determine the second quartile, corresponding to the point in the distribution covering half of the cases—it is another name for the median. The first and third quartiles are determined in the same way, but by finding the points corresponding to 25% and 75% of the cases, respectively.

Variance

If the mean is a good measure of central tendency, then it would seem that a good measure of variability would be the distance each score is away from the mean. Unfortunately, we cannot simply take the average distance of each score from the mean. One property of the mean is that it exactly balances negative and positive distances from it, so if we were to sum the difference between each score in a distribution and the mean of that distribution, it would always sum to zero. What we can do, though, is to square the difference of each score from the mean so the distance retains its value. This is the notion behind the variance as a measure of variability.

The **variance** is the average squared deviation of each case from the mean, so it takes into account the amount by which each case differs from the mean. The equation to calculate the variance is:

$$\sigma^2 = \frac{\sum_{1}^{N}(x - \bar{x})^2}{N}$$

In words, this formula says to take each score and subtract the mean, then square this difference, then square this difference, then sum all of these differences, then divide this sum by N or the total number of scores. We will calculate the variance for the crime rate data from Town A in Exhibit 11.17.

x	$(x - \bar{x})$	$(x - \bar{x})^2$
19.5	$(19.5 - 62.4) = -42.9$	1,840.41
28.2	$(28.2 - 62.4) = -34.2$	1,169.64
35.7	$(35.7 - 62.4) = -26.7$	712.89
41.9	$(41.9 - 62.4) = -20.5$	420.25
63.2	$(63.2 - 62.4) = -0.8$	0.64
75.8	$(75.8 - 62.4) = 13.4$	179.56
92.0	$(92.0 - 62.4) = 29.6$	876.16
95.7	$(95.7 - 62.4) = 33.3$	1,108.89
109.4	$(109.4 - 62.4) = 47.0$	2,209.00
		8,517.44

We can now determine that the variance is:

$$\sigma^2 = \frac{8,517.44}{9}$$

$$\sigma^2 = 946.38$$

The variance of these data, then, is 946.38. The variance is used in many other statistics, although it is more conventional to measure variability with the closely related standard deviation than with the variance.

Standard Deviation

The **standard deviation** is simply the square root of the variance. It is the square root of the average squared deviation of each case from the mean:

$$\sigma^2 = \sqrt{\frac{\sum_{1}^{N}(x - \bar{x})^2}{N}}$$

To find the standard deviation, then, simply calculate the variance and take the square root. For our example, the standard deviation is:

$$\sigma = \sqrt{946.38}$$

$$\sigma = 30.76$$

When the standard deviation is calculated from sample data, the denominator is supposed to be $N - 1$, rather than N, an adjustment that has no discernible effect when the number of cases is reasonably large.

The standard deviation has mathematical properties that make it the preferred measure of variability in many cases. In particular, the calculation of confidence intervals around sample statistics, which you learned about in Chapter 4, relies on an interesting property of normal curves. Areas under the normal curve correspond to particular distances from the mean, expressed in standard deviation units. If a variable is normally distributed, 68% of the cases will lie between plus and minus 1 standard deviation from the distribution's mean, and 95% of the cases will lie between 1.96 standard deviations above and below the mean. Cases that fall beyond plus or minus 1.96 standard deviations from the mean are termed outliers. Because of this property, the standard deviation tells us quite a bit about a distribution, if the distribution is normal. This same property of the standard deviation enables us to infer how confident we can be that the mean (or some other statistic) of a population sampled randomly is within a certain range of the sample mean (see Chapter 4).

CROSSTABULATING VARIABLES

Most data analyses focus on relationships among variables to test hypotheses or just to describe or explore relationships. For each of these purposes, we must examine the association among two or more variables. **Crosstabulation (crosstab)** is one of the simplest methods for doing so. A crosstabulation displays the distribution of one variable for each category of another variable; it can also be called a *bivariate distribution*. Crosstabs also provide a simple tool for statistically controlling one or more variables while examining the associations among others. In the next section you will learn how crosstabs used in this way can help to test for spurious relationships and evaluate causal models. Crosstabulations are usually used when both variables are measured at either the nominal or ordinal level. That is, when the values of both variables are categories.

We are going to provide a series of examples of crosstabulations from our delinquency data. In our first example, the independent variable we are interested in is the youth's gender (V1, see Exhibit 11.2), and the dependent variable is the youth's self-reported involvement in delinquent behavior (DELINQ1). To use the delinquency variable in a crosstabulation, however, we first need to recode it into a categorical variable. We will make three approximately equal categories of self-reported delinquency—low, medium, and high. Using the SPSS recode command, we will create another variable called DELINQ2, which was made from the following recode commands:

$$(0\text{--}2 = 1)$$
$$(3\text{--}13 = 2)$$
$$(14\text{--}118 = 3)$$

Anyone who reported from 0 to 2 delinquent acts is now coded as 1, or low delinquency; anyone reporting from 3 to 13 delinquent acts is now coded as 2, or medium delinquency; and anyone reporting more than 14 delinquent acts is now coded as 3, or high delinquency. If you were to do a frequency distribution of this new variable, DELINQ2, you would see that there are three approximately equal groups.

We are interested in the relationship between gender and delinquency because a great deal of delinquency theory would predict that males are more likely to be delinquent than

Exhibit 11.18   Crosstabulation of Respondents' Gender by Delinquency

		SELF-REPORTED DELINQUENCY			
		Low	Medium	High	Total
	Female	275	182	223	680
		40.4%	26.8%	32.8%	100%
GENDER	Male	175	166	251	592
		29.6%	28.0%	42.4%	100%
	Total	450	348	474	1,272

females. The gender of the youth is the independent variable, and the level of self-reported delinquency is the dependent variable.

Exhibit 11.18 shows the crosstabulation of gender with DELINQ2. Some explanation of this table is in order. Notice that there are two values of gender (male and female) that comprise the two rows of the table, and three values of delinquency (low, medium, and high) that comprise the three columns of the table. Crosstabulations are usually referred to by the number of rows and columns the table has. Our crosstabulation in Exhibit 11.18 is a 2 x 3 (pronounced "two-by-three") table because there are two rows and three columns. Notice also that there are values at the end of each row and at the end of each column. These totals are referred to as the *marginals* of the table. These **marginal distributions** provide the sum of the frequencies for each column and each row of the table. For example, there are 680 females in the data and 592 males. These row marginals should sum to the total number of youths in the data set—1,272. There are 450 youths who are low in delinquency, 348 youths who are medium in delinquency, and 251 youths who are high on the delinquency variable. These column marginals should also sum to the total number of youths in the data set—1,272.

Now notice that there are 2 x 3 or 6 data entries in the table (let's ignore the percentages for now). These data entries are called the *cells* of the crosstabulation and represent the joint distribution of the two variables—gender and delinquency. The table in Exhibit 11.18 has six cells for the joint distribution of two levels of gender with three levels of delinquency. In other words, notice where the value for female converges with the value of low for delinquency. You see a frequency number of 275 in this cell. This frequency is how many times there is the joint occurrence of a female and low delinquency—it shows that 275 females were also low in delinquency. Moving to the cell to the right of this, we see that there are 182 females who were medium in delinquency, and moving to the right again we see that there are 223 females who are high in delinquency. The sum of these three numbers is equal to the total number of females— 680. The row for the males shows the joint distribution of males with each level of delinquency.

What we would like to know is whether there is a relationship or association between gender and delinquency. In other words, are males more likely to be delinquent than females? Because raw frequencies can provide a deceptive picture, we determine whether there is any relationship between our independent and dependent variables by looking at the percentages. Keep in mind that the idea in looking at relationships is that we want to know if variation on the independent variable has any effect on the dependent variable. To determine this, what we always do in crosstabulation tables is to calculate our percentages on each value of the independent variable. For example, notice that in Exhibit 11.18, gender is our independent variable. We calculated our percentages so that for each value of gender the percentages sum to 100% at the end of each row. The percentages for both females and males, therefore, sum to 100% at the end of the row. Now we take a given category of the dependent variable and ask what percentage of each independent variable value falls into that category of the dependent variable. Another way to say this is that we calculate our percentages on the independent variable and compare them on the dependent variable. We compare the percentages for different levels of the independent variable on the same category or level of the dependent variable.

In Exhibit 11.18, for example, notice that 40.4% of the female youths were low in delinquency, but only 29.6% of the males were low. This tells us that females are more likely to be low in delinquency than males. Now let's look at the high category. We can see that 32.8% of the females were high in delinquency and 42.4% of the males were high. Together, this tells us that females are more likely to be low in delinquency and males are more likely to be high in delinquency. There is, then, a relationship between gender and delinquency. Also notice that the independent variable was the row variable, and the dependent variable was the column variable. It does not always have to be this way; the independent variable could just as easily have been the column variable. The important general rule to remember is to always calculate your percentages on the levels of the independent variable (e.g., use marginal totals for the independent variable as denominators) and compare percentages on a level of the dependent variable.

In Exhibit 11.19 we report the same data as in Exhibit 11.18, this time switching the rows and the columns. Now, the independent variable (gender) is the column variable, so we calculate our percentages going down each of the two columns. We then compare percentages across rows. For example, we still see that 40.4% of the females were low in delinquency, whereas only 29.6% of the males were. And 42.4% of the males were high in delinquency, but only 32.8% of the females were high in delinquency.

Exhibit 11.19   Crosstabulation of Respondents' Delinquency by Gender

		GENDER		
		Female	Male	Total
	Low	275 40.4%	175 29.6%	450
SELF-REPORTED DELINQUENCY	Medium	182 26.8%	166 28.0%	348
	High	223 32.8%	251 42.4%	474
	Total	680 100%	592 100%	1,272

Describing Association

A crosstabulation table reveals four aspects of the association between two variables:

- *Existence.* Do the percentage distributions vary at all between categories of the independent variable?
- *Strength.* How much do the percentage distributions vary between categories of the independent variable?
- *Direction.* For quantitative variables, do values on the dependent variable tend to increase or decrease with an increase in value of the independent variable?
- *Pattern.* For quantitative variables, are changes in the percentage distribution of the dependent variable fairly regular (simply increasing or decreasing), or do they vary (perhaps increasing, then decreasing, or perhaps gradually increasing, then rapidly increasing)?

In Exhibit 11.18, an association exists, although we can only say that it is a modest association. The percentage difference at the low and high ends of the delinquency variables is approximately 10 percentage points.

We provide another example of a crosstabulation in Exhibit 11.20. This is a 3 x 3 table that shows the relationship between how morally wrong a youth thinks delinquency is (the independent variable), and his or her self-reported involvement in delinquency (the dependent variable). This table reveals a very strong relationship between moral beliefs and delinquency. We can see that 5.6% of youths with weak moral beliefs are low on delinquency—this increases to 33.8% for those with medium beliefs and to 62.8% for those with strong moral beliefs. At the high end, over two-thirds (72.1%) of those youths with weak moral beliefs are high in delinquency, 29.4% of those with medium moral beliefs are high in delinquency, and only 16.9% of those youths with strong moral beliefs are high in delinquency. Clearly, then, having strong moral beliefs serves to effectively inhibit involvement in delinquent behavior. This is exactly what control theory would have us believe.

Exhibit 11.20 is an example of a negative relationship between an independent and dependent variable. As the independent variable increases (i.e., as one goes from weak to strong moral beliefs), the likelihood of delinquency decreases (one becomes less likely to

Exhibit 11.20   Crosstabulation of Respondents' Morals by Delinquency

		SELF-REPORTED DELINQUENCY			
		Low	Medium	High	Total
	Weak	20 5.6%	79 22.3%	256 72.1%	355 100%
MORALS	Medium	170 33.8%	185 36.8%	148 29.4%	503 100%
	Strong	260 62.8%	84 20.3%	70 16.9%	414 100%
	Total	450	348	474	1,272

Exhibit 11.21   Crosstabulation of Respondents' Study Hours by Certainty of Punishment

		CERTAINTY OF PUNISHMENT			
		Low	Medium	High	Total
	0–3 Hours	126	148	177	451
		27.9%	32.8%	39.2%	100%
NUMBER OF HOURS STUDIED	4–6 Hours	117	113	127	357
		32.8%	31.7%	35.6%	100%
	7+ Hours	129	148	187	464
		27.8%	31.9%	40.39%	100%
	Total	372	409	491	1,272

commit delinquency). The independent and dependent variables move in opposite directions, so this is a negative relationship. The pattern in this table is close to what is called monotonic. In a **monotonic** relationship, the value of cases consistently increases (or decreases) on one variable as the value of cases increases (or decreases) on the other variable. Monotonic is often defined a bit less strictly, with the idea that as the value of cases on one variable increases (or decreases), the value of cases on the other variable tends to increase (or decrease), and at least does not change direction. This describes the relationship between moral beliefs and delinquency. Delinquency is most likely when moral beliefs are low, less likely when moral beliefs are medium, and least likely when moral beliefs are strong.

We present another crosstabulation table for you in Exhibit 11.21. This table shows the relationship between the variable "number of hours studied" and the variable "certainty of punishment" (see Exhibit 11.2). Both variables were originally continuous variables that we recoded into three approximately equal groups for this example. We hypothesize that those youths who study more will have a greater perceived risk of punishment than those who study less, so hours studied is our independent variable and certainty is the dependent variable. Comparing levels of hours studied for those with high certainty, we see that there is not much variation. Of those who did not study very much (0–3 hours), 39.2% were high in perceived certainty. Of those who studied from 4–6 hours, 35.6% were high in perceived certainty and 40.3% of those who studied more than 7 hours per week were high in perceived certainty. Much the same levels prevail at low levels of perceived certainty. Those who do not study very much are no more or less likely to perceive a low certainty of punishment than those who study a lot. Variation in the independent variable, then, is not related to variation in the dependent variable. It looks like there is no association between the number of hours a youth studies and the extent to which he or she thinks punishment for delinquent acts is certain.

You will find when you read research reports and journal articles that social scientists usually make decisions about the existence and strength of association on the basis of more statistics than just percentage differences in a crosstabulation table. A **measure of association** is a type of descriptive statistic used to summarize the strength of an association. There are many measures of association, some of which are appropriate for variables measured at particular levels. One popular measure of association in crosstabular analyses with variables measured at the ordinal level is **gamma.** As with many measures of association, the possible values of gamma vary from –1, meaning the variables are perfectly associated in a negative direction; to 0, meaning there is no association of the type that gamma measures; to + 1, meaning there is a perfect positive association of the type that gamma measures.

Inferential statistics are used in deciding whether it is likely that an association exists in the larger population from which the sample was drawn. Even when the association between two variables is consistent with the researcher's hypothesis, it is possible that the association was just due to chance or to the vagaries of sampling on a random basis (of course, the problem is even worse if the sample is not random). It is conventional in statistics to avoid concluding that an association exists in the population from which the sample was drawn unless the probability that the association was due to chance is less than 5%. In other words, a statistician normally will not conclude that an association exists between two variables unless he or she can be at least 95% confident that the association was not due to chance. This is the same type of logic that you learned about in Chapter 4, which introduced the concept of 95% confidence limits for the mean. Estimation of the probability that an association is not due to chance will be based on one of several inferential statistics, **chi-square** being the one used in most crosstabular analyses. The probability is customarily reported in a summary form such as "$p < .05$," which can be translated as: "The probability that the association was due to chance is less than 5 out of 100 [5%]."

When an association passes muster in this way—when the analyst feels reasonably confident (at least 95% confident) that it was not due to chance—it is said that the association is statistically significant. **Statistical significance** means that an association is not likely to be due to chance, according to some criterion set by the analyst. Convention (and the desire to avoid concluding that an association exists in the population when it doesn't) dictates that the criterion be a probability less than 5%.

But statistical significance is not everything. You may remember from Chapter 4 that sampling error decreases as sample size increases. For this same reason, an association is less likely to appear on the basis of chance in a larger sample than in a smaller sample. In a table with more than 1,000 cases, such as those involving the delinquency data set, the odds of a chance association are often very low indeed. For example, with our table based on 1,272 cases, the probability that the association between gender and delinquency (Exhibit 11.18) was due to chance was less than 1 in 1,000 ($p < .001$)! The association in that table was fairly weak, as indicated by a gamma of .20. Even weak associations can be statistically significant with such a large sample, which means that the analyst must be careful not to assume that just because a statistically significant association exists, it is therefore important. In a large sample, an association may be statistically significant but still be too weak to be substantively significant or important. All this boils down to another reason for evaluating carefully both the existence and the strength of an association.

Controlling for a Third Variable

Crosstabulation can also be used to study the relationship between two variables while controlling for other variables. We will focus our attention on controlling for a third variable in this section, but we will say a bit about controlling for more variables at the section's end. We will examine three different uses for three-variable crosstabulation—identifying an intervening variable, testing a relationship for spuriousness, and specifying the conditions for a relationship. Each of these uses for three-variable crosstabs helps determine the validity of our findings, either by evaluating criteria for causality (nonspuriousness and identification of a causal mechanism) or by increasing our understanding of the conditions required for a relationship to hold—an indication of the crosspopulation generalizability of the findings. All three uses are aspects of **elaboration analysis**—the process of introducing control variables into a bivariate relationship in order to better understand—to elaborate the relationship (Rosenberg, 1968). We will examine the gamma and chi-square statistics for each table in this analysis.

Intervening Variables

We have already discovered that females are less likely to be delinquent than males (Exhibit 11.18). Finding this relationship between gender and delinquency is just the beginning of our work, however. What we would now like to know and investigate is why this relationship exists. What is it about females that makes them less likely to commit delinquent acts than males? Let's first rule out strictly biological factors, and explore some possible social reasons for this gender difference in delinquency. One possibility is that because they are more closely supervised than males, females have fewer opportunities to be delinquent. In other words, females are under more strict parental supervision, and it is because they are under more strict supervision that they are less likely than males to commit delinquency. This possible relationship is shown in Exhibit 11.22. Notice that in this relationship the variable "parental supervision" intervenes between gender and delinquency. It explains why females are at lower risk for delinquency compared to males. To determine whether parental supervision intervenes in the relationship between gender and delinquency, and whether it explains this relationship, we must examine the relationship between gender and delinquency while controlling for differences in parental supervision. If parental supervision intervenes in the gender–delinquency relationship, the effect of controlling for this third variable would be to eliminate, or at least substantially reduce, the original relationship between gender and delinquency.

Exhibit 11.22 Example of an Intervening Variable

Gender $\longrightarrow$ Parental supervision $\longrightarrow$ Delinquency

To examine this possibility, we first recode the parental supervision variable (PARSUPER—see Exhibit 11.2) into two approximately equal levels—weak supervision and strong supervision. We then look at two **subtables** of the gender–delinquency relationship: once under the condition of weak parental supervision and once under the condition of strong parental supervision (Exhibit 11.23). For ease of presentation, we will only report the cell percentages and not the frequencies. What we see is that once parental supervision is controlled, there is no real relationship between gender and delinquency. That is, if males and females have the same amount of supervision from their parents, they do not differ that much in their risk of being delinquent. For example, among females with weak

Exhibit 11.23 Crosstabulation of Respondents' Gender by Delinquency
Within Levels of Parental Supervision

Weak Parental Supervision

		SELF-REPORTED DELINQUENCY			
		Low	Medium	High	Total
	Female	26.1%	27.9%	46.0%	337
GENDER					
	Male	23.2%	27.2%	49.6%	427
	Total				764

$\chi^2 = 1.220$ ($p > .05$) Gamma = .067

Strong Parental Supervision

		SELF-REPORTED DELINQUENCY			
		Low	Medium	High	Total
	Female	54.5%	25.7%	19.8%	343
GENDER					
	Male	46.1%	30.3%	23.6%	165
	Total				508

$\chi^2 = 3.193$ ($p > .05$) Gamma = .136

parental supervision, 46.0% are high in delinquency, and among males with weak parental supervision 49.6% are delinquent. There is less than four percentage points difference between males and females in their risk of being high delinquents under these conditions. Among those with strong parental supervision, 19.8% of the females were high in delinquency and 23.6% of the males were high, less than four percentage points difference.

This percentage analysis is borne out by the chi-square tests and measures of association. Under both the weak and strong levels of parental supervision, the relationship between gender and delinquency is not significant, and gamma is only .067 when supervision is weak and .136 when supervision is strong. In neither case is the obtained gamma very different from zero (indicating no relationship). Collectively, these results would lead us to the conclusion that parental supervision intervenes in the relationship between gender and delinquency. A very important reason females are less delinquent than males, therefore, is that females are under stricter supervision from their parents than males, and strong parental supervision leads to a reduced risk of delinquency.

Extraneous Variables

Another reason for introducing a third variable into a bivariate relationship is to see whether the original relationship is spurious due to the influence of an **extraneous variable,** which is a variable that causes both the independent and dependent variables. The only reason why the independent and dependent variables are related, therefore, is that they both are the effects of a common cause (another independent variable).

Exhibit 11.24 shows what a spurious relationship would look like. In this case, the relationship between x and y exists only because both are the effects of the common cause z. Controlling for z, therefore, will eliminate the x–y relationship. Ruling out possible extraneous variables will help to considerably strengthen the conclusion that the relationship between the independent and dependent variables is causal, particularly if all the variables that seem to have the potential for creating a spurious relationship can be controlled.

Exhibit 11.24 A Spurious Relationship Between x and y

Notice that if a variable is acting as an extraneous variable, then controlling for it will cause the original relationship between the independent and dependent variables to disappear or substantially diminish. This was also the empirical test for an intervening variable. Therefore, the difference between intervening and extraneous variables is a logical one and not an empirical one. In both instances, controlling for the third variable will cause the original relationship to diminish or disappear. There should, therefore, be sound theoretical grounds for suspecting that a variable is acting as an intervening variable, explaining the relationship between the independent and dependent variables.

As an example of a possible extraneous relationship, we will look at the association between a youth's perception of the certainty of punishment and self-reported involvement in delinquency. Deterrence theory should lead us to predict a negative relationship between perceived certainty and delinquency. Indeed, this is exactly what we observe in our delinquency data. We will not show you the crosstabulation table, but when we looked at the relationship between perceived certainty and delinquency we found that 53.2% of youth who were low in certainty were high in delinquency; 39.1% of those who perceived medium certainty were high in delinquency; and only 23.6% of those who perceived a high certainty of punishment were high in delinquency. Youth who believed they would get caught if they engaged in delinquency, then, were less likely to be delinquent. The gamma value for this table was −.382, indicating a moderate negative relationship between perceived certainty and delinquency—exactly what deterrence theory would lead us to expect.

Someone may reasonably argue, however, that this observed negative relationship may not be causal, but instead may be spurious. It could be suggested that what is actually behind this relationship is the extraneous variable, moral beliefs. The argument is that those with strong moral inhibitions against committing delinquent acts think that punishment for morally wrongful actions is certain, *and* refrain from delinquent acts. Thus, the observed negative relationship between perceived certainty and delinquency is really due to the positive effect of moral beliefs on perceived certainty, and the negative effect of moral beliefs on delinquency (see Exhibit 11.25). If moral beliefs are actually the causal factor at work, then controlling for them will eliminate or substantially reduce the original relationship between perceived certainty and delinquency.

Exhibit 11.25 A Spurious Relationship Between Perceived Certainty and Delinquency

To look at this possibility, we examined the relationship between perceived certainty and delinquency under three levels of moral beliefs (weak, medium, and strong). The crosstabulations are shown in Exhibit 11.26. What we can see is that in each of the subtables there is a negative and significant association between the perceived certainty of punishment and delinquency. In two of the three subtables, however, the relationship is weaker than what was in the original table (there the gamma was –.382); we obtained gammas of –.271 and –.197. Under the condition of strong moral beliefs, however, the original relationship is unchanged. What we would conclude from this elaboration analysis is that the variable moral beliefs is not acting as a very strong extraneous variable. Although some of the relationship between perceived risk and delinquency is due to their joint relationship with moral beliefs, we cannot dismiss the possibility that the perceived certainty of punishment has a causal influence on delinquent behavior.

Specification

By adding a third variable to an evaluation of a bivariate relationship, the data analyst can also specify the conditions under which the bivariate relationship occurs. A **specification** occurs when the association between the independent and dependent variables varies across the categories of one or more other control variables. That is, when the original relationship is stronger under some condition or conditions of a third variable and weaker under others.

In criminology, social learning theory would predict that youths who are exposed to peers who provide verbal support for delinquency are at greater risk for their own delinquent conduct. We found support for this hypothesis in our delinquency data set. We examined this relationship by recoding into two approximately equal groups the variable FROPINON (see Exhibit 11.2). The first group had weak verbal support from peers, whereas the second group had strong verbal support. Among those youths who reported that their peers provided only weak verbal support for delinquency, 15% were highly delinquent. Among those with strong verbal support from peers, nearly 58% were highly delinquent. The gamma value for this relationship was .711, a very strong positive relationship. Clearly, then, having friends give you verbal support for delinquent acts (for example, "it's OK to steal"), puts you at risk for delinquency.

It is entirely possible, however, that this relationship exists only when friends' verbal support is backed up by their own behavior. That is, verbal support from our peers might

Exhibit 11.26   Crosstabulation of Perceived Risk by Delinquency Within Levels of Moral
Beliefs

Weak Moral Beliefs

		SELF-REPORTED DELINQUENCY			
		Low	Medium	High	Total
	Low	3.8%	14.7%	81.4%	156
PERCEIVED					
CERTAINTY	Medium	8.6%	27.3%	64.1%	128
	High	4.2%	29.6%	66.8%	71
	Total				355

$\chi^2 = 13.646$ ($p < .001$) Gamma $= -.271$

Medium Moral Beliefs

		SELF-REPORTED DELINQUENCY			
		Low	Medium	High	Total
	Low	22.0%	42.5%	35.4%	127
PERCEIVED					
CERTAINTY	Medium	33.9%	35.6%	30.5%	174
	High	41.1%	34.2%	24.8%	202
	Total				503

$\chi^2 = 13.06$ ($p < .05$) Gamma $= -.197$

Strong Moral Beliefs

		SELF-REPORTED DELINQUENCY			
		Low	Medium	High	Total
	Low	42.7%	28.1%	29.2%	89
PERCEIVED					
CERTAINTY	Medium	58.9%	17.7%	23.4%	107
	High	72.9%	18.3%	8.7%	218
	Total				414

$\chi^2 = 32.23$ ($p = \leq.001$) Gamma $= -.393$

not affect our delinquency when they do not themselves commit delinquent acts, or commit only a very few. In this case, their actions (inaction in this case) speak louder than their words, and their verbal support does not influence us. When they also commit delinquent acts, however, the verbal support of peers carries great weight.

We looked at this possibility by examining the relationship between friends' verbal support for delinquency and a youth's own delinquency within two levels of friends' behavior (FRBEHAVE, see Exhibit 11.2). We recoded FRBEHAVE into two approximately equal groups. In the first group, fewer of one's friends are delinquent (few delinquent friends) than the other (many delinquent friends). This attempt to specify the relationship between friends' opinions and our own delinquency is shown in Exhibit 11.27. What we see is a little complex. When only a few of a youth's friends are also committing delinquent acts, their verbal support still has a significant and positive effect on self-reported delinquency. The gamma value in this subtable is .416, which is moderately strong, but less than the original gamma of .771. When many of a youth's friends are delinquent, however, the positive relationship between peers' verbal support and self-reported delinquency is much stronger, with a gamma of .608. The behavior of our peers, then, only weakly specifies the relationship between peer opinion and delinquency. Clearly, then, what our peers say about delinquency matters even if they are not committing delinquent acts all the time themselves.

Exhibit 11.27 Crosstabulation of Friends' Verbal Support by Delinquency Within Levels of Friends' Delinquent Behavior

Few Delinquent Friends

		SELF-REPORTED DELINQUENCY			
		Low	Medium	High	Total
FRIENDS' VERBAL SUPPORT	Weak	67.3%	23.8%	8.9%	437
	Strong	44.3%	34.3%	21.4%	140
	Total				577

$\chi^2 = 27.374$ ($p < .001$) Gamma = .416

Many Delinquent Friends

		SELF-REPORTED DELINQUENCY			
		Low	Medium	High	Total
FRIENDS' VERBAL SUPPORT	Weak	30.5%	38.5%	31.0%	174
	Strong	7.5%	24.8%	67.4%	521
	Total				695

$\chi^2 = 87.508$ ($p < .001$) Gamma = .608

Our goal in introducing you to crosstabulation has been to help you think about the association among variables and to give you a relatively easy tool for describing association. To read most statistical reports and to conduct more sophisticated analyses of social data, you will have to extend your statistical knowledge. In addition to the statistical techniques we have considered here and the inferential statistics we discussed previously, you should learn about the summary descriptive statistics used to indicate the strength and direction of association. Until you do so, you will find it difficult to state with precision just how strong an association is. You also should learn about a different statistical approach to characterizing the association between two quantitative variables, called regression or correlation analysis. Statistics based on regression and correlation are used very often in social science and have many advantages over crosstabulation, as well as some disadvantages. You will need to take a course in social statistics, however, to become proficient in the use of statistics based on regression and correlation.

ANALYZING DATA ETHICALLY: HOW NOT TO LIE ABOUT RELATIONSHIPS

When the data analyst begins to examine relationships among variables in some real data, social science research becomes most exciting. The moment of truth, it would seem, has arrived. Either the hypotheses are supported or not. But, in fact, this is also a time to proceed with caution, and to evaluate the analyses of others with even more caution. Once large data sets are entered into a computer, it becomes very easy to check out a great many relationships; when relationships are examined among three or more variables at a time, the possibilities become almost endless.

This range of possibilities presents a great hazard for data analysis. It becomes very tempting to search around in the data until something interesting emerges. Rejected hypotheses are forgotten in favor of highlighting what's going on in the data. It's not wrong to examine data for unanticipated relationships; the problem is that inevitably some relationships between variables will appear just on the basis of chance association alone. If you search hard and long enough, it will be possible to come up with something that really means nothing.

A reasonable balance must be struck between deductive data analysis to test hypotheses and inductive analysis to explore patterns in a data set. Hypotheses formulated in advance of data collection must be tested as they were originally stated; any further analyses of these hypotheses that involve a more exploratory strategy must be labeled as such in research reports. Serendipitous findings do not need to be ignored, but they must be reported. Subsequent researchers can try to deductively test the ideas generated by our explorations.

We also have to be honest about the limitations of using survey data to test causal hypotheses. The usual practice for those who seek to test a causal hypothesis with nonexperimental survey data is to test for the relationship between the independent and dependent variables, controlling for other variables that might possibly create spurious relationships. This is what we did by examining the relationship between the perceived certainty of punishment and delinquency while controlling for moral beliefs (Exhibit 11.26). But finding that a hypothesized relationship is not altered by controlling for just one variable does not establish that the relationship is causal; nor does controlling for two, three, or many more variables. There always is a possibility that some other variable that we did not think to control, or that was not even measured in the survey, has produced a spurious relationship between the independent and dependent variables in our hypothesis (Lieberson, 1985). We must always think about the possibilities and be cautious in our causal conclusions.

CONCLUSION

This chapter has demonstrated how a researcher can describe phenomena in criminal justice and criminology, identify relationships among them, explore the reasons for these relationships, and test hypotheses about them. Statistics provide a remarkably useful tool for developing our understanding of the social world, a tool that we can use to test our ideas and generate new ones.

Unfortunately, to the uninitiated the use of statistics can seem to end debate right there—you can't argue with the numbers. But you now know better than that. The numbers will be worthless if the methods used to generate the data are not valid; and the numbers will be misleading if they are not used appropriately, taking into account the type of data to which they are applied. And even assuming valid methods and proper use of statistics, there's one more critical step, for the numbers do not speak for themselves. Ultimately, it is how we interpret and report the numbers that determines their usefulness. It is this topic we turn to in the next chapter.

KEY TERMS

Bar chart
Base *N*
Bimodal distribution
Central tendency
Chi-square
Crosstabulation (crosstab)
Data cleaning
Descriptive statistics
Elaboration analysis
Extraneous variable
Frequency distribution
Frequency polygon
Gamma
Grouped frequency distribution
Histogram
Inferential statistics
Interquartile range
Marginal distributions
Mean
Measure of association

Median
Mode
Monotonic
Negatively skewed
Outlier
Percentage
Positively skewed
Probability average
Quartile
Range
Secondary data analysis
Skewness
Specification
Standard deviation
Statistical significance
Subtables
Unimodal distribution
Variability
Variance

HIGHLIGHTS

• Data-collection instruments should be precoded for direct entry, after verification, into a computer. Use of secondary data can save considerable time and resources, but may limit data analysis possibilities.

- Bar charts, histograms, and frequency polygons are useful for describing the shape of distributions. Care must be taken with graphic displays to avoid distorting a distribution's apparent shape.

- Frequency distributions display variation in a form that can be easily inspected and described. Values should be grouped in frequency distributions in a way that does not alter the shape of the distribution. Following several guidelines can reduce the risk of problems.

- Summary statistics are often used to describe the central tendency and variability of distributions. The appropriateness of the mode, mean, and median vary with a variable's level of measurement, the distribution's shape, and the purpose of the summary.

- The variance and standard deviation summarize variability around the mean. The interquartile range is usually preferable to the range to indicate the interval spanned by cases, due to the effect of outliers on the range. The degree of skewness of a distribution is usually described in words rather than with a summary statistic.

- Crosstabulations should normally be percentaged within the categories of the independent variable. A crosstabulation can be used to determine the existence, strength, direction, and pattern of an association.

- Elaboration analysis can be used in crosstabular analysis to test for spurious and intervening relationships and to identify the conditions under which relationships occur.

- Inferential statistics are used with sample-based data to estimate the confidence that can be placed in a statistical estimate of a population parameter. Estimates of the probability that an association between variables may have occurred on the basis of chance are also based on inferential statistics.

EXERCISES

1. Create frequency distributions from lists in the FBI *Uniform Crime Reports* on characteristics of arrestees in at least 100 cases (cites). You will have to decide on a grouping scheme for the distribution scheme of variables such as race, age, and crime committed, and how to deal with outliers in the frequency distribution.
   a. Decide what summary statistics to use for each variable of interest. How well were the features of each distribution represented by the summary statistics? Describe the shape of each distribution.
   b. Propose a hypothesis involving two of these variables, and develop a crosstabulation to evaluate the support for this hypothesis.
   c. Describe each relationship in terms of the four aspects of an association, after making percentages within each table within the categories of the independent variable. Which hypotheses appear to have been supported?

2. Become a media critic. For the next week, scan a newspaper or some magazines for statistics related to crime or criminal victimization. How many can you find using frequency distributions, graphs, and the summary statistics introduced in this chapter? Are these statistics used appropriately and interpreted correctly? Would any other statistics have been preferable, or useful in addition to those presented?

DEVELOPING A RESEARCH PROPOSAL

Use the General Social Survey data to add a pilot study to your proposal. A pilot study is a preliminary effort to test out the procedures and concepts that you have proposed to research.

1. Review the GSSCRJ2K variable list and identify some variables that have at least some connection to your research problem. If possible, identify one variable that might be treated as independent in your proposed research and one that might be treated as dependent.

2. Request frequencies for these variables.

3. Request a crosstabulation of the dependent variable by the independent variable (if you were able to identify any). If necessary, recode the independent variable to five or fewer categories.

4. Write a brief description of your findings and comment on their implications for your proposed research. Did you learn any lessons from this exercise for your proposal?

WEB EXERCISES

1. Search the Web for a crime-related example of statistics. Using the key terms from this chapter, describe the set of statistics you have identified. What phenomena does this set of statistics describe? What relationships, if any, do the statistics identify?

2. Do a Web search for information on a criminological subject that interests you. How much of the information that you find relies on statistics as a tool for understanding the subject? How do statistics allow researchers to test their ideas about the subject and generate new ideas? Write your findings in a brief report, referring to the Web sites that you found.

SPSS EXERCISES

1. Develop a description of homicide defendants and their sentence length from HOMICIDE.POR. Examine each characteristic with three statistical techniques: a graph, a frequency distribution, and a measure of central tendency.

2. Describe the distribution of each variable, noting any skewness and/or outliers.

3. Collapse the categories for defendant's age (DAGE) and sentence length (PRITIME). Examine the data distributions using a graph and frequency distribution. Does the general shape of the distributions change as a result of changing how the data are measured?

4. Look at the relationship between these two variables. Indicate which variable is the dependent variable and which variable is the independent variable.

5. Run a crosstabulation on these data (use your newly created categorical variables). Be sure to obtain percentiles for categories of the independent variable (either row or column).

6. Propose two variables that might create a spurious relationship between defendant's age and sentence length. Explain your thinking. Propose a variable that might result in a conditional effect of age on sentence length, so that the relationship between age and sentence length would vary across the categories of the other variable. Test these propositions with three variable cross-tabulations. Were any supported? How would you explain your findings?

Chapter 12

REPORTING RESEARCH RESULTS

The goal of research is not just to discover something, but to communicate that discovery to a larger audience—other social scientists, government officials, your teachers, the general public; perhaps several of these audiences. Whatever the study's particular outcome, if the research report enables the intended audience to comprehend the results and learn from them, the research can be judged a success. If the intended audience is not able to learn about the study's results, the research should be judged a failure no matter how expensive the research, how sophisticated its design, or how much of yourself you invested in it.

This conclusion may seem obvious, and perhaps a bit unnecessary. After all, you may think that all researchers write up their results for other people to read. But the fact is that many research projects fail to produce a research report. Sometimes the problem is that the research is poorly designed to begin with and can't be carried out in a satisfactory manner; sometimes unanticipated difficulties derail a viable project. But too often the researcher just never gets around to writing a report. And then there are many research reports that are very incomplete or poorly written, or that speak to only one of several interested audiences. The failure may not be complete, but the project's full potential is not achieved.

Remember that the time for congratulations is when credible results are released and they serve some useful function—not when the research project is first approved. Give careful attention to the research report, whatever type it is, before breaking out the bottle of champagne. And if you've conducted a worthwhile research project, consider whether some of the results might be appropriate for more than one report to different audiences.

The primary goals of this chapter are to help you develop worthwhile reports for any research you conduct and guide you in evaluating reports produced by others. We begin by teaching how to write research proposals, because a formal proposal lays the groundwork for a final research report. The next section highlights problems that are unique to the main types of reports: student papers and theses, journal articles, and unpublished reports for specific clients. The chapter's final sections present suggestions for writing and organizing reports, techniques for displaying statistical results, and ethical issues to be considered.

THE RESEARCH PROPOSAL

Be grateful for those who require you to write a formal research proposal and even more for those who give you constructive feedback. Whether your proposal is written for a professor, a thesis committee, an organization seeking practical advice, or a government agency that funds basic research, the proposal will force you to establish a problem statement and a research plan. Too many research projects begin without a clear problem statement or with only the barest of notions about which variables must be measured or what the analysis should look like. Such projects often wander along, lurching from side to side, then collapse entirely or just fizzle out with a report that is given little attention. So even in circumstances when a proposal is not required, you should prepare one and present it to others for feedback. Just writing your ideas down will help you to see how they can be improved, and feedback in almost any form will help you to refine your plans.

A well-designed proposal can go a long way toward shaping the final research report and will make it easier to progress at later research stages. Every research proposal should have at least five sections, defined as follows:

1. *An introductory statement of the research problem.* Clarify the research question(s) that you are interested in studying and how this question was derived from the existing literature.

2. *A literature review.* Explain your problem in greater detail and build on what has already been reported in the literature on this topic.

3. *A methodological plan.* Detail the methods you will employ (including sample, variables, etc.) along with a discussion of how you will respond to the particular mix of opportunities and constraints you face.

4. *A budget.* Present a careful listing of the anticipated costs.

5. *An ethics statement.* Identify human subjects issues in the research and how you will respond to them in an ethical fashion.

If your research proposal will be competitively reviewed, it must present a compelling rationale for funding. It is not possible to overstate the importance of the research problem that you propose to study (see Chapter 2). If you propose to test a hypothesis, be sure it is one with plausible alternatives: "A boring hypothesis is one which, although likely to be correct, has no credible alternatives" (Dawes, 1995:93).

Case Study: Criminal Victimization of the Elderly

Particular academic departments, grant committees, and funding agencies will have more specific proposal requirements. As an example, Exhibit 12.1 lists the primary required sections of the "Research Plan" for proposals to the National Institutes of Health (NIH), together with excerpts from a proposal one of your authors submitted in this format to the National Institute of Mental Health (NIMH) with colleagues from the Cornell University Medical College (Mark Lachs, M.D.) and Yale University (Christianna Williams). The Research Plan is limited to 25 pages by NIH guidelines. It must be preceded by an abstract (which has been excerpted), a proposed budget, biographical sketches of project personnel, and a discussion of the available resources for the project. Appendixes may include research instruments, prior publications by the authors, and findings from related work. As you can see from Exhibit 12.1, our proposal had several specific aims, all related to criminal victimization among older adults.

So how does a research proposal like this get evaluated? Typically, grants for all government agencies and many nonprofit agencies also include a peer review process whereby other researchers and practitioners in a particular area of expertise will be asked to review your proposal. Based on their recommendations, your proposal either sinks or swims, so to speak. The NIMH review committee approved this particular project for funding, but required two submissions and reviews before funding was awarded (it often takes several resubmissions before even a worthwhile proposal is funded). The committee members recognized the proposal's strengths, but also identified several problems that they believed had to be overcome before the proposal could be funded. The reviewers pointed out several issues they had with the proposal including the following:

> The outcomes of crime considered are too narrow. . . . Number of physician visits, for example, might be a more appropriate outcome variable than nursing home placement to demonstrate increased health care utilization. Nursing home placement may also be confounded. . . . For example, variables such as weak social networks and support could be associated with both crime victimization and nursing home placement. . . . The authors have not considered "short stay" nursing home placement. Conversely, other types of residential living arrangements (e.g., assisted living) do not appear to be included (i.e., nursing home placement is treated as dichotomous). This research considers only reports of crimes made to police and therefore underestimates its prevalence within the cohort. Similarly, the work assumes no cohort members were victimized prior to inception year 1985; some undoubtedly were and this will confound the analysis. . . . Alcohol is a risk factor for victimization in younger individuals yet it is not considered in the proposed research. . . . There is minimal text on psychosocial aspects of stress theory.

If you get the impression that researchers cannot afford to leave any stone unturned in working through procedures in an NIMH proposal, you are right. It is very difficult to

(text continued on p. 382)

Exhibit 12.1 A Grant Proposal to the NIMH

A GRANT PROPOSAL TO THE NIMH

ABSTRACT

Little is known about the epidemiology of crime committed against older
adults, and virtually nothing is known about its health consequences. The
investigators propose linking an established cohort of older adults (The
New Haven EPESE cohort, $n = 2,812$) who have been followed annually with
standardized measures of medical, functional, and psychosocial health for
over a decade, with Police Records from the cohort's catchment area. This
would permit the largest community-based study of crime victimization in
older adults ever conducted, at a fraction of the expense of assembling a
new inception cohort for this purpose. The broad long-term goal of the
research is to identify older adults at highest risk for mortality after
crime so that preventive strategies may be developed and implemented.

RESEARCH PLAN

1. Specific Aims

The specific aims of this research are: (1) to identify risk factors for
crime victimization in an observational cohort of community-dwelling older
adults; (2) to estimate the independent contribution of crime victimization
to erosion of quality-of-life in cohort members after victimization is
measured by (a) the onset of new or worsening functional disability and
(b) a decline in self-perceived health status; (3) to estimate the
independent contribution of crime victimization to increased health care
utilization in cohort members after victimization as measured by (a)
hospitalization and (b) nursing home placement; (4) to estimate the
independent contribution of crime victimization to all-cause mortality in
the cohort after the experience of victimization. A secondary aim of this
research is to determine if gender is an "effect modifier" in influencing
mortality in older adults.

2. Background and Significance

Without question, older adults remain the least studied demographic group
with respect to the epidemiology and impact of crime victimization....
While older adults have relatively low rates of crime victimization
compared to younger adults, when criminal victimization of older adults is
examined more closely, some alarming patterns emerge. For example, recent
research has revealed that older adults suffer violent death from felony-
related homicides perpetrated by strangers at a rate proportionally greater
than younger age cohorts. In addition, it has been found that older
victims of robbery, particularly women, are more likely to sustain injuries
compared to younger victims. Moreover, older victims of violent crime in
general are more likely than younger injured victims to suffer a serious
medical injury that requires hospital or other medical care. Dr. Lachs'
experience in the primary care of older people is consistent with this
literature. For example, he has observed that for many older adults who
are ostensibly well compensated in all spheres (medical, functional, and
psychosocial), a crime victimization can set in motion an inexorable spiral
that may ultimately result in a loss of independence.

The notion that a single event might set into motion a progressive spiral
of decline in many domains for an older adult has a basis in aging theory.
... Normal aging is accompanied by a loss of physiologic reserve in
various systems that need not lead to phenotypic decline.... Rather, when the
organism is taxed through stress, illness, or other factors, this loss of

(Continued)

Exhibit 12.1 (Continued)

physiologic reserve is unmasked.... Crime victimization may be such a precipitating event in the life of an older person. It is a stressful experience that may impact on physical health, mental health, and functional independence.... Stress in general, and stressful life events in particular, have been linked to the onset of illness and other maladaptive behavior by several decades of research at both the individual and societal levels.... While the geriatric literature is rife with examples of mortality and adverse health outcomes following stressful life events...there is virtually no empirical research which examines the impact of crime on health outcomes, mortality, or general quality of life in older people.... The study proposed is the largest and longest longitudinal evaluation of crime, mortality, and quality of life in a well-characterized community-dwelling cohort of older people. It also marries both the medical and criminal justice perspectives bringing together a multidisciplinary team ideally suited to conduct this research and involves a municipal police department at the grassroots level.

Several gaps in our knowledge can be addressed in this research:

- What are the risk factors for crime victimization among older adults? How does medical, functional, and psychosocial health interact with environmental variables (e.g., poverty and social networks) to create a milieu that makes the older person especially vulnerable?
- How does crime victimization influence the need for subsequent nursing home placement? For individuals who escape physical injury from any form of victimization, is there still a quality-of-life toll in the form of new onset functional impairment, social isolation, and subsequent institutionalization months or years after victimization?
- What is the independent contribution of crime victimization to all causes of mortality in older people?
- What role does gender play in influencing the response to crime victimization?

3. Progress Report/Preliminary Studies

In order to determine whether a records linkage between the New Haven EPESE cohort and the City of New Haven's police records was feasible, the investigators conducted a pilot record match between these disparate epidemiological and administrative data sets.... After approval from the institutional review boards at Yale and Cornell, and after development of a carefully devised confidentiality protocol, the investigators received approval from the New Haven Police Department to determine if cohort members had been reported as victims of crime.

A pilot match was undertaken for 200 randomly selected cohort members for a short segment of the follow-up period during which police records were readily available (between 1985 and 1991).... Of the 200 cohort members, there have been 86 police events in 47 cohort members over the 7-year follow-up period. 43% of these were as victims.... These pilot data demonstrate that despite potential technical and bureaucratic obstacles, a records match between the data and police records is indeed feasible.... Additionally, the match rate suggests that ample events have accrued for adequate statistical power.

4. Research Design
Study Sample
The EPESE (Established Population for Epidemiologic Studies of the Elderly) data is an observational cohort of 2,812 older adults living in New Haven who were over the age of 65 in 1982. The study population is based on a stratified cluster sample of 3,337 individuals, 82 percent of whom

responded and agreed to participate.... Members were interviewed yearly in person or by telephone between 1982 and 1990 with an additional in person interview in 1994.

New Haven Police Records
All cohort members who experienced a crime in New Haven and reported the victimization to police will be included in the records match. Typical information on a crime report includes victim characteristics, type of offense, offender characteristics, injuries sustained, and location of the incident along with other information.

Variables
As the specific aims delineate, crime victimization is both a dependent and an independent variable in this research. For the purpose of this research, a cohort member is deemed to have been a crime victim when he or she has experienced any police contact wherein their role in the crime is that of victim and a specific crime incident type is provided. Several independent variables derived from clinical experience and from the criminological literature will serve as independent variables to identify risk factors for crime victimization (dependent variable for specific aim 1) including sociodemographic (age, income, race, sex, etc.), medical (number and type of chronic conditions), functional (ADL impairment, cognitive impairment), and psychosocial (size and quality of social network, depressive symptoms).

For specific aims 2 & 3, criminal victimization will be used along with the other independent variables to predict the outcomes of custodial nursing home placement and mortality

Strategy of Analysis
The initial analysis involves the construction of time failure/survival curves wherein custodial nursing home placement will be the parameter of interest.... Subsequent multivariable analysis will include crime victimization as a time-dependent covariate, with days to nursing home placement after crime victimization as the dependent variable in Cox proportional hazards models.... To achieve the third specific aim to predict all cause mortality, Kaplan-Meier curves will be constructed for victimized and non-victimized groups, and their respective survival over the follow-up period will be compared.... Subsequent multivariable analysis is intended to determine the independent effects of crime victimization on mortality using hierarchical modeling.

5. *Human Subjects*
There is no direct contact with subjects in this research as it is a project that involves the linking of two archival data sets...the major risk in this research is violation of confidentiality with respect to being a crime victim for surviving subjects.... An extensive protocol has been developed such that in the final merged record, EPESE investigators will have no knowledge of which subjects were victims of crime and conversely, police staff will have no knowledge of which of their many crime victims are EPESE cohort members. Ironically, state statutes with respect to crime are more directly concerned with protecting the identify of the alleged perpetrator of crime. For this reason, in the matching process police staff must first ensure that a crime case has no pending legal disposition before releasing the record to the investigators for anonymous abstraction....

6. *Women and Minority Subjects*
The EPESE cohort intentionally over-samples minority subjects, over 20% of whom were non-white at cohort inception. Additionally, women outnumber men in the original cohort 1,647 to 1,143, which is typical of the demography of older adults.

Exhibit 12.2 Material and Forms Required for Research Proposal Submitted to the National Institute of Justice

(1) Standard Form (SF) 424: application for Federal Assistance
(2) Geographic Areas Affected Worksheet
(3) Assurances
(4) Certifications regarding lobbying, debarment, suspension, and other responsibility matters; and drug-free workplace requirements (one form)
(5) Disclosure of lobbying activities
(6) Budget detail worksheet
(7) Budget narrative
(8) Negotiated indirect rate agreement
(9) Names and affiliations of all key persons from applicant and subcontractor(s), advisors, consultants, and advisory board members. Include name of principal investigator, title, organizational affiliation, department (if institution of higher education, address, home, and fax.
(10) Proposal abstract: meant to serve as a succinct and accurate description of the proposed work
(11) Table of contents
(12) Program narrative or technical proposal: Applicants must concisely describe the research goals and objectives, research design, and methods for achieving the goals and objectives. The number of pages in the "program narrative" must not exceed 30 double-spaced pages (margins of a minimum of 1", and no less than 11-point font size).
(13) Privacy certificate
(14) Form 310 (Protection of Human Subjects Assurance Identification/Certification/ Declaration)
(15) Environmental assessment (if required)
(16) References
(17) Letters of cooperation from organizations collaborating in the research project
(18) Resumes
(19) Appendixes (e.g., list of previous NIJ awards, their status, and products)

convince a government agency that a research project is worth the money requested, particularly when the amount requested is large (over $500,000). And that is as it should be: Your tax dollars should be used only for research that has a high likelihood of yielding findings that are valid and useful. But whether you are proposing a smaller project to a more generous funding source or presenting a proposal to your professor, you should scrutinize the proposal carefully before submission and ask others to comment on it. Other people will often think of issues you neglected to consider, and you should allow yourself time to think about these issues and to reread and redraft the proposal. Besides, you will get no credit for having thrown together a proposal as best you could in the face of an impossible submission deadline (or class deadline).

In addition, government funding agencies such as NIMH also ask you to provide many formal statements and certificates—paperwork, paperwork, paperwork! For example, Exhibit 12.2 provides the forms and sections required in a research proposal application to the National Institute of Justice, one of the largest funding agencies for criminological research. Note that the research proposal itself is only one item (item 12) on this list. As you can see, providing the proper forms in the correct order can almost be as much work as writing the proposal itself!

Exhibit 12.3 Decisions in Research

PROBLEM FORMULATION (Chapters 1–2)

1. Developing a research question
2. Assessing researchability of the problem
3. Consulting prior research
4. Relating to social theory
5. Choosing an approach:
   Deductive? Inductive? Descriptive?
6. Reviewing research guidelines

    CHECKPOINT 1
    Alternatives: • Continue as planned.
                  • Modify the plan.
                  • STOP. Abandon the plan.

RESEARCH VALIDITY (Chapters 3–5)

7. Establishing measurement validity:
   • How are concepts defined?
   • Chooose a measurement strategy.
   • Assess available measures or develop new measures.
   • What evidence of reliability and validity is available or can be collected?
8. Establishing generalizability:
   • Was a representative sample used?
   • Are the findings applicable to particular subgroups?
   • Does the population sampled correspond to the population of interest?
9. Establishing causality:
   • What is the possibility of experimental or statistical controls?
   • How to assess the causal mechanism?
   • Consider the causal context.
10. Data required: Longitudinal or cross-sectional?
11. Units of analysis: Individuals or groups?
12. What are major possible sources of causal invalidity?

    CHECKPOINT 2
    Alternatives: • Continue as planned.
                  • Modify the plan.
                  • STOP. Abandon the plan.

RESEARCH DESIGN (Chapters 5–10)

13. Choosing a research design:
    Experimental? Survey? Participant observation?
    Historical, comparative? Multiple methods?
14. Secondary analysis? Availability of suitable data sets?
15. Assessing ethical concerns

    CHECKPOINT III
    Alternatives: • Continue as planned.
                  • Modify the plan.
                  • STOP. Abandon the plan.

(Continued)

Exhibit 12.3   (Continued)

DATA ANALYSIS (Chapter 11)

18. Choosing a statistical approach:
    - Statistics and graphs for describing data
    - Identifying relationships between variables
    - Deciding about statistical controls
    - Testing for interaction effects
    - Evaluating inferences from sample data to the population

        CHECKPOINT 4
        Alternatives: • Continue as planned.
                        • Modify the plan.
                        • STOP. Abandon the plan.

REVIEWING, PROPOSING, REPORTING RESEARCH (Chapter 12)

19. Clarifying research goals
20. Identifying the intended audience
21. Searching the literature and the Web
22. Organizing the text
23. Reviewing ethical and practical constraints

        CHECKPOINT 5
        Alternatives: • Continue as planned.
                        • Modify the plan.
                        • STOP. Abandon the plan.

When you develop a research proposal, it will help to ask yourself a series of questions like those in Exhibit 12.3 (also see Herek, 1995). This checklist is important because it is too easy to omit important details and to avoid being self-critical while rushing to put a proposal together. And it is too painful to have a proposal rejected (or to receive a low grade). It is always best to make sure the proposal covers what it should and confronts the tough issues that reviewers (or your professor) will be sure to spot early.

The series of questions in Exhibit 12.3 can serve as a map to preceding chapters in this book as well as a checklist of decisions that must be made throughout any research project. The questions are organized in five sections, each concluding with a checkpoint at which you should consider whether to proceed with the research as planned, modify the plans, or stop the project altogether. The sequential ordering of these questions obscures a bit the way they should be answered: not as single questions, one at a time, but as a unit—first as five separate stages, and then as a whole. Feel free to change your answers to earlier questions on the basis of your answers to later questions.

The Methodologist's Toolchest™

You may also find it useful when preparing a research proposal to have a computer program identify and review key decisions that you have to make. The Methodologist's

Toolchest™ (Brent & Thompson, 1996) is an expert decision support system containing detailed information on the major components of research proposals. You can review the issues that should be considered for such critical stages as designing a sample, developing measures, and choosing statistics. The software shows you what the alternatives are and asks you which one you prefer. It then can give you feedback to indicate possible consequences of your decision.

This process is represented in Exhibit 12.4. First you see the Toolchest outline of major proposal sections (Exhibit 12.4a). Then you see the different types of threats to validity that you can review, if you are interested (12.4b). Next you see some background information to help you choose a research design, and then feedback indicating the consequences of your design choice for the validity threat on which you focused (history, in the example) (12.4c). The last screens provide suggestions for reducing the threat and a quantitative rating of the extent to which your design has addressed the validity threat (12.4d, 12.4e). Of course, this information and feedback is useful only if you treat it as an additional source of suggestions, not as the ultimate authority. You may sometimes receive inappropriate advice from a system like the Toolchest, because it doesn't understand all the aspects of the research problem. You still must be in charge. Nonetheless, a structured procedure for reviewing decisions and thinking about alternatives can only help improve your proposals.

Exhibit 12.4a   Methodologist's Toolchest™

Exhibit 12.4b

Exhibit 12.4c

Exhibit 12.4d

Exhibit 12.4e

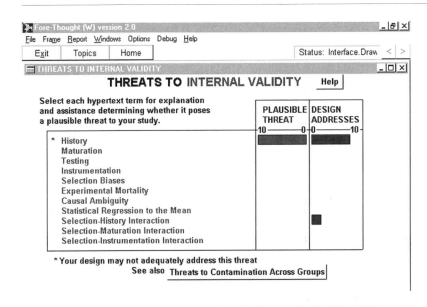

RESEARCH REPORT GOALS

The research report will present research findings and interpretations in a way that reflects some combination of the researcher's goals, the research sponsor's goals, the concerns of the research subjects, and perhaps the concerns of a wider anticipated readership. Understanding the goals of these different groups will help the researcher begin to shape the final report even at the start of the research. In designing a proposal and in negotiating access to a setting for the research, commitments often must be made to produce a particular type of report, or at least cover certain issues in the final report. As the research progresses, feedback about the research from its subjects, sponsoring agencies, collaborators, or other interested parties may suggest the importance of focusing on particular issues in the final report. Social researchers traditionally have tried to distance themselves from the concerns of such interested parties, paying attention only to what is needed to advance scientific knowledge. But in recent years, some social scientists have recommended bringing these interested parties into the research and reporting process itself.

Advance Scientific Knowledge

Most social science research reports are directed to other social scientists working in the area of study, so they reflect orientations and concerns that are shared within this community of interest. The traditional scientific approach encourages a research goal to advance scientific knowledge by providing reports to other scientists. This approach also treats value considerations as beyond the scope of science: "An empirical science cannot tell anyone what he should do but rather what he can do and under certain circumstances what he wishes to do" (Weber, 1949:54).

The idea is that developing valid knowledge about how society is organized or how we live our lives does not tell us how society should be organized or how we should live our lives. There should, as a result, be a strict separation between the determination of empirical facts and the evaluation of these facts as satisfactory or unsatisfactory (Weber, 1949:11). Social scientists must not ignore value considerations, which are viewed as a legitimate basis for selecting a research problem to study. After the research is over and a report has been written, many scientists also consider it acceptable to encourage government officials or private organizations to implement the findings. During a research project, however, value considerations are to be held in abeyance.

Shape Social Policy

Many social scientists seek to influence social policy through their writing. You have been exposed to several examples in this text, including all of the evaluation research cited in Chapter 9. These particular studies, like much policy-oriented social science research, are similar to those that aim strictly to increase knowledge. In fact, these studies might even be considered contributions to knowledge first, and to social policy debate second. What distinguishes the reports of these studies from strictly academic reports is their attention to policy implications.

Other social scientists who seek to influence social policy explicitly reject the traditional scientific, rigid distinction between facts and values (Sjoberg & Nett, 1968). Bellah and colleagues (1985) have instead proposed a model of "social science as public philosophy," in which social scientists focus explicit attention on achieving a more just society:

> Social science makes assumptions about the nature of persons, the nature of society, and the relation between persons and society. It also, whether it admits it or not, makes assumptions about good persons and a good society and considers how far these conceptions are embodied in our actual society.
>
> Social science as public philosophy, by breaking through the iron curtain between the social sciences and the humanities, becomes a form of social self-understanding or self-interpretation. . . . By probing the past as well as the present, by looking at "values" as much as at "facts," such a social science is able to make connections that are not obvious and to ask difficult questions. (p. 301)

This perspective suggests more explicit concern with public policy implications when reporting research results. But it is important to remember that we all are capable of distorting our research and our interpretations of research results to correspond to our own value preferences. The temptation to see what we want to see is enormous, and research reports cannot be deemed acceptable unless they avoid this temptation.

Organize Social Action

For the same reasons that value questions are traditionally set apart from the research process, many social scientists consider the application of research a nonscientific concern. William Foote Whyte, whose *Street Corner Society* (1943) study you encountered in Chapter 7, has criticized this belief and proposed an alternative research and reporting strategy he calls **participatory action research.** Whyte (1991:285) argues that social scientists must get "out of the academic rut" and engage in applied research to develop better understanding of social phenomena.

In participatory action research, the researcher involves some organizational members as active participants. Both the organizational members and the researcher are assumed to want to develop valid conclusions, to bring unique insights, and to desire change.

Dialogue with Research Subjects

Egon Guba and Yvonna Lincoln (1989:44–45) have carried the notion of involving research subjects and others in the design and reporting of research one step further. What they call the **constructivist paradigm** is a methodology that emphasizes the importance of exploring how different stakeholders in a social setting construct their beliefs. This approach rejects the assumption that there is a reality around us to be studied and reported on. Instead, social scientists operating in the constructivist paradigm try to develop a consensus among participants in some social process about how to understand the focus of inquiry, a program that is often evaluated. A research report will then highlight different views of the social program and explain how a consensus can be reached.

Constructivist inquiry uses an interactive research process, in which a researcher begins an evaluation in some social setting by identifying the different interest groups in that setting and the stakeholder groups. The researcher goes on to learn what each group thinks,

Exhibit 12.5 The Circular Process of Uncovering Attitudes and Beliefs

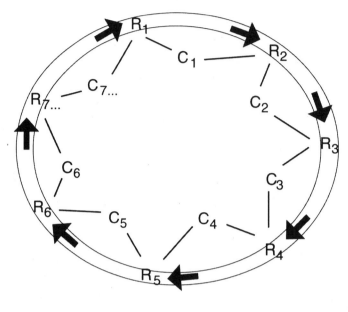

KEY: R = Respondent
      C = Construction

Source: Adapted from Guba & Lincoln, 1989:152.

and then gradually tries to develop a shared perspective on the problem being evaluated (Guba & Lincoln, 1989:42). This process involves four steps that can each be repeated many times in a given study:

1. Identify stakeholders and solicit their claims, concerns, and issues.

2. Introduce the claims, concerns, and issues of each stakeholder group to the other stakeholder groups and ask for their reactions.

3. Focus further information collection on claims, concerns, and issues about which there is disagreement among stakeholder groups.

4. Negotiate with stakeholder groups about the information collected and attempt to reach consensus on the issues about which there is disagreement.

These steps are diagrammed as a circular process in Exhibit 12.5. In this process,

. . . the constructions of a variety of individuals deliberately chosen so as to uncover widely variable viewpoints are elicited, challenged, and exposed to new information and new, more sophisticated ways of interpretation, until some level of consensus is reached (although there may be more than one focus for consensus). (Guba & Lincoln, 1989:181)

The researcher conducts an open-ended interview with the first respondent (R1) to learn about her thoughts and feelings on the subject of inquiry—her "construction" (C1). The researcher then asks this respondent to nominate a second respondent (R2), who feels very differently. The second respondent is then interviewed in the same way, but also is asked to comment on the themes raised by the previous respondent. The process continues until all major perspectives are represented, and then may be repeated again with the same set of respondents.

The final product is a case report:

> A case report is very unlike the technical reports we are accustomed to seeing in positivist inquiries. It is not a depiction of a "true" or "real" state of affairs. . . . It does not culminate in judgments, conclusions, or recommendations except insofar as these are concurred on by relevant respondents.
>
> The case report helps the reader come to a realization (in the sense of making real) not only of the states of affairs that are believed by constructors [research respondents] to exist but also of the underlying motives, feelings, and rationales leading to those beliefs. The case report is characterized by a thick description that not only clarifies the all-important context, but that makes it possible for the reader vicariously to experience it. (Guba & Lincoln, 1989:180–181)

Although this is off the beaten social scientific track, the constructivist approach provides a useful way of thinking about how to best make sense of the complexity and subjectivity of the social world. Other researchers write reports intended to influence public policy and often their findings are ignored. Such neglect would be less common if social researchers gave more attention to the different meanings attached by participants to the same events, in the spirit of constructivist case reports. The philosophy of this approach is also similar to the utilization-based evaluation research approach advanced by Patton (Chapter 9) that involves all stakeholders in the research process.

RESEARCH REPORT TYPES

Research projects designed to produce student papers and theses, applied research reports, and academic articles all have unique features that will influence the final research report. For example, student papers are written for a particular professor or for a thesis committee and often are undertaken with almost no financial resources and in the face of severe time constraints. Applied research reports are written for an organization or agency that usually also has funded the research and has expectations for a particular type of report. Journal articles are written for the larger academic community and will not be published until they are judged acceptable by some representatives of that community (e.g., after the article has gone through extensive peer review).

These unique features do not really match up so neatly with the specific types of research products. For example, a student paper that is based on a research project conducted in collaboration with a work organization may face some constraints for a project designed to produce an applied research report. An academic article may stem from an applied research project conducted for a government agency. An applied research report often can be followed by an academic article on the same topic. In fact, one research study may lead to all three types of research reports, as students write course papers or theses for professors who write both academic articles and applied research reports.

Student Papers and Theses

What is most distinctive about a student research paper or thesis is the audience for the final product—a professor or, for a thesis, a committee of professors. In light of this, it is important for you to seek feedback early and often about the progress of your research and about your professor's expectations for the final paper. Securing approval of a research proposal is usually the first step, but it should not be the last occasion for seeking advice prior to writing the final paper. Don't become too anxious for guidance, however. Professors require research projects in part so that their students can work through, at least somewhat independently, the many issues they confront. A great deal of insight into the research process can be gained this way. So balance your requests for advice with some independent decision making.

Most student research projects can draw on few resources beyond the student's own time and effort, so it is important that the research plan not be overly ambitious. Keep the paper deadline in mind when planning the project, and remember that almost every researcher tends to underestimate the time required to carry out a project.

Group Projects

Pooling your resources with those of several students in a group project can make it possible to collect much more data, but can lead to other problems. Each student's role should be clarified at the outset and written into the research proposal as a formal commitment. Group members should try to help each other out, rather than competing to do the least work possible or to receive the most recognition. Complaints about other group members should be made to the professor when things just can't be worked out among group members. Each group member should have a clear area of responsibility in the final report, and one may want to serve as the final editor.

The Thesis Committee

Students who are preparing a paper for a committee, usually at the M.A. or Ph.D. level, must be prepared to integrate the multiple perspectives and comments of committee members into a plan for a coherent final report. (The thesis committee chair should be the primary guide in this process; careful selection of faculty to serve on the committee is also important.) As much as possible, committee members should have complementary areas of expertise that are each important for the research project—perhaps one methodologist, one specialist in the primary substantive area of the thesis, and one specialist in a secondary area. Theses using data collected by service agencies or other organizations often benefit if an organizational representative is on the committee.

It is very important that you work with your committee members in an ongoing manner, both individually and collectively. In fact, it is vitally important to have a group meeting with all committee members at the beginning of the project to ensure everyone on the committee supports the research plan. Doing this will avoid obstacles that arise due to miscommunication later in the research process.

Journal Articles

It is the **peer review** process that makes preparation of an academic journal article most unique. Similar to a grant review, the journal's editor sends submitted articles to two or three experts—peers—who are asked whether the paper should be accepted more or less as is, revised and then resubmitted, or rejected. Reviewers also provide comments, sometimes quite lengthy, to explain their decision and to guide any required revisions. The process is an anonymous one at most journals: reviewers are not told the author's name, and the author is not told the reviewers' names. Although the journal editor has the final say, editors' decisions are normally based on the reviewers' comments.

This peer review process must be anticipated in designing the final report. Peer reviewers are not pulled out of a hat. They are experts in the field or fields represented in the paper and usually have published articles themselves in that field. It is critical that the author be familiar with the research literature and be able to present the research findings as a unique contribution to that literature. In most cases, this hurdle is much harder to jump with journal articles than with student papers or applied research reports. In fact, most leading journals have a rejection rate of over 90%, so the hurdle is quite high indeed. Of course, there is also a certain luck of the draw in peer review. One set of two or three reviewers may be inclined to reject an article that another set of reviewers would accept (see the next case study). But in general, the anonymous peer review process results in higher quality research reports because articles are revised prior to publication in response to the suggestions and criticisms of other experts.

Criminological and criminal justice research is published in a myriad of journals within several disciplines, including criminology, law, sociology, psychology, and economics. As a result, there is no one formatting style that all criminological literature abides by. If, for example, you are submitting your paper to a psychology-related journal, you must abide by the formatting style dictated by the *Publication Manual of the American Psychological Association.* The easiest way to determine how to format a paper for a particular journal is to examine recent volumes of the journal and format your paper accordingly. To give you a general idea of what a journal article looks like, an article in its entirety has been reprinted in Appendix C, along with an illustration of how to read a journal article.

Despite the slight variations in style across journals, there are typically seven standard sections within a journal article in addition to the title page:

1. *Abstract.* This should be a concise and nonevaluative summary of your research paper (no more than 120 words) that describes the research problem, the sample, the method, and the findings.

2. *Introduction.* The body of a paper should open with an introduction that presents the specific problem under study and describes the research strategy. Before writing this section, you should consider the following questions: What is the point of the study? How do the hypotheses and the research design relate to the problem? What are the theoretical implications of the study, and how does the study relate to previous work in the area? What are the theoretical propositions tested, and how were they derived? A good introduction answers these questions in a few paragraphs by summarizing the relevant argument and the data, giving the reader a sense of what was done and why.

3. *Literature Review.* Discuss the relevant literature in a way that relates each previous study cited to your research—not in an exhaustive historical review. Citation of and specific credit to relevant earlier works is part of the researchers' scientific and scholarly responsibility. It is essential for the growth of cumulative science. This section should demonstrate the logical continuity between previous research and the research at hand. At the end of this section, you are ready to conceptually define your variables and formally state your hypotheses.

4. *Method.* Describe in detail how the study was conducted. Such a description enables the reader to evaluate the appropriateness of your methods and the reliability and the validity of your results. It also permits experienced investigators to replicate the study if they so desire. In this section, you can include subsections that describe the sample, the independent and dependent variables, and the analytic/statistical procedure you will use to analyze the data.

5. *Results.* Summarize the results of the statistical or qualitative analyses performed on the data. It can include tables and figures that summarize findings. If statistical analyses are performed, tests of significance should also be highlighted.

6. *Discussion.* Take the opportunity to evaluate and interpret your results, particularly with respect to your original hypotheses and previous research. Here, you are free to examine and interpret your results as well as draw inferences from them. In general, this section should answer the following questions: What have I contributed to the literature here? How has my study helped to resolve the original problem? What conclusions and theoretical implications can I draw from my study? What are the limitations of my study? What are the implications for future research?

7. *References.* All citations in the manuscript must appear in the reference list, and all references must be cited in the text.

Case Study: Up Close and Personal with Peer Review

In all honesty, your first experience with the peer review process is generally not a pleasant one. In fact, your one-hundredth experience with peer review may not be a very pleasant experience. By this time, however, you will likely have experienced the positive contributions this process can have on your work.

In this section, we will give you an up-close and personal experience with the peer review process. The paper we will use as a case study was written by one of your authors (Bachman, 1996) and was published in the *Journal of Quantitative Criminology.* The title of the paper was "Victim's Perceptions of Initial Police Responses to Robbery and Aggravated Assault: Does Race Matter?"

After many revisions of the paper based on comments from colleagues (both informally and at a professional conference), the paper was submitted to the *Journal of Quantitative Criminology* in the fall of 1994. In early 1995, the editor of the journal, John Laub, gave the author an opportunity to revise and resubmit the article based on three anonymous reviewers' comments. A condensed version of these comments by each of the three reviewers is provided here:

Reviewer A: The paper is a well-framed and well-designed investigation of the relevance of race at a seldom-examined stage in official processing. It pays close attention to theory and methodological issues. Particularly well anticipated were the limitations of the data, namely, victim perceptions of police response. . . . The following should tighten the paper's focus and increase its contribution to the literature: Expand the theoretical relevance of the findings. . . . Moderate conclusions based on findings for the victim's perception of arrest. This variable, more than the others, tells us more about the police communication with victims than it does about their actual behavior. It's also more time dependent on the others; an arrest may be in the offing. . . .

Reviewer B: This manuscript is flawed in two related ways: (1) its reliance on respondent perceptions of police actions; (2) conceptual ambiguity of police response. Each flaw stems from the inappropriate use of National Crime Victimization Survey (NCVS) data. The NCVS data are poorly suited to address detailed questions about police actions. . . . the NCVS data is not representative of police or police agencies. The concept of differential police action by race cannot be meaningfully studied with a nationally representative sample of victims. . . . Variation in police responses across departments is more likely than variation across race of victim/offender. . . . What's the point of controlling for sex? Why not control for weapon use, something that might more plausibly affect police response. . . . The first part of the paper is much too long. . . . Presenting six crosstabulation tables is far too cumbersome. . . . The last complete paragraph on page 27 seems a convoluted attempt to fit results into a cherished theory. . . .

Reviewer C: This is a good paper that makes a significant contribution to the literature on the effects of race on criminal justice processing. . . . The author(s) come close to explicitly discussing the importance of differing frequencies of black on white vs. other combinations, they should flesh this out. If most offenders are in intra-racial criminal events, the observed patterns will have weighted effects on the outcomes of the overall patterns of race and police activity. They may wish to discuss this. . . . Finally, I think the author(s) should include a caveat about the data.

One thing that should be immediately apparent from these comments is the diversity of opinion; if you ask three researchers to judge a manuscript, you typically get three different opinions on its quality. This, of course, is an important part of the process. It is the best way to uncover flaws in the research design and the presentation of results. In this case, two reviewers thought the research made an important contribution to the field while the other thought it was little more than toilet paper. Despite the diversity of opinion, all three reviews helped to improve the final version of the manuscript. But would there be a final version?!?

After more statistical analyses and rewriting, another version of the manuscript was resubmitted to the journal in August of 1995. It was then sent out to the same reviewers along with one additional reviewer. In late October, it received a conditional acceptance; but the paper again had to be revised based on the reviewers' comments. Only if the reviewers' comments and concerns were adequately handled would the paper be published. More rewriting! In December, another version of the manuscript was submitted to the journal and in January of 1996, this version of the paper was finally accepted by the journal. It was published in the final 1996 volume of the journal. And you thought you had it bad when it takes a professor a few weeks to grade and provide comments on a paper! It took this research paper almost two years to finally be published—and this doesn't include the preparation time for the first draft. In the end, however, the final product was significantly better than the first draft originally submitted in 1994. And as a footnote, this was one of the better experiences this author had with publishing! A paper often gets rejected by one or two journals before it is finally accepted for publication.

Applied Reports

Unlike journal articles, applied reports are usually commissioned by a particular government agency, corporation, or nonprofit organization. As such, the most important problem that applied researchers confront is the need to produce a final report that meets the funding organization's expectations. This is called the hired gun problem. Of course, the extent to which being a hired gun is a problem varies greatly with the research orientation of the funding organization and with the nature of the research problem posed. The ideal situation is to have few constraints on the nature of the final report, but sometimes research reports are suppressed or distorted because the researcher comes to conclusions that the funding organization does not like.

Applied reports that are written in a less highly charged environment can face another problem—even when they are favorably received by the funding organization their conclusions are often ignored. This problem can be more a matter of the organization not really knowing how to use research findings than not wanting to use them. And this is not just a problem of the funding organization; many researchers are prepared only to present their findings, without giving any thought to how research findings can be translated into organizational policies or programs.

An Advisory Committee

An advisory committee can help the applied researcher avoid the problems of incompatible expectations for the final report and insufficient understanding of how to use the research results, without adopting the more engaged strategy of Whyte's participatory action research or Guba and Lincoln's constructivist inquiry. An advisory committee should be formed before the start of the project to represent the various organizational segments with stakes in the outcomes of the research. The researcher can use the committee as a source of intelligence about how particular findings may be received and as a sounding board for ideas about how the organization or agency can use research findings. Perhaps most important, an advisory committee can help the researcher work out many problems in research design, implementation, and data collection. Because an advisory committee is meant to comprise all stakeholders, it is inevitable that conflicts will arise between advisory group members. In our experience, however, these conflicts almost invariably can be used to strategize more effectively about the research design and the final product.

Advisory committees are particularly necessary for research investigating controversial issues. For example, after a study conducted in 1999 found that several death row inmates had been wrongly convicted of their crimes, the governor of Illinois placed a moratorium on all death sentences in the state. Other results of the study suggested that the death penalty was handed down unfairly—it found proportionally more minority and poor offenders were sentenced to death than whites and those who could afford hired legal counsel. This caused a great deal of media attention and calls for other states that practice the death penalty to institute similar moratoriums.

As a consequence of this attention, other states have begun to examine their implementation of the death penalty as well. Maryland is one such state. In 2001, the state legislature in Maryland commissioned Raymond Paternoster at the University of Maryland to conduct a study of its practice of the death penalty. The primary goal of the study was to determine whether the administration of the death penalty in the state was affected by the race of the defendant or victim.

At this writing, the results of the study were not yet released, but as you can imagine, they will inevitably be very controversial, regardless of what is found. For example, if racial bias is found, prosecutors may question the study's methodology. Similarly, if racial bias is not found, defense attorneys and other interest groups may also question the study's methodology. To make sure all interests are represented, Paternoster set up an advisory committee before undertaking the study. The advisory committee consists of a group of prosecutors and defense counsel who have had experience in capital cases. They will advise Professor Paternoster on several critical issues, including the years that the study should cover, the sources where information can be found, and the particularly important variables related to sentencing outcomes. Not only will the advisory committee provide substantive input into the research, but by having a broad spectrum of the legal community "on board," it also will lend credibility to the study's findings.

A BIT MORE ON WRITING

"Perfectionism is the voice of the oppressor, the enemy of the people. It will keep you cramped and insane your whole life and it is the main obstacle between you and a shitty first draft." (Lamott, 1994:28)

We often hear lamentations from students such as "It is impossible to know where to begin" or "I have a hard time getting started." To this, we say, begin wherever you are most comfortable but begin early! You don't have to start with the introduction—start in the method section if you prefer. The main point is to begin somewhere and then keep typing, keep typing, and keep typing! It is always easier to rewrite a paper than it is to write the first draft. The fine art of writing is really in the rewriting!

Those of you who began with a research proposal have a head start; you will find that the final report is much easier to write, and more adequate, if you write more material for it as you work out issues during the project. It is very disappointing to discover that something important was left out when it is too late to do anything about it. And we don't need to point out that students (and professional researchers) often leave final papers (and reports) until the last possible minute (often for understandable reasons, including other coursework and job or family responsibilities). But be forewarned: The last-minute approach does not work for research reports.

A successful report must be well-organized and clearly written. Getting to such a product is a difficult but not impossible goal. Consider the following principles formulated by experienced writers (Booth, Colomb, & Williams, 1995:150–151):

- Start with an outline.
- Respect the complexity of the task, and don't expect to write a polished draft in a linear fashion. Your thinking will develop as you write, causing you to reorganize and rewrite.

- Leave enough time for dead ends, restarts, revisions, and so on, and accept the fact that you will discard much of what you write.
- Write as fast as you comfortably can. Don't worry about spelling, grammar, and so on until you are polishing things up.
- Ask all the people whom you trust for their reactions to what you have written.
- Write as you go along, so you have notes and report segments drafted even before you focus on writing the report.

It is important to remember that no version of a manuscript is ever final. As you write, you will get new ideas about how to organize the report. Try them out. As you review the first draft, you will see many ways to improve your writing. Focus particularly on how to shorten and clarify your statements. Make sure each paragraph concerns only one topic. Remember the golden rule of good writing: Writing is revising!

Another useful tip is called reverse outlining. After you have written a first complete draft, outline it on a paragraph-by-paragraph basis, ignoring the actual section headings you used. See if the paper you wrote actually fits the outline you planned. How could the organization be improved?

And perhaps most important, leave yourself enough time so that you can revise, several times if possible, before turning in the final draft.

A well-written research report requires (to be just a bit melodramatic) blood, sweat, and tears and more time than you will at first anticipate. But the process of writing one will help you to write the next. And the issues you consider, if you approach your writing critically, will be sure to improve your subsequent research projects and sharpen your evaluations of others.

Those of you interested in a more focused discussion of writing in general (e.g., grammar, elements of style, emotional aspects of writing) should see Becker (1986), Booth et al. (1995), Mullins (1977), Strunk and White (1979), and Turabian (1967).

DATA DISPLAYS

You learned in Chapter 11 about some of the statistics that are useful in analyzing and reporting data, but there are some additional methods of presenting statistical results that can improve research reports. Combined and compressed displays are used most often in applied research reports and government documents, but they can also help to communicate findings more effectively in student papers and journal articles.

In a **combined frequency display,** the distributions for a set of conceptually similar variables with the same response categories are presented together, with common headings for the responses. For example, you could identify the variables in the leftmost column and the value labels along the top. Exhibit 12.6 is a combined display reporting the frequency distributions in percentage form for five variables that indicate the responses of high school seniors to questions about their delinquent behavior. From this table you can infer several pieces of information besides the basic distribution of self-reported delinquency. You can determine the variation in the cohort's involvement in specific types of delinquent behavior and you can also determine whether this behavior increased or decreased over time (1982–1994). For example, although the majority of seniors reported having an argument or fight with their parents, only a small percentage of students (around 20% on average) reported getting into a fight where a group of their friends were against another

Exhibit 12.6   Combined Frequency Display of High School Seniors Reporting Involvement in Selected Delinquent Activities in the Last 12 Months, United States, 1986–1994

Delinquent Activity	Class of 1987 (N = 3,179)	Class of 1988 (N = 3,361)	Class of 1989 (N = 3,350)	Class of 1990 (N = 2,879)	Class of 1991 (N = 2,627)	Class of 1992 (N = 2,569)	Class of 1993 (N = 2,690)
Argued or had a fight with either of your parents?							
Not at all	8.8	9.7	9.6	9.3	10.0	9.3	12.1
Once	8.5	8.2	8.7	8.8	8.9	8.7	9.4
Twice	12.1	11.0	10.2	12.8	12.7	11.7	12.4
3 or 4 times	23.1	23.7	23.6	23.2	24.7	24.7	20.2
5 or more times	47.5	47.5	47.9	45.9	43.6	45.5	45.9
Taken part in a fight where a group of your friends were against another group?							
Not at all	80.4	80.5	79.7	81.1	79.6	78.7	77.8
Once	11.3	11.1	12.1	11.4	11.2	11.5	11.2
Twice	4.4	4.4	3.9	4.4	5.0	4.4	5.8
3 or 4 times	2.6	2.4	2.4	1.9	2.5	3.2	2.9
5 or more times	1.4	1.6	1.8	1.2	1.7	2.2	2.3
Gotten into trouble with police because of something you did?							
Not at all	75.9	77.5	76.6	75.8	77.4	77.8	90.4
Once	15.3	12.8	13.7	13.2	12.4	11.9	5.9
Twice	4.5	6.2	5.5	6.0	6.0	5.2	1.8
3 or 4 times	2.8	2.4	2.6	3.4	2.7	3.0	1.2
5 or more times	1.5	1.1	1.6	1.6	1.5	2.2	0.6

Source: Monitoring the Future Data provided by Monitoring the Future Project, Survey Research Center, Lloyd D. Johnston, Jerald G. Bachman, and Patrick M. O'Malley, Principal Investigators. Table adapted from *Sourcebook of Criminal Justice Statistics: 1994* (NCJ-154591). Bureau of Justice Statistics, U.S. Department of Justice, Washington, D.C.

group, or getting into trouble with police (around 25% on average). You can also see that the rate of fighting behavior did not change much over the 13-year time period examined; however, the percentage of youth getting into trouble with the police actually decreased.

Compressed frequency displays can also be used to present crosstabular data and summary statistics more efficiently, by eliminating unnecessary percentages (such as those corresponding to the second value of a dichotomous variable) and by reducing the need for repetitive labels. Exhibit 12.7 presents a compressed display used to highlight the results of a survey on attitudes toward problems facing the country by several demographic characteristics. For several problem areas, respondents were asked to tell interviewers if they believed the country was "about the same today," "making progress in this area," or "losing ground" on this area. The percentages displayed are for those respondents who said that they believed the country was "losing ground" on a particular problem area.

Combined and compressed statistical displays present a large amount of data in a relatively small space. To the experienced reader of statistical reports, such displays can

Exhibit 12.7   Compressed Display of Attitudes Toward Problems Affecting the Country Today by Demographic Characteristics, 1995

Question: "Next, as I read you some problem areas, please tell me how you think each is affecting the country today. First, do you think the problem of . . . is about the same today, is the country making progress in this area, or is the country losing ground?"

	Percentage Responding "Losing Ground"		
	Crime	Families Split Up	Drugs
Sex			
Male	71%	73%	60%
Female	82	77	71
Race			
White	77	75	64
Nonwhite	77	75	79
Age			
Under 30 years	73	75	64
30 to 49 years	79	73	63
50 to 64 years	78	77	69
65 years and older	77	76	70
Education			
College graduate	71	71	64
Some college	84	79	67
High school graduate	80	77	66
Less than high school graduate	69	72	66

Source: Interview data from a nationwide sample of 1,800 adults by Princeton Survey Research Associates for the Pew Research Center for The People & The Press. Adapted from the *Sourcebook of Criminal Justice Statistics: 1995* (NCJ-158900). Bureau of Justice Statistics, U.S. Department of Justice, Washington, D.C.

convey much important information. They should be used with caution, however, because people who are not used to them may be baffled by the rows of numbers.

Graphs can also provide an efficient tool for summarizing relationships among variables. Exhibit 12.8 is from the evaluation report of the Children at Risk Program performed by Adele Harrell and her associates (Chapter 9). It presents the percentage of youth who used drugs at different times during the course of the evaluation for both treatment (youth who participated in the program) and control (youth who did not) groups. As you can readily see, compared to youth who did not receive the CAR program, fewer youth who participated in the CAR program used drugs at all times that were measured.

Another good example of the use of graphs to show relationships is provided by a Bureau of Justice Statistics report on age patterns of victims of violent crime (Perkins, 1997). Exhibit 12.9, taken from that report, shows how the rates of violent crimes have varied by particular age groups over time. You can see that whereas violent crime victimization

Exhibit 12.8 Percentage of Children at Risk and Control Youths Reporting Drug Use

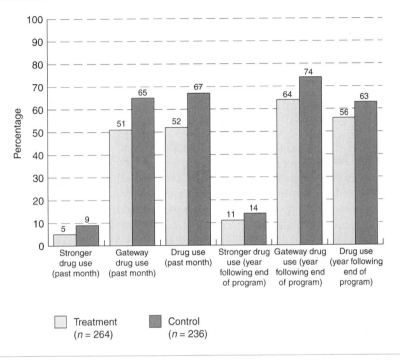

Source: Harrell, A., Cavanagh, S., & Sridharan, S. 1999. *Evaluation of the Children at Risk Program: Results 1 Year After the End of the Program* (NCJ-178914). National Institute of Justice: Research in Brief. Washington, D.C.

Exhibit 12.9 Violent Crime Rates by Age

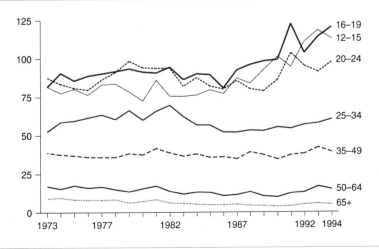

Source: Perkins, C.A. 1997. *Age Patterns of Victims of Serious Violent Crime* (NCJ-162031). Bureau of Justice Statistics. Washington, D.C.

rates have remained relatively stable over time for older age cohorts, younger age cohorts, particularly those under the age of 19, experienced increases in their rate of victimization during the late 1980s and early 1990s.

ETHICS AND REPORTING

It is at the time of reporting research results that the researcher's ethical duty to be honest becomes paramount. Here are some guidelines:

- *Provide an honest accounting of how the research was carried out and where the initial research design had to be changed.* Readers do not have to know about every change you made in your plans and each new idea you had, but they should be informed about major changes in hypotheses or research design.
- *Maintain a full record of the research project so that questions can be answered if they arise.* Many details will have to be omitted from all but the most comprehensive reports, but these omissions should not make it impossible to track down answers to specific questions about research procedures that may arise in the course of data analysis or presentation.
- *Avoid "lying with statistics" or using graphs to mislead.* (See Chapter 10.)
- *Acknowledge the sponsors of the research.* In part, this is so that others can consider whether this sponsorship may have tempted you to bias your results in some way— *and thank staff who made major contributions.*
- *Be sure that the order of authorship for coauthored reports is discussed in advance and reflects agreed-upon principles.* Be sensitive to coauthors' needs and concerns.

Ethical research reporting should not mean ineffective reporting. You need to tell a coherent story in the report and to avoid losing track of the story in a thicket of minuscule details. You do not need to report every twist and turn in the conceptualization of the research problem or the conduct of the research, but be suspicious of reports that don't seem to admit to the possibility of any room for improvement. Social science is an ongoing enterprise in which one research report makes its most valuable contribution by laying the groundwork for another, more sophisticated research project. Highlight important findings in the research report, but use the research report also to point out what are likely to be the most productive directions for future researchers.

CONCLUSION

Good critical skills are essential when evaluating research reports, whether your own or those produced by others. There are always weak points in any research, even published research. It is an indication of strength, not weakness, to recognize areas where one's own research needs to be, or could have been, improved. And it is really not just a question of sharpening our knives and going for the jugular. You need to be able to weigh the strengths and weaknesses of particular research results, and to evaluate a study in terms of its contribution to understanding its particular research question—not whether it gives a definitive answer for all time.

But this is not to say that anything goes. Much research lacks one or more of the three legs of validity—measurement validity, causal validity, or generalizability—and sometimes contributes more confusion than understanding about particular issues. Top journals generally maintain very high standards, partly because they have good critics in the review process and distinguished editors who make the final acceptance decisions. But some daily newspapers do a poor job of screening; and research reporting standards in many popular magazines, TV shows, and books are often abysmally poor. Keep your standards high and your view critical when reading research reports, but not so high or so critical that you turn away from studies that make tangible contributions to the literature—even if they don't provide definitive answers. And don't be so intimidated by the need to maintain high standards that you shrink from taking advantage of opportunities to conduct research yourself.

The growth of social science methods from infancy to adolescence, perhaps to young adulthood, ranks as a key intellectual accomplishment of the 20th century. Opinions about the causes and consequences of crime no longer need depend on the scattered impressions of individuals, and criminal justice policies can be shaped by systematic evidence of their effectiveness.

Of course, social research methods are no more useful than the commitment of the researchers to their proper application. Research methods, like all knowledge, can be used poorly or well, for good purposes or bad, when appropriate or not. A claim that a belief is based on social science research in itself provides no extra credibility. As you have learned throughout this book, we must first learn which methods were used, how they were applied, and whether interpretations square with the evidence. To investigate the social world, we must keep in mind the lessons of research methods.

KEY TERMS

Combined frequency display	Participatory action research
Compressed display	Peer review
Constructivist paradigm	

HIGHLIGHTS

- Proposal writing should be a time for clarifying the research problem, reviewing the literature, and thinking ahead about the report that will be required.

- Relations with research subjects and consumers should be developed in a manner that achieves key research goals and preparation of an effective research report. The traditional scientific approach of minimizing the involvement of research subjects and consumers in research decisions has been challenged by proponents of participatory action research and adherents of the constructivist paradigm.

- Different types of reports typically pose different problems. Authors of student papers must be guided in part by the expectations of their professor. Thesis writers have to meet the requirements of different committee members, but can benefit greatly from the areas of expertise represented on a typical thesis committee. Applied researchers are constrained by the expectations of the research sponsor; an advisory committee from the applied setting can help to avoid problems. Journal articles must pass a peer review by other social scientists and often are much improved in the process.

- Research reports should include an introductory statement of the research problem, a literature review, a methodology section, a findings section with pertinent data displays, and a conclusions section that identifies any weaknesses in the research design and points out implications for future research and theorizing. This basic report format should be modified according to the needs of a particular audience.

- All reports should be revised several times and critiqued by others before they are presented in final form.

- Some of the data in many reports can be displayed more efficiently by using combined and compressed statistical displays.

- The central ethical concern in research reporting is to be honest. This honesty should include providing a truthful accounting of how the research was carried out, maintaining a full record about the project, using appropriate statistics and graphs, acknowledging the research sponsors, and being sensitive to the perspectives of coauthors.

EXERCISES

1. Select a recent article published in a peer-reviewed criminological journal and answer the following questions: How effective is the article in conveying the design and findings of the research? Could the article's organization be improved at all? Are there bases for disagreement about the interpretation of the findings?

2. Formulate a research problem, review the decision checklist (Exhibit 12.3), and write a research proposal. You will find that this is a major project, so you should attempt it only if you will have a month or more to work on it. Alternatively, just answer selected questions from the decision checklist about a research question you would like to pursue.

3. Call a local criminal justice official and arrange for an interview. Ask the official about his or her experience with applied research reports and his conclusions about the value of social research and the best techniques for reporting to practitioners.

4. Rate four criminological journal articles for overall quality of the research and for effectiveness of the writing and data displays. Discuss how each could have been improved.

5. How firm a foundation do social research methods provide for understanding the social world? Stage an in-class debate, with the pro and con arguments focusing on the variability of social research findings across different social contexts and the difficulty of understanding human subjectivity.

DEVELOPING A RESEARCH PROPOSAL

Now it's time to bring all the elements of your proposal together.

1. Organize the proposal material you wrote for previous chapters in a logical order. Based on your research question, select the most appropriate research method as your primary method (Chapters 5–10).

2. To add a multiple method component to your research design, select another research method that could add knowledge about your research question.

3. Rewrite the entire proposal, adding an introduction. Also add sections that outline a budget and state the limitations of your study.

WEB EXERCISES

1. Go to the National Science Foundation's Law and Social Science Program Web site at www.nsf.gov/sbe/ses/law/start.htm. What are the components that the National Science Foundation's Law and Social Science Program looks for in a proposed piece of research? Write a detailed outline for a research proposal to study a subject of your choice to be submitted to the National Science Foundation for funding.

2. Go to the Ethics, Public Policy, and Public Administration site at http://plsc.uark.edu/book/ books/ethics/index.htm. Choose "Cases" and then "Integrity and Separations" (#14). Read the case "Integrity and Separations." Briefly describe the issues surrounding social science research, methods, reporting research results, and ethics in this case. Now return to the home page of the Ethics site. Choose "Set of Questions" and answer the "Questions for Consideration" in terms of the case "Integrity and Separations."

3. Using the Web, find five different examples of criminological research projects that have been completed. Briefly describe each. How does each differ in its approach to reporting the research results? Whom do you think the author(s) of each is "reporting" to (i.e., who is the "audience")? How do you think the predicted audience has helped to shape the author's approach to reporting the results? Be sure to note the Web sites at which you located each of your five examples.

SPSS EXERCISES

1. How do friends' opinions and support for delinquent activities influence levels of delinquency among youth? A combined frequency display of the distributions of a series of YOUTH.POR variables will help you to answer this question.
   a. Obtain a frequency distribution and descriptive statistics for friends' attitudes toward delinquent acts index (FROPINON), index of friends' engagement in delinquent acts (FRBEHAVE), and the delinquency index at time 11 (DELINQ1).
   b. Using the mean as the measure of center, recode the three indexes to measure low and high levels of each variable (e.g., all values below the mean represent low levels of a given variable and all values above the mean represent high levels of the given variable).
   c. Use the percentages in these distributions to prepare a combined frequency display.
   d. Discuss what you have learned about the influence of friends' delinquent tendencies on delinquency levels among youth.

2. Repeat Exercise 1 using the parental index (PARNT2), certainty of punishment index (CERTAIN), and the morality index (MORAL). Note: The scale for the variables of interest in this exercise are measured opposite the delinquency scale. For example, high scores on the parental index indicate high parental supervision, which in theory should correspond with low levels of delinquency. Be sure to place the percentages for DELINQ1 accordingly (make note of the placement of the percentiles for this variable or create more intuitive column labels).

Appendix A

FINDING INFORMATION

ELIZABETH SCHNEIDER

RUSSELL K. SCHUTT

All research is conducted in order to "find information" in some sense, but the focus of this section is more specifically about finding information to inform a central research project. This has often been termed "searching the literature," but the popularity of the World Wide Web for finding information requires that we broaden our focus beyond the traditional search of the published literature. It may sound trite, but we do indeed live in an "information age," with an unprecedented amount of information of many types available to us with relatively little effort. Learning how to locate and use that information efficiently has become a prerequisite for social science.

SEARCHING THE LITERATURE

It is most important to search the literature before we begin a research study. A good literature review may reveal that the research problem already has been adequately investigated; it may highlight particular aspects of the research problem most in need of further investigation; or it may suggest that the planned research design is not appropriate for the problem chosen. It can highlight the strong and weak points of related theories. When we review previous research about our research question, we may learn about weaknesses in our measures, complexities in our research problem, and possible difficulties in data collection. The more of these problems that can be taken into account before, rather than after, data are collected, the better the final research product will be. Even when the rush to "find out" what people think or are doing creates pressure to just go out and ask or observe, it is important to take the time to search the literature and try to reap the benefit of prior investigations.

But the social science literature is not just a source for guidance at the start of an investigation. During a study, questions will arise that can be answered by careful reading of earlier research. After data collection has ceased, reviewing the literature can help to develop new insights into patterns in the data. Research articles published since a project began may suggest new hypotheses or questions to explore.

The best way of searching the literature will be determined in part by what library and bibliographic resources are available to you, but a brief review of some basic procedures and alternative strategies will help you get started on a productive search.

Preparing the Search

You should formulate a research question before you begin the search, although the question may change after you begin. Identify the question's parts and subparts and any related issues that you think might play an important role in the research. List the authors of relevant studies you are aware of, possible keywords that might specify the subject for your search, and perhaps the most important journals that you are concerned with checking. For example, if your research question is, "What is the effect of informal social control on crime?" you might consider searching the literature electronically for studies that mentioned "informal social control" and "crime" or "crime rate" or "violence" and "arrest." If you are concerned with more specific aspects of this question, you should also include the relevant words in your list, such as "family" or "community policing" or even "Northeast."

Conducting the Search

Now you are ready to begin searching the literature. You should check for relevant books in your library and perhaps in the other college libraries in your area. This usually means conducting a search of an online catalog using a list of subject terms. But most scientific research is published in journal articles so that research results can quickly be disseminated to other scientists. The primary focus of your search must therefore be the journal literature.

The journal literature can be searched through paper indexes of research articles that include their abstracts (summaries), such as *Sociological Abstracts* and *Psychological Abstracts,* or using the *Social Science Citation Index,* in which you can find the articles that have cited a particular journal article or book. Articles can be searched in these compilations by subject and by standard indexing keywords, as well as by author, title, journal, and year.

Searching a computerized bibliographic database is by far the most efficient search strategy. The specifics of a database search will vary among libraries and according to your own computer resources (check with your librarian for help). Many libraries provide computerized versions of resources such as *Sociological Abstracts* on CD-ROM and now, more commonly, online via the Internet. Later in this appendix there will be a discussion about searching the Web for information. However, it is important that you start your research using bibliographic databases and then proceed to the Web for supplemental information. The information in databases like *Sociological Abstracts* has been subjected to some type of peer review process prior to being included and indexed in the database; there is no review for much of the information posted on the Web.

After you have accessed the chosen index, either through a computer or in its paper version, you can locate the published articles pertaining to topics identified by your subject terms.

Exhibit A.1   A Search on *Sociological Abstracts Online*

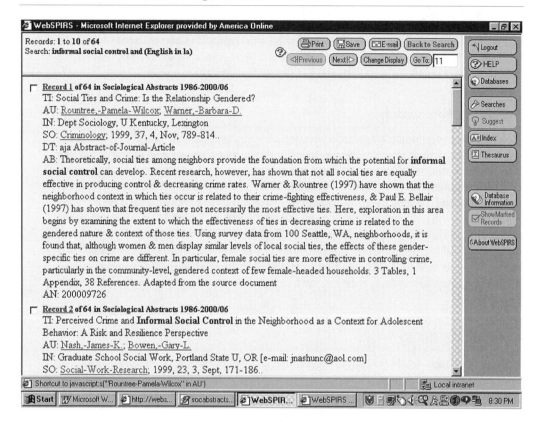

Choose your subject terms very carefully. A good rule is to cast a net wide enough to catch most of the relevant articles with your key terms but not so wide that it identifies many useless citations. For example, a search for "informal social control" would be more successful than a search for "control." You should give most attention to articles published in the leading journals in the field. Your professor can help you identify them. In any case, if you are searching a popular topic, you will need to spend a fair amount of time whittling down the list of citations.

Exhibit A.1 shows the results of a search for articles on "informal social control" in *Sociological Abstracts Online* covering the years 1986 through June 2000 (the database goes back to 1966). Our search for "informal social control" was very straightforward, resulting in 64 English language documents.

Many other bibliographic databases are available. Check with your library, concentrate on the one or two databases that your instructor recommends as most appropriate for your discipline, and try not to get swamped!

One limitation of online databases is that some of them include only relatively recently published sources, so you may have to search for relevant sources in paper volumes or in other computerized sources. A second problem with computerized searching can be the sheer size of the resulting bibliography. For example, searching for "social capital" resulted in 984 citations in *Sociological Abstracts*, 1986–2002. Depending on the database you are working with and the purposes of your search, you may want to limit your search to English language publications, to journal articles rather than conference papers or dissertations (both of which are more difficult to acquire), and to materials published in recent years. Often you should use a more complex strategy that limits your subject search to articles containing certain combinations of words or phrases.

Checking the Results

Now it is time to find the actual articles—and find them you must. You may be tempted to write up a "review" of the literature just based on reading the abstracts, but you will be selling yourself short. Many crucial details about methods, findings, and theoretical implications will be found only in the body of the article. Remember that the authors themselves write the abstracts for their articles, so they may present a sanitized, as well as a very partial, summary of the research in the abstract. To understand, critique, and really benefit from previous research studies, you must read the articles. Don't stop with the articles you identified in your initial search of the *Abstracts* or another index. Always check the bibliographies of the articles that you read for additional relevant sources, and then expand your literature search by reading those articles and books. Continue this process as long as it identifies new and useful sources. You will be surprised (we always are) at how many important articles your initial search missed.

If you have done your job well, you will have more than enough literature as background for your own research, unless it is on a very obscure topic. (Of course, your search also will be limited by library holdings you have access to and perhaps by the time required to order copies of conference papers and dissertations you find in your search.) At this point, your main concern is to construct a coherent framework in which to develop your research problem, drawing as many lessons as you can from previous research. You may use the literature to identify a useful theory and hypotheses to be reexamined, to find inadequately studied specific research questions, to explicate the disputes about your research question, or to summarize the major findings of prior research. Be sure to take notes on each article you read, organizing your notes into the standard sections: theory, methods, findings, conclusions. In any case, write the literature review so that it contributes to your study in some concrete way, and try to avoid a common problem of beginning researchers: Don't feel that you have to discuss an article in your review just because you have read it. Be judicious. You are conducting only one study of one issue, and if you try to relate it to everything that's been studied about related topics it will obscure the value of that study. Don't be diverted from your central concerns by tangential points in other studies.

In this "information age," you should not think of searching the literature as a one-time-only venture—something that you leave behind as you move on to your *real* research. You may encounter new questions or unanticipated problems as you conduct your research or as you burrow deeper into the research of others. Searching the literature to find out what others have found in response to these questions or what steps they have taken to resolve these problems can yield substantial improvements in your own research. There is so much literature on so many topics that it often is not possible to figure out in advance every subject you should search the literature for or what type of search will be most beneficial.

Another reason to make searching the literature an ongoing project is that the literature is always growing. During the course of one research study, whether it takes only one semester or several years, new findings will be published and relevant questions will be debated. Staying attuned to the literature and checking it at least when you are writing up your findings may save your study from being outdated. Of course, this does not make life any easier for researchers. For example, one of your authors was registered for a time with a service that every week sent citations of new journal articles on homelessness to his electronic mailbox. Most were not very important, but even looking over the abstracts for between 5 and 15 new articles each week is quite a chore—that's part of the price we pay for living in the information age!

SEARCHING THE WEB

The World Wide Web and other services available through the Internet provide tools for acquiring vast amounts of information of many different sorts. With the World Wide Web you can search the holdings of libraries around the country as well as the types of bibliographic databases that we have just described. You can also access the complete text of government reports and some conference papers, the text of articles from many newspapers, statements of local government policies, and postings of advocacy groups and individuals on topics of interest. But, it is important to remember that you may also end up with advertisements and third-grade homework assignments when searching the Web.

Connecting to the Web today is relatively simple, but the technology and options available to you are changing very quickly. We recommend talking to a librarian or Information Systems staff member at your school to learn their recommendations or requirements for connecting to the Web.

There are three basic strategies for finding information through the Web: direct addressing, browsing, and searching. For some purposes, you will need to use only one strategy. For other purposes, you will want to use all three.

Direct Addressing

Every Web information source is identified by an address (a uniform resource locator, or URL). If you know the URL of the information source(s) you want to use, you can instruct your browser to go directly to that source. This is by far the most efficient strategy for acquiring information on the Web. Once you have connected to a site, your Internet browser can save the URL as a Bookmark or Favorite.

You may be interested in sites such as those of professional organizations, universities, government publications, and online journals. The American Sociological Association's Web site is www.asanet.org. It lists publications and includes links to sources of social science data. The URL www.annurev.org will help you find abstracts from all volumes of the *Annual Review of Sociology*. This site allows you to download the full text of articles.

Browsing

Many Web sites maintain lists of URLs that pertain to their site or that have been selected because of their relevance and quality. When you visit one of these sites, you can browse their list of related URLs and then go directly to one of these other sites. If you share the interests of the person or organization that maintains such a list, and if they keep their URL list up-to-date, these sites can make Web searches much more efficient. Many government agencies and professional organizations, and some universities and academic departments, now maintain URL lists as part of their own Web sites. For example, the International Sociological Association's Web site, www.ucm.es/info/isa/servers.htm, provides search aids, lists of professional associations, URLs for sociology departments, university catalogs, and data archives. The Web pages of college and university libraries are good places to visit because librarians routinely develop and update lists of recommended Web sites covering many disciplines.

Searching

Search engines are programs that crawl the Web, index its resources (with URLs), and then let you search their database for resources on topics of interest. A few of the popular search engines available today are All the Web, Alta Vista, Google, Infoseek, Lycos, and Yahoo. When using search engines, keep in mind that not all search engines are the same:

- Search engines vary in size.
- Search engines crawl different sites on the Web and so will yield different results.
- Search engines use their own procedures for identifying and indexing Web resources and vary in what type of information is included. For example, some include newspapers whereas others do not.
- Search engines have their own searching syntax and relevance ranking system. You can't jump from one to another and expect it to work the same way.
- No single search engine covers more than one-third of the pages on the Web, and it takes most search engines six months or more to find new Web pages. (Davis, 1999).

Search engines usually provide instructions for basic and advanced searching and it is important to read them. For example, Alta Vista defaults to "or" when two or more terms are put in the search box, so only one of the terms has to appear in a document to be retrieved. Google, on the other hand, defaults to "and," so both terms must show up in a document. Obviously, your search results in these two engines will look very different.

Most search engines perform phrase searching by requiring the search terms to be put in quotation marks. Phrase searching is useful when you want the words you are searching for to be next to each other, such as when you are looking for a concept or a person's name. This is a very effective way to narrow your focus and reduce the number of documents you retrieve. Searching for "informal social control" on Google produced 552 sites, compared to the 234,000 sites retrieved when Google searched informal *and* social *and* control. When searching for names remember to search in both normal and inverted order (i.e., "Russell K Schutt" and "Schutt Russell K."). Including or omitting a middle initial will also affect your search results.

It is a good idea to be well acquainted with two or three search engines; you can rarely rely on just one to meet your needs because all search engines combined cover only about 60% of the Web (Davis, 1999). Your librarian will be able to give you up-to-date information about search engines and their features, advantages, and disadvantages. You can also use metasearch engines such as Dogpile and Metacrawler that offer the advantage of

Exhibit A.2   A Search on "Informal Social Control"

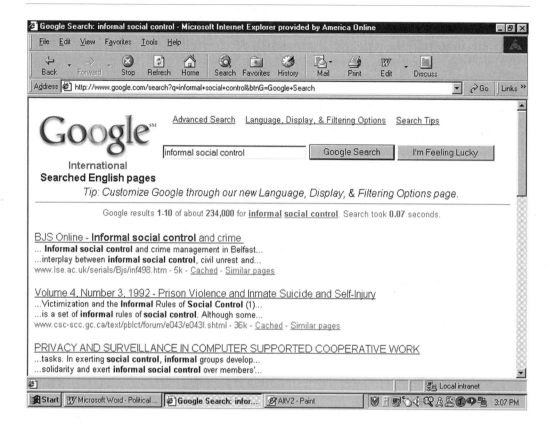

searching numerous search engines at one time. The main disadvantage of metasearch engines is that because different search engines use different searching syntax, searching multiple engines simultaneously may compromise your results.

Exhibit A.2 shows the results from a search we performed on the Web for "informal social control" using Internet Explorer 5.0 as our Web browser and Google as our search engine. You can in the exhibit the framework provided by a Web browser: a box in which you can type a URL for direct addressing; arrows to click to go back or forward between screens; menu items that allow you to edit, download, or print a file; and a Favorites button that you can use to store frequently accessed URLs. (Learning how to organize your Favorites or Bookmarks for quick and convenient use is another skill worth acquiring, but one that will not be taught here.)

Within the Internet Explorer window we find the first information provided by Google: a count of the number of sites found, an annotated list of all the sites, and marginal links to related (or unrelated) sources or advertisements. We also are presented a list of resources that are ordered by a relevancy ranking system.

This screen illustrates the first problem that you may encounter when searching the Web: the sheer quantity of resources that are available. It is a much bigger problem than when searching bibliographic databases. Google, defaulting to using "and" as a connector, found 234,000 documents. Ready to begin? Fortunately, as already discussed, most search engines provide you with "intelligent search" features that help you limit your search to the types of sources in which you are really interested. Clearly that's the approach you would have to take here, and it is well worth your while to invest a little time up front to learn about these features. Remember, a phrase search for "informal social control" produced only 552 documents—a notable improvement. On the Web, less is usually more.

A search on the Web will retrieve information in a variety of formats; some of which are identified below:

- *Newspaper articles*—For example, we found a link to an article that was published in the *Globe and Mail* (Toronto, Ontario).

- *Government policies*—You can find government policies and publications ranging from those done at the city or town level to those written by foreign governments. In our search, we found a book chapter that was published by the National Institute of Justice.

- *Presented papers*—You can often find the complete copy of a formal presentation that was given at a meeting or conference.

- *Classroom lecture notes and outlines; listings from college catalogs*—These are pretty straightforward.

- *Commercial advertisements*—Advertising abounds on the Web and it is especially prolific on search engine pages. Your search engine will even retrieve ads from the Web and list them as results of your search! The boundaries between academic, nonprofit, and commercial information have become very porous.

Remember the following warnings when you conduct searches on the Web:

- *Clarify your goals*—Before you begin the search, jot down the terms that you think you need to search for and a statement of what you want to accomplish with your search. Then you will have a sense of what to look for and what to ignore.

- *Use the best technology*—Take advantage of the more sophisticated search options available to refine your search so that it focuses on what you are really looking for.

- *Quality is not guaranteed*—Anyone can post almost anything, so the accuracy and adequacy of the information you find are always suspect. There's no journal editor or librarian to evaluate quality and relevance.

- *Anticipate change*—Web sites that are not maintained by stable organizations can come and go very quickly. Any search will result in attempts to link to some URLs that no longer exist.

- *One size does not fit all*—Different search engines use different procedures for identifying and indexing Web sites. Some attempt to be all-inclusive whereas others aim to be selective. As a result, you can get different results from different search engines even though you are searching for exactly the same terms. Try to read recent reviews of available search engines to learn how they work before deciding which one to use.

- *Be concerned about generalizability*—You might be tempted to characterize police department policies by summarizing the documents you find at police department Web sites. But how many police departments are there? How many have posted their policies on the Web? Are these policies representative of all police departments? In order to answer all these questions you would have to conduct a research project just on the Web sites themselves.

- *Evaluation, evaluation, evaluation*—As you've already seen, there's a lot of stuff out there, so how do you know what's good? There is help out there in the form of Web sites that contain excellent advice and pointers on how to pick out the good from the bad. You can find one example at www.library.cornell.edu/okuref/ research/webeval/html.

- *Avoid Web addiction*—Another danger of the extraordinary quantity of information available on the Web is that one search will lead to another and another and. . . . There are always more possibilities to explore and one more interesting source to check. Establish boundaries of time and effort to avoid the risk of losing all sense of proportion.

- *Cite your sources*—Using text or images from Web sources without attribution is just as much plagiarism as copying someone else's work from a book or article and pretending that it is your own. Record the Web address (URL), the name of the information provider, and the date for any site from which you obtain material. Include this information in a footnote to the material that you use in a paper. You can find detailed instructions at www.ipl. org/div/farq/netciteFARQ.html.

Appendix B

QUESTIONS TO ASK ABOUT A RESEARCH ARTICLE

1. What is the basic research question or problem? Try to state it in just one sentence. (Chapter 2)

2. Is the purpose of the study explanatory, evaluative, exploratory, or descriptive? Did the study have more than one purpose? (Chapter 1)

3. Was the theoretical framework presented? What was it? Did it seem appropriate for the research question addressed? Can you think of a different theoretical perspective that might have been used? (Chapter 2)

4. What prior literature was reviewed? Was it relevant to the research problem? To the theoretical framework? Does the literature review appear to be adequate? Are you aware of (or can you locate) any important omitted studies? (Chapter 2)

5. How well did the study live up to the guidelines for science? Do you need additional information in any areas to evaluate the study? To replicate it? (Chapter 2)

6. Did the study seem consistent with current ethical standards? Were any trade-offs made between different ethical guidelines? Was an appropriate balance struck between adherence to ethical standards and use of the most rigorous scientific practices? (Chapter 2)

7. What were the major concepts in the research? How, and how clearly, were they defined? Were some concepts treated as unidimensional that you think might best be thought of as multidimensional? (Chapter 3)

8. Were any hypotheses stated? Were these hypotheses justified adequately in terms of the theoretical framework? In terms of prior research? (Chapter 2)

9. What were the independent and dependent variables in the hypothesis or hypotheses? Did these variables reflect the theoretical concepts as intended? What direction of association was hypothesized? Were any other variables identified as potentially important? (Chapter 2)

10. Did the instruments used—the measures of the variables—seem valid and reliable? How did the author attempt to establish this? Could any more have been done in the study to establish measurement validity? (Chapter 3)

11. What were the units of analysis? Were they appropriate for the research question? If some groups were the units of analysis, were any statements made at any point that are open to the ecological fallacy? If individuals were the units of analysis, were any statements made at any point that suggest reductionist reasoning? (Chapter 5)

12. Was the study design cross-sectional or longitudinal, or did it use both types of data? If the design was longitudinal, what type of longitudinal design was it? Could the longitudinal design have been improved in any way, as by collecting panel data rather than trend data, or by decreasing the dropout rate in a panel design? If cross-sectional data were used, could the research question have been addressed more effectively with the longitudinal data? (Chapter 5)

13. Were any causal assertions made or implied in the hypotheses or in subsequent discussion? What approach was used to demonstrate the existence of causal effects? Were all three criteria for establishing causal relationships addressed? What, if any, variables were controlled in the analysis to reduce the risk of spurious relationships? Should any other variables have been measured and controlled? How satisfied are you with the internal validity of the conclusions? (Chapter 5)

14. Was a sample or the entire population of elements used in the study? What type of sample was selected? Was a probability sampling method used? Did the authors think the sample was generally representative of the population from which it was drawn? Do you? How would you evaluate the likely generalizability of the findings to other populations? (Chapter 4)

15. Was the response rate or participation rate reported? Does it appear likely that those who did not respond or participate were markedly different from those who did participate? Why or why not? Did the author(s) adequately discuss this issue? (Chapters 4, 6)

16. Was an experimental, survey, participant observation, or some other research design used? How well was this design suited to the research question posed and the specific hypotheses tested, if any? Why do you suppose the author(s) chose this particular design? How was the design modified in response to research constraints? How was it modified in order to take advantage of research opportunities? (Chapters 5, 9)

17. Was an evaluation research design used? Which type was it? What was the primary purpose of the evaluation? (Chapter 9)

18. Were multiple methods used? Were findings obtained with different methods complementary? (Chapter 10)

19. Was any attention given to social context? To biological processes? If so, what did this add? If not, would it have improved the study? Explain. (Chapters 5, 10)

20. Summarize the findings. How clearly were statistical and/or qualitative data presented and discussed? Were the results substantively important? (Chapters 11, 12)

21. Did the author(s) adequately represent the findings in the discussion and/or conclusions sections? Were conclusions well grounded in the findings? Are any other interpretations possible? (Chapter 12)

22. Compare the study to others addressing the same research question. Did the study yield additional insights? In what ways was the study design more or less adequate than the design of previous research? (Chapters 2, 10, 12)

23. What additional research questions and hypotheses are suggested by the study's results? What light did the study shed on the theoretical framework used? On social policy questions? (Chapters 2, 10, 12)

Appendix C

HOW TO READ
A RESEARCH ARTICLE

The discussions of research articles throughout the text may provide all the guidance you need to read and critique research on your own. But reading about an article in bits and pieces in order to learn about particular methodologies is not quite the same as reading an article in its entirety in order to learn what the research discovered. The goal of this appendix is to walk you through an entire research article, answering the review questions introduced in Appendix B. Of course, this is only one article, and our "walk" will take different turns from one taken by a review of other articles, but after this review you should feel more confident when reading other research articles on your own.

For this example, we will use an article by Alarid, Burton, and Cullen (2000) on gender and crime among felony offenders (reprinted in this volume on pp. C-8–C-31). It focuses on a topic important to explaining the similarities and differences between male and female offending patterns as well as to questions of the generalizability of central criminological theoretical perspectives. Moreover, the article is published in a reputable criminological journal, the *Journal of Research in Crime and Delinquency,* indicating the article makes an important contribution to what is known about the etiology of criminal offending across gender groups.

We have reproduced below each of the article review questions from Appendix B, followed by our answers to them. After each question, we indicate the article page or pages that we are referring to. You can also follow our review by reading through the article itself and noting our comments.

1. *What is the basic research question or problem? Try to state it in just one sentence.* (Chapter 2)

The clearest statement of the research question actually consists of two questions: "[Can] social control and differential association theories . . . help account for participation in crime among young adult male and female felons?" (p. 174 in the original article). Prior to this point, the authors focus on the research problem, describing the limitations of past research and why exploring social control and differential association theories across gender groups among felony offenders is important.

2. *Is the purpose of the study explanatory, evaluative, exploratory, or descriptive? Did the study have more than one purpose?* (Chapter 1)

This study is exploratory in nature. The literature review (pp. 171–174) makes it clear that the primary purpose of this research is exploratory since new ground is being covered based on the limitations of past research. In addition, the problem statement indicates the exploratory character of the study: It "attempts to test the generality of social control and differential association theories to a population that has been infrequently studied" (p. 173).

3. *Was the theoretical framework presented? What was it? Did it seem appropriate for the research question addressed? Can you think of a different theoretical perspective that might have been used?* (Chapter 2)

This study uses two theoretical perspectives, "social control" and "differential association." This framework is very appropriate for the research questions addressed because this study explores the applicability of these theories to adult populations and their generalizability across gender groups. Because the research question focuses specifically on the applicability and generalizability of these specific theoretical perspectives, no other theoretical framework would be applicable.

4. *What prior literature was reviewed? Was it relevant to the research problem? To the theoretical framework? Does the literature review appear to be adequate? Are you aware of (or can you locate) any important omitted studies?* (Chapter 2)

Literature is reviewed from the article's first page until the "method" section (pp. 171–174). All the literature seems relevant to the particular problem as well as the general theoretical framework. The first few paragraphs generalize the findings of several studies that measures of both theories are related to criminal involvement (pp. 171–172). The authors then discuss the limited focus of previous studies and their rationale for selecting social control and differential association as their focus for this study (pp. 172–174). We leave it to you to find out whether any important studies were omitted.

5. *How well did the study live up to the guidelines for science? Do you need additional information in any areas to evaluate the study? To replicate it?* (Chapter 2)

It would be best to return to this question after reading the whole article. The study clearly involves a test of ideas against empirical reality to the extent that reality could be measured; it was carried out systematically and disclosed, as far as we can tell. Because the authors used a sample of newly incarcerated felons, it may be difficult for others to replicate the authors' findings. Drawing from previous research, the authors make some general assumptions about what factors best measure social control and differential association (p. 177). However, in previous studies, those factors measuring social control and differential association have been applied primarily to juvenile populations (p. 172). Intuitively, the same measures or indicators may not be applicable to adult populations (e.g., parental attachment and peer attachment), but we have no empirical evidence of this. The authors also assume respondents' reports of past criminal behavior are valid (pp. 177–178). It appears these are reasonable assumptions, but they are unproved assumptions that could be challenged. This is not in itself a criticism of the research, since some assumptions must be made in any study. The authors specified the meaning of key terms, as required in scientific research. The authors did search for regularities or patterns in their data, thus living up to another guideline. A skeptical stance toward current knowledge is apparent in the literature review and in the authors' claim that "social control and differential association theory appear to have general effects" on young adult felons and across gender groups (pp. 189–190). They encourage the development of new theories but emphasize the importance of "older" theoretical perspectives and their application to underresearched topics (p. 192). The study thus seems to exemplify adherence to basic scientific guidelines and to be very replicable.

6. *Did the study seem consistent with current ethical standards? Were any trade-offs made between different ethical guidelines? Was an appropriate balance struck between adherence to ethical standards and use of the most rigorous scientific practices?* (Chapter 2)

To the best of our knowledge, the study was consistent with current ethical standards. "All data were collected directly from the participants themselves" (p. 175). In accordance with the ASA code of ethics, participation in the study was voluntary, and the participants gave their informed consent to participate. The reporting seems honest and open. The original survey used by the authors is not likely to have violated any ethical guidelines concerning the treatment of human subjects, although it would be necessary to inspect the survey instrument itself to evaluate this.

7. *What were the major concepts in the research? How, and how clearly, were they defined? Were some concepts treated as unidimensional that you think might best be thought of as multidimensional?* (Chapter 3)

There are two key concepts in this study, social control and differential association. These concepts are the focus of the study and are discussed at length. These concepts, however, were not defined so that a layperson would understand what these concepts mean.

8. *Were any hypotheses stated? Were these hypotheses justified adequately in terms of the theoretical framework? In terms of prior research?* (Chapter 2)

Three hypotheses are stated, although they are labeled as theoretical predictions, which are derived from previous research (p. 173). The first hypothesis is that social control will account for variation in offending across gender groups. The second hypothesis is that differential association will account for variation in offending across gender groups. Finally, the third hypothesis is that the effect of the competing theory will be spurious.

9. *What were the independent and dependent variables in the hypothesis(es)? Did these variables reflect the theoretical concepts as intended? What direction of association was hypothesized? Were any other variables identified as potentially important?* (Chapter 2)

The dependent variable for this study is past criminal activity. For purposes of analysis, past criminal behavior is divided into three subscales resulting in four dependent variables: general crime (the total of all criminal activities), violent crime, property crime, and drug crime (p. 177). There are eight independent variables included in this study. The independent variables for the first hypothesis include five social control indicators. These include marital/partner attachment (0 = not married/unattached and 1 = married/attached), attachment to parents (a three-item composite index, higher values represent stronger attachment), attachment to friends (a two-item index, higher values represent stronger attachment), involvement in conventional activities (a two-item index measuring how much free time individual has, higher values represent more free time), and moral belief in the law (measured by a two-item index with higher values representing stronger belief) (pp. 178–180).

The independent variables for the second hypothesis include three indicators of differential association. These include individual definitions toward crime (a five-item index, higher values represent greater tolerance of criminal behavior), others' definitions toward crime (a three-item index, higher values represent greater association with individuals who hold favorable definition toward violating the law), and criminal friends (continuous variable indicating the number of close friends who have broken the law) (pp. 180–182).

Can you identify the variables in the final hypothesis?

10. *Did the instruments used—the measures of the variables—seem valid and reliable? How did the author attempt to establish this? Could any more have been done in the study to establish measurement validity?* (Chapter 3)

The measurement of the dependent variable was straightforward. The authors report the scale used has been identified as a valid and reliable self-report assessment of antisocial behavior (p. 176). In addition, reliability was assessed using Cronbach's alpha method, which indicated the general scale and the subscales are a reliable measure of criminal behavior. The measurement of the independent variables was also straightforward. The authors report the scales used have been identified as valid measures of social control and differential association indicators. In addition, Cronbach's alpha reliability testing shows the measures are reliable.

11. *What were the units of analysis? Were they appropriate for the research question? If some groups were the units of analysis, were any statements made at any point that are open to the ecological fallacy? If individuals were the units of analysis, were any statements made at any point that suggest reductionist reasoning?* (Chapter 5)

The authors sampled young adult, first-time felony offenders sentenced to a residential court-ordered boot camp program. The units of analysis are appropriate for the research question. No statements were made at any point that suggest reductionist reasoning.

12. *Was the study design cross-sectional or longitudinal, or did it use both types of data? If the design was longitudinal, what type of longitudinal design was it? Could the longitudinal design have been improved in any way, as by collecting panel data rather than trend data, or by decreasing the dropout rate in a panel design? If cross-sectional data were used, could the research question have been addressed more effectively with the longitudinal data?* (Chapter 5)

The survey was cross-sectional. The research question could have been addressed more effectively with longitudinal data that followed people from childhood into adulthood, since many of the authors' interpretations reflect their interest in how individuals' past experiences shape their propensity for criminal behavior.

13. *Were any causal assertions made or implied in the hypotheses or in subsequent discussion? What approach was used to demonstrate the existence of causal effects? Were all three criteria for establishing causal relationships addressed? What, if any, variables were controlled in the analysis to reduce the risk of spurious relationships? Should any other variables have been measured and controlled? How satisfied are you with the internal validity of the conclusions?* (Chapter 5)

The explanatory hypotheses indicate that the authors were concerned with causality. However, the lack of previous research on their chosen population suggests an exploratory approach to causality. In order to reduce the risk of spuriousness in the presumed causal relationships, three control variables were included in the analysis: age, race/ethnicity, and gender (p. 188); these variables have been shown to be strongly related to criminal activity. There are other variables that might have created a spurious relationship, but at least several of the most likely contenders have been controlled. For example, some of the differences in social control and differential association measures may be due to social class—that is, individuals who were raised in more affluent families are more likely to have had greater social control in their lives and less opportunity to be involved with individuals who favor, or at least justify, criminal behavior. Income has also been shown to be negatively related to criminal activity—that is, the higher an individual's income, the less likely he or she is to engage in criminal activity.

14. *Was a sample or the entire population of elements used in the study? What type of sample was selected? Was a probability sampling method used? Did the authors think the sample was generally representative of the population from which it was drawn? Do you? How would you evaluate the likely generalizability of the findings to other populations?* (Chapter 4)

The sample was a nonrandom (nonprobability) sample of young, first-time felony offenders. A purposive sampling technique was used when sampling women, the authors "focused [their] efforts on obtaining responses from the entire [female] population . . . in the program over a 15-month period" (p. 175). The authors did not focus on sampling the entire male population; therefore, the authors obtained an availability sample of males sentenced to the program over the same time period. The authors admit the sample is not representative of "felony crimes committed by men and women in prison, [but] closely resembles first-time felony offenders in other shock incarceration programs as an alternative to jail or prison incarceration" (p. 176). Do you believe the authors can generalize their findings to similar populations? Why or why not?

15. *Was the response rate or participation rate reported? Does it appear likely that those who did not respond or participate were markedly different from those who did participate? Why or why not? Did the author(s) adequately discuss this issue?* (Chapters 4, 6)

The response rate was reported. The authors obtained responses from 122 of 124 (or 98.4%) female offenders and 1,031 (or 85.9%) of male offenders (p. 175). With the exception of female offenders, the authors did not discuss differences among those who did and did not participate with the study. Of the two female offenders who did not participate in the study, one did not speak English and the other woman escaped from the facility (p. 175). In general, it is reasonable to believe those who did not participate in the study were not markedly different from those who did participate. The large sample of males and females obtained for this study should have provided good variability.

16. *Was an experimental, survey, participant observation, or some other research design used? How well was this design suited to the research question posed and the specific hypotheses tested, if any? Why do you suppose the author(s) chose this particular design? How was the design modified in response to research constraints? How was it modified in order to take advantage of research opportunities?* (Chapters 6–9)

Survey research was the method of choice and probably was used for this article because it provided the most cost-effective means of gathering data. Survey research seems appropriate for the research questions posed.

17. *Was an evaluation research design used? Which type was it? What was the primary purpose of the evaluation?* (Chapter 9)

This study did not use any type of evaluation research.

18. *Were multiple methods used? Were findings obtained with different methods complementary?* (Chapter 10)

This study used only survey methods.

19. *Was any attention given to social context? To biological processes? If so, what did this add? If not, would it have improved the study? Explain.* (Chapters 5, 10)

Social context is given attention in this study on an individual level. The majority of social control and differential association indicators are measures of social conditions and experiences of the respondents. However, no attention is given to the potential importance of larger social contexts, such as neighborhood or region of the country. Biological factors that may increase the propensity for criminality are not considered in this study.

20. *Summarize the findings. How clearly were statistical and/or qualitative data presented and discussed? Were the results substantively important?* (Chapters 11, 12)

Statistical data are presented clearly using descriptive statistics, examination of bivariate relationships, and multiple regression analysis (a multivariate statistical technique) that highlight the most central findings. No qualitative data are presented. The findings seem substantively important, since they identify social control and differential association theories that can be applied to adult populations across gender groups (pp. 184–188).

21. *Did the author(s) adequately represent the findings in the discussion and/or conclusion sections? Were conclusions well grounded in the findings? Are any other interpretations possible?* (Chapter 12)

The findings are well represented in the discussion and conclusion section (pp. 188–192). The authors point out in their literature review that the focus for testing social control and differential association theories data is often limited to juvenile delinquent populations and frequently fails to consider possible differences between males and females. The findings suggest these theoretical perspectives can be applied to adult criminal populations and are important in explaining variation in criminal behavior across gender groups. You might want to consider what other interpretations of the findings might be possible. Remember that other interpretations are always possible for particular findings—it is a question of the weight of the evidence, the persuasiveness of the theory used, and the consistency of the findings with other research.

22. *Compare the study to others addressing the same research question. Did the study yield additional insights? In what ways was the study design more or less adequate than the design of previous research?* (Chapters 2, 10, 12)

This study investigated the relationship between social control and differential association on a population that had not previously received much attention (young adult felony offenders). This helped the authors to gain additional insights into the influence of social control and differential association on young adults across gender groups.

23. *What additional research questions and hypotheses are suggested by the study's results? What light did the study shed on the theoretical framework used? On social policy questions?* (Chapters 2, 10, 12)

The authors suggest no additional research questions or hypotheses. However, the study does shed light on the importance of "traditional" theoretical perspective in explaining variation in criminal behavior among adults across gender groups. The authors note the importance of new theoretical paradigms but emphasize "that the value of 'older' theoretical perspectives should be remembered and . . . applied to underresearched topics" (p. 192).

Gender and Crime Among Felony Offenders

Assessing the Generality of Social Control and Differential Association Theories

Leanne Fiftal Alarid

Velmer S. Burton, Jr.

Francis T. Cullen

Although often tested empirically on high school samples, differential association and social control theories have only infrequently been used to explain offending by felons. Based on a sample of 1,153 newly incarcerated felons, the authors examine the ability of differential association and social control theories to explain self-reported offending across types of crime and gender groups. Overall, the analyses lend support to both perspectives and suggest that they are "general" theories of crime. It also appears, however, that differential association theory has more consistent effects, especially for men. Parental attachment is a significantly stronger predictor of female than male participation in violent crime. These results indicate that future studies of criminal behavior risk being misspecified if they do not include measures of these "traditional" theories of crime.

Since the 1969 publication of Hirschi's *Causes of Delinquency*, social control or control theory and differential association or "cultural deviance" theory have competed vigorously against one another for the status of the preeminent microlevel sociological theory of crime (see also Kornhauser 1978). Even today, spirited exchanges occur in which the logical and empirical adequacy of the theories is debated (see Akers 1996, 1998; Costello 1997; Hirschi 1996; Matsueda 1988, 1997). These paradigms continue to guide research (see, e.g., Akers 1998; Sampson and Laub 1993) not only because of their theoretical parsimony and elegance but also because they accrue a measure of empirical support (Akers 1996; Krohn 1995).

Although noteworthy exceptions exist, most of the tests of social control and differential association theory have been conducted using self-report surveys on juveniles. Particularly

---

NOTE: Reprinted from the *Journal of Research in Crime and Delinquency,* Vol. 37, No. 2, May 2000, 171-199. © Sage Publications, Inc. A previous version of this article was presented at the 1995 meeting of the Academy of Criminal Justice Sciences.

instructive are empirical studies in which measures of both theories have been incorporated in the analysis. In general, this research suggests that measures of both theories are related to delinquent or adult criminal involvement, although in some studies, the strength of the differential association variables is greater (Benda 1994; Conger 1976; Kandel and Davies 1991; Macdonald 1989; Matsueda 1982; Matsueda and Heimer 1987; McGee 1992; see also Akers 1998; Burton 1991; Krohn 1995).

A key concern, however, is the generality of social control and differential association theories. These perspectives typically have been seen as having the ability to explain various forms of crime for all people (see, e.g., Akers 1998; Sutherland and Cressey 1955; Hirschi 1969; Sampson and Laub 1993). Clearly, the theoretical power of each of these perspectives hinges on their ability to achieve the status of a general theory. Accordingly, a central empirical and thus theoretical issue is whether social control and differential association theories can explain criminal behavior that extends beyond the delinquency found among community samples of youth.

There have been studies conducted on adult samples that have found support for differential association/social learning theory (Akers 1998; Akers and LaGreca 1988, 1991; Akers et al. 1989; Boeringer, Shehan, and Akers 1991; Dull 1983; Orcutt 1987; Tittle, Burke, and Jackson 1986). Research on social control theory with adult samples also suggests that adult social bonds may reduce criminal behavior (Horney, Osgood, and Marshall 1995; Lasley 1988; Sampson and Laub 1993). Even so, the empirical literature assessing whether social control and differential association theories can explain adult criminal behavior remains limited, especially when one searches for studies that include in their analyses measures of both theoretical perspectives.[1] Among the few adult studies testing social control versus differential association theory, the results show mixed support for both perspectives. Thus, two studies using community samples of adults found stronger support for differential association theory (Burton 1991; Macdonald 1989), while another study revealed that social control theory was better able to account for variation in arrests for men and women drug offenders (Covington 1985).

Even with this research, however, there are typically two limitations. First, especially with adult samples, studies often do not explore whether the effects of variables measuring traditional criminological theories vary by gender. Traditional theories have been criticized for their perceived inability to explain female criminality (Adler 1975; Daly and Chesney-Lind 1988; Leonard 1982) and for ignoring how gender-related factors—such as patriarchal power relations—differentially shape the involvement of gender groups in crime (Heidensohn 1985; Messerschmidt 1993) and victimization (Chesney-Lind and Shelden 1992). In turn, it is argued that scholars should formulate separate or different theories of crime for women (Leonard 1982; Messerschmidt 1993; Naffine and Gale 1989; Smart 1976).

Second, tests of social control and differential association theory have only infrequently been conducted on samples that include a high base rate of serious offending. As a result, we have only limited information on whether these theories explain more than relatively minor forms of criminal involvement. As Messner and Rosenfeld (1994:47) note, this "neglect of serious offending by contemporary criminologists" means that it is necessary to employ "other ways of obtaining information from people who commit serious crimes (e.g., they can be interviewed in prison)." Although still not widespread, criminologists increasingly are undertaking tests of criminological theories that employ serious offenders interviewed in prison or in the community (see Covington 1985;

Horney and Marshall 1992; Horney et al. 1995; Longshore, Turner, and Stein 1996; Sampson and Laub 1990, 1993).

Among this body of research on samples of adult offenders, however, research testing social control and differential association theories is rare; research that conducts such studies by gender is virtually nonexistent. The only known exception is Covington's (1985) study of adult heroin addicts in which an attempt is made to explain self-reported total arrests and arrests for property crimes. Covington's analysis revealed that measures of social control were better predictors of women's criminal involvement in property crime and in both men's and women's involvement in overall offending behaviors; differential association measures, however, were able to explain men's property arrests.[2]

In light of the status of the existing research, the current study attempts to test the generality of social control and differential association theories to a population that has been infrequently studied: young adult felons drawn from the inner city. Social control and differential association theories were selected because they have been found, among existing sociological theories, to have the most consistent empirical support in studies of juveniles.[3] Social control theory is also used to explain adult crime in recent important studies (Horney et al. 1995; Sampson and Laub 1993). These theories both predict that their effects will be general—that is, they will account for variation in offending and that this effect will hold for males and females.

These theories also predict that the effects of the competing theory will be spurious (Hirschi 1969). The spuriousness issue is important because most tests with adults have not included measures of both theories (e.g., Horney et al. 1995; Sampson and Laub 1993). As such, findings from previous theoretical tests could be misspecified if the effects of differential association variables account for the findings of social control variables.

Based on previous research on community samples of adults and juveniles that have used both sets of measures, we would anticipate that both variables will have effects. Like members of the community, offenders can be expected to vary in their levels of social control (Horney et al. 1995; Sampson and Laub 1993). We can also expect variation in differential associations and crime-related attitudes. Still, given the lack of previous research testing these theories with a population of offenders extensively involved in crime, the relationship of the theories to criminal involvement remains to be empirically determined.

Thus, the purpose of this article is to test the generality of social control and differential association theories with a sample of young adult felons drawn from the inner city. The study also has the advantage of including males and females. Using a self-report survey, the study examines both overall offending and involvement in specific forms of criminal conduct. By testing the two theories against each other, the central focus will be to discern which theory—if not both theories—can explain variation in offending among young adult men and women felony offenders from an urban area. That is, are social control and differential association theories mainly explanations of juvenile delinquency, or can they help account for participation in crime among young adult male and female felons?

METHOD

The procedures used to test differential association and social control theory with 1,153 felony women and men in a community corrections program have been organized into four categories: (1) data collection, (2) sample characteristics, (3) dependent variables, and (4) independent variables.

Data Collection

Data for this study were gathered from felons sentenced to a residential court-ordered boot camp program in Harris County, Texas, which includes the Houston metropolitan area. The boot camp program was designed for a 17- to 25-year-old male or female adult who had been convicted as a first-time felon and had been sentenced to prison. Offenders were considered for the program by judges as a "last stop before prison." The type of convicted offender (violent, property, or drug) in this program was thus was a reflection of judicial discretion.

The three-month coed program emphasized discipline, physical labor, and drills and offered GED education, life skills, and drug awareness classes. The program housed a maximum capacity of 30 women in one smaller barrack and approximately 240 men in five program barracks, with a sixth housing barrack available for incoming "new boots." Up to 48 men entered the program as a cohort, were housed in the same barracks, and graduated together three months later. Since only about 2 women entered the program every week, there were no distinct female cohorts. Rather, female "new boots" were mixed with more senior women offenders, and the barracks never filled to capacity during the data collection period. For both women and men, the residential stay in the boot camp program was an alternative to jail or prison incarceration. The program was followed by a two-year period of intensive supervision probation in the community (Burton et al. 1993).

Data were collected on participants who entered the boot camp between June 1992 and September 1993. Since a smaller number of women were sentenced to boot camp, we focused our efforts on obtaining responses from the entire population of 124 women in the program over a 15-month time period. Out of the female population in the boot camp program, we were successful at obtaining consent from 122 (or 98.4 percent) of the women. One woman who did not participate could not understand or speak English, while another woman escaped from the facility prior to our weekly visit. Of approximately 1,200 males who entered the program during that time period, we collected questionnaire responses from 1,031 (or 85.9 percent) of the men offenders.

All data were collected directly from the participants themselves, who completed a paper-and-pencil questionnaire in the facility housing barracks within two weeks of their arrival. The male cohorts completed their surveys in a group setting with one trained researcher available to answer questions. The women participants completed their surveys individually with one trained research team member (recall that only two to three women entered the program weekly). We do not believe that the differences in the two data collection methods were significant enough to affect response reliability or validity. The benefits of obtaining a high response rate for the women outweighed any negative effects caused by conducting the men's questionnaire sessions in larger groups. A total of 1,153 usable questionnaires were completed, 10.6 percent by women respondents.

Sample Characteristics

The sample characteristics of the 1,031 men and 122 women indicated that the vast majority lived in the inner city or surrounding urban area at the time of arrest for their most

TABLE C.1: Sample Characteristics

Characteristic	Women (n = 122)	Men (n = 1,031)
Age (17-28 years)	20.6	19.5
Race/ethnicity (percentage)		
African American	44.3	44.4
Caucasian	45.1	31.4
Hispanic	10.7	23.8
Formal education (years)	10.5	10.3
Marital/partner attachment		
(percentage attached)	32.0	35.1
Number of children (percentage)		
None	46.7	69.8
One	30.3	21.3
Two	9.8	6.1
Three or more	13.1	2.9
Median household income (in dollars)	16,800	27,500
Current conviction (percentage)		
Drug	41.8	28.9
Person	19.7	19.5
Property	38.5	51.6

recent conviction. Men and women were both between the ages of 17 and 28 years, with the average age calculated at 19.5 for men and 20.6 years for women. The African American composition of both samples was identical (44 percent). However, there were more Caucasian women (45.1 percent) than men (31.4 percent), and there were more Hispanic men than women (23.8 percent and 10.7 percent, respectively). The amount of formal education completed ranged between 6th grade and three years of higher education, with a mean of a 10th-grade education. Single/unattached women (68.0 percent) and men (64.9 percent) comprised the majority of the sample relative to married and cohabiting women and men.

The demographic differences between the men and women in the sample were number of children, median household income, and current conviction. First, about 46.7 percent of women and 69.8 percent of men had no dependent children. Of all the fathers and mothers, the women more often reported being the primary caretaker and sole financial respondent for the children. As primary caretakers, the women lived in households that generated much lower incomes than men. The median household income for women (most with children) was $16,800, while men's reported annual household income was $27,500.

As for the most recent conviction, crimes of violence were comparably represented by gender; in the sample, 19.7 percent of women and 19.5 percent of men were violent offenders. More women (41.8 percent) than men (28.9 percent) were convicted of a drug offense. Bear in mind that the offense type of each convicted offender (violent, property, or drug) does not represent felony crimes committed by men and women in prison. Even though women are increasingly being sentenced for felony drug offenses as a result of the war on drugs (U.S. Bureau of Justice Statistics 1994; Immarigeon and Chesney-Lind 1993), our sample more closely resembles first-time felony offenders in other shock incarceration programs as an alternative to jail or prison incarceration (MacKenzie and Brame 1994).

Dependent Variables

Dependent variable measures for the analysis were originally derived from Elliott and Ageton's (1980) scale of delinquent behaviors offenses found in the National Youth Survey (NYS). The NYS is currently "the most highly respected self-report assessment of antisocial behavior" (Caspi et al. 1994). We adjusted certain measures to apply to our young adult sample. Respondents were asked whether they had ever committed 35 different deviant and criminal acts (Hindelang, Hirschi, and Weis 1981). Our prevalence dimension of crime measures offense participation or the number of crime types committed. Other researchers have preferred the use of the prevalence measure of variety:

> Variety scores are useful for individual-differences research for several reasons. First, they show the extent of involvement in different types of crimes. . . . Second, they are less skewed than frequency scores. Third, they give equal weight to all delinquent acts, unlike frequency scores, which give more weight to minor crimes that are committed more frequently (e.g., underage drinking) and less weight to serious, less frequent crimes (e.g., rape). (Caspi et al. 1994:170-71)[4]

In the current study, one point was assigned if a respondent admitted involvement in a specific act; if respondents did not admit involvement, no points were assigned. The general crime scale was summed to obtain a composite score, which ranged from 0 to 35. Items in the general crime scale have been employed in previous tests of criminological theories using samples of adults (Burton et al. 1993, 1994, 1998). In addition, we distinguished type of criminal behavior by dividing the offenses into three subscales: violent, property, and drug. Table C.2 shows the means, standard deviations, and reliability for all dependent and independent variables used in the analysis.

Using Cronbach's (1951) alpha method, the 35-item general crime scale was reliable at .82 for women and .90 for men; the 15-item property crime subscale had a reliability level for women and men of .72 and .85, respectively; the 11-item drug subscale was .76 for women and .81 for men; and the 9-item violent crime subscale was reliable for females at .61 and .66 for males (see the appendix for individual offenses included in each subscale and accompanying frequencies separated by gender). Table C.2 shows that men admitted past involvement in an average of nine crimes: three drug offenses, four property crimes, and two violent crimes. Women engaged in an average of nine total crimes: four drug offenses, three property crimes, and two violent crimes. Although the property crime rate differed slightly for men and women, the types of drug offenses and violent crimes committed by both men and women were similar (see English 1993).[5]

Independent Variables

The items used in this study to measure social control and differential association variables were all drawn from previous theoretical tests (see Burton 1991; Burton et al. 1993, 1994, 1998; Fiftal 1993; Matsueda 1982).[6] Participants in our sample responded to

TABLE C.2: Individual Dependent and Independent Variables by Gender

Variable	Number of Items	Women Reliability	Women Mean (SD)	Men Reliability	Men Mean (SD)	Sample F-Ratio
Dependent						
General crime	35	.82	8.57 (5.12) (range: 0-26)	.90	9.49 (6.85) (range: 0-31)	2.06
Violent crime	9	.61	1.64 (1.25) (range: 0-6)	.66	1.72 (1.70) (range: 0-9)	0.27
Property crime	15	.72	2.98 (2.60) (range: 0-11)	.85	4.19 (3.76) (range: 0-17)	11.99**
Drug crime	11	.76	3.96 (2.55) (range: 0-11)	.81	3.62 (2.72) (range: 0-11)	1.68
Independent						
Social control						
Marital/partner attachment	1	—	0.32 (0.47)	—	0.35 (0.48)	0.48
Parental attachment	3	.75	15.25 (2.98)	.64	14.87 (3.02)	1.77
Peer attachment	2	.81	6.84 (2.91)	.73	7.68 (2.79)	9.58**
Involvement	2	.69	6.44 (2.89)	.56	6.09 (2.69)	1.82
Belief	2	.63	8.88 (2.41)	.51	8.11 (2.40)	11.23**
Differential association						
Individual definitions	5	.77	10.97 (4.95)	.62	11.98 (4.52)	5.30*
Others' definitions	3	.71	9.50 (3.79)	.66	10.11 (3.61)	3.11
Criminal friends	1	—	2.87 (1.66)	—	2.77 (1.85)	0.30

*$p < .05$. **$p < .01$.

each item by using a 6-point Likert scale that ranged from *strongly agree* (6) to *strongly disagree* (1). Some responses were recoded so that a high score on an item indicated the presence of differential association or social control. The reliability of each composite independent theory measure was checked by Cronbach's (1951) alpha method. Finally, factor analysis was performed on each composite measure to ensure that each of the individual measures loaded on one factor. The mean, standard deviation, and reliability of each independent variable, separated by gender, can be found in Table C.2.

Social Control Theory

Hirschi's (1969) social control theory was originally formulated to rival differential association or "cultural deviance" theory as an explanation of why some juveniles conform and others engage in delinquency. More recent research has applied this perspective to adult criminality. Social control theory asserts that individuals with strong ties to family and friends (Covington 1985; Sampson and Laub 1990, 1993) will be protected from criminal involvement. In this study, we measure the adult social bond by marital attachment, attachment to parents, attachment to friends, involvement, and belief.[7]

Marital/partner attachment. Attachment to a significant other of the opposite sex by cohabiting or marriage is perceived as providing informal social control by protecting individuals from participation in criminal and other antisocial activities (Rand 1987; Sampson and Laub 1993). In our analysis, we use marital/partner attachment status as one of the adult social bond measures (0 = not married/unattached and 1 = married/attached).

Attachment to parents. We include three items to measure attachment to parents to determine the effect of longstanding connections to parents by gender: "Throughout my life, I have had a lot of respect for my mother and father" (LaGrange and White 1985; Rosenbaum 1987). The second item asks whether respondents have "gotten along" well with their parents throughout their lives. This measure is modified from previous tests of social control (Eve 1978; Simons et al. 1980). The third component states, "My family is the most important thing in my life." The level of reliability for the attachment to parents scale is .75 for women and .64 for men.

Attachment to friends. The bond to friends is an important part of conventional attachment. The items used in the questionnaire yielded a reliability level of .81 for women and .73 for men. Respondents were asked to respond to the following two items: "It is important for me to spend time with my friends," and "My friends are a very important part of my life" (Agnew 1985; Burton 1991; Canter 1982; Friedman and Rosenbaum 1988; Hindelang 1973; Johnson, Marcos, and Bahr 1987; Matsueda 1982; Paternoster and Triplett 1988; Rosenbaum 1987).

Involvement. Involvement in conventional activities is measured by how much free time individuals have (Agnew 1985; Burton 1991; Canter 1982; Johnson 1979; Rosenbaum 1987). The following two items (reliable at .69 for women and .56 for men) were borrowed from Burton's (1991) study: "Between work, family, and community activities, I don't have much free time," and "Before coming here, I had a lot of free time on my hands."

Belief. Finally, the conventional bond is measured by moral belief in the law, specifically in the police, as measured by the following statement: "I have a lot of respect for the police" (Hindelang 1973; Hirschi 1969). The second item, "It is all right to get around the law if you can get away with it," was also used by Hirschi (1969) in previous tests. The two items have a reliability level of .63 for women and .51 for men.

Differential Association Theory

According to Sutherland's (1947) theory of differential association, individuals develop internalized definitions that are favorable or nonfavorable toward violating the law. As individual exposure to procriminal values, patterns, and associates increases, the likelihood of criminal involvement also increases. As in previous studies, we use three differential association variables to measure the likelihood of criminal exposure: individual definitions toward the law, others' definitions toward the law, and number of criminal friends.

Individual definitions toward crime. The five-item scale measuring individual definitions toward crime examined an individual's degree of tolerance for criminal behavior, the moral validity of violating the law, and the level of agreement with committing criminal acts. Cronbach's (1951) alpha reliability for the scale for women is .77 and .62 for men. To measure disapproval toward violating the law, we asked for a response to the following item: "No matter how small the crime, breaking the law is a serious matter" (Akers et al. 1989; Jackson, Tittle, and Burke 1986; Short 1960). A second item, "It is morally wrong to break the law," also assessed anticriminal definitions (see Jackson et al. 1986; Matsueda 1989; Silberman 1976; Tittle et al. 1986). In contrast, to measure adults' willingness to violate the law, three items were included: "Sometimes you just don't have any choice but to break the law" (Krohn, Lanza-Kaduce, and Akers 1984; Short 1960), "If someone insulted me, I would be likely to hit or slap them," and "If breaking the law really doesn't hurt anyone, and you can make a quick buck doing it, then it's really not all that wrong" (Burton 1991).

Others' definitions toward crime. According to Sutherland (1947), criminal behavior is influenced primarily through exposure to other individuals holding definitions favorable toward violating the law. Relying on previous tests of differential association (Akers et al. 1979; Cressey 1953; Dull 1983; Griffen and Griffen 1978; Jaquith 1981; Johnson et al. 1987; Short 1960; Tittle et al. 1986), we included the following item: "Many of the people I associate with think it's okay to break the law if you can get away with it." The second item is designed to determine the type of people (criminal or noncriminal) with whom an individual associates. Thus, respondents were presented with the following item: "Most of the people I associate with would never break the law." In previous research, items similar to this have been related to delinquent involvement (Akers et al. 1989; Krohn et al. 1984; Jackson et al. 1986; Orcutt 1987). Finally, the third item assesses the extent to which individuals are "often in situations where people encourage [them] to do something illegal." This three-item scale has a reliability coefficient of .71 for women and .66 for men.

Criminal friends. Many empirical tests of differential association theory have relied on the number of criminal associates as evidence of interaction with criminal members within an individual's primary group (see, e.g., Akers et al. 1979; Dull 1983; Johnson et al. 1987; Warr and Stafford 1993; Winfree, Griffith, and Sellers 1989). In our study, we apply a measure of the actual number of criminal friends in our model by asking, "In the last 12 months, how many of your five closest friends have done something they could have gotten arrested for?"

FINDINGS

We assessed the bivariate relationships between the eight independent variables and crime by zero-order correlations. Tables C.3 and C.4 show that for the sample as a whole, all three of the differential association variables (individual definitions, others' definitions, and number of criminal friends) were significantly and directly correlated with property, violent, and drug offenses.[8] Similarly, these tables reveal that the social control variables of attachment to parents, involvement in conventional activities, and belief in the law were significantly and inversely correlated with criminal behavior. On the other hand, marriage

TABLE C.3: Zero-Order Correlations of Theoretical Variables and Crime Scales (men)

	General Crime	Violent Crime	Property Crime	Drug Crime	Peer Attachment	Parental Attachment	Marital/ Partner Attachment	Involvement	Individual Belief	Other Definitions	Criminal Definitions	Friends
General crime	1.00											
Violent crime	.75**	1.00										
Property crime	.91**	.60**	1.00									
Drug crime	.80**	.44**	.53**	1.00								
Peer attachment	.15**	.09**	.14**	.13**	1.00							
Parent attachment	-.23**	-.16**	-.22**	-.18**	-.05	1.00						
Marital/partner attachment	-.05	-.01	-.10**	-.00	-.07*	.04	1.00					
Involvement	-.19**	-.12**	-.20**	-.14**	-.10**	-.01	.10**	1.00				
Belief	-.25**	-.24**	-.20**	-.18**	-.02	.21**	-.02	.18**	1.00			
Individual definitions	.27**	.29**	.24**	.18**	.04	-.22**	-.02	-.17**	-.54**	1.00		
Others' definitions	.37**	.32**	.34**	.24**	.02	-.18**	-.07*	-.28**	-.29**	.28**	1.00	
Criminal friends	.39**	.30**	.37**	.29**	.02	-.12**	-.09**	-.22**	-.27**	.27**	.42**	1.00

*$p < .05$. **$p < .01$.

TABLE C.4: Zero-Order Correlations of Theoretical Variables and Crime Scales (women)

	General Crime	Violent Crime	Property Crime	Drug Crime	Peer Attachment	Parental Attachment	Marital/ Partner Attachment	Involvement	Individual Belief	Other Definitions	Criminal Definitions	Friends
General crime	1.00											
Violent crime	.61**	1.00										
Property crime	.86**	.41**	1.00									
Drug crime	.83**	.32**	.50**	1.00								
Peer attachment	.32**	.13	.31**	.27**	1.00							
Parent attachment	-.35**	-.24**	-.33**	-.25**	-.12	1.00						
Marital/partner attachment	-.30**	-.09	-.29**	-.26**	-.20*	.08	1.00					
Involvement	-.26**	-.38**	-.13	-.19*	-.10	-.12	-.07	1.00				
Belief	-.22*	-.17*	-.19*	-.16	-.13	.27**	.10	.09	1.00			
Individual definitions	.28**	.23*	.21*	.24**	.19*	-.20*	-.01	-.16	-.50**	1.00		
Others' definitions	.47**	.35**	.35**	.42**	.17	-.24**	-.00	-.32**	-.18*	.33**	1.00	
Criminal friends	.31**	.22**	.28**	.23**	.03	-.10	-.00	-.13	-.12	.14	.28**	1.00

*$p < .05$. **$p < .01$.

reduced involvement only in property crime, and attachment to peers was positively correlated with all types of crime.[9]

General Criminal Behavior and Gender

Following the bivariate analysis, we used ordinary least squares (OLS) regression to examine the effects of independent variables on dependent variables. The first dependent variable (general crime) was regressed on three control variables (age, race, and gender), five social control variables, and three differential association variables.[10] Race was dummy coded (White vs. non-White), while age was a continuous variable. Regression coefficients were determined with all variables entered simultaneously into the equation. Table C.5 shows the standardized and unstandardized regression coefficients for men and women when both theories were regressed against each other. Gender groups were analyzed both independently and together.

Social control. Table C.5 shows that three out of five social control variables were significantly related to the overall measure of criminal behavior for the sample. Attachment to peers was significantly and positively related to criminal behavior. Attachment to parents and involvement in conventional activities were significantly and inversely related to involvement in criminal behavior. Those who got along well with their parents and considered them an important part of their lives were less likely to engage in criminal behavior. Furthermore, respondents who were immersed in time-consuming activities (i.e., work, family, and community activities) were also less likely to commit crimes.

We conducted a difference of slopes test on the significant unstandardized regression coefficients and their corresponding standard errors to determine if any significant differences existed between men and women. When conducting a hypothesis test of two

TABLE C.5: Effects of Social Control and Differential Association Variables on General Crime: Standardized Betas (unstandardized *B* coefficients) Reported

Variable Name	Women (n = 122)		Men (n = 1,031)		Women and Men (N = 1,153)	
Social control						
Marital/partner attachment						
(0 = not attached)	.21	(2.27)**	.01	(.08)	.02	(.33)
Parental attachment	−.31	(−.53)**	−.09	(−.21)**	−.12	(−.32)**
Peer attachment	.07	(.12)	.06	(.16)*	.07	(.16)*
Involvement	−.24	(−.43)**	−.06	(−.16)*	−.07	(−.18)*
Belief	.03	(.05)	−.06	(−.17)	−.05	(−.15)
Differential association						
Individual definitions	.11	(.11)	.12	(.19)**	.12	(.17)**
Others' definitions	.18	(.31)*	.16	(.31)**	.16	(.30)**
Criminal friends	.16	(.50)*	.26	(.98)**	.26	(.94)**
Control variables						
Age	−.08	(−.15)	.03	(.08)	.01	(.04)
Gender (0 = male)	—	—	—	—	−.05	(−.93)
Race (0 = non-White)	.22	(2.23)**	.19	(2.75)**	.19	(2.64)**
R^2		.51		.29		.30

*$p < .05$. **$p < .01$.

samples of this nature, we relied on the formula suggested by Paternoster et al. (1998). We found that attachment to parents ($z = -2.214$) was a significantly stronger predictor of female ($b = -.533$; $SE = .129$) as opposed to male ($b = -.208$; $SE = .070$) crime participation. On the other hand, there were no significant differences between women and men and the level of involvement as a predictor of criminal participation. The effect, then, of involvement on participation in crime is similar for men and women.

One of the strongest predictors for a woman's involvement in crime was whether she lived with a mate or was married. The significance of this relationship was not in the predicted direction of social control theory, which would hypothesize that family relationships, including marriage, insulate against criminal involvement. On the other hand, marital attachment was not significant for predicting men's criminal behavior.

One factor that was significantly related to men's participation in crime was peer attachment. Young men who were attached to their friends were more likely to engage in criminal behavior—a relationship in the direction opposite to that predicted by social control theory. Other studies have interpreted peer attachment and increased criminal involvement as indirect support for differential association theory, depending on whether the friends were delinquent (Conger 1976).[11]

Differential association. In Table C.5, others' definitions and criminal friends significantly predicted both male and female involvement in crime. A difference of slopes test on criminal friends indicated there were no significant differences between women and men; the effect of criminal friends on participation in crime is similar for men and women.

Individual definitions, although in the expected direction for women, were significant only for men. Furthermore, for men, differential association variables had stronger effects than social control theory variables in predicting their participation in crime. For women, there was some tendency for the social control variables to have stronger effects. The overall explanatory power for both theories in the model for women was $R^2 = .51$ and for men was .29.

Control variables. Race/ethnicity significantly predicted criminal involvement for women and men. Specifically, Anglo men and women were more likely to have been involved in crime than non-White individuals. Age was not a significant predictor of overall rates of criminal behavior. To more precisely measure the nature of gender differences and similarities for overall crime, a separate t-test for independent samples was conducted using unstandardized partial regression coefficients while using gender as the grouping variable. Results indicated that the mean for the men (9.88) was significantly higher than for women (8.56) for the general crime scale.

Type of Criminal Behavior and Gender

Table C.6 shows the contribution of social control and differential association theories to individually and simultaneously explain young men's and women's involvement in drug, property, and violent crimes.

Social control. A consistent and significant predictor of all three crime types for women was parental attachment. Parental attachment was also significant in the direction predicted by social control theory for men's property and violent crime. Attachment to

TABLE C.6: Effects of Social Control and Differential Association Variables on Drug, Property, and Violent Crime: Standardized Betas (and unstandardized coefficients Reported

Variable Name	Drug Crime			Property Crime			Violent Crime		
	Women	Men	Sample	Women	Men	Sam	Women	Men	Sample
Social control									
Marital/partner attachment	.16 (.89)*	.04 (.24)	.06 (.33)*	.21 (1.17)**	-.04 (-.32)	-.02 (-.18)	.08 (.21)	.02 (.07)	.02 (.08)
Parental attachment	-.18 (-.15)*	-.06 (-.05)	-.06 (-.07)*	-.29 (-.26)**	-.10 (-.12)**	-.12 (-.18)**	-.29 (-.12)**	-.06 (-.04)*	-.10 (-.07)**
Peer attachment	-.02 (-.02)	.06 (.06)	.06 (.06)*	.15 (.14)	.06 (.08)*	.07 (.09)*	.01 (.00)	.06 (.04)	.05 (.03)
Involvement	-.22 (-.20)**	-.07 (-.07)*	-.09 (-.08)**	-.10 (-.09)	-.07 (-.10)*	-.07 (-.09)*	-.34 (-.15)**	.01 (.01)	-.02 (-.01)
Belief	.01 (.01)	-.08 (-.09)*	-.07 (-.08)*	.02 (.02)	-.02 (-.03)	-.02 (-.03)	.01 (.01)	-.05 (-.04)	-.04 (-.03)
Differential association									
Individual definitions	.11 (.06)	.08 (.05)*	.09 (.05)*	.06 (.03)	.10 (.08)**	.09 (.08)**	.09 (.02)	.15 (.06)**	.14 (.05)**
Others' definitions	.15 (.18)*	.08 (.06)*	.10 (.08)**	.14 (.21)*	.16 (.16)**	.15 (.15)**	.10 (.03)	.17 (.08)**	.16 (.07)**
Criminal friends	.15 (.22)*	.23 (.34)**	.22 (.33)**	.17 (.23)*	.24 (.50)**	.24 (.48)**	.05 (.04)	.18 (.17)**	.17 (.16)**
Control variables									
Age	.14 (.14)*	.16 (.20)**	.16 (.19)**	-.18 (-.18)*	-.06 (-.11)*	-.08 (-.13)**	-.23 (-.11)**	-.03 (-.02)	-.04 (-.03)
Gender (0 = male)	—	—	.01 (.06)	—	—	-.09(-1.04)**	—	—	-.01 (.07)
Race (0 = non-White)	.44 (2.25)**	.26 (1.51)**	.28 (1.62)**	.03 (.14)	.13 (1.07)**	.12 (.96)**	-.07 (-.17)	.02 (.08)	-.00 (-.00)
R^2	.49	.23	.25	.40	.25	.26	.36	.18	.19

$*p < .05. **p < .01.$

parents served as an effective insulator for men and women against criminal involvement, a finding consistent in delinquency studies (Burton et al. 1995). A difference of slopes test indicated that the effect of parental attachment ($z = -2.136$) was a significantly stronger predictor for women ($b = -.122$; $SE = .036$) than for men ($b = -.036$; $SE = .018$) for violent crime participation. The effect of parental attachment on property crime ($z = 1.62$) is similar for males and females since the difference was found to be not statistically significant.

Lack of involvement in conventional activities significantly predicted men's and women's participation in drug crime, as well as women's violent crime and men's property crime. Difference of slopes tests verified that lack of involvement in activities has similar effects for men's and women's involvement in drug crime and overall crime participation.

Marital attachment significantly predicted women's involvement in drug and property crimes but not in the direction predicted by social control theory. In other words, women who were married or living with a mate or boyfriend were more likely to be involved in drugs and/or property offenses. Marital attachment for men, however, did not insulate against or foster crime.

Differential association. For men, all three measures of differential association theory were significantly and positively related to all three types of crime. Thus, when criminal behavior was separated by type, differential association theory more consistently explained men's participation in drug, property, and violent criminal behaviors than did social control theory. For women, though, both differential association and social control theory were related to explaining female drug and property offenses, while social control variables were stronger predictors of women's participation in violent crime. Difference of slopes tests were conducted to detect significant effects on others' definitions and criminal friends between men and women. None of the differences was statistically significant for participation in property, drug, or overall crime. In other words, the effects of criminal friends and others' definitions on criminal participation were similar for men and women.

Control variables. Of the three control variables, age and race/ethnicity were the most consistent and strongest predictors of differences in rates of offending for men and women. As the age of male and female adults increased, involvement in drug crimes also significantly increased, while male and female property and female violent crimes significantly decreased. Anglo men and women were more likely to have been involved in drug crime than non-White men and women. Also, Anglo men were more likely than were African American and Hispanic men to have been involved in property crime.

The only type of crime that varied by gender was property offenses. Men were more likely than women to have committed crimes against property. For independent samples, *t*-tests were conducted for each of the three subscales, using unstandardized partial regression coefficients. Gender was used in each *t*-test as the grouping variable to more precisely measure the nature of gender differences and similarities for drug, property, and violent offenses. Results confirmed that the mean for the men (4.37) was significantly higher than for women (2.98) for the property crime subscale. However, for drug offenses, there was no difference between men (3.75) and women (3.94). The same held true for the violent crime subscale, in which men (1.77) were found to have a mean similar to that of women (1.64).

DISCUSSION

If psychology is sometimes referred to as the "science of college sophomores," then criminology might earn the label of the "science of high school sophomores"; while psychologists run experiments on their students, criminologists rely, over and over again, on samples of adolescents in school. To be sure, such self-report research is important and has considerably advanced our understanding of crime causation. Nonetheless, the skewness in focusing on adolescents and on minor delinquencies means that the applicability of criminological theory to serious and adult offending for men and women has been examined too infrequently.

A strategy employed episodically to rectify this omission has been to test theories on samples of convicted offenders, who have higher base rates of serious criminality (see, e.g., Covington 1985; Horney et al. 1995; Longshore et al. 1996; Sampson and Laub 1993). Building on this research, we have attempted to assess the generality of social control and differential association theories and to explain self-report crime across gender among first-time convicted felons serving a three-month sentence in a shock probation program, as an alternative to jail or prison incarceration. Several salient results were found.

First, both social control theory and differential association theory appear to have general effects. For the sample as a whole, the support for differential association is especially strong and consistent: The three differential association variables are significantly related to the general crime scale and to the drug, property, and violent crime subscales. Note that many studies that assess differential association use only the single measure of "number of delinquent peers." In a cross-sectional study, the peer-delinquency relationship is subject to the claim of spuriousness—that it is merely a case of "birds of a feather flocking together" (see Hirschi 1969; Gottfredson and Hirschi 1990). In our analysis, however, it is noteworthy that the attitudinal measures of others' definitions and one's own individual definitions also are related to all the crime scales for the sample. Some additional support for differential association theory can be drawn from the positive relationships of peer attachment to all the crime measures for the sample. This result is contrary to Hirschi's (1969) prediction. Furthermore, to the extent that the members of the sample are likely to have delinquent friends, then such attachment might be viewed as an indicator of differential association.

The findings for the social control measures are less impressive but nonetheless offer support for the perspective. Parental attachment had a consistent negative relationship to all of the crime measures for the sample. It appears, therefore, that bonds to parents have continuing effects on serious felons into early adulthood (Sampson and Laub 1993). Furthermore, with the exception of violent crime, involvement in conventional activities was negatively and significantly associated with the crime measures. Previous research on social control theory exploring the relationship between involvement and criminality has revealed mixed findings. While some studies have reported that involvement has few effects on offending (see, e.g., Hirschi 1969), others have found that involvement in conventional activities has a significant and inverse relationship both to minor forms of deviance (Agnew 1985; Friedman and Rosenbaum 1988; Rosenbaum 1987) and to adult offending behavior (Fiftal 1993; Lasley 1988).

Second, the analyses suggest that the "traditional" criminological perspectives can account for offending across the genders. This is not to say, however, that gender-specific theories could not expand our understanding not only of female crime but also of male criminal participation (see, e.g., Chesney-Lind 1989; Hagan 1989; Messerschmidt 1993). Still, the data reveal that differential association and social control variables—albeit with some variation—have similar effects across male and female felons. In fact, for every crime measure, the amount of explained variation is higher for the female sample than it is for the male sample. Furthermore, our results are consistent with a recent meta-analysis of predictors of criminal behavior, which reports that antisocial attitudes/associates and parental/family factors have similar effects for males and females (Andrews and Bonta 1994:68).

Some differences do emerge, however, when analyzing the effects of theoretical variables by gender. We should caution that making interpretations is difficult because the large sample size for the male offenders (1,031 men vs. 122 women) means that the analyses of the males have more power to detect statistically significant relationships. With this caveat stated, it appears that the differential association variables have consistent effects not only across crime types but also across male and female offenders. Only with individual definitions are any gender differences apparent; even here, the relationships, though not significant for women, are in the same direction.

In contrast, the effects of social control variables were stronger for the women than for the men in our sample. We found that the effects of parental attachment significantly and inversely affected males' offending, but the impact of parental attachment on females was significantly stronger for participation in violent offenses. This difference between men and women was not found for property crime, and parental attachment was not significant for male drug crime participation. The effect of a lack of parental attachment as a significant predictor of female violent crime is especially noteworthy for furthering our understanding of female offending.

Covington's (1985) analysis revealed that measures of social control theory were stronger predictors of adult women's criminal involvement. She suggests that as adolescents, females generally are exposed to more parental supervision than male adolescents. Thus, females may be more negatively influenced when familial relations are problematic or when parental supervision is reduced or nonexistent. Covington raises the additional possibility that these findings indicate differential perception of female and male adolescent offending by the juvenile justice system. While male adolescent offending may stem from a variety of causes, "many of the early female [juvenile] arrests may have been based on their detached and unsupervised status as juveniles rather than serious criminality" (Covington 1985:350).

We should note that with the exception of violent crime, being married or attached to a male partner was positively and significantly related to criminal involvement for women. For males, female partner attachment had no effects on any crime scale. The result for males is consistent with Sampson and Laub (1993), who found that marriage only had effects on their sample of former delinquents when marital quality is taken into account (see also Laub, Nagin, and Sampson 1998). Unfortunately, we do not have detailed information on the nature of the marital relationship to disentangle why marriage or attachment fosters criminality.

From a differential association perspective, it may be that the female felons in the sample are involved with men who reinforce their criminality. Research on battered women offenders found that being involved in intimate violent relationships was a main pathway to increasing the risk of offending (Richie 1996). Another possibility is that women from abusive, dysfunctional homes—those who are at a high risk for offending (see, e.g., Chesney-Lind 1989)—attempt to escape family victimization through early marriages and attachments (Miller 1986). These attachments, in turn, influenced the roles these women played in criminal behavior in relation to men (see Alarid et al. 1996). Future research should take into account the quality of the marital relationship, as well as the role that battering and intimate abuse have on subsequent involvement with the criminal justice system.

Another noteworthy finding is that for both males and females, being Caucasian was associated with higher rates of self-reported crime for every scale with the exception of violent offending. These differences could reflect racial differences in criminal justice processing: Compared to minorities, Whites had to have more involvement in self-reported crime before being arrested and incarcerated.

An added finding that may have resulted from decisions made during prosecutorial and judicial case processing was the offending patterns of men and women. While men reported having committed more overall crime than women, particularly more property offenses, women and men did not differ significantly in the type and number of drug and violent crimes. These similarities may mean that judges who sentenced young, first-time felony offenders to shock incarceration as a prison alternative were impartial to gender.

In closing, the analyses reported here lend continuing support to the traditional theories of social control and, especially, differential association/social learning. Importantly, the data support the claim that these are "general" theories, explaining variations in self-report criminality among felony offenders and across men and women. As Cole (1975) demonstrates, however, the fate of crime and deviance theories does not always or usually hinge on their empirical vitality but on whether newer "paradigms" offer fresh research opportunities. New theories, of course, should be welcomed and their explanatory power assessed. But in doing so, we would caution that the value of "older" perspectives should be remembered and, as in our research, applied to underresearched topics.

APPENDIX Prevalence of Self-Reported Criminal Behavior: "Have You Ever . . . ?"

	Women n (%)		Men n (%)	
Property crime subscale (15 items)				
1. Avoided paying at restaurants, the movie theater, etc.?	29	(23.8)	346	(33.7)*
2. Knowingly bought, held, sold stolen property?	50	(41)	531	(51.8)*
3. Taken someone else's vehicle without their permission?	33	(27)	379	(36.9)*
4. Taken anything ($5 or less) from your job?	11	(9)	152	(14.8)
5. Taken anything (between $5 and $50) from your job?	11	(9)	118	(11.5)
6. Taken anything (over $50) from your job?	3	(2.5)	102	(10.0)**
7. Taken anything ($5 or less) from someone (other than work)?	46	(37.7)	317	(31.0)
8. Taken anything (between $5 and $50) from someone (other than work)?	25	(20.5)	306	(30.0)*

9. Taken anything (over $50) from someone else (other than work)?	31	(25.4)	346	(33.7)
10. Damaged/destroyed property belonging to relative/family of origin?	15	(12.3)	166	(16.2)
11. Purposely damaged/destroyed property belonging to an employer?	2	(1.6)	59	(5.7)*
12. Purposely damaged/destroyed property belonging to spouse/partner/friend (someone other than family of origin or an employer)?	22	(18.0)	327	(31.9)**
13. Broken into a building/vehicle?	25	(20.5)	423	(41.2)**
14. Stolen or attempted to steal a motor vehicle?	19	(15.6)	314	(30.6)**
15. Thrown objects at cars/property?	41	(33.6)	419	(40.9)
Drug crime subscale (11 items)				
1. Drank alcoholic beverages before age 21?	92	(75.4)	788	(76.8)
2. Drove a car while drunk?	51	(41.8)	471	(46.0)
3. Bought/provided beer/liquor for someone under 21?	51	(41.8)*	340	(33.2)
4. Had marijuana/hashish?	86	(70.5)**	572	(55.8)
5. Used hallucinogens/LSD?	26	(21.3)	226	(22.0)
6. Had amphetamines?	17	(13.9)	129	(12.6)
7. Had barbiturates?	14	(11.5)	91	(8.9)
Drug crime subscale (11 items)				
8. Had heroin?	6	(4.9)	32	(3.1)
9. Had cocaine?	60	(49.2)**	278	(27.1)
10. Sold marijuana?	34	(27.9)	359	(35.2)
11. Sold hard drugs (cocaine, crack, heroin)?	46	(37.7)	435	(42.5)
Violent crime subscale (9 items)				
1. Been involved in a gang fight?	25	(20.5)	232	(22.6)
2. Used physical force to get money from a relative/family of origin?	4	(3.3)	48	(4.7)
3. Used physical force to get money from someone at work?	1	(0.8)	35	(3.4)
4. Used physical force to get money from someone, a family member, or someone at work?	12	(9.8)	151	(14.7)
5. Hit or threatened to hit a relative/member of family of origin?	42	(34.4)	337	(32.9)
6. Hit or threatened to hit someone at work?	5	(4.1)	144	(14.0)**
7. Hit or threatened to hit friend/partner/spouse?	80	(65.6)**	528	(51.7)
8. Had or tried to have sex with someone against their will?	1	(0.8)	31	(3.0)
9. Attacked someone with the idea of seriously hurting/killing them?	30	(24.6)	264	(25.7)

NOTE: Women, $N = 122$; men, $N = 1,031$.

$*p < .05.$ $**p < .01.$

NOTES

1. There have been several adult tests of social control and differential association measures assessed against deterrence, low self-control, social learning, strain, or subcultural theory measures (see, e.g., Burton et al. 1994; Ginsberg and Greenley 1978; Makkai and Braithwaite 1991; Tittle 1980).

2. Covington's (1985) tests of social control and differential association theories differed from the variables presented in this study. For example, involvement was not included as a social control variable, and individual definitions toward crime were not included as a differential association variable.

3. Strain theory, a fundamental perspective that also offers explanations on criminal behavior, was not included in the final analysis. Although Agnew's (1985) general strain theory has received some empirical support, Merton's social strain theory has received less support in previous studies. We originally included social strain variables that tested relative deprivation and blocked opportunities for both men and women in the data set. The variables measuring blocked opportunities were not reliable (.44) and were not used in the analysis. The variables measuring relative deprivation (reliable at .74) were regressed separately with all dependent crime variables. Relative deprivation was not significant for women for any type of crime and was significant only for male property crime but not for male drug or violent offenses. When relative deprivation was regressed against social control theory and/or differential association theory, relative deprivation had no effect for any type of crime.

4. Incidence data (how many times in the past year) were collected on all criminal behaviors but were not used due to a low reliability of the incidence subscales. The 35-item general crime incidence scale was, however, reliable at .61.

5. We are not suggesting that women are becoming more violent in their criminal involvement, especially as they relate to the women's self-reported involvement of violent crime, particularly the three "hit or threatened to hit" measures in the violent crime subscale (see appendix). The similarities in self-reported crime participation by women and men in our study can be accounted for in part by English (1993:373), who found that incarcerated adult women and men prisoners had similar participation rates for assault, robbery, motor vehicle theft, fraud, and dealing drugs. Our data show, however, that women and men participate in a wide variety of criminal behaviors, from less serious to more serious, which may or may not be related to their conviction offense.

6. A potential weakness of our measures is the varying time frame of our independent and dependent variables (e.g., the time frame for "peer attachment" and "marital attachment" is current, the time frame for "criminal friends" is in the past year, while the time frame for the dependent measure of prevalence is lifetime). We are largely assuming that our measures of our independent variables are relatively stable over time. Furthermore, we believe that our analysis has merit despite these issues. Future research would benefit from longitudinal analysis to determine the stability of theoretical variables over time.

7. Commitment, an element of Hirschi's (1969) social bond, was not used in the analysis due to its low reliability.

8. Men and women were also analyzed separately using correlations between differential association variables with the dependent variables. Our analyses revealed that a significant correlation existed between all variables. For the sample as a whole, the three differential association measures are more highly correlated with each other than are the five measures of social control. This may increase the likelihood of finding greater consistency with differential association measures.

9. When bivariate correlations were analyzed separately by gender, a mixed portrayal emerged for social control variables. Attachment to parents for both men and women was significantly and inversely related to all types of crime. For men, attachment to friends, involvement, and belief were significantly related to all crime types, with the exception of marital attachment, which was significant only for property crime. For women, attachment to friends and marital attachment were related

to drug and property crimes but not violent crime. On the other hand, involvement was significantly related to women's drug and violent crimes but not women's property offenses. Finally, belief was significantly related to women's property crime and violent crime but was not significantly related to women's drug crime.

10. We separately analyzed the control variables with each of the theories before regressing them together as shown in Table C.5. The results of the separate regressions show a significant relationship between age, race, and self-reported offending behavior. Age was inversely related to crime—that is, as age increased, less crime was committed. Men and women of color reported they committed significantly less crime than did Caucasian men and women. When social control theory was introduced into the equation with the three control variables, all social control variables, except for marital attachment, were significantly related to criminal offending. All social control variables were significant in the predicted direction, except for attachment to friends. When social control variables were removed and differential association variables were regressed with the three control variables, all three differential association variables were significantly and directly related to crime in the predicted direction.

11. To detect the presence of an interaction between peer attachment and criminal friends, we introduced a multiplicative term into each regression equation. A hierarchical F-test indicated that an interaction effect was not present for women, but an interaction existed for men for drug, property, and general crime scales (Jaccard, Turrisi, and Wan 1990). The difference between the R^2 values in the main effect and interactive models indicated that the interaction contributed less than 1 percent to each model (.63 percent for drug, .89 percent for general crime, and .90 percent for property offenses).

REFERENCES

Adler, Freda. 1975. *Sisters in Crime: The Rise of the New Female Offender.* New York: McGraw-Hill.

Agnew, Robert. 1985. "Social Control Theory and Delinquency: A Longitudinal Test." *Criminology* 23:47-61.

Akers, Ronald L. 1996. "Is Differential Association/Social Learning Cultural Deviance Theory?" *Criminology* 34:229-47.

———. 1998. *Social Learning and Social Structure: A General Theory of Crime and Deviance.* Boston: Northeastern University Press.

Akers, Ronald L., Marvin Krohn, Lonn Lanza-Kaduce, and Marcia Radosevich. 1979. "Social Learning and Deviant Behavior: A Specific Test of a General Theory." *American Sociological Review* 44:636-55.

Akers, Ronald L., and Anthony LaGreca. 1988. "Alcohol, Contact with the Legal System, and Illegal Behavior among the Elderly." In *Older Offenders,* edited by Belinda Mccarthy and Robert Langworthy. New York: Praeger.

———. 1991. "Alcohol Use among the Elderly: Social Learning, Community Context, and Life Events." In *Society, Culture, and Drinking Patterns Re-Examined,* edited by David J. Pittman and Helene Raskin White. New Brunswick, NJ: Rutgers Center of Alcohol Studies.

Akers, Ronald L., Anthony LaGreca, John Cochran, and Christine Sellers. 1989. "Social Learning Theory and Alcohol Behavior among the Elderly." *Sociological Quarterly* 30:625-38.

Alarid, Leanne Fiftal, Velmer S. Burton, James W. Marquart, Francis T. Cullen, and Steven J. Cuvelier. 1996. "Women's Roles in Serious Offenses: A Study of Adult Felons." *Justice Quarterly* 13:431-54.

Andrews, D. A., and James Bonta. 1994. *The Psychology of Criminal Conduct.* Cincinnati, OH: Anderson.

Benda, Brent B. 1994. "Testing Competing Theoretical Concepts: Adolescent Alcohol Consumption." *Deviant Behavior* 15:375-96.

Boeringer, Scot, Constance L. Shehan, and Ronald L. Akers. 1991. "Social Contexts and Social Learning in Sexual Coercion and Aggression: Assessing the Contribution of Fraternity Membership." *Family Relations* 40:558-64.

Burton, Velmer S. 1991. "Explaining Adult Criminality: Testing Strain, Differential Association, and Control Theories." Ph.D. dissertation, University of Cincinnati.

Burton, Velmer S., Francis T. Cullen, T. David Evans, Leanne Fiftal Alarid, and R. Gregory Dunaway. 1998. "Gender, Self-Control, and Crime." *Journal of Research in Crime and Delinquency* 35:123-47.

Burton, Velmer S., Francis T. Cullen, T. David Evans, and R. Gregory Dunaway. 1994. "Reconsidering Strain Theory: Operationalization, Rival Theories, and Adult Criminality." *Journal of Quantitative Criminology* 10:213-40.

Burton, Velmer S., Francis T. Cullen, T. David Evans, R. Gregory Dunaway, Sesha R. Kethineni, and Gary L. Payne. 1995. "The Impact of Parental Controls on Delinquency." *Journal of Criminal Justice* 23:111-26.

Burton, Velmer S., James W. Marquart, Steven J. Cuvelier, Robert J. Hunter, and Leanne Fiftal. 1993. "The Harris County CRIPP Program: An Outline for Evaluation, Part 1." *Texas Probation* 8:1-8.

Canter, Rachelle J. 1982. "Family Correlates of Male and Female Delinquency." *Criminology* 20:149-67.

Caspi, Avshalom, Terrie E. Moffitt, Phil A. Silva, Magda Stouthamer-Loeber, Robert F. Krueger, and Pamela S. Schmutte. 1994. "Are Some People Crime Prone? Replications of the Personality-Crime Relationship across Countries, Genders, Races, and Methods." *Criminology* 32:163-95.

Chesney-Lind, Meda. 1989. "Girls' Crime and Woman's Place: Toward a Feminist Model of Female Delinquency." *Crime and Delinquency* 35:5-29.

Chesney-Lind, Meda, and Randall G. Shelden. 1992. Girls, *Delinquency, and Juvenile Justice.* Pacific Grove, CA: Brooks/Cole.

Cole, Stephen. 1975. "The Growth of Scientific Knowledge: Theories of Deviance as a Case Study." In *The Idea of Social Structure: Papers in Honor of Robert K. Merton,* edited by Lewis A. Coser. New York: Harcourt Brace.

Conger, Rand. 1976. "Social Control and Social Learning Models of Delinquency: A Synthesis." *Criminology* 14:17-40.

Costello, Barbara. 1997. "On the Logical Adequacy of Cultural Deviance Theories." *Theoretical Criminology* 1:403-28.

Covington, Jeanette. 1985. "Gender Differences in Criminality among Heroin Users." *Journal of Research in Crime and Delinquency* 22:329-53.

Cressey, Donald. 1953. *Other People's Money.* Glencoe, IL: Free Press.

Cronbach, Lee J. 1951. "Coefficient Alpha and the Internal Structure of Tests." *Psychometrika* 16:297-334.

Daly, Kathleen, and Meda Chesney-Lind. 1988. "Feminism and Criminology." *Justice Quarterly* 5:497-538.

Dull, R. Thomas. 1983. "Friend's Use and Adult Drug and Drinking Behavior: A Further Test of Differential Association Theory." *Journal of Criminal Law and Criminology* 74:1608-19.

Elliott, Delbert S., and Suzanne S. Ageton. 1980. "Reconciling Race and Class Differences in Self-Reported and Official Estimates of Delinquency." *American Sociological Review* 45:95-110.

English, Kim. 1993. "Self Reported Crime Rates of Women Prisoners." *Journal of Quantitative Criminology* 9:357-82.

Eve, Raymond. 1978. "A Study of the Efficacy of Interactions of Several Theories for Explaining Rebelliousness among High School Students." *Journal of Criminal Law and Criminology* 69:115-25.

Fiftal, Leanne E. 1993. "Assessing Adult Female Criminality: Testing Differential Association and Social Control Theories." Master's thesis, Sam Houston State University.

Friedman, Jennifer, and Dennis P. Rosenbaum. 1988. "Social Control Theory: The Salience of Components of Age, Gender, and Type of Crime." *Journal of Quantitative Criminology* 4:363-81.

Ginsberg, Irving J., and James R. Greenley. 1978. "Competing Theories of Marijuana Use: A Longitudinal Study." *Journal of Health and Social Behavior* 19:22-34.

Gottfredson, Michael R., and Travis Hirschi. 1990. *A General Theory of Crime.* Stanford, CA: Stanford University Press.

Griffin, Brenda S., and Charles T. Griffin. 1978. "Marijuana Use among Students and Peers." *Drug Forum* 7:155-65.

Hagan, John. 1989. *Structural Criminology.* New Brunswick, NJ: Rutgers University Press.

Heidensohn, Frances M. 1985. *Women and Crime.* New York: Macmillan.

Hindelang, Michael J. 1973. "Causes of Delinquency: A Partial Replication and Extension." *Social Problems* 20:471-87.

Hindelang, Michael J., Travis Hirschi, and Joseph G. Weis. 1981. *Measuring Delinquency.* Beverly Hills, CA: Sage.

Hirschi, Travis. 1969. *Causes of Delinquency.* Berkeley: University of California Press.

———. 1996. "Theory without Ideas: Reply to Akers." *Criminology* 34:249-56.

Horney, Julie, and Ineke Haen Marshall. 1992. "Risk Perceptions among Serious Offenders: The Role of Crime and Punishment." *Criminology* 30:575-94.

Horney, Julie, D. Wayne Osgood, and Ineke Haen Marshall. 1995. "Criminal Careers in the Short-Term: Intra-Individual Variability in Crime and Its Relation to Local Life Circumstances." *American Sociological Review* 60:655-73.

Immarigeon, Russ, and Meda Chesney-Lind. 1993. "Women's Prisons: Overcrowded and Overused." In *It's a Crime: Women and Justice,* edited by Roslyn Muraskin and Ted Alleman. Englewood Cliffs, NJ: Regents/Prentice Hall.

Jaccard, James, Robert Turrisi, and Choi K. Wan. 1990. *Interaction Effects in Multiple Regression.* Newbury Park, CA: Sage.

Jackson, Elton F., Charles R. Tittle, and Mary Jean Burke. 1986. "Offense-Specific Models of the Differential Association Process." *Social Problems* 33:335-56.

Jaquith, Susan M. 1981. "Adolescent Marijuana and Alcohol Use: An Empirical Test of Differential Association Theory." *Criminology* 19:271-80.

Johnson, Richard. 1979. *Juvenile Delinquency and Its Origins: An Integrated Theoretical Approach.* Cambridge, MA: Cambridge University Press.

Johnson, Richard E., Anastasios C. Marcos, and Stephen J. Bahr. 1987. "The Role of Peers in the Complex Etiology of Adolescent Drug Use." *Criminology* 25:323-40.

Kandel, Denise, and Mark Davies. 1991. "Friendship Networks, Intimacy, and Illicit Drug Use in Young Adulthood: A Comparison of Two Competing Theories." *Criminology* 29:441-69.

Kornhauser, Ruth. 1978. *Social Sources of Delinquency.* Chicago: University of Chicago Press.

Krohn, Marvin. 1995. "Control and Deterrence Theories of Criminality." In *Criminology: A Contemporary Handbook,* 2nd ed., edited by Joseph F. Sheley. Belmont, CA: Wadsworth.

Krohn, Marvin, Lonn Lanza-Kaduce, and Ronald Akers. 1984. "Community Context and Theories of Deviant Behavior: An Examination of Social Learning and Social Bonding Theories." *The Sociological Quarterly* 25:353-71.

LaGrange, Randy L., and Helene Raskin White. 1985. "Age Differences in Delinquency: A Test of Theory." *Criminology* 23:19-45.

Lasley, James R. 1988. "Toward a Control Theory of White-Collar Offending." *Journal of Quantitative Criminology* 4:347-62.

Laub, John H., Daniel S. Nagin, and Robert J. Sampson. 1998. "Trajectories of Change in Criminal Offending: Good Marriages and the Desistance Process." *American Sociological Review* 63:225-38.

Leonard, Eileen B. 1982. *Women, Crime, and Society: A Critique of Theoretical Criminology.* New York: Longman.

Longshore, Douglas, Susan Turner, and Judith A. Stein. 1996. "Self-Control in a Criminal Sample: An Examination of Construct Validity." *Criminology* 34:209-28.

Macdonald, Patrick T. 1989. "Competing Theoretical Explanations of Cocaine Use: Differential Association Versus Control Theory." *Journal of Contemporary Criminal Justice* 5:73-88.

MacKenzie, Doris Layton, and Robert Brame. 1994. "Shock Incarceration and Positive Adjustment during Community Supervision: A Multi-Site Evaluation." Presented at the annual meeting of the Academy of Criminal Justice Sciences, June, Chicago.

Makkai, Toni, and John Braithwaite. 1991. "Criminological Theories and Regulatory Compliance." *Criminology* 29:191-220.

Matsueda, Ross L. 1982. "Testing Control Theory and Differential Association: A Causal Modeling Approach." *American Sociological Review* 47:489-504.

———. 1988. "The Current State of Differential Association Theory." *Crime and Delinquency* 34:277-306.

———. 1989. "The Dynamics of Moral Beliefs and Minor Deviance." *Social Forces* 68:428-57.

———. 1997. "'Cultural Deviance Theory': The Remarkable Persistence of a Flawed Term." *Theoretical Criminology* 1:429-52.

Matsueda, Ross L., and Karen Heimer. 1987. "Race, Family Structure, and Delinquency: A Test of Differential Association and Social Control Theories." *American Sociological Review* 52:826-40.

McGee, Zina T. 1992. "Social Class Differences in Parental and Peer Influence on Adolescent Drug Use." *Deviant Behavior* 13:349-72.

Merton, Robert. 1938. "Social Theory and Anomie." *American Sociological Review* 3:672-82.

Messerschmidt, James W. 1993. *Masculinities and Crime.* Lanham, MD: Rowman & Littlefield.

Messner, Steven F., and Richard Rosenfeld. 1994. *Crime and the American Dream.* Belmont, CA: Wadsworth.

Miller, Eleanor M. 1986. *Street Woman.* Philadelphia, PA: Temple University Press.

Naffine, Ngaire, and Fay Gale. 1989. "Testing the Nexus: Crime, Gender, and Unemployment." *British Journal of Criminology* 29:144-56.

Orcutt, James. 1987. "Differential Association and Marijuana Use: A Closer Look at Sutherland (with a Little Help from Becker)." *Criminology* 25:341-58.

Paternoster, Raymond, Robert Brame, Paul Mazerolle, and Alex Piquero. 1998. "Using the Correct Statistical Test for the Equality of Regression Coefficients." *Criminology* 36:859-66.

Paternoster, Raymond, and Ruth Triplett. 1988. "Disaggregating Self-Reported Delinquency and Its Implications for Theory." *Criminology* 26:591-625.

Rand, Alicia. 1987. "Transitional Life Events and Desistance from Delinquency and Crime." In *From Boy to Man: From Delinquency to Crime,* edited by Marvin Wolfgang, Terence P. Thornberry, and Robert M. Figlio. Chicago: University of Chicago Press.

Richie, Beth E. 1996. *Compelled to Crime: The Gender Entrapment of Battered Black Women.* New York: Routledge Kegan Paul.

Rosenbaum, James L. 1987. "Social Control, Gender and Delinquency: An Analysis of Drug, Property and Violent Offenders." *Justice Quarterly* 4:117-32.

Sampson, Robert J., and John H. Laub. 1990. "Crime and Deviance over the Life Course: The Salience of Adult Social Bonds." *American Sociological Review* 55:609-27.

———. 1993. *Crime in the Making.* Cambridge, MA: Harvard University Press.

Short, James F. 1960. "Differential Association as a Hypothesis: Problems of Empirical Testing." *Social Problems* 8:14-24.

Silberman, Matthew. 1976. "Toward a Theory of Deterrence." *American Sociological Review* 41:442-61.

Simons, Ronald L., Martin G. Miller, and Stephen M. Aigner. 1980. "Contemporary Theories of Deviance and Female Delinquency: An Empirical Test." *Journal of Research in Crime and Delinquency* 17:42-57.

Smart, Carol. 1976. *Women, Crime and Criminology: A Feminist Critique.* Boston: Routledge Kegan Paul.

Sutherland, Edwin H. 1947. *Principles of Criminology.* 4th ed. Philadelphia, PA: Lippincott.

Sutherland, Edwin H., and Donald Cressey. 1955. *Principles of Criminology.* Philadelphia, PA: Lippincott.

Tittle, Charles R. 1980. *Sanctions and Social Deviance.* New York: Praeger.

Tittle, Charles, Mary Jean Burke, and Elton Jackson. 1986. "Modeling Sutherland's Theory of Differential Association: Toward an Empirical Clarification." *Social Forces* 65:405-32.

U.S. Bureau of Justice Statistics. 1994. *Special Report, March, 1994.* Washington DC: Government Printing Office.

Warr, Mark, and Mark Stafford. 1993. "Age, Peers, and Delinquency." *Criminology* 31:17-40.

Winfree, L. Thomas Curt, T. Griffiths, and Christine Sellers. 1989. "Social Learning Theory, Drug Use and American Indian Youths: A Cross-Cultural Test." *Justice Quarterly* 6:395-418.

Appendix D

An Introduction to Using SPSS for Windows

Lisa M. Gilman

The Statistical Package for the Social Sciences (SPSS) is one of the most popular statistical software packages used in the social sciences. As you will see, SPSS for Windows is very user friendly. With just a few clicks of the mouse, SPSS enables you to calculate various statistics and create charts and tables for statistical analysis and presentations. This appendix is designed to provide you with a basic introduction to SPSS. Although this introduction can be used with any Windows-based version of SPSS, keep in mind that SPSS is continually being modified. All of the examples provided are conducted using SPSS, version 10. If you are using a different version, you may find some slight differences.

FAMILIARIZING YOURSELF WITH SPSS

Using SPSS for Windows is similar to using other Windows-based applications. First, to access SPSS, you must open the program by double-clicking the left mouse button on the SPSS for Windows icon. If you have SPSS installed on your home computer, this icon will be located in the SPSS file folder. If you are on a computer in your school's computer lab, the icon will likely be located in a folder that contains statistical software or other software programs.

When SPSS begins you will first see the SPSS Data Editor, as shown in Figure D.1. The SPSS Data Editor is where data to be analyzed are entered by hand or data files that have already been created (data set) are loaded in.

The data editor is a data matrix made up of columns and rows. Each column represents a different variable. When data are present in the data editor, the variable names are at the top of each column; when no data are present, the columns read "var." The cases or observations to be analyzed are in the rows, with one observation per row. If you are using the student version of SPSS, you are limited to 50 variables and 1,500 observations. There are no variable/observation limits in the commercial version.

Exhibit D.1   The SPSS Data Editor

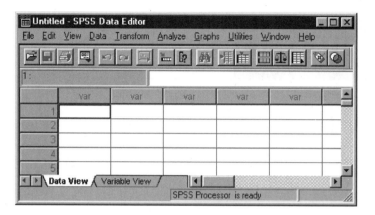

Commands are given to SPSS by clicking the left mouse button on the command you want to execute from drop-down menus, toolbars, and dialog boxes. Across the top of the screen or SPSS window is the menu bar. The menu bar contains the drop-down menus from which most SPSS commands can be run. To access a drop-down menu, you click on the menu title for the command you want to use. For example, if you click on Edit, a new menu will drop down from the menu bar with various edit commands. Familiarizing yourself with what commands are accessible from each drop-down menu will help you feel more comfortable with SPSS. To acquaint you with these menus, a summary of each SPSS drop-down menu is provided in Box D.1.

Box D.1   Summary of SPSS Drop-Down Menus

The **File** menu enables you to open and save data files, import data created by other software, and print the contents of the data editor.

Use the **Edit** menu to cut, copy, and paste data; find data within the open data set; and change options settings.

The **View** menu allows you to change how the data editor looks by changing fonts, turning toolbars on and off, turning grid lines on and off, and turning value labels on and off.

Use the **Data** menu to sort, select, or weight cases.

The **Transform** menu lets you make changes to selected variables, compute new variables, recode the values of existing ones, and replace missing values.

Use the **Analyze** menu to select the statistical procedure you want to use.

The **Graphs** menu allows you to produce a variety of two- and three-dimensional graphical displays of your data for purposes of data analysis and presentation.

Use the **Utilities** menu to obtain information about the variables in the open data set and select a list of variables to appear in dialog boxes.

The **Window** menu lets you switch between SPSS windows or minimize all open SPSS windows.

Use the **Help** menu to access SPSS help topics and run the tutorial.

The second way to communicate with SPSS is via the toolbar, which is just below the menu bar. The toolbar is composed of shortcuts to frequently used commands such as Save File and Print Document. These shortcuts are identified by small pictures or icons. Because all of the commands you will be using are accessible from the drop-down menus, little emphasis is placed on the use of toolbars in this appendix. However, to familiarize yourself with the commands accessible from the toolbar, simply move your mouse over each icon; a small box will appear with the name of the command the icon executes.

When you choose an SPSS command to execute, you are frequently presented with a dialog box. Dialog boxes are the means by which SPSS requests additional information from you for the procedure you want to execute. For example, the dialog box in Exhibit D.2 allows you to set a number of options to display names and descriptions of variables in particular ways. To execute a command, you must click the OK button.

Exhibit D.2   The Options Dialog Box

Another feature in SPSS that you should be familiar with is the SPSS Viewer, also referred to as the Output window. The SPSS Viewer displays the results of each operation executed in SPSS and is divided into two panes. The left pane is referred to as the output navigator. The output navigator contains an outline of everything you asked SPSS to do from the beginning of the session. This pane is good for navigating through the output you have produced. It allows you to easily refer back to any given table or graph. The right pane contains the actual output, such as statistical tables, charts, and text. (See Exhibit D.3.)

Exhibit D.3   The SPSS Viewer

LOOKING AT DATA

Now that you are familiar with SPSS, you can begin playing with data. After you have begun an SPSS session and are in the empty data editor, you must enter your own data or open an existing data set. Entering your own data is beyond the scope of this appendix. Therefore, if you have collected your own data, you may want to refer to the SPSS help file or SPSS user's manual for instructions on entering your own data and defining variables.

To open a data set in SPSS, click on the File drop-down menu. From the File menu, click on Open. Another menu will drop down, asking what type of file you would like to open. Because you are interested in opening a data set for analysis, from the Open sub-menu, click on Data. To simplify instruction, directions such as these will appear in the following form in this appendix:

File → Open → Data

The Open File dialog box, shown in Exhibit D.4, will then open. At this stage, it is necessary to tell SPSS where to look for the file you want to open ("Look in"), the type of file you want to open ("Files of type"), and the name of the data file you want to open ("File name"). When you are done identifying the data set you want to open, click Open. Your selected data file will open in the data editor.

Exhibit D.4   The "Open File" Dialog Box

Now, following the steps outlined above, open the data file NCS91.POR from the disk that came with the textbook. As shown in Exhibit D.5, the variable name is at the top of each column (note that SPSS limits this name to only eight characters). Each row corresponds to a single observation (robbery victims in this case). Browse the data in the data window. At first glance, the data do not appear to make sense. Respondent 1 has the value 3 for AGE, the value 2 for COMPLETE, the value 3 for EDUC, the value 6 for INCOME, and the value 2 for SEX. These values represent a coding scheme in which response categories of each variable are assigned a numerical value so that SPSS can understand the data.

Exhibit D.5   The SPSS Data Editor with NCS91.POR Data

	age	complete	educ	income	sex
1	3.00	2.00	3.00	6.00	2.00
2	1.00	1.00	1.00	6.00	2.00
3	1.00	1.00	1.00	1.00	1.00
4	5.00	2.00	2.00	5.00	1.00
5	2.00	1.00	3.00	1.00	1.00

To better understand this, click on the Variable View tab at the bottom of the data editor. As shown in Exhibit D.6, the variables are now listed by row and the columns represent variable characteristics. Browse the variable list and the characteristics of each variable. Look at the column labeled Values. Click on the Values cell that corresponds with the variable SEX (row 5). The Value Labels dialog box opens to reveal the coding scheme for respondent/victim's sex: 1 stands for "Male" and 2 for "Female." These are referred to as *value labels* and are used to identify the values assigned to the given response categories for each variable. (Note: If the variable is continuous in nature, such as age or income, value labels are not necessary.) To close the Value Labels dialog box, click OK. Now return to the data by clicking on the Data View tab at the bottom of the data editor.

Exhibit D.6   The SPSS Data Editor in Variable View

Looking at the variable characteristics can be useful when you are trying to understand what the variables are and how they are measured (whether they are continuous or categorical variables). However, when you are primarily interested in the value labels, there are three additional ways to view this information. The most common way is looking at a codebook. A codebook contains information pertinent to each variable in a data set. If you collect your own data, you should create a codebook for yourself based on the original survey instrument for future reference.

If there is no codebook available for the data set you are working with, you can produce a basic codebook yourself using SPSS.

Utilities → File Info

This command will open the SPSS Viewer, with a detailed list of all the variables in the open data file. Box D.2 shows a sample of the "File Info" output.

Box D.2   File Info Output

Name	Position
SEX	Sex 5
Measurement Level:	Ordinal
Column Width: 8 Alignment:	Right
Print Format:	F8.2
Write Format:	F8.2

Value Label

1.00 Male
2.00 Female

Another way you can see the value labels is to simply turn the value labels on.
View → Value Labels
This command turns the variable labels on in the data window. Now, as you can see in Exhibit D.7, respondent 1 is 25–34 years old (AGE), was the victim of an attempted robbery (COMPLETE), has completed some college (EDUC), has an income over $50,000 (INCOME), and is female (FEMALE).

Exhibit D.7   The SPSS Data Editor With Value Labels

Keep in mind that not everyone sampled in any given survey will be willing to answer everything. In these instances the respondent's answer (or lack thereof) is coded as a *missing value*. Missing values are values used by the researcher to refer to data that are not present for whatever reason or to ambiguous responses. Missing values are identified from the variable view screen under "missing." In addition, these values are frequently assigned value labels identifying them as missing or unknown. For some statistical calculations, SPSS ignores missing values and calculates the statistic based on the responses of the other respondents.

ANALYZING DATA

Now that you have an open data file and are somewhat familiar with the data, you can begin describing the data in statistical terms. This appendix covers four techniques for analyzing data: frequency distributions, graphs, crosstabulations, and comparing means.

A *frequency distribution* is a table that displays how many and what percentage of observations fall into given categories for the variable of interest. The goal of frequency distributions is to summarize the data so that they are easy to understand.

Using the NCS91.POR data file, compute a frequency distribution for the variable SEX (victim's sex).

Analyze → Descriptive Statistics → Frequencies

The Frequencies dialog box will open, allowing you to indicate which variable you would like frequencies of. This is shown in Exhibit D.8. To move the variable from the variable list on the left to the Variable(s) box on the right, you need to scroll down the list of variables until you find the variable you are interested in, click on the variable name to highlight it, and then click on the arrow in the middle. When you have moved the variable(s), click OK to produce the frequency table in the SPSS Viewer, as shown in Exhibit D.9.

Exhibit D.8   The Frequencies Dialog Box

Exhibit D.9   A Frequency Table

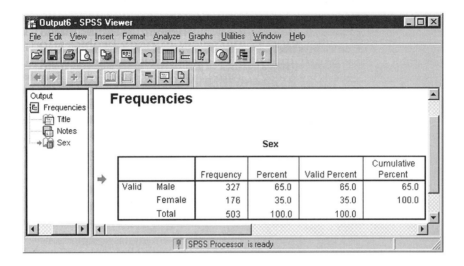

You can produce the same results using a *bar chart*. A bar chart graphically displays how many and what percentage of observations fall into given categories for the variable of interest. Go ahead and produce a bar chart for victim's sex to look at the percentage of respondents who fit into each category.

Graphs → Bar → Simple → Define

When requesting a bar chart, you must place the variable that you are interested in analyzing in the Category Axis box. For this example, the bars should represent "% of cases"; this option can be selected from the top portion of the dialog box, as shown in Exhibit D.10. After you have made your selection, click OK to create the bar chart. (See Exhibit D.11.)

Exhibit D.10   Defining a Bar Chart

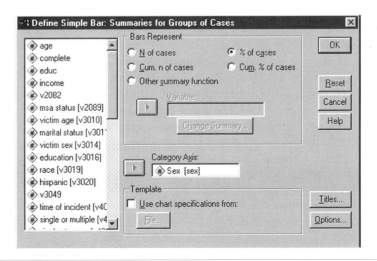

Exhibit D.11 A Bar Chart

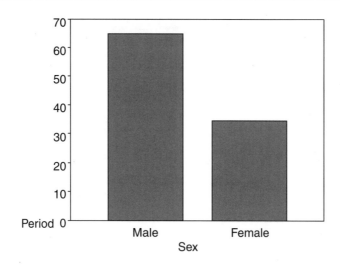

Frequency distributions and bar charts are good for describing the distribution of the variables in the data set. However, to examine the relationship between two variables, a different set of statistical techniques are necessary. Two such techniques are covered here. The first, *crosstabulations,* enables you to look at the relationship between two categorical variables (nominal or ordinal). For example, say you want to look at the relationship between homicide victim provocation (the victim provoked the event) and whether or not the homicide defendant was convicted. Your research question may be, "Does victim provocation decrease the likelihood of conviction?" You can explore this using the crosstabulation feature in SPSS. Open HOMICIDE.POR and request a crosstab for the variables PROVOKE and CONVICT.

Analyze → Descriptive Statistics → Crosstabs

In addition to indicating what variables you want SPSS to put in the crosstab table, you can indicate that you want SPSS to calculate percentages for the independent variable. To select the appropriate percentages, you must open the Cell Display dialog box by clicking the Cells button (see Exhibit D.12). You should know what variable is the independent variable and what variable is the dependent variable. In this example, victim provocation (column) is the independent variable and conviction (row) is the dependent variable—victim provocation is hypothesized to influence conviction; therefore, column percentages are requested. It makes no difference to SPSS where you place your dependent and independent variables. However, to interpret the table correctly to assess the relationship between the variables of interest, it is important that the appropriate percentages are calculated. When you are done selecting the appropriate percentages, click Continue. If you are familiar with statistics, you may want SPSS to calculate chi-square. You can choose this option by clicking the Statistics button. After you have chosen your statistics and cell options, click OK to have SPSS create the crosstab table.

Exhibit D.12 The Crosstabs and "Cell Display" Dialog Boxes

The results of the requested table are shown in Exhibit D.13. As you can see, 84% of homicides in which there was no victim provocation resulted in a conviction, compared to only 67% of homicides where provocation was involved. So it does appear that victim provocation decreases the likelihood of conviction for homicide defendants. You may want to further explore this relationship by choosing a control variable such as race of the defendant, prior criminal history, or victim/offender relationship. To do this, choose your control variable and place it in the Layer window near the bottom of the Crosstabs dialog box.

Exhibit D.13 A Crosstabs Table

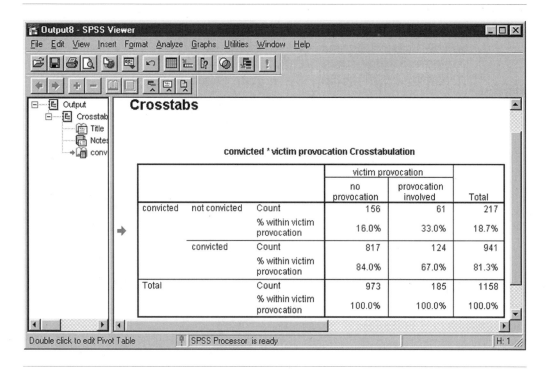

When the relationship of interest involves an interval/ratio (continuous) level variable, comparing the means of the outcome (dependent) variable is necessary. Say, for example, you are interested in comparing the sentence length of male and female homicide defendants. Research question: On average, for the crime of homicide, do women receive a shorter sentence than men? Let's find out!

Analyze → Compare Means → Means

When the Means dialog box opens, you need to tell SPSS what your dependent and independent variables are. As shown in Exhibit D.14, the dependent variable is incarceration term in days (PRITIME), and the independent variable is sex of the defendant (SEX). After selecting the variables of interest, click OK to have SPSS calculate the means for each variable.

Exhibit D.14 The Means Dialog Box

The output, as seen in Exhibit D.15, reflects that, on average, female homicide defendants are sentenced to a term of about 11,449 days (31.37 years), compared to about 16,518 days (45.25 years) for male homicide defendants. So the answer to the research question is, "Yes, on average, women convicted of homicide often receive a shorter sentence than do men convicted of homicide." Of course, keep in mind that there may be extraneous factors influencing the sentencing decision, such as prior criminal record, victim provocation, victim/offender relationships, and the race of the defendant or the victim, or the difference may simply be due to chance. Further analysis, which is beyond the scope of this appendix, would be necessary to evaluate these possibilities.

Exhibit D.15 The Calculated Means Report

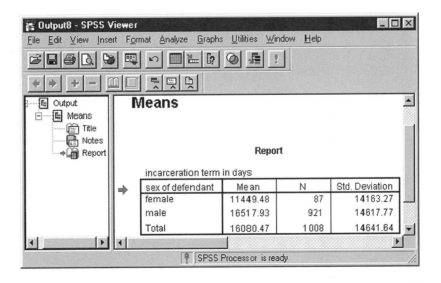

Selecting Cases

In some instances it may be necessary to select cases that meet a specific criterion for purposes of analysis. For instance, you may have a rather large data set that you want a random sample from, or you may want to look at only a particular group such as females. Open YOUTH.POR, then:

Data → Select Cases

The Select Cases dialog box (Exhibit D.16) has a number of options. If you want to include only those cases that meet a certain criterion, such as only females, you would select the "If condition is satisfied" option and click the If button to define what characteristic you would like to limit your sample to. Exhibit D.17 shows the Select Cases: If dialog box. For this example, the cases selected are only those cases in which the respondent is female; V1 is the variable "sex of respondent," and females are coded 0. When done, click Continue, then OK. Only those cases selected will be included in subsequent analyses. Cases not selected are identified in SPSS with a slash mark through the row number on the left of the data editor.

Exhibit D.16 The "Select Cases" Dialog Box

Exhibit D.17 The "Select Cases If" Dialog Box

If you wanted to choose a random sample from your data, you would select the "Random sample of cases" option from the main Select Cases dialog box and click on the Sample button to identify what percentage of cases you want to include for analysis. The Select Cases: Random Sample dialog box will open, requesting the sample size you desire (see Exhibit D.18). Click Continue. If you want to save the selected sample as a new data set for future analysis, you should tell SPSS to delete unselected cases. This is done by selecting "deleted" from the "Unselected Cases Are:" option near the bottom of the Select Cases dialog box (see Exhibit D.16).

Exhibit D.18 The "Select Cases: Random Sample" Dialog Box

Recoding Variables

In some instances, it may be necessary to recode variables to analyze the data in a specific way. Not all variables are coded as we want them to be coded. For example, we may want to look at the relationship between amount of television viewing and level of delinquency. To explore this relationship, we would recode the variable measuring the number of hours per week the respondent watches television (V21) into a dichotomous variable measuring frequent and infrequent television viewing, using the mean as the measure of center. In other words, we want to collapse everyone who watches television less than the average number of hours per week into a single category, and everyone who watches television more frequently than the average collapsed into another category.

The first step is to obtain the mean number of hours per week high school students watch television based on the sample of high school youth in YOUTH.POR. To calculate the mean, request a frequency distribution for the variable V21; be sure to click the Statistics button and select "Mean" as the measure of central tendency. Click Continue, then OK.

Analyze → Descriptive Statistics → Frequencies

The next step is telling SPSS that you want to recode a variable:

Transform → Recode → Into Different Variables

Before we can tell SPSS to create a new variable based on our specifications, we must indicate what our old variable is. In the Recode into Different Variables dialog box (see Exhibit D.19) select V21 and click the arrow to move the variable to the Numeric Variable → Output Variable window. Because SPSS will create a new variable based on the new coding scheme, we must tell SPSS what the name of the new variable is going to be ("Name"). For this example, I have named the new variable "tv." After you enter a name, you must click Change or the new variable will not be created.

Exhibit D.19 The "Recode into Different Variables" Dialog Box

The next step is to specify what the old and new values are. Click the Old and New Values button to define these parameters. The Recode into Different Variables: Old and New Values dialog box will open. This dialog box is where you specify how you want to code the new variable.

The left side of the dialog box is where old values are specified; on the right is where the new values are specified. After you indicate what the old values were and tell SPSS what the new values will be, you need to click the Add button to put the recode specifications in the Old → New box. For this example, as shown in Exhibit D.20, a range was specified to identify those respondents who watch television less than average; 11.8 or fewer hours of television viewing per week is coded as 1 and represents infrequent television viewing. Watching television frequently is defined as watching television more often than average. Therefore, the range includes anyone who watches television at or above the mean number of hours watched per week for this sample; 11.81 (the mean) and up are coded as 2 to represent frequent television viewing. When all your recode specifications are completed, click Continue to exit the dialog box, then click OK to execute the recode command. If there are missing data in your data set, it is important that you identify these and code them accordingly. Frequently, missing values are coded as 99. If you did not identify this value as a missing value, SPSS would include it in the second TV viewing category. That's an awful lot of television viewing for one week! After executing the command, it is always a good idea to obtain a frequency distribution to look at the distribution of your new variable to check for abnormalities.

Exhibit D.20 The "Recode into Different Variables: Old and New Values" Dialog Box

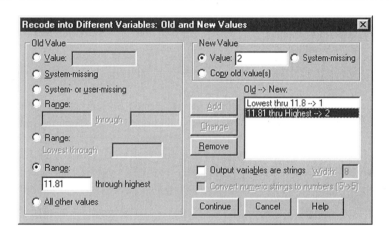

If you look at the frequency distribution for TV viewing in Exhibit D.21, you will notice that there are no value labels. If someone who is unfamiliar with how you coded your data looked at this output, he or she would not be able to understand what 1 and 2 mean.

Exhibit D.21 TV Viewing Frequency Distribution

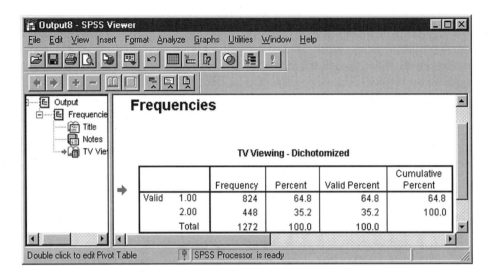

To assign value labels to your new variable, click on the variable name ("tv" in this example). This will bring you to the Variable View screen. Click on the Labels cell for the new TV Viewing variable. The Variable Labels dialog box will open (see Exhibit D.22). Type the number "1" in the Value box, and type in a value label in the Value Label box. Do the same thing for the frequent television viewing category. Now you can examine the data and determine whether there is a relationship between the amount of television watched and levels of delinquency.

Exhibit D.22 Value Labels in the "Variable Labels" Dialog Box

After you have created new variables, or made any changes to your data that you do not want to lose, you should save your work. To save the data file, click:

   File → Save As

In the Save As dialog box, indicate where you want to save the file ("Save in"), give your file a name, and click Save (see Exhibit D.23).

Exhibit D.23 The "Save As" Dialog Box

CONCLUSION

At this point you should be familiar with SPSS and able to complete all the exercises included in this book. Remember, the more you practice, the more comfortable you will be with SPSS. If you have trouble, don't be afraid to refer to the SPSS help file or Statistical Tutor (which are available from the Help drop-down menu), your instructor, or the computer lab consultant.

Appendix E

TABLE OF RANDOM NUMBERS

Line/Col.	(1)	(2)	(3)	(4)	(5)	(6)	(7)	(8)	(9)	(10)	(11)	(12)	(13)	(14)
1	10480	15011	01536	02011	81647	91646	69179	14194	62590	36207	20969	99570	91291	90700
2	22368	46573	25595	85393	30995	89198	27982	53402	93965	34095	52666	19174	39615	99505
3	24130	48360	22527	97265	76393	64809	15179	24830	49340	32081	30680	19655	63348	58629
4	42167	93093	06243	61680	07856	16376	39440	53537	71341	57004	00849	74917	97758	16379
5	37570	39975	81837	16656	06121	91782	60468	81305	49684	60672	14110	06927	01263	54613
6	77921	06907	11008	42751	27756	53498	18602	70659	90655	15053	21916	81825	44394	42880
7	99562	72905	56420	69994	98872	31016	71194	18738	44013	48840	63213	21069	10634	12952
8	96301	91977	05463	07972	18876	20922	94595	56869	69014	60045	18425	84903	42508	32307
9	89579	14342	63661	10281	17453	18103	57740	84378	25331	12566	58678	44947	05585	56941
10	85475	36857	43342	53988	53060	59533	38867	62300	08158	17983	16439	11458	18593	64952
11	28918	69578	88231	33276	70997	79936	56865	05859	90106	31595	01547	85590	91610	78188
12	63553	40961	48235	03427	49626	69445	18663	72695	52180	20847	12234	90511	33703	90322
13	09429	93969	52636	92737	88974	33488	36320	17617	30015	08272	84115	27156	30613	74952
14	10365	61129	87529	85689	48237	52267	67689	93394	01511	26358	85104	20285	29975	89868
15	07119	97336	71048	08178	77233	13916	47564	81056	97735	85977	29372	74461	28551	90707
16	51085	12765	51821	51259	77452	16308	60756	92144	49442	53900	70960	63990	75601	40719
17	02368	21382	52404	60268	89368	19885	55322	44819	01188	65255	64835	44919	05944	55157
18	01011	54092	33362	94904	31273	04146	18594	29852	71585	85030	51132	01915	92747	64951
19	52162	53916	46369	58586	23216	14513	83149	98736	23495	64350	94738	17752	35156	35749
20	07056	97628	33787	09998	42698	06691	76988	13602	51851	46104	88916	19509	25625	58104
21	48663	91245	85828	14346	09172	30168	90229	04734	59193	22178	30421	61666	99904	32812
22	54164	58492	22421	74103	47070	25306	76468	26384	58151	06646	21524	15227	96909	44592
23	32639	32363	05597	24200	13363	38005	94342	28728	35806	06912	17012	64161	18296	22851
24	29334	27001	87637	87308	58731	00256	45834	15398	46557	41135	10367	07684	36188	18510
25	02488	33062	28834	07351	19731	92420	60952	61280	50001	67658	32586	86679	50720	94953
26	81525	72295	04839	96423	24878	82651	66566	14778	76797	14780	13300	87074	79666	95725
27	29676	20591	68086	26432	46901	20849	89768	81536	86645	12659	92259	57102	80428	25280
28	00742	57392	39064	66432	84673	40027	32832	61362	98947	96067	64760	64584	96096	98253
29	05366	04213	25669	26422	44407	44048	37937	63904	45766	66134	75470	66520	34693	90449
30	91921	26418	64117	94305	26766	25940	39972	22209	71500	64568	91402	42416	07844	69618
31	00582	04711	87917	77341	42206	35126	74087	99547	81817	42607	43808	76655	62028	76630
32	00725	69884	62797	56170	86324	88072	76222	36086	84637	93161	76038	65855	77919	88006
33	69011	65797	95876	55293	18988	27354	26575	08625	40801	59920	29841	80150	12777	48501

(Continued)

Appendix E (Continued)

Line/Col.	(1)	(2)	(3)	(4)	(5)	(6)	(7)	(8)	(9)	(10)	(11)	(12)	(13)	(14)
34	25976	57948	29888	88604	67917	48708	18912	82271	65424	69774	33611	54262	85963	03547
35	09763	83473	73577	12908	30883	18317	28290	35797	05998	41688	34952	37888	38917	88050
36	91567	42595	27958	30134	04024	86385	29880	99730	55536	84855	29080	09250	79656	73211
37	17955	56349	90999	49127	20044	59931	06115	20542	18059	02008	73708	83317	36103	42791
38	46503	18584	18845	49618	02304	51038	20655	58727	28168	15475	56942	53389	20562	87338
39	92157	89634	94824	78171	84610	82834	09922	25417	44137	48413	25555	21246	35509	20468
40	14577	62765	35605	81263	39667	47358	56873	56307	61607	49518	89656	20103	77490	18062
41	98427	07523	33362	64270	01638	92477	66969	98420	04880	45585	46565	04102	46880	45709
42	34914	63976	88720	82765	34476	17032	87589	40836	32427	70002	70663	88863	77775	69348
43	70060	28277	39475	46473	23219	53416	94970	25832	69975	94884	19661	72828	00102	66794
44	53976	54914	06990	67245	68350	82948	11398	42878	80287	88267	47363	46634	06541	97809
45	76072	29515	40980	07391	58745	25774	22987	80059	39911	96189	41151	14222	60697	59583
46	90725	52210	83974	29992	65831	38857	50490	83765	55657	14361	31720	57375	56228	41546
47	64364	67412	33339	31926	14883	24413	59744	92351	97473	89286	35931	04110	23726	51900
48	08962	00358	31662	25388	61642	34072	81249	35648	56891	69352	48373	45578	78547	81788
49	95012	68379	93526	70765	10593	04542	76463	54328	02349	17247	28865	14777	62730	92277
50	15664	10493	20492	38391	91132	21999	59516	81652	27195	48223	46751	22923	32261	85653
51	16408	81899	04153	53381	79401	21438	83035	92350	36693	31238	59649	91754	72772	02338
52	18629	81953	05520	91962	04739	13092	97662	24822	94730	06496	35090	04822	86772	98289
53	73115	35101	47498	87637	99016	71060	88824	71013	18735	20286	23153	72924	35165	43040
54	57491	16703	23167	49323	45021	33132	12544	41035	80780	45393	44812	12515	98931	91202
55	30405	83946	23792	14422	15059	45799	22716	19792	09983	74353	68668	30429	70735	25499
56	16631	35006	85900	98275	32388	52390	16815	69298	82732	38480	73817	32523	41961	44437
57	96773	20206	42559	78985	05300	22164	24369	54224	35083	19687	11052	91491	60383	19746
58	38935	64202	14349	82674	66523	44133	00697	35552	35970	19124	63318	29686	03387	59846
59	31624	76384	17403	53363	44167	64486	64758	75366	76554	31601	12614	33072	60332	92325
60	78919	19474	23632	27889	47914	02584	37680	20801	72152	39339	34806	08930	85001	87820
61	03931	33309	57047	74211	63445	17361	62825	39908	05607	91284	68833	25570	38818	46920
62	74426	33278	43972	10119	89917	15665	52872	73823	73144	88662	88970	74492	51805	99378
63	09066	00903	20795	95452	92648	45454	09552	88815	16553	51125	79375	97596	16296	66092
64	42238	12426	87025	14267	20979	04508	64535	31355	86064	29472	47689	05974	52468	16834
65	16153	08002	26504	41744	81959	65642	74240	56302	00033	67107	77510	70625	28725	34191
66	21457	40742	29820	96783	29400	21840	15035	34537	33310	06116	95240	15957	16572	06004

Line/Col.	(1)	(2)	(3)	(4)	(5)	(6)	(7)	(8)	(9)	(10)	(11)	(12)	(13)	(14)
67	21581	57802	02050	89728	17937	37621	47075	42080	97403	48626	68995	43805	33386	21597
68	55612	78095	83197	33732	05810	24813	86902	60397	16489	03264	88525	42786	05269	92532
69	44657	66999	99324	51281	84463	60563	79312	93454	68876	25471	93911	25650	12682	73572
70	91340	84979	46949	81973	37949	61023	43997	15263	80644	43942	89203	71795	99533	50501
71	91227	21199	31935	27022	84067	05462	35216	14486	29891	68607	41867	14951	91696	85065
72	50001	38140	66321	19924	72163	09538	12151	06878	91903	18749	34405	56087	82790	70925
73	65390	05224	72958	28609	81406	39147	25549	48542	42627	45233	57202	94617	23772	07896
74	27504	96131	83944	41575	10573	08619	64482	73923	36152	05184	94142	25299	84387	34925
75	37169	94851	39117	89632	00959	16487	65536	49071	39782	17095	02330	74301	00275	48280
76	11508	70225	51111	38351	19444	66499	71945	05422	13442	78675	84081	66938	93654	59894
77	37449	30362	06694	54690	04052	53115	62757	95348	78662	11163	81651	50245	34971	52924
78	46515	70331	85922	38329	57015	15765	97161	17869	45349	61796	66345	81073	49106	79860
79	30986	81223	42416	58353	21532	30502	32305	86482	05174	07901	54339	58861	74818	46942
80	63798	64995	46583	09765	44160	78128	83991	42865	92520	83531	80377	35909	81250	54238
81	82486	84846	99254	67632	43218	50076	21361	64816	51202	88124	41870	52689	51275	83556
82	21885	32906	92431	09060	64297	51674	64126	62570	26123	05155	59194	52799	28225	85762
83	60336	98782	07408	53458	13564	59089	26445	29789	85205	41001	12535	12133	14645	23541
84	43937	46891	24010	25560	86355	33941	25786	54990	71899	15475	95434	98227	21824	19585
85	97656	63175	89303	16275	07100	92063	21942	18611	47348	20203	18534	03862	78095	50136
86	03299	01221	05418	38982	55758	92237	26759	86367	21216	98442	08303	56613	91511	75928
87	79626	06486	03574	17668	07785	76020	79924	25651	83325	88428	85076	72811	22717	50585
88	85636	68335	47539	03129	65651	11977	02510	26113	99447	68645	34327	15152	55230	93448
89	18039	14367	61337	06177	12143	46609	32989	74014	64708	00533	35398	58408	13261	47908
90	08362	15656	60627	36478	65648	16764	53412	09013	07832	41574	17639	82163	60859	75567
91	79556	29068	04142	16268	15387	12856	66227	38358	22478	73373	88732	09443	82558	05250
92	92608	82674	27072	32534	17075	27698	98204	63863	11951	34648	88022	56148	34925	57031
93	23982	25835	40055	67006	12293	02753	14827	22235	35071	99704	37543	11601	35503	85171
94	09915	96306	05908	97901	28395	14186	00821	80703	70426	75647	76310	88717	37890	40129
95	50937	33300	26695	62247	69927	76123	50842	43834	86654	70959	79725	93872	28117	19233
96	42488	78077	69882	61657	34136	79180	97526	43092	04098	73571	80799	76536	71255	64239
97	46764	86273	63003	93017	31204	36692	40202	35275	57306	55543	53203	18098	47625	88684
98	03237	45430	55417	63282	90816	17349	88298	90183	36600	78406	06216	95787	42579	90730
99	86591	81482	52667	61583	14972	90053	89534	76036	49199	43716	97548	04379	46370	28672
100	38534	01715	94964	87288	65680	43772	39560	12918	86537	62738	19636	51132	25739	56947

Source: Beyer, 1968.

Appendix F

HYPERRESEARCH™

*A Software Tool for
Qualitative Data Analysis*

ANN DUPUIS

You may have noticed the computer CD bundled with this book, and wondered what's on it. The short answer is: The CD includes a demo version of the HyperRESEARCH software (for both Macintosh and Windows), including an electronic manual and a full set of tutorials with all necessary support and sample files.

For the long answer, please read on.

WHAT IS HYPERRESEARCH?

HyperRESEARCH is a software tool for qualitative data analysis, developed by ResearchWare, Inc. (www.researchware.com). It is one of several CAQDAS packages available. (CAQDAS is an acronym for computer-assisted qualitative data analysis software.) Like many CAQDAS programs, HyperRESEARCH's essential capabilities are for qualitative analysis—code-and-retrieve data analysis features, report-generating capabilities, multimedia support (for data including graphics, video, and audio as well as text), and theory-building tools. These features are packaged within an easy-to-use package that helps you, the user, take control.

NOTE: Ann Dupuis is a Technical Support and Documentation Specialist at ResearchWare, Inc. (support@researchware.com). This appendix is copyright ©2002 by ResearchWare, Inc. HyperRESEARCH™ is a trademark of ResearchWare, Inc.

A demo version of HyperRESEARCH is available on the accompanying CD. (You also can download HyperRESEARCH from www.researchware.com.) This version of the software is fully functional; however, you are limited to using "demo mode," which places limits on the size of your study (your Master Code List is limited to 75 code names, you may have only seven cases, and you may apply only 50 code instances to each case). You can purchase a "license key" from ResearchWare, Inc. or any of its reseller partners to unlock the software (lift the restrictions imposed in demo mode).

If you are a student, you may find that the free demo version of the software is adequate to your needs while you learn how to conduct qualitative research. If you are an instructor, you should note that the demo version of HyperRESEARCH is free for you and your students to use. ResearchWare, Inc. also has a promotional program in which qualifying educators will receive a free license key to unlock the unrestricted version of HyperRESEARCH for their own use. Visit its Web site at www.researchware.com for more information.

Exhibit F.1   HyperRESEARCH Basic Interface: Study Window, Code List Editor, Source Window, and Annotation Window; Not Shown: Hypothesis Tester, Report Generator, Code Map, and Other Specialized Functions

A QUICK TOUR OF HyperRESEARCH

This introduction to HyperRESEARCH briefly shows the major features of the software. For a more in-depth, step-by-step look at how HyperRESEARCH facilitates qualitative data analysis, it is recommended that you use the tutorials on the CD. You can install HyperRESEARCH on your computer and follow the step-by-step tutorials to learn first hand how to use the software. The CD includes sample research materials and HyperRESEARCH studies you can use in conjunction with the tutorials, or to explore the software's capabilities on your own.

HyperRESEARCH's Flexible
Structure and Point-and-Click Interface

HyperRESEARCH allows you to organize your data in many ways. A study consists of one or more cases (a case is the unit of analysis in a HyperRESEARCH study) (Exhibit F.2). You decide what a case will represent, such as an individual, a time period, or a focus group. HyperRESEARCH allows you to choose your codes and code relationships, the depth of your analysis, and the source of your data (i.e., text, graphic, audio, and video sources). HyperRESEARCH allows you to apply codes for multiple sourcefiles to a single case (or a single source file to multiple cases). You also can assign multiple codes to any chunk of source material.

Exhibit F.2   Graphic Representation of the Structure of a HyperRESEARCH Study

HyperRESEARCH's point-and-click interface features pull-down menus, click-and-drag selection, and keyboard shortcuts for those who prefer keyboard commands to mouse clicks.

The Study Window

The Study window is the main HyperRESEARCH window, where your cases and code references are displayed. The Study window also shows you how many cases are currently in your study, and how many code instances have been applied to the current case (Exhibit F.3).

You can view the code references of one case at a time. Each code reference consists of a code name (from your Master Code List, entered into the Code List Editor), the source file name, the source type (text, audio, video, graphic), and a code reference (HyperRESEARCH's reference points for recalling the source material).

With the View Source option selected, clicking on any code reference will recall the underlying source material. HyperRESEARCH will open the file in a Source window, with the underlying source material highlighted.

Exhibit F.3   Study and Source Windows Showing Highlighted Code and Source Material

While working in your Study window, you also can manipulate your code instances. The Codes menu offers a variety of commands you can use with your codes, including duplicating code instances (applying additional codes to the same source material referenced by the original code), recoding (changing the code name applied to the referenced source material), and deleting (removing one or more specific code instances from the case) (Exhibit F.4).

Exhibit F.4 Codes Menu Showing Options Available While Working With Code Instances in the Study Window

You can also sort the code instances in your study by name, by reference, by type, by source file, or by any combination of these criteria.

The Select Cases and Select Codes commands allow you to concentrate on subsets of your cases and codes. These powerful commands facilitate quick review of themes and patterns in your data and coding. Used in conjunction with the report generator and the hypothesis tester, code and case selections allow you to temporarily ignore extraneous data when generating reports or testing hypotheses.

You may select codes by name, by type (text, audio, etc.), by criteria (including Code Proximity functions), or via the Code Map. The codes you select will appear in the Study window. Codes not included in the selection will be hidden from view. You can recall them at any time by altering your code selection parameters (Exhibit F.5).

The Code List Editor

The Code List Editor allows you to create, view, and manipulate your Master Code List. You can add codes, edit codes (with changes being reflected in the individual code references throughout your study), and enter detailed definitions or descriptions for your master codes (Exhibit F.6).

You can use the Code List Editor to enter a Code Description for any of your master codes. It's great for quick reference when deciding exactly which code to apply to a source chunk, especially when several researchers are working on the same study.

Exhibit F.5   Study Window Showing Codes Selected By Name (All Other Codes Are Hidden)

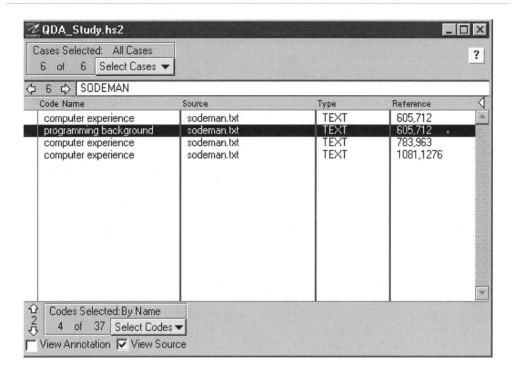

Exhibit F.6   The Code List Editor, Showing a Code Description

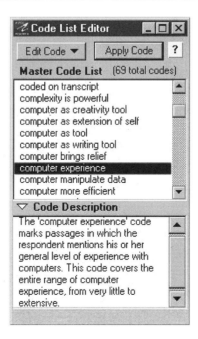

Any changes you make to the Master Code List will be reflected in the individual code instances applied to the cases in your study. Thus, if you wish to rename all instances of a master code throughout your study, you would use the global Rename command available from the Edit Code menu in the Code List Editor.

To affect specific code instances, rather than all codes throughout your study, use the main Codes menu commands in conjunction with individual code instances in the Study window.

The Source Windows

HyperRESEARCH has four Source window types, one for each of the four types of source material (text, graphics, audio, and video). Displayed reports include hyperlinks to underlying source material. HyperRESEARCH's ability to work with multiple data types, such as text, graphic, audio, and video sources, provides the flexibility to integrate all of the data necessary to conduct your research.

The Text Source Window

The text Source window displays text files. You can customize the Font Settings (typeface and size) and also choose whether to Display Codes in Context (code names appear in the left margin). This window is fully resizable and movable.

HyperRESEARCH 2.5 allows you to select any chunk of text (from one character to an entire file) and apply any number of codes to it. Text source files also can be split into multiple pages, if you wish (Exhibit F.7).

Exhibit F.7   Source Window (Text)

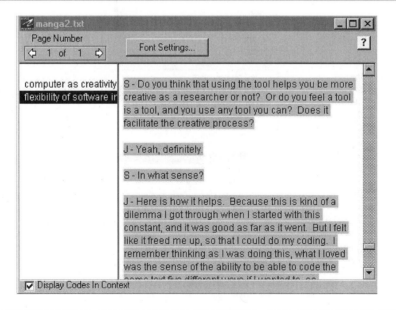

View your codes adjacent to the source material by using Display Codes In Context. The material can be sent to a printer with the codes appearing in the left margin. The Codes In Context feature also can be turned off, maximizing the space available for text (with no margin for viewing code names).

To select text for coding, simply click and drag over the desired chunk. Then use the Code List Editor to apply one or more codes to the source selection.

The Graphic Source Window

The graphic Source window allows you to display still images (.gif, .jpg, or similar graphic files) and assign codes to selected portions of the image (Exhibit F.8).

Exhibit F.8   Source Window (Graphic)

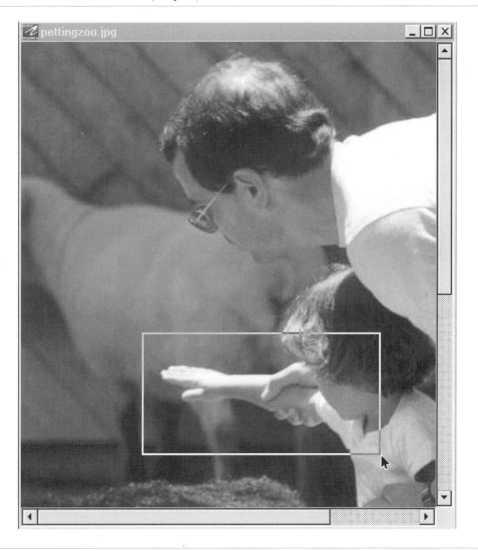

To select a portion of a graphic for coding, click and drag from one corner of a rectangular chunk to the opposite corner. Then use the Code List Editor to apply one or more codes to the graphic selection.

The Movie Source Window

The movie Source window displays movie files (with their audio tracks, if any) using Apple's QuickTime software. You can select and code any number of frames, which can be replayed when recalling the source material from the Study window or in a hyperlinked report (Exhibit F.9).

Exhibit F.9   Source Window (Video)

To select a video segment for coding, simply click and drag along the slide track while holding down the Shift key. Alternatively, position the slide bar at the beginning of the desired segment, then hold the Shift key down and click on the Play button. Release the Shift key when you reach the end of the desired segment.

After you have selected a video segment, you can fine-tune your selection. The video window controls offer frame-by-frame precision.

As with text selections, you can apply more than one code to a given chunk.

The Audio Source Window

The audio Source window uses Apple's QuickTime software to allow you to play back an audio file and select portions for coding. Viewing the coded source material of an audio file (either by selecting the code reference on the Study window with the View Source feature active, or clicking on a hyperlinked code reference in a report) recalls and replays the selected portion of the audio track (Exhibit F.10).

Exhibit F.10 Source Window (Audio)

The audio Source window controls are identical to the video Source window controls.

The Annotation Window

The Annotation window allows you to add a memo or annotation to any code reference in your study. Unlike a Code Definition, which applies to a master code, an Annotation is specific to an individual code reference and its underlying source material (Exhibit F.11).

Exhibit F.11 Annotation Window

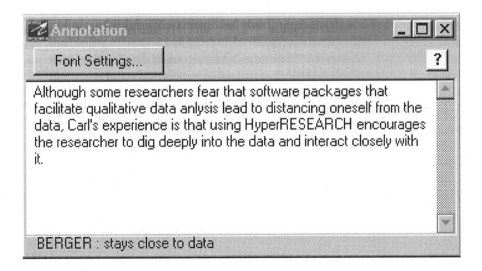

To annotate a code, select a code reference on a case card, choose the Annotate command, and add up to 32,000 characters of information per reference. Annotations can be used as a built-in memo system. All annotations are fully editable and can be included in reports.

The Report Window

The Report window presents the report generation options. Use this window to customize the data you wish retrieved for a given report.

Generate custom reports and display them on your screen or save them as text to output to a word processor, spreadsheet, or statistical package. Hyperlinked reports allow you to click on any code reference to view the source material (Exhibit F.12).

Exhibit F.12 Report Window Showing Report Element Options

In addition to specifying which elements you wish included in a report, you can use the Select Cases and Select Codes commands to specify precisely which cases and codes you wish included in the report. Generate a report that includes all codes across your entire study, or report on any subset of cases and codes.

If you choose any report elements from the right column (Master Case List through Master Source File List), the report generator will also display a header page with the specified information (Exhibit F.13).

Exhibit F.13 Report Display Window with Header Information

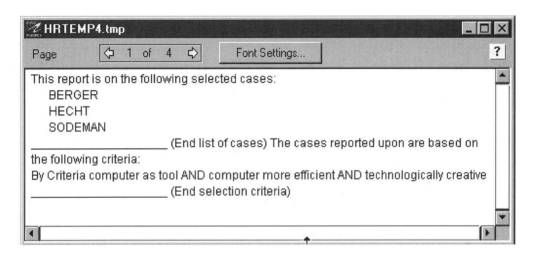

The body of the report will present results based on the current selection of cases and code instances in your Study window. You may choose to include the source material and any annotations for reported codes as well as the code names themselves.

If the Hyperlinks elements are all included, the code reference lines will actually be hyperlinks. Clicking on a code reference (e.g., "MACKEY used hand methods before 1 TEXT 13109,13334 mackey.txt") will open the underlying source material in a Source window. This allows you to view the source material in the context of the rest of the file if you wish (Exhibit F.14).

Exhibit F.14 Report Display Window Showing Hyperlinked Code References
and Source Material

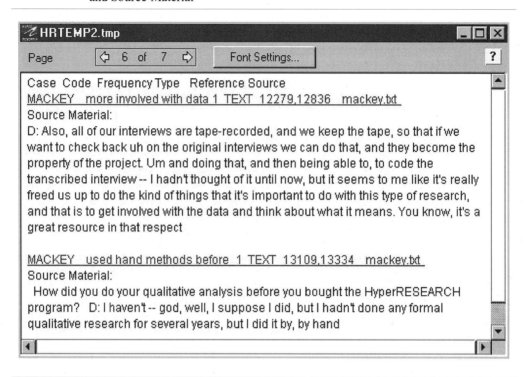

You can save report settings (including the current selection of cases and codes in your study) to run the same report again. You also can export the generated report to a text file, which you can work further with in a word processor or other program.

LEARNING MORE ABOUT THE BASICS

We've covered the basics of HyperRESEARCH: coding and retrieving, code manipulation, and generating reports. You may want to stop reading now, and start experimenting with the software itself. Tutorials One through Four on the CD offer step-by-step "walk-throughs" for the procedures for starting a study (or opening an existing one), coding source material, manipulating code instances, and generating reports. Tutorial Five covers coding and retrieving graphic, video, and audio source material. After you've mastered these procedures, you'll be ready for the more advanced and specialized capabilities HyperRESEARCH offers.

For an introduction to HyperRESEARCH's advanced features (covered in depth in Tutorials Six and Seven), read on.

ADVANCED FEATURES

In addition to the basic code-and-retrieve features HyperRESEARCH offers, there are several more advanced features available.

Autocoding

With Autocode, you can automatically assign a code to multiple sources and multiple cases, looking for several phrases or words in a single pass. Specify a number of characters, words, or lines before and/or after the found phrases to be included in the chunk selected for autocoding.

First you assign source files to the proper cases. Then you specify the phrase (or phrases) to search for and how much surrounding source material to include (Exhibit F.15).

Exhibit F.15   Autocode (Phrases) Window Set to Select Entire Paragraphs
Around Each Occurrence of the Specified Phrases, in Selected Sources

Finally, you select the codes to apply to the matching source materials (Exhibit F.16).

Exhibit F.16 Autocode (Code) Window With Code Names to Assign

The Autocode button becomes active when all necessary parameters are supplied. HyperRESEARCH will apply the selected code or codes to all instances of the selected phrase it finds, and place the code references in the Study window for the specified cases.

Autocoding is best used as a first-pass tool, to earmark certain sections of your textual data for more precise coding. You may wish to use separate code names for autocoded passages (such as the "autocode phobic" code name in the example pictured in Exhibit F.16). These code names would then be replaced with final code names (such as "evidence of computer phobia") when you examine the actual source material and select a more precise segment of text to code.

Code Proximity Searches

HyperRESEARCH lets you conveniently reference overlapping code instances with Code Proximity searches. One of several code- and case-selection tools available, the

Code Proximity functions will seek out specific relationships between two code names (Exhibit F.17).

Available functions are:

- *Equals*—The code references for "code 1" and "code 2" match exactly. With text files, the starting and ending character placement for the source material selection will be exactly the same for the code references being compared.
- *Excludes*—The source material for "code 1" completely excludes any source material coded with "code 2." There are no overlapping characters, pixels, or video or audio segments.
- *Includes*—The source material for "code 1" completely includes the source material for "code 2." For example, a textual selection of two paragraphs coded with "code 1" will include the source material for "code 2" if "code 2" has been applied to one of those paragraphs (and no other source material outside the selection for "code 1").
- *Overlaps*—The source material for "code 1" overlaps one or more characters coded with "code 2." Code references that qualify for the equals or includes functions will also qualify for the overlaps function. However, the matches for overlaps don't need to be as specific as those for includes or equals. Coded text segments that share even one character can qualify as overlapping. With graphics, video, and audio files, the overlapping of even one pixel or time segment is enough to qualify for the overlaps function.

Exhibit F.17 Selection of Codes Based on Code Proximity Functions

You can use the Code Proximity functions to select subsets of your codes or subsets of your cases, based on the relative placement of the codes segments within your source files.

The Code Map Window

The Code Map window allows you to explore graphic representations of the relationships between your master codes. You can group codes in any way you wish, and visually link master code names to one another. Arrange your codes visually to indicate code families, trees, or networks (Exhibit F.18).

Exhibit F.18   The Code Map Window

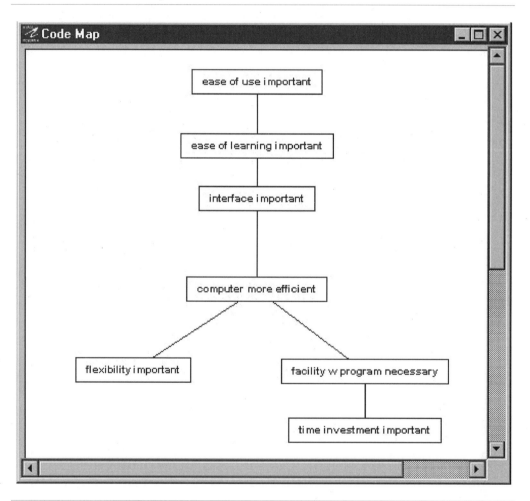

You can select codes using your Code Map and apply that selection to the Study window, which will then display only those code references corresponding to the selected master codes. Selections of mapped codes can be made by selecting each code individually, or by selecting one code and then expanding the selection based on code links. In Exhibit F.18, commanding HyperRESEARCH to select all codes within two links of the "computer more efficient" code would select everything but "ease of use important."

Thus, the Code Map can be used as a visually oriented code selection tool as well as a visualization tool.

The Hypothesis Window

The Hypothesis Tester is an "expert system" that helps you build theories and test them against the codes you've applied to your data. Like the Report Generator, the Hypothesis Tester consists of two windows: the Hypothesis Test window and a Report Display window.

The Hypothesis Test window includes a section that displays the current Hypothesis Test Rules, and a section that allows you to edit those rules (Exhibit F.19).

Exhibit F.19   The Hypothesis Window Showing Part of a Hypothesis Rule List

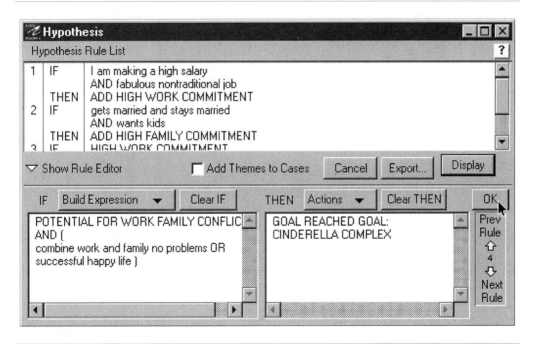

When the Hypothesis Rule List is complete, you can Export the hypothesis test report to a text file, or Display it to the Report Display window. You can also save the hypothesis for later use, or open an already-constructed hypothesis (Exhibit F.20).

Exhibit F.20 The Hypothesis Menu

Although the Hypothesis Tester may seem complicated at first, at its heart it's another way to examine your cases, looking for combinations of the presence and/or absence of code names. It utilizes Boolean expressions (delineating the code combinations to search for with the use of logical AND, OR, and NOT) and can also utilize the Code Proximity functions to look specifically for coded segments that overlap one another.

You can also use the Hypothesis Tester to add Theme codes to your case. Say you'd like to find every case that has been coded with both "gets married and stays married" and "wants kids." You'd like to apply the code "high family commitment" to each relevant case.

You could do this by selecting cases by criteria ("gets married and stays married" AND "wants kids"). You could then go to each selected case and either duplicate one or more "gets married and stays married" and "wants kids" with the "high family commitment" code, or you could open the relevant source file, select a passage (possibly one related to those already coded), and apply the "high family commitment" code directly.

Alternatively, you can do this by creating a hypothesis test that does essentially the same thing. Such a test would have one rule:

IF ("gets married and stays married" AND "wants kids") THEN ADD CODE "HIGH FAMILY COMMITMENT".

(Using all capital letters for the code name helps distinguish it as a Theme code.)

With the Add Themes to Cases option checked, running this hypothesis test would tell HyperRESEARCH to find any case that had one or more instances of "gets married and stays married" and also one or more instances of "wants kids" already coded to it. HyperRESEARCH would then add the "HIGH FAMILY COMMITMENT" code name as a Theme code. This code would not point to any specific source file or source material. It would, however, be considered in any Select Cases or Select Codes command, and would show up on your Reports (provided you chose to include Theme types as a Report Element) (Exhibit F.21).

Exhibit F.21   Study Window With Theme Code "HIGH FAMILY COMMITMENT" Applied

Code Name	Source	Type	Reference
successful happy life	Interview 6.txt	TEXT	221,276
gets married and stays married	Interview 6.txt	TEXT	736,836
wants kids	Interview 6.txt	TEXT	891,948
combine work and family no problems	Interview 6.txt	TEXT	1086,1205
works in traditional field	Interview 6.txt	TEXT	1633,1776
takes major responsibility for family work	Interview 6.txt	TEXT	1483,1872
successful happy life	Interview 6.txt	TEXT	1779,1872
concern about getting old	Interview 6.txt	TEXT	2,218
HIGH FAMILY COMMITMENT	Cinderella Complex.hhp	THEME	2

LEARNING MORE ABOUT HYPERRESEARCH

The best way to learn more about HyperRESEARCH is to dive right into the materials on the CD. Install the software (both Macintosh and Windows versions are included), print out the tutorials (at least Tutorials One through Four, which cover the basics), and play around with the sample studies (the Cinderella Study and the Qualitative Data Analysis Study).

You also can visit ResearchWare's Web site at www.researchware.com. You'll find instructions there on how to join the HyperRESEARCH email discussion list. The Web site also lists events (workshops, conferences, and trade shows), links for online resources for qualitative data analysis, and more.

Welcome to the world of CAQDAS!

REFERENCES

Abbott, Andrew. 1992. "From Causes to Events: Notes on Narrative Positivism." *Sociological Methods,* 20 (May): 428–455.

Abbot, Andrew. 1994. "History and Sociology: The Lost Synthesis." Pp. 77–112 in *Engaging the Past: The Uses of History Across the Social Sciences.* Durham, NC: Duke University Press.

Abel, David. 2000. "Census May Fall Short at Colleges." *The Boston Sunday Globe,* March 26, pp. B1, B4.

Abrams, Philip. 1982. *Historical Sociology.* Ithaca, NY: Cornell University Press.

Adair, G., T. W. Dushenko, and R. C. L. Lindsay. 1985. "Ethical Regulations and Their Impact on Research Practice." *American Psychologist,* 40: 59–72.

Agnew, R. 1986. "Work and Delinquency Among Juveniles Attending School." *Journal of Criminal Justice,* 9: 19–41.

Alarid, Leanne Fiftal, Velmer S. Burton, Jr., and Francis T. Cullen. 2000. "Gender and Crime Among Felony Offenders: Assessing the Generality of Social Control and Differential Association Theories." *Journal of Research in Crime and Delinquency,* 37: 171–199.

Alfred, Randall. 1976. "The Church of Satan." Pp. 180–202 in *The New Religious Consciousness,* edited by Charles Glock and Robert Bellah. Berkeley: University of California Press.

Altheide, David L. and John M. Johnson. 1994. "Criteria for Assessing Interpretive Validity in Qualitative Research." Pp. 485–499 in *Handbook of Qualitative Research,* edited by Norman K. Denzin and Yvonna S. Lincoln. Thousand Oaks, CA: Sage.

Alvarez, Alex. 2000. *Governments, Citizens, and Genocide.* Bloomington: Indiana University Press.

American Psychiatric Association. 1994. *Diagnostic and Statistical Manual of Mental Disorders,* 4th ed. (*DSM IV*). Washington, DC: American Psychiatric Association.

American Sociological Association. 1997. *Code of Ethics.* Washington, DC: American Sociological Association.

Anderson, Elijah. 1990. *Streetwise: Race, Class, and Change in an Urban Community.* Chicago: University of Chicago Press.

Anderton, Douglas L., Richard E. Barrett, and Donald J. Bogue. 1997. *The Population of the United States.* New York: Free Press.

Anglin, M. D., D. Longshore, and S. Turner. 1999. "Treatment Alternatives to Street Crime: An Evaluation of Five Programs." *Criminal Justice and Behavior,* 26(2): 168–195.

Archer, Dane and Rosemary Gartner. 1984. *Violence and Crime in Cross-National Perspective.* New Haven, CT: Yale University Press.

Asmussen, Kelly J. and John W. Creswell. 1995. "Campus Response to a Student Gunman." *Journal of Higher Education,* 66(5): 575–591.

Babbie, Earl and Fred Halley. 1995. *Adventures in Social Research: Data Analysis Using SPSS for Windows.* Thousand Oaks, CA: Pine Forge Press.

Babbie, Earl, Fred Halley, and Jeanne Zaino. 2000. *Adventures in Social Research: Data Analysis Using SPSS v. 9.0 and 10.0 for Windows 95/98.* Thousand Oaks, CA: Pine Forge Press.

Babor, Thomas F., Robert S. Stephens, and G. Alan Marlatt. 1987. "Verbal Report Methods in Clinical Research on Alcoholism: Response Bias and Its Minimization." *Journal of Studies on Alcohol,* 48(5): 410–424.

Bachman, Ronet. 1992. *Death and Violence on the Reservation: Homicide, Family Violence, and Suicide in American Indian Populations.* Westport, CT: Auburn House.

Bachman, Ronet. 1996. "Victim's Perceptions of Initial Police Responses to Robbery and Aggravated Assault: Does Race Matter?" *Journal of Quantitative Criminology,* 12: 363–390.

Bachman, Ronet. 2000. "A Comparison of Annual Incidence Rates and Contextual Characteristics of Intimate Perpetrated Violence Against Women from the National Crime Victimization Survey (NCVS) and the National Violence Against Women Survey (NVAWS)." *Violence Against Women,* 6(8): 839–867.

Bachman, Ronet and Raymond Paternoster. 2003. *Statistics for Criminology and Criminal Justice,* 2nd ed. New York: McGraw-Hill.

Bachman, Ronet, Raymond Paternoster, and Sally Ward. 1992. "Rationality of Sexual Offending: Testing a Deterrence/Rational Choice Conception of Sexual Assault." *Law and Society Review,* 26: 401–432.

Bachman, Ronet and Linda Saltzman. 1995. "Violence Against Women: Estimates from the Redesigned National Crime Victimization Survey." *Bureau of Justice Statistics Special Report.* Washington, DC: U.S. Department of Justice.

Bachman, Ronet and Bruce Taylor. 1994. "The Measurement of Rape and Family Violence by the Redesigned National Crime Victimization Survey." *Justice Quarterly,* 11: 702–714.

Bailey, William C. 1990. "Murder, Capital Punishment, and Television: Execution Publicity and Homicide Rates." *American Sociological Review,* 55 (October): 628–633.

Bainbridge, William Sims. 1989. *Survey Research: A Computer-Assisted Introduction.* Belmont, CA: Wadsworth.

Bandura, Albert, Dorothea Ross, and Sheila A. Ross. 1963. "Imitation of Film-Mediated Aggressive Models." *Journal of Abnormal and Social Psychology,* 66: 3–11.

Barringer, Felicity. 1993. "Majority in Poll Back Ban on Handguns." *The New York Times,* June 4, p. A14.

Becker, Howard S. 1958. "Problems of Inference and Proof in Participant Observation." *American Sociological Review,* 23: 652–660.

Becker, Howard S. 1963. *The Outsiders: Studies in the Sociology of Deviance.* New York: Free Press.

Becker, Howard S. 1986. *Writing for Social Scientists.* Chicago: University of Chicago Press. (This can be ordered directly from the American Sociological Association, 1722 N Street NW, Washington, DC 20036, 202–833–3410.)

Bellah, Robert N., Richard Madsen, William M. Sullivan, Ann Swidler, and Steven M. Tipton. 1985. *Habits of the Heart: Individualism and Commitment in American Life.* New York: Harper & Row.

Bennet, Lauren, Lisa Goodman, and Mary Ann Dutton. 1999. "Systematic Obstacles to the Criminal Prosecution of a Battering Partner: A Victim Perspective." *Journal of Interpersonal Violence,* 14: 761–772.

Berk, Richard A., Alec Campbell, Ruth Klap, and Bruce Western. 1992. "The Deterrent Effect of Arrest in Incidents of Domestic Violence: A Bayesian Analysis of Four Field Experiments." *American Sociological Review,* 57: 698–708.

Best, Joel and David F. Luckenbill. 1990. "Male Dominance and Female Criminality: A Test of Harris's Theory of Deviant Type-Scripts." *Sociological Inquiry,* 60: 71–86.

Beyer, William H. (Ed.). 1968. *CRC Handbook of Tables for Probability and Statistics,* 2nd ed. Boca Raton, FL: CRC Press.

Binder, Arnold and James W. Meeker. 1993. "Implications of the Failure to Replicate the Minneapolis Experimental Findings." *American Sociological Review,* 58 (December): 886–888.

Black, Donald J. (Ed.). 1984. *Toward a General Theory of Social Control.* Orlando, FL: Academic Press.

Blau, Peter M. and Judith R. Blau. 1982. "The Cost of Inequality: Metropolitan Structure and Violence Crime." *American Sociological Review,* 47: 114–129.

Bollen, Kenneth A., Barbara Entwisle, and Arthur S. Alderson. 1993. "Macrocomparative Research Methods." *Annual Review of Sociology,* 19: 321–351.

Booth, Wayne C., Gregory G. Colomb, and Joseph M. Williams. 1995. *The Craft of Research.* Chicago: University of Chicago Press.

Botein, B. 1965. "The Manhattan Bail Project: Its Impact in Criminology and the Criminal Law Process." *Texas Law Review,* 43: 319–331.

Bourgois, Philippe, Mark Lettiere, and James Quesada. 1997. "Social Misery and the Sanctions of Substance Abuse: Confronting HIV Risk Among Homeless Heroin Addicts in San Francisco." *Social Problems,* 44: 155–173.

Braga, A. A., D. L. Weisburd, E. J. Waring, L. G. Mazerolle, W. Spelman, and F. Gajewski. 1999. "Problem-Oriented Policing in Violent Crime Places: A Randomized Controlled Experiment." *Criminology,* 37(4): 541–580.

Brame, R. and D. L. MacKenzie. 1996. "Shock Incarceration and Positive Adjustment During Community Supervision: A Multisite Evaluation." In *Correctional Boot Camps: A Tough Intermediate Sanction,* edited by D. L. MacKenzie and E. E. Herbert (NCJ 157639). Washington, DC: National Institute of Justice, U.S. Department of Justice.

Brener, Nancy D., Thomas R. Simon, Etienne G. Krug, and Richard Lowry. 1999. "Recent Trends in Violence-Related Behaviors Among High School Students in the United States." *Journal of the American Medical Association,* 282(5): 133–147.

Brent, Edward and Alan Thompson. 1996. *Methodologist's Toolchest™ for Windows: User's Guide and Reference Manual.* Columbia, MO: Idea Works.

Bridges, George S. and Joseph G. Weis. 1989. "Measuring Violent Behavior: Effects of Study Design on Reported Correlates of Violence." Pp. 14–34 in *Violent Crime, Violent Criminals,* edited by Neil Alan Weiner and Marvin E. Wolfgang. Newbury Park, CA: Sage.

Broder, David S. 2000. "Don't Toy with the Census." *Washington Post,* April 4, p. A29.

Bureau of Justice Statistics. 1994. *Sourcebook of Criminal Justice Statistics: 1994.* (NCJ 154591). Washington, DC: U.S. Department of Justice.

Bureau of Justice Statistics. 1995. *Sourcebook of Criminal Justice Statistics: 1995* (NCJ-158900). Washington, DC: U.S. Department of Justice.

Bureau of Justice Statistics. 2002. "Nation's Violent Crime Victimization Rate Falls 10 Percent." Press Release, September 9, 2002. www.ojp.usdoj.gov/bjs/pub/press/cv01pr.htm.

Burt, Martha R. 1996. "Homelessness: Definitions and Counts." Pp. 15–23 in *Homelessness in America,* edited by Jim Baumohl. Phoenix: Oryx Press.

Bushman, Brad J. 1995. "Moderating Role of Trait Aggressiveness in the Effects of Violent Media on Aggression." *Journal of Personality and Social Psychology,* 69(5): 950–960.

Bushway, S. and P. Reuter. 1997. "Labor Markets and Crime Risk Factors." In *Preventing Crime: What Works, What Doesn't, What's Promising,* edited by L. W. Sherman, D. Gottfredson, D. MacKenzie, J. Eck, P. Reuter, and S. Bushway. Unpublished report by the Department of Criminology and Criminal Justice, University of Maryland.

Butterfield, Fox. 1996a. "After 10 Years, Juvenile Crime Begins to Drop." *The New York Times,* August 9, pp. A1, A25.

Butterfield, Fox. 1996b. "Gun Violence May Be Subsiding, Studies Find." *The New York Times,* October 14, p. A10.

Butterfield, Fox. 1997. "Serious Crime Decreased for Fifth Year in a Row." *The New York Times,* January 5, p. 10.

Buzawa, Eva S. and Carl G. Buzawa. 1996. *Domestic Violence: The Criminal Justice Response,* 2nd ed. Thousand Oaks, CA: Sage.

Campbell, Donald T. and M. Jean Russo. 1999. *Social Experimentation.* Thousand Oaks, CA: Sage.

Campbell, Donald T. and Julian C. Stanley. 1966. *Experimental and Quasi-Experimental Designs for Research.* Chicago: Rand McNally.

Campbell, Richard T. 1992. "Longitudinal Research." Pp. 1146–1158 in *Encyclopedia of Sociology,* edited by Edgar F. Borgatta and Marie L. Borgatta. New York: Macmillan.

Campbell, T. T. and D. W. Fiske. 1959. "Convergent and Discriminant Validity by the Multi-Trait, Multi-Method Matrix." *Psychological Bulletin,* 56: 126–139.

Cantor, David. 1984. *Comparing Bounded and Unbounded Three and Six Month Reference Periods in Rate Estimation.* Washington, DC: Bureau of Social Science Research.

Cantor, David. 1985. "Operational and Substantive Differences in Changing the NCS Reference Period." Pp. 125–137 in *Proceedings of the American Statistical Association, Social Statistics Section.* Washington, DC: American Statistical Association.

Cao, L., A. Adams, and V. J. Jensen. 1997. "A Test of the Black Subculture of Violence Thesis: A Research Note." *Criminology,* 35(2): 367–379.

Cavender, Gray and Lisa Bond-Maupin. 2000. "Fear and Loathing on Reality Television: An Analysis of *America's Most Wanted* and *Unsolved Mysteries*." Pp. 51–57. In *Criminology: Perspectives,* edited by Steven Cooper. Bellvue, WA: Coursewise Publishing.

Chamlin, Mitchell B. and John K. Cochran. 1997. "Social Altruism and Crime." *Criminology,* 35(2): 203–228.

Cloward, Richard and Lloyd E. Ohlin. 1960. *Delinquency and Opportunity: A Theory of Delinquent Gangs.* New York: Free Press.

Coffey, Amanda and Paul Atkinson. 1996. *Making Sense of Qualitative Data: Complementary Research Strategies.* Thousand Oaks, CA: Sage.

Cohen, L. E. and M. Felson. 1979. "Social Change and Crime Rate Trends: A Routine Activity Approach." *American Sociological Review,* 44: 588–608.

Coleman, James S. and Thomas Hoffer. 1987. *Public and Private High Schools: The Impact of Communities.* New York: Basic Books.

Coleman, James S., Thomas Hoffer, and Sally Kilgore. 1982. *High School Achievement: Public, Catholic, and Private Schools Compared.* New York: Basic Books.

Converse, Jean M. 1984. "Attitude Measurement in Psychology and Sociology: The Early Years." Pp. 3–40 in *Surveying Subjective Phenomena* (vol. 2), edited by Charles F. Turner and Elizabeth Martin. New York: Russell Sage Foundation.

Cook, Philip J. and John H. Laub. 1998. "The Epidemic in Youth Violence." In *Youth Violence: Crime and Justice* (vol. 24), edited by Michael Tonry and Mark H. Moore. Chicago: University of Chicago Press.

Cook, Thomas D. and Donald T. Campbell. 1979. *Quasi-Experimentation: Design and Analysis Issues for Field Settings.* Chicago: Rand McNally.

Cooper, Harris and Larry V. Hedges. 1994. "Research Synthesis as a Scientific Enterprise." Pp. 3–14 in *The Handbook of Research Synthesis,* edited by Harris Cooper and Larry V. Hedges. New York: Russell Sage Foundation.

Core Institute. 1994. "Core Alcohol and Drug Survey: Long Form." Carbondale, IL: FIPSE Core Analysis Grantee Group, Core Institute, Student Health Programs, Southern Illinois University.

Corse, Sara J., Nancy B. Hirschinger, and David Zanis. 1995. "The Use of the Addiction Severity Index with People with Severe Mental Illness." *Psychiatric Rehabilitation Journal,* 19(1): 9–18.

Costner, Herbert L. 1989. "The Validity of Conclusions in Evaluation Research: A Further Development of Chen and Rossi's Theory-Driven Approach." *Evaluation and Program Planning,* 12: 345–353.

Crossen, Cynthia. 1994. "How 'Tactical Research' Muddied Diaper Debate." *The Wall Street Journal,* May 17, pp. B1, B9.

Czaja, Ronald and Bob Blair. 1995. *Survey Research.* Newbury Park, CA: Pine Forge Press.

Dannefer, W. Dale and Russell K. Schutt. 1982. "Race and Juvenile Justice Processing in Court and Police Agencies." *American Journal of Sociology,* 87 (March): 1113–1132.

Davies, Paul. 1993. "The Holy Grail of Physics." *The New York Times Book Review,* March 7, pp. 11–12.

Davis, James A. and Tom W. Smith. 1992. *The NORC General Social Survey: A User's Guide.* Newbury Park, CA: Sage.

Davis, Ryan. 1999. "Study: Search Engines Can't Keep Up With Expanding Net." *The Boston Globe,* July 8, pp. C1, C3.

Dawes, Robyn. 1995. "How Do You Formulate a Testable Exciting Hypothesis?" Pp. 93–96 in *How to Write a Successful Research Grant Application: A Guide for Social and Behavioral Scientists,* edited by Willo Pequegnat and Ellen Stover. New York: Plenum Press.

Decker, Scott H. and Barrik Van Winkle. 1996. *Life in the Gang: Family, Friends, and Violence.* Cambridge, England: Cambridge University Press.

Denzin, Norman K. and Yvonna S. Lincoln. 1994. "Introduction: Entering the Field of Qualitative Research." Pp. 1–17 in *Handbook of Qualitative Research,* edited by Norman K. Denzin and Yvonna S. Lincoln. Thousand Oaks, CA: Sage.

Diamond, Timothy. 1992. *Making Gray Gold: Narratives of Nursing Home Care.* Chicago: University of Chicago Press.

Dillman, Don A. 1978. *Mail and Telephone Surveys: The Total Design Method.* New York: Wiley.

Dillman, Don A. 1982. "Mail and Other Self-Administered Questionnaires." Chapter 12 in *Handbook of Survey Research,* edited by Peter Rossi, James Wright, and Andy Anderson. New York: Academic Press. Reprinted on pp. 637–638 in Delbert C. Miller, 1991. *Handbook of Research Design and Social Measurement* (5th ed.). Newbury Park, CA: Sage.

Dillman, Don A. 2000. *Mail and Internet Surveys: The Tailored Design Method,* 2nd ed. New York: John Wiley & Sons.

Dillman, Don A., James A. Christenson, Edwin H. Carpenter, and Ralph M. Brooks. 1974. "Increasing Mail Questionnaire Response: A Four-State Comparison." *American Sociological Review,* 39 (October): 744–756.

Dixon, J. and Al J. Lizotte. 1987. "Gun Ownership and the Southern Subculture of Violence." *American Journal of Sociology,* 93: 383–405.

Dolnick, Edward. 1984. "Why Have the Pollsters Been Missing the Mark?" *The Boston Globe,* July 16, pp. 27–28.

Duggan, Paul, Michael D. Shear, and Marc Fisher, 1999. "Killers Fused Violent Fantasy, Reality." *The Washington Post,* April 22, p. A1.

Dunford, Franklyn W., David Huizinga, and Delbert Elliott. 1990. "The Role of Arrest in Domestic Assault: The Omaha Police Experiment." *Criminology,* 28: 183–206.

Durkheim, Emile. 1897 (1951). *Suicide.* New York: Free Press.

Ehrlich, I. 1975. "The Deterrent Effect of Capital Punishment: A Question of Life and Death." *American Economic Review,* 65: 397–417.

Elliott, D. and S. Ageton. 1980. "Reconciling Race and Class Differences in Self-Reported and Official Estimates of Delinquency." *American Sociological Review,* 45: 95–110.

Elliott, Delbert A., David Huizinga, and Suzanne S. Ageton. 1985. *Explaining Delinquency and Drug Use.* Newbury Park, CA: Sage.

Ellison, C. G. 1991. "An Eye for an Eye? A Note on the Southern Subculture of Violence Thesis." *Social Forces,* 69: 1223–1239.

Emerson, Robert M. (Ed.). 1983. *Contemporary Field Research.* Prospect Heights, IL: Waveland Press.

Emerson, Robert M., Rachel I. Fretz, and Linda L. Shaw. 1995. *Writing Ethnographic Fieldnotes.* Chicago: University of Chicago Press.

Erikson, Kai T. 1966. *Wayward Puritans: A Study in the Sociology of Deviance.* New York: Wiley.

Erikson, Kai T. 1967. "A Comment on Disguised Observation in Sociology." *Social Problems,* 12: 366–373.

Farrington, David P. 1977. "The Effects of Public Labeling." *British Journal of Criminology,* 17(2): 112–125.

Felson, Richard B., Allen E. Liska, Scott J. South, and Thomas L. McNulty. 1994. "The Subculture of Violence and Delinquency: Individual versus School Context Effects." *Social Forces,* 73(1): 155–174.

Fenno, Richard F., Jr. 1978. *Home Style: House Members in Their Districts.* Boston: Little, Brown.

Fink, Arlene. 1998. *Conducting Research Literature Reviews: From Paper to the Internet.* Thousand Oaks, CA: Sage.

Fleury-Steiner, Benjamin. 2003. *Jurors' Stories of Death: How America's Death Penalty Invests in Inequality.* Ann Arbor: University of Michigan Press.

Forero, Juan. 2000. "Census Takers Top '90 Efforts in New York City, with More to Go." *The New York Times,* June 12, p. A29.

Fowler, Floyd J. 1988. *Survey Research Methods* (rev. ed.). Newbury Park, CA: Sage.

Fowler, Floyd J. 1995. *Improving Survey Questions: Design and Evaluation.* Thousand Oaks, CA: Sage.

Fraker, Thomas and Rebecca Maynard. 1987. "Evaluating Comparison Group Designs with Employment-Related Programs." *Journal of Human Resources,* 22(2): 194–227.

Freedman, David A. 1991. "Statistical Models and Shoe Leather." Pp. 291–313 in *Sociological Methodology* (vol. 21), edited by Peter V. Marsden. Oxford: Basil Blackwell.

Gallup, G. 1986. *Public Opinion,* 1985. Wilmington, DE: Scholarly Resources Press.

Garner, Joel, Jeffrey Fagan, and Christopher Maxwell. 1995. "Published Findings from the Spousal Assault Replication Program: A Critical Review." *Journal of Quantitative Criminology,* 11: 3–28.

Glaser, Barney G. and Anselm L. Strauss. 1967. *The Discovery of Grounded Theory: Strategies for Qualitative Research.* London: Weidenfeld and Nicholson.

Glashow, Sheldon. 1989. "We Believe That the World Is Knowable." *The New York Times,* October 22, p. E24.

Gleick, James. 1990. "The Census: Why We Can't Count." *The New York Times Magazine,* July 15, pp. 22–26, 54.

Glover, Judith. 1996. "Epistemological and Methodological Considerations in Secondary Analysis." Pp. 28–38 in *Cross-National Research Methods in the Social Sciences,* edited by Linda Hantrais and Steen Mangen. New York: Pinter.

Goffman, Erving. 1961. *Asylums: Essays on the Social Situation of Mental Patients and Other Inmates.* Garden City, NY: Doubleday.

Goldenberg, Sheldon. 1992. *Thinking Methodologically.* New York: HarperCollins.

Goldfinger, Stephen M., Russell K. Schutt, Larry J. Seidman, Winston M. Turner, Walter E. Penk, and George S. Tolomiczenko. 1996. "Self-Report and Observer Measures of Substance Abuse Among Homeless Mentally Ill Persons in the Cross-Section and Over Time." *The Journal of Nervous and Mental Disease,* 184(11): 667–672.

Goleman, Daniel. 1993a. "Placebo Effect Is Shown to Be Twice as Powerful as Expected." *The New York Times,* August 17, p. C3.

Goleman, Daniel. 1993b. "Pollsters Enlist Psychologists in Quest for Unbiased Results." *The New York Times,* September 7, pp. C1, C11.

Goleman, Daniel. 1995. *Emotional Intelligence.* New York: Bantam Books.

Gordon, Raymond. 1992. *Basic Interviewing Skills.* Itasca, IL: Peacock.

Gregg v. Georgia, 428 U.S. 153 (1976).

Griffin, Larry J. 1993. "Narrative, Event-Structure Analysis, and Causal Interpretation in Historical Sociology." *American Journal of Sociology,* 98 (March): 1094–1133.

Grinnell, Frederick. 1992. *The Scientific Attitude* (2nd ed.). New York: Guilford Press.

Grossman, David C., Jolly J. Neckerman, Thomas D. Koepsell, Ping-Yu Liu, Kenneth N. Asher, Kathy Beland, Darin Frey, and Frederick P. Rivara. 1997. "Effectiveness of a Violence Prevention Curriculum among Children in Elementary School: A Randomized Controlled Trial." *The Journal of the American Medical Association,* 277(20), 1605–1612.

Groves, Robert M. 1989. *Survey Errors and Survey Costs.* New York: Wiley.

Groves, Robert M. and Mick P. Couper. 1998. *Nonresponse in Household Interview Surveys.* New York: Wiley.

Groves, Robert M. and Robert L. Kahn. 1979. *Surveys by Telephone: A National Comparison with Personal Interviews.* New York: Academic Press. As adapted in Delbert C. Miller, 1991. *Handbook of Research Design and Social Measurement* (5th ed.). Newbury Park, CA: Sage.

Gruenewald, Paul J., Andrew J. Treno, Gail Taff, and Michael Klitzner. 1997. *Measuring Community Indicators: A Systems Approach to Drug and Alcohol Problems.* Thousand Oaks, CA: Sage.

Guba, Egon G. and Yvonna S. Lincoln. 1989. *Fourth Generation Evaluation.* Newbury Park, CA: Sage.

Guba, Egon G. and Yvonna S. Lincoln. 1994. "Competing Paradigms in Qualitative Research." Pp. 105–117 in *Handbook of Qualitative Research,* edited by Norman K. Denzin and Yvonna S. Lincoln. Thousand Oaks, CA: Sage.

Gubrium, Jaber F. and James A. Holstein. 1997. *The New Language of Qualitative Method.* New York: Oxford University Press.

Hadaway, C. Kirk, Penny Long Marler, and Mark Chaves. 1993. "What the Polls Don't Show: A Closer Look at U.S. Church Attendance." *American Sociological Review,* 58 (December): 741–752.

Hagan, John. 1994. *Crime and Disrepute.* Thousand Oaks, CA: Pine Forge Press.

Hage, Jerald and Barbara Foley Meeker. 1988. *Social Causality.* Boston: Unwin Hyman.

Hagedorn, John. 1988. *People and Folks.* Chicago: Lake View Press.

Hamilton, V. Lee and Joseph Sanders. 1983. "Universals in Judging Wrongdoing: Japanese and Americans Compared." *American Sociological Review,* 48 (April): 199–211.

Haney, C., C. Banks, and Philip G. Zimbardo. 1973. "Interpersonal Dynamics in a Simulated Prison." *International Journal of Criminology and Penology,* 1: 69–97.

Hantrais, Linda and Steen Mangen. 1996. "Method of Management of Cross-National Social Research." Pp. 1–12 in *Cross-National Research Methods in the Social Sciences,* edited by Linda Hantrais and Steen Mangen. New York: Pinter.

Harding, Sandra. 1989. "Value-Free Research Is a Delusion." *The New York Times,* October 22, p. E24.

Harrell, A., S. Cavanagh, and S. Sridharan. 1999. *Evaluation of the Children at Risk Program: Results 1 Year After the End of the Program* (NCJ 178914). Washington, DC: National Institute of Justice, U.S. Department of Justice.

Heckathorn, Douglas D. 1997. "Respondent-Driven Sampling: A New Approach to the Study of Hidden Populations." *Social Problems,* 44: 174–199.

Heimer, Karen and Stacy De Coster. 1999. "The Gendering of Violent Delinquency." *Criminology,* 37(2): 277–318.

Herek, Gregory. 1995. "Developing a Theoretical Framework and Rationale for a Research Proposal." Pp. 85–91 in *How to Write a Successful Research Grant Application: A Guide for Social and Behavioral Scientists,* edited by Willo Pequegnat and Ellen Stover. New York: Plenum Press.

Hirsch, Kathleen. 1989. *Songs from the Alley.* New York: Doubleday.

Hirschel, J. David, Ira W. Hutchison, III, and Charles W. Dean. 1992. "The Failure of Arrest to Deter Spouse Abuse." *Journal of Research in Crime and Delinquency,* 7–33.

Ho, D. Y. R. 1996. "Filial Piety and Its Psychological Consequences." Pp. 155–165 in *Handbook of Chinese Psychology,* edited by M. H. Bond. Hong Kong: Oxford University Press.

Holmes, Steven A. 1994. "Census Officials Plan Big Changes in Gathering Data." *The New York Times,* May 16, pp. A1, A13.

Hoover, Kenneth R. 1980. *The Elements of Social Scientific Thinking* (2nd ed.). New York: St. Martin's Press.

Horney, Julie, D. Wayne Osgood, and Ineke Haen Marshall. 1995. "Criminal Careers in the Short-Term: Intra-Individual Variability in Crime and Its Relation to Local Life Circumstances." *American Sociological Review,* 60: 655–673.

Horney, Julie and Cassia Spohn. 1991. "Rape Law Reform and Instrumental Change in Six Urban Jurisdictions." *Law and Society Review,* 25: 117–153.

Huberman, A. Michael and Matthew B. Miles. 1994. "Data Management and Analysis Methods." Pp. 428–444 in *Handbook of Qualitative Research,* edited by Norman K. Denzin and Yvonna S. Lincoln. Thousand Oaks, CA: Sage.

Humphrey, Nicholas. 1992. *A History of the Mind: Evolution and the Birth of Consciousness.* New York: Simon & Schuster.

Humphreys, Laud. 1970. *Tearoom Trade: Impersonal Sex in Public Places.* Chicago: Aldine.

Hunt, Morton. 1985. *Profiles of Social Research: The Scientific Study of Human Interactions.* New York: Russell Sage Foundation.

Irwin, John. 1970. *The Felon.* Englewood Cliffs, NJ: Prentice Hall.

James, T. S. and J. M. Granville. 1984. "Practical Issues in Vocational Education for Serious Juvenile Offenders." In *Violent Juvenile Offenders: An Anthology,* edited by R. Mathias, P. DeMuro, and R. Allison. San Francisco, CA: National Council on Crime and Delinquency.

Janesick, Valerie J. 1994. "The Dance of Qualitative Research Design: Metaphor, Methodolatry, and Meaning." Pp. 209–219 in *Handbook of Qualitative Research,* edited by Norman K. Denzin and Yvonna S. Lincoln. Thousand Oaks, CA: Sage.

Jervis, Robert. 1996. "Counterfactuals, Causation, and Complexity." Pp. 309–316 in *Counterfactual Thought Experiments in World Politics: Logical, Methodological, and Psychological Perspectives,* edited by Philip E. Tetlock and Aaron Belkin. Princeton, NJ: Princeton University Press.

Johnson, Dirk. 1997. "Party Animals in Fraternities Face the Threat of Extinction." *The New York Times,* May 15, pp. A1, A29.

Johnson, Holly. 1996. *Dangerous Domains: Violence Against Women in Canada.* Toronto: Nelson Canada.

Johnston, Lloyd D., Jerald G. Bachman, and Patrick M. O'Malley. 1994. *Sourcebook of Criminal Justice Statistics: 1994* (NCJ-154591). Washington, DC: Bureau of Justice Statistics, U.S. Department of Justice.

Kamin, Leon. 1974. *The Science and Politics of IQ.* Potomac, MD: Erlbaum.

Kandakai, Tina L., James H. Price, Susan K. Telljohann, and Carter A. Wilson. 1999. "Mothers' Perceptions of Factors Influencing Violence in Schools." *Journal of School Health,* 69(5): 189–205.

Kaufman, Sharon R. 1986. *The Ageless Self: Sources of Meaning in Late Life.* Madison: University of Wisconsin Press.

Kershaw, Sarah. 2000. "In a Black Community, Mistrust of the Government Hinders Census." *The New York Times,* May 16, p. A20.

Kifner, John. 1994. "Pollster Finds Error on Holocaust Doubts." *The New York Times,* May 20, p. A12.

"Killers Fused Violent Fantasy, Reality." 1999. *The Washington Post,* April 22, p. A-1.

King, Gary, Robert O. Keohane, and Sidney Verba. 1994. *Scientific Inference in Qualitative Research.* Princeton, NJ: Princeton University Press.

Kobelarcik, E. L., C. A. Alexander, R. P. Singh, and G. M. Shapiro. 1983. "Alternative Reference Periods for the National Crime Survey." In *Proceedings of the American Statistical Association: Section on Survey Methods.* Washington, DC: American Statistical Association.

Koegel, Paul. 1987. *Ethnographic Perspectives on Homeless and Homeless Mentally Ill Women.* Washington, DC: Alcohol, Drug Abuse, and Mental Health Administration, Public Health Service, U.S. Department of Health and Human Services.

Kohn, Melvin L. 1987. "Cross-National Research as an Analytic Strategy." *American Sociological Review,* 52: 713–731.

Kohut, Andrew. 1988. "Polling: Does More Information Lead to Better Understanding?" *The Boston Globe,* November 7, p. 25.

Kraemer, Helena Chmura and Sue Thiemann. 1987. *How Many Subjects? Statistical Power Analysis in Research.* Newbury Park, CA: Sage.

Krauss, Clifford. 1996. "New York Crime Rate Plummets to Levels Not Seen in 30 Years." *The New York Times,* December 20, pp. A1, B4.

Krueger, Richard A. 1988. *Focus Groups: A Practical Guide for Applied Research.* Newbury Park, CA: Sage.

Kubey, Robert. 1990. "Television and the Quality of Family Life." *Communication Quarterly,* 38 (Fall): 312–324.

Kuhn, Thomas S. 1970. *The Structure of Scientific Revolutions* (2nd ed.). Chicago: University of Chicago Press.

Kvale, Steinar. 1996. *Interviews: An Introduction to Qualitative Research Interviewing.* Thousand Oaks, CA: Sage.

Labaw, Patricia J. 1980. *Advanced Questionnaire Design.* Cambridge, MA: ABT Books.

LaLonde, Robert J. 1986. "Evaluating the Econometric Evaluations of Training Programs with Experimental Data." *The American Economic Review,* 76: 604–620.

Lamott, Anne. 1994. *Bird by Bird: Some Instructions on Writing and Life.* New York: Anchor Books.

Langford, Terri. 2000. "Census Workers in Dallas Find the Well-Off Hard to Count." *The Boston Globe,* June 1, p. A24.

Larson, Calvin J. 1993. *Pure and Applied Sociological Theory: Problems and Issues.* New York: Harcourt Brace Jovanovich.

Larson, Calvin J. and Gerald R. Garrett. 1996. *Crime, Justice and Society* (2nd ed.). Dix Hills, NY: General Hall.

Lavrakas, Paul J. 1987. *Telephone Survey Methods: Sampling, Selection, and Supervision.* Newbury Park, CA: Sage.

Lazarsfeld, Paul F. and Anthony R. Oberschall. 1965. "Max Weber and Empirical Research." *American Sociological Review* (April): 185–199.

Lempert, Richard. 1989. "Humility Is a Virtue: On the Publicization of Policy-Relevant Research." *Law and Society Review,* 23: 146–161.

Lempert, Richard and Joseph Sanders. 1986. *An Invitation to Law and Social Science: Desert, Disputes, and Distribution.* New York: Longman.

Lieberson, Stanley. 1985. *Making It Count: The Improvement of Social Research and Theory.* Berkeley: University of California Press.

Lieberson, Stanley. 1991. "Small N's and Big Conclusions: An Examination of the Reasoning in Comparative Studies Based on a Small Number of Cases." *Social Forces,* 70: 307–320.

Lieberson, Stanley. 1992. "Einstein, Renoir, and Greeley: Some Thoughts About Evidence in Sociology." *American Sociological Review,* 57 (February): 1–15.

Linsky, Arnold, Ronet Bachman, and Murray Straus. 1995. *Stress Culture and Aggression in the United States.* New Haven, CT: Yale University Press.

Lipsky, Michael. 1980. *Street-Level Bureaucracy.* New York: Russell Sage Foundation.

Litwin, Mark S. 1995. *How to Measure Survey Reliability and Validity.* Thousand Oaks, CA: Sage.

Lofland, John and Lyn H. Lofland. 1984. *Analyzing Social Settings: A Guide to Qualitative Observation and Analysis* (2nd ed.). Belmont, CA: Wadsworth.

Lofland, John and Lyn H. Lofland. 1995. *Analyzing Social Settings: A Guide to Qualitative Observation and Analysis* (3rd ed.). Belmont, CA: Wadsworth.

Loth, Renee. 1992. "Bush May Be Too Far Back, History of Polls Suggests." *The Boston Globe,* October 25, p. 19.

Lynch, James P. 1996. "Clarifying Divergent Estimates of Rape from Two National Surveys." *Public Opinion Quarterly,* 60: 410–430.

Lynch, Michael and David Bogen. 1997. "Sociology's Asociological 'Core': An Examination of Textbook Sociology in Light of the Sociology of Scientific Knowledge." *American Sociological Review,* 62: 481–493.

MacKenzie, D. L. 1994. "Results of a Multisite Study of Boot Camp Prisons." *Federal Probation,* 58(2): 60–66.

MacKenzie, D. L., R. Brame, D. McDowall, and C. Souryal. 1995. "Boot Camp, Prisons and Recidivism in Eight States." *Criminology,* 33(3): 401–430.

MacKenzie, D. L. and A. Piquero. 1994. "The Impact of Shock Incarceration Programs on Prison Crowding." *Crime and Delinquency,* 40(2): 222–249.

MacKenzie, D. L. and C. Souryal. 1995. "Inmate Attitude Change During Incarceration: A Comparison of Boot Camp with Traditional Prison." *Justice Quarterly,* 12(2): 125–150.

MacKenzie, D. L. and C. Souryal. 1996. "Multisite Study of Correctional Boot Camps." In *Correctional Boot Camps: A Tough Intermediate Sanction,* edited by D. L. MacKenzie and E. E. Herbert (NCJ 157639). Washington, DC: National Institute of Justice, U.S. Department of Justice.

Mangione, Thomas W. 1995. *Mail Surveys: Improving the Quality.* Thousand Oaks, CA: Sage.

Marini, Margaret Mooney and Burton Singer. 1988. "Causality in the Social Sciences." Pp. 347–409 in *Sociological Methodology,* vol. 18, edited by Clifford C. Clogg. Washington, DC: American Sociological Association.

Martin, Lawrence L. and Peter M. Kettner. 1996. *Measuring the Performance of Human Service Programs.* Thousand Oaks, CA: Sage.

Martin, Linda G. and Kevin Kinsella. 1995. "Research on the Demography of Aging in Developing Countries." Pp. 356–403 in *Demography of Aging,* edited by Linda G. Martin and Samuel H. Preston. Washington, DC: National Academy Press.

Matt, Georg E. and Thomas D. Cook. 1994. "Threats to the Validity of Research Syntheses." Pp. 503–520 in *The Handbook of Research Synthesis,* edited by Harris Cooper and Larry V. Hedges. New York: Russell Sage Foundation.

Maxwell, Joseph A. 1996. *Qualitative Research Design: An Interactive Approach.* Thousand Oaks, CA: Sage.

Mayr, Ernst. 1982. *The Growth of Biological Thought: Diversity, Evolution, and Inheritance.* Cambridge, MA: Harvard University Press.

McDowall, D., C. Loftin, and B. Wiersema. 1992. "A Comparative Study of the Preventive Effects of Mandatory Sentencing Laws for Gun Crimes." *The Journal of Criminal Law and Criminology,* 83(2): 378–391.

McLellan, A. Thomas, Lester Luborsky, John Cacciola, Jeffrey Griffith, Frederick Evans, Harriet L. Barr, and Charles P. O'Brien. 1985. "New Data from the Addiction Severity Index: Reliability and Validity in Three Centers." *The Journal of Nervous and Mental Disease,* 173(7): 412–423.

Menand, Louis. 2001. *The Metaphysical Club: A Story of Ideas in America.* New York: Farrar, Straus, and Giroux.

Merton, Robert K. 1938. "Social Structure and Anomie." *American Sociological Review,* 3: 672–682.

Merton, Robert K., Marjorie Fiske, and Patricia L. Kendall. 1956. *The Focused Interview.* Glencoe, IL: Free Press.

Messner, Steven F. and Richard Rosenfeld. 1994. *Crime and the American Dream.* Belmont, CA: Wadsworth.

Miczek, Klaus A., Joseph F. DeBold, Margaret Haney, Jennifer Tidey, Jeffrey Vivian, and Elise M. Weerts. 1994. "Alcohol, Drugs of Abuse, Aggression, and Violence." Pp. 377–570 in *Understanding and Preventing Violence: Vol. 3, Social Influences,* edited by Albert J. Reiss, Jr., and Jeffrey A. Roth. Washington, DC: National Academy Press.

Milgram, Stanley. 1965. "Some Conditions of Obedience and Disobedience to Authority." *Human Relations,* 18: 57–75.

Milgram, Stanley. 1974. *Obedience to Authority: An Experimental View.* New York: Harper & Row.

Mill, John Stuart. 1872. *A System of Logic: Ratiocinative and Inductive* (8th ed.), vol. 2. London: Longmans, Green, Reader, & Dyer.

Miller, Delbert C. 1991. *Handbook of Research Design and Social Measurement* (5th ed.). Newbury Park, CA: Sage.

Miller, Susan. 1999. *Gender and Community Policing: Walking the Talk.* Boston: Northeastern University Press.

Mills, C. Wright. 1959. *The Sociological Imagination.* New York: Oxford University Press.

Mohr, Lawrence B. 1992. *Impact Analysis for Program Evaluation.* Newbury Park, CA: Sage.

Monkkonen, Eric H. 1994. "Introduction." Pp. 1–8 in *Engaging the Past: The Uses of History Across the Social Sciences.* Durham, NC: Duke University Press.

Moore, Joan W. 1978. *Homeboys: Gangs, Drugs, and Prison in the Barrios of Los Angeles.* Philadelphia: Temple University Press.

Moore, Joan W. 1991. *Going Down to the Barrio: Homeboys and Homegirls in Change.* Philadelphia: Temple University Press.

Morin, Richard. 1999. "Unconventional Wisdom: New Facts and Hot Stats from the Social Sciences." *Washington Post,* September 5, p. B5 (Outlook section).

Mosher, Clayton, J., Terance D. Miethe, and Dretha M. Phillips 2002. *The Mismeasure of Crime.* Thousand Oaks, CA: Sage.

Mueser, Kim T., Paul R. Yarnold, Douglas F. Levinson, Hardeep Singhy, Alan S. Bellack, Kimmy Kee, Randall L. Morrison, and Kashinath G. Yadalam. 1990. "Prevalence of Substance Abuse in Schizophrenia: Demographic and Clinical Correlates." *Schizophrenia Bulletin,* 16(1): 31–56.

Mullins, Carolyn J. 1977. *A Guide to Writing and Publishing in the Social and Behavioral Sciences.* New York: Wiley.

National Institute of Alcohol Abuse and Alcoholism. 1994. "Alcohol-Related Impairment." *Alcohol Alert,* 25 (July): 1–5.

National Institute of Alcohol Abuse and Alcoholism. 1995. "College Students and Drinking." *Alcohol Alert,* 29 (July): 1–6.

National Institute of Alcohol Abuse and Alcoholism. 1997. "Alcohol Metabolism." *Alcohol Alert,* 35 (January): 1–4.

National Opinion Research Center (NORC). 1992. *The NORC General Social Survey: Questions and Answers.* Chicago: National Data Program for the Social Sciences. Mimeographed.

National Victim Center and the Crime Victims Research and Treatment Center. 1992. *Rape in America: A Report to the Nation.* Arlington, VA: Author.

Navarro, Mireya. 1990. "Census Questionnaire: Link to Democracy and Source of Data." *The New York Times,* March 25, p. 36.

Needleman, Carolyn. 1981. "Discrepant Assumptions in Empirical Research: The Case of Juvenile Court Screening." *Social Problems,* 28 (February): 247–262.

Newport, Frank. 2000. "Popular Vote in Presidential Race Too Close to Call." Princeton: The Gallup Organization. 12/13/00. www.gallup.com/poll/releases/pr001107.asp.

Nie, Norma H. and Lutz Erbring. 2000. *Internet and Society: A Preliminary Report.* Palo Alto, CA: Stanford Institute for the Quantitative Study of Society.

Nisbett, Richard E. and Dov Cohen. 1996. *Culture of Honor: The Psychology of Violence in the South.* Boulder, CO: Westview Press.

Oberschall, Anthony. 1972. "The Institutionalization of American Sociology." Pp. 187–251 in *The Establishment of Empirical Sociology: Studies in Continuity, Discontinuity, and Institutionalization,* edited by Anthony Oberschall. New York: Harper & Row.

Olzak, Susan, Suzanne Shanahan, and Elizabeth H. McEneaney. 1996. "Poverty, Segregation, and Race Riots: 1960 to 1993." *American Sociological Review,* 61: 590–613.

Orcutt, James D. and J. Blake Turner. 1993. "Shocking Numbers and Graphic Accounts: Quantified Images of Drug Problems in the Print Media." *Social Problems,* 49 (May): 190–206.

Orshansky, Mollie. 1977. "Memorandum for Daniel P. Moynihan. Subject: History of the Poverty Line." Pp. 232–237 in *The Measure of Poverty. Technical Paper I: Documentation of Background Information and Rationale for Current Poverty Matrix,* edited by Mollie Orshansky. Washington, DC: U.S. Department of Health, Education, and Welfare.

Padilla, Felix M. 1992. *The Gang as an American Enterprise.* New Brunswick, NJ: Rutgers University Press.

Papineau, David. 1978. *For Science in the Social Sciences.* London: Macmillan.

Pate, Anthony M. and Edwin E. Hamilton. 1992. "Formal and Informal Deterrents to Domestic Violence: The Dade County Spouse Assault Experiment." *American Sociological Review,* 57: 691–697.

Paternoster, Raymond. 1991. *Capital Punishment in America.* New York: Lexington Books.

Paternoster, Raymond, Robert Brame, Ronet Bachman, and Lawrence W. Sherman. 1997. "Do Fair Procedures Matter? The Effect of Procedural Justice on Spouse Assault." *Law & Society Review,* 31(1): 163–204.

Patton, M. Q. 1997. *Utilization Focused Evaluation: The New Century Text* (3rd ed.). Thousand Oaks, CA: Sage.

Pepinsky, Harold E. 1980. "A Sociologist on Police Patrol." Pp. 223–234 in *Fieldwork Experience: Qualitative Approaches to Social Research,* edited by William B. Shaffir, Robert A. Stebbins, and Allan Turowetz. New York: St. Martin's Press.

Perkins, Craig. 1997. *Age Patterns of Victims of Serious Violent Crime.* Washington, DC: U.S. Department of Justice, Bureau of Justice Statistics.

Phillips, Derek L. 1971. *Knowledge from What? Theories and Methods in Social Research.* Chicago: Rand McNally.

Posavac, E. J. and R. G. Carey. 1997. *Program Evaluation: Methods and Case Studies.* Upper Saddle River, NJ: Prentice Hall.

Powell, Kenneth E., Lois Muir-McClain, and Lakshmi Halasyamani. 1995. "A Review of Selected School-Based Conflict Resolution and Peer Mediation Projects." *Journal of School Health,* 65(10): 426–432.

Presley, Cheryl A., Philip W. Meilman, and Rob Lyerla. 1994. "Development of the Core Alcohol and Drug Survey: Initial Findings and Future Directions." *Journal of American College Health,* 42: 248–255.

Punch, Maurice. 1994. "Politics and Ethics in Qualitative Research." Pp. 83–97 in *Handbook of Qualitative Research,* edited by Norman K. Denzin and Yvonna S. Lincoln. Thousand Oaks, CA: Sage.

Purdy, Matthew. 1994. "Bronx Mystery: 3d-Rate Service for 1st-Class Mail." *The New York Times,* March 12, pp. 1, 3.

Putnam, Israel. 1977. "Poverty Thresholds: Their History and Future Development." Pp. 272–283 in *The Measure of Poverty. Technical Paper I: Documentation of Background Information and Rationale for Current Poverty Matrix,* edited by Mollie Orshansky. Washington, DC: U.S. Department of Health, Education, and Welfare.

Radin, Charles A. 1997. "Partnerships, Awareness Behind Boston's Success." *The Boston Globe,* February 19, pp. A2, B7.

Ragin, Charles C. 1987. *The Comparative Method: Moving Beyond Qualitative and Quantitative Strategies.* Berkeley: University of California Press.

Ragin, Charles C. 1994. *Constructing Social Research.* Thousand Oaks, CA: Pine Forge Press.

Regoli, R. M. and J. D. Hewitt. 1994. "Delinquency in Society: A Child-Centered Approach." New York: McGraw-Hill.

Reiss, Albert J., Jr. 1971. *The Police and the Public.* New Haven, CT: Yale University Press.

Reiss, Albert J. and Jeffrey A. Roth. 1993. *Understanding and Preventing Violence.* Washington, DC: National Academy Press.

Reynolds, Paul Davidson. 1979. *Ethical Dilemmas and Social Science Research.* San Francisco: Jossey-Bass.

Richards, Thomas J. and Lyn Richards. 1994. "Using Computers in Qualitative Research." Pp. 445–462 in *Handbook of Qualitative Research,* edited by Norman K. Denzin and Yvonna S. Lincoln. Thousand Oaks, CA: Sage.

Richardson, Laurel. 1995. "Narrative and Sociology." Pp. 198–221 in *Representation in Ethnography,* edited by John Van Maanen. Thousand Oaks, CA: Sage.

Riedel, Marc. 2000. *Research Strategies for Secondary Data: A Perspective for Criminology and Criminal Justice.* Thousand Oaks, CA: Sage.

Rise, Eric W. 1995. *The Martinsville Seven: Race, Rape, and Capital Punishment.* Charlottesville, VA: University Press of Virginia.

Rives, Norfleet W., Jr., and William J. Serow. 1988. *Introduction to Applied Demography: Data Sources and Estimation Techniques.* Sage University Paper Series on Quantitative Applications in the Social Sciences, series no. 07-039. Newbury Park, CA: Sage.

Rosen, Lawrence. 1995. "The Creation of the Uniform Crime Report: The Role of Social Science." *Social Science History,* 19: 215–238.

Rosenbaum, David E. 2000. "Seeking Answers, Census Is Raising Privacy Questions." *The New York Times,* April 1, pp. A1, A9.

Rosenberg, Morris. 1968. *The Logic of Survey Analysis.* New York: Basic Books.

Rosenfeld, Richard, Timothy M. Bray, and Arlen Egley. 1999. "Facilitating Violence: A Comparison of Gang-Motivated, Gang-Affiliated, and Nongang Youth Homicides." *Journal of Quantitative Criminology*, 15(4): 496–516.

Rossi, P. H. and H. E. Freeman. 1989. *Evaluation: A Systematic Approach* (4th ed.). Newbury Park, CA: Sage.

Ruback, R. Barry and Paula J. Vardaman. 1997. "Decision Making in Delinquency Cases: The Role of Race and Juveniles' Admission/Denial of the Crime." *Law and Human Behavior*, 21(1): 47–69.

Rubin, Herbert J. and Irene S. Rubin. 1995. *Qualitative Interviewing: The Art of Hearing Data.* Thousand Oaks, CA: Sage.

Rueschemeyer, Dietrich, Evelyne Huber Stephens, and John D. Stephens. 1992. *Capitalist Development and Democracy.* Chicago: University of Chicago Press.

Ruggles, Patricia. 1990. *Drawing the Line: Alternative Poverty Measures and Their Implications for Public Policy.* Washington, DC: The Urban Institute Press.

Sampson, Robert J. 1987. "Urban Black Violence: The Effect of Male Joblessness and Family Disruption." *American Journal of Sociology,* 93 (September): 348–382.

Sampson, Robert J. and John H. Laub. 1990. "Crime and Deviance over the Life Course: The Salience of Adult Social Bonds." *American Sociological Review,* 55 (October): 609–627.

Sampson, Robert J. and John H. Laub. 1993. "Structural Variations in Juvenile Court Processing: Inequality, the Underclass, and Social Control." *Law and Society Review,* 27(2): 285–311.

Sampson, Robert J. and Janet L. Lauritsen. 1994. "Violent Victimization and Offending: Individual-, Situational-, and Community-Level Risk Factors." Pp. 1–114 in *Understanding and Preventing Violence: Vol. 3, Social Influences,* edited by Albert J. Reiss, Jr., and Jeffrey A. Roth. Washington, DC: National Academy Press.

Sampson, Robert J. and Stephen W. Raudenbush. 1999. "Systematic Social Observation of Public Spaces: A New Look at Disorder in Urban Neighborhoods." *American Journal of Sociology,* 105: 603–651.

Sampson, Robert J., Stephen W. Raudenbush, and Felton Earls. 1997. "Neighborhoods and Violent Crime: A Multilevel Study of Collective Efficacy." *Science,* 277: 918–924.

Sanchez-Jankowski, Martin. 1991. *Islands in the Street.* Berkeley: University of California Press.

Saretsky, H. "The OEO P. C. Experiment and the John Henry Effect," *Phi Delta Kappan,* 53: 579–581 (1972).

Schnelle, J. F., R. E. Kirchner, J. W. Macrae, M. P. McNess, R. H. Eck, S. Snodgrass, J. D. Casey, and R. H. Uselton, Jr. 1978. "Police Evaluation Research: An Experimental and Cost-Benefit Analysis of a Helicopter Patrol in a High Crime Area." *Journal of Applied Behavior Analysis,* 11: 11–21.

Schorr, Lisbeth B. and Daniel Yankelovich. 2000. "In Search of a Gold Standard for Social Programs." *The Boston Globe*, February 18, p. A19.

Schuman, Howard and Stanley Presser. 1981. *Questions and Answers in Attitude Surveys: Experiments on Question Form, Wording, and Context.* New York: Academic Press.

Schutt, Russell K. and M. L. Fennell. 1992. "Shelter Staff Satisfaction with Services, the Service Network and Their Jobs." *Current Research on Occupations and Professions,* 7: 177–200.

Schutt, Russell K., Suzanne Gunston, and John O'Brien. 1992. "The Impact of AIDS Prevention Efforts on AIDS Knowledge and Behavior Among Sheltered Homeless Adults." *Sociological Practice Review,* 3(1): 1–7.

Schwandt, Thomas A. 1994. "Constructivist, Interpretivist Approaches to Human Inquiry." Pp. 118–137 in *Handbook of Qualitative Research,* edited by Norman K. Denzin and Yvonna S. Lincoln. Thousand Oaks, CA: Sage.

Scull, Andrew T. 1988. "Deviance and Social Control." Pp. 667–693 in *Handbook of Sociology,* edited by Neil J. Smelser. Newbury Park, CA: Sage.

Sechrest, Lee and Souraya Sidani. 1995. "Quantitative and Qualitative Methods: Is There an Alternative?" *Evaluation and Program Planning,* 18: 77–87.

Seidman, Larry J. 1997. "Neuropsychological Testing." Pp. 498–508 in *Psychiatry* (vol. 1), edited by Allan Tasman, Jerald Kay, and Jeffrey Lieberman. Philadelphia: W. B. Saunders.

Seltzer, Richard A. 1996. *Mistakes That Social Scientists Make: Error and Redemption in the Research Process.* New York: St. Martin's Press.

Shadish, William R. 1995. "Philosophy of Science and the Quantitative-Qualitative Debates: Thirteen Common Errors." *Evaluation and Program Planning,* 18: 63–75.

Shaw, Clifford, R. and McKay, Henry D. 1942. *Juvenile Delinquency and Urban Areas.* Chicago: University of Chicago Press.

Shepherd, Jane, David Hill, Joel Bristor, and Pat Montalvan. 1996. "Converting an Ongoing Health Study to CAPI: Findings from the National Health and Nutrition Study." Pp. 159–164 in *Health Survey Research Methods Conference Proceedings,* edited by Richard B. Warnecke. Hyattsville, MD: U.S. Department of Health and Human Services.

Sherman, L. W. 1992. *Policing Domestic Violence: Experiments and Dilemmas.* New York: Free Press.

Sherman, L. W. 1997. "Thinking About Crime Prevention." In *Preventing Crime: What Works, What Doesn't, What's Promising,* edited by L. W. Sherman, D. Gottfredson, D. MacKenzie, J. Eck, P. Reuter, and S. Bushway. Unpublished report by the Department of Criminology and Criminal Justice, University of Maryland.

Sherman, L. W. and Richard A. Berk. 1984. "The Specific Deterrent Effects of Arrest for Domestic Assault." *American Sociological Review,* 49: 261–272.

Sherman, L. W. and E. G. Cohn. 1989. "The Impact of Research on Legal Policy: The Minneapolis Domestic Violence Experiment." *Law and Society Review,* 23: 117–144.

Sherman, L W., P. Gartin, and M. Buerger. 1989. "Hot Spots of Predatory Crime: Routine Activities and the Criminology of Place." *Criminology,* 27: 27–56.

Sherman, L. W., D. Gottfredson, D. MacKenzie, J. Eck, P. Reuter, and S. Bushway. 1997. *Preventing Crime: What Works, What Doesn't, What's Promising.* Unpublished report by the Department of Criminology and Criminal Justice, University of Maryland.

Sherman, L. W., Douglas A. Smith, Janell D. Schmidt, and Dennis P. Rogan. 1992. "Crime, Punishment, and Stake in Conformity: Legal and Informal Control of Domestic Violence." *American Sociological Review,* 57: 680–690.

Short, James F., Jr. and Ivan Nye. 1957–1958. "Reported Behavior as a Criterion of Deviant Behavior." *Social Problems,* 5: 207–213.

Simon, Rita J. and Sandra Baxter. 1989. "Gender and Violent Crime." Pp. 171–197 in *Violent Crime, Violent Criminals,* edited by Neil Alan Weiner and Marvin E. Wolfgang. Newbury Park, CA: Sage.

Sjoberg, Gideon (Ed.). 1967. *Ethics, Politics, and Social Research.* Cambridge, MA: Schenkman.

Sjoberg, Gideon and Roger Nett. 1968. *A Methodology for Social Research.* New York: Harper & Row.

Skinner, Harvey A. and Wen-Jenn Sheu. 1982. "Reliability of Alcohol Use Indices: The Lifetime Drinking History and the MAST." *Journal of Studies on Alcohol,* 43(11): 1157–1170.

Skocpol, Theda. 1984. "Emerging Agendas and Recurrent Strategies in Historical Sociology." Pp. 356–391 in *Vision and Method in Historical Sociology,* edited by Theda Skocpol. New York: Cambridge University Press.

Sobell, Linda C., Mark B. Sobell, Diane M. Riley, Reinhard Schuller, D. Sigfrido Pavan, Anthony Cancilla, Felix Klajner, and Gloria I. Leo. 1988. "The Reliability of Alcohol Abusers' Self-Reports of Drinking and Life Events That Occurred in the Distant Past." *Journal of Studies on Alcohol,* 49(2): 225–232.

Sosin, Michael R., Paul Colson, and Susan Grossman. 1988. *Homelessness in Chicago: Poverty and Pathology, Social Institutions and Social Change.* Chicago: Chicago Community Trust.

Specter, Michael. 1994. "Census-Takers Come Calling and Get a Scolding." *The New York Times,* March 3, p. A4.

Stewart, David W. 1984. *Secondary Research: Information Sources and Methods.* Beverly Hills, CA: Sage.

Stout, David. 1997. "Officials Are Starting Early in Their Defense of the 2000 Census." *The New York Times,* March 23, p. 37.

Straus, M. 1979. "Measuring Intrafamily Conflict and Violence: The Conflict Tactics (TC) Scale." *Journal of Marriage and the Family,* 41: 75–88.

Straus, Murray A. and Richard J. Gelles. 1990. *Physical Violence in American Families: Risk Factors and Adaptations to Violence in 8,145 Families.* New Brunswick, NJ: Transaction Publishers.

Strunk, William, Jr., and E. B. White. 1979. *The Elements of Style* (3rd ed.). New York: Macmillan.

Sudman, Seymour. 1976. *Applied Sampling.* New York: Academic Press.

"Survey on Adultery: 'I Do' Means 'I Don't.'" 1993. *The New York Times,* October 19, p. A20.

Tannenbaum, F. 1938. *Crime in the Community.* New York: Columbia University Press.

Tarnas, Richard. 1991. *The Passion of the Western Mind: Understanding the Ideas That Have Shaped Our World View.* New York: Ballantine.

Thorne, Barrie. 1993. *Gender Play: Girls and Boys in School.* New Brunswick, NJ: Rutgers University Press.

Thrasher, Frederic. 1927. *The Gang: A Study of 1,313 Gangs in Chicago.* Chicago: University of Chicago Press.

Tjaden, Patricia and Nancy Thoennes. 2000. "Extent, Nature, and Consequences of Intimate Partner Violence." In *Findings from the National Violence Against Women Survey* (NCJ 181867). Washington, DC: National Institute of Justice, U.S. Department of Justice.

Toby, Jackson. 1957. "Social Disorganization and Stake in Conformity: Complementary Factors in the Predatory Behavior of Hoodlums." *Journal of Criminal Law, Criminology and Police Science,* 48: 12–17.

Tonry, Michael and Mark H. Moore. 1998. *Youth Violence: Crime and Justice* (vol. 24). Chicago: University of Chicago Press.

Tufte, Edward R. 1983. *The Visual Display of Quantitative Information.* Cheshire, CT: Graphics Press.

Turabian, Kate L. 1967. *A Manual for Writers of Term Papers, Theses, and Dissertations* (3rd ed., rev.). Chicago: University of Chicago Press.

Turner, Charles F. and Elizabeth Martin (Eds.). 1984. *Surveying Subjective Phenomena* (vols. I and II). New York: Russell Sage Foundation.

Tyler, T. 1990. *Why People Obey the Law.* New Haven, CT: Yale University Press.

U.S. Bureau of the Census. 1999. *United States Census 2000, Updated Summary: Census 2000 Operational Plan.* Washington, DC: U.S. Department of Commerce, Bureau of the Census.

U.S. Bureau of the Census. 2000a. "Census Bureau Directory Says 92 Percent of U.S. Households Accounted For; Thanks President and Vice President for Message to Census Workers." *United States Department of Commerce News,* May 31. www.census.gov/Press-Release/www/2000/cb00cn41.html.

U.S. Bureau of the Census. 2000b. "U.S. Commerce Secretary William M. Daley Delegates Decision to Census Bureau on Adjusting Census 2000." *United States Department of Commerce News,* June 14. www.census.gov/Press-Release/www/2000.

Vaillant, George E. 1995. *The Natural History of Alcoholism Revisited.* Cambridge, MA: Harvard University Press.

van de Vijver, Fons and Kwok Leung. 1997. *Methods and Data Analysis for Cross-Cultural Research.* Thousand Oaks, CA: Sage.

Van Maanen, John. 1982. "Fieldwork on the Beat." Pp. 103–151 in *Varieties of Qualitative Research,* edited by John Van Maanen, James M. Dabbs, Jr., and Robert R. Faulkner. Beverly Hills: Sage.

Venkatesh, Sudhir Alladi. 1997. "The Social Organization of Street Gang Activity in an Urban Ghetto. *American Journal of Sociology,* 103: 82–102.

Vidich, Arthur J. and Stanford M. Lyman. 1994. "Qualitative Methods: Their History in Sociology and Anthropology." Pp. 23–59 in *Handbook of Qualitative Research,* edited by Norman K. Denzin and Yvonna S. Lincoln. Thousand Oaks, CA: Sage.

Vigil, James Diego. 1988. *Barrio Gangs.* Austin: University of Texas Press.

Wallace, Walter L. 1971. *The Logic of Science in Sociology.* Chicago: Aldine.

Wallace, Walter L. 1983. *Principles of Scientific Sociology.* New York: Aldine.

Wallerstein, J. S. and Wyle, C. J. 1947. "Our Law-Abiding Law Breakers," *Probation,* 25: 107–112.

Walters, Pamela Barnhouse, David R. James, and Holly J. McCammon. 1997. "Citizenship and Public Schools: Accounting for Racial Inequality in Education for the Pre-and Post-Disfranchisement South." *American Sociological Review,* 62: 34–52.

Watson, Charles G., Curt Tilleskjor, E. A. Hoodecheck-Schow, John Pucel, and Lyle Jacobs. 1984. "Do Alcoholics Give Valid Self-Reports?" *Journal of Studies on Alcohol,* 45(4): 344–348.

Watson, Roy E. L. 1986. "The Effectiveness of Increased Police Enforcement as a General Deterrent." *Law and Society Review,* 20(2): 293–299.

Weatherby, Norman L., Richard Needle, Helen Cesari, Robert Booth, Clyde B. McCoy, John K. Waters, Mark Williams, and Dale D. Chitwood. 1994. "Validity of Self-Reported Drug Use Among Injection Drug Users and Crack Cocaine Users Recruited Through Street Outreach." *Evaluation and Program Planning,* 17(4): 347–355.

Webb, Eugene, Donald T. Campbell, Richard D. Schwartz, and Lee Sechrest. 1966. *Unobtrusive Measures: Nonreactive Research in the Social Sciences.* Chicago: Rand McNally.

Weber, Max. 1949. *The Methodology of the Social Sciences* (translated and edited by Edward A. Shils and Henry A. Finch). New York: Free Press.

Weber, Robert Philip. 1985. *Basic Content Analysis.* Beverly Hills, CA: Sage.

Wechsler, Henry, Andrea Davenport, George Dowdall, Barbara Moeykens, and Sonia Castillo. 1994. "Health and Behavioral Consequences of Binge Drinking in College: A National Survey of Students at 140 Campuses." *JAMA: The Journal of the American Medical Association,* 272(21): 1672–1677.

Weisburd, D., L. Maher, and L. Sherman. 1992. "Contrasting Crime General and Crime Specific Theory: The Case of Hot Spots of Crime." *Advances in Criminological Theory,* 4: 45–69.

Weisburd, David, Stanton Wheeler, Elin Waring, and Nacy Bode. 1991. *Crimes of the Middle Class: White-Collar Offenders in the Federal Courts.* New Haven, CT: Yale University Press.

Weiss, C. H. 1977. "Introduction." In *Using Social Research in Public Policy Making,* edited by C. H. Weiss. Lexington, MA: D. C. Heath.

Wells, L. Edward and Joseph H. Rankin. 1991. "Families and Delinquency: A Meta-Analysis of the Impact of Broken Homes." *Social Problems,* 38 (February): 71–93.

Whyte, William Foote. 1943. *Street Corner Society: The Social Structure of an Italian Slum.* Chicago: The University of Chicago Press.

Whyte, William Foote. 1991. *Social Theory for Social Action: How Individuals and Organizations Learn to Change.* Newbury Park, CA: Sage.

Widom, Cathy Spatz. 2000. "Childhood Victimization: Early Adversity, Later Psychopathology." *National Institute of Justice Journal* (NCJ JR000242). Washington, DC: National Institute of Justice, U.S. Department of Justice.

Williams, Christine and E. Joel Heikes. 1993. "The Importance of Researcher's Gender in the In-depth Interview: Evidence from Two Case Studies of Male Nurses." *Gender and Society,* 7: 280–291.

Wilson, William Julius. 1987. *The Truly Disadvantaged: The Inner City, the Underclass, and Public Policy.* Chicago: University of Chicago Press.

Wolcott, Harry F. 1995. *The Art of Fieldwork.* Walnut Creek, CA: AltaMira Press.

Wolfgang, Marvin E. and F. Ferracuti. 1967. *The Subculture of Violence.* London: Tavistock.

Wright, Richard and Scott Decker. 1994. *Burglars on the Job: Streetlife and Residential Break-ins.* Boston: Northeastern University Press.

Zaret, David. 1996. "Petitions and the 'Invention' of Public Opinion in the English Revolution." *American Journal of Sociology,* 101: 1497–1555.

Zelditch, M., Jr. 1962. "Some Methodological Problems of Field Studies." *American Journal of Sociology,* 67: 566.

Zielbauer, Paul. 2000. "2 Cities Lag Far Behind the U.S. in Heeding the Call of the Census." *The New York Times,* April 21, p. A21.

Glossary/Index

Note: Page numbers followed by *e* indicate a reference to an exhibit.